We dedicate this handbook to one of our contributors, John T. Warren, Associate Professor of Communication Pedagogy in the Department of Speech Communication at Southern Illinois University, Carbondale, who passed away on April 2, 2011.

John represented the best of critical intercultural communication work: thoughtful, incisive, evocative, compassionate, and always in pursuit of transformative change. He produced the most influential scholarship and his legacy will continue to live on in his students, colleagues, and all those he encountered. We will greatly miss John, our friend and colleague.

Rona Tamiko Halualani and Thomas K. Nakayama

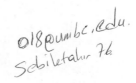

Handbooks in Communication and Media

This series aims to provide theoretically ambitious but accessible volumes devoted to the major fields and subfields within communication and media studies. Each volume sets out to ground and orientate the student through a broad range of specially commissioned chapters, while also providing the more experienced scholar and teacher with a convenient and comprehensive overview of the latest trends and critical directions.

The Handbook of Children, Media, and Development, *edited by Sandra L. Calvert and Barbara J. Wilson*

The Handbook of Crisis Communication, *edited by W. Timothy Coombs and Sherry J. Holladay*

The Handbook of Internet Studies, *edited by Mia Consalvo and Charles Ess*

The Handbook of Rhetoric and Public Address, *edited by Shawn J. Parry-Giles and J. Michael Hogan*

The Handbook of Critical Intercultural Communication, *edited by Thomas K. Nakayama and Rona Tamiko Halualani*

The Handbook of Global Communication and Media Ethics, *edited by Robert S. Fortner and P. Mark Fackler*

The Handbook of Communication and Corporate Social Responsibility, *edited by Øyvind Ihlen, Jennifer Bartlett, and Steve May*

The Handbook of Gender, Sex, and Media, *edited by Karen Ross*

The Handbook of Global Health Communication, *edited by Rafael Obregon and Silvio Waisbord*

The Handbook of Global Media Research, *edited by Ingrid Volkmer*

The Handbook of Global Online Journalism, *edited by Eugenia Siapera and Andreas Veglis*

The Handbook of Communication and Corporate Reputation, *edited by Craig E. Carroll*

Forthcoming

The Handbook of International Advertising Research, *edited by Hong Cheng*

The Handbook of Critical Intercultural Communication

Edited by

Thomas K. Nakayama
and Rona Tamiko Halualani

WILEY-BLACKWELL

A John Wiley & Sons, Ltd., Publication

This paperback edition first published 2013
© 2013 Blackwell Publishing Ltd.

Edition history: Blackwell Publishing Ltd (hardback, 2010)

Blackwell Publishing was acquired by John Wiley & Sons in February 2007. Blackwell's publishing program has been merged with Wiley's global Scientific, Technical, and Medical business to form Wiley-Blackwell.

Registered Office
John Wiley & Sons Ltd, The Atrium, Southern Gate, Chichester, West Sussex, PO19 8SQ, UK

Editorial Offices
350 Main Street, Malden, MA 02148-5020, USA
9600 Garsington Road, Oxford, OX4 2DQ, UK
The Atrium, Southern Gate, Chichester, West Sussex, PO19 8SQ, UK

For details of our global editorial offices, for customer services, and for information about how to apply for permission to reuse the copyright material in this book please see our website at www.wiley.com/wiley-blackwell.

The right of Thomas K. Nakayama and Rona Tamiko Halualani to be identified as the authors of the editorial material in this work has been asserted in accordance with the UK Copyright, Designs and Patents Act 1988.

Library of Congress Cataloging-in-Publication Data

The handbook of critical intercultural communication / edited by Thomas K. Nakayama, Rona Tamiko Halualani.
    p.   cm. – (Handbooks in communication and media)
    Includes bibliographical references and index.
    ISBN 978-1-1184-0008-1 (pbk.: alk paper)
    1. Intercultural communication–Handbooks, manuals, etc.   I. Nakayama, Thomas K.
    II. Halualani, Rona Tamiko.
    HM1211.H34 2010
    303.48'2–dc22

                                                    2010034204

A catalogue record for this book is available from the British Library.

Cover image: *Constructive Signs 1* by Ignacio Auzike, oil on canvas, 2006. Photo © Getty Images.
Cover design by Simon Levy

Set in 10/13pt Galliard by SPi Publisher Services, Pondicherry, India
Printed and bound in Malaysia by Vivar Printing Sdn Bhd

Contents

Notes on Contributors

Bryant Keith Alexander is Professor of Performance, Pedagogy and Culture in the Department of Communication Studies at California State University Los Angeles, and currently serves as the Associate Dean of the College of Arts and Letters. His published essays have appeared in a wide variety of scholarly journals and books including: *Men and Masculinities: Critical Concepts in Sociology*, the *Handbook of Performance Studies*, the Third Edition of the *Handbook of Qualitative Research*, the *Handbook of Critical and Indigenous Methodologies*, and the *Handbook of Communication and Instruction*. He is the coeditor of *Performance Theories in Education: Pedagogy, Identity and Reform* (Erlbaum, 2008) and the author of *Performing Black Masculinity: Race, Culture and Queer Identity*.

Brenda J. Allen is a Professor of Communication and Associate Dean in the College of Liberal Arts and Sciences at the University of Colorado Denver. Her research and teaching areas are organizational communication, diversity, and critical pedagogy. Among her numerous publications is a groundbreaking book entitled *Difference Matters: Communicating Social Identity*. She conducts workshops and presents keynote speeches on diversity, empowerment, mentoring, presentational speaking, and teamwork.

Karen Lee Ashcraft is an Associate Professor at the University of Utah. Her research addresses organizational communication and, specifically, examines organizational forms and occupational identities as they intersect with relations of power and difference. Her work has appeared in such outlets as *Communication Monographs, Communication Theory, Management Communication Quarterly*, and *Administrative Science Quarterly*; and her current project examines how gender, race, and sexuality become pivotal to the evolution of professional identity.

Bernadette Marie Calafell is Associate Professor in the Department of Communication Studies at the University of Denver. Her research converges around issues of performance, rhetoric, and intersectionality, particularly within

Chicana/o and Latina/o communities. In 2009 she was awarded the Lilla A. Heston Award for Outstanding Research in Oral Interpretation and Performance. Her publications include essays in the *Journal of International and Intercultural Communication, Critical Studies in Media Communication, Text and Performance Quarterly, The Communication Review, Cultural Studies ⇔ Critical Methodologies,* and *Communication, Culture, and Critique.* She recently coedited (with Shane T. Moreman) a special issue of *Text and Performance Quarterly* on "Latina/o Performativities." She is also author of the book *Latina/o Communication Studies: Theorizing Performance.*

Aimee Carrillo Rowe is Associate Professor of Rhetoric and GWSS (Gender, Women's and Sexuality Studies) and is Executive Director of POROI (Project on the Rhetoric of Inquiry) at the University of Iowa. Her teaching and writing address the politics of representation and feminist alliances, third world feminism, and whiteness and antiracism. Her book *Power Lines: On the Subject of Feminist Alliances,* offers a coalitional theory of subjectivity as a bridge to difference-based alliances. Her writing appears primarily in interdisciplinary outlets such as *Hypatia, Radical History Review,* and *NWSA Journal.*

Guo-Ming Chen is Professor of Communication Studies at the University of Rhode Island. Currently, Chen is the executive director of International Association for Intercultural Communication Studies and the coeditor of *China Media Research.* His research interests are in intercultural/organizational/global communication. Chen has published numerous articles and books. His research has appeared in *Journal of Cross-Cultural Psychology, Communication Yearbook, Journal of Psychology, International and Intercultural Communication Annual, Communication Quarterly,* and others.

Victoria Chen is Professor in the Communication Studies Department at San Francisco State University. Her research interests include the construction of cultural identity, public dialogue facilitation, commemorative rituals, and the theory of the coordinated management of meaning (CMM). Her work has appeared in *Research on Language and Social Interaction, International and Intercultural Communication Annual, Human Systems,* and other anthologies. She is the coeditor of *Our Voices: Essays in Culture, Ethnicity, and Communication.*

Hsin-I Cheng is Assistant Professor of Communication at Santa Clara University. Her research interests include culture and identity, immigration, diasporic communities, and border crossing in the context of transnationalism. Specifically she is interested in unpacking various interactive processes of identity crafting (e.g., intersections of ethnicity, class, gender, race, nationality) in relation to geopolitical arrangements (e.g., colonial and imperial legacy, neoliberal consumerism). She is the author of *Culturing Interface: Identity, Communication, and Chinese Transnationalism.* Her research has appeared in *Journal of International and Intercultural Communication,* and *Intercultural Communication and Language.*

Leda Cooks is a Professor in the Department of Communication at the University of Massachusetts, Amherst. Her research has focused on the ways identities are created, negotiated, and re-membered in a variety of (inter)cultural contexts, from performances of travel and sojourn, to public schools and university classrooms. Her work draws from scholarship in critical/cultural studies, performance studies, critical pedagogy, social constructionism and intercultural/interracial communication. Current research looks at the tensions between intergroup dialogue and advocacy for social justice, constructions of (im)mobile cultural identities in food/travel television, and negotiations of community in community based learning. Her essays and research have appeared in *Communication Education, Communication Theory, Feminist Media Studies, Text and Performance Quarterly, Michigan Journal of Community Service Learning, Academic Exchange Quarterly, Review of Education, Pedagogy, and Cultural Studies,* and the *International and Intercultural Communication Annual.*

Melissa L. Curtin is adjunct Assistant Professor and Coordinator of Special Projects in Language, Culture and Communication at the University of California, Santa Barbara, where she teaches in the Department of Linguistics and Department of Communication and also coordinates interdisciplinary projects related to culture and communication. Her research interests include language, discourse and social semiotic processes of identification; semiotic landscapes and politics of place; theories and practices of cultural adjustment; and ethnographic theory and methods. Her research has appeared in *Seeking Identity: Language in Society* and *Linguistic Landscape: Expanding the Scenery.*

Sara DeTurk is an Associate Professor of Communication at the University of Texas at San Antonio. Her research interests include identity, cultural ideologies about difference, social change, social justice activism, intergroup alliances, and intergroup dialogue. Her work has appeared in *Communication Education, Communication Quarterly,* the *Qualitative Research Journal,* the *Journal of Business and Management,* and the *Journal of Intergroup Relations.*

Jolanta A. Drzewiecka is Associate Professor of Intercultural Communication in the E. R. Murrow College of Communication at Washington State University. Her research interests focus on questions about identity constructions and representations through national, ethnic, and racial terms. She is particularly interested in the claims to belonging individuals advance to, through, and against specific culturally significant Others. Her work has been published in *Communication Theory, Communication Quarterly, International and Intercultural Annual, Southern Journal of Communication* and other communication journals.

Deanna L. Fassett is Associate Professor of Communication Studies at San José State University. She is coauthor of *Critical Communication Pedagogy* and coeditor of the forthcoming *SAGE Handbook of Communication and Instruction.* Her research has appeared in *Communication Education, Text and Performance Quarterly,* and *Communication and Critical/Cultural Studies.*

Lisa A. Flores is an Associate Professor at the University of Colorado Boulder. She writes at the intersections of rhetorical studies, critical race studies, and critical intercultural communication. Her recent work emphasizes questions of dominance as it explores the ways in which masculinity and whiteness maintain their hegemonic status, even when seemingly threatened. She has published in such places as *Critical Studies in Media Communication, Text and Performance Quarterly*, and *Communication and Critical Cultural Studies*.

Radhika Gajjala, is Professor of Communication and Cultural Studies, and Director of Women's Studies at Bowling Green State University, Ohio. Her book *Cyberselves: Feminist Ethnographies of South Asian Women*. She coedited South Asian Technospaces and Webbing Cyberfeminist Practice.

Alberto González is Professor of Communication in the Department of Communication at Bowling Green State University. His research and teaching interests include the following: intercultural rhetoric, political discourse of Mexican Americans, and popular music as a mode of communication. His research has appeared in various journals including *The Quarterly Journal of Speech, Southern Communication Journal, Communication Quarterly, Intercultural Communication Studies, and Journal of Latinos and Education*. He is coeditor of *Our Voices: Essays in Culture, Ethnicity, and Communication*.

Rona T. Halualani is Professor of Communication Studies at San José State University. She is the author of *In the Name of Hawaiians: Native Identities and Cultural Politics*. Her work on critical intercultural communication studies, identity, cultural politics, and intercultural contact has been published in *Journal of International and Intercultural Communication, International Journal of Intercultural Relations, Communication and Critical Cultural Studies*, and *International and Intercultural Communication Annual*.

Marouf Hasian is a Professor in the Department of Communication at the University of Utah. His areas of interest include postcolonial studies, critical memory studies, law and rhetoric, and genocide studies. His work has appeared in several journals, including *Critical Studies in Media Communication*, the *Quarterly Journal of Speech*, and *Western Journal of Communication*.

Ronald L. Jackson II, Professor and Head of African American Studies, is one of the leading communication and identity scholars. His research examines how theories of identity relate to intercultural and gender communication. In his teaching and research, he explores how and why people negotiate and define themselves as they do. Additionally, his research includes empirical, conceptual, and critical approaches to the study of masculinity, identity negotiation, Whiteness, and Afrocentricity. He is coeditor of the *Journal Critical Studies in Media Communication*, past president of the Eastern Communication Association, and author of nine books and dozens of scholarly essays.

Etsuko Kinefuchi is Assistant Professor of Communication Studies at the University of North Carolina at Greensboro. Her research centers on cultural and racial identity construction, representation, and negotiation in national and transnational contexts as well as community building across differences. Her work has been published in *Critical Studies in Media Communication*, *Journal of International and Intercultural Communication*, *International and Intercultural Communication Annual*, *Intercultural Communication: A Reader*, and *Readings in Intercultural communication: Experience and Contexts*.

Wendy Leeds-Hurwitz is Director of the Center for Intercultural Dialogue in Washington, D.C., and Professor Emerita of Communication at the University of Wisconsin-Parkside. She received her M.A. and Ph.D. degrees from the University of Pennsylvania. Her specializations are intercultural communication, language and social interaction, ethnography of communication, semiotics, communication theory, childhood socialization, history of the discipline, interdisciplinarity, and higher education pedagogy. Her major publications include the books *Communication in Everyday Life*, *Semiotics and Communication*, *Wedding as Text*, and *Rolling in Ditches with Shamans*; the edited collections *Social Approaches to Communication*, *From Generation to Generation*, *Socially Constructing Communication*, and *The Social History of Language and Social Interaction Research*; and the co-edited collection *Socially Constructing Communication*.

Lara Lengel is Professor and Chair, Department of Communication Studies at Bowling Green State University. She began her research on women in intercultural and transnational contexts when she was a Fulbright Scholar and American Institute of Maghreb Studies Fellow in Tunisia (1993–1994). Her books, *Intercultural Communication and Creative Practice: Music, Dance, and Women's Cultural Identity*, *Casting Gender: Women and Performance in Global Contexts*, and articles in *International and Intercultural Communication Annual*, *Feminist Media Studies*, *Gender & History*, *Text and Performance Quarterly*, *Global Media Journal*, and *Journal of Communication Inquiry* address gender and women in transnational contexts, critical intercultural communication studies, performance studies, and feminist ethnography.

Tracy Marafiote is an Assistant Professor at the State University of New York at Fredonia. Working from the perspectives of cultural studies, critical intercultural and environmental communication, her research examines the intersections of gender, race, class, and nature. Current studies focus on the impact of cultural forces and identities on the environment, intercultural relations, and social change. She has published in *Environmental Communication: A Journal of Nature and Culture*, *The Environmental Communication Yearbook*, and the *Journal of the Northwest Communication Association*.

Judith N. Martin is Professor of Intercultural Communication in the Hugh Downs School of Human Communication at Arizona State University. Her principle research interests focus on the role of culture in online communication; interethnic and interracial communication, as well as sojourner adaptation and re-entry. She has published numerous research articles in communication journals as well as other disciplinary journals and has coauthored three textbooks in intercultural communication.

Scott C. Martin is Professor of History and American Culture Studies and Chair of the Department of History at Bowling Green State University. Scott's books include *Demon of the Domestic Sphere: Temperance, Gender and Middle-Class Ideology, 1800–1860, Cultural Change and the Market Revolution in America, 1789–1860*, and *Killing Time: Leisure and Culture in Southwestern Pennsylvania, 1800–1850*. His research on gender and cultural studies, social and cultural history, and alcohol and drug policy have appeared in *Journal of Family History, Social History of Alcohol and Drugs, International Journal of the History of Sport, Journal of the Early Republic,* and *Journal of Social History.*

S. Lily Mendoza is Associate Professor of Culture and Communication in the Department of Communication and Journalism at Oakland University. Her research interests include theories of identity and subjectivity, cultural politics in national, post- and transnational contexts, dynamics of cross-cultural theorizing, discourses of indigenization, race, and ethnicity and Filipino and Filipino American studies. She is the author of *Between the Homeland and the Diaspora: The Politics of Theorizing Filipino and Filipino American Identities* and has published in various anthologies and intercultural communication journals.

Yoshitaka Miike is Associate Professor in the Department of Communication at the University of Hawai'i, Hilo. Inspired by Dr. Molefi Kete Asante's Afrocentric idea, he has proposed and developed the metatheory of Asiacentricity as an alternative paradigm for the study of Asian cultures and communication. He is the recipient of a 2004 Distinguished Scholarship Award from the International and Intercultural Communication Division of the National Communication Association for the 2003 Outstanding Article of the Year. He coedited *The Global Intercultural Communication Reader* and guest-edited three journal special issues on Asian communication theory. He currently serves as a consulting editor of *Intercultural Communication Studies* and as an editorial board member of *China Media Research.* He has reviewed numerous manuscripts for national and international journals including *Asian Journal of Communication, Communication Yearbook, Howard Journal of Communications, International and Intercultural Communication Annual,* and *Journal of Multicultural Discourses.*

Dreama G. Moon is Professor of Intercultural Communication in the Department of Communication at California State University, San Marcos. In her scholarly work, she is interested in the social construction of domination and the ways in which both dominant and nondominant group members negotiate, acquiesce to, and oppose domination. Her research broadly focuses on how dominant ideologies, such as white supremacy, classism, and sexism, are reproduced in and by communication as well as how they are contested, disrupted, and resisted. Her research has appeared outlets such as the *Communication Quarterly, Howard Journal of*

Communication, International and Intercultural Communication Annual, and *Communication and Critical/Cultural Studies.*

Shane T. Moreman is Associate Professor in the Department of Communication at California State University, Fresno. His research mainly concerns Latina/o populations, but more generally it involves critical intercultural approaches to the communicative and performative aspects of all cultural identity expression and interaction. He has publications in *Communication and Critical/Cultural Studies, Text and Performance Quarterly, Journal of International & Intercultural Communication, Liminalities, The Communication Review* and *Theatre Journal.* In 2008, he received "Latina/o Scholar of the Year" from the Latina/o Communication Studies Division of the National Communication Association.

Richard Morris is Professor of Ethnic Studies in the College of Interdisciplinary Arts and Sciences at Arizona State University. His books, essays, and poetry typically deal with cultural relations between Native nations and incursive states. His research has received international and national recognition in several academic and Native disciplines.

Jamie Moshin is in the Department of Communication at the University of Washington. His work lies at the intersection of (critical) rhetoric, cultural studies and discourse analysis. His research focuses on notions of race, identity, whiteness, ethnicity, masculinity, and discourse. In particular, he focuses on the discursive construction and representation of American Jewishness. He is currently at work on a dissertation on postrace and the "new Jew," specifically looking at the Jewish discursive appropriation of African American rhetorical devices and discursive identifiers.

Thomas K. Nakayama is Professor and Chair of Communication Studies at Northeastern University. He was a Fulbrighter at the Université de Mons-Hainaut in Belgium. He was founding editor of the *Journal of International and Intercultural Communication* (vols. 1–3). He has edited a number of publications, including *Transforming Barbed Wire: The Incarceration of Japanese Americans in Arizona During World War II,* and *Whiteness: The Social Communication of Identity.* He has coauthored two books on intercultural communication. His work on issues of race, gender, sexuality and nationality has appeared in a variety of journals, including *Critical Studies in Mass Communication, Quarterly Journal of Speech, Communication and Critical/Cultural Studies, Communication Theory, Journal of Communication, Text and Performance Quarterly* and the *Howard Journal of Communications.*

Kent A. Ono is Professor in and Chair of the Department of Communication at the University of Utah. University of Illinois at Urbana-Champaign. In addition to authoring *Contemporary Media Culture and the Remnants of a Colonial Past,* coauthoring *Asian Americans and the Media* and *Shifting Borders: Rhetoric, Immigration, and California's Proposition 187,* he has edited *Asian American Studies after Critical Mass* (2005, Blackwell) and *A Companion to Asian American*

Studies and has coedited *Enterprise Zones: Critical Positions on* Star Trek. He is currently cowriting a book entitled, *Critical Intercultural Communication*.

Jim Perkinson is a long-time activist and educator from inner city Detroit, currently teaching as Professor of Social Ethics at the Ecumenical Theological Seminary and lecturing in Intercultural Communication Studies at the University of Oakland (Michigan). He is the author of *White Theology: Outing Supremacy in Modernity* and *Shamanism, Racism, and Hip-Hop Culture: Essays on White Supremacy and Black Subversion*, and has written extensively in both academic and popular journals on questions of race, class, and colonialism in connection with religion and urban culture. He is in demand as a speaker on a wide variety of topics related to his interests and a recognized artist on the spoken-word poetry scene in the inner city.

Raka Shome (Ph.D, University of Georgia) served as the Inaugural Margaret E. and Paul F. Harron Endowed Chair in Communication (2011–2012) at Villanova University. Prior to this she taught at London School of Economics, Arizona State University, and University of Washington, and was a Visiting Scholar at NYU. Her research on whiteness, transnationality, gender, postcoloniality, and non-Western modernities has been published in numerous leading journals in communication and cultural studies. She has delivered talks nationally and internationally on the subject of race, culture, and transnationality.

Kathryn Sorrells is an Associate Professor in the Department of Communication Studies at California State University, Northridge. Kathryn combines approaches from critical, cultural studies, feminist and postcolonial perspectives to investigate and teach about issues of culture, gender, race, class and social justice. Kathryn is the recipient of numerous national, state, and local awards for founding and directing the *Communicating Common Ground Project*, an innovative community action research project that allows CSUN students the opportunity to develop creative alternatives to intercultural and interethnic conflict. She is the author of *Globalizing Intercultural Communication* (forthcoming) and has published a variety of articles related to intercultural communication, globalization, and social justice.

William J. Starosta, Howard University, teaches coursework in intercultural communication, qualitative research, and rhetoric. He has held elective office in two professional societies. He is founding editor of the *Howard Journal of Communications* and presently researches inter-ethnic conflict, intercultural rhetoric, and intercultural communication theory.

Melissa Steyn is Director of Intercultural and Diversity Studies and an Associate Professor in the Sociology Department at the University of Cape Town. She is best known for her work on whiteness and white identity in postapartheid South Africa. Melissa is author of *Whiteness Just Isn't What is Used to Be: White Identity in a Changing South Africa* which won the 2002 outstanding book award in the International and Intercultural Communication Division, NCA. She has coedited *The Prize and the Price: Shaping Sexualities in South Africa* (vol. 2), *Performing*

Queer: Shaping Sexualities in South Africa (vol. 1), *Under construction: Race and identity in South Africa Today* and *Cultural Synergy in South Africa: Weaving Strands of Africa and Europe.* Her published research in Communication journals has appeared in *Communication Theory, Communication Quarterly,* and the *International Journal of Intercultural Relations.*

Crispin Thurlow is Associate Professor of Communication based at the University of Washington (Seattle, USA) where he also holds adjunct positions in Linguistics and Interdisciplinary Arts & Sciences. His most recent books are *Tourism Discourse: Language and Global Mobility* and *Semiotic Landscapes: Language, Image, Space.*

Yukio Tsuda is Professor of International Language Policy, Global Communication, and English Language Education at the University of Tsukuba, Japan. His research interests include the following: The Hegemony of English and its impact on languages and cultures; language policy; English language education policies. His publications are mostly in Japanese, except for *Language Inequality and Distortion* and several articles. He published a number of books in Japanese, among which are *Eigo Shihai-no Kouzou* and *Eigo Shihai-to Kotoba-no Byoudou* (The Hegemony of English and Linguistic Equality).

John T. Warren was an Associate Professor of Communication Pedagogy in the Department of Speech Communication at Southern Illinois University, Carbondale. His books include *Performing Purity: Whiteness, Pedagogy, and the Reconstitution of Power, Casting Gender: Women and Performance in Intercultural Contexts* (coedited with Laura Lengel), and *Critical Communication Pedagogy* (coauthored with Deanna L. Fassett).

Acknowledgments

This handbook – a special contribution to intercultural communication studies – would not have been possible without the support, advice, and direction of many colleagues, friends, and loved ones. We especially recognize those scholars who dared to question and challenge traditional approaches to intercultural communication – those such as Molefi Kete Asante, Wenshu Lee, Alberto González, Marsha Houston, William Starosta, Guo-Ming Chen, Mary Jane Collier, Judith Martin, Kent Ono, Dreama Moon, Leda Cooks, Gust Yep, Victoria Chen, and Dolores Tanno, among others. Their bold "first steps" in creating a space for critical intercultural communication studies has been essential for the engagement of culture and intercultural discourses and dimensions through power, cultural politics, and justice. Today, there is a vibrant critical mass of scholars – many of whom are contributors to this handbook – who are intrigued and deeply vested in the interrogation of interculturalities through tropes and modes of power, positionality, context, and agency and committed to transforming the conditions in which we live for the better of us all and especially for those who are neglected, marginalized, and forgotten.

Our sincerest thanks go to all of the contributors of this handbook who submitted wonderful critical works and displayed great patience and kindness during the long process of creating this edited collection.

We also recognize the support of our colleagues at San Jose State University and Arizona State University for their encouragement, advice, and valued perspectives. Our partners – Kung and David, respectively – were incredible as they provided unwavering support and love during the tenure of this project, giving up "quality time" with us.

This handbook had been envisioned by us for many years, but it took the outreach and guidance of Elizabeth Swayze, Jayne Fargnoli, and Margot Morse at Wiley-Blackwell to make it a reality. Margot Morse took wonderful care of us during the entire process and her patience with us was constant.

We would like to make a special tribute of this handbook – a project born of the critical spirit to interrogate, challenge, protest, and demand change – to a special scholar and mentor who embodied such a spirit – Leah VandeBerg. Leah was a constant teacher, ally, and advocate of critical projects and helped to inform Rona's perspective and role as a critical scholar in communication studies. It is through Leah that she began to envision what should and could be possible in our intercultural worlds.

Rona Tamiko Halualani and Thomas K. Nakayama

1

Critical Intercultural
Communication Studies
At a Crossroads

Rona Tamiko Halualani
and Thomas K. Nakayama

Standing at the Crossroads

Many of us dare to go where others steer clear: across and through the junctures and ruptures of historical authority, formidable structures, and power forces that touch our encounters, relationships, and everyday lives; inside the fragmentations and displacements of cultural groups and identities – ours and those of others for whom we care; in and around the contours of our intersecting positionalities in relation to surrounding ideologies and hegemonies of society, and deep within the struggles over power among cultural groups, members, and dominant structures and forms. We have traversed these trajectories in the overlap among corollary areas such as rhetorical, cultural, critical, and feminist studies, critical communication pedagogy, organizational communication, media studies, performance studies, race and ethnic studies, and intercultural communication studies, with a wonderful diversity in approach and theoretical position and a unified, steadfast focus on culture, communication, and power. Such important work has emerged and converged into a vibrant and burgeoning body of scholarship and political engagements that we refer to as "critical intercultural communication studies."

Critical intercultural communication studies represents an exciting, productive, and rapidly growing area of inquiry within the field of intercultural communication in the larger Communication discipline and one that connects with and joins other situated fields in Communication (rhetorical, cultural, critical, and feminist studies, critical communication pedagogy, organizational communication, media studies, race and ethnic studies, interpersonal communication, performance studies, among others). This area foregrounds issues of power, context, socio-economic relations and historical/structural forces as constituting and shaping culture and intercultural communication encounters, relationships, and contexts (Collier *et al.*, 2001; Martin and Nakayama,

The Handbook of Critical Intercultural Communication, edited by Thomas K. Nakayama and Rona Tamiko Halualani. © 2010 Blackwell Publishing Ltd.

1999; Mendoza, Halualani, and Drzewiecka, 2003; Starosta and Chen, 2001, 2003). According to Martin and Nakayama (2000), a critical perspective is defined as one that addresses issues of macro contexts (historical, social, and political levels), power, relevance, and the hidden and destabilizing aspects of culture. These scholars explain that the critical perspective seeks to "understand the role of power and contextual constraints on communication in order ultimately to achieve a more equitable society" (p. 8). Moreover, a critical perspective in intercultural communication requires that we "understand how relationships emerge in historical contexts, within institutional and political forces and social norms that often invisible to some groups" and how intercultural communication relations are "constrained and enabled by institutions, ideologies, and histories" (Collier, 2002, pp. 1–2, see Lee *et al.*, 1995).

Although to some extent, scholars in the field have imagined and envisioned what critical intercultural communication studies can be (see e.g., Collier *et al.*, 2001; Martin and Nakayama, 1997, 2000; Moon, 1996; Ono, 1998; Starosta and Chen, 2001), we have not fully engaged and explored such imaginings in terms of the diverse theoretical strands and foci, the unifying points of convergence, and the stakes involved that constitute critical intercultural communication studies. We are situated in a unique moment – at a crossroads if you will – to reflect back on the steps it took to get here, take stock of where we are, and where we need to go.

Looking Back

In reflecting back, several junctures paved the way for the emergence of an area of study generally termed as "critical intercultural communication studies." In their genealogy, Halualani, Mendoza, and Drzewiecka (2009) trace the significant junctures and moves that paved such a way. They discuss the importance of scholars' calls (Asante, 1980; González and Peterson, 1993; Prosser, 1969; Smith, 1979; Lee *et al.*, 1995; Mendoza, 2005; Moon, 1996) for closer attention to historical specificity and contextual grounding in intercultural studies. Overlapping this stretch of time was a period in which several critiques of the predominant theoretical construct of culture as nation circulated (see e.g., Altman and Nakayama, 1992; Asante, 1980; González and Peterson, 1993; Moon, 1996; Ono, 1998; Smith, 1981). Yet another juncture that occurred was the rise of works that argued for the retheorizing of culture as "sites of struggle" based on power relations and ideologies (Collier *et al.*, 2001; Cooks, 2001; Martin and Nakayama, 1999; Moon, 1996; Starosta and Chen, 2001). These junctures gradually opened up and stretched the boundaries of intercultural communication inquiry and research and ignited new, complex questions about culture and communication.

These historical moves should also be contextualized in terms of the prevailing tide of knowledge formation in the field of intercultural communication in the areas of scholarly research (in the field's journals and monographs) and textbook materials. We contend that through this body of knowledge, intercultural communication was proscribed in a very specific way: as a privatized, interpersonal (one on one), equalized and neutral encounter/transaction between comparable national group members (and in some cases, racial/ethnic group members within a nation) and as such, in terms of individual (interpersonal) skill development to bridge equalized differences among cultures regardless of the context, setting, or historical/ political moment.

For instance, from the 1980s to the mid-1990s, academic journal articles dedicated to a focus on intercultural communication as well as scholarly monographs and books, primarily framed culture as nation and relied on postpositivist (cultural measurement) approaches (as argued by González and Peterson, 1993; Martin and Nakayama, 1999; Moon, 1996). There also grew a steady rise of intercultural communication textbooks and readers written for lower division undergraduate students that focused on a survey of intercultural communication concepts. The majority of these successful and multieditioned textbooks focused on an interpersonal approach to intercultural communication, emphasizing individual and group-centered attitudes and communication skills. While useful and important in its own right, such an approach glosses over the larger macro-micro process of intercultural communication, or the ways in which larger structures of power (governmental, institutional, legal, economic, and mediated forces) intermingle with microacts and encounters among/within cultural actors and groups.

In response, there have been several academic critiques of the intercultural communication field and the theoretical and methodological shortcomings of the traditional social scientific and interpretive paradigms that have dominated the field historically. Among these are works that have raised overlooked questions about the relationship between and among culture, communication, and politics, in terms of situated power interests, historical contextualization, global shifts and economic conditions, different politicized identities in terms of race, ethnicity, gender, sexuality, region, socioeconomic class, generation, and diasporic positions (e.g., Collier, 1998; Drzewiecka, 1999; González, Houston, and Chen, 1994; González and Peterson, 1993; Hall, 1992; Halualani, 1998, 2000; Lee *et al.*, 1995; Martin and Nakayama, 1999; Martin *et al.*, 1998; Mendoza, 2000; Moon, 1996; Ono, 1998; Smith, 1981). According to these critiques, a power-based perspective not only fills a void but also meets the demands of many scholars, instructors, and students who are intrigued with larger macro processes that inform intercultural relations. Likewise, in the field, scholars have been calling for a perspective – known as "critical intercultural communication studies" on intercultural communication ("the fifth moment") – through a power-based lens especially within the last fourteen years (see e.g., Collier, 1998; Collier *et al.*, 2001; González and Peterson, 1993; Lee *et al.*, 1995; Martin and Nakayama, 1999; 2000; Moon, 1996; Ono, 1998; Smith, 1981; Starosta and Chen, 2001). What followed suit from these critiques were numerous identifications of gaps in knowledge, calls to fill voids in research, and the explicit need to approach intercultural communication in a dramatically different way. This "taking stock" phase has elucidated significant questions that have not been fully engaged. These questions form the road ahead or the "forks" in the road that need to be confronted. We call your attention to these questions located at this crossroads.

Lingering Questions and Forks in the Road

In order for critical communication studies as an area of study to further grow, develop, and stay relevant (historically, politically), there are several lingering questions regarding the nature, key assumptions, lines of work and collaboration with other schools of thought, and challenges for the future of critical intercultural communication that need to be faced.

What does it mean to do critical intercultural work in communication?

The aforementioned critiques of the field underscore the need for a critically infused approach to culture and communication but do not fully articulate what this means in terms of larger goals and the role of a critical intercultural communication scholar. Indeed, many initial summaries of a critical perspective describe the larger goal of a critical intercultural communication approach as "making change," "to push against the grain of the status quo," and to "interrogate dominant power relations and structures" (Martin and Nakayama, 1997, 1999; Moon, 1996). But what does this mean for us as scholars in terms of framing and conducting our research? How do you begin to engage power when the stakes involve the larger goals of liberation, justice, voice and the power to name, the dismantling of legacies of colonialist oppression, and a culture's self-determination? And with what larger objective in mind: as an intellectual project only or one that progresses into a form of advocacy, activism, and or action effort? It is important to designate what our work is aspiring to be and do and our unique role as academics, scholars, educators, intellectuals, activists, and practitioners. We can, perhaps, take a cue from cultural studies and Stuart Hall's (1996) reading of Gramsci's concept of the "organic intellectual" who must "work on two fronts at one and the same time":

> On the one hand, we had to be at the very forefront of intellectual theoretical work because, as Gramsci says, it is the job of the organic intellectual to know more than the traditional intellectuals do: really know, not just pretend to know, not just to have the facility of knowledge, but to know deeply and profoundly ... the second aspect is just as crucial: that the organic intellectual cannot absolve himself or herself from the responsibility of transmitting those ideas, that knowledge, through the intellectual function, to those who do not belong, professionally, in the intellectual class. And unless those two fronts are operating at the same time, or at least unless those two ambitions are part of the project of cultural studies, you can get enormous theoretical advance without any engagement at the level of the political project. (Hall, 1996, p. 268)

As "organic intellectuals" and critical intercultural communication scholars, we must navigate through and stay true to the highest quality of analyzing power and paving the way to transgress and break down that with which we interrogate.

Furthermore, might we also gain from cultural studies the reconceptualization of culture and intercultural communication contexts, discourses, and cases as *political projects* that require inquiry, investigation, historicization, reflexivity about one's interests and location, and translation for other audiences, purposes, and uses (Hall, 1996)? That is, our engagements of culture, power, and intercultural communication represent projects with urgencies and much at stake for real people and having real consequences. Political projects also connote a continuous line of work, change, and commitment to them; these are not fixed, one-time dalliances with a topic. Instead, these projects are sustained works that are continually pursued, worked on, and traced. In this way, critical intercultural scholars can better craft timely responses and strategies for how to interrupt dominant conditions and constructions of power. How we approach this question requires not just more dialogue among scholars but also more attempts to make visible (in published, online, performative forms and demos) the full cycle of critical intercultural communication as political projects (from inquiry to analysis to reflection to praxis).

> *What is the unique role that only critical intercultural communication scholarship is meant to take up and the area that a critical perspective is uniquely designed and equipped to shed light on? And what are the larger assumptions and tenets of such work?*

Critical intercultural communication studies is best suited to pay close attention to and follow how macro conditions and structures of power (the authority of History, economic and market conditions, formal political sphere, institutional arenas, and ideologies) play into and share microacts/processes of communication between/ among cultural groups/members. Critical perspectives have always been finely attuned to revealing great insight on the larger, hidden (beneath-the-surface) and visible (what we see but take-for-granted given its naturalized appearance) aspects of power that constitute intercultural communication encounters and relations. Such a view has been obscured through the field's chronically singular focus on interpersonal acts between intercultural interactants and two-group comparisons along scales that are presumed to be culturally shared and equivalent. A critical perspective's penchant for tracing the historical specificity and globalized economic conditions surrounding and constituting intercultural contexts is especially useful given that history, economics, and power have always positioned cultural group members and their identities disproportionately to one another within and across contexts. There is likely much more by way of dimensions, layers, and intersections of power (and aspects that we have yet to fully recognize and understand) that can be revealed and unpacked through a critical perspective. Thus, there are limitless possibilities for what critical intercultural communication studies can shed light on in terms of intracultural and intercultural relations on local–global levels. The truth of the matter is that we may not even realize the full potential of this perspective and what it can uncover about culture and intercultural dimensions. It is an exciting time to fully explore the possibilities and take in all of the different views.

Moreover, through such a view, critical intercultural communication studies holds recast, loosely defined assumptions about **culture, communication**, and **inter-culturality** in relation to power.

Culture

First, as Halualani, Drzewiecka, and Mendoza (2003) argue, a critical intercultural perspective retheorizes *culture as an ideological struggle* between and among competing vested interests, a move that requires us to go beyond empiricist explanations to account for the constitution of intercultural interactions within the constraints of historic power relations. In other words, there needs to be a move away from an unproblematized description and characterization of culture as given, or as an essential (natural/internal) set of traits or characteristics or psychological tendencies possessed by a group of individuals merely by virtue of their geographically "belonging together" (Halualani, Drzewiecka, and Mendoza, 2003). Several scholars have previously argued that it is important instead to turn to conceptualizing culture through power and "contest the notion of 'culture' as unproblematically shared" (Moon, 1996, p. 75). In their dialectical explication of intercultural communication, Martin and Nakayama (2000) explain that "culture ... is not just a variable, nor benignly socially constructed but a site of struggle where various communication meanings are constructed ..." (p. 8). In other words, they argue that cultures are differentially positioned in relationship to one another within societal structures, material conditions, power relations and as such, culture becomes a field of forces where competing interests vie for dominance and control (Halualani, Drzewiecka, and Mendoza, 2003).

There is a necessary theoretical move, then from "culture" to "ideology," or from understanding culture as a neutral, innocent place to one always and already implicated in power relations where differently positioned subjects and social entities (e.g., the nationstate) compete for advantage and control of the process of meaning production (Halualani, Drzewiecka, and Mendoza, 2003). This entails, too, analyzing cultural meanings and practices in the context of particular subjects' interests and positionings vis-à-vis the ideological operation of power within a specific given social formation.

Culture is therefore an assemblage of meanings and representations that are vested with or are reified and spoken via different power interests, most notably by dominant structures (nationstate and its arms, law and governance, institutions, the economy, and the media) and cultural groups themselves (Hall, 1985). Thus, to say that culture is "a site of struggle" is to point to the process whereby competing interests (dominant structures and cultural communities) shape different representations of culture from different positionalities of power (Hall, 1980, 1985). The view then of culture as a set of socially created/shared meanings and practices must always go hand-in-hand with attention to the structures of power (government, law and court system, economy and modes of production, education, and the media) that attended its constitution (Halualani, Drzewiecka, and Mendoza, 2003). This reconceptualization of culture does not mean that individuals are then merely passive consumers of culture; rather, in their quotidian performance of it, they participate in actively creating and recreating meanings that are made available to them by competing ideologies.

Communication

Culture as a site of struggle imbues "communication" not as some equalizing, neutral channel of expression that is widely reproduced in the field of communication studies; communication is not just a way of speaking, a set of utterances. Communication involves the creation, constitution, and intertwining of situated meanings, social practices, structures, discourses, and the nondiscursive. Culture is therefore a larger social formation constituted by communicative meaning-making practices (or dialectical exchanges among meanings, practices, and structures). *Communication, then, encompasses the processes and practices of articulation.* For example, Hall (1980) in his well-cited and very important essay, suggests a different way of conceptualizing communication via a four-part theory of communication (different from content analysis), particularly for mass communication research and media studies. He complicates and retheorizes the process of communication as in mass communication(s) research in which there is a circulation circuit or loop with a linear set-up between the sender, message, and receiver. Rather than being a linear, equivalent process, he argues for a structured conception of the different moments as a "complex structure of relation" (During, 1993, p. 91). As described by Slack (1996), the process of communication had been theorized as the mechanism whereby correspondence between meanings is encoded (the what) and the effects that meaning generates is guaranteed. Hall challenged this, arguing that there are no intrinsic identities in a neutralizing, de-historizing process. Instead, the components of the process (e.g., sender, receiver, message, meaning) are themselves articulations, without necessarily essential meanings – thus, we are compelled to rethink communication as largely a process not of correspondence but of articulation – that there is more within communication than a reliable model of encoding/decoding (as Hall demonstrates and Morley, 1980 with television news as well). So, what happens is that if every component or meaning in the process of communication is itself an articulation, then they are relatively autonomous moments, in which no one moment can fully guarantee the next with which it is articulated (Hall, 1980, p. 129) – so autonomy is somewhat relative (much like Althusserian structuralism) and breaks articulation from a necessary noncorrespondence risk, thereby demonstrating that some articulations are located differently (in particular specific locations) and thus vested with different degrees of power and privilege. Through communication as articulation, we should analyze how particular meanings, practices, discourses (systems of meanings, messages, and symbols as well as practices of speaking) institutions, and relations – are all somewhat autonomous but organized into unities that are effective, which may be relatively disempowering and enabling (and with these practices as lines of tendential force). Theorizing communication in this way offers some interesting methodological detours and strategic paths. In this way, the specificity of communication allows for examining how these forces

at a certain moment, yield intelligible meanings, enter the circuits of culture – the field of cultural practices – that shape the understandings and conceptions of the

world of men and women in their ordinary everyday social calculations, construct
them as potential social subjects and have the effect of organizing the ways in which
they come to or form consciousness of the world. (Hall, 1989, p. 49).

Studying/participating in communication in terms of a struggle to mean and to
connect meanings, involves a process of rearticulating contexts, that is of "examining
and intervening in the changing ensemble of forces (or articulations that create and
maintain identities that have real concrete effects. "Understanding a practice involves
theoretically and historically (re)-constructing its context" (Grossberg, 1992, p. 55).
The goal is not to situate a phenomenon in a context, but to map a context, mapping
the very identity that brings the context into focus – context is not something out
there "within which practices occur or which influence the development of practices.
Rather identities, practices, and effects generally, constitute the very context within
which they are practices, identities, or effects" (Grossberg, 1992, p. 125).

Interculturality

The notion of "intercultural" may be too reminiscent of a traditional view of an
equal line or exchange between cultural groups – a notion that the critical perspective quickly challenges and de-mystifies. Instead, a critical perspective reconceptual-
izes the terms "intercultural" and "intracultural" as broad spatial metaphors through
which to analyze more fully the relationship between culture, identity, and power.
Such a broadening transforms the notion of "inter" from connoting actual interaction between culturally different "dialogue partners" to the intersecting layers of
cultural, discursive, and signifying practices that constitute power relations within
and around groups. Instead, " 'inter' and 'intra' could symbolize temporarily useful
spatial metaphors for re-thinking how culture involves contested sites of identification as opposed to others and the resulting political consequences" (Halualani,
Mendoza, and Drzewiecka, 2009, p. 17). Interculturality as a metaphor and movement of power represents a form of articulation and communication that sutures
into place as a homology the seemingly natural linkages between a place, group, and
subjectivity (Lavie and Swedenburg, 1996). This notion could be productively
deployed to examine the different relations of power within and across contexts.

We must keep in mind that the assumptions above are mediated by and read
through the different histories, conjectures, discourses, and theoretical positions
held within a context or surrounding a group. There is a diversity of history, politics, stakes, and power interests involved but a united in these aforementioned
presuppositions.

*How does a critical framing of intercultural scholarship change the nature of theorizing
and methodological practice?*

As a result of the macro-micro focus of critical intercultural communication, the
roles of theory and method become complicated. How do we "build" or identify

theory with such moving contexts and factors such as history, structures, and economics? Rather than the pasting of theoretical molds onto different contexts, embracing the notion of "theorizing" could prove useful. Similar to cultural studies, a critical scholar looks into a setting with a particular philosophical lens to examine culture and power, and this "context," or the combination of metacontext and analyzed setting then informs a theoretical formation about the setting. As another movement, the theoretical framework bears meaning upon the analyzed setting. For example, a scholar who believes that the struggle around politically created culture exists predominantly among lower class ethnic women because of their multiple oppressions of gender, race, and class, will approach contexts of ethnic female communities. With their own philosophical assumptions, the researcher would delve into such a context and analyze its specific material conditions and history. From this critical exploration, the scholar can propose a type of theoretical framework based on examined specificities (e.g., histories, experiences, economics, social relations) about the field of forces in that context. Perhaps, the scholar would develop a theoretical notion that ethnic women resist dominant Anglo patriarchal culture in their "talk" about oppressive meanings and texts and use this construct to critically analyze the "culture." This theoretical framework and resulting critical analysis would then seep back into and inform the analyzed setting by uncovering its underlying cultural practices. As a result, critical work recognizes that there is no theory in advance and no social process of culture without some theoretical sense-making; it travels through a trajectory of theory from and towards context (e.g., metacontext and the studied setting) (Grossberg, 1993).

Methodologically speaking, examining macro to micro dimensions requires varied tools and processes (for e.g., discourse analysis, political economy, in-depth interviewing, oral histories, auto/ethnography, performance and narrative analysis, and surveys). The vast array of theorizings and methods suitable for critical analyses further complicates the "heuristic" and dialogic functions of this kind of intellectual work. But, alas, the goal is to not merely build or propagate research for its own sake but rather to yield multiple insights over time that can be shared and discussed in degree and by historical moment within, through, and across contexts and through postcolonial comparison (as it allows).

What are some key dimensions or foci of critical intercultural research and what does such a perspective yield in terms of insight, inquiry, and analysis of culture and intercultural communication?

There is still much we do not know about critical intercultural communication studies and what it can do and proffer. For instance, we need to uncover the major macro aspects that can be looked at through this perspective and what can still be learned about specific cultural and intercultural communication phenomena and contexts, ones that have not been engaged before or ones that have for too long been studied in a particular way and can be viewed differently through a critical lens. More specifically, there are topics that can be engaged for key insights not yet uncovered in other approaches, topics such as race, language inequalities, local-to-global articulations, diasporas, and much more. By exploring and contributing to this area of critical intercultural communication studies, our conclusions and theorizings about culture and intercultural communication can be furthered.

> *How do we take the larger collection of critical intercultural communication research, informed by multiple theoretical and perspectival traditions and spread across various fields of communication scholarship and outside disciplines, and engage these works in meaningful and productive dialogue around insights, conclusions, and question-probing and provide these with a deeper, integrated focus to have important metacritical conversations that characterize the continual development of perspectives and forms of scholarship (as even in the case of critical theory, cultural studies work, postcolonial perspectives, feminist studies, among others)?*

The idea is to not "police" or discipline the boundaries of critical intercultural communication studies or create some grand narrative but to stake out some positions and meeting points to build a diverse community with webs of connection, convergence, and vested stakes. With rich critical intercultural work spread out across disciplines, regions, institutions, conferences, and publication outlets (by graduate students, junior faculty, and advanced stage faculty), how we as a larger community amass together the collected insights and political projects and create a vehicle through which we share, communicate, converse, and push each other on our projects, can help stretch our analyses and interventions towards our aims for justice, liberation, and meaningful, transformative change.

> *How do we not let our academic need to trace, name, identify, and record critical scholarship and its varied nature smother or undermine a necessary and key focus on historical specificity, contextualization, situated power dynamics, and fluid theorizings in critical work?*

We understand the academic obsession for boundary delineation and identification of positions (especially in the United States). However, it is key for us to consider how such a need to name, identify, and solidify may in fact suffocate that with which we critique in terms of the larger contextualizations and situated power dynamics that constitute such phenomena. Reconciling these often conflicting aspects of critical work merits more attention and careful movement so that the political projects (and the larger aims of these) always take priority.

> *How does such work link up to, contrast and interact with intercultural scholarship from other paradigmatic perspectives? Or does it and does it even have to?*

Martin and Nakayama (1999) have long pushed for a dialogic approach in the field of intercultural communication among paradigmatic schools of thought so as to stretch the collective knowledge in the field. Indeed, linkages among the postpositivist, interpretive, and critical approaches can magnify great insight on culture and intercultural communication especially in terms of multilayered contexts that involve privatized experience, perception, and behavior and larger structures, conditions, and histories. But we must also ask ourselves about the areas in which these approaches depart and collide. There is no denying that there are fundamental differences in assumptions about culture and communication and the goals of intellectual work. To constantly feel the pressure of folding in to and accommodating (or dialoguing with) other perspectives may inadvertently weaken the potency of critical analyses and engagements and risk defusing and domesticating politically charged projects. We should at least ask what the risks are to our own work as critical scholars with political projects when we do this. Some may have tangled with the question of how to dialogue with a perspective that has historically reproduced and reified colonialist myths and images of a cultural group and ones that she or he is trying to dismantle in their work. Can we align with dominant arms of Science and Governmental Classifications that have so persistently punished a group, a people, or a land for whom/which we are advocating? The question may actually be not whether or not to link up or dialogue but when it is appropriate and useful to the contexts and groups with which/whom we work and focus on. Ultimately, critical scholars must face head-on the tricky issue of interacting and collaborating with other colliding perspectives and at what cost.

What are the future directions of critical intercultural communication work and pathways that need to be continually revisited and others that have been sorely neglected?

Through these forks in the road, we stand at the crossroads of critical intercultural communication studies with even more questions about what the future holds for the area and for the engaged political projects. Our future cannot be tentatively mapped out without doing the painstaking work of traversing this crossroads (and the forks we still face). This handbook is our concerted attempt to broach several of these lingering questions and delineate a path through which there is continued inquiry, dialogue, debate, and energy on this road.

This Handbook of Critical Intercultural Communication

What we as intercultural scholars and contributors have noted is that there has yet to be a more definitive move in intercultural communication as a field to go beyond critique to sustained production of new knowledge on intercultural communication phenomena (and not just conceptualizations) based on a critical perspective. A possible reason for this lacuna may be the lack of clarification of what this perspective is all about, what its constitutive elements are including its theoretical and methodological possibilities. The aim of this handbook therefore is to push critical intercultural communication studies into the next necessary phase for the intercultural communication field: the articulation and explication of the critical paradigm in intercultural communication.

This *Handbook of Critical Intercultural Communication* stands as one of the first collections that features all works and projects through the critical intercultural communication studies perspective in communication studies. As a focused collection, it aims to tour what might be the constitutive elements of a critical theoretical tradition in intercultural communication scholarship. While some areas of communication have made more definitive moves towards theorizing communication from a critical perspective, notably media studies, rhetoric, organizational communication, and performance studies, intercultural communication remains at the threshold of this paradigmatic challenge.

Compared to other intellectual courses, the theoretical and contextual range of critical intercultural communication studies has not been fully delineated, articulated, or explored, although scholars have argued for its creation since the 1970s. (There are also several critiques that call for, but do not explicitly detail a critical intercultural communication perspective, e.g., González and Peterson, 1993; Smith, 1981, with the exception of Martin and Nakayama, 2000.) As this intellectual course is still developing and taking shape and is in dire need of delineation, a *Handbook of Critical Intercultural Communication* is designed to serve as a consolidated resource of essays that highlight critical intercultural communication studies, its historical inception, logics, terms, and possibilities. In addition, it will also serve as a valuable tool to help graduate students, scholars, and faculty members showcase, articulate, and imagine what kinds of work can constitute and speak to the area of critical intercultural communication studies. Our companion will be one of the first volumes to sketch out the intellectual terrain of critical intercultural communication studies in terms of the following: (a) revisiting and reengaging important scholars and their key works (which have been updated and recast for today) that enabled such a course of study and (b) presenting works that demonstrate the new and vibrant possibilities of engaging culture and intercultural relations and contexts in a "critical" way. It is our hope that this *Handbook of Critical Intercultural Communication* will help scholars revisit, assess, and reflect on the formation of critical intercultural communication studies and where it needs to go in terms of theorizing, knowledge production, and social justice engagement. Our handbook will also highlight the contemporary issues and debates that are shaping the area of critical intercultural communication studies. The handbook is organized in terms of four main sections: (a) critical junctures and reflections, (b) critical dimensions, (c) critical topics, and (d) critical visions. Part interludes punctuate the handbook with specified contexts for each of these main portions.

The first part of the handbook will highlight the formative critical moments and "junctures" through which a critical perspective first emerged and "took flight" within intercultural communication. In unique fashion, this part includes current reflections and insights of influential intercultural communication scholars such as Alberto González, Dreama G. Moon, Wendy Leeds-Hurwitz, William J. Starosta and Guo-Ming Chen, Leda Cooks, Judith N. Martin and Thomas K. Nakayama, Kent A. Ono, and S. Lily Mendoza, who wrote original essays that created the impetus for a critical line of inquiry. As opposed to merely including the reprints of these essays, these scholars have contributed present-day reflections and updated insights on those essays and their thoughts in the current moment about the critical turn in intercultural communication studies (in terms of the questions – What does it mean to do critical work? What is the unique role that only critical intercultural communication scholarship is meant to take up? And what are the larger assumptions and tenets of such work?). This section serves the purpose of referring back to several key works that historically shaped a critical orientation to intercultural communication studies while at the same time adding a new spin to these works through the contemporary/postreflections of the authors.

With critically incisive work from Raka Shome, Kathryn Sorrells, Yoshitaka Miike, Aimee Carrillo Rowe, Crispin Thurlow, Yukio Tsuda, Melissa L. Curtin, Marouf Hasian, and Jolanta A. Drzewiecka, the second part of the handbook highlights key dimensions – theorizing, language and hierarchies of meaning and value, and historical memory – that constitute and drive a critical perspective of intercultural communication. Such dimensions touch on the main aspects that a critical work is well suited to uncover and interrogate such as politically situated theorizing, historical context, ideologies and hegemonies, structural/material and interactional forms of power.

Next, the handbook features significant and urgent topics and subjects within critical intercultural communication studies and represents examples of critical works and political projects that form the larger body of this area. Indeed, these works represent actual case studies and specific political projects that focus on different cultural groups/contexts from a critical intercultural perspective. Such work collectively demonstrates the dynamic and politicized nature of the critical intercultural communication studies perspective as presented in specific studies (and begin to answer the recurring questions – What is a critical intercultural communication study and what does it look like?). As a unique feature of this book, the authors present mini-case studies and incorporate reflexive comments on the goals and assumptions they made in their political projects so that the reader can understand the complexities of theorizing and researching issues of cultural politics and communication.

Topics presented in this section, such as gender, race intersections, disability/ability/subjectivity, inclusion/exclusion, assimilation and coculturation, diasporas and diasporic politics, postcolonialism, globalization, intercultural training and dialogue frameworks, and alliances with other fields of critical communication studies, represent ongoing, contemporary concerns of critical intercultural communication scholars. Here many scholars with intersectional identity locations and research interests across fields in and out of the Communication discipline (such as Lara Lengel and Scott C. Martin; Ronald L. Jackson II and Jamie Moshin; Bryant Keith Alexander; Jim Perkinson; Bernadette Marie Calafell and Shane Moreman; Lisa A. Flores, Karen Lee Ashcraft, and Tracy Marafiote; John T. Warren; Deanna L. Fassett; Richard Morris; Victoria Chen; Etsuko Kinefuchi; Radhika Gajjala; Melissa Steyn; Hsin-I Cheng; Sara DeTurk; and Brenda J. Allen) speak to these concerns with a specific context in mind and directly link this concern to a critical perspective and the insights, risks, and consequences that follow from taking up such a view.

Finally, we as editors of this collection conclude the handbook with a delineation of what the intellectual course of critical intercultural communication studies will come to be in the future. It is our hope to envision, imagine, and aspire for what critical intercultural communication studies can become and do for the world.

References

Altman, K., and Nakayama, T. (1992) The fallacy of the assumption of a unitary culture. Paper presented at the annual meeting of the Speech Communication Association, Chicago.

Asante, M.K. (1980) Intercultural communication: An inquiry into research direction. *Communication Yearbook*, 4, 401–410.

Collier, M.J. (1998) Researching cultural identity: Reconciling interpretive and postcolonial perspectives, in *International and Intercultural Communication Annual XXI: Communication and Identity*, (eds A. González and D. Tanno), Sage, Thousand Oaks, CA, pp. 122–147.

Collier, M.J. (2002) Transforming communication about culture: Critical new directions, in *International and Intercultural Communication Annual, 24*, (ed. M.J. Collier), Sage, Thousand Oaks, CA, pp. 1–8.

Collier, M.J., Hegde, R.S., Lee, W.S. *et al.* (2001) Dialogue on the edges: Ferment in communication and culture, in *Transforming Communication about Culture: Critical New Directions, International and Intercultural Communication Annual, 24*, (ed. M.J. Collier), Sage, Thousand Oaks, CA, pp. 219–280.

Cooks, L. (2001) From distance and uncertainty to research and pedagogy in the borderlands: implications for the future of intercultural communication. *Communication Theory*, 11, 339–351.

Drzewiecka, J.A. (1999) Immigrant identity formations: Between cultures, nations, and politics. Doctoral dissertation. Arizona State University.

During, S. (1993) *The Cultural Studies Reader*, Routledge, London.

González, A., Houston, M., and Chen, V. (eds) (1994) Introduction in *Our Voices: Essays in Culture, Ethnicity, and Communication*, Roxbury Publishing Co., Los Angeles, pp. xiii–2.

González, A., and Peterson, T.R. (1993) Enlarging conceptual boundaries: A critique of research in intercultural communication, in *Transforming Visions: Feminist Critiques in Communication Studies* (ed. S.P. Bowen), Hampton Press, New York, pp. 249–278.

Grossberg, L. (1992) *We Gotta Get Out of This Place: Popular Conservatism and Postmodern Culture*, Routledge, New York.

Grossberg, L. (1993) Cultural studies and/in new worlds. *Critical Studies in Mass Communication*, 10, 1–22.

Hall, S. (1980) Encoding, decoding, in *Culture, Media, Language*, (eds S. Hall, D. Hobson, A. Lowe *et al.*), Hutchinson, London, pp. 128–139.

Hall, S. (1985) Signification, representation, ideology: Althusser and the poststructuralist debates. *Critical Studies in Mass Communication*, 2, 91–114.

Hall, S. (1989) Ideology and communication theory, in *Rethinking Communication, Vol.1, Paradigm Issues*, (eds B. Dervin, L. Grossberg, B. O'Keefe *et al.*), Sage, Thousand Oaks, CA, pp. 40–52.

Hall, S. (1992) Theories of culture and communication. *Communication Theory*, 1, 50–70.

Hall, S. (1996) Cultural studies and its theoretical legacies, in *Stuart Hall: Critical Dialogues in Cultural Studies*, (eds D. Morley and K.H. Chen), Routledge, London, pp. 262–275.

Halualani, R.T. (1998) Seeing through the screen: The struggle of culture, in *Readings in Cultural Contexts* (eds J.N. Martin, T.K. Nakayama, and L.A. Flores) Mayfield, Mountain View, CA, pp. 264–275.

Halualani, R.T. (2000) Rethinking 'ethnicity' as structural-cultural project(s): Notes on the interface between cultural studies and intercultural communication. *International Journal of Intercultural Relations*, 24, 579–602.

Halualani, R.T., Drzewiecka, J.A., and Mendoza, S.L. (2003) "Culture as struggle": Retheorizing from a critical intercultural communication perspective. Unpublished paper.

Halualani, R.T., Mendoza, S.L., and Drzewiecka, J.A. (2009) Critical junctures in intercultural communication studies: A review. *The Review of Communication Journal*, 9 (1), 17–35.

Lavie, S., and Swedenburg, T. (1996) Introduction: Displaclement, diaspora, and geographies of identity, in *Displacement, Diaspora, and Geographies of Identity* (eds S. Labvie and T. Swedenburg). Duke University Press, Durham, pp. 1–25.

Lee, W.S., Chung, J., Wang, J., *et al.* (1995) A sociohistorical approach to intercultural communication. *Howard Journal of Communications*, 6, 262–291.

Martin, J.N., and Nakayama, T.K. (1997) *Intercultural Communication in Contexts*, Mayfield, Mountain View, CA.

Martin, J.N., and Nakayama, T.K. (1999) Thinking about culture dialectically. *Communication Theory*, 9, 1–25.

Martin, J.N., and Nakayama, T.K. (2000) *Intercultural Communication in Contexts*, 2nd edn, Mayfield, Mountain View, CA.

Martin, J.N., Nakayama, T.K., and Flores, L.A. (1998) A dialectical approach to intercultural communication, in *Readings in Cultural Contexts*, Mayfield, Mountain View, CA, pp. 5–14.

Mendoza, S.L. (2000) Between the homeland and the diaspora: The politics of theorizing Filipino and Filipino American identities, Doctoral dissertation, Arizona State University.

Mendoza, S.L. (2005) Tears in the archive: Creating memory to survive and contest empire, in *Among US: Essays on Identity, Belonging, and Intercultural Competence*, rev. edn (eds R. Lustig and J. Koester), Pearson, Boston, MA, pp. 233–254.

Mendoza, S.L., Halualani, R.T., and Drzewiecka, J.A. (2003) Moving the discourse on identities in intercultural communication: Structure, culture, and resignifications. *Communication Quarterly*, 50 (3/4), 312–327.

Moon, D.G. (1996) Concepts of "culture": Implications for intercultural communication research. *Communication Quarterly*, 44, 70–84.

Morley, D. (1980) *The "Nationwide" Audience: Structure and Decoding*, BFI, London.

Ono, K.A. (1998) Problematizing "nation" in intercultural communication research, in *Communication and Identity across Cultures* (eds D. Tanno and A. González), Sage, Thousand Oaks, CA, pp. 34–55.

Prosser, M.H. (1969) *Sow the Wind and Reap the Whirlwind: Heads of State Address the United Nations*, vol. 1 and 2, William Morrow, New York.

Slack, J.D. (1996) The theory and method of articulation in cultural studies, in *Stuart Hall: Critical Dialogues in Cultural Studies* (eds D. Morley and K.H. Chen), Routledge, London, pp. 112–127.

Smith, A.G. (1981) Content decisions in intercultural communication. *Southern Speech Communication Journal*, 47, 252–262.

Smith, A.L. (1979) *Rhetoric of Black Power*, Greenwood, Westport, CT.

Starosta, W.J., and Chen, G.-M. (2001) A fifth moment in intercultural communication?: A dialogue. Paper presented at the meeting of the National Communication Association, Atlanta, GA.

Starosta, W.J., and Chen, G.-M. (2003) *Ferment in the Intercultural Field: Axiology/Value/ Praxis – International and Intercultural Communication Annual*, 26, Sage, Thousand Oaks, CA.

Part I

Critical Junctures and Reflections In Our Field
A Revisiting

Introduction to Part I

New trajectories and lenses on the macro structures and conditions of power in relation to the microcommunication practices in intercultural contexts, emerged out of the critical turn in intercultural communication studies. Much of this can be credited to several key scholars who dared to question accepted positions and proclaimed "truths" around culture, intercultural communication, nation, intercultural theorizing, and intercultural inquiry. For example, Wendy Leeds-Hurwitz (1990) provided one of the few historicizations of the field of intercultural communication and grounded it in the economic and political realities of the time. Likewise, two of the most notable scholars who pushed for a critical perspective in the field, Judith N. Martin and Thomas K. Nakayama (2000) presented a compelling case for a dialogic approach to intercultural communication, one that made necessary a space for a perspective to help "understand the role of power and contextual constraints on communication in order ultimately to achieve a more equitable society" (p. 8). In her critical genealogy of culture in the field, Dreama G. Moon (1996) powerfully traced how intercultural communication scholarship had employed specific constructs of culture in different historical periods and constructs that related to the political and economic ideologies prevailing in those moments. She illustrated how various forms of research did not merely approach the culture the way "it is" but rather worked off of a specific conceptualizing and framing of culture shaped by history, context, and politics. As one of the first critiques of the intercultural communication field, Alberto González and Tarla Rai Peterson (1993) contributed a feminist critique of past intercultural communication, arguing that such work never took seriously the ways in which power positions, value-laden perspectives, and reigning ideologies play into intercultural encounters and relationships. Kent A. Ono (1998) continued such important work by problematizing the field's preoccupation with, overreliance on, and ultimate reification of the construct of culture as nation, which obscured the complexities found within and across nations (as in shifting national identity politics, emerging transnational formations, and intercultural relations within – and that often belied – national frameworks). As another example, S. Lily Mendoza (2005) in one of the most important pieces about theorizing in critical intercultural communication, delves into difficult terrain: the conundrum of recasting our analyses of culture and intercultural contexts through a focus on power relations, historical situatedness, and positionality but in a way that does not dismiss or exclude collective representations or reframings. For Mendoza, a critical retheorizing requires close attention to the situated politics and power dynamics at hand (who is involved, in what historical and political moment, articulated by whom, in what positioning, and in terms of what is at stake). Using the notion of "borderlands," Leda Cooks (2001) pushes the field of intercultural communication to consider and enact critical scholarship that starts from the presupposition point of (in)differences, inequalities, and unequal positionings in intercultural relations as opposed to a presumed point of equality and mutual understanding. Finally, after historicizing the critical turn in the field to the 1980s, William J. Starosta and Guo-Ming Chen (2003) boldly name the emergence of a fifth moment in the field, or rather the formation of a critical perspective among the dominant research paradigms (positivist/postpositivist, interpretive) in intercultural communication. While urging the field to reexamine itself in light of and through a critical perspective, these scholars (among several others not featured here) paved the way for an explicitly critical turn in intercultural communication studies, one that would be a mainstay for continued growth, evolution, and revision.

In the first part of this handbook, we return to these scholars and their insights in new essays through which they reflect upon and update their aforementioned analyses that greatly impacted critical intercultural communication studies. Such a revisiting stands as a rare treat through which we can take in first hand the current ideas, conclusions, and retrospectives of these influential scholars as they both look to the past and the future of critical intercultural communication.

References

Cooks, L. (2001) From distance and uncertainty to research and pedagogy in the borderlands: Implications for the future of intercultural communication. *Communication Theory*, 11, 339–351.

González, A., and Peterson, T.R. (1993) Enlarging conceptual boundaries: A critique of research in intercultural communication, in *Transforming Visions: Feminist Critiques in Communication Studies*, (ed. S.P. Bowen), Hampton Press, New York, pp. 249–278.

Leeds-Hurwitz, W. (1990) Notes on the history of intercultural communication: The Foreign Service Institute and the mandate for intercultural training. *Quarterly Journal of Speech*, 76, 262–281.

Martin, J., and Nakayama, T.K. (2000) *Intercultural Communication in Contexts*, Mountain View, CA: Mayfield.

Mendoza, S.L. (2005) From a theory of certainty to a theory of challenge: Ethnography of an intercultural communication class. *Intercultural Communication Studies*, 14, 82–99.

Moon, D.G. (1996) Concepts of "culture": Implications for intercultural communication research. *Communication Quarterly*, 44, 70–84.

Ono, K.A. (1998) Problematizing "nation" in intercultural communication research, in *Communication and Identity across Cultures*, (eds D. Tanno and A. González), Sage, Thousand Oaks, CA, pp. 34–55.

Starosta, W.J., and Chen, G.-M. (2003) "Ferment" an ethic of caring and the corrective power of dialogue, in *International and Intercultural Communication Annual 26: Ferment in the Intercultural Field: Axiology/Value/Praxis*, (eds W.J. Starosta and G.-M. Chen), Sage, Thousand Oaks, CA, pp. 3–23.

2

Writing the Intellectual History of Intercultural Communication

Wendy Leeds-Hurwitz

Critical intercultural communication, like most theoretical approaches, means different things to different people. At its heart, a critical perspective addresses issues of macro contexts, one implication being that we must study the contexts of our own research efforts.[1] It is naïve to think that the best ideas magically float to the top to become accepted practice; there are always more concrete explanations for why specific ideas seemed relevant or useful at a specific moment in time.[2] All critical approaches, including critical intercultural communication, are about questioning the status quo. It is worth the effort to learn the history of our own assumptions, to consider when it is time to change them.

My own research is more appropriately described as interpretive than critical, but there are at least some shared assumptions.[3]

1 Reality is socially constructed, and people are active interpreters of their social environment.
2 Selves and relationships are dynamic, emergent concepts, maintained or changed through communication in multiple social situations.
3 Cultures result from the negotiated creation and shared use of symbols and meanings.
4 Intercultural communication occurs when individuals using different cultural symbols and meanings interact; thus intercultural communication often involves a mismatch of codes.

Some years ago I published an article entitled "Notes in the History of Intercultural Communication: The Foreign Service Institute and the mandate for intercultural training" (Leeds-Hurwitz, 1990). This was never intended to be a complete or definitive history of intercultural communication; rather, my intention was to write several related "Notes" on the history of intercultural communication which, when

The Handbook of Critical Intercultural Communication, edited by Thomas K. Nakayama and Rona Tamiko Halualani. © 2010 Blackwell Publishing Ltd.

taken together, would tell the whole story of how this part of the discipline of communication developed. As often happens, I got side-tracked into other projects, and did not return to this one. To move a little further along that path, I would like now to document some of the other strands that should be considered when writing the history of intercultural communication.

Intellectual history is inherently critical because it questions *why* we do what we do. Disciplinary history in particular asks: *why do we study what we study (and not something else) in the ways in we study it (and not other ways)?* In the history documented here, three more specific questions are at issue.

1   Why do intercultural scholars so often assume that each culture has a set of characteristics shared by all members equally (even though much research has demonstrated that cultures are not typically homogeneous)?
2   Why do intercultural scholars so often focus only on psychological characteristics (even though there are many other aspects of culture that could be the emphasis of study)?
3   Why do intercultural scholars so often assume that it is adequate to interview members of a culture living outside their culture as typical representatives of that culture (even though typical members of a culture stay within it, and do not choose to live elsewhere)?

These questions will be answered in the remainder of this chapter. The short answer to all three is that a study of the anthropological precursors to intercultural communication research, especially the research traditions known as national character, culture and personality, and culture at a distance studies, have led to a set of assumptions many current researchers take for granted, rather than questioning how they came to appear to be so obvious, and whether they are the best assumptions for us now. These approaches were historically necessary in the 1930s and 1940s, but 80 years later, it is certainly time to question their appropriateness for the current international context.

In what follows, I will outline people and organizations that have been important in the history of intercultural communication, but which are generally ignored by current scholars. One obvious question is why these people and organizations have been so thoroughly forgotten by communication scholars, when they helped to establish the direction of our work today. I will return to that question after introducing them.

In these pages, Edward Hall, and the Foreign Service Institute in the late 1940s-early 1950s, will not be a concern, since that is the part of the story already published (Leeds-Hurwitz, 1990). Instead, the focus here will be on the period immediately preceding that part of the story, the late-1930s and 1940s, describing a strand of research that did not lead directly to intercultural communication, but that still shared basic concerns and assumptions with it. The 1930s and 1940s are important because the first application of anthropological concepts, such as culture, to real modern-day problems of interaction between members of different cultures occurred then. It is worth talking about this bit of history today because most people in communication do not know much, if anything, about this work, despite its influence on our practices today.

used ethngraphs)

Anthropology in the 1930s and 1940s

By World War II, anthropology as a unique discipline had become an accepted part of the university core; the department at Columbia University in New York, under the direction of Franz Boas, was the central hub (Darnell, 2001; Leeds-Hurwitz, 2004a; Murray, 1994). Anthropologists used ethnography as one of their main methods, traveling the globe to document a wide variety of cultures (Leeds-Hurwitz, 2004b). During war time, however, anthropologists unable to engage in the traditional fieldwork, that would have taken them outside the United States, had to develop new ways to examine cultures (Cassidy, 1982). Of the 300 anthropologists in the country at the time "all but a half dozen were involved in some aspect of the war effort" (Mead, 1968, p. 90). Margaret Mead is the best-known and most influential of this group. As she herself explained, "I am sometimes introduced to audiences as a pioneer in the application of cultural anthropology to the conduct of international affairs" (1968, p. 89). While not stated in the vocabulary of intercultural communication as studied today, her central concern, understanding cultural differences and the impact these have on the interactions between members of different cultures, was obviously quite similar.

In addition to Mead, a core group of anthropologists including Ruth Benedict, Gregory Bateson, Geoffrey Gorer, Douglas Haring, Clyde Kluckhohn, David Mandelbaum, and Rhoda Metraux participated during the war years in an overlapping series of organizations, committees, institutes, and conferences that permitted them to spend time on the projects they considered significant. These attracted an overlapping group of anthropologists and psychologists, together with sociologists, philosophers, and others. Eliot Chapple has suggested that Mead's strength "was in the building of networks, cliques and systems" (quoted in Howard, 1984, p. 231), and she used this ability to ensure that scholars first found ways to contribute to the war effort, and then after the war ended to continue the research they had begun. While it has been suggested that Bateson specifically desired "a patchwork of institutional ties" (Howard, 1984, p. 220), for most scholars it was then, as now, more typical to join a single university and conduct research under their auspices. So my investigations reveal not only connection of the content to intercultural communication, but also serve as a case study in how to design and conduct large-scale research investigations over a long period of time and by a group of scholars rather than a single individual. Lawrence Frank, a psychologist and close friend and long-time collaborator of Mead's, seems to have been at the nexus of these various efforts, generally in cooperation with Mead; further investigation will have to document his training and interests, his institutional affiliation with the Rockefeller Foundation, and his substantial interest in multidisciplinary, problem-oriented research in greater detail than is possible here.

A provocative comment characterizing one of the organizations to be described here suggests that "It didn't end up as a bureaucracy. It ended in a point of view" (Howard, 1984, p. 233; describing the Committee on Food Habits). In other words, the goal was never to establish a single organization that would continue indefinitely, but rather to use various organizations for short time periods as vehicles to pursue various research agendas. This was uncommon in the 1930s as it is today. For reasons of national security, many of the research projects listed in this chapter were not discussed publicly at length and did not result in formal publications. When working for the OSS (Office of Strategic Services, the predecessor organization to the CIA), presentation of research results to outsiders is not particularly encouraged. For these reasons, it is difficult to completely unravel the tight network of structures invented by this cohort of scholars, and this task will take far more time than I have yet spent. At this time my goal is only to outline the major strands.

Three theoretical concepts were integral to all of this research: "culture and personality," "national character," and "culture at a distance" studies. "Culture and personality" refers to a combination of anthropological and psychological insights, developed in the 1920s, largely under the direction of Edward Sapir, leading later to what was termed "psychological anthropology" (Bock, 1980). "National character" studies combined a background of culture and personality research with immediate wartime needs. As explained by Mead: "The term 'national character' was traditionally applied rather loosely to the body of writing that sought to interpret the people of a nation as distinguished from their history, literature, arts, or philosophy" (1961, p. 15; see also Gorer, 1950). The people within national boundaries were viewed as essentially homogeneous in this model; the assumption of a "national character" implied that everyone in a particular nation shares certain core characteristics (clearly no longer a typical assumption in today's multicultural world).

The national character studies then spawned the "culture at a distance" projects, involving different individuals at different points in time, but primarily Mead, Benedict, Bateson, Metraux, Gorer, and Haring again, as well as Martha Wolfenstein, Natalie Joffe, Nicholas Calas, Jane Belo (Cassidy, 1982, p. 45; Mead, 1951, p. 75), and later, Kluckhohn and Weston LaBarre (Mead, 1961, p. 16). Culture at a distance refers to the effort to learn about members of particular cultures (again, viewed at that time as synonymous with countries) without actually traveling to them. Instead, former members of a culture were questioned, and media products were examined, for what they could tell about the assumptions of the culture's members.

Having identified the central players and some of the basic concepts I will now sort out the major organizations, the portfolio each one took, when each was active, and who were the significant members in each. The story as told here will actually start with one key organization, because it was the most influential, and longest lived, then moves on to earlier and later smaller organizations.

CIR/IIS

In 1940, over an informal meal after a session of the American Anthropological Association, Mead and Rhoda Metraux, together with a few others, invented the *Council on Intercultural Relations* (Howard, 1984, p. 224); it was formally established in 1941, and included Frank, Bateson, Benedict, Gorer, Edwin Embree,

Alfred Metraux, and Philip Moseley, among others (Mead, 1959, p. 351; Howard, 1984, p. 225). The Council "gradually emerged as an independent entity with various linkages in the Washington years," overseeing multiple clusters of scholars (Howard, 1984, p. 225).

It later was formally incorporated under the name *Institute for Intercultural Studies* (Mead, 1953b, p. 97). The Institute's goal was "to combine a policy orientation with national character research" (Lipset, 1982, p. 170). Scholars at the Institute attempted "to develop a series of systematic understandings of the great contemporary cultures so that the special values of each might be maintained and enhanced in the postwar world" (Mead, 1959, p. 562). They used recent immigrants, refugees, war prisoners, literature, films, newspapers, travelers' accounts, and government propaganda as resources in producing studies of "culture at a distance." These were widely circulated, first in mimeograph form, listing the Institute for Intercultural Studies as publisher, and then, as publications in an eclectic series of venues.

These studies documented typical norms of interaction and values within a single culture (interpreted as meaning a single country) at a time. The "national character" studies had impact on later research within intercultural communication, which often began with the assumption that documenting standard behavior and assumptions for members of a single culture at a time was the first (sometimes the only) goal in the study of intercultural interaction. Occasionally these studies investigated actual intercultural encounters, that is, the behavior of individuals from different cultural backgrounds when thrown together. As Benedict stated: "I believed that by serious study of learned cultural behavior we could achieve a better international understanding and make fewer mistakes in international communication" (quoted in Modell, p. 298). A later goal of the Institute's research was to describe "areas of agreement which can be used as a background for the acceptance of differences" (Mead, 1948, p. 210), more directly foreshadowing research into intercultural encounters.

Mead's (1948) description of the interactions between US soldiers and British civilians served as a prototypical case study, and was presented to students in the early days of intercultural communication as an example of the sort of applied focus this area of study encouraged. In fact, it became something of an apocryphal tale: I remember hearing the story in graduate school from Ray Birdwhistell (in the 1970s at the University of Pennsylvania), long before I actually read a published version.

Let me present a brief summary of this research, as written by Mead a few years later, for those who have never heard about it, since it is the perfect example of what the national character studies could lead to in terms of intercultural investigation. Mead begins by describing the problem of the relations of US soldiers to British girls in Britain in wartime, when most of the British men were overseas. Enormous misunderstanding and mutual ill-feeling resulted from the contrast in the ways of rearing British and US adolescents for dealing with sexual advances. In the United States, the boy is permitted great initiative, but the girl is trained to be able to exercise such a strong veto upon his importunities that he can trust her to impose an external check upon them. In Britain, on the other hand, the girl is reared to a certain protective shyness but has an expectation of yielding to the determined advances of a man, who will discipline his impulses in appropriate ways. The combination in wartime Britain of large numbers of US young men, accustomed to ask for a great many more favors than they expected to receive, and a group of girls trained to say yes when asked did not necessarily result in a greater number of illegitimate children than is usual when troops are quartered in any community; yet it produced great friction between British and Americans (Mead, 1951, p. 83; the full story is told in Mead, 1944).

The fact that Mead, an American, was married to Bateson, who was British, may well have helped bring the issue to her attention. Birdwhistell, who worked closely with Mead in the 1950s, never published but often described for students his own follow-up research on comparable differences between courtship patterns displayed by northerners and southerners in the United States. Again, the fact that he was raised in the south but spent much of his career in the north could only have helped him to notice the differences in assumptions between these cultural groups. Notice, however, that his story was different from Mead's in one significant way: he was looking at differences within a country, rather than between countries, demonstrating that he viewed countries as heterogeneous rather than homogeneous.

The Institute for Intercultural Studies was important because it was one of the longest lasting of the organizations discussed here (it only disbanded in 2009). Even so, it was only one of a surprisingly large set of organizations created by anthropologists as tools in their investigation of issues related to intercultural communication. Brief descriptions of the others follow.

BIE

The *Bureau for Intercultural Education* had as its stated goal "to promote cultural diversity through the schools of America" (Modell, 1983), and Benedict worked with others through the late-1930s in this effort. They emphasized the process of integrating new immigrants into mainstream American culture, using the insights of anthropology.

CNM

The *Committee for National Morale* was organized by Arthur Upham Pope in 1939 in an attempt "to mobilize what would now be called the 'behavioral sciences' for the war effort" (Mead, 1959, p. 557). By 1939 Mead, Bateson, Frank, Chapple, Erik Erickson and Lockhardt were among those who worked with the Committee (Bock, 1980, p. 108, Cassidy, 1982, p. 42; Mead, 1961, p. 17). Bateson tried to devise ways for members to "use their scientific and intellectual professional skills, as distinguished from spy-skills, cross-culturally" (as quoted in Howard, 1984, p. 223).

CSPR

The *Conference on Science, Philosophy and Religion in their Relation to the Democratic Way of Life* "stressed an interdisciplinary approach to ethical problems" (Mead, 1959, p. 558). This was established in 1939 by Lewis Finkelstein and Lyman Bryson. By their second conference in 1940, they attracted not only Boas, but also Paul Tillich, Albert Einstein, and other stars (Howard, 1984, p. 220), so this group moved far beyond the core group of anthropologists.

OWI/OSS

Once World War II became a reality, the anthropologists became more directly involved, and many went to Washington to formally join the *Office of War Information*. This group included Mead, Gorer, Bateson, Benedict, Kluckhohn, and Dorothy Leighton (Mead, 1961, p. 17). An overlapping group ended up working for the *Office of Strategic Services*, including Bateson, Levy, Murray, and Kurt Lewin (Mead, 1961, p. 18). OSS was, as previously noted, the precursor to the CIA.

CFH

The *Committee for the Study of Food Habits*, attached to the National Research Council, documented differences in assumptions as to what were appropriate foods across racial and ethnic groups within the United States, and helped set the stage for how to manage in case severe food shortages occurred during wartime. Mead was the Executive Secretary from 1942 to 1945, taking a formal leave of absence from her usual institutional home at the American Museum of Natural History in New York, to move to Washington, DC, for the duration of the war (Howard, 1984, pp. 227–228; Mead, 1953b, p. 98).

RCC

Research in Contemporary Cultures was the term for the series of culture at a distance projects, begun under the direction of Benedict at Columbia University in 1947, as an outgrowth of the war efforts (Cassidy, 1982, p. 45). Benedict directed the project from 1947 to 1948, and then Mead took it over from 1948 to 1949 (Mead, 1951, p. 77). The initial research was paid for by a grant from the Office of Naval Research (Mead and Metraux, 1953, p. v; for details of the project, see Mead, 1953b), and then continued in a series of successor projects.

SSC/SCC

Studies in Soviet Culture, conducted at the American Museum of Natural History, funded by the Rand Corporation, 1948–1950, directed by Mead (Mead, 1951, p. 77; Mead and Metraux, 1953, p. v); and *Studies in Contemporary Culture*, also funded by

the Office of Naval Research, under the auspices of the Center for International Studies
at the Massachusetts Institute of Technology (Mead and Metraux, 1953, p. v).

The major players in RCC and the successor groups, in addition to Benedict and
Mead, were Metraux, Gorer, Wolfenstein, Ruth Bunzel, and Nathan Leites, (Mead,
1953a, p. 8). In total, there were some 120 scholars involved between 1947 and
1951; records of the results of these projects were kept by the Institute for
Intercultural Studies (Mead and Metraux, 1953, p. 451–453).

Other groups

There were additional links to the *Institute of Human Relations* at Yale University,
especially through Gorer, Sapir, John Dollard, and Harry Stack Sullivan (Mead,
1951, p. 77; 1961, p. 17); to the *Hanover Human Relations Seminar* of 1934
(Mead, 1961, p. 17); to the *Social Science Research Council Study on Cooperation
and Competition* of 1935 (Mead, 1961, p. 17); to the *Russian Research Center*,
Harvard University, 1947-1952, directed by Kluckhohn (Mead, 1951, p. 77); and
to the *Society for the Psychological Study of Social Issues* (Mead, 1961, p. 17).

Implications

What are the connections of this group of war-period applied anthropologists
to intercultural communication? Mead (1951) described such applied work in
anthropology as being required by "the urgent need to devise better methods of
co-operation between national groups and within national groups which are torn by
regional, class, or ideological conflicts" (p. 76). First, this is still one of the goals of
much intercultural communication research today; we have made less progress in the
last 60 years than might have been hoped when this task was begun. Towards that
goal, the 1930s studies utilized research methods still used by intercultural communication scholars: informant interviews; extensive life histories; study of fiction and films
produced within a culture; study of oral narratives produced within a culture; analyzing interaction patterns, including gender roles and parent-child interactions (Mead
and Metraux, 1953). In addition to research methods, some of the basic assumptions
of this group were similar or identical to those held by scholars of intercultural
communication today. Specifically, it is assumed by members of both groups that:

> all cultural behavior is mediated by human beings who not only hear and speak and com-
> municate through words, but also use all their senses, in ways that are equally systematic,
> to see and to project what they see in concrete forms – in design, costume, and architec-
> ture – and to communicate through the mutual perception of visual images; to taste and
> smell and to pattern their capacities to taste and smell, so that the traditional cuisine of a
> people can be as distinctive and as organized as a language. (Mead, 1953a, p. 16)

It is further a basic assumption of much intercultural research then as now that
"every human being embodies in an individual form the culture or cultures within

which he has been reared and within which he lives" (Mead, 1951, p. 73). At both points in time, this justified the use of small numbers of informants: if all members of a culture learn all of the essentials of their own culture, the need for extensive research into different segments of a society is minimized. Of course, this approach only works in a homogeneous society, but that was assumed to be reasonable until surprisingly recently by the vast majority of researchers.

Geoffrey Gorer lists a series of postulates taken for granted in the national character studies, and several of these are quite similar to modern assumptions.[4] Of Gorer's list, the five having greatest overlap are these:

1 human behavior is understandable;
2 it is predominantly learned;
3 "In all societies the behavior of the component individuals of similar age, sex, and status shows a relative uniformity in similar situations;"
4 "All societies have an ideal adult character;" and
5 "The habits established early in the life of the individual influence all subsequent learning" (Gorer, 1953, pp. 77–78).

I would argue that these statements characterize a substantial portion of intercultural communication work through very recent times.

In addition to similar assumptions like these, there are shared theoretical concepts, such as *culture*. Mead (1953a) defined culture as "the total shared, learned behavior of a society or a subgroup" (p. 22), a definition that would be amenable to most intercultural communication scholars today. Obviously such essential concepts in intercultural communication as *ethnocentrism* also come from anthropology, though that particular concept was not a central focus in the study of culture at a distance since it did not actually examine interaction between members of different cultures. Also, there are common emphases in topics studied, most especially the "analysis of the patterns of interaction between individuals or groups of individuals" (Mead, 1951, p. 79). This is best exemplified in Mead's own study of US soldiers and British civilians, described in some detail previously, although she usually cites Bateson as having greatest interest in the topic.

In sum, I would argue that some of the precursor research necessary to the later establishment of intercultural communication was conducted by anthropologists in the overlapping groups surrounding Margaret Mead and the Institute for Intercultural Studies through the 1930s and 1940s. Some of the assumptions are the same, as are some specific theoretical terms, research methods, and topics investigated.

Conclusion

Why should today's communication scholars (and specifically, critical intercultural communication scholars) care about some largely forgotten projects conducted by an overlapping group of anthropologists in the 1930s and 1940s? The broad answer: one of the tenets of critical scholarship is the focus on historical context – something not only required when we embark upon a specific research project, but also when we reflect upon and begin to question the academic endeavor in which we take part. Thus, we must study the history of our own disciplinary traditions and assumptions. The more immediate answer: it is my argument that the research and assumptions of the particular group of scholars in the 1930s and 1940s documented in these pages have substantially influenced the current study of intercultural communication. If their work can in fact be shown to have influenced ours, we must be willing to spend at least a little time examining the history of our assumptions, and how they have developed over time. Multiple strands of research have influenced what we study today and how we study it; the fact that we have forgotten some, if not most, is no excuse to continue to ignore this work. Modern scholars can benefit from studying the past because it will help to reveal why we study what we do, and why we use the methods that we do. A critical approach to intercultural communication certainly implies this sort of reflexivity. Knowing our own history permits decisions about whether some of our assumptions should perhaps be revised, or whether they still serve researchers well. If modern-day researchers continue to do in the present what our predecessors did in the past, it should at least be the result of a deliberate choice.

What exactly was the influence of the 1930s research on intercultural communication research today? National character research is never named in early intercultural communication writings, but it had substantial impact on the assumptions of Edward Hall, who then influenced the assumptions of other, later scholars. Early intercultural communication research, at least into the 1990s, and some of the current work as well, takes for granted that each country has a typical set of patterns of communicating that can be described; this is a direct use of the concept of national character, even though this is no longer the accepted term. Scholars in the early days of intercultural communication did not, as we do today, seek to understand the various constituent groups in each country, or across national boundaries, let alone study the cosmopolitans who move easily between cultures and countries (Pearce, 1989); rather each country was seen as a monolithic whole. While the national character studies made sense in the early days of understanding other groups, they limited the growth of intercultural communication research, which now sees each country as more heterogeneous. Is it possible that countries have become more heterogeneous, or is it the case that we simply are more likely to recognize the heterogeneity that has always been present? I would argue that both statements are true: yes, the world is becoming more heterogeneous (due to such factors as ease of travel), but yes also to the suggestion that scholars did not look for heterogeneity initially, and so did not document it when they found it. In either case, the easy match between culture and nation is now out of date (Ono, 1998).

Culture at a distance studies are never named as a precursor to intercultural communication research, but the assumption that you could adequately understand a culture without actually traveling to the group responsible for its development and maintenance was taken for granted as unquestioned and unquestionable for a surprisingly long time. At least anthropologists moved from studying culture at a distance (by other names initially) to the practice of on-site, in-person ethnography, and only returned to accepting the study of cultures at a distance under wartime duress.[5] Just as the anthropologists of the 1930s used recent immigrants and travelers as a resource, so intercultural communication in the 1960s and 1970s (and sometimes much later) assumed the use of foreign students and expatriates as adequate and sufficient resources to learning all that was necessary to understanding another culture. Once travel was not constrained due to war, such second-hand sources became less justifiable, but they had become an easy and accepted method of gathering data, were taken for granted as appropriate, and their use unquestioned for decades. It is my argument here that one reason for this unquestioning acceptance was the prior research in culture at a distance that came before intercultural communication as we know it today. Critical intercultural communication scholars, such as Mendoza, Halualani and Drzewiecka (2002), who now question the assumption that national identity controls communication behavior (as must be the case if international students are appropriate informants for all communication behavior in their home countries) can look to the research in the 1930s and 1940s documented here for an explanation of the origins of that assumption. *It is through knowing our own past history that we learn to question the assumptions we take for granted, and to discover their origin.*

Now it is time to return to the question of *why* the early precursors have been so thoroughly ignored by intercultural communication scholars today. I can postulate several reasons. First, most of this work was conducted by anthropologists, therefore communication scholars did not see it as their heritage but someone else's, and have felt free to ignore it. Second, Mead and her colleagues used organizations as tools to facilitate their research, not ends in themselves. The result was that few of these organizations have lasted, and few have lived on in the collective memory of the academy; it is not only communication scholars who do not know about much about the work documented in this chapter, but most anthropologists as well. Third, several of the projects described here were conducted as part of foreign policy; they were understood to be applied anthropology, conducted for particular immediate purposes, rather than being traditional research conducted in order to document truth for future generations. Much of the work described here thus never was made widely available, so it is not surprising that it was not widely read and remembered. When research is not made readily available (sometimes even when it is), its impact is severely minimized.

These facts explain why the current generation of intercultural scholars is ignorant of the research studies listed earlier, yet they do not justify their deletion from the record. We need to know our past, not for its own sake, but so that we learn why we study what we do in the ways we do, and so that we can consider making changes to our current assumptions and practices based on what we discover. Presumably some of what was appropriate in the 1930s will still be appropriate in the new century, but at least some of it is outdated and in desperate need of revision.

The historical moment of the 1930s and 1940s does not closely resemble the historical moment of today; to ignore that fact means not taking the assumptions of critical scholarship seriously. The implication is that, while all academics should spend time learning the history of research that underlies their own endeavors, it is particularly important for critical scholars.

Notes

1 This is not the place to supply an extensive list of work in the area, but a few relevant sources are Collier (2001); Martin and Nakayama (2000); Starosta and Chen (2003).
2 Sources directly addressing intercultural communication include Lee *et al.* (1995); and Leeds-Hurwitz (1990, 1993, 2010).
3 See Leeds-Hurwitz (1993) for further discussion of these assumptions within intercultural communication.
4 The entries omitted in this summary specifically concern the learning of children, and have not been followed up as they might.
5 See Leeds-Hurwitz (2004b) for details of the early days of ethnographic practice.

References

Bock, P.K. (1980) *Continuities in Psychological Anthropology: A Historical Introduction*, W.H. Freeman, San Francisco.
Cassidy, R. (1982) *Margaret Mead: A Voice for the Century*, Universe, New York.
Collier, M.J. (ed.) (2001) *Transforming Communication about Culture: Critical New Directions, International and Intercultural Communication Annual*, 24, Sage, Thousand Oaks, CA.
Darnell, R. (2001) *Invisible Genealogies: A History of Americanist Anthropology*, University of Nebraska Press, Lincoln.
Gorer, G. (1950) The concept of national character. *Science News*, 18, 105–122.
Gorer, G. (1953) National character: Theory and practice, in *The Study of Culture at a Distance*, (eds M. Mead and R. Metraux), University of Chicago, Chicago, pp. 57–82.
Howard, J. (1984) *Margaret Mead: A Life*, Simon and Schuster, New York.
Lee, W. S., Chung, J., Wang, J., and Hertel, E. (1995) A sociohistorical approach to intercultural communication. *Howard Journal of Communications*, 6, 262–291.
Leeds-Hurwitz, W. (1990) Notes in the history of intercultural communication: The Foreign Service Institute and the mandate for intercultural training. *Quarterly Journal of Speech*, 76, 262–281.
Leeds-Hurwitz, W. (1993) Tendances actuelles de la recherche en communication interculturelle: Aux Etats-Unis [Research trends in intercultural communication: In the United States], in *Dictionnaire critique de la communication, Tome 1* [*Critical dictionary of communication, Vol. 1*] (ed. L. Sfez) Presses Universitaires de France, Paris, pp. 500–501.
Leeds-Hurwitz, W. (2004a) *Rolling in Ditches with Shamans: Jaime de Angulo and the Professionalization of American Anthropology*, University of Nebraska Press, Lincoln.
Leeds-Hurwitz, W. (2004b) Ethnography, in *Handbook of Language and Social Interaction* (eds K. Fitch and R. Sanders), Lawrence Erlbaum, Mahwah, NJ, pp. 327–353.

Leeds-Hurwitz, W. (2010) The emergence of language and social interaction research as a specialty, in *The Social History of Language and Social Interaction Research: People, Places, Ideas*, (ed. W. Leeds-Hurwitz), Hampton Press, Cresskill, NJ, pp. 3–60.

Lipset, D. (1982) *Gregory Bateson: The Legacy of a Scientist*, Beacon, Boston.

Martin, J.N., and Nakayama, T.K. (2000) *Intercultural Communication in Contexts*, Mayfield, Mountain View, CA.

Mead, M. (1944) *The American Troops and the British Community*, Hutchinson, London.

Mead, M. (1948) A case history in cross-national communications, in *The Communication of Ideas*, (ed. L. Bryson), Institute for Religious and Social Studies, New York, pp. 209–229.

Mead, M. (1951) The study of national character, in *The Policy Sciences: Recent Developments in Scope and Method*, (eds. D. Lerner and H.D. Lasswell), Stanford University, Stanford, CA, pp. 70–85.

Mead, M. (1953a) The study of culture at a distance, in *The Study of Culture at a Distance*, (eds M. Mead and R. Metraux), University of Chicago, Chicago, pp. 3–53.

Mead, M. (1953b) The organization of group research, in *The Study of Culture at a distance*, (eds M. Mead and R. Metraux), Chicago: University of Chicago, pp. 85–101.

Mead, M. (ed.) (1959) *An Anthropologist at Work: Writings of Ruth Benedict*, Avon, New York.

Mead, M. (1961) National character and the science of anthropology, in *Culture and Social Character: The Work of David Riesman Reviewed*, (eds S.M. Lipset and L. Lowenthal), Free Press, Glencoe, IL, pp. 15–26.

Mead, M. (1968) The importance of national cultures, in *International Communication and the New Diplomacy*, (ed. A.S. Hoffman), Indiana University, Bloomington, pp. 89–105.

Mead, M., and Metraux, R. (eds) (1953) *The Study of Culture at a Distance*, University of Chicago, Chicago.

Mendoza, S.L., Halualani, R.T., and Drzewiecka, J.A. (2002) Moving the discourse on identities in intercultural communication: Structure, culture, and resignifications. *Communication Quarterly*, 50 (3/4), 312–327.

Modell, J. (1983) *Ruth Benedict: Patterns of Life*, University of Pennsylvania, Philadelphia.

Murray, S.O. (1994) *Theory Groups and the Study of Language in North America: A Social History*, John Benjamins, Amsterdam.

Ono, K.A. (1998) Problematizing "nation" in intercultural communication research, in *Communication and Identity across Cultures*, (eds D. Tanno and A. Gonzalez), Sage, Thousand Oaks, CA, pp. 34–55.

Pearce, W.B. (1989) *Communication and the Human Condition*, Southern Illinois Press, Carbondale.

Starosta, W.J., and Chen, G.-M. (eds) (2003) *Ferment in the Intercultural Field: Axiology/value/praxis, International and Intercultural Communication Annual*, 26, Thousand Oaks, CA: Sage.

3

Critical Reflections on Culture and Critical Intercultural Communication

Dreama G. Moon

As excited as I was to be in my very first graduate class on Intercultural Communication, by the end of student introductions I was quite confused and convinced I had made a terrible mistake in giving up a successful career in nonprofit human service organizations to become an intellectual. Working with people in prison, and with domestic violence and sexual assault victims showed me how social inequities can often mean life and death. When beginning my graduate education, I chose Intercultural Communication as a field as I imagined that it was sure to be compatible with my interests in social change. In that first class, I was surprised to learn that many people envisioned intercultural communication as being mostly about study abroad and traveling to exotic locations where "they" learned about "them." I heard few speak of social inequality, human rights, and other issues about which I was passionate. It seemed that culture was seen as synonymous with nation and that culture usually signified somewhere else outside the United States. No one seemed to imagine the United States as a cultural space worthy of (and in need of) critical attention. These ideas seemed to be repeated in most of the literature we read that semester.

I wondered how it was that intercultural communication came to be configured in this (what seemed to me) apolitical and ahistorical manner. Given its roots in the United States, I was curious as to how intercultural communication scholarship seemingly escaped being influenced by the various freedom struggles of the 1960s and 1970s. To try to understand, I embarked on an in-depth study of the discipline. How did this field of inquiry come to be? What were the field's interests? What were its passions? I was curious to learn what the accepted "truths" were in intercultural communication and more importantly, how these ideas came to hold sway. I conducted a genealogical investigation of the field, a decision heavily influenced by Leeds-Hurwitz's (1990) piece on intercultural communication and Foucault's (1972) notions of power and knowledge.

The Handbook of Critical Intercultural Communication, edited by Thomas K. Nakayama and Rona Tamiko Halualani. © 2010 Blackwell Publishing Ltd.

As I assessed the genealogy (Foucault, 1972) of the field from its inception through the early-1990s, it became clear that Edward Hall's experience at the Foreign Service Institute played a pivotal role in terms of how "culture" came to be defined and by extension, studied in the field. Hall himself reports his frustration with the governmental insistence that "culture" be treated as an instrumental set of rules or "cookbook" that white US American trainees could learn quickly then bring to bear as they pursued their assignments in foreign countries (Hall, 1956). The legacy of Hall's experience, according to Leeds-Hurwitz (1990), was the creation of an agenda for intercultural communication as a field of inquiry which included comparative approaches to the study of culture primarily defined in terms of national boundaries and a preference for microanalysis (and the commiserate lack of attention to structural influences and/or "dialogue" between micro and macro practices).

However, the field was not always thus. In my analysis of the literature, I noted that the aforementioned agenda began to crystallize around 1980. Prior to that, the field entertained more heterogeneous notions of culture, approaches to its study were more varied, and scholarship was more engaged with social and political issues of the time. Drawing on Foucault (1972), I argued that 1980 represented a "disjuncture" in the field (perhaps related to the rise of conservatism around the world and insistence for "intellectual rigor" as defined by positivism; Casmir and Asuncion-Lande, 1990, p. 282). As I read the scholarship produced in the 1980s, I identified some clear trends. First, I observed that "culture" had become primarily defined as "nationstate" and assessed almost completely quantitatively. This led to the development of many notions including individualistic versus collectivist cultures, high and low context cultures, and other sorts of generalizations about massive populations of peoples. Second, I noted that intercultural communication was studied from a primarily interpersonal/microanalytic approach and generally did not attend to structural issues. This is problematic in that over-focusing on micro practices encourages us to ignore how structural constraints push and pull such practices, and conversely, how micro practices can reinscribe or even be used to oppose and change structural configurations. Third, analyses of how power operates in intercultural contact of all sorts were absent. It seems clear that assuming such contact takes place in a power-neutral context is bound to make one miss the intricacies of how intercultural relations play out. As a result of this assessment, I came to see that intercultural communication developed in the midst of World War II as a tool of imperialism and that much of its foundations were infused with a colonial perspective. More seriously, I did not see that social justice and equity were of great import to intercultural scholarship.

As a result of my analysis, I suggested some directions that intercultural communication scholars might entertain in order to broaden the field. Those ideas included moving beyond the "culture = nation" formula to constructions that take into account power plays and minority perspectives; developing more complex notions of cultural identity especially those that attend to the political nature of identification processes; attending to communication processes within groups, particularly those that are socially dominant; rethinking foundational concepts (such as adaptation, competence, and sojourning) in the field from the perspective of the

"Other" and understanding our investment in continuing to frame these concepts in traditional ways; and including popular culture as a site for examining representations of intercultural communication. In short, I argued for the adoption of a critical inter/cultural practice that I believed could contain all of these elements and more, and which could enhance intercultural theory and practice in a number of ways. Undergirding this notion of critical inter/cultural communication is a deep and abiding commitment to social justice and equity.

Since 1996, others have expanded our understanding of what might constitute a critical inter/cultural practice. In the last decade, the "critical turn" in intercultural communication has changed the face of the field in a number of noteworthy ways. In the next section, I review intercultural communication scholarship published in our disciplinary journals and noting some of the ways in which critical scholarship has made important innovations to the field.

Intercultural Communication, 1997–2007

Much has changed in the field of intercultural communication since the "Concepts of 'Culture'" essay and I have been anxious to revisit its development. In that essay, I relied on the *Index to Journals in Communication Studies Through 1990* (Matlon, 1992) to identify articles published in the field using the key term "intercultural communication" as a descriptor, arguing that given that the *Index* was published by the Speech Communication Association (now the National Communication Association), it provided a reasonable indicator of what was then understood as "intercultural communication" within the communication discipline. In that search, I located 102 articles published between 1951 and 1990. My approach to the current project had to be modified as the *Index* is no longer published. I decided to continue the focus on journal articles using the key term "intercultural communication" and broadened the search to include journals published by both the National Communication Association and the International Communication Association. Although many of us publish in outlets other than those offered by our professional associations, the journals endorsed by and published by our two major disciplinary associations should reflect the breadth of our field and suggest what types of work garner attention in the form of publication. In other words, a field publishes what is important to it and its members.

Focusing on the years 1997–2007 (10 years after publication of the "Concepts" essay) and using the Academic Search Premier and Communication and Mass Media Complete databases, I identified 1051 articles using the search term "intercultural communication" of which only 68 (fewer than 10%) of which were published in our associations' journals. Although I realize that scholars often use other words (e.g., interracial, international, cross-cultural) to situate work that many would identify as "intercultural," I tried to stick as closely as possible to the process that I employed in the "Concepts" essay. In addition, given that scholars suggest key terms to use for describing their work, the focus on the key term "intercultural communication" is a clear indicator of how authors position the work in the field.

Of the 68 essays that I reviewed, the overwhelming majority reflected the trends noted by Leeds-Hurwitz (1990) and observed by myself in the "Concepts" essay. For example, well over a fourth of the essays (29% or 20 out of 68) are grounded in a variable analytic tradition in which culture is defined in terms of national citizenship or in terms of Hofstede's individualism/collectivism framework; just under one-third use comparative approaches (18 of the 68) in which two or more national cultures are compared and contrasted on some variable of interest (i.e., self-construal); and little attention is given to structural influences or power dynamics. The foci of much intercultural communication scholarship continues to place emphasis on individualism-collectivism, low-context/high-context, interpersonal processes, intercultural competence, and adaptation from traditional points of view. As I examined the literature more closely, critical impulses emerged (although the authors themselves may not have acknowledged them as such). In the next section, I discuss six trends identified in my analysis of these texts that illustrate the impact that the "critical turn" in intercultural communication has made to the field.

Contributions of the "Critical Turn"

My review of the intercultural scholarship published between 1997 and 2007 uncovered six areas to which critical scholars have made useful contributions. These areas include (1) historicizing the field, (2) conceptualizations of culture, (3) theoretical/conceptual development, (4) expansion of foundational concepts, (5) critique of dominant ideologies, and (6) pedagogy as critical praxis.

Historicizing the field

One of the most interesting occurrences I observed is the proliferation of histories of the field (Cooks, 2001; Dresner, 2006; Rogers, 1999; Kim, 2005). For most, Leeds-Hurwitz's (1990) historical piece has been viewed as the "official" history of the development of the field and its intellectual legacy (Cooks, 2001; Moon, 1996; Rogers, 1999). This agenda-setting legacy left us with a highly constrained (and constraining) notion of culture, and a penchant for comparative microanalyses grounded in such notions.

While my "Concepts" essay offered a critique of this agenda, more recently intercultural scholars have uncovered other influences that give us alternative ways of thinking about the field and its possibilities (Carbaugh and Berry, 2001; Cooks, 2001; Rogers, 1999; Kim, 2005). This is a highly important work as "to create a history, to have the authority to shape and give voice to the story, has implications for not only the past and present, but gives important impetus to how future stories are told" (Cooks, 2001, p. 342). For example, Rogers (1999) noted how Simmel's notion of the stranger has informed current day intercultural communication inquiry, especially work dealing with uncertainty reduction theory which Rogers sees as foundational to the field of intercultural communication. In response,

Cooks (2001) levied a stinging critique, arguing that the notion of stranger has enabled intercultural communication scholars to ignore unequal power differentials inherent in intercultural contact and instead assume a neutral playing field and equal stakes in reducing uncertainty. Rather than seeing uncertainty reduction theory as foundational, Cooks instead observes that this and similar theories are "noteworthy for their lack of attention to the material circumstances and consequences of actually embodied interaction" (p. 343).

As an intercultural communication scholar, it is exciting to see intellectual debates such as this. Rather than accepting a master narrative that centers the work of one or two prominent scholars, other stories of origin and influence offer multiple ways of "seeing" the field's past and thus, multiple ways of envisioning its future. The proliferation of historical narratives discourages the formation of "official" rules and points of view and provides contested ways of understanding the field's inception as well as its current moment.

Conceptualizing culture

In addition to historically diverse readings of the field, a second trend noted in the sampled texts involves how the ways in which we conceptualize culture have changed (Kim; 2005; Rogers, 1999). From its original signification of nationstate, the meaning of culture been broadened to include gender, race, ethnicity, sexual orientation, social class, and other identifications that affect and are affected by interaction. In the body of the literature reviewed, culture was defined as nationality in many of the essays; however, culture was also conceptualized in terms of race (Cooks, 2003; Covarrubias, 2007; Foeman, 2006; Gorham, 2006; Halualani *et al.*, 2006; Harris, 2003, 2004; Hoerl, 2007; Martin and Davis, 2001), gender (Mulac, Bradac, and Gibbons, 2001), and ethnicity (Rinderie, 2005).

While the nationstate is still often taken as a unit of analysis in intercultural communication research, critical intercultural communication has offered other constructions of culture that do not rely on notions of sharedness. The unifying theme here is the treatment of culture as "imagined, constituted in communication, and constrained by social structures and ideologies over a trajectory of time by people and institutions" (Collier, 2002, p. xi). The framing culture as a site of struggle and contestation rather than comprised of shared values, behaviors, and attitudes introduced by Martin and Nakayama's (1997) important text, *Intercultural Communication in Contexts*, is now taken for granted by critical intercultural scholars and is one of our most important contributions to the study of intercultural communication. The move from viewing culture as unproblematically shared and relatively stable to one that acknowledges culture as a contested zone and thus in flux opens up new possibilities for intercultural scholars, allowing us to understand that rather than being comprised of "a reality," culture is a space of competing realities embedded in power relations with all but the dominant or hegemonic version getting short shrift. In coming to understand how and why this occurs allows scholars to engage the operations of power and structural influences on intercultural communication processes and possibilities.

Given the critique levied against equating culture with nation, it is surprising that so much of the published work continues to draw on this construction (e.g., Barnett and Eunjung, 2005; Bresnahan *et al.*, 2005; Callahan, 2005; Cai and Fink, 2002; Carbaugh and Berry, 2001; Chen, 1997; Crabtree, 1998; Drake, 2001; Fitch and Morgan, 2003; Heinz, 2004; Lee and Choi, 2005; Matveev, 2004; McCann and Honeycutt, 2006; Manusov, Winchatz, and Manning, 1997; Miller, 2002; Nishishiba and Ritchie, 2000; Oetzel and Ting-Toomey, 2003; Oetzel *et al.*, 2001; Ota, Giles, and Somera, 2007; Park and Levine, 1999; Scott, 2000; Sellnow, Liu, and Venetter, 2006; Tasaki and Min-Sun, 1999; Wurtz, 2005). Using nation as a unit of analysis hides more than it illuminates by forcing researchers to "discover" unifying principles (i.e., individualism) that "describe" whole populations (Ono, 1998). These "discoveries" are likely to be stereotypes that the people supposedly identified by them would not recognize. Ono strongly claims that "blanket stereotypes of a society ... is a move toward controlling the people in that country" (p. 198). In this he means that the stereotypes are used to differentiate the culture under investigation from US culture where the differentiation is usually noted for the purposes of arguing for US superiority. To make matters worse, these stereotypes are often taught to naïve students as tools for survival in a global economy and who one day may need to communicate with the persons so described by the stereotypes.

In the view of critical scholars, this approach ill prepares students to address the complexities of the global condition. While typically nationstates are thought of as a geographic space in which politics, ethnicity, and culture coincide, in today's world this is less and less the case. In fact, few true nationstates exist. In today's economic and war-torn climate, we can expect to see an increase in migrating populations as new markets are sought and as people leave their current home countries in search of work and/or safety. Critical scholars argue that a more complex world needs more complex ways of understanding its populations.

Theoretical development

A third area to which critical intercultural scholars have contributed is to the field's conceptual development. In particular, I noted at least three critical theoretical innovations in the examined set of texts: Martin and Nakayama's (1999) dialectics, Martinez's (2006) phenomenological extension of dialectics, and Orbe's (1998) cocultural theory. Taking on the notion of polarizing "paradigm wars," Martin and Nakayama (1999) advocate for the possibility of inter-paradigmatic dialogue and collaboration. As a way of actualizing such a possibility, they offer dialectics as an approach to culture and communication stating that "[it] offers us the possibility of engaging multiple, but distinct, research paradigms. It offers us the possibility of seeing the world in multiple ways and to become better prepared to engage in intercultural interaction" (p. 13). Such an approach reinterprets intercultural interaction as a dynamic and changing process that transcends facile dichotomies and "resists fixed, discrete bits of knowledge (Martin and Nakayama, 1999, p. 14). In other words, the dialectical approach to the study of intercultural communication "makes explicit the dialectical tension between what previous research topics have been studied (cultural differences, assumed static nature of culture, etc.) and what should be studied (how cultures change, how they are similar, importance of history)" (Martin and Nakayama, 1999, p. 19). Seeking a method of dealing with the complexities of racial and ethnic difference in scholarly inquiry, Martinez (2006) demonstrates how semiotic phenomenology can particularize the dialectical approach both theoretically and practically.

One last important contribution from critical intercultural scholars has been the development of Orbe's (1998) cocultural theory. Working out of muted group and phenomenological traditions, Orbe outlines communication strategies that marginalized group members' use in interactions with dominant group members. As members of marginalized groups must develop strategies for communicating and negotiating with those from more socially powerful groups, this work can help us understand how power works in intercultural interactions from minority perspectives which are all too often ignored in traditional intercultural communication research. Orbe's work on cocultural theory has been crucial to the shift away from traditional descriptors of subordinated cultures (i.e., subculture) to the term "coculture" which draws attention to the diversity of influential cultures that exist in the United States while acting as a sanction to the use of past terms such as "sub-culture" which call up and/or rely on notions of hierarchy, superiority, and inferiority.

Reimaging foundational concepts

Over the past 10 years, scholars have devoted a fair amount of energy toward questioning and rethinking foundational concepts such as intercultural communication competence, cultural adaptation, and cultural identity through a critical lens. As I mentioned earlier, a number of the works reviewed addressed the important notion of intercultural communication competence (e.g., Arasaratnam, 2006; Blake and Kaplowitz, 2001; DeTurk, 2001; Matveev, 2004; Neuliep and McCroskey, 1997; Quinlisk, 2004; Zhu and Valentine, 2001). As Collier (1998) observes, "competence ... is a construct based on implicit privilege ... Who decided the criteria? ... Competent or acceptable on the basis of what social and historical context? To assume that ontological interlocutors negotiate mutual rules of appropriate conduct is to deny the power of ideology, historical structures, and limitations in the field of choices" (p. 142). In this line of inquiry, new models of intercultural competence have been developed which identify competence as comprised of empathy, motivation, attitude toward other cultures, experience and listening (Arasaratnam, 2006). Although the initial development of the measures was drawn from individuals of multiple cultural perspectives, continued development of the measures have been tested on mostly White US undergraduate students. Challenges to the notion of competence have been made by critical scholars. For example, DeTurk (2001) draws on the work of Dace and McPhail (1998) to challenge the notion of empathy as a skill or competency. Traditionally intercultural communication research has taken the presence of empathy as an important indicator of intercultural competence. DeTurk persuasively argues that any conceptualization of empathy across cultures or social groups of any kind must take into account power differentials. In fact, "mutually enhancing interaction between unequals is not probable... In fact, conflict is inevitable" (Miller, 1992, p. 79).

In addition to intercultural competence, scholars in this sample also paid a fair amount of attention to studying cultural adaptation (Chen 1997; Hammer *et al.*, 1998; Kassing, 1997; Neuliep and McCroskey, 1997; Neuliep and Ryan, 1998; Roach and Olaniran, 2001; Yang and Rancer, 2003). Most of these studies are concerned with issues related to reducing uncertainty and apprehension. Recently, traditional approaches to the study of cultural adaptation have relied on the notions of interpersonal saliencies, intergroup saliencies, communication message exchange, and host contact conditions as explanatory and predictive measures of cultural adaptation (Hammer *et al.*, 1998). Critical scholars have attempted to problematize the notion of adaptation as a power-neutral, linear process. For instance, my work on "passing" was an attempt to politicize the notion of cultural adaptation and to unhinge it from traditional portrayals as a relatively seamless neutral process through which migrants come to take on the behaviors, attitudes, and values of the dominant culture (Moon, 1998, 2000). By conceptualizing adaptation as a process of identity negotiation and as a dynamic process of resistance and acquiescence to dominant notions of who "we" are (or should be), with all of this taking place within relations of power, the metaphor of "passing" can be invoked in order to rethink adaptive processes as potentially disruptive, contested, and transformative.

Last, cultural identity continues to be a popular focus in intercultural research (Kim, 2007). As I have pointed out, cultural identity tends to still be manifested as national identity or in terms of collectivism/individualism and low-high context. Despite this, the reimaging of culture has also inspired and necessitated the rethinking of identification processes and how we think about cultural identity. Rather than think in terms of "sharedness" or "stability," critical intercultural communication scholars are more likely to examine cultural identity through tropes of "displacement," "struggle," and "resistance" (Flores, 2001; Hegde, 1998). The historization of intercultural communication has pushed the field beyond the notion of identity and identification as given or natural to one that encourages attention to the historical and political processes that produce them (Mendoza, Halualani, and Drzewiecka, 2002). Mendoza *et al.* (2002) argue that intercultural scholars need to analyze both ends of identity construction – "its structural determinations, on the one hand, and its ongoing, open-ended, unforeclosed re-creation and re-construction, on the other" (p. 313). Critical scholars have moved beyond a focus on isolated cultural groupings to "scrutinize intersections of nationality, race, ethnicity, gender, and classes" (Collier, 2001, p. xii). By attending to notions of intersectionality, scholars are more likely to produce knowledge that is specific and local, rather than abstract and overly generalized. In addition, we are more likely to be able to observe how issues of power and privilege may play out in intercultural interactions. In this way, identification can be seen as both voluntary and imposed, both embraced and struggled over and with, both rejected and claimed.

Critique of dominant ideologies

The field has increasingly witnessed an interrogation of dominant ideologies and their implications for intercultural inquiry which have opened up new and exciting agendas for the future of the field. In identifying what they call the "white problem" in intercultural communication studies, Nakayama and Martin (2007) articulate the ways in which the history of the development of intercultural communication studies in the United States centered and became infused with the interests of white hegemony which continue to taint our scholarship and teaching today. More specifically, they argue that this centering of whiteness has influenced intercultural communication in at least three ways: by implicitly defining American as "white"; by ignoring transnational relationships developed through migration, displacement, colonialization, and imperialism; and by overlooking the voices and experiences of marginalized Americans They advocate a postcolonial intercultural communication as a corrective for these gaps that would de-center whiteness and include postcolonial notions of culture and identity and a deeper reflexivity on the part of white scholars as they study the "Other."

As they and others have made apparent, in many ways intercultural communication remains ensconced in colonial perspectives that de-humanize "others" and which implicitly (and perhaps explicitly) support and reproduce US imperialism. In the body of work reviewed, I noted moves designed to rectify the "white problem" by rendering the ways in which dominance works in intercultural interactions and by supplying counter-memories to offset hegemonic memories of dominant-subordinate relations, especially in the US context (Cooks, 2003; Covarrubias, 2007; Crabtree, 1998; Halualani *et al.*, 2006; Hoerl, 2007). In this literature, whiteness is taken as a "set of rhetorical strategies employed to construct and maintain a dominant White culture and identities" (Cooks, 2003, p. 246) and critical scholars are interested in explicating the form and impact of such strategies in cultural and intercultural contexts. Much of this work is tied to a social justice framework that understands that contact alone will not ensure global awareness and sensitivity (Crabtree, 1998).

Pedagogy and the activist turn

A last area that has enjoyed a notable amount of scholarly attention is intercultural pedagogy. One of the aspects of critical theoretical approaches that I find valuable is the insistence that theory and praxis be fused. Critical intercultural scholars have devoted a fair amount of thought regarding how one can successfully bring this point of view to the classroom. The availability of textbooks that include or are written from a critical perspective (e.g., Martin and Nakayama, 1997) has made this task somewhat easier. Of the essays that I reviewed, 15 addressed issues dealing with the intercultural classroom. In particular, these scholars are interested in using intercultural theory and insights as strategies for challenging students' levels of prejudice and their sensitivity to racial issues in particular (Cooks, 2003; Harris, 2003), and their overall worldviews in general (Martin and Davis, 2001). The conundrum for critical scholars is how to help students "unlearn" ways of thinking about the world that bolster the status quo and envision alternative ways of thinking about the world that challenge it. This interest in imaging the classroom as a potential site for social change is central to critical pedagogy and is especially relevant as we reflect on more traditional approaches to understanding the acquisition of intercultural skills and their relevance for real world interactions. Related to this is the manner in which we define relevant concepts and attempt to measure them. For example, in traditional intercultural work on intercultural competence, empathy is seen as the central characteristic to "competent and effective intercultural communication" (Broome, 1991, p. 235). Unfortunately, traditional pre- and posttests of empathy after exposure to courses with a diverse focus have not always supported the idea that diversity matters in terms of increasing students' levels of empathy (Carrell, 1997). Rather than assuming that diversity does not matter in terms of content, instructor identity, and approach, critical intercultural scholars argue that it is perhaps our pedagogical strategies for teaching intercultural communication that require our attention.

One of the most intriguing and timely developments spawned from the critical turn in intercultural communication has been the inclusion of whiteness in the intercultural curriculum. For example, Martin and Davis (2001) observed that intercultural communication scholars have "rarely explicitly studied the cultural patterns of white people" but instead have done so "under the rubric of 'Americans' " (p. 298). For intercultural educators, the tendency for US Americans (and others) to invoke a white face when imaging the word "American" has been one of the most deeply problematic assumptions to unpack. As a corrective, Martin and Davis suggest four areas of study that could be fruitfully integrated into the undergraduate intercultural communication classroom: the historical "whitening" of some US immigrant groups and the role of history in understanding the social and political development of whiteness, white privilege, the discursive and communication patterns of US whites, and representations of whiteness in popular culture. These have proved to be extremely fruitful areas of study and have led to the writing of two excellent texts dealing with such relationships in pedagogical settings (Cooks and Simpson, 2007; Warren; 2003).

Dialogue on the (Disciplinary) Edges

In my examination of the intercultural communication work published from 1997 through 2007, it seems clear that critical scholars have made pivotal contributions to the intercultural inquiry. To reiterate, critical work has broadened the ways in which we think about, define, and study culture. Critical scholars have contributed theoretical innovations to the field, offering ways of theorizing intercultural ideas in intersectional and complex manners. Along the way, we have reworked and rethought foundational concepts such as adaptation, competence, and identity that read in power-differentials and structural constraints. Most importantly, we have levied a deep interrogation of dominant ideologies such as whiteness and the myriad of ways that such worldviews play out in intercultural contact at all levels of interaction. Last, we have taken the critical impulse to the classroom, imagining it as a space of change, and have worked to develop pedagogies that empower students and provide them with ways of changing their worlds. Critical scholars can be proud of these valuable insights and contributions.

On the other hand, it has been difficult for critical scholars to engage most "traditional" intercultural scholars (I apologize for the binary distinction and use it only to distinguish scholars who work out of a critical theoretical tradition from those who do not) in intellectual conversation in consequential ways (Ono, 1998). When I reflect on who attends which conferences panels at professional conferences or who cites whom in published work, it appears that a kind of one-way communication often occurs with critical scholars attempting to engage "traditional" scholarship in conversation while their own work is generally ignored by more "traditional" scholars (with a few notable exceptions of course). My evidence for this is primarily anecdotal but let me elaborate on this point as I believe that it highlights an important gap in the intellectual community of intercultural scholars that does not bode well for the future of critical intercultural studies both domestically and globally.

The first piece of evidence I want to note is the observation that few "traditional" intercultural scholars utilize insights about intercultural communication offered by critical work. In my review of the references cited lists of the 68 published articles examined as part of this project, I note that critical work is seldom cited by "traditional" scholars while the reverse is less true. For example, all but three of the articles based in the critical tradition reviewed here cited "traditional" scholars, while only three of the "traditional" articles included reference to the work of critical scholars and even then the reference tended to be cursory. This pattern may be partly explainable by the usual graduate school experience. Given that critical scholars are trained in "traditional" graduate programs, we must know and engage a broad spectrum of ideas across a variety of paradigmatic approaches and thus come to see the value of multiple perspectives which we often incorporate in our work. The reverse is not true. A student can easily complete a graduate program without ever being exposed to a piece of work written from a critical perspective. And, in fact, the general devaluation of critical paradigms in many graduate programs reduces the likelihood of students seeking out this work on their own. This tendency then may affect future ways of thinking about the value of multiparadigmatic approaches and the value of reading work outside one's research tradition.

In addition and perhaps relatedly, publishing critical scholarship in mainstream peer-reviewed outlets has proven challenging (Calafell and Moreman, 2009; Hendrix, 2005). For example, of the 68 articles published in our profession's mainstream journals reviewed for this chapter, fewer than 20 of them could be accurately as "critical". In main part, positivist views and treatment of intercultural communication continue to dominate our field's academic journals while critical scholars have been forced to seek alternative outlets for publication of their work, outlets overlooked by my approach. For example, two extremely important outlets for critical intercultural communication scholarship have historically been the *International and Intercultural Communication Annual* and *Howard Journal of Communication*. In addition, many other important pieces of critical scholarship are located outside peer-reviewed outlets such as edited volumes and textbooks. With the addition of new journals such as *Critical/Cultural Studies* and the *Journal of Intercultural and International Communication*, critical scholars have had more opportunity to disseminate their work in the field's outlets. Due to the difficulty in finding publication outlets, critical work has tended to be engaged most often by those who have deliberately sought it out rather than one being able to skim a recent copy of a journal and easily access a variety of ideas and approaches including critical ones.[1]

A last observation I would like to offer is what I can only label as the intellectual dismissal often extended to critical work by "traditional" scholars. This dismissal is expressed in a multitude of ways including failure to acknowledge that a critical perspective in intercultural communication exists (this can be seen in failures to include the contributions of this tradition in historical overviews of the field with the notable exception of Kim, 2007); or when acknowledging that a critical tradition exists, to dismiss it as irrelevant or unimportant (I heard this in at two different graduate programs I attended: "and then there's the critical paradigm but we won't be discussing that"); and to fail to take seriously insights derived from critical work as discussed above (and thus to include them in your own work).

I find this type of academic dismissal most disturbing and would like to offer a couple of examples. The first involves a roundtable submission to NCA and a reviewer's response. Composed of both emerging and established mostly critical (but including a couple of well-known "traditional") scholars, the panel was to explore the future of intercultural communication in a time of economic and institutional instability. One reviewer wrote, "Overall, I do not find much theoretical or methodological contribution coming from this session." As a reviewer, I am not aware that roundtables must meet standards regarding the development of theoretical and/or methodological innovations. Most generally roundtable discussions are focused on specific topics of interest, state/future of the field discussions, and so forth and are not constructed to engage in theory building (although they often may). The fact that the reviewer found it necessary to make a snide remark regarding the potential outcomes of such a discussion seems mean-spirited at the least.

A second example regards a forum published in the 1998 *International and Intercultural Communication Annual*. The forum topic was the notion of "nation-state" for which James Chesebro (1998) wrote an essay to which Kent Ono and Carley Dodd responded with Chesebro having final comments. When reading the forum, I was most struck by Chesebro's lack of engagement with Ono's ideas and his thinly veiled attacks on Ono's character and motivations. It resonated with some of my experiences in graduate school as I tried to be a critical scholar in an increasingly unfriendly-to-critical academic environment.

In my view, Ono's response to Chesebro's essay clearly illustrated his intellectual engagement with the ideas. Ono carefully challenged evidence offered by Chesebro, identified points of agreement and divergence, and articulated a cogent argument regarding how he saw Chesebro's underlying assumptions of the "nationstate" as problematic. Conversely, Chesebro opened his response to Ono with the following: "Kent Ono uses my chapter on cultural change as an opportunity to promote his specific political and ideological agenda" (p. 216). Chesebro goes on to say, "Although Mr. Ono is worried that my chapter will 'unwittingly' promote an ideological position he dislikes, he does little to underscore the ideological position he himself argues for, nor does he offer the kind of reasons and evidence for his position that one might expect in an academic exchange (pp. 216–217). After reducing Ono's carefully crafted essay to nonacademic ideological positioning, Chesebro continues go to chastise Ono for "pretending" to be objective and unbiased.

This sort of contradictory and emotive response of "traditional" scholars to challenges posed by critical scholars to their work is one that unfortunately I have observed on any number of occasions as well as been victim to. The animosity underlying such responses indicates that something is going on here other than simple intellectual disagreement. To disagree with another's ideas requires serious engagement of those ideas which most read as an indicator of professional and intellectual respect. Debate is something that pushes a field to grow and thus should be welcomed. To attack a colleague's supposed "agenda" rather than to address their argument suggests the existence of deep, underlying paradigmatic tensions. Similar to Calafell and Moreman (2009, p. 128) observation in regards to the reception of autoethnography in performance studies, "The inability of academia to honor various types of knowledge production and theory serves as a huge impediment" to furthering the field.

As we ponder the "critical turn" in intercultural communication, the observations I have made about the reception of the turn should be kept in mind. Part of the way one can trace the influence of a tradition is by counting how many times that tradition is used or engaged in publications. If we were to use this method, given the above observations, I might be inclined to say that talk about something called "the critical turn" in intercultural communication research is somewhat overstated. Certainly given the preference in the field both domestically and globally to hold on to concepts such as national culture, uncertainty reduction, and individualism/collectivism, one cannot argue that critical scholars have set off a paradigmatic revolution in the Kuhnian sense. Another way that one might assess the importance or significance of a school of thought is by the level of resistance to it by the mainstream. One might recall the reception that other ideas which have questioned accepted ways of thinking about something have garnered throughout history. If we take this measure, then the critical turn has evidently posed some deep challenges to the field's normative approach to intercultural inquiry.

In the critical essay "Dialogue on the Edges," Collier *et al.* (2001) describe how they came to settle on the use of the metaphor of "edges" in conceptualizing their cyber-dialogue about intercultural communication inquiry. Their ultimate decision to use the term "edges" to connote the liminality, fluidity, multidirectionality, and contested nature of critical intercultural communication is especially apropos when one considers the state of our published work and the engagement of this work by the rest of the field. Speaking from the edges can be an extremely powerful position. Edginess questions what is most taken for granted; it motivates us to think and to imagine something better than currently exists; moreover, it unsettles us, pushes us to consider previously undreamed-of possibilities. Too, edginess can be a self-corrective measure to absorption into unself-reflexive ways of thinking about the world, the people in it, and possibilities of relationships among us. Perhaps it is this edginess that has enticed some "traditional" scholars who have incorporated "paradigmatic borrowing" and multiparadigmatic collaboration as strategies to both enhance their own work and provide a path out of the woods of polarized paradigm thinking that other intercultural scholars can follow (Martin and Nakayama, 1999). As examples I can think of how the work of Mary Jane Collier and Judith Martin (long-standing and highly-respected scholars) has been enhanced by their engagement of critical approaches and in turn, how their work has grown in its appeal to intercultural scholars of many traditions. These scholars (and others) evidence the cross-paradigmatic conversation called for by Martin and Nakayama.

Cleary "edginess" alone is insufficient to address the (increasing?) polarization of "traditional" and critical scholarship in the field. The dialectical approach outlined by Martin and Nakayama (1999) offers us the possibility of engaging multiple, but distinct, research paradigms in ways that permit us to see the world in complex and varied ways and become better prepared to engage in and study intercultural interaction. Such a process of engagement will not be easy as they note, "Whereas there cannot be any easy fit among … paradigmatic differences, it is important that we not only recognize these differences, but also seek ways that these epistemological differences can be productive rather than debilitating (p. 19). Refusal to address this issue deprives our field of robust intellectual engagement essential for its growth and evolution and thus remains the next great challenge for critical scholars to take on.

Notes

1   In case you may be tempted to think that low numbers of published critical work might be attributed to problems with the search terms used in this essay, let me clarify my process. As I mentioned earlier, many critical intercultural scholars may use key words other than "intercultural communication" to locate their work. To explore this possibility, I ran additional searches of the Academic Search Premier and Communication and Mass Media Complete and databases using other key phrases including "cross-cultural communication." In using this key term, I located five essays published in association journals. I also did the same with the search term, "culture and communication" and in that search, I located 12 articles published in association journals, most of which deal with media effects and discourses. Of these additional 17 articles, perhaps three or four were written from a critical perspective. Thus, even when expanding the search terms used, critical scholarship remains a small percentage of published work.

References

Arasaratnam, L.A. (2006) Further testing of a new model of intercultural communication competence. *Communication Research Reports*, 23 (2), 93–99.

Barnett, G.A., and Eunjung, S. (2005) Culture and the structure of the international hyperlink network. *Journal of Computer-Mediated Communication*, 11 (1), 217–238.

Blake, A.G., and Kaplowitz, S.A. (2001) Sociolinguistic inference and intercultural coorientation: A Bayesian model of communicative competence in intercultural interaction. *Human Communication Research*, 27 (3), 350–381.

Bresnahan, M.J., Levine, T.R., Shearman, S.M. *et al.* (2005) A multi-method multi-trait validity assessment of self-construal in Japan, Korea, and the United States. *Human Communication Research*, 31 (1), 33–59.

Broome, B.J. (1991) Building shared meaning: Implications of a relational approach to empathy for teaching intercultural communication. *Communication Education*, 40, 235–249.

Cai, D.A., and Fink, E.L. (2002) Conflict style differences between individualist and collectivists. *Communication Monographs*, 69 (1), 67–88.

Calafell, B.M., and Moreman, S.T. (2009) Envisioning an academic readership: Latina/o performativities per the form of publication. *Text and Performance Quarterly*, 29 (2), 123–130.

Callahan, E. (2005) Cultural similarities and differences in the design of university web sites. *Journal of Computer-Mediated Communication*, 11 (1), 239–273.

Carbaugh, D., and Berry, M. (2001) Communicating history, Finnish and American discourses: An ethnographic contribution to intercultural communication inquiry. *Communication Theory*, 11 (3), 352–347.

Carrell, L.J. (1997) Diversity in the communication curriculum: Impact on student empathy. *Communication Education*, 46 (4), 234–245.

Casmir, F.I., and Asuncion-Lande, N.C. (1990) Intercultural communication revisited: Conceptualization, paradigm-building, and methodological approaches, in *Communication Yearbook, 12*, (ed. James A., Anderson), Sage, Newbury Park, CA pp. 278–309.

Chen, L. (1997) Verbal adaptive strategies in U.S. American dyadic interactions with U.S. American or East-Asian partners. *Communication Monographs*, 64 (4), 302–323.

Chesebro, J.W. (1998) Distinguishing cultural systems: Change as a variable explaining and predicting cross-cultural communication, in *International and Intercultural Communication Annual, 21*, (eds Dolores V. Tanno and Alberto González), Sage, Thousand Oaks, CA, pp. 177–192.

Collier, M.J. (1998) Researching cultural identity: Reconciling interpretive and postcolonial approaches, in *Communication and Identity across Cultures*, (eds D. Tanno and A. González) Sage, Thousand Oaks, CA, pp. 122–147.

Collier, M.J. (2001) Transforming communication about culture: An introduction, in *International and Intercultural Communication Annual, 24*, (ed. M.J. Collier), Thousand Oaks, CA, Sage, pp. ix–xix.

Collier, M. (2002) Transforming communication about culture: An introduction, in *Transforming Communication about Culture: Critical New Directions*, (ed. M. Collier), Sage, Thousand Oaks, CA, p. ix.

Collier, M., Hegde, R.S., Lee, W. *et al.* (2001) Dialogue on the edges, in *International and Intercultural Communication Annual, 24*, (ed. M.J. Collier), Sage, Thousand Oaks, CA, pp. 219–280.

Cooks, L. (2001) From distance to uncertainty to research and pedagogy in the Borderlands: Implications for the future of intercultural communication. *Communication Theory*, 11 (3), 339–352.

Cooks, L. (2003) Pedagogy, performance, and positionality: Teaching about whiteness in interracial communication. *Communication Education*, 52 (3/4), 245–257.

Cooks, L.M., and Simpson, J.S. (eds) (2007) *Whiteness, Pedagogy, Performance: Dis/placing Race*. Lexington Books, Lanham, MD.

Covarrubias, P. (2007) (Un)biased in Western theory: Generative silence in American Indian Communication. *Communication Monographs*, 74 (2), 265–271.

Crabtree, R.D. (1998) Mutual empowerment in cross-cultural participatory development and service learning: Lessons in communication and social justice from projects in El Salvador and Nicaragua. *Journal of Applied Communication Research*, 26 (2), 182–209.

Dace, K.L., and McPhail, M.L. (1998) Crossing the color line: From empathy to implicature in intercultural communication, in *Readings in Intercultural Contexts*, (eds J.N. Martin, T.K. Nakayama, and L.A. Flores), Mayfield, Mountain View, CA, pp. 455–463.

DeTurk, S. (2001) Intercultural empathy: Myth, competency, or possibility for alliance-building? *Communication Education*, 50 (4), 374–385.

Drake, L.E. (2001) The culture-negotiation link. Integrative and distributive bargaining through an intercultural communication lens. *Human Communication Research*, 27 (3), 317–349.

Dresner, E. (2006) Davidson's philosophy of communication. *Communication Theory*, 16 (2), 155–172.

Fitch, F., and Morgan, S. (2003). "Not a lick of English": Constructing the ITA identity through student narratives. *Communication Education*, 52 (3/4), 297–310.

Flores, L.A. (2001) Challenging the myth of assimilation: A Chicana feminist response, in *Constituting Cultural Difference through Discourse*, (ed. M.J. Collier), Sage, Thousand Oaks, CA, pp. 26–46.

Foeman, A.K. (2006) "Yo! What's it like to be Black?": An exercise to help students deepen the content of cross-cultural dialogue. *Communication Teacher*, 20 (2), 40–43.

Foucault, M. (1972) *The Archaeology of Knowledge*, Pantheon Books, New York.

Gorham, B.W. (2006) News media's relationship with stereotyping: The linguistic intergroup bias in response to crime news. *The Journal of Communication*, 56 (2), 289–308.

Hall, E.T. (1956) Orientation and training in government for work overseas. *Human Organization*, 15, 4–10.

Halualani, R.T., Fassett, D.L., Morrison, J.H.T.A. *et al.* (2006) Between the structural and the personal: Situated sense-makings of "race." *Communication and Critical/Cultural Studies*, 3 (1), 70–93.

Hammer, M.R., Wiseman, R.L., Rasmussen, J.L. *et al.* (1998) A test of anxiety/uncertainty management theory. The intercultural adaptation context. *Communication Quarterly*, 46 (3), 309–326.

Harris, T.M. (2003) Impacting student perceptions of and attitudes toward race in the interracial communication course. *Communication Education*, 52 (3/4), 311–317.

Harris. T.M. (2004) Interracial communication. *Communication Teacher*, 18 (4), 132–135.

Hegde, R. (1998) Swinging the trapeze: The negotiation of identity among Asian Indian immigrant women in the United States, in *Communication and Identity across Cultures*, (eds D. Tanno and A. González), Sage, Thousand Oaks, CA, pp. 34–55.

Heinz, B. (2004) The world in one semester: International communication partners. *Communication Teacher*, 18 (3), 87–90.

Hendrix, K.G. (2005) An invitation to dialogue: Do Communication journal reviewers mute the race-related research of scholars of color? *Southern Journal of Communication*, 70, 329–345.

Hoerl, K. (2007) Mario Van Peebles's Panther and popular memories of the Black Panther Party. *Critical Studies in Mass Communication*, 24 (3), 206–227.

Kassing, J.W. (1997) Development of the intercultural willingness to communicate scale. *Communication Research Reports*, 14 (4), 399–407.

Kim. Y.Y. (2005) Inquiry into intercultural and development communication. *The Journal of Communication*, 55 (3), 564–577.

Kim, Y.Y. (2007) Ideology, identity, and intercultural communication: An analysis of differing academic conceptions of cultural identity. *Journal of Intercultural Communication Research*, 36 (3), 237–253.

Lee, W.N., and Choi, S.M. (2005) The role of horizontal and vertical individualism and collectivism in online customers' responses toward persuasive communication on the Web. *Journal of Computer-Mediated Communication*, 11 (1), 317–336.

Leeds-Hurwitz, W. (1990) Notes on the history of intercultural communication: The Foreign Service Institute and the mandate for intercultural training. *Quarterly Journal of Speech*, 76, 262–281.

Manusov, V., Winchatz, M., and Manning, L. (1997) Acting out our minds: Incorporating behavior into models of stereotype-based expectancies for cross-cultural interactions. *Communication Monographs*, 64 (2), 119–140.

Martin, J.N., and Davis, O.I. (2001) Conceptual foundations for teaching about whiteness in intercultural communication classes. *Communication Education*, 50 (4), 298–313.

Martin, J.N., and Nakayama, T.K. (1997) *Intercultural Communication in Contexts*, Mayfield, Mountain View, CA.

Martin, J.N., and Nakayama, T.K. (1999) Thinking dialectically about culture and Communication. *Communication Theory*, 9 (1), 1–25.

Martinez, J.M. (2006) Semiotic phenomenology and intercultural communication scholarship: Meeting the challenge of racial, ethnic, and cultural difference. *Western Journal of Communication*, 70 (4), 292–310.

Matlon, R.J. (1992). *Index to Journals in Communication Studies through 1990*, Speech Communication Association, Annandale, VA.

Matveev, A.V. (2004) Describing intercultural competence: In-depth interviews with American and Russian managers. *Qualitative Research Reports in Communication*, 5, 55–62.

McCann, R.M., and Honeycutt, J.M. (2006) A cross-cultural analysis of imagined interactions. *Human Communication Research*, 32 (3), 274–301.

Mendoza, S.L., Halualani, R.T., and Drzewiecka, J.A. (2002) Moving the discourse on identities in intercultural communication: Structure, culture, and resignifications. *Communication Quarterly*, 50 (3/4), 312–327.

Miller, A.N. (2002) The exploration of Kenyan public speaking patterns with implications for the American introductory public speaking course. *Communication Education*, 51 (2), 168–183.

Miller, J.B. (1992) Domination and subordination, in *The Social Construction of Difference: Race, Class, Gender, and Sexuality,* (ed. P.S. Rothenberg), St. Martin's Press, New York, pp. 73–80.

Moon, D.G. (1996) Concepts of "culture": Implications for intercultural communication research. *Communication Quarterly,* 44 (1), 70–84.

Moon, D.G. (1998) Performed identities: Passing as an inter/cultural discourse, in *Readings in Cultural Contexts* (eds J.N. Martin, T.K., Nakayama, and L.A. Flores), Mayfield, Mountain View, CA, pp. 322–330.

Moon, D.G. (2000) Interclass travel, cultural adaptation, and "passing" as a disjunctive inter/cultural practice, in *International and Intercultural Communication Annual, 23,* (eds Y.Y. Kim and W.B. Gudykunst), Sage, Thousand Oaks, CA, pp. 215–240.

Mulac, A., Bradac, J.J., and Gibbons, P. (2001) Empirical support for the gender-as-culture hypothesis. An *intercultural* analysis of male/female language differences. *Human Communication Research,* 27 (1), 121–152.

Nakayama, T.K., and Martin, J.N. (2007) The "white" problem in intercultural communication research and pedagogy, in *Whiteness, Pedagogy, Performance: Dis/placing Race* (eds Leda M. Cooks and Jennifer S. Simpson), Lexington Books, Lanham, MD, pp. 111–13.

Neuliep, J.W., and McCroskey, J. (1997) The development of a U.S., and generalized ethnocentrism scale. *Communication Research Reports,* 14 (4), 385–398.

Neuliep, J.W., and Ryan, D. J. (1998). The influence of intercultural communication apprehension and socio-economic orientation on uncertainty reduction during initial cross cultural encounters. *Communication Quarterly,* 46 (1), 88–99.

Nishishiba, M., and Ritchie, L.D. (2000) The concept of trustworthiness: A cross-cultural comparison between Japanese and U.S. business people. *Journal of Applied Communication Research,* 28 (4), 347–369.

Oetzel, J.G., and Ting-Toomey, S. (2003) Face concerns in interpersonal conflict: A cross-cultural empirical test of the face negotiation theory. *Communication Research Reports,* 30 (6), 599–624.

Oetzel, J., Ting-Toomey, S., Masumoto, T. *et al.* (2001) Face and facework in conflict: A cross-cultural comparison of China, Germany, Japan, and the United States. *Communication Monographs,* 68 (3), 235–259.

Ono, K.A. (1998) Problematizing "nation" in intercultural communication research, in *International and Intercultural Communication Annual, 21,* (eds Dolores V. Tanno and Alberto González), Sage, Thousand Oaks, CA, pp. 193–22.

Orbe, M.P. (1998). *Constructing Co-Cultural Theory: An Explication of Culture, Power, and Communication,* Sage, Thousand Oaks, CA.

Ota, H., Giles, H., and Somera, L. (2007) Beliefs about intra-and intergenerational in Japan, the Philippines, and the United States. *Communication Studies,* 58 (2), 173–188.

Park, H.S., and Levine, T.R. (1999) The theory of reasoned action and self-construal: Evidence from three cultures. *Communication Monographs,* 66 (3), 199–218.

Quinlisk, C.C. (2004) Communicator status and expectations in intercultural communication: Implications for language learning in a multicultural community. *Communication Research Reports,* 21 (1), 84–91.

Rinderie, S. (2005) The Mexican diaspora: A critical examination of signifiers. *Journal of Communication Inquiry,* 29 (4), 294–316.

Roach, K.D., and Olaniran, B.A. (2001) Intercultural willingness to communicate and communication anxiety in international teaching assistants. *Communication Research Reports*, 18 (1), 26–35.

Rogers, E.M. (1999) Georg Simmel's concept of the stranger and intercultural communication research. *Communication Theory*, 9 (1), 58–74.

Scott, J.C. (2000) Differences in American and British vocabulary: Implications for international business communication. *Communication Quarterly*, 63 (4), 27–39.

Sellnow, D., Liu, M., and Venetter, S. (2006) When in Rome, do as the Romans do: A comparative analysis of Chinese and American new teachers' compliance-gaining strategies. *Communication Research Reports*, 23 (4), 259–264.

Tasaki, K., and Min-Sun, K. (1999) The effects of social status on cognitive elaboration and post-message attitude: Focus on self-construals. *Communication Quarterly*, 47 (2), 196–214.

Warren, J.T. (2003) *Performing Purity: Whiteness, Pedagogy, and the Reconstitution of Power*, Peter Lang, New York.

Wurtz, E. (2005) Intercultural communication on Web sites: A cross-cultural analysis of Web sites from high-context cultures and low-context cultures. *Journal of Computer-Mediated Communication*, 11 (1), 274–299.

Yang, L., and Rancer, A.S. (2003) Ethnocentrism, intercultural communication apprehension, intercultural willingness-to-communicate, and intentions to participate in an intercultural dialogue program: Testing a proposed model. *Communication Research Reports*, 20 (2), 189–190.

Zhu, Y., and Valentine, D. (2001) Using a knowledge-based approach to develop student intercultural competence in industry. *Communication Quarterly*, 64 (3), 102–109.

4

Reflecting Upon "Enlarging Conceptual Boundaries: A Critique of Research in Intercultural Communication"

Alberto González

Scholarly Landscape

The late-1980s and early-1990s were exciting years in communication studies, especially for those who studied culture and communication. Many influential works came from outside of communication. At that time, Gloria Anzaldúa's (1987) book, *Borderlands/*La Frontera: *The New Mestiza* was still a tremendous inspiration with her accessible depictions of hybrid identity and border culture. Similarly, the critique of feminist theory by bell hooks in *Feminist Theory: From Margin to Center* (1984) provided a model for examining scholarly and pedagogical emphases within communication studies. Other authors such as Patricia Hill Collins (1991) and Ruth Behar (1993) were fresh voices that examined the politics of theory and cultural interpretation. I still fondly recall the excitement that ran through my department when someone, somehow (this was before web sites!) had obtained a copy of the course syllabus for an ethnography course taught by Professor Behar at the University of Michigan.

Within communication, critical perspectives transformed notions of rhetoric and culture. For example, Ramie McKerrow's (1989) essay on "Critical Rhetoric: Theory and Praxis," Dwight Conquergood's (1991) essay, "Rethinking Ethnography: Towards a Critical Cultural Politics" and James Carey's (1992) book *Communication as Culture*: *Essays on Media and Society* left me wondering how to read these treatments even as I knew that I was allied with their alternative notions of liberation, drama, and dialogue.

Tarla Rai Peterson and I were assistant professors at Texas A & M University in the late-1980s. Tarla's interests spanned rhetoric, the environment, and gender studies, while my interests spanned rhetoric, culture, and intercultural communication. The two of us had worked with Marty Medhurst on an edited book, *Communication & the Culture of Technology* (1990). Through this project Tarla and I found that we

The Handbook of Critical Intercultural Communication, edited by Thomas K. Nakayama and Rona Tamiko Halualani.   © 2010 Blackwell Publishing Ltd.

worked well together and had a common sensibility toward academe. It seemed that the time was right to examine feminist criticism in communication from an intercultural perspective. We asked: If communication is to move from what we called "privileged Anglo-masculine analyses of culture, social structures and behavior," (González and Peterson, p. 251) to a feminist analysis of culture and intercultural relations, what would that look like? Fortunately, our department encouraged and supported collaboration and critical inquiry. We presented our initial approach to this question at the Speech Communication Association National Convention in 1989. The paper was called "Unexplored Possibilities for a Feminist Perspective in Intercultural Communication Inquiry." In 1990, Tarla and I presented a follow-up paper called, "Entreé in Gender Research: Responsibilities, Difficulties and Potential" at the Conference on Research in Gender and Communication in Atlanta, Georgia. It was at this conference that we met Sheryl Perlmutter Bowen and Nancy Wyatt. Sheri and Nancy would soon coedit *Transforming Visions: Feminist Critiques in Communication Studies* (1993) in which "Enlarging Conceptual Boundaries: A Critique of Research in Intercultural Communication" would appear.

Before our chapter was to land in *Transforming Visions*, we attempted to publish our work in a mainstream communication journal. I do not have a record of the journal to which we sent the paper, but I do have the review (pers. comm. February 5, 1991). The reviewer found the notion of exploring linkages between feminist and intercultural perspectives interesting. However, the reviewer stated, "I must say in all candor that I have some problems with this paper. First, a feminist perspective as defined by González *et al.* is inherently judgmental. A perspective that is inherently judgmental – relying on terms like domination, oppression, radicalizing – is, in my view, incompatible with an intercultural perspective." The reviewer went on to give the core purpose of intercultural study (italics are in the original): "The thrust of intercultural communication, from my perspective, is to *describe* cultural phenomena: it is not supposed to *evaluate* cultural events." The reviewer concluded by saying that the paper "could be improved if the evaluative terms were removed [and] a value neutral approach was taken."

This review was instructive on so many levels! Foremost, this review taught us that intercultural communication scholars who thought and wrote from critical perspectives were not considered intercultural scholars. Someone who began with a descriptive premise for intercultural communication excluded critical scholars by definition. This explained the frustration of many communication scholars – particularly African American and Latino/as – that was expressed on many panels at both regional and national communication conventions. The review exposed the incredible tension created by the proliferation of interdisciplinary critical inquiry outside communication studies and the conservative and defensive nature of communication studies.

For many of us, this divide was about more than a difference in research method or research perspective – it was about inclusion and the "real" role of the gateway positions within academe. I return to the nature of gateways below.

This review also taught us that we had to make a strong a statement about the status of intercultural communication research. We had the opportunity to do this when Sheri Bowen and Nancy Wyatt issued the call for submissions to *Transforming Visions*.

Writing "Chapter 9"

One of the goals of what was to become "Chapter 9" in *Transforming Visions,* was to depict the fragmented status of intercultural scholarship. This is why we provided an overview of intercultural communication that advanced three categories of research: the Cultural Measurement Branch, the Cultural Description Branch, and the Cultural Criticism Branch. Our naming of these categories as "branches" was deliberate. We wanted to convey an organic and changing quality to the research in these categories. We wanted to avoid "pure," "ideal," or "classic" instances of intercultural study. Like cultures, the research about them adapts to and contests new influences and partici-pants in sometimes unpredictable ways. Besides, our original choice of three research "camps" sounded too militaristic and there was enough discord already.

The main goal was to begin to redefine what counted as intercultural communi-cation research. By placing these research programs under the same heading of "intercultural communication" we wanted to legitimize *to the field* if not to our-selves the kinds of studies that many scholars of color were doing that creatively blended notions of gender, race and ethnicity, communication, and culture. Regardless of the prevailing perception, we wanted to seat scholars such as William Gudykunst, Gerry Philipsen, and Molefi Asante at the same intercultural table (though they might be positioned at opposite ends of the table).

We also wanted to make the case that writing from a feminist perspective did not entail a narrow and predetermined cultural judgment. First, we argued that the calls by traditional interculturalists for an ethic of cultural acceptance and inclusion were com-patible with feminist critiques of domination. Second, we wanted to show that having a feminist perspective did not preclude the critic – or relieve the critic – from interpret-ing how women "make sense of their own reality" (González and Peterson, 1993, p. 266) in ways they would recognize and authorize. We pointed to examples of qualita-tive data gathering from diaries, women's autobiographies, poems, and ethnography and to textual analysis from more conventional sources of public communication to illustrate the possibilities for a grounded approach to feminist intercultural inquiry.

In writing this section on research, we did not want to appear to be appeasing the traditionalists, or to be trying to gain their approval, we simply wanted to show that their dismissal of critical perspectives as illustrated by our paper reviewer, was both wrong and limiting.

Next Steps

There was another lesson taught by the review of our submission. Editorships clearly reflect the preferences of editors and influence what readers come to accept as appro-priate questions, topics, and methods in a research area. Editors can encourage or discourage lines of inquiry and while this seems like an observation that any master's student can recite, there was so much new critical literature being published that we naïvely thought communication studies was keeping pace. We were wrong.

By the early 1990s, I realized that to expand the range of who and what people read about intercultural communication I would have to gain some of the gatekeeping positions that were so obviously influential. Emboldened by hooks' (1989) new book *Talking Back: Thinking Feminist, Thinking Black*, I concluded that communication studies was an entity *with which I could interact*. Still, I was afraid. While presenting a paper (González, 1993) at the Kenneth Burke Society Convention held in Airlie, Virginia, I asked a close friend Dolores Tanno, then at California State University, San Bernardino, if she would like to co-edit the *International and Intercultural Communication Annual*. The *Annual* was published by Sage for the Speech Communication Association. It was the premier outlet for intercultural research. She agreed and so began the saga of gaining the editorship.

Throughout the 1980s, the *Annual* had been dominated by the Cultural Measurement Branch. The themes seemed repetitive and did not reflect the vibrancy of activity that I knew existed. My goal was to hold an intervention by proposing new themes for each volume and sending the calls for submissions to the very writers who felt excluded from mainstream publication venues. These themes were designed to invite participation from scholars working in all three Branches. Though initially we were judged not qualified to edit the *Annual* the Publications Board of SCA eventually accepted my proposal.

We produced three volumes: *Politics, Communication, and Culture* (González and Tanno, 1997), *Communication and Identity across Cultures* (Tanno and González, 1998), and *Rhetoric in Intercultural Contexts* (González and Tanno, 1999). I am pleased that contributors included emerging scholars who are prominent now as well as scholars who were already well established in intercultural research.

At the same time that "Enlarging Conceptual Boundaries: A Critique of Research in Intercultural Communication" was accepted for inclusion in *Transforming Visions*, Marsha Houston, then at Tulane University and Victoria Chen, then at Denison University and I had committed to editing an intercultural anthology for Roxbury Press. We called it *Our Voices: Essays in Culture, Ethnicity, and Communication* (González, Houston and Chen, 1994). The idea for the book was Marsha's. Her thought was to provide intercultural perspectives and experiences that were readily and repeatedly available at communication conventions, but not in journals or books. We dedicated the book "To those who spoke unheard before us." Never one to mince words with friend or foe, however, Marsha's admonition to contributors was essentially, "Let's say what we want to about culture in this book and then move on."

Like "Enlarging Conceptual Boundaries: A Critique of Research in Intercultural Communication" this anthology was another critique of mainstream intercultural literature. Though I was not familiar at the time with Linda Alcoff's (1991) essay, "The Problem of Speaking for Others," she articulated what we believed was a weakness in intercultural research. Using her terms, we believed that intercultural studies and texts were "about" us (the cultural others) rather than "with" us. We remained silent but were spoken "for" by the permanent authorities that occupied privileged locations within the academy. *Our Voices* remains our attempt to speak for ourselves featuring varying aspects of economic class, ethnicity, gender, religion, and nationality. There was no desire to present a unified African American, Chinese or Latino perspective. We wanted readers to encounter the diversity of voices within these labels rather than the monolithic presentations of cultures found in the texts at the time.

We pitched the book to several major publishers of communication texts, but the acquisition editors always questioned our vision for the book: "Don't you want to include more communication theory? Don't you want established researchers among the contributors? Are the personal experiences of the authors cultural? Don't you think that a white researcher should write the foreword in order to bring credibility to the collection?" Roxbury Publishing was an independent company in Los Angeles with a small book list. We give credit at every opportunity to Claude Teweles for giving us complete control over the direction of the anthology through four editions. Without his trust in us, *Our Voices* might never have been published.

As the first edition of *Our Voices* emerged in 1994 – populated with scholars early in their careers – we proclaimed the need for imitators. With additional collections, more of our voices would be shared. Always be careful what you ask for.

Conclusion

This period of time from the late-1980s through the mid-1990s saw the activation of a network of critical scholars. At that juncture, many of us chose to engage our academic organizations by serving on editorial boards, becoming program planners, forming new units within SCA (now the National Communication Association), editing books and journals and running for various leadership positions. In addition to delivering new content, we wanted to deliver a sense of inescapability. Our critique of the mainstream in communication studies played a small role in fueling a larger scholarly activism that by 2010 clearly has resulted in greater diversity in what is read in intercultural communication.

The interest in race, ethnicity, and intercultural communication has intensified. The program on whiteness studies continues with the Cooks and Simpson (2007) collection as a recent example. Recently, the *International and Intercultural Communication Annual* became a quarterly journal with Thomas K. Nakayama as inaugural editor. A second edition of the Orbe and Harris (2008) text on *Interracial Communication* is now available.

It is important to note that coalitions always underlie novel responses to intellectual or professional exigencies. Key allies such as Professors James Chesebro, Ramie McKerrow, William Starosta, Judith Trent, and others provided encouragement and opportunities to many who pursued new critical cultural writing and research. Much of the productivity of the 1990s was facilitated by their efforts.

I have described the development of just one book chapter. That chapter and other important works – many described in this volume – found their way into graduate course readings and research projects. These early critiques now play the role of points of departure for current critical work.

References

Alcoff, L. (1991) The problem of speaking for others. *Cultural Critique*, 20, 5–33.

Anzaldúa, G. (1987) *Borderlands*/La Frontera: *The New Mestiza*, Spinsters/Aunt Lute Book Company, San Francisco.

Behar, R. (1993) *Translated Woman: Crossing the Border with Esperanza's Story*, Beacon Press, Boston, MA.

Bowen, S.P., and Wyatt, N. (1993) *Transforming Visions: Feminist Critiques in Communication Studies*, Hampton Press, Cresskill, NJ.

Carey, J.W. (1992) *Communication as Culture: Essays on Media and Society*, Routledge, New York.

Collins, P.H. (1991) *Black Feminist Thought: Knowledge, Consciousness, and the Politics of Empowerment*. Routledge, New York.

Conquergood, D. (1991) Rethinking ethnography: Towards a critical cultural politics. *Communication Monographs*, 58, 179–194.

Cooks, L.M., and Simpson, J.S. (eds.) (2007) *Whiteness, Pedagogy, Performance: Dis/Placing Race*, Lexington Books, Lanham, MD.

González, A. (1993) Kenneth Burke, otherness, and Mexican American rhetoric. Kenneth Burke Society Second National Triennial Convention, Airlie, VA.

González, A., Houston, M., and Chen, V. (1994) *Our Voices: Essays in Culture, Ethnicity, and Communication*, Roxbury Press, Los Angeles.

González, A., and Peterson, T.R. (1993) Enlarging conceptual boundaries: A critique of research in intercultural communication, in *Transforming Visions: Feminist Critiques in Communication Studies*, (eds S.P. Bowen and N. Wyatt), Hampton Press, Cresskill, NJ, pp. 249–278.

González, A., and Tanno, D.V. (1997) *Politics, Communication, and Culture. International and Intercultural Communication Annual*, 20, Sage, Thousand Oaks, CA.

González, A., and Tanno, D.V. (1999) *Rhetoric in Intercultural Contexts. International and Intercultural Communication Annual*, 22, Sage, Thousand Oaks, CA.

hooks, b. (1984) *Feminist Theory: From Margin to Center*, South End Press, Boston, MA.

hooks, b. (1989) *Talking Back: Thinking Feminist, Thinking Black*, Temple University Press, Philadelphia, PA.

McKerrow, R.E. (1989) Critical rhetoric: Theory and praxis. *Communication Monographs*, 56, 91–111.

Medhurst, M.J., González, A., and Peterson, T.R. (1990). *Communication & the Culture of Technology*, Washington State University Press, Pullman, WA.

Orbe, M.P., and Harris, T.M. (2008) *Interracial Communication: Theory into Practice*, 2nd edn, Sage, Los Angeles.

Tanno, D.V. and González, A. (1998) *Communication and Identity across Cultures. International and Intercultural Communication Annual*, 21, Sage, Thousand Oaks, CA.

5

Intercultural Communication and Dialectics Revisited

Judith N. Martin and Thomas K. Nakayama

Ten years ago, we identified and described four distinct paradigms of culture and communication research (functionalist, interpretive, critical humanist, and critical structuralist) based on their metatheoretical assumptions and explored strategies for constructive interparadigmatic discussions (Martin and Nakayama, 1999). We then proposed a new way – a dialectical approach – to conceptualize and study intercultural communication. We suggested that a dialectic perspective could guide future research in two ways. First, as a trans-paradigmatic methodology for study-ing culture and communication phenomena and second, as a conceptual frame-work for understanding intercultural communication practice. In this essay we again survey current culture and communication research through a paradigmatic lens, assess the current contributions of a dialectical approach to the study of culture and communication and offer new directions for incorporating a dialectic perspective into our research.

After 10 years, revisiting the contemporary terrain of intercultural communication seems warranted. The field has exploded in many different directions that have opened up the very notion of "intercultural" communication. In some ways, the term itself, "intercultural," tends to presume the interaction between discrete and different cultures. We know, however, that cultures have always been in contact and that the notion of cultural difference hides and masks the very ways that cultures have already influenced each other. So rather than cultural difference, our inclination is to put that concept into dialectical tension with cultural similarity to highlight the hybrid and heterogeneous character of all cultures. Ten years later, the very problem of conceptualizing "intercultural communication" remains as vibrant and relevant as ever.

The Handbook of Critical Intercultural Communication, edited by Thomas K. Nakayama and Rona Tamiko Halualani. © 2010 Blackwell Publishing Ltd.

Current Paradigmatic Approaches

Our original article identified four paradigms (functionalist, interpretive, critical humanist, and structural humanist) that defined the contours of research in the area. A more recent review of extant culture and communication research reveals that the original taxonomy still guides inquiry in this area[1] and there seem to be three emerging trends: (1) a continuing critique of Western paradigmatic research traditions, (2) a burgeoning body of literature focused on postcolonial approaches within the two critical paradigms, and (3) a growing trend of what we termed interparadigmatic borrowing, leading to a blurring of paradigmatic assumptions.

Functionalist paradigm

The functionalist paradigm, perhaps more commonly referred to now as postpositivist, still dominates much of culture and communication scholarship with foundations in social psychological research (Barnett and Lee, 2002; Gudykunst, 2003; Gudykunst *et al.*, 2005; Hofstede, 1991). From this perspective, culture is often viewed as a variable, defined *a priori* by group membership, many times on a national level, and includes an emphasis on the stable and orderly characteristics of culture, and the relationship between culture and communication is usually conceptualized as causal and deterministic (Martin and Nakayama, 1999). That is, group membership and the related cultural patterns (e.g., values like individualism–collectivism) can theoretically predict communication behaviors including conflict styles (Ting-Toomey and Oetzel, 2002), face concerns (Ting-Toomey, 1994, 2005), conversational constraints (M.S. Kim, 2005), conversational style (Kim *et al.*, 1996), anxiety/uncertainty management strategies (Gudykunst, 2005), and accommodation strategies (Gallois *et al.*, 1995; Gallois, Ogay and Giles, 2005, Giles, Coupland and Coupland, 1991).

Interpretive paradigm

Scholars who conduct culture and communication research in the interpretive paradigm are concerned with understanding the world as it is, and describing the subjective, creative communication of individuals, usually using qualitative research methods. This work is largely based on the philosophical foundations of contemporary phenomenology (Merleau-Ponty, 1962), hermeneutics (Dilthey, 1976, Gadamer, 1976, 1989; Schleiermacher, 1977), and symbolic interactionism (Mead, 1934). Interpretivism emphasizes the "knowing mind as an active contributor to the constitution of knowledge" (Mumby, 1997, p. 6). Culture, in the interpretive paradigm, is generally seen as socially constructed and emergent, rather than defined *a priori*, and it is not limited to nationstate collectives; interpretivists emphasize the stable, orderly characteristics of culture, reflecting an assumption of the social world as cohesive, ordered, and integrated (Martin and Nakayama, 1999). The relationship between culture and communication is seen as more reciprocal than causal, where culture may influence communication but is also constructed and enacted through communication. Communication is often viewed as patterned codes that serve a communal, unifying function (Carbaugh, 1988a, 1988b, 1990; Hall, 1992; Philipsen, Coutu and Covarrubias, 2005).

The strongest exemplars of such research continue to be the ethnography of communication studies conducted by Donal Carbaugh and colleagues, studies of how social/cultural identities are intricately intertwined with communicative codes (Carbaugh, 1996); and how these communicative codes vary from culture to culture and often lead to misunderstandings in intercultural interactions (Carbaugh, 2005; Carbaugh and Berry, 2001). For example, studies have focused on the communication contrasts between Russian and US American, Blackfeet Indian and white US Americans, as well as comparisons of Finnish and US Americans patterns of conversational speech and silence. A second major interpretive research program is based on the Communication Theory of Identity (Hecht, 1993; Jung and Hecht, 2004; Hecht *et al.*, 2005). For example, Witteborn's (2004) study of Arab women's expressions of cultural identity before and after 9/11, Golden, Niles and Hecht (2002) study of Jewish American Identity and Ribeau, Hecht and Jackson's (2003) study of African-American identity.

As we noted in our earlier essay, there are a few research programs like Y.Y. Kim's (2002, 2005, 2008) that do not fit neatly into one paradigm. Although she designates her systems-based theory of cultural adaptation as distinctive from both functionalist and interpretive paradigms (Y.Y. Kim, 1988), one could argue that her theory is based primarily on functional social psychological research on cultural adaptation, and has generated primarily functionalist research.

The rise of the critical paradigm and its influence on research in other paradigms has been dramatic. For critical scholars, culture is not a benignly socially constructed variable, but a site of struggle where various communication meanings are contested within social hierarchies – the ultimate goal is to examine systems of oppression and work for system change. Critical scholars in the two remaining paradigms vary in their emphasis either focusing on the "consciousness" as the basis for a radical critique of society, or structural relationships within a realist social world (Burrell and Morgan, 1988, p. 34).   *Com there of it*

Critical humanist paradigm

Critical humanist research has much in common with the interpretive viewpoint, as both assume that reality is socially constructed and emphasize the voluntaristic characteristic of human behavior. However, critical humanist researchers conceive this voluntarism and human consciousness as dominated by ideological superstructures and material conditions that drive a wedge between them and a more liberated consciousness. Within this paradigm, the point of academic research into cultural differences is based upon a belief in the possibility of changing uneven, differential ways of constructing and understanding other cultures.

Founded largely upon the work by Althusser (1971), Gramsci (1971, 1978), and the Frankfurt school (Habermas 1970, 1981, 1987; Horkheimer and Adorno,

consciousness as dominated by ideological
superstructures and material conditions

1988; Marcuse, 1964), critical humanist scholars attempt to work toward articulating ways in which humans can resist the societal forces. One prominent strand of research focuses on the construction of cultural identities in intercultural settings, identifying ways that individuals negotiate relations with the larger discursive frameworks; for example, Nakayama's (1997) description of the competing and contradictory discourses that construct identity of Japanese-Americans, Flores (1994, 2003) work on Chicana and Chicano immigrant identities and Lee's (1999) essay on Chinese women's identities all explore the contradictory and competing ways in which identity is constructed. Other examples of research in this paradigm are critical rhetorical studies, for example, Nakayama and Krizek's (1995) study of the rhetoric of Whiteness. Finally, there is also a growing body of popular culture studies that explore how media and other messages are presented and interpreted (and resisted) in often conflicting ways (e.g., Delgado, 2002).[2]

Of particular interest to culture and communication scholars is postcolonial scholarship. Postcolonial studies, based on Edward Said's work (1979, 1994) examine power relations in the transnational global world, concerned with the effects and affects of colonialism that accompanied or formed the underside of colonialism (Ashcroft, Griffiths and Tifflin, 1995; Diaz, 2003; Dirlik, 1994; Hegde, 1998c; Quayson, 2000; Schwarz, 2000: Shome, 1996; Shome and Hegde, 2002). While much of critical theory work has focused on disenfranchised groups, based on race, gender, sexual orientation *within* nationstates, postcolonial scholarship provides an historical and international depth to the understanding of cultural power. As noted by Shome and Hegde (2002), postcolonial scholars study issues of race, class, gender, sexuality and nationality that are of concern to contemporary critical scholarship, by situating these phenomena within geopolitical arrangements, and relationship of nations and their inter/national histories" (p. 252).

This scholarship is represented primarily within the critical humanist paradigm which stresses the importance of change and conflict in society. Based largely on work by Foucault and Spivak, postcolonial researchers have explored the ways that marginalized voices can speak and under what conditions. For example, in her work with battered Asian women, Supriya (1996, 2002) explores the conditions that both allow and disallow these women to speak about their experiences and the construction of their identities within a culturally different dominant environment in Chicago. How people navigate identities within the historical contexts of Euro-American domination around the world is reflected in this scholarship whether these people have migrated to new places or not. For example, Darling-Wolf's (2004) exploration of how Japanese women negotiate notions of attractiveness/ beauty within forces of US colonialism and cultural imperialism, Kraidy's (2002) and Kraidy and Murphy's (2008) discussion of cultural hybridity and Hegde's (1998a, 1998b) studies of Asian women and immigrants, as well as Hall's (1985) study of hybridity and Caribbean identity underscore the complex ways that new subjectivities are (re)produced and deployed. Whereas Hall relies more on Foucault, Supriya's work rests more on Spivak, but both are concerned with questions of identity and hybridity in the aftermath of the forces of colonialism and imperialism.

By focusing on the ways that these experience and negotiate these forces, postcolonialism can be a type of critical humanism.

Critical structuralist paradigm

Critical structuralist research also advocates change – but from an objectivist and more deterministic standpoint. Whereas the critical humanists forge their perspective by focusing upon "consciousness" as the basis for a radical critique of society, the critical structuralists concentrate upon structural relationships within a realist social world (Burrell and Morgan, p. 34). Largely based upon the structuralist emphasis of Western Marxists (Gramsci, 1971, 1978; Lukács, 1971; Volosinov, 1973), this approach emphasizes the significance of the structures and material conditions that guide and constrain the possibilities of cultural contact, intercultural communication, and cultural change. Within this paradigm, the possibilities for changing intercultural relations rest largely upon the structural relations imposed by the dominant structure (Mosco, 1996). Here, culture is conceptualized as societal structures. These scholars largely examine economic aspects of industries that produce cultural products (e.g., advertising, media) and how some industries are able to dominate the cultural sphere with their products (Fejes, 1986; Meehan, 1993). For example, Roth (2001) examines a range of ways that the material world influences intercultural communication, from the medium of communication (e.g., more choice due to technological advances but these structures also shape the quality and type of interaction) as well as the larger structural contexts, such as international trade and globalization (e.g., McDonaldization and Coca-colonization of cultures).

The impact of the critical research (emphasizing history, power relations, and societal forces/contexts) is increasingly incorporated into positivist and interpretive research (Collier *et al.*, 2002; Halualani, Mendoza and Drzewiecka, 2009; Nakayama and Martin, 2007), extending the work of a few earlier scholars who noted the important role of power dynamics within intercultural communication (Casmir, 1993; Folb, 1982; Houston, 1992; Pennington, 1989). In addition, critical sensibilities concerning research methodologies can be seen in various calls for culture and communication scholars in all paradigms to examine the consequences of power differentials between researchers and researched and how researchers' positions and privilege constrain their interpretations of research findings (Collier, 2006; González, 2000; González and Krizek, 1994; Martin and Butler, 2001; Moon, 1996; Tanno and Jandt, 1994). The influence of critical thought is also seen in the increasing calls for researchers to address issues of social justice, and demand that research be relevant to everyday communicators. As scholar-activists, our research should ultimately work to improve the lives of those we seek to understand (Broome *et al.*, 2005; Thurlow, 2004).

Finally a number of scholars point to the ethnocentrism in much of communication research, including culture and communication scholarship, and offer alternative foundations for research endeavors (Asante, 1987). More than 20 years ago Ishii (1984) noted the limitations of western theorizing in intercultural communication and called for more indigenous perspectives. Gordon (1998/1999) also critiqued

marginalized voice can speak, under w/conditions

the ethnocentric western bias in communication theorizing, cautioning that the communication theory developed in the United States should not become the communication theory for the world and called for multicultural communication perspectives to be generated and shared internationally. Many scholars have heeded these exhortations, resulting in a "multicultural turn in communication theory" (Miike 2007, p. 272). For example, Min Sun Kim (2002) has critiqued Western bias in the positivistic communication research on self-related variables (e.g., communication styles, self disclosure, conflict styles) and called for a shift from an Anglo-centered field to one that questions the pervasive European-American belief in the autonomous individual: "we need to recognize one major stumbling block in knowledge production in Western contexts: a cultural view that the individual, *a priori*, is separate and self-contained, and must resist the collective" (Miike, 2007, p. 283).

Miike (2003, 2004, 2006) has written extensively on how Asiacentric epistemological, ontological, and methodological traditions might transform Eurocentric communication research into culturally reflexive and sensitive theories and practice. These sentiments are echoed by other scholars such as Gordon (2007) who identifies four areas that have been insufficiently attended to within the dominant (i.e., US American) communication theory: (1) the "relational" self, (2) human "feeling" and the human "body," (3) "nature" and "spirit" and (4) more "communal" and less "agentic" discourses. He calls for scholars from around the world to enrich the "communication" conversation (p. 89). Commenting on Gordon's call, Ishii (2007) further describes the deep philosophical and religious foundations that undergird many Asian communication insights and suggests that the "introduction of Asian scholarly paradigms to their Western counterparts is increasingly expected to serve as a new illuminating signpost for the further healthy development of the challenging discipline of communication studies and education" (p. 108). It remains to be seen whether these calls will result in new paradigms or whether the Asiacentric scholarship will be incorporated into current communication conceptualization and research endeavors.

Beyond the Paradigms

Our 1999 essay identified four research strategies for productively managing discourse across the paradigmatic divide: liberal pluralism, interparadigmatic borrowing, multiparadigmatic collaboration, and a dialectic perspective.

Liberal pluralism acknowledges the value of each paradigmatic perspective, that each contributes in some unique way to our understanding of culture and communication. Recent researchers have adopted this perspective – as ways of helping us think about various communication topics. For example, research on cultural identity can be described as falling into particular paradigmatic approaches (Yep, 2003).

A second and more frequent position is that of *interparadigmatic borrowing*. This position is also strongly committed to paradigmatic research, but recognizes potential complementary contributions from other paradigms. Researchers taking this position listen carefully to what others say, read research from other paradigms, and integrate some concerns or issues into their own research. As noted earlier, the influence of critical scholarship is now seen throughout positivist and interpretive scholarship – as issues of history, context and power relations are incorporated into much of current research (Halualani, Mendoza and Drzewiecka, 2009). One example is Collier's (and colleagues) recent work that incorporates notions of history and power differentials in ongoing studies of interethnic relationships (Thompson and Collier, 2006) and cultural identity (Collier, 2005). This borrowing is analogous to a traveler abroad learning new cultural ways (e.g., learning new expressions) that they incorporate into their lives back home. However, the researcher, while borrowing, is still fundamentally committed to research within a particular paradigm.

A third position is *multiparadigmatic collaboration*. This approach is not to be undertaken lightly. It is based on the assumption that any one research paradigm is limiting, that all researchers are limited by their own experience and worldview (Deetz, 1996; Hammersly, 1992), and that different approaches each have something to contribute. Unlike the other positions, it does not privilege any one paradigm and attempts to make explicit the contributions of each in researching the same general research question. Though this sounds good, it is fraught with pitfalls. Deetz (1996) warns against "teflon-coated multiperspectivalism" that leads to shallow readings (p. 204). Others have warned against unproductive synthetic (integrative) and additive (pluralistic, supplementary) approaches (Deetz, 1996; Hall, 1992). We suggested in our original essay that culture and communication scholars are particularly well positioned for interparadigmatic dialogue and multiparadigmatic collaboration, since these approaches remind us of our interdisciplinary foundations, when anthropologists like E.T. Hall used linguistic frameworks to analyze nonverbal interaction – a daring and innovative move (Leeds-Hurwitz, 1990).

Interparadigmatic dialogue now seems quite common as noted above, while multiparadigmatic collaboration (collaborative research in multicultural teams) is more challenging and less common. Our own collaboration focusing on questions of white identity ("What does being White mean communicatively in the United States today?)" led to a series of studies, a type of rotation among incompatible orientations and led to some insights about the meaning of Whiteness in the United States today (Nakayama and Krizek, 1995; Martin *et al.*, 1996).

A fourth position is a *dialectic perspective*. Like multiparadigmatic research, this position moves beyond paradigmatic thinking, but is even more challenging in that it seeks to find a way to live with the inherent contradictions and seemingly mutual exclusivity of these various approaches. That is, a dialectic approach accepts that human nature is probably both creative and deterministic; that research goals can predict, describe, and change; that the relationship between culture and communication is, most likely, both reciprocal and contested. Dialectic offers intercultural communication researchers a way to think about different ways of knowing in a more comprehensive manner, while retaining the significance of considering how we express this knowledge. In our original essay, we did not advocate any single form of dialectic as "No single dialectical form can satisfy epistemological needs within the complexity of multiple cultures. To reach for a singular dialectical form runs counter to the very notion of dialectical because dialectical thinking depends so closely on the habitual everyday mode of thought which it is called on to transcend, it can take a number of different and apparently contradictory forms" (Jameson, 1971, p. 308).

A dialectical approach offers us the possibility of "knowing" about intercultural interaction as a dynamic and changing process. We can begin to see epistemological concerns as an open-ended process, as a process that resists fixed, discrete bits of knowledge, which encompasses the dynamic nature of cultural processes.

A second contribution of our original essay was to propose a dialectical perspective to understanding intercultural interaction, summarized in the next section.

A Dialectical Approach to Studying Intercultural Interaction

A dialectical perspective on intercultural communication practice emphasizes several important notions (Bakhtin, 1981). First, a dialectical approach focuses on the relational, rather than individual aspects and persons. This means that one becomes fully human only in relation to another person and that there is something unique in a relationship that goes beyond the sum of two individuals. Second, the most challenging aspect of the dialectical perspective is that it requires holding two contradictory ideas simultaneously, contrary to most formal education in the United States. This notion, well known in Eastern countries as based on the logic of "soku," ("not-one, not-two"), emphasizes that the world is neither monistic nor dualistic (Nakayama, 1973, pp. 24–29). Rather, it recognizes and accepts as ordinary, the interdependent and complementary aspects of the seeming opposites (Yoshikawa, 1987, p. 187). Finally, it also underscores the dynamic character of culture, as well as our knowledge about cultures and communication. As these dialectical tensions shift – driven by many different forces, including globalization, economics, politics, natural disasters and so on – our knowledge of 'others' also shifts as our own reasons for knowing about others change. Hence, what we "know" is never fixed or stable.

In our original essay we noted that interpersonal communication scholars had applied a dialectical approach to relational research (Baxter, 1988,1990; Baxter and Montgomery, 1996; Montgomery, 1992) and current interpersonal researchers have continued this strong research tradition, identifying two types of dialectics: internal dialectics that operate between two people and external dialectics that operate between the couple and the larger society: (autonomy-connection, novelty-predictability, openness–closedness) (Baxter and Montgomery, 1996).

We identified six similar dialectics that seem to operate interdependently in intercultural interactions: cultural–individual, personal/social–contextual, differences–similarities, static–dynamic, present–future/history–past, and privilege–disadvantage dialectics. These dialectics are neither exhaustive nor mutually exclusive but represent an ongoing exploration of new ways to think about face-to-face intercultural interaction and research (Martin and Nakayama, 1999).

Cultural–individual dialectic

Some of our behavior is idiosyncratic (individual) and some behaviors reflect cultural influences. A dialectical perspective reminds us that people are both cultural group members and individuals and intercultural interaction is characterized by both.

Personal–contextual dialectic

A dialectical perspective emphasizes the relationship between personal and contextual communication. There are some aspects of communication that remain relatively constant over many contexts. There are also aspects that are contextual. That is, people communicate in particular ways in particular contexts (e.g., professors and students in classrooms), and messages are interpreted in particular ways. Outside the classroom (e.g., at football games or at faculty meetings), professors and students may communicate differently, expressing different aspects of themselves. Intercultural encounters are characterized by both personal and contextual communication.

Differences–similarities dialectic

A dialectical approach recognizes the importance of similarities and differences in understanding intercultural communication. There has been a tendency to over-emphasize group differences in traditional intercultural communication research – in a way that sets up false dichotomies and rigid expectations. However, a dialectical perspective reminds us that difference and similarity can coexist in intercultural communication interactions.

Static–dynamic dialectic

The static-dynamic dialectic highlights the ever-changing nature of culture and cultural practices, but also underscores our tendency to think about these things as constant. So thinking about culture and cultural practices as both static and dynamic helps us navigate through a diverse world and develop new ways of understanding intercultural encounters.

Present–future/history–past dialectic

A dialectic in intercultural communication exists between the history–past and the present–future. Much of the functionalist and interpretive scholarship investigating culture and communication has ignored historical forces. Other scholars added history as a variable in understanding contemporary intercultural interaction, for example, Stephan and Stephan's (1996) prior intergroup interaction variable that influences degree of intergroup anxiety. In contrast, critical scholars stress the importance of including history in current analyses of cultural meanings. A dialectical perspective suggests that we need to balance both an understanding of the past and the present.

Privilege–disadvantage dialectic

As individuals, we carry and communicate various types of privilege and disadvantage, the final dialectic. The traditional intercultural communication research mostly ignores issues of privilege and disadvantage although these issues are central in critical scholarship. Privilege and disadvantage may be in the form of political, social position, or status. Individuals may be simultaneously privileged and disadvantaged, or privileged in some contexts and disadvantaged in others.

In our original essay, we argued that the dialectical approach represented a major epistemological move in our understanding of culture and communication, as it makes explicit the dialectical tension between what previous research topics have studied (cultural differences, assumed static nature of culture, etc.) and what should be studied (how cultures change, how they are similar, importance of history).

Current Dialectical Research

A review of recent research reveals at least four ways in which scholars have incorporated the notion of "thinking dialectically" about culture and communication in contemporary communication (and related) scholarship and practice: (1) as a rationale supporting the concept of the fluidity and complexity of culture or the dynamic relationship between culture and communication; (2) as a metatheory/methodological way to study/conceptualize the notion of culture and intercultural communication. The third and fourth incorporate the specific six intercultural dialectics, as a framework (3) for studying or (4) for teaching about intercultural communication phenomena.

A Rationale for Supporting the Fluidity and Complexity of Culture/Communication

For some scholars, the contribution of the dialectic approach to the study of culture and communication seems to be as a rationale for supporting the concept of the fluidity and complexity of culture or the dynamic relationship between culture and communication. For example, Chuang (2003) mentions our dialectical approach as a way to avoid essentializing others in intercultural encounters.

Similarly, Rodriguez (2002) proposes the notion that human beings are *culturing* beings. He cites our dialectic framework as one of several that represents a new way of looking at culture as complex and dynamic, challenging the commonly held view that cultures are stable and homogenous. He contends that by "verbing" our understanding of culture, we acknowledge the pervasive ambiguity in contemporary global realities, acknowledge that "human beings are fundamentally relational beings with a striving and potentiality for communion with the world and each other" (p. 9). Further, he suggests that *culturing* shows the evolving and changing nature of all cultures – as humans negotiate the "quantum tensions" of chaos and order, ambiguity and meaning, homogeneity and diversity, stability and instability (p. 9). He concludes that acknowledging this complexity and the interconnectedness of all humans can imply a moral potentiality and a new way of understanding human beings and intercultural communication theory.

A Methodological Strategy for Studying Culture and Communication Phenomena

To our knowledge, and perhaps not surprisingly, few researchers have taken up the challenge to use a dialectic approach as a transparadigmatic way to conduct research. The only one to date is Martinez's (2006), "Semiotic Phenomenology and intercultural communication scholarship: Meeting the challenge of racial, ethnic, and cultural difference". In this essay, she argues that it may be easy to take a conscious shift toward thinking dialectically about culture and communication, but it is also important – and very difficult – to take a dialectical perspective in the preconscious and unconscious aspects of how we perceive other cultures. She challenges scholars to take "a much more robust theoretical and practical specification of how cultural perception drives our thinking and acting as scientists and scholars (p. 295).

Her challenge necessitates crossing paradigms to understand this complexity. She turns to Peirce (1958) to begin that robust theoretical and practical specification.

More commonly, scholars use the dialectic perspective as a way to integrate critical and interpretive perspectives. For example, Collier (2005) acknowledges her move from what was more prescriptive scholarship (with attention to intercultural competence), to now integrating both interpretive and critical orientations in studies of cultural identities and communication (p. 242). For example, one study, integrating interpretive and critical paradigms, investigated how black and white interracial couples' discourse reveal larger social structures and how cultural identity issues related to race are negotiated between partners (Thompson and Collier, 2006). They describe the contributions of each paradigm to their study. The interpretive perspective – characterized by an intersubjective view of cultural identities as constituted and maintained through communication – aids in descriptions of how individuals enact a variety of identifications and go about "doing being" (Sacks, 1984). It also honors the unique voices of the coresearchers – the interracial couples. A critical perspective calls attention to a variety of structural forces in these interracial relationships: social institutions including marriage and the family; ideologies such as whiteness and norms of individualism; and contexts ranging from historical events and political climate to norms governing interaction in the work-place and social conversation. They conclude that the critical/interpretive dialecti-cal perspective results in a comprehensive analysis "based on the constraints of social structures within the context of emergent, situated, relational conduct" (p. 491).

Sorrells (2003) employs a similar dialectical orientation to critical and interpretive approaches in her study of how Navajo women potters negotiate meanings of tradi-tion and cultural representation in their artistry. As she notes "working between and across paradigms in a dialectical fashion enables engagement in a critical process of questioning assumptions, methods and ways of interpretation used in each approach." A critical approach provides theories for understanding the political dimensions of communication processes while the primary goal of interpretive research is to understand and describe human communication: "The two approaches complement each other; each approach provides a partial but necessary understand-ing the negotiation of meanings and representation process" (p. 25).

Scholars in other disciplines also use the notion of dialectic approaches to sup-port multiparadigmatic approaches to research. Shalhoub-Kevorkian (2006) inves-tigates Palestinian children's experiences in the conflict zone during the construction of the Israeli Separation Wall. She used qualitative research methods (focus group discussions, participant observation data as well as the children's photographs and their written compositions). She notes that

> using these critical and interpretative approaches has helped me to work between and across paradigms in a way that Martin and Nakayama (1999) have defined as "dialec-tic". It enables me to engage in a critical process of questioning the assumptions and methods I am using to process the data and ways of interpretation (see also Trinh, 1991) while taking into account the political dimensions inherent to any process of understanding (p. 1108).

Using this dialectic approach allows her to contextualize the immediate moment(s) as these children speak in their own voices through their narratives and photos, as well as the "extended scene." The result is that the children and their experiences are seen more complexly, not only as passive victims of political violence, but also as agents of change and mobilization.

In a study investigating the patterns of medical waste management in a Bangladeshi city, Hassan *et al.* (2008) employed qualitative questionnaires and in-depth inter-views. They note our dialectic approach was used to confirm the credibility of sto-ries and examine the "cross-case themes" gathered from in-depth interviews. The term "dialectic" is a set of questions for trying to understand the empirical reality rather than a set of pre-designed answers which "presents a way of thinking about intercultural communication that allows for a very rich understanding" (p. 3).

Many communication scholars recognize the utility of a dialectical approach in studying communication, often seen in very general terms as a "tension" particularly in interpersonal communication. For example, several disparate studies cite the dia-lectical approach as a way of understanding complex meaning construction in cultural and intercultural contexts. For example, Dutta-Bergman (2004) investigated meanings around health issues among the Santalis, a marginalized people in India by way of in-depth focus groups and interviews as well as community meetings and team-building exercises. He takes a "cultured centered" approach and in his analysis employs our dialectical approach "as a way of justifying meaning construction as a dynamic cultural process with possibility for coexistence of multiple and often contradictory meanings." This enabled him to meet the objective of developing "an understanding of the complexity of meanings constructed around health rather than drawing neatly packaged stable constructs that might inform one-way campaigns of health communication" (p. 241). He identifies four key dialectics that operate interdependently and often simultaneously: tradition–modernization, structural limits–individual agency, despair–hope, and assimilation–resistance. The dialectical perspective enables one to understand "the richness of the cultural space and locating health within cultural, social, economical and political contexts" (p. 259).

Similarly, Collins, Villagran and Sparks (2007) investigate the barriers to communication about cancer prevention and treatment along the United States/Mexico border. Again, using participants' narratives from in-depth interviews they noted the dialectical tensions that arose from the participants' narratives. For example the patients' understanding of the causes and cures for cancer are negotiated between the tensions of *bienestar* (well-being) and religious beliefs. In addition, their Mexican identity interacts with structural barriers that reinforce disparities for some United States immigrants. They note how "the analysis of these dialectical tensions stresses the contradictory and sometimes oppositional nature of communication and provides insight into strategies by which people negotiate tensions to make sense of their experience and/or justify choices" (p. 335).

Finally, in an in-depth study of Korean cultural values and communication patterns, Shim, Kim and Martin (2008) describe how their Korean interviewees communicate their culture in daily life, as they try to reconcile the old and new, the traditional and contemporary, and Confucianism and capitalism that are often at odds. For example, they note how young Koreans in particular experience a dialectical tension in their personal and professional lives as they attempt to hold true to traditional Confucian values of collectivism and at the same time embrace Western individualism.

The Six Dialectics as a Framework for Studying Intercultural Communication

A number of scholars have used the six dialectics as a framework to study intercultural phenomena from a variety of theoretical perspectives – rhetorical, interpersonal, autoethnographic, ethnographic and so forth – either as sensitizing concepts to use in initial data analysis or as a way to explain findings.

Probably the most comprehensive is Chen's (2002) essay exploring dialectical tensions in intercultural romantic relationships. She assumes that intercultural relationships are both interpersonal and intercultural and attempts to understand the interface between the individual and the relationship on one hand, and the relationship and the (national/ethnic/racial) culture on the other. To further understanding, she juxtaposes Baxter's six relational dialectics (three internal, three external) with our intercultural dialectics (primarily difference–similarity, individual–cultural, and personal–social) and shows how these dialectical tensions can be played out in intercultural relationships. She chooses these three intercultural dialectics because they present fundamental contradictions in communication between individuals (internal), between individuals and their culture of the partners (external) and between individuals and their respective cultures (external).

She concentrates primarily on issues of information sharing, interdependence, and variability. She takes a developmental approach, showing how a shift in a particular dialectic in a relationship can trigger another shift, thereby developing the relationship, moving it forward (or backward). For example, in examining how internal information sharing is played out in the openness–closedness relational dialectic in intercultural relationship – because of the difference–similarity dialectic, partners in intercultural relationship may look rather differently on how much information should be shared (openness–closedness) depending on their cultural background. Being more or less open may be viewed negatively or positively by the other partner, and is constantly negotiated in tension with the difference–similarity dialectic, moving the relationship forward (or not). She continues this type of analytic framework for the remaining relational dialectics: autonomy–connection, separation–integration, predictability–novelty and conventionality–uniqueness. In conclusion she notes that the dialectical approach offers a coherent understanding of the intricacies of intercultural relationships.

A recent study by Cools (2006) – like Chen (2002) – combines the relational dialectics of Baxter and Montgomery (1996) and the intercultural dialectic in a study of the relationship communication of six heterosexual intercultural couples living in Finland. Through analysis of in-depth interview data she identifies a variety of cultural challenges faced by these intercultural couples as well as the existence of two intercultural relational dialectics: privilege–disadvantage, and belonging–exclusion.

Another use of the six intercultural communication dialectics is from a very different research tradition – a rhetorical study. Brown (2004) analyzed the film *The Horse Whisperer* to show how three interrelated US American myths (the agrarian, the wisdom of the rustic, and the frontier myth) reflect a larger tension between the western myth and the metropolitan – both vying to dominate US social reality. He uses the six intercultural dialects as a way to analyze the dynamic nature of cultural processes – showing the dynamic interplay of ideologies. For example, the differences–similarities dialectic focuses on the relationship between the differences among cultural groups, but also the similarities that unite individuals across cultures. Annie (the mother) and Tom (the horse whisper trying to help Annie's daughter's damaged horse) represent individuals from two different cultural groups who appear to adhere to opposing cultural values. For example, the metropolitan

reflect g fansie
larger the western
between

myth is defined by values such as living a complex/complicated lifestyle. In the metropolitan myth, the individual is apart from nature and dominates nature. Meanwhile, the western myth is composed of the agrarian, wisdom of the rustic, and frontier myths. The interrelated myths place value on being in harmony with nature, living off the land, having patience, and simplifying life to its most important elements. In the western myth, the individual is part of nature and the "circle-of-life" philosophy. Despite the cultural differences between Annie and Tom, they do find similarities that unite them. Both characters are united in trying to rehabilitate Pilgrim (the damaged horse) and repair Annie's relationship with her daughter. In the process of uniting to solve Annie's problems, both characters become united by love, which teeters on an extramarital romance. The attributes of love and the physical attraction experienced between Annie and Tom momentarily transcend the cultural differences that separate them (Brown 2004, p. 290).

Another more peripheral (to dialectics) study examined the turning points and dialectical interpretations of first generation college (FGC) student experiences in the United States (Orbe, 2008). Using interview and questionnaire data, Orbe employs the dialectic as a way to understand the complex ways in which FGC students negotiate and perform multiple aspects of their identities. He uses a variety of dialectics, only two of ours: differences–similarities (and he has 2 sub-dialectics – ordinary–special, peripheral–central) – he seems to use the dialectic, not to characterize communication but as a theoretical concept that encourages us to see the variation/heterogeneity within the group that he is studying (FGC students).

He concludes that the dialectic "provides a framework to understand how the personal and social identities of FGC students are negotiated over time amid a number of other tensions which speaks to the necessity of understanding identity negotiation as a complex process experienced by multidimensional beings" (Orbe, 2008, p. 92).

The Six Dialectics as a Framework for Teaching Intercultural Communication

incorporated into the
extant literature
DA is incorporated

A final way that a dialectical approach is incorporated into extant literature involves using the six dialectics as a framework for teaching about intercultural communication. For example, Fong and Chuang (2003)'s *Communicating Ethnic and Cultural Identity* presents our dialectics with respect to understanding ethnic and cultural identity. In Yep's chapter "Approaches to cultural identity: Personal notes from an autoethnographical journey," he describes the three paradigmatic approaches to identity (Social Science, Interpretive and Critical) and then proposes that our dialectical approach provides a more comprehensive way at looking at the complex construct of cultural identity. Through autoethnography he illustrates the complex, fluid, contextual, and political nature of his own multiracial/ethnic cultural identity.

A more general textbook focused on international business, *Communicating Globally: Intercultural Communication and International Business* (Schmidt *et al.*,

2007) provides an overview of Baxter and Montgomery's work and also our dialectics as a framework for learning about intercultural communication encounters. Similarly, Rimmington and Alagic (2008) in *Third Place Learning: Reflective Inquiry Into Intercultural and Global Cage Painting* uses our dialectic framework and the six dialectics as a lens for understanding intercultural interactions, pointing out that the dialectics are useful in preventing misunderstandings resulting from the effects of preconceived notions of cultural others. This book is for educators interested in teaching about cultural diversity and the approach is based on the cage painting metaphor for "dialogic coconstruction of meaning and understanding of multiple perspectives", encouraging "reflection and bodymindful inquiry" into one's worldview-third place learning" (p. xi).

Thurlow (2004) also uses the dialectical framework as a way to help students resist a naïve and utopian view of intercultural communication as possibly perfect and easy. He warns that we should not "lure our students into saccharine, uncritical lullabies of international harmony and world peace" (p. 213). He furthers suggests that our thinking (and teaching) should be more oriented to the personal and political – that one teaching strategy for achieving a more experiential and critical orientation toward interculturality and difference is through autobiographical writing – stories of the intercultural everyday.

Gengui and Yuqing (2008) take our dialectical approach (particularly the similarities–differences dialectic) and use it to frame instruction about nonverbal communication in intercultural encounters "The dialectical philosophy highlights the importance of having an integrated teaching programme of both the cultural differences and similarities in an educational curriculum" (p. 121). They note that overemphasizing differences or neglecting similarities can lead to stereotyping and prejudice and conclude that their students find it easy to focus on similarities (not really recognizing cultural differences in nonverbal behavior) while teachers want to focus on differences and ignore similarities. They conclude that "a dialectic perspective is both important and practical to the teaching of kinemics and proxemics for intercultural communication" (p. 126).

Future of the Dialectical Perspective

Our retrospective on the dialectical approach over the past 10 years shows that there is much more to be explored to demonstrate the utility and opportunity here for pushing the boundaries and conceptualization of intercultural (and international) communication. The dynamic epistemological claims of scholars in intercultural communication need to be better understood. How do we know what know and when do we know it? What do we know about other cultures – or even our own cultures? – and what kinds of knowledge do we have? In whose interest is this kind of cultural knowledge, as opposed to knowing other kinds of knowledge?

A dialectical approach helps us to emphasize that cultures are not fixed in how we describe them, know about them, and see them as 'different' – the relational

He warns that the definition of dialectical approach

aspect to our own culture and selves can be foregrounded. A dialectical approach emphasizes that cultures and cultural knowledge are always shaped in relationship to other cultures. By emphasizing a dialectical approach, we can help avoid stereotyping others and misusing that kind of knowledge in cultural interactions.

A dialectical approach is also helpful to explore the heterogeneity (in tension with homogeneity) of various cultures. As a dialectical approach underscores the many relational aspects of cultures (both within and without), it can be powerful in understanding how gender, sexuality, race/ethnicity, age, religion and other cultural forces can help define and change cultures. Dialectical perspective might be a very useful tool in thinking about other cultures in far more complex ways.

A dialectical perspective can expose hierarchies and power relations in cultures and how cultures present themselves and are defined. The dialectical tension between defining a culture from within and from the outside is well-worth further exploration in understanding how a culture is defined. For example, the St. Patrick's parade in Boston won a 1995 US Supreme Court decision that allows them to exclude gay and lesbian groups from participation (Drake, 2009). In his speech at Columbia University, the president of Iran, Mahmoud Ahmadinejad, claimed that "In Iran, we don't have homosexuals, like in your country" (CBS News, 2007). A dialectical perspective can highlight the processes by which some people are included in a culture or cultural events and which ones are not. A dialectical approach asks who is included and who is not and how? Sometimes the exclusion comes from within. For example, the bartender from South Philadelphia who speaks Italian to his friends but says he does not speak Italian, or some people who identify as Catholics yet use birth control. A dialectical perspective does not determine who "really" is or is not a member of a cultural community – but it highlights the tensions over how those boundaries are drawn.

A dialectical perspective, then, asks us to think about cultures as not simply dynamic, but about how these cultures change. What kinds of forces shape cultures? What role do global economics play? Religions? Language communities? We can hardly begin to list the many forces that have shaped cultures. Similarly, our call for a dialectical perspective also means that there are many more dialectical tensions to be discussed and utilized to understand culture and communication better. Our list of some dialectical tensions was never meant to be exhaustive. Rather, we begin with a call for more work on dialectical approaches to culture and communication.

Finally, what would a dialectical study look like? We are often asked to describe a dialectical study. It is important to note that a dialectical approach is not a method, but a perspective. It is not driven by a particular set of methodological rules. Perhaps no single study can encompass what needs to be done in taking a dialectical perspective. Perhaps we need to work in collaboration with others – using multiple methodological and theoretical approaches – to understand culture and communication better. Perhaps a single study cannot do multiple methodologies and theories well. Our call for a dialectical perspective is a call for this scholarly collaboration, as there is no one approach that can begin to encompass the complexity of culture and communication.

Notes

1 In our earlier essay, we noted the emerging postmodern approach in communication studies (Best and Kellner 1991, Mumby, 1997). At this point, it seems that only a few culture and communication scholars have embraced this paradigmatic research trajectory (Chuang, 2003).

2 We should note here that the question of scholarly boundaries we identified in our earlier essay still remain. That is, critical voices have been (and are) present in other areas of communication scholarship that overlap with culture and communication studies, for example, critical ethnography (Conquergood, 1991), critical rhetoric (McKerrow, 1989), performance studies (Lengel, 2005). Though this topic is beyond the scope of this essay, these questions remain: What is the appropriate focus for the study of culture and communication? Will cultural studies, critical ethnography, and so forth, be incorporated along with intercultural communication research to form a larger area of study? Or, will intercultural communication researchers simply borrow some of their ideas and retain more narrow boundaries?

References

Althusser, L. (1971) *Lenin and Philosophy and Other Essays* (trans. B. Brewster), New York, Monthly Review Press.

Asante, M.K. (1987) *The Afrocentric Idea*, Temple University Press, Philadelphia.

Ashcroft, B., Griffiths, G., and Tifflin, H. (1995) *The Postcolonial Studies Reader*, Routledge, London.

Bakhtin, M.M. (1981) *The Dialogic Imagination: Four Essays by M.M. Bakhtin* (eds M. Holquist, trans. C. Emerson and M. Holquist), University of Texas Press, Austin, TX.

Barnett, G.A., and Lee, M. (2002) Issues in intercultural communication research, in *Handbook of International and Intercultural Communication*, 2nd edn (eds. W.B. Gudykunst and B. Mody), Sage, Thousand Oaks, CA, pp. 275–290.

Baxter, L.A. (1988) A dialectical perspective on communication strategies in relationship development, in *A Handbook of Personal Relationships* (ed. S.W. Duck), John Wiley and Sons, Inc, New York, pp. 257–273.

Baxter, L.A. (1990) Dialectical contradictions in relationship development. *Journal of Social and Personal Relationships*, 7, 69–88.

Baxter, L.A., and Montgomery, B. (1996) *Relating: Dialogues and Dialectics*, Guilford Press, New York.

Best, S., and Kellner, D. (1991) *Postmodern Theory: Critical Interrogations*, Guilford Press, New York.

Broome, B.J., Carey, C., De La Garza, S.A. *et al.* (2005) "In the thick of things": A dialogue about an activist turn in intercultural communication, in *Taking Stock in Intercultural Communication: Where to Now?*, (eds. W.J. Starosta and G.-M. Chen), National Communication Association, Washington, DC, pp. 145–175.

Brown, T.J. (2004) Deconstructing the dialectical tensions in *The Horse Whisperer*: How myths represent competing cultural values. *Journal of Popular Culture*, 38 (2), 274–295.

Burrell, G., and Morgan, G. (1988) *Sociological Paradigms and Organizational Analysis*, Heinemann, Portsmouth, NH.

Carbaugh, D. (1988a) Comments on "Culture" in Communication Inquiry. *Communication Reports*, 1, 38–41.

Carbaugh, D. (1988b) *Talking American*, Ablex, Norwood, NJ.

Carbaugh, D. (ed.) (1990) *Cultural Communication and Intercultural Contact*, Erlbaum, Hillsdale, NJ.

Carbaugh, D. (1996) *Situating Selves: The Communication of Social Identities in American Scenes*, SUNY Press, Albany, NY.

Carbaugh, D. (2005) *Cultures in Conversations*, Routledge, New York.

Carbaugh, D., and Berry, M. (2001) Communicating history, Finnish and American discourses: An ethnographic contribution to intercultural communication inquiry. *Communication Theory*, 11 (3), 352–366.

Casmir, F.L. (1993) Third-culture building: A paradigm shift for international and intercultural communication. *Communication Yearbook*, 16, 407–428.

CBS News (2007) "Ahmadinejad Questions 9/11, Holocaust" September 24, 2007. http://www.cbsnews.com/stories/2007/09/24/national/main3290972.shtml

Chen, L. (2002) Communication in intercultural relationships, in *Handbook of International and Intercultural Communication*, 2nd edn, (eds. W.B. Gudykunst and B. Mody), Sage, Thousand Oaks, CA, pp. 241–258.

Chuang, R. (2003) Postmodern critique of cross-cultural and intercultural communication, in *International and Intercultural Communication Annual, 26: Ferment in the Intercultural Field*, (eds W.J. Starosta and G.-M. Chen), Sage, Thousand Oaks, CA, pp. 24–35.

Collier, M.J. (2005) Theorizing cultural identification: Critical updates and continuing evolution, in *Theorizing about Intercultural Communication*, (ed. W.B. Gudykunst), Sage, Thousand Oaks, CA, pp. 235–256.

Collier, M.J. (2006) Cultural positioning, dialogic reflexivity, and transformative third spaces. *Western Journal of Communication*, 70 (4), 263–269.

Collier, M.J., Hegde, R.S., Lee, W., Nakayama, T.K. and Yep, G.A. (2002) Dialogue on the edges: Ferment in communication and culture, in *International and Intercultural Communication Annual, 24: Transforming Communication about Culture*, (ed. M.J. Collier), Sage, Thousand Oaks, CA, pp. 219–280.

Collins, D., Villagran, M.M., and Sparks, L. (2007) Crossing borders, crossing cultures: Barriers to communication about cancer prevention and treatment along the U.S./Mexico border. *Patient Education and Counseling*, 71, 333–339.

Conquergood, D. (1991) Rethinking ethnography: Towards a critical cultural politics. *Communication Monographs*, 58, 179–195.

Cools, C.A. (2006) Relational communication in intercultural couples. *Language and Intercultural Communication*, 6 (3&4), 262–274.

Darling-Wolf, F. (2004) Sites of attractiveness: Japanese women and westernized representations of feminine beauty. *Critical Studies in Media Communication*, 21 (4), 325–345.

Deetz, S. (1996) Describing differences in approaches to organization science: Rethinking Burrell and Morgan and their legacy. *Organization Science*, 7, 119–207.

Delgado, F. (2002) Mass-mediated communication and intercultural conflict, in *Readings In intercultural Communication*, 2nd edn, (eds J. Martin, T. K. Nakayama and L. Flores), McGraw-Hill, New York, pp. 351–360.

Diaz, A.R. (2003) Postcolonial theory and third wave agenda. *Women and Language*, 24 (1), 10–17.

Dilthey, W. (1976) *Selected Writings* (ed. and trans. H.P. Rickman). Cambridge University Press, New York.

Dirlik, A. (1994) The postcolonial aura: Third World criticism in the age of global capitalism. *Critical Inquiry*, 20, 328–356.

Drake, J.C. (2009, March 13) St. Patrick's parade a political quandary. *The Boston Globe.* http://www.boston.com/news/local/massachusetts/articles/2009/03/13/st_patricks_parade_a_political_quandary/ (accessed May 13, 2010)

Dutta-Bergman, M.J. (2004) The unheard voices of Santalis: Communicating about health from the margins in India. *Communication Theory*, 14 (3), 237–263.

Fejes, F. (1986) *Imperialism, Media and the Good Neighbor: New Deal Foreign Policy and United States Shortwave Broadcasting to Latin America*, Ablex, Norwood, NJ.

Flores, L.A. (1994) Creating discursive space through a rhetoric of difference: Chicana feminists craft a homeland. *Quarterly Journal of Speech*, 82 (2), 142–156.

Flores, L.A. (2003) Constructing rhetorical borders: Peons, illegal aliens, and competing narratives of immigration. *Critical Studies in Media Communication*, 20 (4), 362–387.

Folb, E. (1982) Who's got the room at the top? Issues of dominance and nondominance in intracultural communication, in *Intercultural Communication: A Reader*, (eds L.A. Samovar and R.E. Porter), Wadsworth, Belmont, CA, pp. 132–141.

Fong, M., and Chuang, R. (2003) *Communicating ethnic and cultural identity*, Rowman and Littlefield, Lanham, MD.

Gadamer, H.G. (1976)*Philosophical Hermeneutics*, (ed. and trans, D.E. Linge), University of California Press, Berkeley.

Gadamer, H.G. (1989) *Truth and Method*, Crossroad Publishing, New York.

Gallois, G., Giles, H., Jones, E. *et al.* (1995) Accommodating intercultural encounters: Elaborations and extensions, in *Intercultural Communication Theory*, (ed. R.L. Wiseman), Sage, Thousand Oaks, CA, pp. 115–147.

Gallois, G., Ogay, T., and Giles, H. (2005) Communication Accommodating Theory, in *Theorizing about Intercultural Communication*, (ed. W.B. Gudykunst), Sage, Thousand Oaks, CA, pp. 121–148.

Gengui, L. and Yuqing, L. (2008) Using dialectical approach to study kinemics and proxemics for the education of Intercultural Communication. *CELEA journal*, 31 (4), 121–126.

Giles, H., Coupland, N., and Coupland, J. (eds) (1991) *Contexts of Accommodation: Developments in Applied Sociolinguistics*, Cambridge University Press, Cambridge, UK.

Golden, D.R., Niles, T.A., and Hecht, M.L. (2002) Jewish American identity, in *Readings in Intercultural Communication* (eds J.N. Martin, T.K. Nakayama, and L.A. Flores), McGraw-Hill, Boston, MA, pp. 44–51.

González, M.C. (2000) The four seasons of ethnography: A creation-centered ontology for ethnography, *International Journal of Intercultural Relations*, 24, 623–650.

González, M.C., and Krizek, R. (1994) *Indigenous ethnography*. Annual meeting of the Western Communication Association, San Jose, CA.

Gordon, R. (1998/1999) A spectrum of scholars: Multicultural diversity and human communication theory. *Human Communication: Journal of the Asian and Pacific Communication Association*, 2 (1), 1–7.

Gordon, R.D. (2007) Beyond the failures of Western communication theory. *Journal of Multicultural Discourses*, 2 (2), 89–107.

Gramsci, A. (1971) *Selections from the prison notebooks*, (trans. Q. Hoare and G.N. Smith), New York: International.

Gramsci, A. (1978) *Selections from Cultural Writings*, Cambridge, MA: Harvard University Press.

Gudykunst, W.B. (ed.) (2003) *International and Intercultural Communication*, Sage, Thousand Oaks, CA.

Gudykunst, W.B. (2005) An anxiety/uncertainty management (AUM) theory of effective communication: Making the mesh of the net finer, in *Theorizing about Intercultural Communication*, (ed. W.B. Gudykunst), Sage, Thousand Oaks, CA, pp. 281–322.

Gudykunst, W.B., Lee, C.M., Nishida, T., and Ogawa, N. (2005) Theorizing about intercultural communication, in *Theorizing about Intercultural Communication*, (ed. W.B. Gudykunst), Sage, Thousand Oaks, CA, pp. 3–32.

Habermas, J. (1970) On systematically distorted communication. *Inquiry*, 13, 205–218.

Habermas, J. (1981) Modernity versus postmodernity. *New German Critique*, 22, 3–14.

Habermas, J. (1987) *The Theory of Communicative Action: Lifeworld and System, vol. 2*, (trans. T. McCarthy), Beacon Press, Boston, MA.

Hall, B.J. (1992) Theories of culture and communication. *Communication Theory*, 2, 50–70.

Hall, S. (1985) Signification, representation, ideology: Althusser and the post-structuralist debates. *Critical Studies in Mass Communication*, 2, 91–114.

Halualani, R.T., Mendoza, S.L., and Drzewiecka, J.A. (2009) "Critical" junctures in intercultural communication studies: A review. *The Review of Communication*, 9 (1), 17–35.

Hammersly, M. (1992) *What's Wrong with Ethnography?* Routledge, Chapman and Hall, New York.

Hassan, M.M., Ahmed, S.A., Rahman, K.A., and Biswas, T.K. (2008) Pattern of medical waste management: Existing scenario in Dhaka City, Bangladesh, *BMC Public Health*, 8:36, http://www.biomedcentral.com/1471-2458/8/36 (accessed May 13, 2010)

Hecht, M.L. (1993) A research odyssey: Towards the development of a Communication Theory of Identity. *Communication Monographs*, 60, 76–82.

Hecht, M.L., Warren, J.R., Jung, E., and Krieger, J.L. (2005) A communication theory of identity: Development, theoretical perspective and future directions, in *Theorizing about Intercultural Communication*, (ed. W.B. Gudykunst), Sage, Thousand Oaks, CA, pp. 257–278.

Hegde, R. (1998a) Translated enactments: The relational configurations of the Asian Indian immigrant experience, in *Readings in Intercultural Communication* (eds J.N. Martin, T.K. Nakayama, and L.A. Flores), McGraw-Hill, Boston, MA, pp. 315–322.

Hegde, R. (1998b) Swinging the trapeze: The negotiation of identity among Asian Indian immigrant women in the United States, in *Communication and Identity across Cultures*, (eds D.V. Tanno and A. González), Sage, Thousand Oaks, CA, pp. 34–55.

Hegde, R.S. (1998c) A view from elsewhere: Locating difference and the politics of representation from a transnational feminist perspective. *Communication Theory*, 271–297.

Hofstede, G. (1991) *Cultures and Organizations: Software of the Mind*, McGraw-Hill, New York.

Horkheimer, M., and Adorno, T. (1988) *Dialectic of Enlightenment* (trans. J. Cumming), Continuum, New York.

Houston, M. (1992) The politics of difference: Race, class and women's communication, in *Women Making Meaning*, (ed. L.F. Rakow), Routledge, Chapman, and Hall, New York, pp. 45–59.

Ishii, S. (1984) *Enryo-sasshi* communication: A key to understanding Japanese interpersonal relations. *Cross Currents*, 11 (1), 49–58.

Ishii, S. (2007) A western contention of Asia-centred communication scholarship paradigms: A commentary on Gordon's paper. *Journal of Multicultural Discourses*, 2 (2), 108–114.

Jameson, F. (1971) *Marxism and Form*, Princeton University Press, Princeton, NJ.

Jung, E., and Hecht, M.L. (2004) Elaborating the communication theory of identity: Identity gaps and communication outcomes, *Communication Quarterly*, 52 (3), 265–283.

Kim, M.-S. (2002) *Non-Western Perspectives on Human Communication*, Sage, Thousand Oaks, CA.

Kim, M.-S. (2005) Culture-based conversational constraints theory: Individual- and culture-level analyses, in *Theorizing about Intercultural Communication*, (ed. W.B. Gudykunst), Sage, Thousand Oaks, CA, pp. 93–117.

Kim, M.-S., Hunter, J.E., Miyahara, A., Horvath, A.-M., Bresnahan, M., and Yoon, H.-J. (1996) Individual vs. culture level dimensions of individualism and collectivism: Effects on preferred conversational styles. *Communication Monographs*, 63, 28–49.

Kim, Y.Y. (1988) On theories in intercultural communication, in *Theories in Intercultural Communication*, (eds Y.Y. Kim and W.B. Gudykunst), Sage, Beverly Hills, CA, pp. 11–21.

Kim, Y.Y. (2002) Adapting to an unfamiliar culture: An interdisciplinary overview, in *Handbook of International and Intercultural Communication*, (eds. W.B. Gudykunst and B. Mody), Sage, Thousand Oaks, CA, pp. 259–273.

Kim, Y.Y. (2005) Adapting to a new culture: An integrative communication theory, in *Theorizing about Intercultural Communication*, (ed. W.B. Gudykunst), Sage, Thousand Oaks, CA, pp. 375–400.

Kim, Y.Y. (2008) Intercultural personhood: Globalization and a way of being. *International Journal of Intercultural Relations*, 32 (4), 301–304.

Kraidy, M.M. (2002) Hybridity in cultural globalization. *Communication Theory*, 12, 316–339.

Kraidy, M.M., and Murphy, P.D. (2008) Shifting Geertz: Toward a theory of translocalism in global communication studies. *Communication Theory*, 18 (3), 335–355.

Lee, W.S. (1999) One Whiteness veils three uglinesses: From border-crossing to a womanist interrogation of colorism, in *Whiteness: The Communication of Social Identity*, (eds T.K. Nakayama and J.N. Martin), Sage, Thousand Oaks, CA, pp. 279–298.

Leeds-Hurwitz, W. (1990) Notes on the history of intercultural communication: The Foreign Service Institute and the mandate for intercultural training. *Quarterly Journal of Speech*, 76, 262–281.

Lengel, L. (2005) *Intercultural Communication and Creative Practice: Music Dance and Women's Cultural Identity*, Praeger, Westpoint, CT.

Lukács, G. (1971) *History and Slass Consciousness: Studies in Marxist Dialectics*, (trans. R. Livingston), MIT Press, Cambridge, MA.

Marcuse, H. (1964) *One Dimensional Man*, Beacon Press, Boston, MA.

Martin, J.N., and Butler, R.L.W. (2001) Toward an ethic of intercultural communication research, in *Transcultural Realities: Interdisciplinary Perspectives on Cross-Cultural Relations*, (eds W.H. Milhouse, M.K. Asante, and P.O. Nwosu), Sage, Thousand Oaks, CA, pp. 283–298.

Martin, J.N., Krizek, R.L., Nakayama, T.K., and Bradford, L. (1996) Exploring Whiteness: A study of self-labels for White Americans. *Communication Quarterly*, 44, 125–144.

Martin, J.N., and Nakayama, T.K. (1999) Thinking dialectically about culture and communication. *Communication Theory*, 9, 1–25.

Martinez, J.M. (2006) Semiotic Phenomenology and intercultural communication scholarship: Meeting the challenge of racial, ethnic, and cultural difference. *Western Journal of Communication*, 70 (4), 292–310.

McKerrow, R. (1989) Critical rhetoric: Theory and praxis. *Communication Monographs*, 56, 91–111.

Mead, G.H. (1934) *Mind, Self, and Society*, University of Chicago Press, Chicago.

Meehan, E.R. (1993) Rethinking political economy: Change and continuity. *Journal of Communication*, 43 (4), 105–116.

Merleau-Ponty, M. (1962) *Phenomenology of Perception* (trans. C. Smith), Routledge and Kegan Paul, London.

Miike, Y. (2003) Toward an alternative metatheory of human communication: An Asiacentric vision. *Intercultural Communication Studies*, 12 (4), 39–63.

Miike, Y. (2004) Rethinking humanity, culture, and communication: Asiacentric critiques and contributions. *Human Communication*, 7 (1), 67–82.

Miike, Y. (2006) Non-Western theory in Western research? An Asiacentric agenda for Asian communication studies. *Review of Communication*, 6 (1/2), 4–31.

Miike, Y. (2007) An Asiacentric reflection on Eurocentric bias in Communication theory. *Communication Monographs*, 74 (2), 272–278.

Montgomery, B.M. (1992) Communication as the interface between couples and culture. *Communication Yearbook*, 475–507.

Moon, D.G. (1996) Concepts of culture: Implications for intercultural communication research. *Communication Quarterly*, 44, 70–84.

Mosco, V. (1996) *The Political Economy of Communication*, Sage, Thousand Oaks, CA.

Mumby, D.K. (1997) Modernism, postmodernism, and communication studies: A rereading of an ongoing debate. *Communication Theory*, 7, 1–28.

Nakayama, N. (1973) *Mujunteki, sosoku no ronri*, Hyakkaen, Kyoto, Japan.

Nakayama, T.K. (1997) Disorienting identities: Asian Americans, history, and intercultural communication, in *Our Voices: Essays in Ethnicity, Culture, and Communication*, 2nd edn, (eds. A. González, M. Houston, and V. Chen), Roxbury, Los Angeles, pp. 14–20.

Nakayama, T.K., and Krizek, R.L. (1995) Whiteness: A strategic rhetoric. *Quarterly Journal of Speech*, 81, 291–309.

Nakayama, T.K., and Martin, J.N. (2007) The "White problem" in intercultural communication research and pedagogy, in *Whiteness, Pedagogy and Performance: Dis/placing Race*, (eds L.M. Cooks and J.S. Simpson), Lexington Books, Lanham, MD.

Orbe, M.P. (2008) Theorizing multidimensional identity negotiation: Reflections on the lived experiences of first-generation college students. The intersections of personal and social identities. *New Directions for Child and Adolescent Development*, 120, 81–95.

Peirce, C.S. (1958) *The Collected Papers of Charles Sanders Peirce*, vols 1–8, (eds. C. Hartshorne, P. Weiss, and A. Burks), Harvard University Press, Cambridge, MA.

Pennington, D.L (1989) Interpersonal power and influence in intercultural communication, in *Handbook of International and Intercultural Communication*, (eds. M.K. Asante and W.B. Gudykunst), Sage, Thousand Oaks, CA, pp. 261–274.

Philipsen, G., Coutu, L.M., and Covarrubias, P. (2005) Speech codes theory: Restatement, revisions, and response to criticisms, in *Theorizing about Intercultural Communication*, (ed. W.B. Gudykunst), Sage, Thousand Oaks, CA, pp. 55–68.

Quayson, A. (2000) Postcolonialism and postmodernism, in *A Companion to Postcolonial Studies*, (eds. H. Schwarz and S. Ray), Blackwell, Malden, MA, pp. 87–111.

Ribeau, S.A., Hecht, M.L., and Jackson, R.L. (2003) *African American Communication: Exploring Identity and Culture*, Lawrence Erlbaum Associates, Mahwah, NJ.

Rimmington, G.M., and Alagic, M. (2008) *Third Place Learning: Reflective Inquiry into Intercultural and Global Cage Painting*, IAP, Charlotte, NC.

Rodriguez, A. (2002) Culture to culturing: Re-imagining our understanding of intercultural relations. *Intercultural Communication*, 5, 2–11.

Roth, K. (2001) Material culture and intercultural communication. *International Journal of Intercultural Relations*, 25 (5), 563–580.

Sacks, H. (1984) On doing "being ordinary," in *Structures of Social Action: Studies in Conversation Analysis*, (eds J.M. Atkinson and J. Heritage), Cambridge University Press, Cambridge, pp. 413–429.

Said, E. (1979) *Orientalism*, Vintage Books, New York.

Said, E. (1994) *Culture and Imperialism*, Vintage Books, New York.

Schleiermacher, F.D.E. (1977) *Hermeneutics: The Handwritten Manuscripts* (trans. J. Duke and J. Forstman), Scholars Press for the American Academy of Religion, Missoula, MT.

Schmidt, W.V., Conaway, R.N., Easton, R.S., and Wardrope, W.J. (2007) *Communicating Globally: Intercultural Communication and International Business*, Sage, Thousand Oaks, CA.

Schwarz, H. (2000) Mission impossible: Introducing postcolonial studies in the US academy, in *A Companion to Postcolonial Studies*, (eds H. Schwarz and S. Ray) Blackwell, Malden, MA, pp. 87–111.

Shalhoub-Kevorkian, N. (2006) Negotiating the present, historicizing the future: Palestinian children speak about the Israeli separation wall. *American Behavioral Scientist*, 49 (8), 1101–1124.

Shim, Y.-J., Kim, M.-S., and Martin, J.N. (2008) *Changing Korea: Understanding Culture and Communication*, Peter Lang, New York.

Shome, R. (1996) Postcolonial interventions in the rhetorical canon: An "other" view. *Communication Theory*, 6 (1), 40–59.

Shome, R., and Hegde, R. (2002) Postcolonial approaches to communication: Charting the terrain, engaging the intersections. *Communication Theory*, 12, 249–270.

Sorrells, K. (2003) Embodied negotiation: Commodification and cultural representation in the U.S. Southwest, in *Intercultural Alliances: Critical Transformation*, (ed. M.J. Collier), Sage, Thousand Oaks, CA, pp. 17–47.

Stephan, W.G., and Stephan, C.W. (1996) *Intergroup Relations*, Westview Press, Boulder, CO.

Supriya, K.E. (1996) Confessionals, testimonials: Women's speech in/and contexts of violence. *Hypatia*, 11, 92–106.

Supriya, K.E. (2002) *Shame and Recovery: Mapping Identity in an Asian Women's Shelter*, Peter Lang, New York.

Tanno, D.V., and Jandt, F.E. (1994) Redefining the "other" in multicultural research. *Howard Journal of Communications*, S, 36–54.

Thompson, J., and Collier, M.J. (2006) Toward contingent understanding of intersection identifications among selected U.S. interracial couples: Integrating interpretive and critical views. *Communication Quarterly*, 54 (4), 487–506.

Thurlow, C. (2004) Relating to our work, accounting for our selves: The autobiographical imperative in teaching about difference. *Language and Intercultural Communication*, 4 (4), 209–228.

Ting-Toomey, S. (ed.) (1994) *The Challenge of Facework: Cross Cultural and Interpersonal Issues*, State University of New York Press, Albany.

Ting-Toomey, S. (2005) The matrix of face: An updated face-negotiation theory, in *Theorizing about Intercultural Communication*, (ed. W.B. Gudykunst), Sage, Thousand Oaks, CA, pp. 71–92.

Ting-Toomey, S., and Oetzel, J.G. (2002) Cross-cultural face concerns and conflict styles: current status and future directions, in *Handbook of International and Intercultural Communication*, 2nd edn, (eds. W.B. Gudykunst and B. Mody), Sage, Thousand Oaks, CA, pp. 153–164.

Trinh, T.M.H. (1991) *When the Moon Waxes Red: Representation, Gender and Cultural Politics*, Routledge, London.

Volosinov, V.N. (1973) *Marxism and the Philosophy of Language*, (trans. L. Matejka and I. R. Titunik), Harvard University Press, Cambridge, MA.

Witteborn, S. (2004) Of being an Arab woman before and after September 11: The enactment of communal identities in talk. *Howard Journal of Communications*, 15, 83–98.

Yep, G.A. (2003) Approaches to cultural identity: Personal notes from an autoethnographical journey, in *Communicating Ethnic and Cultural Identity*, (eds M. Fong and R. Chuang), Rowman and Littlefield, Lanham, MD, pp. 69–83.

Yoshikawa, M.J. (1987) The double-swing model of intercultural communication between the East and the West, in *Communication Theory: Eastern and Western Perspectives*, (ed. D.L. Kincaid), Academic Press, San Diego, CA, pp. 319–329.

6

Reflections on "Problematizing 'Nation' in Intercultural Communication Research"

Kent A. Ono

When Dolores Tanno asked me to write a piece responding to an essay by James Chesebro for the twenty-first volume of the *Intercultural Communication Annual*, at first I hesitated. Despite the fact that Dolores was one of my scholarly heroes, and despite the fact that I knew I would need to publish more in order to get tenure at UC Davis and that writing an essay for the Annual would help, and despite the fact that it was an honor to have been asked to write a response to an essay written by such a prominent figure in the field as Chesebro, I wavered. Not only had I not been trained as an "intercultural communication scholar" (I was a rhetorician, after all), but the idea of responding to a piece by James Chesebro was a daunting prospect.

In this brief essay, first, I want to tell a story about how my response emerged, in part to demonstrate that ideas do not come ready made, and also to show how critical work emerges, often in unusual ways, and sometimes without a lengthy literature from which to build one's theory. Second, I discuss the central ideas in the essay that I think still have relevance to critical intercultural communication today.[1] Finally, before concluding, I provide a rejoinder to Chesebro's response to my response to his essay, as a way of furthering the conversation.

History of My Essay

I was, at the time Dolores asked me to write the essay, an Assistant Professor at UC Davis, one without the necessary ethos, I thought, to be a credible respondent. Not only was this the first time I had been asked to respond to an essay in print, but here I was being asked to respond to a senior scholar's work, and not any senior scholar, either. At the time, Chesebro was President of the National Communication Association, and was recognized as one of the most complete

The Handbook of Critical Intercultural Communication, edited by Thomas K. Nakayama and Rona Tamiko Halualani.   © 2010 Blackwell Publishing Ltd.

scholars in the field. Since I did not consider myself an intercultural communication scholar at the time and was critical of much of the work I had read (as is clear by the arguments I ended up making in my published response to Chesebro. This essay is in part a story of my journey to becoming a *critical* intercultural communication scholar), what right did I have responding to Chesebro, and what could I say that would be of value? Equally intimidating was the fact that I held Professor Chesebro in high esteem, having read his essays on television and Kenneth Burke as a graduate student and consulted his edited book, *Gayspeak: Gay Male and Lesbian Communication* (Chesebro, 1981), on numerous occasions.

Dolores and I had more than one conversation about my writing an essay before I reluctantly agreed to write the piece. I remember her trying to set my mind at ease by telling me that a second scholar, Carley Dodd, would also be writing a response to Chesebro's essay. Still reluctant, but encouraged by the fact that Dolores continued to think it important that I write the piece, and knowing that as a fellow person of color she likely recognized the hesitant feelings I might be having about writing it, I agreed. I did not know what she saw in me or my work or why she thought I would be appropriate for this specific task, but her encouragement helped give me the confidence and strength necessary to agree to write the essay.

Next came the task of reading Chesebro's article. Dolores sent me a version of the essay. At that point in the process, his article was only available to me in text form, having not yet been typeset, or printed. I worked from his draft, carefully reading it, jotting down notes, and beginning to formulate my own ideas. I read relevant articles but spent most of my time thinking about what to say and how to respond. Perhaps because I was teaching a full course load in fall 1996, perhaps because I was beginning my fourth year at UC Davis pretenure, perhaps because the deadline to submit the piece was very short, perhaps also because I was still getting my grounding as a scholar in the discipline, the piece is more defensive and the tone less generous than I would like to think it would be were I to have written it today.

Writing an essay that challenges basic and fundamental assumptions of a discipline such as that of intercultural communication, in part because one finds certain assumptions, as well as the carrying out of research based on those assumptions, sometimes troubling and at other times offensive, is not unique for those from marginalized backgrounds and perspectives. Moreover, making such a challenge from a marginalized position may mean, as it did for me: (1) developing an alternative approach without the benefit of having significant historical or theoretical examples on which to draw, and (2) establishing that there is something wrong with the key tenets of traditional scholarship that requires change. Coming from outside the field and working in a new scholarly area, rather than building a theory with the benefit of a wealth of published information, my approach was to build theory organically; hence, I built a case out of alternative approaches to research. The hard part, however, was summoning the courage to challenge widely held beliefs and ideas about scholarship and finding the words and ideas with which to convey that challenge (since in many ways what one wants to say has either not yet been articulated, or at least has not been discussed widely). In retrospect, my hesitation in writing the article made sense.

While intercultural communication had been around for some time, *critical* intercultural communication scholarship was in its bare infancy. From my current historical perspective, by critical intercultural communication, I mean the retheorization of intercultural communication that in part developed out of cultural studies and critical theory scholarship. In particular, critical intercultural studies foregrounds, or at least acknowledges as relevant, political and cultural dimensions of communication within and across cultural groups. Critical intercultural communication stresses the significance of cultural identity as a dimension of both communication and the study of culture. Critical intercultural communication also typically emphasizes theory as germane to praxis, even as practical. It builds ideas, concepts, and theories across academic divisions, hence is *transdisciplinary*. Critical intercultural communication sees the personal not only as a part of research but also as a constitutive dimension of scholarship in the academy. In taking the personal seriously, critical intercultural communication acknowledges the rhetorical and performative dimensions of everyday life and foregrounds questions generally understood to be central to the humanities generally. Activism and experience, themselves, may be integral to theorizing. In fact, social change and shifts in power may be the end goal, and theories may develop directly from social praxes. Typically, critical intercultural communication resists and challenges normative assumptions about academic life that have a tendency to stifle curiosity, identity, creativity, and openness to and interest in difference.

At the time Dolores asked me to write the essay, however, even basic positions about what critical intercultural communication was had not yet been taken, and theoretical concepts had not been developed in print. Who could have imagined at that very early point that 13 years later critical intercultural communication would be so vibrant an area of research as to warrant an entire collection, one that includes this essay by me reflecting on my earlier piece?[2]

In short, it was clear to me that writing the essay I had agreed to write would be difficult. On October 9, 1996, I wrote a letter to Dolores, after she had kindly read a draft of my piece and had given me comments. In my letter to her I wrote, "I am feeling a bit better about this draft, but I still feel I lack some further background on the intercultural issues Chesebro discusses." Feeling that the essay required more research, but not knowing quite where to turn, I searched once more for relevant articles but again found few. Then, it occurred to me that, even though not much had been written, I could contact people who had been attempting to make critical arguments within communication and intercultural communication, such as Carole Blair, Wenshu Lee, Tom Nakayama, and Rona Halualani. They, too, were at a loss for resources and could think of little published on the topic. My conversations with them, however, helped me to realize just how little published research was out there taking a critical intercultural communication studies approach. I was running out of time; the deadline for the essay submission was quickly approaching. I worked swiftly, focusing my attention primarily on making arguments that emerged directly from reading Chesebro's text, brought in what little scholarship I had been able to gather, and built from ideas I had resulting from my conversations with Carole, Wenshu, Tom, and Rona. NCA 1996 was fast approaching. I got the essay into shape and sent it to Dolores on November 6, 1996, to be published in 1998.

Central Ideas in the Essay

Let me say at the outset that, in retrospect, some of my main points were not specific to Chesebro's article. My critiques could have been written about any number of intercultural essays produced during the same time period or even before it. Thus, it was not just to Chesebro's work I was responding but also to the broader field of intercultural communication. For instance, I challenged Chesebro's argument that nations should be compared culturally, but by no means was he alone in making such comparisons. Comparing nations was basic to communication research and, to some extent, a defining approach to intercultural communication research. Chesebro's own review of literature demonstrated just how accepted a "nation-state" approach to intercultural communication had been up until that point.

Despite how commonplace a national approach to scholarship was, thinking about the concept of the nationstate critically was new within communication studies and to intercultural communication, more specifically. While Chesebro and I both viewed the nation as a social construction, my way of viewing it is as a figure, or a symbol, that can be and often is used in a strategic manner to mobilize peoples' interests, ideas, and activities, even ways of being, differs significantly from Chesebro's view of the nation as a social construction. The taken-for-grantedness of the nationstate in Chesebro's and other intercultural work of the time suggests the level of acceptance people have with the way the world is organized, implying the degree to which "the nation," perhaps even more so than "the people," was (and still is) a commonplace of US-American life.[3]

Additionally, discussing nations the way Chesebro did fits squarely within a field with a liberal humanist foundation. Such a foundation is evident in intercultural and cross-cultural communication research that has drawn heavily from research in psychology, cultural behavior and behavioral management, and cross-cultural relations. The values of such a tradition encourage scholars to learn about others, provide goodwill when possible, share (or "exchange") information and ideas, and in general tolerate difference. In this same vein, Chesebro's article was written in good faith, hoping to improve knowledge across cultures. As he wrote, "as cultures are compared and contrasted to each other on an increasing number of dimensions, the unique identity of each cultural system begins to emerge" (Chesebro, 1981, p. 178).

Finally, Chesebro's comparison of nations' similarities and differences, rather than on racial structure and attitudes, reflects the lack of broad discussion and theorization of race as a constitutive dimension of communication research in the field as a whole.

To be clear then, Chesebro could not have drawn on critical intercultural research in formulating his arguments about cross-cultural comparisons. Indeed, I, myself, was not able to draw on that research in writing my response to his article, since that research did not exist at the time. Our dialogue in these essays was, after all, prior to most publications on transnationalism, postcolonialism, whiteness, and critical race theory in communication. His essay was written when the Critical/ Cultural Division of the National Communication Association was a concept, not a reality, and, thus, well before the *Journal of Communication and Critical/ Cultural Studies* and the *Journal of International and Intercultural Communication* came onto the scene.

Key points from the original essay

As I look back on my essay, I make three key points that still have relevance to critical intercultural communication studies today:

First, it is problematic to use the nationstate as the primary basis for cultural comparison, because, as Benedict Anderson has suggested, nationstates are imaginary formations. As constructs, nationstates necessarily have limited explanatory power, especially when attempting to represent the diversity of ideas, opinions, lifestyles, and behaviors of people. Not unlike the building of nationstates, the recurrent discursive representation of nationstates as coherent entities and as stable and fixed formations often serves to reify notions of difference and commonality – rather than put them into question, as critical intercultural communication seeks to do – rendering nations a problematic standard for cultural comparison.

Absolutely, it is still the case that people do refer to nations every day as if they exist. The word "nation," therefore, is not *just* another household word. It is one of the many *houses* like cities or states that moors us to planet Earth. Because it helps position us as individual subjects within our daily lives, and in relation to people, institutions, and spaces, and plays a significant role in articulating identities, the reification and naturalization of the nation also occurs on a daily basis across disparate social spaces. It is this habitual referencing or citation – its *citationality* – that renders nation a seemingly uncontestable, indisputible part of reality.[4] However, the concretization of nations through daily reification should not keep us from maintaining, intellectually, that nations are very much fictions.

Gayatri Spivak famously described the "worlding" of "the Third World" as a strategic act of signification, as a discursive act imperial cultures did to produce a particular kind of power relationship between the imperial nation and subjects of "distant cultures, exploited but with rich intact literary heritages waiting to be recovered, interpreted, and curricularized in English translation" (Spivak, 1985, p. 262). Worlding is not unlike what we might call *nationing*; however, whereas in Spivak's approach, worlding refers to something an empire does to establish its power relationship with people it generalizes as of a particular kind or type, we define nationing here as the production of a power relationship that aims to put in place a particular worldview for those conceived of as members of the nation who will, in the future, do the labor of maintaining the nation.

As the late Michael McGee might have asked about nations, "When was the last time you saw a nation walking up your driveway?" Nations can be conceptually useful sometimes, such as when nations allow for the delivery of social justice (sometimes a rare event). However, the taken for grantedness of nations, the automatic way subjects often think of nations as protecting "us" from outsiders and determining our social identities (e.g., rendering us patriotic to only one flag in the world) make them obstacles, too. Thus, for example, a nation may play a role in inhibiting filial relations and communications with those demarcated as *outside of a given nationstate*, precisely because this would be regarded as communing with members of *other* nations and not with one's own.

Today, the degree to which nations have become naturalized is indeed troubling and renders their use for the purposes of cultural comparison problematic. Comparing the United States with Iraq, for instance, would, by suggesting those living in Iraq have cultural identities that are alike in some fundamental, national way, seriously abrogate scholarly responsibility to study such fundamental tensions within Iraq and the United States such as religious, ethnic, gendered, and classed ones. Moreover, in the case of Iraq, thinking of it as a nationstate may mean having to overlook the degree to which the "people" are not one and the same as those in charge of its government, even as "heads of state," and what they say are often taken to be symmetrically interrelated with the objectives of the abstract polity circumscribed by the nation. As Shohat and Stam have written, "The nation of course is not a desiring person but a fictive unity imposed on an aggregate of individuals, yet national histories are presented as if they displayed the continuity of the subject-writ-large" (Shohat and Stam, 1994, p. 101). It is precisely this kind of abstraction, this attempt to identify a unifying principle that applies to all cases equally, to subsume individuals, groups, and individual and group thought and action to the nation, through the figure of the nationstate, that evacuates cultural analysis of the obligation to understand and search for cultural complexity and that, one might argue, helped rationalize the United States' invasion of Iraq in the first place and the continued efforts by the United States to control paternally the people living there.

Since writing my essay, work in transnational communication studies and transnational studies more broadly has blossomed.[5] That work, often written by people living in a country other than the one where they were born, really challenges nation-centered analysis. The rich, complex, and vast criss-crossing of national boundaries both by people and by capital has intensified and fundamentally altered the space for cultural analysis and comparison. For, national politics still do exist, and as the recent formation of the Republic of Kosovo suggests, desires for nationhood and for independence continue, despite the powerful role that transnational politics, capital, and power now play. In short, while it would be folly to suggest that one can ignore the nationstate, it is important to understand the way the nationstate functions in relation to transnational capitalism and corporations.

Second, many theoretical concepts used to compare cultures historically have limited analytical or heuristic value today, despite having been used repeatedly over

time in intercultural communication research and in other fields. Here, I am thinking of the binaristic concepts developed primarily by Geert Hofstede, Harry
Triandis, and by paid cross-cultural educators like Edward T. Hall (1959) such as
individualist/collectivist, low context/high context, authoritativeness/obedience,
and masculine/feminine. It is important to note that current use of these terms
seems to have been little informed by the transformation of thinking about culture
following the civil rights era of the 1950s through the 1970s. Thus, when used
these concepts often function simply as stereotypes. As Voronov and Singer (sum-
marizing Sinha and Tripathi) write:

> When a whole culture or society is pigeonholed in dichotomous categories (e.g.,
> masculine–feminine, active–passive, or loose–tight), subtle differences and qualitative
> nuances that are more characteristic of that social entity may be glossed over. Such
> descriptive labels evoke unduly fixed and caricature-like mental impressions of cul-
> tures or societies rather than representative pictures of their complexities. Also, pre-
> senting cultures in black-or-white terms not only clouds one's understanding of them
> but inevitably leads to good–bad comparisons (Voronov and Singer, 2002, p. 461).

Thus, conceiving of culture in terms of binaries about nations facilitates the differentiation of self from others and does so by affirming, and confirming, binaries,
ones often reputed to be linked to nature, hence rendering them resistant to
change, that serve to facilitate the concept of self-preservation over communal and
the preservation of society as ideals.

As my original article suggests, such stereotypes also can help create and maintain contemporary power relations. They can promote and reify a particular and
peculiar kind of *Western gaze*. Such abstractions can be used to privilege a particular perspective, a vantage point of the Westerner, the citizen of the United States,
white European Americans, people with legal and political legitimacy within a first-
world nationstate, those who invent the grounds for cultural comparison from a
subjective and limited point of view. Representation studies have demonstrated
that assumptions are built into representations and, thus, that representations make
sense within particular social, cultural, and historical contexts. Those who invoke
the nation, those figureheads who stand in for the national government, and those
who simply benefit from a national way of thinking may do so inadvertently but
nevertheless, through actions and discourse, play a role in the maintenance of a
particular relation of power.

Additionally, whether aware of it or not, subjects may inadvertently take on a
white, masculine, heterosexist, US, European, or Western perspective, without recognizing that such a position of power to name, define, and represent has the
potential to create and maintain problematic, stereotypical assumptions based on
US colonial, historical imaginings across East/West, North/South dimensions.
This power-effect should remind us that the power to name and describe is inter-
linked with cultural capital and privilege. Those with the power to name, and in this
case to compare, have the power, as do baseball umpires, to "call them they way

they see them," with their own particular ideas, attitudes, and perspectives informing the ultimate representation of a given culture and its relationship to them.

Additionally, however, employing a Western gaze also has the potential to incur tremendous costs. For instance, those using this Western gaze may accept unequal power relations as a given and therefore may overlook important dimensions of the cultural relationship, as well as the positive dimension of the Other. Additionally, objectification of the other may ultimately prevail over the Other's humanity, since already available categories exist that make further understanding, exploration, and curiosity unnecessary. Finally, because of this objectification of the Other, a full and complex understanding of humanity, and of the Self, becomes less realizable, sapping humanity from those invoking this objective gaze and reducing the complexity of human life to simple, formulaic understandings that may also reduce meaningfulness.

In part, concepts that function to produce simplistic understandings of other cultures and their differences from those in the West emerged because of a lack of scholarship recognized by those in the Western academy as germane to the study of culture, and a lack of cultural analysis that questioned and challenged the ideologically laden assumptions of US scholarship. However, since my essay was written, work on cultural perspectives and "the gaze," as well as work that simply retheorizes relationships with a much broader conception of identities, has been produced.[6]

A third argument I make in the earlier essay is that historically the field of communication, and arguably the sciences, social sciences, and humanities more broadly has produced theory that aims to be universally applicable. This tendency to universalize and strive for theories with universal applicability is problematic and may result in scholars attempting to produce and justify scholarship that is dependent on problematic assumptions about national similarities and difference. This critique clearly goes beyond a critique of Chesebro's argument and beyond the field of intercultural communication to a critique of "universalist" theory and its presumptions in scholarship, more broadly. Theories that aim for universality, as so many have argued persuasively, necessarily maintain culturally specific assumptions and perspectives. Thus, while they may appear to be universal, because they aspire to apply to every case, in fact they obscure the degree to which such universalizing assumptions and ideals are deeply ideological and specific and not universal at all but in fact are narrowly subjective. Questions that help us make sense of the problems with theories that universalize include: Why is generalizing across experiences necessary? In making such generalizations, what aspects of specificity are overlooked or covered over? What justifies a generalizing principle rather than a particular one? That is, whether it is an argument that all people should have human rights or that queer identities should be valued everywhere, equally, such universalist notions, no matter how apparently obvious they may be to those who advance them, are far more complicated when discussed within the context of a multiplicity of cultural spaces, and not just the ones from which such ideas emerge.

It is not, of course, that having a theory that applies to everyone is a problem. The problem is that employing theories as if they are fact, are irrefutable, and explain everything for everyone, without taking the academic step of specifying the ground on which those theories are formed, noting their potential limited scope and applicability, and admitting alternative views exist (or even focusing primarily on those alternative views), by not identifying the cases that do not apply because of their unusualness, distinctness, uniqueness, or oddity weakens the theory and means it is *less* objective than it would be otherwise.[7] Thus, I am not arguing that universality as a stance does not have usefulness. Rather, I am suggesting that in articulating a universal position that it not be conceived either as the only position or that it serve to marginalize theories that argue the opposite stance of, say, case-specific examples. More germane to the study of nations, universality is the abstracting step that leads to the generalization of people's ideas and interests as "national" ones.

Rebuttal to Chesebro's Response to My Article

Since I did not get an opportunity to respond to Chesebro's response to my response to his essay, I am pleased to have the opportunity now to address some of the points he makes there. For those interested in the debate, having a response from me might be helpful, since our dialogue there took place at an important turning point in the field of intercultural communication, just as the vibrant subfield of critical intercultural studies was beginning to emerge.

The main critique I level against Chesebro, to which he did not respond in his rebuttal to my essay, is of his use of literature, not his main argument that change should be an important variable in cross-cultural comparison. I say on p. 195, "DCS's primary limitations stem from problems in the literature used as the basis for the study" (Ono, 1998). I suggest that there does exist work within cultural studies in particular that helps to put some of key assumptions about nation and culture that Chesebro's article articulates into question. I then also suggest that it is surprising that given the tremendous amount of cultural studies work that exists, which would have helped strengthen the analysis in the article, that Chesebro somehow bypassed that scholarship entirely.

Another challenge I make to Chesebro in the article is that scholarship he cites and relies upon does not conceive of the people under study themselves as offering valid perspectives with which outsiders might understand them. This issue goes beyond self-reports by interviewees. Rather, the point I did not make as clearly as I would have liked is that without an understanding of worldviews, without an understanding of cultural complexity and cultural syncretism, without an in-depth understanding of cultural difference, not much of value can be said about people by outsiders.

While he was only reviewing work on cross-cultural international communication in that section, my critique of his use of Liebes's work was that Liebes assumes that the ways nonUS Americans view US television conforms entirely to the stereotypes that exist in the United States and the West about those outside it. Her work suffers from a problem of much cultural work prior to critical intercultural studies and that is trying to understand people by reproducing what we already know about them. Without realizing it, ideological assumptions about cultures other than one's own come to be used as a basis for cultural comparison. Because the lens of Western knowledge mediates the researcher's apprehension of difference, and because that difference is understood through the language, discourse, and ideological structures common in the West, there was reason to question and challenge not only Liebes's research, but also Chesebro's use of it. Additionally, I was troubled by the theoretical assumption Chesebro makes that the differences Liebes found could be understood as "national" versus ideological differences, when in fact one of my main arguments was that what are conceived of as national characteristics in studies that compare nations are in fact ideological ones.

Words like "a culture" and "a collective" suggest that while Chesebro defines culture as socially constructed, he also constitutes concrete national differences in his language and relies on troubling notions of national differences as informative of cultural ones. Perhaps the part of his essay that I found most problematic was on p. 182, where, after defining culture as socially constructed, he defends a "nation-state" model for ascertaining and evaluating cultural differences. He writes "In terms of the practical, we need to study nation-state cultures. In an ideal world, we might examine cultures regardless of nation-state boundaries. But data and understandings are now linked to and collected by nation-states, not by cultural systems" (Chesebro, 1998, p. 182). He goes further to defend what he calls Triandis's production of "stereo-types as hypotheses of national character" (Chesebro, 1998, p. 182). Such a position is highly surprising, given Chesebro's evident support through his own work of research on multicultural communication.

In retrospect, Chesebro's primary argument that "change" ought to be a key variable for cultural comparison is a good one. While his interest is in change being a predictor of a technological or progressive society, a despotic one, or a conservative one, and while his own work rightly challenges the United States for having possibly become conservative over time, since I now have a second chance, I would say that change should be a fundamental part of intercultural analysis for the reasons Chesebro gives. Additionally, however, change should be a central concept for understanding cultural identities, lives, and bodies unfamiliar to a given scholar. There is an historical tendency to conceive of "others" as fixed in time and as "Europe, alone and unaided ... as the 'motor' for progressive social change" (Shohat and Stam, 1994, p. 2). Shohat and Stam tell a story from the film *Het Dak Van de Walvis* of a French anthropologist who studies Indians returning home to Europe in despair after finding out that Indians change their names each month and invent an entirely new vocabulary every day (Shohat and Stam, 1994, p. 44). One could imagine the researcher's frustration at not being able to objectify them, render them legible or fixed. Their dynamism and commitment to change flies in the face of colonialism's need to render them artifactual, lifeless, and timeless. The very concept of the "Third World," Shohat and Stam suggest, was framed as referring to nations as "'backward,' 'underdeveloped,' and 'primitive'" (Shohat and

Stam, 1994, p. 25). In part, this is why Native Americans are often represented in traditional, historical plains Indian clothing (usually not even historically accurate), and Asians are represented as wearing traditional kimonos (Japanese) or peasant clothing (Chinese), rather than as living, breathing, human beings within rapidly changing global contexts.

Conclusion

During a time when so much is happening on worldwide scale, when economics has gone global, and when transnational exchanges of labor and capital, not to mention world travel, is at unprecedented highs, rethinking the nation and what it means for the study of communication, and what the nation's role will be in burgeoning subfields like critical intercultural communication studies is highly necessary. While earlier approaches to intercultural communication may have conceived of the nation in particular ways, ways that researchers still find useful today, in order to stay current and therefore to be heuristically significant, readapting tools for cultural analysis is required.

While mine is only one among many essays that people consider central to the early emergence of critical intercultural communication studies, perhaps in the way I tell the story, people can learn about the process of publication, speaking from the margins, rethinking fields and beginning new ones, and understand better some of the stakes involved in doing critical intercultural communication today. Perhaps this essay is but one more attempt to rethink key concepts like nation anew, in hopes that further dialogue and theorization rethinks the grounds for this essay, as well.

Notes

1 While it is beyond the scope or focus of this essay (and certainly footnote) to discuss all precursors to, contributors to, and builders of critical intercultural communication studies, it is possible to define at least some central dimensions of what has become a reconception of intercultural communication, as well as a field of communication that has theoretical and practical dimensions that adequately render it a field in and of itself. One would be remiss not to notice that from the mid-1990s to the present, scholars at and emerging from Arizona State University's communication department have been at the forefront of developing critical intercultural communication. For full details of these publications see Further Reading.

2 The fairly recent emergence of the *Journal of International and Intercultural Communication* (National Communication Association) and the appointment of Thomas Nakayama as its inaugural editor, suggests the current centrality of critical intercultural communication studies research, even as the journal publishes both traditional and critical work.

3 Michael McGee's famous essay about "the people" suggested the degree to which the people was an ideograph that was and could be used rhetorically to exert influence.

McGee, himself, was fond of saying, "All people try very hard to live up to the stereotype of their choice." By using "people" in this way, McGee invited his listeners to see themselves as one of the people, to understand the people to be definitive of what humans are, and to (suggestively) imply that there was a generalizing entity, the people, about which universal-like claims could be made. The power generated invoking the notion of the people to make grand claims that appeared to apply to the largest number of social members was, as McGee noted so eloquently and definitively, rhetorically produced. So, too, is the power behind "the nation." Those successful at invoking the concept of the nation, and on its taken for grantedness, can, potentially, seem to have access to a highly broad notion of the broader society. However, in invoking the nation, what one, in fact does, is cover over the vastly different ways individuals and individual groups live their lives. Critical intercultural communication departs from a nation-based model of communication precisely because a nation-based model has a tendency to generalize behavior; whereas, critical cultural communication seeks to radically empiricize that reality. By radical empiricism, I mean that critical intercultural communication sees the discourse of the nation as something that people do and do not buy into, based on their social circumstances. Personal experiences, in everyday life, may or may not allow someone to wish to identify with national discourses. It is true that a very large number of people, who we might call "national subjects" might try very hard to live a life in accordance with what they view as the ideal behavior of a citizen of the nation. Yet, their economic, health, personal, interpersonal, and more generally life circumstances may allow them, to a greater or lesser degree, to imagine themselves to be part of that ideal national subjectivity. Indeed, people may opt either to be national members, and hence accept invitations to understand themselves to be a part of this larger project, or not to be members of what they understand to be definitive of that collectivity. Part of what critical intercultural communication aims to do, then, is to seek to define what is actually meaningful to people within their historical, cultural, political contexts, not what is taken for granted as meaningful to the nation. Critical intercultural communication seeks to find out what is important to people, not what is assumed to be important about their everyday lives and the social connections they make.

4   For instance, in Judith Butler's (1993) discussion of the performative, she suggests that "it is not because an intention successfully governs the action of speech, but only because action echoes prior to actions, and *accumulates the force of authority through the repetition or citation of a prior, authoritative set of practices*" (pp. 226–227).

5   For more on transnationalism in the field, see Shome, and Hegde (2002), Appadurai (1996), Moallem, Kaplan, and Alarcon (1999). Also, especially as it relates to politics and communication, see Ono (2005).

6   I am thinking here of work such as Rony (1996) which does a wonderful job of critically examining the anthropological gaze. Also of note is works such as Halberstam (1998) and Sloop (2004) both of which trouble discrete notions of gender and sexuality and by doing so fundamentally problematize scholarly approaches that "gender" nations as masculine and feminine.

7   In her essay, Sandra Harding (1993) argues for "strong objectivity," suggesting that scientists historically have promoted a notion of "objectivity" that, in fact, is not very objective and has tended to disregard people who are marginalized when applied. Her argument is that by specifying one's social position, or "standpoint," stronger, not weaker, objectivity is rendered possible.

References

Appadurai, A. (1996) *Modernity at Large: Cultural Dimensions of Globalization*, University of Minnesota Press, Minneapolis.

Butler, J. (1993) *Bodies that Matter: On the Discursive Limits of "Sex,"* Routledge, New York.

Chesebro, J. (1981) *Gayspeak: Gay Male and Lesbian Communication*, The Pilgrim Press of the United Church, New York.

Chesebro, J.W. (1998) Distinguishing cultural systems: Change as a variable explaining and predicting cross-cultural communication, in *Communication and Identity across Cultures: International and Intercultural Communication Annual, 21*, (eds. V. Dolores, T. Tanno and A. González), Sage, Thousand Oaks, CA, pp. 177–192.

Halberstam, J. (1998) *Female Masculinity*, Duke University Press, Durham, NC.

Hall, E.T. (1959) *The Silent Language*, Doubleday and Company, New York.

Harding, S. (1993) Rethinking standpoint epistemology: What is "Strong Objectivity"? in *Feminist Epistemologies*, (eds Linda Alcoff and Elizabeth Potter), Routledge, New York, pp. 49–82.

Moallem, M., Kaplan, C., and Alarcon, N. (eds) (1999) *Between Woman and Nation. Nationalisms, Transnational Feminisms and The State*, Duke University Press, Durham, NC.

Ono, K.A. (1998) Problematizing "nation" in intercultural communication research, in *Communication and Identity across Cultures: International and Intercultural Communication Annual, 21*, (eds. V. Dolores, T. Tanno and A. González), Sage, Thousand Oaks, CA, pp. 193–202.

Ono, K.A. (2005) From nationalism to migrancy: The politics of Asian American Transnationalism. *Communication Law Review* 5 (1), http://commlawreview.org/Archives/v5i1/From%20Nationalism%20to%20Migrancy.pdf (accessed May 18, 2010).

Rony, F.T. (1996) *The Third Eye: Race, Cinema, and Ethnographic Spectacle*, Duke University Press, Durham, NC.

Shohat, E., and Stam, R.S. (1994) *Unthinking Eurocentrism: Multiculturalism and the Media*, Routledge, New York.

Shome, R., and Hegde, R. (2002) Culture, communication, and the challenge of globalization. *Critical Studies in Media Communication*, 17 (2), 172–189.

Sloop, J.M. (2004) *Disciplining Gender: Rhetorics of Sex Identity in Contemporary U.S. Culture*, University of Massachusetts Press, Boston.

Spivak, G., and Chakravorty, G. (1985) Three women's texts and a critique of imperialism, in *"Race," Writing, and Difference*, (ed. H.L. Gates, Jr.), University of Chicago Press, Chicago, pp. 262–280.

Voronov, M., and Singer, J. (2002) The myth of individualism-collectivism: A critical review. *Journal of Social Psychology*, 142 (4), 461–480.

Further Reading

Allen, B.J. (2003) *Difference Matters: Communicating Social Identity*, Waveland, Long Grove, IL.

Calafell, B.M. (2007) *Latina/o Communication Studies: Theorizing Performance*, Peter Lang, New York.

Cheng, H.-I. (2008) *Culturing Interface: Identity, Communication, and Chinese Transnationalism*, Peter Lang, New York.

Delgado, F.P. (1998). When the silenced speak: The textualization and complications of Latina/o identity. *Western Journal of Communication*, 62 (4), 420–438.

Flores, L.A. (1996) Creating discursive space through a rhetoric of difference: Chicana feminists craft a homeland, *The Quarterly Journal of Speech*, 82 (3) 142–156.

González, A., Houston, M., and Chen, V. (eds) (2000) *Our Voices: Essays in Culture, Ethnicity, and Communication*, Roxbury, Los Angeles.

Halualani, R.T. (2002) *In the Name of Hawaiians: Native Identities and Cultural Politics*, University of Minnesota Press, Minneapolis.

Hecht, M.L. (ed.) (1998) *Communicating Prejudice*, Sage, Thousand Oaks, CA.

International and Intercultural Communication Annual (particularly the 1997, 1998, 2000, 2001, 2002, 2003, 2006, and 2007 editions).

Kraidy, M.M. (2005) *Hybridity, or the Cultural Logic of Globalization*, Temple University Press, Philadelphia.

Martin, J. (ed) (2000) Special issue. *International Journal of Intercultural Relations*, 24.

Martin, J.N., and Nakayama, T.K. (1997) *Intercultural Communication in Contexts*, Mayfield, Mountain View, CA.

Martin, J.N., Nakayama, T.K., and Flores, L.A. (eds) (1998) *Readings in Intercultural Communication*, McGraw-Hill, Boston, MA.

Martinez, J. (2000) *Phenomenology of Chicana Identity and Experience*, Rowman and Littlefield, Lanham, MD.

Mendoza, S. (2001) *Between the Homeland and the Diaspora: The Politics of Theorizing Filipino and Filipono American Identities*, Routledge, New York.

Mendoza, S.L., Halualani, R.T., and Drzewiecka, J.A. (2002) Moving the discourse on identities in intercultural communication: Structure, culture, and resignifications. *Communication Quarterly*, 50 (3/4), 312–327.

Moon, D.G. (1996) Concepts of "culture": Implications for intercultural communication research. *Communication Quarterly*, 44 (1), 70–84.

Nakayama, T.K. (1994) Show/down Time: "Race, gender, sexuality and popular culture," *Critical Studies in Mass Communication*, 11 (June), 162–179.

Nakayama, T.K., and Krizek, R.L. (1995) Whiteness: A strategic rhetoric, *Quarterly Journal of Speech*, 81, 291–309.

Nakayama, T.K., and Martin, J.N. (eds) (1998) *Whiteness: The Communication of Social Identity*, Sage, Thousand Oaks, CA.

Shome, R. (1996) Race and popular cinema: The rhetorical strategies of whiteness in City of Joy. *Communication Quarterly*, 44 (4), 502–518.

Shome, R., and Hegde, R.S. (2002) Culture, communication, and the challenge of globalization. *Critical Studies in Media Communication*, 19 (2), 172–189.

Warren, J. (2001) Doing whiteness: On the performative dimensions of race in the classroom. *Communication Education*, 50, 91–109.

7

Reflections on "Bridging Paradigms: How Not to Throw Out the Baby of Collective Representation with the Functionalist Bathwater in Critical Intercultural Communication"

S. Lily Mendoza

But there is a moment when [hegemony] always declares itself to be universal and closed, and that is the moment of naturalization. That's the moment when it wants its boundaries to be coterminous with the truth, with the reality of history. And that is always the moment which, I think, escapes it. That's my hope. Something had better be escaping it.

(Hall, 1997, p. 68)

The purpose of theorizing is not to enhance one's intellectual or academic reputation but to enable us to grasp, understand, and explain – to produce a more adequate knowledge of – the historical world and its processes; and thereby to inform our practice so that we may transform it.

(Hall, 1988, p. 36)

The article, "Bridging Paradigms" (Mendoza, 2005), which is the subject of this reflection piece, is one I've written in the spirit of what Hall invokes in the above epigraphs – that theorizing has a purpose beyond mere intellectual pursuit and that part of its crucial task is to give an adequate accounting of the operation of symbolic power and expose its pretensions to naturalness and its arbitrary foreclosures. Indeed, if, as Lemert (1999, quoting Bradley) notes, "one of the primary functions of societal institutions is to conceal the basic nature of the society, so that the individuals that make up the power structure can pursue the business of consolidating and increasing their power untroubled by the minor carpings of a dissatisfied peasantry" (p. 2), then the task of symbolic/ideological critique becomes ever more urgent in a world where, anymore, the primary mode of legitimation has become increasingly that of media "spin" and manipulation of the image. The task then for critical intercultural communication is clear. To the extent that the discipline's domain is in the realm of the

The Handbook of Critical Intercultural Communication, edited by Thomas K. Nakayama and Rona Tamiko Halualani. © 2010 Blackwell Publishing Ltd.

symbolic – in particular, the reading, interpretation, performance, enactment, negotiation, and legitimation of the text (and reality) of difference – it behooves us as
critical intercultural communication scholars to learn to equip ourselves to do this
kind of symbolic work with greater savvy and sophistication, one befitting the growing savvy and sophistication of ideological mystification abroad in our world today.

In much of my work, the particular site of ideological interrogation closest to
home has been the very practice and politics of intercultural theorizing, in particular,
the question having to do with the seeming impossibility of rapprochement between
the old functionalist modes of analysis and the deconstructive critique as articulated
in the posttheory discourses, notably, postmodernism, poststructuralism, and postcolonialism. At the time of writing, although the turn to deconstructive and post-
structuralist theorizing was then still relatively new in intercultural communication
and offered many exciting theoretical possibilities for the discipline, I began to notice
a curious phenomenon: the new paradigm's rapid hegemonization in many circles of
scholarship. I found it curious because with its rise to dominance, I noted – not
without much irony given the critique's own injunction against all forms of closure
and totalization – what seemed to be the closing down of thought in the very process of its unqualified embrace in many quarters in the academy. Evidence of this was
not so much in published pieces where greater accountability demanded more care
in one's expression, but mostly in informal venues, that is, in conferences and classrooms where the rolling of eyes and groans of incredulity directed toward those
perceived still to operate within the by-now largely discredited language of "essentialism" (or what was knee-jerked as naïve realism or positivism) betrayed the condescension of those who saw themselves possessed of the ultimate theoretically correct
position toward those who had yet "to see the light," as it were. Such phenomenon
of the devolution of formerly insurgent discourses into new disciplinary formations
once they attain what I call "theoretical hegemony"(policing communicative expression and precluding dissent) became the subject of my book, *Between the Homeland
and the Diaspora: The Politics of Theorizing Filipino and Filipino American Identities*
(Mendoza 2002/2006). In it I wrote:

> Such moments of theoretical, ideological, and paradigmatic triumph when power
> condenses into monopolistic centers in the realm of the symbolic, I submit, constitute
> dangerous moments in the life of a scholarly community. And this is true even where
> success is originally fought for and won in the name of democratic or liberatory
> imperatives. Indeed history is replete with examples of how the articulation of any
> social or discursive order to dominant power results [almost] invariably not only in
> smug arrogance and self-congratulatory poses on the part of its architects, but in a
> stance that makes self-reflexivity and interrogation extremely difficult, if not alto-
> gether impossible. (Mendoza, 2002/2006, p. 4)

In "Bridging Paradigms," I examine more closely the implications and challenges
posed by the rise to hegemony of the anti-essentialist critique for the theorization
of identity struggles within critical intercultural communication.[1] In many ways,
although the critique served as a welcome development in the field in the way it

enabled analysis to move away from reductive, variable analytic, and positivistic modes of explanation toward more politicized understandings of the key concepts in the field (e.g., identity, nation, culture, communication, ethnicity, race, etc.), still, in practice, the deconstructive perspective was not exempt from the pitfall of reification. One particular challenge it poses is how now to account adequately for the struggles of minoritized communities whose discourse is often couched in identitarian (essentialist) rhetoric. I ask in this regard: With the radical suspicion of all essentialist and identitarian politics, is there sense in continuing the project of cultural "description" that aims at collective representation of differing groups for purposes of establishing intercultural understanding? Furthermore,

> [i]s there space in a regime of unbridled deconstruction for "re-constructive" theoriz-ing? If so, how might one engage in this practice differently without falling into the poststructuralist "crime" (and very real dangers) of essentialism? Is there a way we can save the baby of collective representation from getting thrown out with the bathwater of functionalism? And what is our investment in doing so? (Mendoza, 2005, p. 239)

In the article, I sought to extend the important contributions of such key theorists as Spivak (1996) ("strategic essentialism"), Butler (1995) ("contingent founda-tions"), and West (1995a) ("identity from above and identity from below") by arguing that the task of analysis requires some kind of "bridging" work, one that would take seriously deconstruction's own dictum and underscore the contingency of its own perspective by refusing to freeze it into a mere formalism. For this, I proposed the need for dynamic translation work, suggesting Hall's theory (and method) of articulation as a helpful analytical framework for this purpose.

In what follows, since much of my work in this regard has been metatheoretical in nature (i.e., theorizing about the politics of theorizing), I wish to situate the "Bridging" piece within the larger context of my personal background and history, and in the process, articulate not only the stakes for me in this line of inquiry but also to map out key directions coming out of it that I find crucial for the future of intercultural communication if it is to intervene effectively (and in relevant ways) in the world and make a difference.

From the beginning, "bridging" for me has been the overarching metaphor for what I understand intercultural communication scholars do. To bridge is to strad-dle worlds – whether by choice or by force – and to be compelled to find a way of connecting the two in ways that make sense.

My entry into intercultural communication studies was compelled by just such a need. As a postcolonial Filipina, I needed to find a way to make sense of things in my crazy world growing up – the jarring disconnect between my cognitive world as shaped by decades of tutelage in Western philosophy and Protestant liberalism[2] and that other wordless world at the fringes of my consciousness intuited only by a kind of bodily knowing, a differing psychic desire, and the puzzling refusal of my tongue to entirely acquiesce to colonial English despite its imposition in Philippine schools as the official medium of instruction.[3] I recall writing naïvely in my statement of purpose as an applicant to an intercultural graduate program in the United States, "One need not have traveled to another country to experience culture shock; two (or three or even more) cultures can reside inside oneself without ever finding rational integration." Indeed it was the search for such integration – a way out of the psychic distress of not being able to feel at home in oneself brought on by the disconnect – that, as I now see looking back, first pulled me into intercultural communication as a field of study. Intercultural communication pioneer E.T. Hall (1976), writing on the intricacies of synchronous body rhythms of both human and nonhuman groups as in and of themselves unique and complex systems of communication, gave me a way of speaking of what is perhaps the most insidious effect of colonial domination: the throwing of a people out of synch with themselves so that they no longer know how to be. Early Filipino scholars speak of it in terms of a split psyche – the interior struggle of the Filipino caught between the anarchic freedoms of animist enchantment and the endless calculations of sin and redemption; between the call of the *duendes* and other spirit beings in the natural world and the admonition (at least for the educated) to rest one's faith in science and empirical proof; and between the free energy exchange of unbounded selves (in the indigenous notion of *kapwa* as "shared being") and the containment of the abstract individual in the Euro-Western Enlightenment discourse on the self (cf. Norbert Elias' 1994/2000 notion of *homo clausus* or the autonomous individual). I was to learn that such dimensions of splitting were only a few in an endless litany of contrasts between indigenous Filipino subjectivity, on the one hand, and that of the modern West, on the other.

Searching for a way to make sense of the two clashing worlds so I didn't end up schizophrenic entailed a torturous journey. Although the encounter of cultures need not be inherently problematic where difference is negotiated in a relation of mutual exploration and curiosity, in a dominating context where takeover and control of the other is part of the ongoing dynamic, the encounter invariably devolves into conflictual relations and becomes psychically wrenching especially for the dominated. Thus, given my Protestant upbringing, my journey began with a rationalistic moralism that effectively individualized the colonial malaise, reduced it to an inherent weakness of character, and encouraged a profound internalization of blame (as well as shame). The result was an inability to function unself-consciously, always feeling like one was constantly under surveillance. The self-preoccupation that followed became a mode of survival in a regime that perpetually called into question one's whole existence (I learned later on that the syndrome had a name: *colonial narcissism*). If the default condition, historically, of human beings is to look at the world through an ethno-culturally rooted vision, trained and coded in intimate, intricate and adaptive relationship with their environment, that of the colonized is effectively a training in reverse – into a way of seeing "from without," by way of the surveilling gaze of a hostile Other rooted elsewhere in a different ethic of relations.

To be thrown out of synch then, to go back to Hall's formulation, is to be compelled to a lifelong psychic search for "a way back" – if ever such were possible – to one's lost primal rhythm; or failing that, to struggle to make sense of the dis-ease and perhaps make it yield syncopated beats for creative self-recreation through such tactics as transcoding, code switching, and translation. Indeed native peoples forcibly assimilated into modernity's logic but who nonetheless retain deep ties to their cultural traditions become adept at the latter, often subverting the imperial code through subconscious performances of subtle (and not-so-subtle) transcripts of resistance, often enacted under the radar of colonialism's surveilling gaze.

My own rigorous socialization into Western modes of cognition, first, under the tutelage of American missionaries and Peace Corps Volunteers and subsequently through the disembodied oeuvre of Western ideology via the academic disciplines, left no other door open for me than the resolution of the crisis at an intensely conscious level, that is, through the avenue of theorizing that Spivak and Harasym (1987) refer to as a way of "worlding the world." The intervention of Filipino scholars working in psychology and anthropology, positing a systematic contrast between "Filipino native culture," on the one hand, and the intruding "Western/ North American culture," on the other – although still largely functionalist in orientation – was the opening opportunity for me. Understanding the clash in logics between the two diametrically opposed lifeways as being at the root of my experience – and not an inherent pathology in "the Filipino character" – was powerful, effectively de-naturalizing the aberrations of the colonial condition as well as communalizing what was formerly deemed merely as a personal/individual malaise. Later, new historiographic readings of Philippine-US relations (*Bagong Kasaysayan*) also relativized for me the purported superiority of North American modes of subjectivity even as it displaced the question of ethical valuation from that of a reified notion of "nature" (who or what Filipinos supposedly "are") onto the terrain of the encounter and its attendant "intercultural" conditions. Most fundamental and crucial, of course, was the question of who actually invaded (killed, raped, and pillaged) whom – becoming vigilantly clear in remembering the terms of imposition and the mode of narration that legitimized the dominating violence.

Thus, it is the case that from where I sit the question of intercultural communication can never be separate from the history and politics of encounter. Philippine historians, for example, note that indigenous inhabitants of the Philippine islands have always maintained lively contact with the outside world in the form of inter-island trading with neighbors long before the coming of Europe and the West. However, it was not until the forcible takeover of the colonial powers that violence, conflict, and resistance began to characterize their encounter with others.

Such personal background and history has pushed me to engage intercultural communication theorizing from a different place than that which presumes neutrality in the encounter of peoples – a stance that for me would belie the long history of modernity consisting mostly of European takeover of indigenous peoples' land, resources, and bodies in various projects of colonial (and corporate) theft and plunder. When I first came to graduate communication studies in the US, I was told by one professor that I "raise great philosophical questions but do not 'do communication' enough." Indeed, what do questions of history, politics, culture, and identity have to do with communication? Where communication was assumed to be mainly about innocent meaning exchanges between self-willed, autonomous, and rational individuals interacting mostly on a level playing field, why would anyone focus on anything other than face-value interpretation of talk and the minute psychodynamics of interpersonal relationships?

However, to grow up postcolonial, to be positioned as "other" and to be cast as anomaly or "outlaw" or otherwise to fall outside the norm, is precisely to be denied the luxury of such a circumscribed and acontextual (and I would say, ultimately disingenuous) understanding of what happens in the encounter of bodies within any given time and place. It is to be compelled always – if one were to survive at all with any kind of integrity – to do the hard work and discipline of ideological analysis and the labor of unpacking the layers of symbolic mystification that make up control of the conceptual scheme by those in power. On the other hand, it is also to be susceptible to hailings by other ways of being and knowing – if not consciously, then by a kind of bodily knowing encoded in the inchoate motions of a submerged historical subjectivity that auspiciously carry within them kernels of a different report on the world than that supplied by the prevailing ideology. Such differing subjectivity, I submit, although fraught with the dis-ease of psychic fracturing, bears the potential gift of double seeing (Du Bois, 1961) – a gift at the heart of which is the capacity to inhabit the ambivalence of two-ness (or plural being) in ways that can rework the violence (of domination) into resources for vitality, beauty, and creative re-invention of one's violently dismembered world.

Key then to gaining insight into the workings of dominant power in intercultural relations is learning to listen, first and foremost, to bearers of such alternative subjectivities – those, in the words of Bhabha (1994), "who have suffered the sentence of history" (p. 172), for whom the dominant ideology does not work. It means willingness to hear an often tentatively expressed and guardedly nuanced "minority report" – whether coming from those embedded by suffering and marginalization in minority positions or from those who, though themselves not personally marginalized, have become privy to such experience through critical alliance with those who are. This is not to take a naïvely nativist position or uncritically to valorize the minority position as such, but to underscore a priority. To the extent that the project of mastery and domination – whether in the mode of one form or another of ethno-cultural supremacy or the global corporatist bureaucracy – is invariably invested in keeping the present order of things intact through control of the means of symbolic (re)production by which legitimacy is secured, it behooves those of us committed to a vision of communication as liberatory practice to learn from those others whose mastery of the subtlest workings of power has been key to their survival.

Nowhere is such deep listening to the perspective from below more sorely needed than in the normative discourse of intercultural communication theorizing today. Although the last decade-and-a-half has seen much more commitment to cultural and historical contextualization in analyses of situations involving intercultural interaction (cf. Broome *et al.*, 2005; Collier *et al.*, 2001; Halualani, 2002; Mendoza, 2002/2006; Nakayama and Martin, 1999; Shome and Hegde, 2002 to mention only a few), what remains unquestioned despite all efforts to critique dominant power is the overarching logic of modernity that clearly and univocally undergirds theoretical analysis in the field thus far. The presumption is glaring. Despite the fact that 99% of our species' history has been lived differently – in diverse, ecologically adaptive lifestyles based on a mode of existence that did not presume scarcity or "economics" as the organizing principle of human life – and that up until the fifteenth century, a quarter of the globe still lived in that ecologically adaptive mode before the project of colonial/imperial/corporate genocide began systematically extinguishing such, today we neither know nor care to know about such alternative lifestyles. This is notwithstanding evidence that such lifestyles' record of sustainability, by all counts, is arguably vastly more humane, less given to violence and rapacious greed and far more egalitarian than that of "civilization." Modern ignorance (and arrogance) treats any suggestion that something worthwhile might be learned from that protracted, unrecorded bulk of our species' history as not only preposterous but downright scandalous, so much so that any attempt to open up serious conversation about the subject becomes next to impossible. Indeed one wonders if the representation of that whole way of life (based on hunting and foraging, communal sharing, immediate return, and a land-based subsistence economy) only in debased, primitivist narratives or as mere "pre-history" (i.e., only a prelude to history which is the real deal) in the majority of academic and popular discourses is not motivated precisely by a strangely desperate need to preclude its consideration as a legitimate vision of human life and perhaps even potentially desirable.

Yet, our present time is instructive. For the first time, there is growing suspicion not only among so-called environmental zealots but serious scholars from various fields that the global crises we face today are no longer (were they ever?) merely cultural but civilizational in their proportions: global warming, peak oil, depletion of natural resources, species extinction, population overshoot, nuclear proliferation, toxic pollution, and more recently, the threat of global economic collapse. Even in public discourse, talk of civilizational collapse (e.g., Diamond, 2005; Heinberg, 2002; Jensen, 2006; Klare, 2002; Ruppert, 2004; and Simmons, 2005 to mention only a few) and the reaching of "tipping points" are rife. Indeed, to the extent that modernity has finally succeeded in hegemonizing its unilinear logic of settlement, progress, development, and the re-engineering of nature in service of growth, efficiency, and wealth accumulation around the globe, the world has become effectively singular in its logic and trajectory despite the cultural particularities yet extant among various human groups. Faced with the reality of a finite planet, such cultural logic with its drive toward unlimited growth and expansion can only mean one thing – increasing competition over fast diminishing resources. Given such, it may be fair to say that, ultimately, it is the absurd and patently false premise of ever-increasing economic betterment promised to *all* that is the most formidable Gordian knot troubling intercultural encounter, and not the more starkly dissonant registers of difference organized by race, ethnic, and gender codes that simultaneously mask and inchoately legitimize the great shell game of global capital, in reality ever only privileging a few at the expense of the many. To try then to grapple with the problematic of difference (and the encounter of difference) without its grounding in the last instance in economics and politics, at least since modernity's metastasis onto the global stage, is to fall into mere culturalism and to fail to grasp what is really going on.

At the risk of sounding reductive and sweeping, I can only in small measure suggest the gravity of the theoretical lacuna identified and in barest outline figure the urgency and depth of the challenge its redress poses for intercultural communication scholarship. In what follows, I can present but provisional thoughts on where critical intercultural communication needs to go next if it is not to suffocate in irrelevance. I offer them here in the form of talking points[4] – my own version of what Hall (1996) calls "thinking at the limit" (p. 242).

1   We cannot conduct business as usual. We face challenges today of global and catastrophic proportions that are a direct result of what scientists call the outstripping, by unbridled human consumption, of the earth's carrying capacity, that is, of the planet's capacity to sustain life as invented by us modern humans. In a context of increasing competition over diminishing resources – fossil fuel, food, and other supplies – intercultural relations can only become increasingly more violent and coercive. As ecofeminist Sharon D. Welch (1985) notes ruefully, "We stand on the brink of extinction through nuclear holocaust or ecological disaster, a species whose greatest achievement in the last century has been the perfection of the art of genocide" (p. 88).

2   More than ever, ideological war – knowledge leveraging politics – serves as the key site for dominant groups to strive to preserve their advantage. In the words of critical race theorist Goldberg (1993): "To control the conceptual scheme ... is to rule the world" (p. 9). It is worth noting, however, that even symbolic power has its limits, and today there is a growing consensus that we are fast reaching a threshold that even symbolics cannot fully mask: the physical limit of the earth's capacity to sustain our species' long-term survival. (We are, after all, not (yet) cyborgs, but bodies of flesh and blood just pretending to be exempt from the limits of raw nature.)

3   Given this context of scholarship, there is a crucial need for an alternative vision for how to live in a world increasingly devastated by the project of modernity – a project ruthlessly devoted to re-engineering nature in service of a few (or more specifically, in the interest of corporate global capital). Without such a vision, critical scholars are bereft of any basis – save for what's already given in the dominant critical discourse – for critique of what's going on and for re-imagining a different future.

    In the discourse of critical theory, the vision that is invoked is cast in unimpeachable terms: social justice, gender and racial equality, empowerment, peace, and so forth. But, often, what is meant by these is simply a fight for a "just share" of the pie of privilege – an "equal cut" of the pile of stolen goods, cast as "entitlements" under the rubrics of upward mobility, development, progress, and so on. What is damning is that not many understand that the very condition for the possibility of the few enjoying such privilege is precisely the deprivation of the vast majority from having any share in it at all.

Author Ahmed (2007) remarks that today a different demand is sounding out from various indigenous peoples around the world. While Third World liberation movements of the last century struggled mainly to achieve political independence and material advancement by embracing Western modernity (i.e., demanding a "fair" share of the stolen pie), he notes that today, "indigenous movements of this century question and reject the main foundations of the worldview of the Enlightenment" (n.p.). They now believe its promise is empty and want nothing to do with it.

4   Over the last few years, I, too, have become convinced of the same. I am no longer interested in the Enlightenment promise of individual liberty and formal equality. Rather, I want to invest whatever remains of my energy in exposing the mystifying effects of such an emphasis, the price exacted by its enactment in practice, the ideological justifications invented for its desirability, and all the fetishistic meanings invested in its successful marketing around the globe even while visiting terror on those who dare disagree with its priority. My concern rather is to do justice to the repressed memories and wise practices of our ancestors whose arts of sustainability begin to emerge today as far more compelling and trustworthy than the short-sighted plundering that our own imperative of growth-at-any-cost is now exhibiting (cf. Brennan, 2000; Jensen, 2000/2004; Quinn, 1992; Sahlins,1998; Shepard, 1998; Zerzan, 2005).

5   In light of this growing realization, I have lost interest in merely tinkering with the system and striving to make it better here and there, in "training students for success" so they can join the army of the world's exemplary workers and global consumers. I am convinced that the system itself needs fundamental alteration, that its logic (of rapacious control and domination, limitless consumption and growth, unbridled individualism and competition, arrogant homocentrism and narcissism) is bankrupt. The more the poor peoples of the world are inserted into its agenda and made to hope in its promise, the more their own and the earth's degradation will continue.

Someone has said that we modern humans are a peculiar kind of creature. We are the only species who, when confronted with evidence that something doesn't work, resort to doing more and more of the same, instead of abandoning the hopeless endeavor and trying something else altogether. Of course one must recognize that the system *does* work, for an elite few, if in the short run (cf. Naomi Klein's reference to the "global green zone" increasingly becoming the paradigm of the century – the wealthy with their gated communities, back-up generators, and stocks of bottled water while everywhere else is ruin and devastation).

6   What has this meant for my own research trajectory? Much of my recent work has been devoted to an attempt to query modernity itself as the taken-for-granted baseline for communication theory, and instead work to:

- grasp modernity as a constricting monovision that truncates concern for any other life form than the human;
- understand modernity as a discursive formation whose scant few centuries of duration hardly qualifies it as time-tested and credible in the crucible of human evolution;
- map the ideological and historical morphology of the epoch in terms of its particular symbolic inventions, reifications of time, disciplines of representation, productions of hierarchy and domination, and so on;
- track its extant mechanisms and forms of exclusion (e.g., abjected forms of rationality, alternative ways of being human); and
- recuperate the suppressed histories of nonmodern humans (including the unsung stories of indigenous peoples who continue to resist incorporation into modernity's ruthless logic or erasure inside the digits of the market), their heterogeneous ways of being and their modes of communication, and ask deep questions about what such excavated histories have to teach us.

For the short term, it means paying the price of momentarily being unable to produce work for publication as usual because the reeducation takes energy and time. It entails immersing oneself in a whole new idiom, and developing the capacity to hear the alternative languages (the hidden transcripts, the gestural hesitancies, the subtle sonorities, etc.) of those who have been silenced by us modern humans in the genocidal project of human takeover of the planet.

Ultimately, it means for me a radical recontextualization of everything I have ever learned within the only world my Western liberal education has taught me – the world of abstraction and scientific rationalism, of the endless play of signification and representation, of words manipulated on the tongue and etched on the page, of disembodied thought and sound bytes and strokes on the keyboard. Perhaps the challenge now is to open myself up to a whole new way of being and seeing, to relearn once more the forgotten wordless language of my ancestors – the language of dreams, of ancient memory, of dance, of spirit-beings, of body on body communication unafraid of intimacy beyond the word.

Thus, the bridging function I see myself taking on as a critical intercultural communication scholar at this juncture of crisis is bridging to that other ancient world of the indigenous and rediscovering its longings and witness inside my body and my own culture. It is, as well, to work to recover a bridge of ritual and myth and for a mobilization of science toward listening to what other life forms know about living in very specific local ecologies and understanding that their being is integral to human *being* – an intelligence grasped in indigenous communities of old as a "world of spirit" offering communications delicate and crucial to the long-term viability of the entire ecology in an enduring ethic of reciprocity.

Bridging to those indigenous communities and, through them, bridging to plant and animal life, is finally for the sake of a third task of bridging, which seeks to open a future alternative to modernity's policies of genocide and hospitable to the mutuality that originally (and for eons) governed human life on the planet.

Such an agenda demands that I become what the late intercultural communication scholar Barnlund, at the 1990 Summer Institute of Intercultural Communication, insistently identified as a "violator" of disciplinary boundaries. Indeed, the very question that our species' survival raises calls precisely into question the old academic division of labor that today serves as a barrier to comprehending the whole picture. To be a critical intercultural communication scholar in our time is to perform an interstitial role, to straddle worlds, cultures, and social formations and attend not only to their distinct particularities but also to their interconnections. It is to refuse the fragmentation of perception and knowledge that effectively keeps the workings of dominant ideology intact and virtually intractable. Such bridging work necessarily entails the synthetic (integrative) exercise of combining disparate knowledges that alone makes contextual analysis possible. And, as far as contexts go, I find of utmost relevance the ubiquity of corporate colonization (Deetz, 1992) that drives much of what is going on in our world today – from the increasing incidence of violence and war, the intensifying competition over fast-diminishing resources, the frenzied movement of peoples, resources, and labor across borders, the forcible opening up of national and local places to the logic of the market, the creative innovating, in the cultural sphere, of hybrid forms of popular culture around the globe in service of consumption-driven corporate ideology to the rise of local and global resistance movements seeking a different order of co-existence on an increasingly crowded and finite planet.

Equally urgent is the imperative of opening up the space of representation in our scholarship to alternative visions of human life as a way out of the impasse of the current moment. To the extent that the fast disappearing witness to that ancient way of life with their differing logics, temporalities, subjectivities, and relations to place-based ecologies today represent the only remaining real "other" of globalized modernity, I ask whether their unceremonial passing should not be marked – beyond tears and mourning – with a clear-eyed understanding of what it is that we lose with their untimely demise. Are we better off regarding them merely as surplus populations whose insistence on their "anachronistic" way of life (certainly not the fact that they happen to sit on top of much-coveted natural resources!) is to be blamed for their consignment to the dustbin of history? Does it make us rest easy to accept that it is simply the fate of "retrogressive life-modes" to give way to "evolutionary progress"? Or do we have courage enough to admit that their demise is neither accidental nor unrelated to our flourishing, that in the calculus of a finite planet ill-suited to a modality of life wedded to the pursuit of infinite growth and expansion, their lives and ours intimately collide in what writer Quinn (1992) calls the paradigmatic relation between cultures of "leaving" and cultures of "taking"? What happens if we begin to track seriously the politics of that quintessential intercultural relation, not only in the distant past, but in the current moment? How might we de-naturalize the elaborate "explaining story" (Quinn, 1992, p. 44) that taker cultures tell to legitimize their plunder and their amassing of "cargo"[5] at the expense of the flourishing of others? What if, for once, we become willing to crack open our categories of thought and begin really to listen and understand deeply what our (taker cultures') ascendency has meant for all leaver peoples around the globe – they who are now pushed to the brink of extinction, along with other species-beings in nature, by our rapacious greed and demand for more? What new theorizations of the politics of intercultural communication might emerge? How might such deep listening to the excluded voices of modernity potentially reconfigure the field and reshape our goals and priorities as critical intercultural communication scholars?

These are questions that demand radical re-imagination of what is legitimate to study and what receives priority emphasis in intercultural communication problematics. For me, assuming the categories and premises of modernity as the unquestioned ground on which alone to analyze the politics of encounter is no longer (if it ever was) an option in the present time. My own colonial history, my deepening immersion into the lifeworlds and language(s) of an-other community of species-beings, along with the looming question of ecological survival has radically altered the calculus for me. The call is sounded out ... and there may not be much time.

Notes

1 This is a concern shared on a larger scale by West (1995b) when he notes,

> The major shortcoming of Derrida's deconstructive project is that it puts a premium on a sophisticated ironic consciousness that tends to preclude and foreclose analyses that guide action with purpose ... His works and those of his followers too often become rather monotonous, Johnny-one-note rhetorical readings that disassemble texts with little attention to the effects and consequences these dismantlings have in relation to the operations of military, economic and social powers (p. 163).

2 A legacy of the United States' colonial occupation of the Philippines from 1902–1946 that saw the massacre of half a million to a million Filipinos and reorienting the country's economy and political institutions to service US colonial interests.

3 I talk about this experience growing up colonized in greater detail in "Tears in the Archive: Creating Memory to Survive and to Contest Empire" (Mendoza, 2005/2006).

4 Based on a paper titled, "Doing Scholarship in a Time of War" presented at the 2007 National Communication Association held in Chicago, Illinois.

5 The term used by Yali, a New Guinean querying Jared Diamond, to describe the material goods first brought by Europeans to the area, thus: "Why is it that you white people developed so much cargo and brought it to New Guinea, but we black people had little cargo of our own?" (Diamond, 1997, p. 14)

References

Ahmed, B. (2007) Burying Columbus in Palestine. *Al-Ahram Weekly Online*. October 25–31, http://weekly.ahram.org.eg/2007/868/op122.htm (accessed May 14, 2010).

Bhabha, H. (1994) *The Location of Culture*, Routledge, London.

Brennan, T. (2000) *Exhausting Modernity: Grounds for a New Economy*, Routledge, London and New York.

Broome, B.J., Carey, C., De La Garza, S.A. *et al.* (2005) In the thick of things: A dialogue about the activist turn in intercultural communication, in *Taking Stock in Intercultural Communication: Where to Now?: International and Intercultural Communication Annual, 28,* (eds. W.J. Starosta and G.-M. Chen), National Communication Association, Washington, DC, pp. 145–175.

Butler, J. (1995) Contingent foundations: Feminism and the question of "postmodernism," in *Feminist Contentions: A Philosophical Exchange (Thinking Gender)*, (eds. S. Benhabib, J. Butler, D. Cornell *et al.*), Routledge, New York, pp. 35–57.

Collier, M.J., Hegde, R.S., Lee, W. *et al.* (2001) Dialogue on the edges: Ferment in communication and culture. *Transforming Communication about Culture: Critical New Directions, International and Intercultural Communication Annual 24*, (ed. M.J. Collier), Sage, Thousand Oaks, CA, pp. 219–280.

Deetz, S.A. (1992) *Democracy in an Age of Corporate Colonization: Developments in Communication and the Politics of Everyday Life*, State University of New York Press, Albany.

Diamond, J. (1997) *Guns, Germs and Steel: The Fate of Human Societies*, W.W. Norton & Company, New York.

Diamond, J. (2005) *Collapse: How Societies Choose to Succeed or Fail*, The Penguin Group, New York.

Du Bois, W.E.B. (1961) *The Souls of Black Folk*, Fawcett Publications, Inc., New York.

Elias, N. (1994/2000) *The Civilizing Process: Sociogenetic and Psychogenetic Investigations*, Blackwell, Malden, MA.

Goldberg, D.T. (1993) *Racist Culture: Philosophy and the Politics of Meaning*, Blackwell, Oxford.

Hall, E.T. (1976) *Beyond Culture*, Doubleday, New York.

Hall, S. (1988) The toad in the garden: Thatcherism among the theorists, in *Marxism and the Interpretation of Culture*, (eds C. Nelson and L. Grossberg), University of Illinois Press, Urbana, pp. 35–73.

Hall, S. (1996) When was "the post-colonial"? Thinking at the limit, in *The Post-Colonial Question: Common Skies, Divided Horizons*, (eds I. Chambers and L. Curtis), Routledge, London, pp. 242–260.

Hall, S. (1997) Old and new identities, old and new ethnicities, in *Culture, Globalization, and the World-System*, (ed. A.D. King), University of Minnesota Press, Minneapolis, pp. 41–68.

Halualani, R.T. (2002) *In the Name of Hawaiians: Native Identities and Cultural Politics*, University of Minnesota Press, Minneapolis, MN.

Heinberg, R. (2002) *The Party's Over: Oil, War, and the Fate of Industrial Societies*, Consortium Book Sales and Dust, Minneapolis, MN.

Jensen, D. (2000/2004) *A Language Older Than Words*, Chelsea Green Publishing Company, White River Junction, VT.

Jensen, D. (2006) *End Game: The Problem of Civilization*, Seven Stories Press, New York.

Klare, M.T. (2002) *Resource Wars: The New Landscape of Global Landscape*, Owl Books, New York.

Lemert, C. (1999) Social theory: Its uses and pleasures, in *Social Theory: The Muticultural and Classic Readings* (ed. C. Lemert), Westview Press, Boulder, CO, pp. 1–20.

Mendoza, S.L. (2002/2006) *Between the Homeland and the Diaspora: The Politics of Theorizing Filipino and Filipino American Identities*, Routledge, New York and London; University of Santo Tomas Publishing House, Manila.

Mendoza, S.L. (2005) Bridging paradigms: How not to throw out the baby of collective representation with the functionalist bathwater in critical intercultural communication, in *Taking Stock in Intercultural Communication: Where to Now? International and Intercultural Communication Annual 28*, (eds W.J. Starosta and G.-M. Chen), National Communication Association, Washington, DC, pp. 237–256.

Mendoza, S.L. (2005/2006) Tears in the archive: Creating memory to survive and contest empire, in *Among US: Essays on Identity, Belonging, and Intercultural Competence*, (eds R. Lustig and J. Koester), Pearson, Boston, MA, pp. 233–245.

Nakayama, T., and Martin, J. (1999) *Whiteness: The Communication of Social Identity*, Sage, Thousand Oaks.

Quinn, D. (1992) *Ishmael*, Bantam Books, New York.

Ruppert, M. (2004) *Crossing the Rubicon: September 11 and the Decline of American Empire at the End of the Age of Oil*, New Society Publishers, Gabriola Island, British Columbia, Canada.

Sahlins, M. (1998) The original affluent society, in *Limited Wants, Unlimited Means: A Reader on Hunter-Gatherer Economics and the Environment*, (ed. J. Gowdy), Island Press, Washington, DC, pp. 5–41.

Shepard, P. (1998) A post-historic primitivism, in *Limited Wants, Unlimited Means*, (ed. J.M. Gowdy), Island Press, Washington, DC, pp. 281–325.

Shome, R., and Hegde, R. (2002) Postcolonial approaches to communication: Charting the terrain, engaging the intersections. *Communication Theory*, August, 249–270.

Simmons, M.R. (2005) *Twilight in the Desert: The Coming Saudi Oil Shock and the World Economy*, John Wiley & Sons, Inc., Hoboken, NJ.

Spivak, G.C. (1996) Subaltern studies: Deconstructing historiography, in *The Spivak Reader: Selected Works of Gayatri Chakravorty Spivak*, (eds D. Landry and G. MacLean), Routledge, New York, pp. 203–235.

Spivak, G.C., and Harasym, S. (eds) (1987) *The Postcolonial Critic: Interviews, Strategies, Dialogues*, Routledge, New York.

Welch, S. (1985) *Communities of Resistance and Solidarity: A Feminist Theology of Liberation*, Orbis, Maryknoll, New York.

West, C. (1995a) A matter of life and death, in *The Identity in Question*, (ed. J. Rajchman) Routledge, New York, pp. 15–31.

West, C. (1995b) The New Cultural Politics of Difference, in *The Identity in Question*, (ed. J. Rajchman), Routledge, New York, pp. 147–171.

Zerzan, J. (ed.) (2005) *Against Civilization*, Feral House, Los Angeles.

8

Revisiting the Borderlands of Critical Intercultural Communication

Leda Cooks

What does it mean to study communication?

What does it mean to study culture?

Why should we study intercultural communication?

These three questions are well-represented in the first chapter of most intercultural communication textbooks, but, we might ask, what do these questions foreground and what is left out? Many of our textbooks describe the study of communication as the study of the transference or exchange of meaning. This traditional definition would seem to cover most attempts to send and receive messages, and thus to coordinate the symbolic constructions necessary for *cultures* to survive – leading to the frequent defining of the latter as the bank into which such meanings are deposited (or rejected). Yet, the realization that some meanings survive while others are rejected, and that some have the power to define a culture by deciding who and what means something is not immediately clear to students of communication. Thus, the answer to last question is dependent on the how the first two are framed.

Moreover, as James Carey (1989) has explained, most definitions of communication, based as they are in the US history of nation-building and industrial expansion, highlight metaphors of transportation and movement and thus privilege conveyance meanings for communication over those that highlight acts of communion or ritual.[1] A decade earlier, Michael Reddy (1979) had argued that Claude Shannon and Warren Weaver's (1949) widely used transference model of communication metaphorically presented communication as a conduit or channel through which words are containers for meaning. According to this model, ideas or thoughts are implanted into words, conveyed through language and extracted into the minds of

The Handbook of Critical Intercultural Communication, edited by Thomas K. Nakayama and Rona Tamiko Halualani. © 2010 Blackwell Publishing Ltd.

those who receive or retrieve the message. In his wide-ranging metaphoric analyses, John Durham Peters (1999) notes that throughout Western philosophy the communication of ideas has been imagined as *reaching* out (to the hope of consubstantiation and dread of solipsism), *containing* (keeping information in or away from others) and I would add, ever *moving* onward. Echoing the concerns of Emmanuel Levinas, Jurgen Habermas, John Dewey, and Martin Heidegger, among many other structuralist and poststructuralist philosophers, Peters observes that "the task is to find an account of communication that erases neither the curious fact of otherness at its core nor the possibility of doing things with words" (Peters, 1999, 21).

This "curious fact of otherness" at the root of most philosophical questions of communication is perhaps more obviously questioned in studies of communication between/among cultures. Yet, it remains important to keep in mind that where we in intercultural communication (ICC) *move* (theoretically speaking) with this question is closely connected to the metaphors we employ.[2] With this metaphorical framework in mind, in this chapter I wish to connect the three questions posed above – and their related perspectives and consequences, ethical and pedagogical implications – to the work being carried out by critical scholars in intercultural communication. In the space that follows I set the context for critical research in intercultural communication and then review some themes from an earlier essay on this topic (Cooks, 2001)[3] in light of concepts that have been developed in more recent critical intercultural and international scholarship. I offer these impressions not as an inclusive summary of all that critical intercultural work has contributed but as some useful ideas to consider. Later, I look at the role of the aesthetic in critical research in ICC, both as a hegemonic tool of appropriation as well as an opening for critique outside the bounds of academic form. Carrying on this notion of the aesthetic I look finally at the potential of performance *as* critical ICC pedagogy.

Setting the Context for Critical Scholarship in ICC

My concern then and now with the ethical implications of academic study was spurred by the oft stated and yet seemingly conflicting goals of liberal education and the academy: the seeking of truth and the notion of the good society (Blitz, 2004). On the surface this hardly seems to be a bad notion and certainly most communication scholars are in favor of both goals, yet critical scholars in the field are wary. Should we to commit to the truth as an objective reality we might very well sacrifice those whose cultural truths (and very existences) did not register as variables for analysis or, perhaps worse, we might assume that their truths needed only to be adjusted to our own. Related to this idea, if in the past we sought to make our society better through the study of intercultural communication, the history of the field seemed to indicate that our concern lay primarily in the temporary adjustment for difference – a difference registered through its foreignness from a white, male, majority US cultural center.

This concern, even preoccupation, with difference led to an increasing focus on the cultures of "others" while the position, perspective and body of the researcher remained invisible. As mentioned in my 2001 essay, Leeds-Hurwitz (1998) among others, traces the history of the ICC field to the study of other cultures (in particular Edward Hall's work in this area) for the purposes of helping US Foreign Service Personnel manage their assignments more effectively. Hall's scholarship – while actually more complex in its theory than its inclusion as part of a unit on nonverbal behaviors might represent – addressed those with the mobility and privilege to travel to and from "other" spaces/people. Although early research and teaching cautioned against US ethnocentricity, the focus of the warning was on individual (rude) behaviors that violated Western ideas of civility. Epistemological, theoretical and structural inequalities and social change were rarely addressed. The lack of focus on who named or authored the bodies, communication and cultures of others did not mean that self-reflection was not called for, or that the behavior of the US dominant culture was never a focus. Indeed, attention to behaviors such as the use of space, or directness and amount of talk, matters of manners, and so forth, ran throughout the research of the past (almost) four decades.[4] What was missing from the concentration on behavior, however, was a deeper look at the questions posed at the start of this essay from the perspective of those in dominant positions in the academy and in the culture at large.

Based on these frustrations, in my 2001 essay I made a case for an alternative approach to intercultural communication that begins with sites of (in)difference and inequality and works toward an understanding of similarities. In no way did I intend to simplify the complex flows of power that cover over privilege of the dominant groups in the name of tolerance and multiculturalism; instead my concern was that ideas about and frameworks for understanding difference emanated from a center that was unaware/ignorant of its epistemological assumptions and the consequent power of defining difference *in terms of* differentiation in degrees from a objectively scientific center.

As with many others then and now, I was influenced by the early work of Stuart Hall, whose encoding/decoding model (1973), offered a critique of the linear sender, message receiver models that focused not on the objective fidelity of the content of a message but on the ways dominant meanings for messages (i.e., accessible to the mainstream of society) were secured, resisted, or negotiated by (media) audiences who did not necessarily identify or align themselves with the dominant discourses of cultural identities. Hall's shift toward "the articulation of connected practices" (Hall, 1973, p. 128) demonstrated the various ways culturally dominant discourses could secure the center, even as those defined outside the center redeployed the discourses for their own uses. ICC scholars (myself included) interested in the ways interaction across cultural boundaries solidified or exposes gaps and junctures in the dominant discourses of nationality, culture and identity built on his model to study face to face as well as mediated discourses.

Situating our teaching and research in the overlapping and in-between spaces of centers and peripheries, privilege and marginalization, dominance and oppression, comfort and struggle, and so on, I argued for a view from the borderlands. I observed that:

(a) Borders, although socially constructed, involve a range of (inter)actions and are enacted with a particular consequentiality and (b) we encounter the borders of culture and discipline, of history and identity not as immutable scientific fact but as a dynamic, discursive force that both constrains and enables mobility and social relations. (Cooks, 2001, p. 346)

The 2001 essay was a call for the communication discipline, and intercultural communication in particular, to acknowledge its history *as* ontology and epistemology at a time when several histories of the field were being re-written. I contemplated what a shifted epistemology (from center to borderlands) might look like, what problems and problematics might emerge and how our research as well as our teaching might address this shift. In other words, what happens when the culture part of intercultural communication is not defined by the (under-theorized) center but those excluded from it? Borders and borderlands are complex spaces where bodies overlap and cultures and identities are never pure or easy. Identities always exist in multiplicities, and our early attempts to capture and analyze intercultural contact for the purposes of theory development had drawn broad strokes and simplified "culture" for the purposes of data analysis. Building on Durara's (1996) ideas about national borders, I focused on three degrees of border permeability: (1) the dense borders of public cultures; (2) sifting borders of a community's social geography; and (3) fluid and intimate borders of our inter/personal relationships. Border identities, then, are interconnected and tightened or loosened as we move from inter/personal identity constructions in-relation-to others to the institutions that support (or do not) those constructions.

Extending from these borderlands, one could view the arbitrariness with which boundaries were constructed within our discipline. Were there easy distinctions to be made between interpersonal relationships studied in interpersonal communication courses and research and those in intercultural communication? Did group communication, health communication, conflict communication, and organizational communication (among other commonly offered courses) not, by definition, include communication among peoples from differing cultures? What about teaching intercultural communication? Under what sub-disciplinary boundaries was this concern to be located? My critique of the disciplinary (theoretical and methodological) distinctions made among communication processes which were complex, contextual, and overlapped among subfields led me to rethink the differences and boundaries constructed in intercultural communication in terms of degrees of permeability. As I stated then:

Viewing our research in such a way allows for conceptualization of categories that obscure the traditional lines of positivist versus interpretivist, quantitative versus qualitative, and intercultural research versus interpersonal (organizational, group) research. Instead, we can see that intercultural research on difference can define and legitimate borders and boundaries of difference while assuming the taken-for-granted nature of their identity. If we are to examine research in ICC in terms of the degree of density or sedimentation of the boundaries it creates, we get a view of the ways marginality and difference are constructed as part of a dominant discourse (of scientific research, of academia, of nation), that reaffirms boundaries already constructed (in terms of uncertainty, competence, etc.) (Cooks, 2001, p. 347)

Critical scholarship in communication has, in many ways, addressed similar issues in the time since I issued this call for borderlands. My call built on and was joined by several other scholars in the field who were working to theorize a way out of the culture, nation, and communication boxes which confined researcher/ researched identities and limited our voices in the field. Our concern was linking communication theory with the situations in which we and others found ourselves – as privileged scholars and sojourners attempting to be reflexive and reciprocal in our research, as bodies othered both inside and outside of academia, as trying to create a space of critique that opened other spaces for inquiry and other authors and subjects for that inquiry. We were working (albeit with different degrees of power, access, and success) to create a space to consider difference not as differentiations from a center but on its own terms. Rejecting a postmodern relativism, however, we had as one purpose (of many) building alliances across cultures toward social change.

Notably, and perhaps obviously, critical research and pedagogy has long found a more comfortable home in the junctures between disciplinary boundaries and for these reasons much critical scholarship exposes the labor of boundary work in favor of structural change. The very interdisciplinarity of such work, located as it is in between cultural studies, anthropology, radical education, critical race studies, postcolonial studies, globalization studies, and so forth, worked against its institutionalization in the communication discipline in the form of publication outlets, graduate and undergraduate course offerings, textbooks and most importantly, academic positions. Nonetheless, in the late-twentieth century, a critical agenda for research and teaching in ICC was forming around several of the issues outlined above. In particular, scholars in intercultural communication such as Brenda Allen, Mary Jane Collier, Fernando Delgado, Alberto González, Ronald L. Jackson II, Judith Martin, Dreama Moon, Mark Orbe, William Starosta, Tom Nakayama and Gust Yep (among many others) called for a commitment on the part of critical scholars to: (1) address the structural inequalities and biased perspectives of traditional intercultural research; (2) be more self-reflexive in their theorizing in ICC that manifested in a commitment to decentering their own research; (3) recognize the complexities of communication processes and power dynamics that are unstable and unevenly mark privilege even as we work to define identities and cultures for social justice and change; (4) destabilize disciplinary boundaries and demonstrate the overlap among intercultural, interpersonal, organizational, group, health, and communication; and (5) conduct theory and research both inside and outside academia that addresses and is applicable to social struggle and works toward social change. Building on these commitments, in what follows I return to the themes from my earlier essay to address current critical work in ICC.

Current Critical Scholarship in ICC:
A View from the Borderlands

Drawing connections from my 2001 essay to the current research in critical intercultural communication offers a different, albeit partial painting of the field as a series of interconnected tensions, sometimes building up, sometimes breaking down sediment, destabilizing the national territories of citizenship, diaspora, refugee, rethinking social geographies in terms of bodies and spaces, and the fluidity and interrelatedness of personal identities such as age and sexuality, race and class, ability and gender. Broadly speaking, much of the critical research in communication has called for more connections between the micropolitics of everyday life and the macropolitical implications of state and nation, and yet when such work is attempted detailed analysis is often sacrificed. Researchers (and here I include my own work) might conduct a study of an intercultural interaction using discourse analytic methods that get at the status shifts and interruptions of power as usual, but when the analysis broadens out to include larger structural dynamics and national/cultural identities, the complexities often flatten into oppressor–oppressed relations and opportunities for changing dynamics disappear. Here for the sake of illustration, I implicate some critical discourse analytic studies that address racist talk, ethnography of communication studies that attempt to address structural inequalities, and autoethnographic work that dwells more in the personal than with the relationship between the personal and the structural. On the other side, I include some cultural studies researchers and political economists who make a half-hearted attempt at analyzing interaction – either summing up, paraphrasing or leaving passages wholly without analysis while spending considerable time on the structural and material implications of the interaction. Much of the difficulty with any such analysis stems from the rigidness of structural conceptions of space, place and identity from which critical analysis is conducted.

Several critical scholars (notably several authors in this volume) have found that by focusing on in-between spaces (boundaries and borderlands) they can circumvent the micro/macro dichotomies for a concentration on the ways communication forms more or less dense identities, relations, organizations, communities, and nations. Their focus is often on the language or interactions used to establish (degrees of) similarity or difference and to accomplish, if temporarily, spaces for identification and resistance. Even among those (cultural) studies that do not focus specifically on interaction, language is nonetheless at the core of critique. Communication and culture are viewed as socially constructed in these studies, and thus intercultural interaction is positioned as a dynamic field through which cultural discourses and identities are privileged, maintained, challenged, and so on. Important to this perspective is the prefix *inter-* as the connecting point of relational sense-making. In other words, difference and culture are both structural and relational, and words which locate self in-relation-to other are also located in *this* space at *this* time with a history both specific to the relationship and generalized to the language used to define and categorize self and other.

The dense borders of public culture or history are still the focus of the majority of research on concepts of nation and national identity. Still, the interconnectedness between global and local in intercultural communication is increasingly assumed, and questions of who is included/excluded in definitions of first/third world are often asked. While any number of critical articles could serve as examples of this movement, I wish to mention three studies that highlight the tensions globalization brings to theorizing intercultural/international difference. In the first study, an essay entitled, "Rethinking Nationality in the Context of Globalization" Stephen Crofts Wiley (2004) focuses in particular on the difficulties with the concept of nation both as a unit for variable analytic study as well as an idea that is always-already assumed in intercultural/international research. Crofts Wiley is careful to assert that the nation as a concept is not going away, but that it needs to be retheorized as the construct that it is in light of globalization. He organizes studies of the nation into five broad perspectives: mainstream mass communication theory; critical nation-based theory; relational theory (postcolonial and neoimperial); globalization theory; and contexualist theory (Crofts Wiley, 2004, p. 79). Notably, his perspectives fall along a continuum from what I would call the dense notions of nation as boundaries containing internally homogenous peoples to the contextual idea of nation as "a logic of social and spatial organization" (Crofts Wiley, 2004, p. 79). From the standpoint of critical intercultural communication, these perspectives are articulated in our everyday talk about identities and thus are linked less to actual physical geographical spaces than cultural identifications or what Crofts Wiley sees as recirculated and appropriated logics (public, commercial, bureaucratic, gender, etc.). For instance, he asks "How is Americanness distributed across the planet? – and conversely, how is it distributed within the borders of the political and administrative territory with which it is nominally identified?" (Crofts Wiley, 2004, p. 92). His conceptualization, too, brings mediated representations into the realm of the interpersonal and intercultural, as media is increasingly acknowledged as an (in)visible voice in interaction (e.g. Drzewiecka, 2002). The essay tacks back and forth from the borders of public cultures to the social geographies that form them. Although Crofts Wiley does not examine the interactions that might produce such logics, we see that interaction could fit well into his framework as a unit of analysis.

Also connecting the density of public cultures to the more pliable boundaries of social geography is Raka Shome's (2003) essay entitled "Space Matters: The Power and Practice of Space." Shome's article examines the border between the US and Mexico and presents "illegal" bodies located on that border as complex and uncontained, both mobile and fixed as "immigrants," they are always on the move. She presents several premises: that spaces are complex, intricate and interconnected; that space is a product of social relations even as spatial structures help to constitute them; that material space does not possess inherent power but is a result of networks. Shome demonstrates convincingly both the power of certain bodies in certain places to disrupt material relations as well as the ability of space to affix certain social identities. Although her concern is mostly with marginalized/border identities, her work incorporates many of David Harvey's (1996) arguments for the connections of space and capital in an age of globalization. Harvey offers that while objective "space" (here, borders) exists, particular understandings of space need to be theorized from the standpoint of material practices and the flow of capital. While I favor a more flexible and discursive understanding of spaces of and for identity practices, her essay overlaps strongly with my own discussion of borderlands and highlights the materiality of bodies in the movement back and forth along lines of density/fluidity.

Revisiting my earlier argument – that intercultural research has been conducted from a privileged center from which difference has been constructed – there arises the postmodern, transnational "problem" that center and periphery are increasingly overlapping so to render both ideas meaningless. Indeed, this is the line of reasoning put forward by Richard Rogers (2006) in an article entitled, 'From Cultural Exchange to Transculturation: A Review and Reconceptualization of Cultural Appropriation." Rogers defines appropriation as "the use of a culture's symbols, artifacts, genres, rituals or technologies by members of another culture" (Rogers, 2006, p. 474), noting that some form of appropriation is inevitable when cultures come into contact. Rogers observes that theories of cultural appropriation take a variety of forms, including cultural exchange, cultural domination, cultural exploitation and finally, transculturation. Cultural exchange assumes an equal back and forth flow of ideas and resources from one culture to another. Cultural dominance describes the hegemonic influence of dominant cultures in those that are subordinate (while not ascribing total appropriation or subordination, but possibilities for simultaneous domination and resistance). Cultural exploitation is more easily defined as the use of one culture's symbolic and material resources by another without "reciprocity, permission and/or compensation" (Rogers, 2006, p. 477). Transculturation implies a much more complicated set of relationships, where constant contact dilutes the boundaries of national cultures. Globalization challenges the boundaries of culture and introduces instead a network of relationships. Rogers states that, "the challenge for cultural, critical media, critical rhetorical, and intercultural communication studies is to re-conceptualize culture as radically relational or dialogic" (2006, p. 499). Again we can observe the densities and fluidities inherent in each category as both culture and appropriation lose their stability as isolatable concepts.

In a similar vein, in my earlier essay I stated that, "an alternative perspective on culture asks how people are organized socially according to local conceptions of cultural identities, and thus how resources, both material and social, are distributed across people who engage such identities or are made sense of according to such categories" (Cooks, 2001, p. 347). Still, as Crofts Wiley's and Shome's articles make clear, if we are to entertain the idea of complexity and overlap in border spaces, then intercultural scholarship must necessarily address the tensions between homeland and diasporic spaces in more depth and specifically as they impact the personal spaces of everyday life.

Certainly, critical intercultural studies that address diasporic communities and "home" as dialogic, nostalgic intercultural *spaces* have increased in the past several years, perhaps due to the recognition on the part of journal reviewers and editors that forces of mobility, technology, and globalization are increasing such communities, and that communication within and across such communities is changing the dynamics and definitions of *intercultural* work. In other words, the old boundaries have shifted once again and, where concepts such as "homeland," "nationalism," and "citizenship" are no longer clear, the idea of borderlands is increasingly coming into focus.

Although many critical authors in globalization studies, postcolonial studies, and diaspora studies recognize the complexities of diaspora in a time of globalization,[5] I am interested here particularly in ICC scholars who recognize diasporic identities as a product and process of intercultural communication (see for instance, Drzewiecka, 2002; Halualani, 2002; Mendoza, 2002). That is, communication as a process of naming – of recognition of self and other in interaction. Implied in this focus on intercultural communication is a simultaneous understanding of the complexities of intracultural conflict over cultural means and meanings. Too, these studies refuse a stable and coherent relationship between identities and home-spaces, either (im)planted in land, blood, or nationalism. I believe that such studies map the social geographies of borderlands to demonstrate both their dynamic qualities as well as their often contradictory ties to more "permanent" social boundaries. Given space limitations, I wish to briefly outline one exemplary study due to its deliberate focus on authenticity.

In "Connecting Hawaiians: The Politics of Authenticity in the Hawaiian Diaspora," Rona Halualani (2002) theorizes cultural identity through discourses of authenticity among Hawaiians in Hawai'i and Hawaiians on the mainland. Halualani looks how terms such as *aina* (land), *koko* (blood) and indigeneity are shared across the two groups while what and how they signify identity differ in important ways. Halualani's focus on language use in interaction complicates the usual theorizing of relationships between "native" and Diaspora by demonstrating the ways "home" spaces and "blood" relations become part of a narrative that measures authenticity in terms of the "true" preservation of a coopted native identity. Among the diasporic group members she interviews and observes, nativeness or indigeneity is articulated not by the boundaries of geography but through narratives of kinship to Hawaiian royalty. In discussing the implications of her study for future research in ICC, Halualani notes that "membership" and authenticity must be studied relationally and in light of contextual changes and migration patterns.

As a boundary marker, authenticity holds different densities in different contexts and can move from a discourse of indigeneity and essentialism in public culture to performances of personal identity that move in and out of identity categories. We must be careful, however, of what identity sees and what is seen. As Hall (1997) observes about the English:

The English "eye" sees everything else but is not so good at seeing itself actually looking at something. It becomes coterminous with sight itself ... [I]t is strongly centered; knowing where it is, what it is, it places everything else ... To be English is to know yourself in relation to the French, and the hot-blooded Mediterraneans, and the passionate traumatized Russian soul. You go round the entire globe: when you know what everybody else is, then you are what they are not (pp. 20–21).

Thus, the determination of cultural authenticity, whether the strategic goal of critical research on identity or a source of postmodern critique, remains central to the work of critical communication scholars. The ability to define one's own (racial, gender, ethnic, cultural) identity is increasingly in play for those who have the technology, economic means, and social capital to do so. Yet for those whose identities are always already defined, "authentic" identity is both critical for survival and socially dangerous.

This observation brings us to the last, most fluid and intimate of the boundaries: those personal identities that are engaged at the borders of cultural and social acceptability. As this personal, often private, boundary interacts and overlaps with the other two, we begin to see how the intimate details of border relationships are framed as social and public "problems" where boundaries may be set between us and them. In my previous essay I mentioned the possibilities of combining social constructionist research on identity with postcolonial scholarship as a way to analyze interactions in the borderlands. Here I add the critique of the micro-macro studies mentioned above: a critical framing of intercultural interaction often simplifies differences where their construction is often more complicated, and layers of privilege and oppression are uneven. How might we get at the complexities of interpersonal discourses without sacrificing an analysis of power dynamics?[6] In looking at communication among those from differing cultures, critical ICC scholars must ask whether our purpose is to discover the range of possible cultural variations or to narrow down the categories for the purpose of theorizing differences.

I offer that it is the heuristics of the latter that has constrained the ICC field, including those critical scholars concerned with the ways the cultures of marginalized groups have been appropriated by the dominant culture. Whether our concern is with legitimating (and publicizing) our cause through social scientific methods or establishing solidarity to define better, and thus establish a base to unify our position and our argument, we must be careful not to close down opportunities for exploration while defending our critique. Other strictly held determinations such as privilege and oppression, while important to exploring the dynamics and discourses of power, have in many cases prevented a detailed analysis of the multiple status moves present in any interaction. Perhaps we lose sight of the flexibilities of identities in discursive formations, an articulation conceptualized by Foucault as "a discursive practice [that] establishes an *interactive* relation between otherwise heterogeneous elements (institutions, techniques, social groups, perceptual organizations, relations between various discourses)" (1972, p. 72).

Too, how might we be more reflexive in analyzing the imposition of our moral imperative as critics on the subjects/objects of our critique? The limitations of our frameworks as well as our "critical morality" must be reflected upon, as well as the relationship between the critic and the "reality" being critiqued. There are, of course, many densities to consider: the density (valence?) of our emotional invest-ments, the densities of words and language both within and across cultural bound-aries, the density of our scholarly positions, and so forth. As we move through intercultural spaces and places, Lash and Urry (1994) suggest that we emphasize the role of subjectivity and self-reflexive critique in the formation of identity through aesthetic social practices. Picking up on Lash and Urry's argument for the aesthetic amid the "signs" (semiotics) of globalization – and my own concerns with the critical imperative for social change, the need for critical reflection on our own academic forms and formalism and the possibilities for doing so – I turn to Shugart's (2003) discussion of the aesthetic and finally to a call for performance studies as critical ICC pedagogy.

A Critical Aesthetic

In an essay entitled, "An Appropriating Aesthetic: Reproducing Power in the Discourse of Critical Scholarship," Helene Shugart (2003) critiques the conform-ity of critical rhetorical work to an aesthetic that objectifies, essentializes, and fet-ishizes those whom it intends to recognize and empower. In particular, she is moved by the uneasiness she senses in the "fit" between the ethical and moral com-mitment of critical scholarship and the hegemony of the form. Shugart explores also, for instance, the ways critical scholars conform to expectations for (a) citation and (b) methods of analysis. In the former case, critical rhetoricians are often expected to cite scholarship that does not necessarily build or extend their analysis but as confirmation and legitimation of their ideas. In the latter case, the language and forms of methods of analysis serve to separate the critic as subject from the object of analysis in order to secure the aesthetic assumed and expected in "seri-ous" academic scholarship.

Although Shugart does not explore the full complexities of the aesthetic[7] in this article, she does look at the relationship between the critic, critique and the "reality" of oppression in order to raise the ethical question of "critique to what ends?" The critic may seek to recognize hegemonic relations in the dominant culture, to advo-cate for those voices are not present in our research, or to argue against inequity and for social change, but our work also must conform to the academic code in order to be published. Shugart cites scholars who may recognize the limits of the form in their work but do not attempt to move beyond their (academic) critique; indeed, she herself does not challenge expectations for form in her own essay criticizing the same.[8] While Shugart and others have discussed the demands to publish and, dare I add, the desire for publications as a major force for a particular aesthetic, I also include teaching (and our own graduate training) as a major hegemonic force for an appropriating aesthetic. In addition to the challenges for critical scholars listed above, for critical intercultural communication scholars we might include expectations for social scientific methodologies and methods of analysis that proscribe the study of cultural interaction from a particularly Western frame. A certain distance from the text, interaction, and/or ethnographic site is assumed as appropriately objective, just as a certain personal/relational distance from one's subjects ensures neutrality.

These challenges may be met with a somewhat different response to the idea of the aesthetic; that is, through bringing to light in our scholarship and teaching the use of form for form's sake. It is this contest to, and celebration of, form that distinguishes the study of performance. Performance calls attention to the spaces and moments of action (process), recognizes acts as meaningful through "restored behavior" (repetition), seeks new forms of action through the movement among aesthetic practices and the study of them (creativity), and studies the punctuation and flow of both the sacred and mundane, marked and unmarked presentations of culture and identities (event).

Critical ICC scholars have included the study of performance in their work (e.g., Alexander, Nakayama, Madison, Jackson, Johnson) although few have discussed the reasons why a turn to the aesthetic and performance could advance our theorizing and pedagogy in this area. I engage this discussion as well as my own practices of critical intercultural communication in this last section of this chapter.

Critical Intercultural Communication Pedagogy and Performance

In my 2001 essay, I discussed the possibilities for a pedagogy that viewed intercultural communication from the borderlands. My focus was on the questions we might pose and the curricula we might introduce in order to shift the emphasis from the center to the borderlands. Looking at where we are as a field now, it seems evident that communications technology, along with a greater acceptance and availability of critical texts, has opened up the field to include more, if not all, voices. With more intercultural interaction opportunities availed to the dominant culture via changing demographics and greater mobility as well as the Internet, university students can test the viability of intercultural theories for themselves. Yet, amid the increasing possibilities for our intercultural communication pedagogy, our teaching methods and research on teaching are restricted again by a pedagogical aesthetic that situates knowledge firmly in the mental capacities of cultural participants. In focusing on culture as abstraction, located in the mind and not the body, students (and teachers) learn to separate the subject (self) and object (other) of culture. The threads that bind and blur cultures, agency and embodiment, get lost in our heady desire to have knowledge of the Other without intimately knowing much about our own (especially dominant) culture.

Performance studies critiques and celebrates the aesthetic through both acknowledging and transcending cultural forms. It is particularly concerned with questioning and blurring artistic, disciplinary and social/cultural boundaries. Barbara Kirshenblatt-Gimblett (1999) observes:

> Performance Studies ... is not only intercultural in scope and spirit, but also challenges aesthetic hierarchies and analyzes how they are formed. Performance Studies encompasses not only the most valorized, but also least valued, cultural forms within these hierarchies ... By theorizing embodiment, event, and agency in relation to live (and mediated) performance, Performance Studies can potentially offer something of a counterweight to the emphasis in Cultural Studies on literature and media and on text as an extended metaphor for culture (p. 1).

Although Performance Studies, too, can uphold and celebrate dominant and oppressive cultural performances and performativities, its focus on bodies in space opens up critical analysis to locations of and for embodiment, possibilities for meaning outside textual forms and reflection on one's own scholarly body (Cooks, 2007). Through its intentional blurring of boundaries, performance studies adds to critical intercultural communication (CIC) a concentration on the social construction of cultural forms as both expected and enacted. Moreover, through a focus on the embodiment of boundaries and borders (physical and social geographies) performance studies situates bodies in spaces that may/not be creatively and critically engaged. Although CIC as with all critical scholarship runs the danger of remaining in the abstract, a grounding in critical performance studies allows communication scholars to direct their attention to the power embedded in the mundane, in the ways bodies inhabit spaces and languages (refuse to) locate their (in)visibility.

For our pedagogy, this means teaching and learning about embodiment as the performance of cultural identity. Discussion in class of which or whose bodies are mobile or fixed, in what spaces or contexts, as well as class performances of culturally (in)appropriate behaviors provides a format for agency, creativity and cultural critique. Moreover, it allows teacher and students to take risks in classroom by putting their body "on record" and by sharing the depth of feeling that often comes with such disclosure of what was "always-already" there. Addressing critical intercultural communication and its pedagogy specifically, it is important to discuss the embodiment of privilege, albeit never complete across all spaces and purposes, alongside any discussion of the performance of intercultural similarities and differences. Moreover, in teaching about intercultural conflict, performance studies offers a view from the borderlands by addressing specifically the ways differences are embodied in social and cultural spaces.

I do not offer a view from the borderlands or performance studies as antidotes, but I have found my own challenges, comforts, joys, and continued intercultural education through performance work in my classes and in marginalized communities outside the university. By "performance," I mean the continued focus on our bodies as spaces for the enactment of culture. By "work" I mean teaching community based learning courses and carrying out research in the classroom and community that advocates change in academia. I also attempt research that both confronts the aesthetics of academic forms and that is (sometimes) publishable – acknowledging the relative safety of my position as a white female academic from which to resist oppressive voices while retaining my own.[9]

Conclusion; What's at Stake?

For critical scholars in intercultural communication, to address the "curious fact of otherness" often means asking the aesthetic questions of meaning and form as they impact ethical questions about struggle and change. If our goal as critical academics is one of finding the truth, then we must run the risk that it is not our own truth that we might find. If our goal is the "good society" then again we must estimate the value of our research toward that goal. We must continue to ask of ourselves the harder questions about our own struggles as academics who both want to work for change and wish to have a career – or at least a stable livelihood – in institutions that uphold hegemonic relations and the privileges of the dominant culture.

If we question both the idea of a "Truth" or even "truths," then we might also turn to different metaphors for communication and otherness than transportation or even communion mentioned at the start of this chapter. Many scholars of globalization refer to networking and flow as new metaphors for intercultural communication. I acknowledge the importance of connecting points and transient subjectivities and add to these the metaphors of borders and performance. Neither is new to us an interpretation for communication and/or otherness, but both add something that the others do not. Borderlands address a sense of in-betweeness and overlapping boundaries of identities and communal spaces and the tensions of embodiment and location. Performance is not only about the staged presentations of self and other but the imposition of form upon substance and the recreation of substance through form.

In this essay I have presented several ideas for consideration as we contemplate the nature and the future of critical intercultural communication. Where my previous essay was concerned with the boundaries that separated center-periphery, self and other, similarity and difference, and the intercultural communication field from all others in the discipline, this essay acknowledges some movement away from binaries due to the increasingly obvious influences of mobility, technology, and globalization in the early-twenty-first century. Still, as some gaps shrink, others continue to grow and, as rich and poor grow further apart, other cultural identity issues become more divisive as well. The field of critical intercultural communication has embraced cultural and postcolonial studies, political economy, globalization studies and, to some extent, a social constructionist perspective. As scholars and pedagogues facing a dizzying array of opportunities for education, it seems imperative to start with questioning aesthetics – as form, interpretation, creativity, and opportunity for change.

As I have indicated throughout this essay, critical intercultural communication for me is not only about critiquing hegemony and the politics of culture as it has been construed; rather, it is about the enactment and embodiment (inhabitation) of these ideas as power: the power conveyed through naming and categorizing "others," the agency that occurs with/in bodily (in)visibility, and the oppression that occurs when one's body is always already marked. CIC is also about those spaces where power opens up spaces for multiplicity, for multiple identifications that confuse our categories and make messes where tidy theories are called for. CIC research focuses on the mundane often understudied moments of interaction when race, ethnicity and culture are unremarkable, and yet cultural identities are marked as self or other.

This essay, and the earlier one calling for a view from the borderlands, hopes to contribute to this growing body of theory and practice, reflection not only on the ways in which borders and boundaries are constructed but on their densities and fluidities, both discursive and nondiscursive. Acknowledging the irony of an academic call for analysis *beyond* discourse, I ask rather for a look at what we always-already know as injustice and oppression, and *also* a sideways glance at what forms of resistance and agency might be going on "behind the teacher's (ethnographer's, research's) back" as it were. Such a call is nothing new in critical research, but as discourses of identity proliferate, questions of the *usefulness* of authenticity remain and as intercultural communication teachers and researchers, we must ask *to whom* as well as *for what* are such concepts (and associated essentialisms) useful. This requires a seriousness of purpose as well as openness to creativity and play, awareness of the moral imperative or our work as well as its ubiquitous nature, and ultimately the connections among mind, body, and emotion that inform our work. Further, we need to make the connections, in our theorizing, teaching, and research between what we create, maintain and resist in our conversations on campus and in the community with the larger social and cultural foundations of our talk. I have endeavored to show the ways many CIC scholars are engaging in this work, and to show the places where our theories and research need to move. Such a task is far more intimidating (and, I argue, necessary) than ever before, as intercultural communication is no longer a subcategory of the discipline but indeed, IS the discipline of communication.

Notes

1 Importantly, as he notes, Carey's metaphors illustrate the history of the study of communication in the United States, and so are situated within that history. Presumably other national histories and other less recognized cultural and diasporic histories within the United States would lead to similar or different metaphors.

2 More thorough metatheoretical analyses and critiques of definitions of communication can be found elsewhere and are beyond the scope of this essay. See, for instance Peters (1999) and Shepherd, St. John and Striphas (2006).

3 Henceforth referred to as the "2001 essay."
4 Dreama Moon (2002) highlights some research in the 1970s that expressed concern with dominant cultural systems and critiqued the cultural bias in the field. However, she notes that in the 1980s intercultural communication began to focus on nationality as culture and to focus once again on producing "intercultural rule books" (p. 15).
5 See, Ahmed, Appadurai, Benhabib, Bhabha, Chow, Escobar, Radhakrishnan, and many, many more.
6 I recognize the contributions of Critical Discourse Analysis (see Fairclough, Norman 1995) but find too that the form simplifies and thus constrains a nuanced analysis of interaction.
7 Arguably, the aesthetic has been a concern of philosophy from the time of Socrates. Western philosophers (e.g. Nietzsche, Heidegger, Foucault) have variously concerned themselves with the relationship between interpretation and reality via aesthetics as human capacity for creativity that is located both in and beyond language.
8 Nor, should I add, do I – although elsewhere I have experimented with form (see Further Reading).
9 Self-reflexivity does not insure either critical theorizing or action, and my own relative cultural dominance ensures the moral requirement of making a choice.

References

Blitz, M. (2004) Liberal education and liberalism. *The Good Society*, 13 (3), 45–48.

Carey, J. (1989) *Communication as Culture*, Routledge, New York.

Cooks, L. (2001) From distance and uncertainty to research and pedagogy in the borderlands: Implications for the future of intercultural communication. *Communication Theory*, 11 (3), 339–351.

Cooks, L. (2007) Accounting for my teacher's body: What can I teach, what can we learn?. *Feminist Media Studies*, 7 (3), 299–312.

Crofts Wiley, S. (2004) Rethinking nationality in the context of globalization. *Communication Theory*, 14 (1), 78–96.

Drzewiecka, J.A. (2002) Collective memory, media representations and barriers to intercultural dialogue, in *Intercultural Alliances: Critical Transformation*, (ed. M.J. Collier), Sage, Thousand Oaks, CA, pp. 189–220.

Durara, P. (1996) Historicizing national identity or who imagines what and when, in *Becoming National: A Reader*, (eds G. Eley and R. Grigor Suny), Oxford University Press, New York and Oxford, pp. 158–175.

Fairclough, N. (1995). *Critical Discourse Analysis*, Addison Wesley, Boston, MA.

Foucault, M. (1972) *The Archaeology of Knowledge*, (trans. A.M. Sheridan), Tavistock Press, London.

Hall, S. (1973) *Encoding and Decoding in the Television Discourse*, Centre for Contemporary Cultural Studies, University of Birmingham, Birmingham.

Hall, S. (1997) The local and the global: Globalization and ethnicity, in *Culture, Globalization and the World-System: Contemporary Conditions for the Representation of Identity*, (ed. A.D. King), University of Minnesota Press, Minneapolis, pp. 19–41.

Halualani, R. (2002) Connecting Hawaiians: The politics of authenticity in the Hawaiian diaspora, in *Intercultural Alliances: Critical Transformation*, (ed, M.J. Collier), Sage, Thousand Oaks, CA, pp. 221–248.

Harvey, D. (1996) *Justice, Nature and the Geography of Difference*, Blackwell, Cambridge, MA.

Kirshenblatt-Gimblett, B. (1999) Performance Studies, Rockefeller Foundation, Culture and Creativity, www.nyu.edu/classes/bkg/issues/rock2.htm (accessed May 14, 2010).

Lash, S., and Urry, J. (1994) *Economies of Signs and Space*, Sage, London.

Leeds-Hurwitz, W. (1998) Notes on the history of intercultural communication: The Foreign Service Institute and the Mandate for Intercultural Training, in *Readings in Cultural Contexts*, (eds J.N. Martin, T.N. Nakayama, and L.A. Flores), Mayfield, Mountain View, CA, pp. 15–29.

Mendoza, S.L. (2002) Bridging theory and cultural politics: Revisiting the indigenization-poststructuralism debates in Filipino and Filipino American Struggles for identity, in *Intercultural Alliances: Critical Transformation*, (ed, M.J. Collier), Sage, pp. 249–277.

Moon, D.G. (2002) Thinking about "Culture" in intercultural communication, in *Readings in Intercultural Communication: Experiences and Contexts*, 2nd edn, (eds J.N. Martin, T.K. Nakayama, and L.A. Flores) McGraw-Hill, New York, pp. 13–20.

Peters, J.D. (1999) *Speaking into the Air: A History of the Idea of Communication*, University of Chicago Press, Chicago.

Reddy, M.J. (1979) The conduit metaphor: A case of frame conflict in our language about language, in *Metaphor and Thought*, (ed. I. Andrew Ortony), Cambridge University Press, Cambridge, pp. 284–324.

Rogers, R.A. (2006) From cultural exchange to transculturation: A review and reconceptualization of cultural appropriation, *Communication Theory*, 16, 474–503.

Shannon, C.E., and Weaver, W. (1949) *A Mathematical Model of Communication*, University of Illinois Press, Urbana, IL.

Shepherd, G.J., St. John, J., and Striphas, T.G. (2006) *Communication as …: Perspectives on Theory*, Sage, Thousand Oaks, CA.

Shome, R. (2003) Space matters: The power and practice of space, *Communication Theory*, 13 (1), 39–56.

Shugart, H. (2003). An appropriating aesthetic: reproducing power in the discourse of critical scholarship, *Communication Theory*, 13 (3), 275–303.

Further Reading

Anzaldúa, G. (1987). *Borderlands/LaFrontera*, San Francisco, Aunt Lute Books.

Ashcraft, K., and Allen, B. (2003), Racial foundations of organizational communication. *Communication Theory*, 13 (1), 5–38.

Brah, A. (1996) *Cartographies of Diaspora: Contesting Identities*, Routledge, New York.

Clifford, J. (1988). *The Predicament of Culture*, Harvard University Press, Cambridge, MA.

Conquergood, D. (1991), Rethinking ethnography: Towards a critical cultural politics. *Communication Monographs*, 58, 141–156.

Cooks, L.M., and Simpson, J. (eds) (2007) *Dis/Placing Race: Whiteness, Performance and Pedagogy*, Rowman and Littlefield, Lanham, MD.

de Certeau, M. (1984) *The Practice of Everyday Life* (trans. S. Rendall), University of California Press, Berkeley.

Hall, S. (1986) Introduction: Who needs identity?, in *Questions of Cultural Identity*, (eds S. Hall and P. Du Gay), Sage, London.

Kraidy, M. M. (2002). Hybridity in cultural globalization. *Communication Theory*, 12, 316–339.

Marcus, G.E., and Fisher, M.J. (1986). *Anthropology as Cultural Critique*, University of Chicago Press, Chicago.

Martin, J.N., and Nakayama, T.K. (1999) Thinking dialectically about culture and communication, *Communication Theory*, 1, 1–25.

Nakayama, T., and Martin, J. (1999). *Whiteness: The Communication of Social Identity*, Sage, London.

Visweswaran, K. (1994) *Fictions of Feminist Ethnography*, University of Minnesota Press, Minneapolis.

9

Expanding the Circumference of Intercultural Communication Study

William J. Starosta and Guo-Ming Chen

STAROSTA: I was guest lecturing for a class at a neighboring university, when the instructor asked me how the two of us started to work together. It seemed highly improbable to him that we could find common ground, or that we could learn to work across our cultural differences. Yet, we have worked together and I, at least, have grown from my exchanges with you. It is not for me to say whether, or how, you may have changed over the years.

During our two decades of association, either the field of intercultural communication has been changing rapidly, or else maybe just my own perspectives have shifted. I don't know which is truer, that the field has transformed around me, or if my own orientation toward intercultural communication has changed, while the field remained about the same.

We have written about the changing character of the field. Do some aspects of what we have discussed particularly resonate with you, or are they mostly scholarly abstractions to you?

CHEN: All phenomenal existence is conditioned by the two opposite but complementary forces of *yin* and *yang*. Unfortunately, after a half-a-century of development, the study of intercultural communication continues to be dominated by the concept of "difference," while "similarity" remains unnoticed. Although as humans "we must be born twice: once to a physical mother; and once to a social/cultural one" (Thayer, 1987, p. vii) that differentiates us by skin color and cultural values, deep down we are as similar as twin brothers. It is this bipolar coexistence of *yin* and *yang* leading our way of finding the similarities within the differences and recognizing the two sides of a coin through a meaningful dialogue. It is also the union of difference and similarity as a formation of polar tension that causes the rotational movement of our dialogue.

We must change during the course of the rotation. Our dialogue is a practice of self-analysis, which not only reflects the change of us, but also the transformation

The Handbook of Critical Intercultural Communication, edited by Thomas K. Nakayama and Rona Tamiko Halualani. © 2010 Blackwell Publishing Ltd.

of intercultural communication study. Ah, change itself is the only constant phenomenon of the universe.

Before we move on, let me first listen to your point of view regarding the specific
aspects of change in the study of intercultural communication.

STAROSTA: I feel our conversations force us to suspend our personal sense of the real
in order to entertain the sense of reality as our dialogic partner finds it. *Yin* and
yang have now given our conversations parameters they did not always have.

I began my study of intercultural communication as a positivist for whom cultures
did not change; at least, they did not do so rapidly, allowing critics to describe what
(essentially) *is* in lawful terms: Greeks communicate as Greeks, and Germans as
Germans. Their culture is evident from their rhetoric. Black Germans? Punjabi
Indian workers in Athens? Native Americans and African Americans at home? Back
then, that was considered "interracial," not intercultural. The field wrestled for so
many years with foundational definitions.

Our dialogue (Starosta and Chen, 2003a) called this a first "moment," a time of
positivist, foundational orientation. It was not until I studied for a year in India,
and worked in a historically Black university, that I realized that a nation has many
voices, not just one. I saw how these voices can be mismatched in the public sphere,
forcing persons even within the same nation to listen across cultures. This moved
me through an ethnographic (postpositivist) moment to a postmodern one of
many voices, and on to critical analysis. I was told, but had not yet internalized,
that being white and male defined me, and gave me privilege.

Did I find "difference" to be the key to understanding intercultural communication? I think I did. I had seen interaction falter and fail because of differing discourse
practices. Cultural difference started out as self-evident for me. I committed myself
to communicology, improving practice to make intercultural interaction "work."
A catalog of essentialized cultural differences, expressed mostly as binaries, made
this commitment possible.

Positionality? Reflexivity? Whiteness? Multiply readable texts? That took time to
learn, because I had to experience some of what I taught in order to understand it.
I look back now and do not recognize that early me; that early me seems an alien;
or maybe I am the alien now?

Ummm, you raise so many questions. Are *yin* and *yang* real for me? I think
maybe they are a part of a third culture that has emerged while we interacted, and
I treat them "as if " they are real. True, I had studied them in the abstract, and had
even been graded on them; but they seem more real now that we interact. I am
listening when you say we are as twins, not really different, but we still are as head
and tail of a coin. Are *yin* and *yang* empirically-verifiable categories, or analytic
tools, or does our thinking and interacting construct a way of looking at the world
that seems to work? The appearance of "paradox" carries us on to a fifth moment
of research; by the time I understand it, it will again have changed.

CHEN: Difference leads to alienation. It exists not only in communication process,
but also in the study of communication. However, the communication gap caused
by differences can only be bridged by the similarities embedded in the two

interactants. The moment of making efforts to understand differences is also the moment to seek similarities between the two. The premise for the _yin_ and _yang_ argument is that the pure _yin_ won't grow, and the pure _yang_ won't produce. Without the _yang_ component in _yin_ and the _yin_ component in _yang_, the coin formed by the head and tail won't function well. It is this holistic, interconnected worldview from my own culture that has been agonizing to me since I stepped into the field of intercultural communication.

As a "foreign student," an "other," an "it," a "yellow Asian," and an "alien" since almost three decades ago in the United States of America, I have been facing so many alienating experiences in daily life interactions just because I am different from "them" in the way I look and the way I talk. While working hard to understand and resolve the differences between me and them, I changed myself to treat the differences by adopting their confrontational style in order to sooth my hurting feeling of alienation. I am not sure if this way of tackling differences helps my counterparts understand me better and accept me more, but I know that it won't help me escape from the hurting of alienation. Being aware of or even being sensitive enough to cultural differences may alleviate the psychological tension inside, but it seems it won't guarantee that the awareness and sensitivity can lead to behavioral effectiveness in a real intercultural encounter.

Moreover, as a student, researcher, and educator of intercultural communication for so many years, I continue to be puzzled by whether the either-or mode embedded in the confrontational style of problem solving can induce a productive communication. To me, this either-or mode equates the isolation between pure _yin_ and pure _yang_, which mirrors the dialectical replacement of each other, rather than the dialogical unification of the _yin_ and _yang_ as _Tai Chi_ or the head and tail of a coin. Thus, I am still wondering if a philosophy of intercultural communication, built on the nature of interpenetration and identification of _yin_ and _yang_ (i.e., the two interactants) can be developed to unlock the mystery of intercultural communication, and through which interactants can avoid being victimized by the mere facts of research findings or by currently fashionable and legitimatized practice in the academic and research community.

The development (or different moments as we previously discussed) of intercultural communication study also reflects this unfortunate dialectical transformation of imbalanced _yin_ and _yang_. I attended an NCA–2007 program about the new directions in intercultural communication research, sponsored by the International and Intercultural Division, in which one of the authors reported that her study of NCA publications over the past 10 years showed that about 80% of intercultural communication related articles were based on a critical/interpretive paradigm. The trend is understandable if we check the development of social sciences study after 1990s. However, what worries me is not the shift from the discovery to critical/interpretive paradigm, but the either-or trend that tends to push the other side away. The lack of reconciliation, cooperation, and interpenetration of different paradigms is unhealthy to the development of any disciplines, including (intercultural) communication.

I remain as a student in doing and researching intercultural communication, and I am always wondering if a state of harmonious coexistence of the intercultural communication study can be reached. Without this sense and practice of coexistence among the different, I don't think a healthy research community or a healthy daily life intercultural communication can be attained and without this coexistence, I'll continue to carry the burden of being labeled as an empiricist by the critical/interpretive followers, and vice versa, though the reality is that I am both or neither one. This intellectual alienation, plus the alienated feeling in the process of daily intercultural communication, makes me a double-alienated or double-marginalized person. Quite sad, isn't it?

STAROSTA: You've never before been this open about your own positionality; before, you have insulated your position with philosophy. To see you step out from your writing as a person is very powerful for me. I am sorry that you must deal with this dynamic.

Sadly, life on the hyphen is a place of immense alienation. So many writers and commentators have discussed the intergenerational strain for Amy Tan's mother–daughter dyads, or the sense of nonbelonging, the clear sense of being on the "frontier," for Mexicans in the United States. Wei Sun and I (2006) reported on in-depth interviews with Asian American professionals, most of whom reported "invisibility," something paralleling your "sadness."

It is part of the fifth and sixth moments to see that something around us has allowed a sense of alienation, of either-or, of nonbelonging, to grow. But it is also an expectation of those moments that we search for ways to unify, to bring us together, to speak to both our separateness and our commonality. I hope the very same moments that you see as dividing us will provide avenues of reinscribing, of writing new texts that are inclusive enough to speak also to our similarities.

"Both-and" is the core paradox of multiculturalism. At the same time as we try to reduce the projection of difference among various cultural populations, we want to recognize and respect differences of origin. W.E.B. Du Bois' (1903) *Souls of Black Folk* says about "double consciousness":

> One ever feels his two-ness, … an American, a Negro; two souls, two thoughts, two unreconciled strivings; two warring ideals in one dark body … The history of the American Negro is the history of this strife, … this longing to attain self-conscious manhood, to merge this double self into a better and truer self, in this merging he wishes neither of the old selves to be lost. He would not Africanize America, for America has too much to teach the world and Africa. He would not bleach his Negro soul in a flood of white Americanism, for he knows that the Negro blood has a message for the world. He simply wishes to make it possible for a man to be both a Negro and an American (p. 3).

Yin and *yang*, apart and together. If I am right that the intercultural field was born out of a sense of difference, it is well past time to enlarge the circumference of intercultural communication study to allow not only for similarity, but to rebuild what has been taken away through projecting negative difference and essentialism, through all the binaries.

CHEN: This "double consciousness" concept may confuse those hyphenated groups. If we only require, say, African or Asian Americans to foster two souls, two thoughts, or to be black/yellow/brown and white, it may improve communication in interethnic/minority interaction (e.g., between Italian Americans and Korean Americans) because of their experience living in two different cultures, but it may not help to reach an effective communication in interracial interaction (e.g., between African Americans and white Americans) for their counterpart is only living in a single culture. It sounds like that the burden of reaching intercultural understanding is imposed more to the hyphenated groups. Don't you think so?

In my opinion, the emphasis of studying differences should be treated as a means rather than the end of intercultural communication inquiry. I don't mean to devalue the study of cultural differences, instead, it is very important to understand and be sensitive to cultural differences, but it should just serve as the first step of reaching intercultural communication competence (Chen, 2007; Chen and Starosta, 1996). These cognitive and affective abilities referring to intercultural communication should be reinforced by looking into the universal human nature, in other words, what we want is not merely the reality structured by the social products via communication, we have to push one step further to visualize the "human" behind the web of the socially structured meanings. Only when the face of all of us as humans emerges can intercultural communication overpower the differences embedded in skin color, beliefs and values, or other cultural, religious, geographical, or economical influences.

I do agree that it is high time to expand the circumference of intercultural communication study, especially at the moment of facing the inescapable impact of the globalization trend (Chen, 2008). One of the subjects deserving deliberation here is "cultural identity." "Identity" in recent years has become a magic concept in the inquiry of intercultural communication. For some reason, I sense that the trend seems as though it won't lead us to anywhere. We advocate the importance of establishing, authenticating, or negotiating our own cultural identity in the intercultural communication process, but by tightly holding one's own cultural identity, how can we reach out to penetrate into others' identities? I am worried that the study of cultural identity might have shown a bias of encouraging people to weave a stronghold like a cocoon or a wall, which thrusts us into the dead end of intercultural interaction. I dream that someday I can see a topic like "beyond cultural identity" appear in the research community. Hope I don't sound too cynical. It just represents my personal opinion based on the observation, and I wish I could provoke more discussions on this subject.

STAROSTA: There is identity, there is similarity; there is difference, there is ambiguity. Ambiguity is a strategic resource of words that stands apart from the nature of things themselves, and enables people to function together. No two persons are the same, even when they are from the same family, from the same culture, from the same immediate environment. But language allows them to speak as though they are the same, and to act together. Intercultural communication begins when persons enter other cultural environments, where they lose the power to define themselves, if they ever really had it.

What is identity? Is it a fixed self-description that happens because we speak it, because we assert it, because we believe in it? Or, contrarily, is identity what some-one else calls us, someone makes us, someone considers or names us? One person's migrant worker is another's undocumented worker is a third person's cultural invader is a fourth person's illegal alien, and is a fifth's fellow human being. I don't see the chance to define the self and to live by that definition as being easy for someone from another culture.

You offer that perhaps cultural identity research "won't lead us to anywhere." You suggest that one can "hold one's own cultural identity" apart from the cultural identity of another. If words were things, if saying a thing is so would make it so, then I could see the "stranger" defining his or her own identity. But dual con-sciousness rests on the idea that I know first from Andrea Rich (1973): we can enact our identity only so far as the host culture allows. We can say what we are, but the larger society must ultimately validate our assertion of identity. Otherwise, we are not the thing we say we are. Hence your frustration, and that of others who experience dual consciousness.

Ambiguity of identity, ambiguity of culture, is at the heart of what you call "interpenetration" of cultures. I don't expect such interpenetration to be easily measurable, since it will change by context, by task, by linguistic choice, and by level of tolerance. The tolerance for ambiguity or readiness to gloss differences to build on similarities is central to aligning our cultural practice with the expectations of *yin* and *yang*.

The critical literature allows that the mainstream can assert an identity fairly easily, because their cultural variance is not very great, and they expect that others should adopt their culture. At the same time, they may prevent others from joining completely. An identity, in these cases, is a site of contestation, of push and pull. This gives us the frontier, the place where no identity is fixed, where identity constantly shifts. It gives the stranger a longing to identify, but erects barriers to such identification. I take this to be what you mean, that "the burden of reaching intercultural understanding is imposed more on the hyphenated group." If so, I think you are quite right.

I find myself, as a student of communication, documenting the process by which a newcomer negotiates difference, asserts an identity, moves closer to or farther from the mainstream, and generally discovers too late that the power to define identity rests with the mainstream more than it does with the stranger. You hope we will realize that "what we want is not merely the reality structured by the social products via communication, we have to push one step further to visualize the 'human' behind the web of the socially structured meanings." Maybe you are treating these socially structured meanings as neutral occurrences. The wish to state an identity lies with the stranger; the power to accept that definition of iden-tity lies with the native. It is the native, in this situation, who must look beyond the traditional definition to "find the humanness" of the stranger.

We are starting at the same point, I think, even if we do not end at the same place: It is unfair to place the burden of dual consciousness on the stranger, but often that happens. We ask the international student or business person to adapt to difference, but then stand in the way of that adaptation and when the other wants to retain a sense of cultural origin, we tell them, "love it or leave it." Mainstream culture does not make it easy for those different in appearance or speech to become the same, to find similarity. Your description of *yin* and *yang* stems from what ought to be, what is the ideal. It is immensely painful for me to see the use of language to separate what is, at heart, the same. People assert difference for a reason; either to hold on to cultural power (the "centrism") or in cultural self-defense, in response to oppression, to prevent being overwritten by the dominant culture.

What later "moments" tell us is that one can focus on what is, or on what ought to be. Seldom are these two the same. Only through a struggle does the mainstream find cause to permit similarity to be located between the newcomer and the resident of long standing. We turn to social constructionism and to intercultural rhetoric to offer hope to find words and categories that express our similarity, while respecting our difference, that is, to harmonize us.

I am not sure from your comments what role you assign the intercultural communication researcher. Is such a researcher a facilitator and a change agent? Does this researcher call attention when persons drift apart in their definitions, and facilitate their interpenetration? Does the researcher stand at a distance, or become an active participant in the process of finding similarity within difference?

CHEN: A researcher should locate or position her/himself in the continuum formed by the basic and applied research at the two ends, though I personally tend to prefer that a researcher should remain as a researcher only. A researcher's study may facilitate social change, but I think very few scholars can be a successful researcher and a change agent at the same time. This is a dilemma the critical/cultural study must face. A critical study scholar can be a powerful agent instigating social change by identifying the culturally and historically situated hidden structure of an oppressed group through his/her study, but to be an activist in pushing the change of a social situation is another issue. A person who endeavors to play both a good researcher and a successful activist for social change may only prove to be a mediocre player on both sides. This may just reflect my own bias, but I would like to seek an answer for how to bridge the gap between a pure researcher and an activist.

Let's move back to the issue of the critical turn of intercultural communication study. Difference must be defined by the social interaction, and cultural identity can only emerge from the differences seen or felt by the interactants in the process of intercultural communication. I found that the pursuit or study of cultural identity is a very important impetus for the rising of the critical paradigm in the study of intercultural communication after 1990s. Fox example, the study of "whiteness" (Avant-Mier and Hasian, 2002; Jackson, 1999; Jackson and Heckman, 2002; Jackson, Shin and Wilson, 2000; Nakayama and Krizek, 1995; Martin and Nakayama, 1999); the counteraction to Eurocentrism (Asante, 1980, 2007; Chen, 2006; Chu, 1988; Dissanayake, 2003, 2006; Miike, 2003, 2007); diaspora (Drzewiecka, 2002; Drzewiecka and Halualani, 2002; Halualani, 2003, 2008; Mendoza, 2002); or the critical approach to ethnicity, gender, and race (Hegde,

1998; Jackson and Dangerfield, 2002; Lee, 1998; Moon, 1999; Park, 2002; Reich, 2002) is largely based on the search for one's cultural identity, either a straight or hyphenated one. I am sure you have much to say about this critical turn from a historical perspective and want to add your reflection or critic on the scholarly contributions in this specific area.

STAROSTA: I find a tension between the individual and the collective. There can be no true individual, since each person is enculturated into some larger grouping; but there can be no complete loss of the self into the social other (Hinduism, Buddhism, Sufism, and some other philosophies say we *can* completely lose ourselves in the Absolute). Identity comes to float somewhere between the individual and the collective.

The first research moment thought that everyone should move in a single direction, but that some groups were more backward, more underdeveloped, further behind than others on the way to that common destination. Two notions, that is, categories of persons and a linear path to sameness, dominated researcher thinking. A second moment introduced relativism, where the things people did as cultural and gendered entities made sense in their context. A certain essentialism of identity still dominated the researchers' thinking, but difference did not always have to be negative, and not everyone needed to be on the way to the same place.

A third moment located different voices within what appeared at first to be single groups. Not everyone within the same national frame, as one example, had to have the same identity.

A fourth moment concentrated on power relationships. Someone was always ready to write their definitions and narratives onto other persons, to their selfish advantage. The targeted persons might acquiesce either out of weakness or out of a low level of awareness. But their definition was not their own, their identity was largely inscribed by powerful others. They learned to internalize oppression; even in the absence of overt pressure by the powerful they facilitated genderism and racism.

A fifth moment aimed at self-definition, at the assertion of an identity that provided dignity and purpose. This was a moment of consciousness raising and activism, of action research, of praxis.

Newer moments blur the earlier ones. They allow for the creation of coalitions; for the presence of multiple identities; for the confusing of gender and cultural and national definitions. Globalization, queer theory, and research on complicity all call into question the right or ability of others to define one's own identity. Identity becomes fluid and hard to locate.

If it deserves its own moment, I will not say, but it seems to me that reinscription projects now are starting to surface. My own participation in these projects falls under the heading of Centrisms (Starosta and Chen, 2003b). It may be possible for someone to define a place where they want to be, and to build and to maintain that place, to their presumed benefit. The act of asserting a Centrism opens the possibility of oppressing other persons again, of course.

The fourth moment and beyond (by my counting, since other persons may see more or fewer moments) would call upon researchers to consider activism. That seems a difficult choice, for you. Hyphenated identities, life on the margins of social groups, become the concern of researchers in the third moment and beyond. In your mind, does this categorization scheme help our discussion at all?

CHEN: Thank you for the precise description of the developmental history of the different moments from the perspective of identity study. Identity may be approached from different aspects and by different methodologies (Mendoza, Halualani and Drzewiecka, 2003; Shin and Jackson, 2003) but the critical line of inquiry on the subject is the one that shapes the fifth moment of the study of inter-cultural communication. Since the trend is only running at its early stage, I would like to raise a few challenges faced by the scholars in this area.

First, when I was seeking an answer for how to bridge the gap between a pure researcher and an activist, I only looked at it from the scholarship perspective rather than as an ideology. As an intercultural communication researcher and a hyphenated man, I, like you, adopt a critical cultural approach to the study of identity and work hard to instigate the possible social change for improving the unequal condition in different ethnic or racial groups, but I have to face the most fundamental question for being as a researcher. I am wondering how far a researcher can go toward becoming an activist while can still remain successful in scholarship. I have no problem to say that I can be a good scholar and an advocate of social change, but I have to confess that to be a good scholar and a competent activist at the same time is far beyond my reach. I am wondering how many scholars in the critical study group can be effective at being both a scholar and activist. Before the answer for bridging the gap between a pure researcher and an activist is sought, I don't think we can be satisfied with what we have accomplished so far in improving the intercultural communication.

Second, the process of building an identity is also a process of excluding or excommunicating one's counterpart, in other words, the self-definition or assertion of an identity, as you described this as the goal of the fifth moment, might provide us with dignity and purpose, but it might as well lose our sight by deiden-tifying the other and shrinking us from committing ourselves to what coexistence or intercultural communication should be. When every individual or group becomes a center, this world may evolve into an ocean filled with hundreds of thousands of dead islands. As you said, "The act of asserting a Centrism opens the possibility of oppressing other persons again, of course." This should mean that identity searching is a double-edged sword. How to manage this double-edged sword should be a riddle we need to unfold.

Third, phrases such as "multiple identities" or "fluid identity" are infected by the semantic ambiguity. If we say that identity is a defined personal or cultural space in which we only communicate with a small number of members whose beliefs are consistent with ours, then how could we well conceptualize all these different iden-tities based on a compatible or equal footing; especially when we are moving, or let the identity float, from this space to that space, do we have to dilute or even cancel the former identity? Theoretically, if we do embrace and advocate the ideas of "mul-ticultural person," "multiple identities," or "multiple centers," I am wondering when we are in action, how do we unify or disassociate this "multi' with a hyphen?

Self examination is critical during the course of developing a sound personal, cultural, or academic identity. I raise the above questions aiming to serve as a stimulus for self reflection for the study of identity from the critical cultural perspective. I hope you won't frown on my intentional thought-provoking challenges.

STAROSTA: These are excellent observations and questions. It is by facing the hardest questions that arise from these moments that we affirm or move beyond each moment. Because I name and number these moments, it does not mean that I am clear about where I stand with respect to them. I feel a pull from multiple directions, often determined by the person with whom I am coauthoring at a certain time.

You raise so very many points. I am sure to oversimplify them in my answers. You twice raised the difficulty or even the impossibility of serving both as sound researcher and as strong social activist. Filmmakers, as one example, can research prison conditions or civil rights marches, and then create a documentary on these conditions. Santiago-Valles (2003) writes not only on the moral necessity of performing applied research that grows out of a thorough understanding of the community's conditions, but of the possibility of doing so. The researcher learns to tell the community's narrative in a way that community recognizes, and then brings this telling to an audience that has yet to see the problem through authentic eyes. First, then, I think some researchers have done some of what you ask about; though most do not.

Second, I think collaboration across cultures on a research project helps to keep a certain fidelity and credibility part of intercultural research. We make a mistake to try to research alone. Each distinct cultural perspective adds a lens by which to understand the communication, leading to a double-emic view of the thing (Starosta and Chen, 2000). That double emic view can lead to better listening, to adopting a critical perspective on the process, to reforming the process, or to improving interunderstanding among the interactants (Chen and Starosta, 2005; Starosta and Shi, 2007) I think always that it should be motivated by a sense of the need to ameliorate the problems posed by differences, and to lower differences in power. The reduction of a sense of difference is an end I have seen you advocate.

Then you raise the dialectic nature of identity. To say what I am, I may have to say what you are. To say what you are, I may have to say what I am. I agree with you on this point; our identity is not a stand-alone quantity, it results from a give-and-take interaction with the attributions of others.

We are far too interconnected to expect to move to monasteries, take a vow of silence, and live in perpetual isolation. Except for those seeking a fixed and eternal relationship with a fixed truth, there is no point to this pursuit; we are social creatures, who grow through the process of symbolic interactionism. Consequently, our truth also shifts from interaction to interaction, from situation to situation, from historical moment to historical moment. I have seen persons who speak so fluently in a foreign language that they are mistaken for natives. For a fleeting moment, they are not natives; rather, they are something in between local and international. Relationships also change. At some point, when a German or Spaniard or Hindi speaker invites us linguistically to move to a less formal, more familiar level of address, we enter into a different sort of relationship with the other. Yes, asserting our identity separates us; but the separation holds the seeds of reuniting us, at a level beyond national culture.

I guess I do not see differences as walls, but rather as what a cell biologist would call a semi-permeable membrane. Some elements can pass through the barriers, but others do not or cannot and perhaps should not. The barriers can filter out viruses while still allowing the cell to get nutrients. We need the wisdom to recognize the difference between what heals us and what destroys us.

Finally, you return to my words about the linguistic resources of ambiguity. Here I am thinking out loud; I haven't given this enough thought to offer a firm answer. I would say this. When a sojourner leaves his or her place of origin, either physically or psychologically, and goes elsewhere, s/he is not in anything approaching complete control of the interactions that will be encountered with the other. Research suggests that the sojourner adapts best by reaching a point of equilibrium between the familiar and the new. The new teaches adaptation skills; the familiar gives comfort for the stress of encounter. As the sojourner dips into both the old and the new, I am not prepared to name that person's identity; I do not see it as being stable enough to let me do so.

A North African student was given a job interview in which the hiring committee clearly expected an "African" applicant to be "black." They subsequently called the student's professor to see if she could say if the applicant was "black" or not. Instead, she answered, "An interesting question. What did he say when you asked him?" I guess I might call him hyphenated, a person on a frontier, a multicultural person. But what would he call himself?

CHEN: I greatly appreciate your thoughtful responses to the questions I raised, which not only account for your position, but also enlighten me much, and should well inform the readers, too. I'd like to make a few more points for us to continue to ponder here.

First, a documentary on the poor prison conditions produced by a filmmaker is a good example for an applied research project. It is like what a scholar can do by producing a publishable paper advocating social change, but this is not what I conceive of as the meaning of an "activist." To me, an activist is the one who leads, for example, civil rights marchers, a person not only holding a pen, but also holding a sword. I probably have an inaccurate perception of the meaning of an activist. If we accept my interpretation of an activist, critical approach scholars, in addition to instigating social change, will have to change the academic culture too.

Second, your double-emic view of interaction has a great potential in reaching a better understanding in intercultural communication. From the methodological perspective, for the sake of argument, this double-emic process of looking into one's counterpart's position during interaction seems a way to achieve intersubjectivity. Will this approach provide a channel to connect to the etic perspective? In other words, for example, the third culture building model, similar to the double-emic approach, may serve as an etic view applied to the two involved cultures in the interaction.

Finally, yes, we are social creatures. As human beings we must be born in some culture and grow in communication. Through communication we have to learn how to participate in the web of meaning woven by another way of coding the world, in each moment of intercultural communication research, scholars endeavored to offer valuable views on how to more effectively move forward in this participation process. Now it is the moment for scholars of the critical approach to offer us, as you said, "the wisdom to recognize the difference between what heals us and what destroys us." Isn't it?

As in our previous dialogues, we attempted to answer the questions we raised on the study of intercultural communication, but they always ended up stirring up more new questions, instead of feeling frustrated on this kind of outcome, I feel encouraged, because this is why I continue to be optimistic for the development of intercultural communication study. An academic field without facing stimulating questions or ferment is like a plant without roots which can only stop growing. Our spirit of facing the challenges fosters in us creative courage, which helps us discover new forms on which a sound field of intercultural communication can be built, and I hope this effort can "bring into existence new kinds of being that give harmony and integration" (May, 1975, p. 169).

STAROSTA: Qualitative research, by its nature, changes everyone it touches. It forces the researcher to listen in a way that was not possible earlier, and to try earnestly to reproduce the authentic words of those who were studied without losing their power. It causes the respondents or coresearchers to talk about matters that they had not previously been made to explain or to clarify, and to render their perceptions in a way that becomes intelligible to the researcher. It leads to partnerships between the two parties, where the researcher presents findings to the press, the government, or to the academic community. The published narrative or performance, if powerfully rendered, evokes changes in many who encounter it in ways too many to be quantified. Is this "activism"? It depends on whether we have to stand in front of a column of tanks in Tiananmen Square or chain ourselves to a public building in order to count as an activist. There seem to me to be many levels and grades of activism, and only some of them place us immediately at risk.

I usually cannot easily separate words from social actions. Words that do not ameliorate the human condition have the effect of perpetuating it. Many political activists who fear censorship if they speak as journalists become novelists or poets, their words speak to social conditions and relationships in a way that tears at the soul. They would not have such power unless they had somehow probed (researched) the authentic voices of those they depict. The sixth moment opens many new ways to apply or to perform our research. Collaboration allows some of us to actively listen across cultures, while others among us perform the lessons that we learn.

The double emic approach may be purely descriptive, saying, "Here are two ways this matter can be viewed," but I hope it will be carried to the level of prescription. I would like to think that the clarity that comes from seeing two (or more) ways to authentically describe a matter could allow a critic to more deeply appreciate the discourse, and to see more accurately and empathically than does either participant on his or her own. That should lead to humane criticism, and should promote synergistic (proionic) solutions that are more than the sum of the individual parts. The option that you suggest is that the researcher who stands in between, who hears multiple voices without judging them, can promote intersubjectivity and interunderstanding among the parties. This is true. The process could be replicated elsewhere, and has an etic aspect. However general is the process, though, the content remains culture(s) specific.

Is "now" the time to discern (or to practice?) the difference between what heals us and what destroys us? I try to live in the present, though I am a product of the past, perhaps innumerable pasts. For me, then there is no time but "now" to learn how to heal and not to destroy; and to act on that understanding.

It is always difficult for me to dialog with you, but it is fulfilling. There are some positions I would be tempted to overlook or to gloss, that you make me examine more closely and to credit. There are moments when I would take off in a flight of fancy, but you return me back to earth. Dialogue for me is a great corrective. While it limits me, it eventually also teaches me how to transcend. Frustrating? Yes, this process is frustrating; but it also brings me hope. If I can steer my way through our exchanges, I believe I will find a richer understanding at the end of my sojourn.

What we do in a formal academic exchange, intercultural interactants do, or could do, or should do in every place, at all times, across all cultures. If this process works successfully, we add to our repertoire, to our possibilities, through our dialogue. I dare to suggest, we may even transform the other, while we are ourselves being transformed. If I am right that makes us both, in some sense at least, into "activists," though neither of us lifts a sword.

CHEN: Nice points you have made. Before we wrap up this intense dialogue, I think it is a good idea for us to recapitulate the issues we raised from the critical perspective. As an emerging paradigm for the study of intercultural communication, the critical perspective has to not only deal with those ambiguous research concepts faced by previous paradigms, but also provide a new insight and direction for the study and development of the field. The issues we discussed in this dialogue can be generally summarized into the "tensions between dichotomized categories." Implicitly, we referred to the tensions of individual versus group, subjectivity versus objectivity, and mono-paradigm versus multi-paradigm, and explicitly we explored the tensions of difference versus similarity and researcher versus activist, and we used the *yin* and *yang* model to theorize the tensions between those dichotomies. Here I would like to further explicate the *yin* and *yang* model, which I think can serve as a possible guideline for critical researchers to follow.

I think a critical researcher must recognize that *yin* and *yang* are the two sides of a coin dictating that differences are in similarities and that they should learn how to search for similarities in differences by holding the attitude of "harmony without uniformity." In other words, all situations are stages of change and transformation, and any new perspectives are never without affinities to previous perspectives. Thus, opposition and fellowship complement one another. It is the opposites that provide an opportunity for critical scholars to understand themselves, and fellowship that helps them find their space of scholarship, either as a researcher or activist. Only through the complementary force of *yin* and *yang*, like the periodical ebb and flow of tide and the succession of day and night, can the efforts of critical scholars that continue the past and pass something on to the future be completed.

In a nutshell, the emergence of the critical perspective of intercultural communication study illustrates an epistemological advance, which is embedded in the historical continuity of scholarship based on the work in everyday interaction from different paradigms, in the continuum of the past, the present and the future, no matter which aspect, for example, liberal pluralism, interparadigmatic borrowing, mulitparadigmatic collaboration or critical dialectic (Martin and Nakayama, 1999) one takes, the critical perspective, like functionalist or interpretative perspective, must face similar fundamental questions of the intellectual inquiry. Although the critical perspective tends to be more useful in handling the ambivalence of the dichotomy thinking in the study of intercultural communication, it is still demanding more research dealing with the connections, relationalities, tensions, and contractions between the dichotomies. Moreover, other concepts, such as appropriateness, hybridity, boundary, and translation, still remain untapped in the intercultural communication study from the critical perspective. All these challenges indicate that in order to make contributions to the running river of intellectual inquiry, the critical perspective will need to continue to explain phenomena that previous paradigms were unable to explain, to provide a new research strategy or methodological procedure for gathering evidence to support the perspective, and to suggest new problems for solution in the process of intercultural communication (Kuhn, 1962).

You have been in the field for a long time, I am sure you would also like to wrap up our dialogue by showing your final comments on the intercultural communication study from the critical perspective.

STAROSTA: "We must change during the course of the rotation." As I read your earlier words, I picture the flipping of a coin. Sometimes it shows "heads," sometimes "tails," but it remains one coin, not two. You write of "harmony without uniformity." A false ontology separates one coin into differences.

My thinking, like yours, returns to writing on dialectic (e.g., Cargile, 2005; Gershenson, 2005; Martin and Nakayama, 2005) that the only way we can come to parse some cultural practice or element is by means of an implicit or explicit comparison to its contrary, to the thing in its absence, to an opposing element. As you say, for years critical scholars rejected the dichotomization of cultural knowledge into two essences, each of which was absent from the other: high or low culture, individual or collective, verbal or nonverbal cultures, touching or nontouching cultures seemed measurable, but led only towards laws and control, not toward praxis. Perhaps the rendering of scholars as oriented toward either measuring or promoting change; the belief that those on the hyphen must choose either one culture or the other; the belief in a single and essentialist location for nation and for individual identity, the belief that different research paradigms are incommensurable, all share a common weakness. Those who work from difference choose fixity over change. Intercultural communication researchers should be studying fluidity, tensions, shifting definitions and boundaries, temporary alliances across difference, or cultural morphing, and we should be on the alert for those moments when one centrism stands poised to "flip" into another.

References

Asante, M.K. (1980) Intercultural communication: An inquiry into research directions, in *Communication Yearbook, 4,* (ed. D. Nimmo), Transaction, New Brunswick, NJ, pp. 401–410.

Asante, M.K. (2007) Communicating Africa: Enabling centricity for intercultural engagement. *China Media Research,* 3 (3), 70–75.

Avant-Mier, R., and Hasian, M. (2002) In search of the power of whiteness: A genealogical exploration of negotiated racial identities in American's ethnic past. *Communication Quarterly,* 50, 391–409.

Cargile, A.C. (2005) Describing culture dialectically, in *Taking Stock in Intercultural Communication: Where to Now?* (eds W.J. Starosta and G.-M. Chen), Sage, Thousand Oaks, CA, pp. 99–123.

Chen, G.-M. (2006) Asian communication studies: What and where to now. *The Review of Communication,* 6 (4) 295–311.

Chen, G.-M. (2007) A review of the concept of intercultural effectiveness, in *The Influence of Culture in the World of Business,* (ed. M. Hinner) Peter Lang, Germany, pp. 95–116.

Chen, G.-M. (2008) Intercultural communication, in *Communication Studies,* (in Chinese), (ed. S. Lu), Ren Min University Press, Beijing, pp. 194–217.

Chen, G.-M., and Starosta, W.J. (1996). Intercultural communication competence: A synthesis. *Communication Yearbook,* 19, 353–383.

Chen, G.-M., and Starosta, W.J. (2005) *Foundations of Intercultural Communication,* University Press of America, Lanham, MD.

Chu, G.C. (1988) In search of an Asian perspective of communication theory, in *Communication Theory: The Asian Perspective,* (ed. W. Dissanayake), Asian Mass Communication Research and Information Center, Singapore, pp. 204–210.

Dissanayake, W. (2003) Asian approaches to human communication: Retrospect and prospect, *Intercultural Communication Studies,* 30 (1), 27–30.

Dissanayake, W. (2006) Postcolonial theory and Asian communication theory: Toward a creative dialogue. *China Media Research,* 2 (4), 1–8.

Drzewiecka, J.A. (2002) Reinventing and contesting identities in constructive discourses: Between diaspora and its others. *Communication Quarterly,* 50, 1–23.

Drzewiecka, J.A., and Halualani, R.T. (2002) The structural-cultural dialectic of diasporic politics. *Communication Theory,* 12, 340–366.

Du Bois, W.E.B. (1903) *Souls of Black Folk,* A.C. McClurg and Co., Chicago.

Gershenson, O. (2005) Postcolonial discourse analysis and intercultural communication: Modeling the connections, in *Taking Stock in Intercultural Communication: Where to Now?* (eds W.J. Starosta and G.-M. Chen), Sage, Thousand Oaks, CA, pp. 124–144.

Halualani, R.T. (2003) The Hawaiian diaspora: Dis/connections between home and diasporic site, *International and Intercultural Communication Annual,* 25, (ed. M.J. Collier), Sage, Thousand Oaks, CA, pp. 221–248.

Halualani, R.T. (2008) "Where exactly is the Pacific?": Global migrations, Diasporic movements, and intercultural communication. *Journal of International and Intercultural Communication*, 1, 3–22.

Hegde, R.S. (1998) Swinging the trapeze: The negotiation of identity among Asian Indian immigrant women in the United States, in *Communication and Identity across Cultures*, (eds D.V. Tanno and A. González), Sage, Thousand Oaks, CA, pp. 34–55.

Jackson, R.L. (1999) White space, white privilege: Mapping discursive inquiry into the self. *Quarterly Journal of Speech*, 85 (1) 38–54.

Jackson, R.L., and Dangerfield, C. (2002) Defining black masculinity as cultural property: An identity negotiation paradigm, in *Intercultural Communication: A Reader*, (eds L. Samovar and R. Porter), Wadsworth, Belmont, CA, pp. 120–130.

Jackson, R.L., and Heckman, S. (2002) Perceptions of White identity and White liability: An analysis of White student response to a college campus racial hate crime. *Journal of Communication*, 52, 434–450.

Jackson, R.L., Shin, C., and Wilson, S. (2000) The meaning of whiteness. *World Communication*, 29 (1), 69–86.

Kuhn, T.S. (1962) *The Structure of Scientific Revolutions*, University of Chicago Press, IL.

Lee, W.S. (1998) Patriotic breeders or colonized converts: A postcolonial feminist approach to antifootbinding discourse in China, in *Communication and Identity across Cultures*, (eds D.V. Tanno and A. González), Sage, Thousand Oaks, CA, pp. 11–33.

Martin, J.M., and Nakayama, T.K. (2005) *Experiencing Intercultural Communication: An Introduction*, McGraw-Hill, Boston, MA.

May, R. (1975) *The Courage to Create*, Bantam, Bantam.

Mendoza, S.L. (2002) *Between the Homeland and the Diaspora: The Politics of Theorizing Filipino and Filipino American Identities*, Routledge, New York.

Mendoza, S.L., Halualani, R.T., and Drzewiecka, J.A. (2003) Moving the discourse on identities in intercultural communication: Structure, culture, and resignifications. *Communication Quarterly*, 50 (3/4), 312–327.

Miike, Y. (2003) Beyond Eurocentrism in the intercultural field: Searching for an Asiacentric paradigm, in *Ferment in the Intercultural Field: Axiology/Value/Praxis*, (eds W.J. Starosta and G.-M. Chen), Sage, Thousand Oaks, CA, pp. 243–276.

Miike, Y. (2007) An Asiacentric reflection on Eurocentric bias in communication theory, *Communication Monographs*, 74 (2) 272–278.

Moon, D. (1999) White enculturation and bourgeois ideology: The discursive production of "Good (white) Girls," in *Whiteness: The Communication of Social Identity* (eds T. Nakayama and J. Martin), Sage, Thousand Oaks, CA, pp. 177–197.

Nakayama, T., and Krizek, R. (1995) Whiteness: A strategic rhetoric. *Quarterly Journal of Speech*, 81, 291–309.

Nakayama, T., and Martin, J. (eds) (1999) *Whiteness: The Communication of Social Identity*, Sage, Thousand Oaks, CA.

Park, P.S. (2002) Negotiating identity in raced and gendered workplace interactions: The use of strategic communication by African American woman senior executives within dominant culture organizations. *Communication Quarterly*, 50, 251–268.

Reich, N.M. (2002) Towards a rearticulation of women-as-victims: A thematic analysis of the construction of women's identities surrounding gendered violence. *Communication Quarterly*, 50, 292–311.

Rich, A.L. (1973) *Interracial Communication*, Barnes and Noble, New York.

Santiago-Valles, W.F. (2003) Intercultural communication as a social problem in a glo-balized context: Ethics of praxis research techniques, in *Ferment in the Intercultural Field: Axiology/Value/Praxis*, (eds W.J. Starosta and G.-M. Chen), Sage, Thousand Oaks, CA, pp. 57–90.

Shin, C.I., and Jackson, R.L. (2003) A review of identity research in communication theory: Reconceptualizing cultural identity, in *Ferment in the Intercultural Field: Axiology/Value/Praxis*, (eds W.J. Starosta and G.-M. Chen), Sage, Thousand Oaks, CA, pp. 211–240.

Starosta, W.J, and Chen, G.-M. (2000) Listening across diversity in global society: An intro-duction, in *Communication and Global Society*, (eds G.-M. Chen and W.J. Starosta), Peter Lang, New York, pp. 1–16.

Starosta, W.J., and Chen, G.-M. (2003a) "Ferment," an ethic of caring, and the corrective power of dialogue, in *International and Intercultural Communication Annual, 26*, (eds W.J. Starosta and G.-M. Chen), Sage, Thousand Oaks, CA, pp. 3–23.

Starosta, W.J., and Chen, G.-M. (2003b) On theorizing difference: Culture as centrism, in *International and Intercultural Communication Annual, 26*, (eds W.J. Starosta and G.-M. Chen), Sage, Thousand Oaks, CA, pp. 277–287.

Starosta, W.J., and Shi, L. (2007) Alternate perspectives on Gandhian communication ethics. *China Media Research*, 3 (4), 7–14.

Sun, W., and Starosta, W.J. (2006) Perceptions of minority invisibility and model minority status among Asian American professionals. *The Howard Journal of Communications*, 17 (2), 119–142.

Thayer, L. (1987) *On Communication: Essays in Understanding*, Ablex, Norwood, NJ.

Part II

Critical Dimensions in Intercultural Communication Studies

Introduction to Part II

Critical intercultural communication studies takes a cue from critical perspectives across multiple disciplines and areas of study (feminist theory, postcolonial studies, cultural studies, critical theory, queer theory, critical race theory, critical media studies, among others) to pay close attention to larger frameworks that envelop contexts, discourses, and issues. These frameworks can be thought of as key "dimensions" of interest for a critical intercultural approach, dimensions that are present in every political project but in varied form. Three key dimensions stand out prominently as focal points for critical intercultural communication studies and are featured in this next section.

The first dimension has to do with the complexities of theorizing from a critical intercultural perspective in global, transnational, indigenous, and intersectional contexts (as elucidated by Raka Shome, Kathryn Sorrells, Yoshitaka Miike, and Aimee Carrillo Rowe). Here these scholars remind of us of the unique challenge in reading, analyzing, and making sense of historically specific and politically situated (temporally, structurally) contexts and phenomena. To take external and abstract theoretical models and cases and paste these onto other contexts and examples would in many ways be an act of violence against the very spirit of critical work (to transform, transgress, and dismantle oppressive conditions of power); it would reinscribe a dominant cover that smothers the embedded voices, power interests, and takes of a community, culture, and political project. How we go about drawing insights and making conclusions, how we approach theorizing in varied contexts is a serious challenge for critical intercultural communication studies. These scholars demonstrate that rather than tacking on theory from elsewhere, the specific context should lead the way following the pace and pattern of the movement of history, economics, power interests, geopolitics, international histories, intersectional relations, and culturally specific frameworks at hand.

Another key dimension – language and its hierarchies of meanings and value – poses a significant problem for critical intercultural communication scholars with the solidifying global order of preferred languages and their valorization (and vested reproduction) on a world scale (as discussed by Yukio Tsuda) and the vast and dynamic range of interwoven meanings, differences, inequalities, and ideological remnants present within and around language forms (formal language structures, everyday talk, emergent speech codes and expressions) (as traced by Crispin Thurlow). In their provocative essays, Tsuda and Thurlow venture into terrain that intercultural communication studies has been slow to uncover: the concrete and contextually specific power moves within and around language (micro to macro) and the larger (macro) hegemonic assumptions, practices, and installments that naturalize the self-proclaimed authority and supremacy of English. Language in form, function, political effect and consequence is certainly much more than we have made it out to be; it is more than a channel, display, and system of expression separate from any structure and condition of power and influence. Language creates power and is created by power.

In the interface among culture, power, and immigration, Melissa L. Curtin provides a much needed perspective on the role of power, structural forces, and historical context in groups' cultural adjustment to the United States context. Here she challenges traditional assimilation and acculturation theoretical models by arguing for the incorporation of a critical theory of coculturation, which stands as a useful vehicle for scholars who wish to link individual factors and processes to structural and historical structures and conditions.

Finally, the dimension of historical memory captures the daunting and yet delicate challenges we face in the field of intercultural communication: to examine and uncover communication relations and meanings within historically specific and politically grounded moments and contexts. Through a focus on historical memories and knowledges, critical intercultural communication scholars are positioned well to fully interrogate cultures and intercultural communication cases through an eye on gained/naturalized power interests over time, communication discourses and identity constructions that have become reified by dominant power interests and have either been ideologically cemented or are inoculated in seemingly new forms to represent progressive change, and the struggle over cultural/ethnic/religious/political loyalties over time (which has prevailed, which is marginalized, and the negotiations among these). In their richly detailed and grounded essays, Jolanta A. Drzewiecka and Marouf Hasian demonstrate what it means to foreground historical memories and knowledges in intercultural contexts and the level and magnitude of insight and implication such analyses bring to bear on larger questions about how we remember the past given present cultural political demands and needs and the positioning (from past to present) of cultural groups within and across national and diasporic contexts. Examining the key dimensions of theorizing contexts of power, language and its constitutive and surrounding politics, and historical memories enables critical intercultural communication work to be as nuanced, contextually meaningful, illuminating, and transformative as it strives to be.

10

Internationalizing Critical Race Communication Studies
Transnationality, Space, and Affect

Raka Shome

*My point is that a strategic practice of criticism will ask whether the moment
of normalization of a paradigm is not also the moment when it is necessary to
reconstruct and reinterrogate the ground of the questions themselves through
which it was brought into being in the first place.*

David Scott (1999, p. 8).

Postcolonial Disturbances

This essay seeks to problematize the "critical" in critical intercultural communication studies, particularly, studies on race, through the framework of postcolonial
studies. In particular, it argues that the "critical" turn in intercultural communication studies, while having accomplished important tasks such as centralizing the
relationship between culture, communication, and power, remains limited in its
impulse by being largely US centered in its orientation. Critical intercultural communication studies too often reflect an approach to race that does not adequately
foreground the fact that race itself is caught in the politics of the "international;"[1]
that race is and always has been a transnational political phenomenon that is imbricated in a politics of spatiality and affectivity (although these are not the only
dimensions of a transnational framework on race). Consequently, we often find in
critical intercultural communication studies an implicit tendency to territorialize
race where race becomes synonymous with the boundaries of the nationstate.
Such a framework ends up shoring and maintaining a US centered ethos in our
understanding of race.

Before proceeding further, I want to contextualize my own position in the field
of critical "intercultural" communication studies. (I place "intercultural" within

The Handbook of Critical Intercultural Communication, edited by Thomas K. Nakayama and
Rona Tamiko Halualani. © 2010 Blackwell Publishing Ltd.

quotations because, as I discuss later, I believe the term and what it connotes is limiting for today's world. For now, I use the term to refer to a field within communication studies in order to articulate my own position within it). I position myself as a postcolonial scholar in critical intercultural communication studies. To say this differently, I am always interested in examining how larger intersecting histories and geopolitics of race, nation, and transnationality come together in the production of colonial legacies and practices – past and present. Given my own stance as a postcolonial critic, I am thus committed to investigating the cultural politics of the "international" in the articulation of racial and colonial regimes and subject positions.

In intercultural communication scholarship, "critical" intercultural studies have been largely concerned with issues of power and cultural politics – this is what the 'critical' in critical intercultural studies at one level means. What postcolonial communication studies adds to critical intercultural communication studies is that it insists on the importance of recognizing the connections between cultural power and larger geopolitical relations and international histories as they come to inform unequal power relations between different cultural groups and identities, and their practices and imaginations. Or, to say this differently, postcolonial communication studies is not just interested in studying power relations and inequities between dominant and marginal cultures; at one level it always attempts to connect and situate these inequities, and the intimacies that inform them, within depths of international histories and geopolitics as they inform interactions between cultural groups and identities (Halualani and Drzewiecka, 2002; Grossberg, 2002; Kraidy, 2002, 2005; Parameswaran, 2002, 2007; Shome, 1996, 1998, 2006a, 2006c, 2006d; Shome and Hegde, 2002). Thus, a postcolonial scholar typically remains committed to exploring the power relations of the global and their frequent colonial operations as they inform micro and macro politics of power in different historical contexts (and I use the term 'historical' broadly to mean both past and present times). This is what makes a postcolonial stance so necessary and urgent in intercultural communication studies for such a stance invites a recognition of the always already presence of geopolitical relations in any national or local context.

Riding on the wave of the "critical" turn in intercultural communication studies in National Communication Association (NCA), this essay seeks to contribute to its terrain by troubling the "critical" impulse through the framework of the "international." Put another way, this essay invites communication scholars working on race to interrogate the US centered intellectual boundaries within which we often theorize race and in doing so, end up excluding perspectives and populations (including those within the US) whose racial becoming straddles multiple (and colliding) geographies and trajectories, multiple nations and their diasporas, and multiple (and often colliding) dreams and despairs. It should be noted here that I do not suggest that there is somehow only one theoretical framework for engaging in the "international." Indeed, in the field of cultural studies today, especially with the emergence of the Association of Cultural Studies (ACS), there is an ongoing discussion about what the "international" in our theorization of culture, and in our attempts to produce cross-border knowledge, may mean (see Abbas and Erni, 2005; Ang and

Stratton, 1996; Chen, 1996; Fornas, 2010; Morris, 2006; Shome, 2009). Still, the logic of the "international" *critically* deployed is so predominantly absent in critical theorizations of race in intercultural communication in the United States that in reading the literature it almost feels at times that race is a national(ist) construct.

I have been associated in various ways with the NCA since 1992. While admittedly much has changed in terms of demographics within the association, it is still the unfortunate case however – at least for the most part – that work on race that privileges recognition in our field is usually work that speaks to US racial categories and frames of identification. If your theorizing on race and colonialism emerge from non-US worlds, you become "international." That is, unless one can be a "recognizable" minority or speak through frameworks that relate to "recognizable" US centered racial categories (Asian American, Latin American, African American, Native American, Pacific Islander) one can feel confident about constantly being on the margins or considered "international." Consider even the name of the division in NCA – Intercultural and International Communication Division. The adjoining "and" between the two terms "intercultural" and "international" is minimally dangerous; the "and" in between makes little sense (as the international is always intercultural and vice versa). In separating the two terms, we reproduce an intellectual imagination that sees the international as somehow separate from the intercultural (which in communication studies at least seems to signify work on domestic cultures).

Even today it is troubling to find how racial identities that are not US citizens are subject to all kinds of disciplining in the academy–which are sometimes benign and sometimes not so benign. Such disciplining can take various forms such as marking you for how you speak (accent), minimizing you for your very different cultural assumptions about things such as sociality and collegiality (and the construct of collegiality needs constant interrogation for it is written by US norms of sociality and professionalism); or sometimes not even bothering to sensitively reflect on whether your assumptions and practices might have anything to do with national differences – for so frozen we become in our engagements with race that we are able to conceive it only in relation to logics of US modernity; disciplining your writing style (especially if it does not reflect American trained English); in practices of employment and hiring decisions (we tend to be far more comfortable with minorities who we recognize as legitimate US minorities), and so much more.[2]

I want to also note that such disciplining does not come only from the white dominant culture; it can often come from US "minorities" themselves who, despite occupying a certain position of marginality, nonetheless are still socialized and articulated by US frameworks, and who are far better equipped (being citizens) to relate to and play by the rules of the dominant (white) culture, and who sometimes can perform a condescension towards those whose supposed "origins" are from the "third world" (a category that in reality does not exist anymore but is still resorted to in US dominant culture). Such practices of disciplining consequently result in a certain nationalization of race that is problematic. This is a nationalization that rarely acknowledges that domestic US minorities, in relation to the larger global playing field of racial and political dominance, can themselves occupy privileged positions when seen transnationally. It also rarely acknowledges that domestic minorities themselves while arguing for racial difference within the US can however also remain unreflexive about modes of cultural otherness that are related to geopolitical and historical logics that ensue from other modernities. Making a similar comment in her critique of US centered multiculturalism and identity politics, Gayatri Spivak (1999) once despairingly noted that: "I cannot comment on the ethico political agenda of silencing the critical voice of the South by way of a woman of color in the North" (p. 389). Spivak's statement succinctly captures the fact that the category "woman of color" in which so much of critical race and multicultural feminism has invested its energy in US race studies becomes somewhat meaningless unless we are willing to stretch and situate it across the macro and micro cultural, historical, spatial, temporal, and economic relations that connect and disconnect the symbolic, material, emotional, and psychic lives of human beings in unequal ways in diverse parts of the world (Shome, 2006b).

Race Troubles: Troubling US Centeredness in our Racial Lenses

If the US becomes the implicit framework in our theorizing of culture, in our relationships to each other, and in our privileging of race, then we are in trouble. We are in trouble not only because such an ethos perpetuates a problematic national/ international binary in our theorizations of culture and race, but also because: (1) we implicitly stabilize the relationship between race and nation; (2) we fail to recognize that the cultural politics of the United States – given United States' dominance in the global sphere – does not begin or end with the US; (3) we dangerously reproduce an unwitting nationalism in our scholarship; and (4) we show little interest in racial politics in other parts of the world and in doing so, reinforce an US centered introversion, insularity, and arrogance that plagues everyday living in the US.

It is this frequently unmarked US nation-centeredness in critical race communication studies that I want to trouble and disrupt, from other worlds and other modalities. My impulse to trouble race in critical intercultural communication studies arises not merely from the fact that in our discipline, as mentioned earlier, those whose "origins" are elsewhere somehow do not find legitimate and recognized points of identification in our field. There is an important sociological reason as well. There is now a growing recognition that race in the twenty-first century is in crisis. At a centuries' end and another one's beginning what race is, how we should study it, how we should teach it, and so on, needs significant rethinking, if not overhauling. Howard Winant (2004) notes that "it is no secret that much of what is taught about race is outmoded" (p. 69) and that complex dynamics of globalization have resulted in new racial formations that centralize the importance of "internationalizing" race in any discussions of it in the twenty-first century. However, Winant despairingly notes that such attempts at internationalizing race too often "disturbs and alienates more locally and nationally oriented scholars whose commitments to specific racially defined communities and to equality and justice are focused on domestic US racial conditions" (p. 72).

If our times are such that any national politics is itself an outcome of, as well as, contributes to, larger global politics (although this has been true to some extent of all times) then race studies in the US, and in particular critical race studies in communication, by retaining its focus only on domestic racial matters, ends up unwittingly domesticating race. We cannot understand, for instance, the racial politics of US immigration without connecting it to racial immigration policies in other parts of the world. Why for instance are there so many more asylum seekers in the United Kingdom than in the United States? Why is US immigration policy far more selective than that of the United Kingdom? While answering these questions is not the specific purpose of this paper, it bears mentioning nonetheless that these issues themselves are connected to divergent global histories of colonialism that have produced complex racial formations in different national contexts. These formations themselves are situated in relations of the "international." Indeed, we cannot even understand the crisis of race in the twenty-first century in the US – by which I mean the complex, unpredictable, and divergent ways in which race itself in localized in particular contexts, territories, geographies, and modalities and our frequent inadequacy to provide a vocabulary to capture such processes – without looking at racial formations in worlds beyond the United States as well.

Why for instance does a phenomenon like Katrina receive worldwide attention and funding from so many parts of the world (despite the initial neglect towards Katrina shown by the US government and the racial implications of that), but in 2002, when there were horrible Hindu-Muslim riots in Gujrat (India), and Muslims were butchered and abused in horrific ways by Hindu fundamentalists, there was little attention given to this incident in the US media as well as much of the Western world in general. Surely it is not just because Katrina was a natural disaster. Could it possibly also have anything to do with the fact that in dominant global racial and cultural radar screens, some minority bodies, given their national positioning in larger geopolitics, invite more recognition of their mistreatment by their nation-states but not others? Could it be the case that certain "historical wounds" (Chakrabarty, 2006, p. 77) and certain instances of historical negligence already function within recognizable frames of reference (this inviting humanitarian action towards them) but not others? How can we even talk about race without recognizing that the politics of race are simultaneously imbricated in a situation of unequal transnational relations – of space, visibility, and history? I cannot even remember how many times I have been told in our field that my work is "international" even though I do critical race studies but a domestic US minority scholar whose work may be focused on recognizable US racial categories is somehow a "domestic" scholar of US race studies. One does not need to beat the drums here anymore to note the troubling binary of national/international at play here, or the presence of a nationalized "common sense" through which race is categorized in critical race studies in the field of Communication in the United States.

It must be asserted here that a transnational perspective is not incommensurate with localized or nation based contexts (i.e., conceptually nation/local and the transnational are not oppositions). To examine the cultural politics of a local context does not mean that the context is outside transnational relations. Transnationality is not an abstraction. Transnational relations can only manifest themselves in situated local contexts. The issue however is how we understand the nation or the local. If in examining, say, the racial politics of the nation (say the United States), we do not adequately address how such politics itself may be an outcome of, and intersect with, larger transnational relations, then we end up reifying the nation (or the local). If however, we understand the nation (and its cultural politics) as always intersecting with larger transnational relations that may inform a particular national context in a given moment, then we end up adopting a transnational framework in our analyses. So, to say this again, a transnational perspective should not be seen as having nothing to do with the nation or the local – as it sometimes tends to be wrongly assumed. Rather, a transnational framework invites us to recognize that however local, and situated, a cultural politics might be, it is always inflected (whether we explicitly recognize it or not) by numerous connections and disconnections of the "global."

There are some other issues at stake here too, issues that become especially salient in contemporary neoliberalism as its rationalities increasingly individualize and privatize race and consequently invite us to see race in contemporary times as seemingly having little to do with structural power relations (we are 'postracial' now!). If minimally, scholarship on race is about interrogating possibilities of "freedom" from racism (Gilroy, 2004) and exploring possibilities of agency, then it must be recognized that issues such as agency and freedom are not abstractions. Or put another way, where and how one experiences agency or not has to do with the way in which one's body and identity are situated in larger transnational relations of power that always inform race in a "local" context (Shome, 2003). Consequently, the very interpretive tools and frameworks that we may use in critical race studies in communication in the United States to theorize race and racial agency clearly cannot make sense in other contexts. As obvious as this point may be, it needs reemphasizing. Unless we can also focus on how race functions in other contexts, we would end up normalizing critical and interpretive tools that remain marked by US centered logics that do not adequately connect race to power relations of the global and can therefore dangerously present those logics in ways that would suggest that their functioning is bounded by the nation. It is important to point out that what I am advocating is not a "comparative" cultural analysis. These days we tend to see a lot of endorsement of comparative cultural analysis. However, as Kaplan and Grewal (2002) have suggested, the problem with the notion of "comparative" is that it considers nations as units separate from each other, that elides the processes and power relations of geopolitical connections and disconnections that inform the nation at any given moment.

For all the above reasons, I want to trouble the "critical" in critical intercultural communication studies by crossing to a different geography – London, United Kingdom. In some ways, this paper is a product of this "crossing" (I moved to

London from the United States in 2006 after 16 years in the United States) that is transatlantic, historical, geopolitical, personal, emotional, and much more. Like all crossings, it was fluid and painful, coherent and incoherent, territorialized and deterritorialized, global and local, fraught with unlearnings and relearnings, and without a beginning and an end. In many ways the crossing through which I rethink the limits of race in US race studies in Communication is one that began long back and has travelled many maps and fields of dwelling (territorial and discursive, spatial and historical) in my life time (the British Empire, India, Middle East-Oman, Hong Kong, United States, London). It is thus constantly interrupted by many other colliding crossings and their histories that are an outcome of numerous "others" I have encountered in my multiple crossings). It is these multiple and often colliding crossings that forever force upon me the fact that the very performativity of race is geopolitical, spatial, affective, and always already transnational. Having constantly been in motion (and yet sometimes not having as much agency as I would like over the "motion") I, like many, simply cannot engage race through a boundedness in which race fits neatly with territorial, material, and discursive lines of the nation.

This essay seeks to contribute to a limited, but gradually growing, literature in critical cultural communication studies in the United States that has begun addressing the importance of recognizing that transnational connections and disconnections inform racial and cultural politics in any local/national context. In US communication studies, works of scholars (noted here not in any order of priority) such as Dilip Gaonkar, Toby Miller, Arvind Rajagopal, Michael Curtin, Angharad Valdivia, Marwan Kraidy, Radhika Parameswaran, Nitin Govil, Soyini Madison, Anandam Kavoori, Sujata Moorti, Divya McMillan, Hemant Shah, Shanti Kumar, Aswin Punathambekar, Shakuntala Rao, and Radha Hegde, among others have begun probing and theorizing such issues in various ways. Here I am mentioning scholars situated in US communication studies primarily because it is US communication scholarship that tends to be so US centered (and these scholars constitute some exceptions and are hence being noted) while communication scholars beyond the US engage in far more transnational theorizing of their cultural contexts. Further, this essay is meant to trouble the nation-centric impulses of US 'intercultural' communication studies. The recognition offered by this growing group of scholars is that the structures, flows, and regimes of the global inform the power relations of a national/local context and vice versa, such that the distinction between the national and the international does not really hold.

In what follows, there are two arguments that I will advance in order to argue for a transnational framework in our theorizing of race. First, I want to emphasize the important of a spatial perspective in theorizing race. I find the spatial turn useful in rethinking race because racial agency (itself an ever shifting category) is centrally tied to a politics of space and place. How we experience race, how we are made and unmade by race has to do with the spatial relations of race (that are also material relations) that inform a context (a place) in a particular moment. Such spatial relations I suggest are always already transnational. Second,

I want to insist on the importance of an affective dimension in theorizing race. This move follows emerging works in cultural theory that recognize affect as an important site through which to theorize the politics of culture (for instance works of scholars such as Sara Ahmed, Lawrence Grossberg, and Ann Cvetkovich among others).

From Other Worlds, Other Frames and Other Desires

Race, space, and the transnational

Race is spatialized. This is not a novel assertion to the extent that scholarship in critical geography and anthropology has for a while now argued for the importance of a spatial perspective on culture. In communication studies too, such a spatial move has been made (Conley and Dickinson, 2010; Greene, 2010; Grossberg, 1996; Hay, 2005; Shome, 2003). Far less has been written however, on the intersections of race, space, and the transnational. If we live in a time in which, due to shifts in immigration policies of so many nationstates, and flows and restrictions of bodies in transnational relations of power, new cartographies of belonging are being staged, then race, as a cartography of belonging, has to be rethought through a transnational spatial perspective. Such rethinking necessitates a recognition not only that race is contextual but what exactly the "context" of race is in a given moment is one that can only be understood by acknowledging that the context of race is always an outcome of convergences and divergences of transnational relations in a given moment. The thing is that, as many have already argued, we live in a time where "insides" and "outsides" of power cannot be clearly defined. Who is outside and who is inside systems of global power cannot be theorized through neat binaries anymore. Thus, to state that to be nonwhite is necessarily to be outside is a statement logic is anachronistic for the spatial configurations of the transnational cannot be determined in advance. The politics of the transnational is a "politics without guarantees" (to use Stuart Hall's celebrated phrase); it is a politics that has to do with one's placement in a given context of transnationality, and the relationalities that inform them...

Aihwa Ong has argues that today we are witnessing "new arrangements [of power] that cannot be accommodated by a universalizing theory of the postcolonial" (1999, p. 35). Similarly, Inderpal Grewal's (2005) recent work has advanced the notion of "transnational connectivities" (p. 14) that, in my reading, suggests the importance of examining the ways in which particular transnational relations of power connect (or not) in the production of identities, discourses, imaginations, and situated practices. Grewal (2005) has been particularly interested in the relation between biopolitics and geopolitics. She writes that

> geopolitics is not simply a matter of the international conflicts between nation-states but rather must be understood not simply, as Gearoid Tuathali has suggested, in

terms of what might be seen as "geo-power" (that is the "ensemble of technologies or power concerned with the governmental production and management of territorial space") but also in terms of how these technologies produce subjects of these territories and the means to regulate them (Grewel, 2005, p. 19).

What I am theoretically building towards is the assertion that given that race is also a biopolitical category – to understand race today, to experience what may be called the intricate intimacies of race – we have to situate race in a framework of transnational connections (or disconnections) through which to understand how race is territorialized in particular ways in a particular context; how larger geopolitics inform the biopolitics of race, which is at the same time a politics of space, territoriality, and colliding modernities.

For instance, Ong (2006) has noted how in modes of neoliberal governmentality expatriate talents constitute a form of movable entitlement. Many non-Western racial subjects, often falling under the category of "highly skilled migrants" (a category used in the Border and Immigration Agency's classification in the United Kingdom) – have far more entitlements and benefits in particular national contexts into which they move due to professional reasons, while citizens or other migrants in that same national context, considered to be of a lesser economic value to the nationstate, do not have the same kind of agency or recognition from the state. "[T]he intersection of politics of inclusion and of exclusion creates situations in which talented expatriates are incorporated as prototype ideal citizens, while low-skill migrants brought in for labor extraction are politically excluded" (Ong, 2006, p. 21). In other words, the issue to recognize here is how nationstates rewrite and manage their space and technologies of territoriality in order to make the nation more globally competitive while at the same time restage the nation through new modes of neoliberal flexibility and inflexibility that result in differential management of populations within the same racial group. In such a context, who is inside and who is outside, who belongs and who does not belong, often becomes difficult to determine simply along racial lines. It is in such a context of neoliberal management of space and articulation of populations that a discussion of race in contemporary times must be placed.

For instance, the South Asian cultural identity or space is transnationally situated; diasporic and mobile South Asian communities are found in western nations such as the United Kingdom or the United States. In these spatial contexts, we cannot theorize a South Asian identity as necessarily being an "other" in global systems of power and governmentality. To offer a brief example, technology today functions as a site or regime through which global talent flows into the West. India provides one of the largest pools of highly skilled technology migrants who are brought into these nations with high salaries and attractive perks. The spatial relations within which these migrants are situated enable them to have a sense of agency that is significantly different from other populations in the same cultural category. Securing visas and other transnational documents of passage are never a problem for this group that constitutes globally mobile technotalent. Similarly, the likes of Indian entrepreneur Laxmi Mittal situated in London – reportedly the third richest man in the world owning possibly the most expensive house in the planet – also occupy a privileged spatial relation to the nationstate (both the United Kingdom and India) and flows of globalization. Bollywood movie stars regularly "move" as it were into the space of London, hosting large events, attending Bollywood movie premiers, and shooting films, all of which bring in big revenue into the nation (both the United Kingdom as well as India).

Yet, at the same time, in London there are South Asian communities who are significantly underprivileged and occupy a very different relation with the nation – for instance, Bangladeshis on the lower rungs of society are found usually in convenience stores, ethnic food markets, or *desi* restaurants. Or there are "Asian gangs" who have become a dominant category today in the police quarters of London, and Britain more generally. The phrase "Asian gangs," a construct of the dominant culture, refers to South Asian youth engaged in unlawful activities that are portrayed by the media as being sites of "terror" or moral panics. A recent online BBC News report noted plans of Metropolitan Police to create a new unit to tackle "British Asian criminal gangs" (Choudhury, 2004). Religion complicates this scenario as well. As in the United States since 9-11, the figure of the terrorist has become synonymous with the figure of the Muslim in London. Europe especially in the last few years has witnessed a great rise in anti-Muslim sentiments and sensibilities. The controversy over the Mohammed cartoons in the Danish press was a prime example of this. Other examples include the continuous politics around "veiling." Veils are worn by many South Asian Muslim women in the United Kingdom, although not only. In 2006, former Foreign Secretary Jack Straw stated that the veil makes open communication difficult. Straw referred to the veil as constituting a "visible statement of separation and of difference." This sparked a nationwide controversy over veiling and brought to the surface the national resentment towards Muslims in the United Kingdom. In schools in Britain, controversies continue to break out over whether teachers should be allowed to wear the veil in the classroom. Most recently (in 2010), with a parliamentary committee in France recommending partial banning of the veil in public places in France, and Nicholas Sarkozy loudly declaring that the veil is "not welcome" in France, the debate in the neighboring United Kingdom has been reignited leaving many to wonder if the United Kingdom will follow in the trail of its neighbor across the channel.

In such a context, where the South Asian cultural identity (and many South Asians are Muslims) is multiply situated across unequal spatial relations that disciplines their bodies in differential and unequal ways in transnational relations of culture, it becomes difficult to theorize a South Asian cultural identity as always being an "other" without looking at larger spatial relations. The likes of Mittal and Bollywood bodies cross borders with ease because the very context – cultural and economic – through which they are articulated manifests particular spatial connections through which the territoriality of India and that of the United Kingdom come together in particular ways in the production of their own contemporary, but always linked, modernities. On the other hand, "Asian gangs" in the

United Kingdom are criminalized for often having connections to criminal activity in their own communities in India, Bangladesh, Pakistan, Sri Lanka and so forth. Their international link is subject to modes of disciplining that illustrate how the juridical powers of multiple nationstates come together in the regulation of "Asian gangs" in the United Kingdom. The larger issue is to recognize the very different ways in which diverse multiplicities within the South Asian cultural identity are diversely and unequally territorialized through different modes of "transnational connectivity" in the same nation space.

How then does one talk about a South Asian cultural identity in the United Kingdom realize of course that there is no homogenous or authentic South Asian identity but given that it is a community that is geopolitically recognized through particular frames of history, I am here using the term South Asian to refer to a particular historical group whose constitution of course is internally fractured by geopolitical complexities). Is it always an "other" in modes and spaces of colonialism in the same way? When Shilpa Shetty was subject to racism on the reality show "Big Brother," in the United Kingdom, her body, in that moment, was subject to particular modes of disciplining and violence but her transnational Bollywood "capital" over night made her a "global" star. Such stardom does not compensate for the racism. Rather, it illustrates the complex ways in which her body is "placed" in particular spatial relations of transnational connectivity and differentially navigates regimes of otherness (as she was "othered" in the context of Big Brother) as well as those of dominance (she became a global star). The argument being offered here emphasizes Doreen Massey's (2005) assertion that thinking about the spatial (and here I would say thinking about race spatially).

> in a particular way can shake up the manner in which certain political questions are formulated, can contribute to political arguments already under way, and – most deeply – can be an essential element in the imaginative structure which enables in the first place an opening up to the very sphere of the political (p. 9).

Given that London is a space of multiple modernities and their collisions, we cannot take a category such as "South Asian" in London for granted and racialize it through a homogeneous modality of "otherness." There is no guarantee today that a particular cultural identity will necessarily experience discipline and punishment, agency and freedom, in similar ways just by virtue of occupying that cultural identity.

Thus, to theorize race today is to recognize that it can be limiting to begin with race in the first place. Rather, we have to examine the ways in which neoliberal flows of globalization connect and disconnect spaces, territories, geographies and imaginaries, and how such connections differentially territorialize and deterritorialize the same cultural identity in not just unequal, but often, opposing ways. This requires an approach where we begin to examine how particular cartographies of belonging and power produce and situate a cultural identity (say a South Asian identity) in often colliding (although always intersecting) ways in regimes of neoliberalism. The site of race today itself is "multi-sited" (to use George Marcus' well known term) where the multiness is situated in a politics of global convergences and divergences that constitute a particular racial cartography in a given context.

Such an assertion invites an additional recognition that the transnational is a product of multiple and colliding modernities, and their linkages and tensions. This argument that race functions within transnational assemblages of power is not new, given the transnational move that now dominates the literature in cultural studies. What I want to argue (and through that hopefully extend the transnational move) is that too often in the literature on transnationalism, when race is considered transnationally, the analysis frequently takes on a linear dimension. That is, when transnationality is evoked in the theorization of a particular racial community, it too often takes a binary form. We tend to focus on one particular racial community and then theorize its transnational connections in relation *to one* modernity, one dominant culture, or one diasporic crossover.

For example, there is now a lot of work on South Asian cultural products crossing over to the United States and scholars have examined such issues in relation to global flows through which "South Asia" as an imaginary as well as a cultural and material practice travels to the United States. While such work has offered influential insights that have advanced transnational perspectives on race – especially in relation to the South Asian diaspora–, the limitation has been that such work has often ended up conceiving the transnational through one linkage and often through a dualism (for instance, conceiving South Asian transnationality in relation only to Anglo cultural spaces). To understand the racialized space of the transnational, to theorize the politics of cultural belonging in globalization, to map the cartographies of cultural situatedness in neoliberalism, one also has to examine the politics of a particular cultural identity (including that of its territorialization) in relation to multiple other intersecting cultural histories that have flown into the United States from 'other worlds. That is, in a given national context, the transnational relations that inform a particular cultural identity themselves are multiple and situated at the intersection of multiple modernities whether recognized or not. In the United States for example, while Indian diasporic relations are predominantly understood in relation to intersections between India and the (white) United States, the fact of the matter is that the diasporicness of Indians in the United States are forged through connections that are related not just to the white US culture but also other racial and immigrant groups, and their international histories as they circulate in and trouble the US national sphere. The point to bear in mind is that innumerable intersecting geopolitical and historical relations of diverse immigrant groups constitute the space of the Unites States and it is within this space that the diasporicness of Indians in the United States is negotiated. Paul Gilroy (2004) writes that

> simple, mechanical conceptions of racial difference now offer no plausible therapy capable of salving the visceral anxieties and pre-political concerns that speak to the currency of "race" and absolute ethnicity ... Repudiation of ... dualistic pairings –black/

white, settler/native, colonizer/colonized – has become an urgent political and moral task. Like the related work of repairing the damage they have so evidently done, it can be accomplished via a concept of *relation*. *This idea refers historians and critics of racism to the complex, tangled, profane and sometimes inconvenient forms of interdependency* (p. 42) (italics added).

This point is especially important I feel for our discipline in the United States. Too often our scholarship assumes a singular modernity or linkage in theorizations of race and diaspora. However, modernity is not singular; it is, as some scholars have been arguing for a while, multiple and colliding. It is in the spaces between these multiplicities and collisions that we often witness unpredictable convergences between geopolitics (larger structural shifts and changes in relations between nationstates) and biopolitics (the production of subjects, governance of populations, the demarcation of space and bodies). Additionally, we also witness complex racial "intimacies" produced through those convergences. I use the term intimacies here broadly to mean the everyday practices of belonging, through which our racial identities are intimately anchored in particular spatial contexts and the numerous histories and cultural groups that also constitute that context to which we remain intimately connected as well (whether recognized or not).

For instance, to understand the racial biopolitics of South Asian identity in the place of London in relation to larger transnational spatial relations, one also has to situate that identity in relation to the flows of other immigrant bodies into London in recent years and the spatial relations within which those bodies are situated, to fully understand how South Asian bodies are racialized in particular ways but not others. London today is populated by East Europeans. Polish migrant workers populate the place of London and are usually found in domestic jobs. In comparison you do not find as many South Asians in domestic jobs. You find South Asians far more in ethnic grocery stores, given the exoticism of South Asian cuisine that has simultaneously become relatively mainstream in the United Kingdom. You also find them, as noted earlier, in discourses about "youth gangs" and "Muslim fundamentalism." The famous Finsbury Park mosque in North London – which is one of London's largest mosques – has been the focus of Scotland Yard police attention for a long time as a place that potentially breeds terrorists – and terrorists today are generally associated with parts of South Asia. The mosque however serves a diverse population of Bangladeshis, Pakistanis, Algerians, and Egyptians – yet it has come into the discourse of terror in ways that that simplify the multiplicities of cultural relations that inform Mosque – both as space and place.

In a different mode, other ethnic groups such as Turkish Cypriots have a different placement in the spatial relations that make up London. For instance, Turkish Cypriots, an invisible and marginalized community, have complained about the marginalization they experience from the larger British community as well as Greek Cypriots. One focus of the complaints also has been that their mobility and ability to connect back home is restricted by the nationstate as there are no flights into North Cyprus from the United Kingdom. This is a consequence of the invasion of

Northern Cyprus by Turkey in 1974 that resulted in the isolation of Northern Cyprus by the international community. In 2007 the Turkish Cypriot community organized an online petition campaign asking Tony Blair "to support the recent application to the UK Civil Aviation Authority for direct flights between London and Ercan airport in northern Cyprus" (Northern Cypriot Community, 2007). The struggle still goes on. This is a different instance of spatial positioning of an ethnic community in London, which is the result of a different geopolitical and historical struggle than that of South Asians.

Other ethnic communities face different challenges. For example, the African Caribbean community has historically been racialized and disciplined in particular ways associated with danger and are subject to all kinds of police disciplining. The murder of Stephen Lawrence (sometimes seen as Britain's Rodney King) in 1993 by white youths, and the failed police investigation that followed pointed to serious institutional racism in the police force and sparked one of the most publicized race discussions in Britain that put the entire British justice system on public trial.

So what do these brief examples have to do with my larger argument about the racialization of South Asian body politics in connection to a relational perspective on space (Massey, 2005)? To understand the racial positioning of the category "South Asian" in London and the United Kingdom, one has to theorize its placement (itself a heterogeneous matter) in relation to the placement of *other ethnic and immigrant communities as well*. This relationality should not be conceived just as a matter of recognizing difference in relation to other immigrant communities. Rather, such a perspective requires us to confront the different historical and global power relations that inform space of London (and the United Kingdom in general) in relation to its diverse immigrant groups. For example, when I, as a person of South Asian culture, experience race, experience the space of race in London, and experience my body in that space of race, I can only do so in relation to these numerous other transnational intersections – of religion, of discourses of terror, of different immigration relations (and their underlying histories) that constitute other ethnicities, and that position those ethnic bodies in London in ways different to mine. Consequently how I experience my racial agency has to be understood not just in relation to the dominant white culture but in relation to these numerous other ethnic communities, and their colliding and intersecting histories, and the different ways in which those histories are territorialized by, and in, the nation.

Consider here also the recent instances of hostility between Asian and African-Caribbean communities in Birmingham, England. The hostility stems from many sources – particularly the anger that the African-Carribbean community feels towards Asians (who dominate the running of grocery and food stores). The fears that are often expressed by the African-Caribbean community is that "they" are taking over. Sentiments such as "we've have centuries of slavery. Now the Asians want to take over here" or "they throw change at us as if we're lower class citizens" reflect a growing resentment towards Asians in the Afro-Carribbean community (Townsend, 2005). On the other hand the Asian community replies with responses such as "we can work 16 hours a day. We pay tax. We own the shops. They're jealous" (Townsend, 2005). While the media often frames such sentiments as examples of "racism" between minority communities (mistaking racism for prejudice), the larger issue here has to do with the very different spatial relations and placements of these two communities in the space of the United Kingdom.

I want to end this section thus by reemphasizing that the study of race in communication studies must be spatialized. Race must be situated in transnational spatial relations and connections but this is not to say however that race has to be reduced to space. We need surely to avoid spatial reductionism but we do need to recognize space as a central technology of power in the constant making and unmaking of race.

Race, affect, and the transnational

The field of otherness is an affective field

In a fairly recent essay Harding and Pribram (2004) argue that "emotions have tended to be ignored or denigrated within Western philosophical and scientific traditions" (p. 863). It would be fair to say that this is true of our field as well. In our field, Grossberg has been one of the few scholars who has consistently argued for the importance of theorizing affect and emotions as sites of power (Grossberg 1992, 1996). Grossberg is widely known for having critiqued cultural studies for its overemphasis on meaning/signification and discourse at the expense of overlooking other planes of power. Explaining "affect" as a type of "psychic energy," Grossberg (1992) discusses it as "the strength of investment" (in Harding and Pribram, 2004, p. 873) "people have in their practices, identities, experiences, everyday life and so on" (Harding and Pribram, 2004, p. 873) that influences what is important to an individual, what s/he values, and the emotional intensity that structures those values. In many ways, this is an extension and reworking of Raymond Williams theory of "structures of feeling." Structures of feeling or affect are one of the ways in which power and subjectivity are articulated, reproduced, resisted, or mobilized.

Building on the moves made by scholars such as Lawrence Grossberg (1992, 1996), Sara Ahmed (2004a, 2004b), Ann Cvetkovich (1992), Jennifer Harding and Deidre Pribram (2004) I want to argue that theorizing affect is or should be important in theorizations of race. In asserting that the field of emotions/affect is political and in inviting us to recognize the relation between affect and otherness, Sara Ahmed (2004a) asks us to

> reflect on the processes whereby "being emotional" comes to be seen as a characteristic of some bodies and not others ... In order to do this, we need consider how emotions operate to "make" and "shape" bodies as a forms of actions, which also involve orientation towards others. ... [e]motions shape the very surfaces of bodies, which take shape through repetition of actions over time, as well as through orientation towards and away from others (p. 4).

Ahmed's work is particularly influential in understanding the relationship between affect and race.

Affect matters in the theorization of race, for it enables us to move beyond discursive/constructionist understandings of race that reduce it merely to significations/representations to one that enables us to probe deeper in order to address the feelings (and their structures) that shape the relation between the other and the nonother in ways that frees otherness from being a monolithic category. Such an understanding invites us to recognize that the spatial, geopolitical, and historical parameters *that produce otherness also simultaneously secure certain affective planes of belonging and nonbelonging* through such production. This consequently makes racial otherness not just a white/nonwhite issue (in Anglo dominated contexts) but something far more complex and unpredictable.

Let me explicate this further. In London I do not always "feel" like a South Asian. I "feel" like an American (and I am not suggesting that "American" is a monolithic category or that there is one "feeling" about Americanness but that there are dominant narratives of Americanness through which I, as a South Asian disporic subject who has lived in the United States for most of her adult life, have been interpellated as well). I do not always "feel" like a South Asian in London because South Asians are so easily identified with Bangladeshis and Pakistanis in the East End. To be South Asian in London is a very different experience for me than to occupy that same category in the United States. My spatial and historical positioning in the United States through which I now re-engage my postcolonial position in London makes it difficult for me to "feel" like a South Asian in London even though in the United States I always have "felt" like a South Asian (which is what I am). The feelings/emotions through which I make sense of, and invest in, my identity are themselves an outcome of a particular territorialization (in the United States) through which I am now again being reterritorialized and deterritorialized in London. The larger issue here is this: how do our spatial and geopolitical positionings secure in us particular affects through which we make sense of our identities and through that sense making produce affective responses to "others" that reinforce their social position as "others." Theorizing the relation between otherness and affect is not easy; it is not easy because it invites us to consider the planes of emotions that themselves are products of historical and geopolitical situatedness through which we secure our subjectivities and experience our identities.

For communication scholars, affect as a theoretical construct, is difficult to deal with because it is not about signification and our field is about studying signification. I argue, however, that if critical race communication studies limits itself primarily to the study of the *discourse* of race, it misses out a lot of the complexities of contemporary globalization where otherness is as much an affective field (consider the relation between "affect" and the geopolitical violence generated after 9-11 by US imperialism) as it is a discursive field.

Further, *affect is also informed by transnational relations and thinking of race as a field of affect is to think of it transnationally.* Amanda Wise and Selvaraj Velayutham (2006) advance the notion of "transnational affect." They define it as "the circulation of bodily emotive affect between transnational subjects and between subjects and symbolic fields which give qualitative intensity to vectors and routes thus reproducing belonging to and boundaries of transnational fields" (p. 3). This is an important line of thought for internationalizing critical race studies in communication. Minimally this complex statement invites us to recognize that not only are our feelings central to how we experience our racial positioning and racial spaces, but also that the affects which inform racial relations are themselves "vectors" and "routes through which racial belonging is secured in particular contexts and moments.

So, for instance, with the example of the tense racial relations between Afro–Caribbeans and Asians in Birmingham cited earlier, what informs this relationship is also a transnational affective politics. The emotions between the two groups that produce the tense racial situation have to be located in transnational relations of history and geography. The Afro-Carribbean community's history (and the affective relations that constitute that history) in relation to the United Kingdom has produced a particular placement of that community in the nationstate which is very different from Asians in the United Kingdom The emotions that drive their relationship have passed through routes and vectors of feeling that are an outcome of different modernities and the collisions of those modernities with British imperial modernity. Such collisions have shaped their history, identity, and placement in the contemporary colonial British space. Thus to adequately understand the often hostile relationship between the Afro-Caribbeans and Asians is to listen beyond the echoes of their current anger in order to hear the hauntings, feelings, dreams and despairs that histories of imperialism have suppressed in these communities but that always lurks behind the anger.

To recognize the intersection between race and affect, to recognize that race is affective, is to ask questions such as: What affects do we criminalize (and hence racialize) and what do we legitimize? How does affect function as a site of transnational connections and disconnections? The discourse of terrorism produces fear – that fear produces distance between Muslims and the rest of us. That distance, that fear, that anxiety, however has to be understood as an outcome of, contemporary geopolitics and transnational governmentality of territories and spaces that led up to 9-11 and are continuing. What today has produced the figure of the Muslim male as a site that generates fear from the public that results in all kinds of disciplining of the Muslim male body is a transnational field of collisions and connections of diverse modernities, geopolitics, histories, economies, religions, and much more. To understand the racial affects that are produced by the figure of the Muslim – hate, fear, terror – is therefore to see this affective field as a site of transnational governmentality that *territorializes* (in acts of capture of terrorists by the nationstate; through surveillance mechanisms of security through which the Muslim male body is hunted down in various nationstates) and *deterritorializes* the Muslim male body (for instance, Muslim male bodies when wrongly apprehended can often be denied entry into nations, or thrown into captivity – as in the case of Guantanamo Bay – whereby they run the risk of becoming stateless).

One might ask here the following: why should critical intercultural communication scholars be at all concerned with affect given that the topic is outside the realm of signification, and hence outside the object of our scholarship? I want to argue that the study of affect matters for communication scholars because the affective field is political. The emotions that inform the politics of culture – love, hate, disgust, fear – constitute the basis through which larger social structures are mobilized. Long before the study of affect opened up in cultural studies, Frantz Fanon in that now famous paragraph from *Black Skin, White Masks* (1991) was precisely pointing to the centrality of affect in the experience of race. In that famous and poignant paragraph where Fanon invokes a frightened white child saying to its mother "Look, a Negro ... Mama, see the Negro! I'm frightened," (pp. 111–112). Fanon was pointing to how the child's fear of his black body becomes the site through which the "corporeal schema crumbled, its place taken by a racial epidermal schema." As Fanon writes, he could no longer laugh at this fear "because I already knew that [behind it] there were legends, stories, history and above all historicity" (p. 112).[3] Our structures of communication produce affects and affects inform the politics of communication – of seeing, naming, classifying, and disciplining. Why some bodies produce fear in us have to do with how those bodies have acquired particular significations through history that invite certain affective responses towards them but not others. Thus, at one level to think of culture transnationally is also to think of it affectively.

While staying on the point of affect, but digressing a little, I want to take this opportunity (in my impulse to argue for the importance of the 'international' in our research practices) to invite scholars in the field of communication to recognize how affect functions as a political site in our academic structures. For instance, the discomfort and unease that we may feel towards colleagues from non-US countries, the feelings that may be generated in us when we hear them speaking "differently," or expressing themselves through affective norms that we in the United States are socialized to delegitimize, the confusion we may feel when we see them embracing assumptions about "professionalism" that disturb our neoliberal rationalities through which we conceive of work and the workplace, all play a big part in recognizing that structures of collegiality are not value free; they are indeed too often nationalistically situated. I have become interested in the construct of "collegiality" because *collegiality too often functions as an affective (and violent) instrument that determines how we should belong and perform ourselves in the academy.* (I also remain suspicious of attempts to normalize notions of collegiality through rigid US centered norms of sociality given that the US academy is populated by continuous transnational flows of people, ideas, and economic exchanges). Indeed, it would be worth doing a study on how US nationalism is inadvertently protected and stabilized in the US academy in the name of "collegiality."[4]

For instance, in some South Asian cultures – people are socialized to express their emotions far more than in US cultures; in many Asian cultures, notions of privacy are culturally different than in the United States. Consequently, one may find Asian colleagues to be far more chatty and direct (and I am particularly thinking of South Asian – and in particular– Indian cultures). US colleagues, potentially evaluating such intercultural encounters through their tight normative framework of privacy, civility, and "professionalism" may find that to be strange. I myself have some experience of this. When I first entered the United States, I used to be quite surprised to see how notions of friendship and their normative frameworks differed from my own culture. Having been raised in India, we have always quite easily revealed ourselves (as that is valued in friendship) to "friends;" we are chatty with acquaintances as that is seen as being friendly. In the United States it took me a while to recognize that Americans do not reveal themselves too easily – even to "friends" (and there always seems a need to "put on a happy face" and show all is going fine) and that despite the filmsy façade of American friendliness, pleasantries, and confidence, there is always such a need not to reveal oneself too much (and yet ironically an entire commercial industry of talk shows have based their business on trivial confessionals). If you are "chatty" with acquaintances, or show your emotions easily, you can be misunderstood as not being "professional." As I have recently argued (Shome, 2009), those from other modernities who may function out of different affective structures and express themselves through affective norms that defy or challenge the rigid and repressive affective order of the US academy, too often can find themselves labeled through affective constructs such as "uncivil," "emotional," "angry" or "strange". Feminist scholars have long made the argument that women and minorities find themselves constructed in such ways in the academy. I argue that international scholars in the US academy find themselves to be the subject of even more intense affective disciplining – given the lack of awareness or interest that US born academics often tend to have about other cultures and their affective expressions and norms.

If the discipline of communication is truly interested in internationalizing itself in a *critical* manner, it must pay attention to the affective norms through which we discipline bodies, identities, speaking, and professional styles, of those from other modernities in our academic contexts. Instead of just marking how those from other modernities "feel" to us, what affects they provoke in us (for instance discomfort,) we need to flip the scenario and ask how American scholars and the affective structures of the US academy *seem to "them"*? (Much could be said about how the American academy may seem to colleagues from "other worlds"). What affects are produced in scholars from other modernities inhabiting the space of the US academy when they experience the nationcentric norms of the US academy? Indeed, this would truly be a moment of a critical transnational reflection where we begin not from the United States but from other modernities looking into the US academy.

The larger point is that it is important to recognize that the academy is a highly politicized transnational affective field through which a community and its norms of performance are enabled. Paying attention to what emotions and affects from other modernities we permit in the academy, what meanings we give to them, becomes an ethical responsibility if we are to reflexively forge a transnational community of scholars committed to the process of understanding and challenging the violent communicative structures that shape our world today. If international scholars find themselves affectively disciplined in the tight spaces of the US academy, then we will be perpetuating an affective global field that dominates the world today, especially after 9-11, in which increasingly US sentiments and feelings about the world are being made to count while other feelings, other emotions, other expressions and other longings are simply hunted and chased out in the name of civility and "clash of civilizations." I end with an invitation to US situated scholars in our field to reflect on the politics of affective disciplining in the academy, in our structures of collegiality, in our norms of sociality, and in our professional practices as we critically engage with the "international" – the international body and its affects and emotions.

Notes

1 I place "international" within quotation marks because the "international" itself is a complicated category. That is, to be ' "international" is not to resort to a territorial linear additive logic of the world; one can be "international" even while focusing on a local context. The internationalizing efforts advocated in this essay have to do with uneven global power relations as they inform local contexts and vice versa. My use of the quotation marks around the term "international" invokes this complexity of the international and refuses a simplistic spatially linear notion of it, or a notion that simplistically sees it in a neat binary relation with the nation. Whether we acknowledge it or not "international" relations always inform any particular national/local context and vice versa.

2 For a provocative discussion of academic practices and protocols in a different context, I invite readers to also look at the work of Meaghan Morris, especially 2005.

3 In a different context, Sara Ahmed (2004a) also offers a very provocative discussion of this famous section in Fanon's work in order to theorize the relationship between the politics of fear and race.

4 I have engaged in an elaborate discussion of some of these issues in Shome (2009).

References

Abbas, A., and Erni, J. (2005) Introduction: Internationalizing cultural studies, in *Internationalizing Cultural Studies*, (eds A. Abbas and J. Erni), Blackwell, Malden, MA, pp. 1–12.

Ahmed, S. (2004a) *The Cultural Politics of Emotion*, Edinburgh University Press, Edinburgh.

Ahmed, S. (2004b) Affective economies. *Social Text*, 22 (20), 117–139.

Ang, I., and Stratton, J. (1996) On the impossibility of a global cultural studies, in *Stuart Hall: Critical Dialogues in Cultural Studies*, (eds K. Chen and D. Morley), Routledge, New York, pp. 361–391.

Chakrabarty, D. (2006) History and the politics of recognition, in *Manifestos for History*, (eds K. Jenkins, S. Morgan and A. Munslow), Routledge, New York, pp. 77–87.

Chen, K. (1996) Not yet the postcolonal era: The (super) nation-state and the transnationalism of cultural studies: Response to Ang and Stratton. *Cultural Studies*, 10, 37–70.

Choudhury, B. (2004) Scotland Yard tackles Asian crime gangs, June 15, http://news.bbc.co.uk/2/hi/uk_news/3808165.stm (accessed May 18, 2010).

Conley, D., and Dickinson, G. (2010) Textural democracy. *Critical Studies in Media Communication*, 27 (1), 1–7.

Cvetkovich, A. (1992) *Mixed Feelings*, Rutgers University Press, New Brunswick.

Fanon, F. (1991) *Black Skin, White Masks*, New York: Grove Press.

Fornas, J. (2010) Continents of cultural studies-unite in diversity! Comparing Asian and European experiences. *Inter-Asia Cultural Studies*, 11 (2), 214–220.

Gilroy, P. (2004) *Postcolonial Melancholia*, Columbia University Press, New York.

Greene, R. (2010) Labor, location and transnational literacy. *Critical Studies in Media Communication*, 27 (1), 105–110.

Grewal, I. (2005) *Transnational America*, Duke University Press, Durham.

Grossberg, L. (1992) *We Gotta Get Out of This Place*, Routledge, New York.

Grossberg, L. (1996) *Dancing In Spite of Myself*, Duke University Press, Durham.

Grossberg, L. (2002) Postscript. *Communication Theory*, 12 (3), 367–370.

Hay, J. (2005) Between cultural materialism and spatial materialism: James Carey's writing about communication, *in Thinking with James* Gray, (eds. C. Robertson and J. Packer), Peter Lang, New York, pp. 29–55.

Halualani, R., and Drzewiecka, J. (2002) Structural-cultural dialectic of diasporic politics. *Communication Theory*, 12 (3), 340–366.

Harding, J., and Pribram, D. (2004) Losing our cool. *Cultural Studies*, 18 (6), 863– 883.

Kaplan, C., and Grewal, I. (2002) Transnational practices and interdisciplinary feminist scholarship: Reconfiguring women's and gender studies, in *Women's Studies on Its Own*, (ed. R. Wiegman), Duke University Press, Durham, pp. 66–81.

Kraidy, M. (2002) Hybridity in cultural globalization. *Communication Theory*, 12 (3), 316–339.

Kraidy, M. (2005) *Hybridity, or the Cultural Logic of Globalization*. Temple University Press, Philadelphia.

Massey, D. (2005) *For Space*, Sage, Thousand Oaks, CA.

Morris, M. (2005) Humanities for taxpayers: Some problems. *New Literary History*, 36, 111–129.

Morris, M. (2006) Chair's letter. *Newsletter of the Association of Cultural Studies*, vol. 3.

Northern Cypriot Community (2007) www.embargoed.org/press_releases (last accessed March 15, 2008).

Ong, A. (1999) *Flexible Citizenship*, Duke University Press, Durham.

Ong, A. (2006) *Neoliberalism as Exception: Mutations in Citizenship and Sovereignty*, Duke University Press, Durham.

Parameswaran, R. (2002) Local culture in global media. *Communication Theory*, 12 (3), 287–315.

Parameswaran, R. (2007) The other side of globalization: Communication, culture, and postcolonial critique. *Communication, Culture, and Critique*, 1 (1), 116–125.

Scott, D. (1999) *Refashioning Futures: Criticism after Postcoloniality*, Princeton University Press, Princeton, NJ.

Shome, R. (1996) Postcolonial interventions in the rhetorical canon: An "other" view. *Communication Theory*, 6 (1), 40–59.

Shome, R (1998) Caught in the term "postcolonial": Why the "postcolonial" still matters. *Critical Studies in Mass Communication*, 15 (2), 203–212.

Shome, R. (2003) Space matters: The power and practice of space. *Communication Theory*, 13 (1), 39–56.

Shome. R. (2006a) Interdisciplinary research and globalization. *Communication Review*, 9, 1–36.

Shome, R. (2006b) Transnational feminism and communication studies. *Communication Review*, 9, 255–267.

Shome, R. (2006c) Challenges of international women of color in the United States: The complicated "rights" of belonging in globalization, in *Social Justice and Communication Scholarship*, (ed. O. Swartz), Lawrence Erlbaum, Mahwah, NJ, pp. 105–126.

Shome, R. (2006d) Thinking through the diaspora: Call centers, India, and a new politics of hybridity. *International Journal of Cultural Studies*, 9 (1), 105–125.

Shome, R. (2009) Postcolonial reflections on the "internationalization" of cultural studies. *Cultural Studies*, 29, 694–719.

Shome, R., and Hegde, R. (2002) Postcolonial approaches to communication: Charting the terrain, engaging the intersections. *Communication Theory*, 12 (3), 249–270.

Spivak, G. (1999) *A Critique of Postcolonial Reason*, Harvard University Press, Cambridge, MA.

Townsend, M. (2005) Blacks complain of Asian racism. October 30, www.majorityrights.com/index.php/weblog/comments/blacks_complain_of_asian_racism (accessed May 18, 2010).

Winant, H. (2004) *The New Politics of Race: Globalism, Difference, Justice*, University of Minnesota Press, Minneapolis.

Wise, A., and Velayutham, S. (2006) Towards a typology of transnational affect. Centre for Research on Social Inclusion, Working paper, 4, Marquarie University.

11

Re-imagining Intercultural Communication in the Context of Globalization

Kathryn Sorrells

Today, our world is "home" to nearly 7 billion people. Increasingly, we – the 7 billion people of the globe – find our everyday lives, our work, and our wages, as well as our identities and imaginations interconnected and interdependent. In the past 30 years, revolutionary changes in communication and transportation technologies have coalesced with neoliberal economic and political policies to dramatically accelerate the interaction and inter-relationship among people from different ethnic and racial cultures, religious cultures, class cultures, and different national and regional cultures around the world (Appadurai, 1996; Grewal, 2005; Yúdice, 2003). Deeply rooted in the history of colonization, the forces of globalization have catapulted people, symbolic forms, practices and ideas from different cultures into shared and contested physical and virtual spaces in homes, relationships, schools, neighborhoods, the workplace and in political alliance and activism in unprecedented ways.

Globalization is a complicated and contested concept with multiple and layered meanings, which is understood and experienced in a broad array of ways by individuals and groups with different interests, positionalities and points of view. While the term "globalization" came into common usage in the, 1990s to describe our rapidly changing world, the various factors and forces that constitute and shape globalization have been in play for a much longer time (Nederveen Pieterse, 2004). Synthesizing various perspectives (Appadurai, 1996; Inda and Rosaldo, 2002; Stiglitz, 2002), I define *globalization* as the complex web of economic, political, and technological forces that have brought people, cultures, cultural products, and markets, as well as beliefs, practices and ideologies into increasingly greater proximity to and con/ disjunction with one another within inequitable relations of power. The word "globalization" is used here to address both the *contested processes* that contribute to and the vastly *inequitable conditions* of living in our contemporary world.

The Handbook of Critical Intercultural Communication, edited by Thomas K. Nakayama and Rona Tamiko Halualani. © 2010 Blackwell Publishing Ltd.

In this chapter, I draw attention to the context of globalization and reveal the distinctly complex, contradictory, and inequitable conditions in which intercultural communication occurs today. I propose four areas of focus to re-imagine the study and practice of intercultural communication to address both the harsh challenges and the creative possibilities inherent in our contemporary global context. I begin by sketching out the theoretical foundations, assumptions, and unique perspective offered by a critical approach for re-imagining the study of intercultural communication in the context of globalization. Then, several scenarios are introduced to provide the background and exigency for situating intercultural communication in the context of globalization and employing a critical perspective. To address the complex, contradictory and contested nature of the global context, I elaborate four areas of focus to re-imagine the practice and study of intercultural communication. The chapter culminates with a brief discussion of intercultural praxis, which integrates the four areas of focus as we re-envision intercultural communication in the context of globalization.

Foundations and Assumptions

The proposal to re-imagine intercultural communication in the context of globalization is grounded in and informed by cultural studies (Appadurai, 1996; Tomlinson, 1999; Winant, 2001), postcolonial (Said, 1978; Spivak, 1988; Young, 2001) and feminist theories (Alexander and Mohanty, 2003; Butler, 1993; hooks, 1992), as well as research on globalization from various disciplinary perspectives (Inda and Rosaldo, 2002; Nederveen Pieterse, 2004; Stiglitz, 2002; Yúdice, 2003), studies on transnationalism and migration (Grewal, 2005; Ong, 1999; Smith and Guarnizo, 2006; Toro-Morn and Alicea, 2004) and critical pedagogy (Freire, 1998; McLaren and Farahmandpur, 2004). This transdisciplinary approach complements existing critical research in communication studies and intercultural communication as referenced throughout the chapter.

In re-imagining intercultural communication in the context of globalization, I assume an overtly critical and "political" perspective as it is not possible to take a neutral, disinterested position in talking and theorizing about or engaging in intercultural communication. Every participant in an intercultural interaction, every cultural text, or cultural product that is read or consumed and every attempt to enact and theorize interpersonal and intergroup interactions, relationships, identities, alliances, and conflicts is situated in particular historical, social, economic, and political contexts; consequently, we cannot remove ourselves from the convergence of conditions and forces that constitute our lives and intercultural relations in the context of globalization (Collier *et al.*, 2001; Shome and Hegde, 2002a). Similarly, I assume a posture of examination and critique regarding the context and consequences of theory making and knowledge construction/production. The field of intercultural communication is rooted in Western, White perspectives, colonial modes of thinking and imperial knowledge production (Asante, 1987; Miike, 2003; Mendoza, 2005). Masking these underpinnings obscures the role power plays in processes of representation and the construction of knowledge as well as how the intercultural field continues to serve neocolonial and imperialist interests.

Additionally, aligning with foundational assumptions from critical approaches, I challenge the false dichotomy of theory and activism by pairing critical knowledge construction with informed action for social change. Broome *et al.* (2005) envision the intercultural field taking an "activist turn" that links our scholarly efforts with "action that attempts to make a positive difference in situations where people's lives are affected by oppression, domination, discrimination, racism, conflict, and other forms of cultural struggle due to differences in race, ethnicity, class, religion, sexual orientation, and other identity markers" (p. 146).

Therefore, taking a critical intercultural perspective means that I must situate my understanding of and actions regarding intercultural communication within an interconnected web of social, political, economic, and historical contexts. Intercultural communication does not occur in a vacuum outside relationships of power. Whether in interpersonal, group, community, organizational, or nationstate interactions, uneven power relations, historically constituted and constantly renegotiated, frame and inform intercultural communication. For me, making structural inequities explicit, revealing how institutional and discursive systems work to advantage some and disenfranchise others and emphasizing the complex and contradictory nature of our positionalities in different contexts is crucial. It is also vital to highlight the full human agency of individuals and groups who negotiate inequities, making choices even when options are limited and who create meaningful lives in the midst of devastating conditions. I encourage us all to challenge the tendency to reduce the complexity of actors in the global context to simplistic categories of victims, heroes, demons, or saviors. Several questions emerge as pivotal from a critical intercultural perspective: First, who benefits materially and symbolically from existing relations of power and who is served by how we make sense of inequitable power arrangements? Second, how are current inequities linked to colonial, postcolonial and imperial conditions? Third, what role can each of us play within our spheres of influences to challenge inequities and create a more socially just world? Conscious of the how knowledge construction in the field of intercultural communication can serve white, male, heteronormative, Western, colonial, and imperialist agendas, I strive to engage in scholarly, pedagogical and community processes and practices that not only challenge and resist hegemony but proactively create spaces for inclusive coproduction of knowledge and collaborative activism. Thus, this chapter on re-imagining the field of intercultural communication is an invitational gesture to engender critical insight, scholarly self-reflection, and innovative alternatives and to motivate individual and collective action towards social justice.

Intercultural Communication in the Context of Globalization

The frequent and multidirectional movement of capital, commodities, services, information, labor, and ideologies in the context of globalization are driven by shifts in international economic policies and global political governance that have taken place since World War II and that have accelerated dramatically since the 1980s (Stiglitz,

2002). Economic liberalization, also known as "free" trade, is the cornerstone of neoliberalism. Neoliberalism is based on government deregulation, a shift of responsibility from the public sector to individuals and the privatization of public space, issues, industries, and resources (Harvey, 2005). Characterized by a growth in multinational corporations, an intensification of international trade and international webs of production, distribution, and consumption and the displacement of hundreds of thousands of people from their homes, jobs, and countries, neoliberal globalization has exponentially increased and dramatically impacted intercultural interactions worldwide. As anthropologists Jonathan Xavier Inda and Renato Rosaldo (2002) claim, "it is a world of culture in motion. It is a world where cultural subjects and objects – that is, meaningful forms such as capital, people, commodities, images, and ideas – have become unhinged from particular localities" (p. 11). Culture, in the context of globalization, is de-territorialized, where cultural subjects (people) and cultural objects (film, food, traditions and ideas) are uprooted from their "situatedness" in particular physical, geographic locations and re-territorialized, or re-inserted in new, multiple and varied geographic localities (Appadurai, 1996).

In the context of neoliberal globalization, wealth concentration has intensified and economic inequity exacerbated both within and across nations resulting in vastly disparate access to resources and deepening racial inequities (Toro-Morn and Alicea, 2004). Today, 15% of the people on our planet wake up each morning assured of instantaneous communication with others around the globe (Wellman and Haythornthwaite, 2002), while more than 50% of the world's population lives below the internationally defined poverty line, starting their day without the basic necessities of food, clean water, and shelter (United Nations, 2004). In an era of instant messages and global communication, about, 1 billion or, 26% of the adult population worldwide do not have the skills to read and write (UNESCO, 2006). Today, for every dollar an average white family owns in the United States, the average family of color has less than a dime, magnifying the racial wealth gap accrued from centuries of discriminatory and exclusionary laws and practices (Lui *et al.*, 2006). In our global context, families, friends, migrants, tourists, business people, and strangers come closer together more rapidly than ever before in the history of human interaction; yet, some have the privilege of experiencing intercultural interactions through leisure, recreation, and tourism, while other people travel far from home out of economic necessity and basic survival. Indeed, we live in a world in motion–propelled, disrupted, inspired, and constrained by powerful forces. Globalization has dramatically altered the context for understanding, theorizing and engaging in intercultural communication. In each scenario below, consider how the context of globalization shapes intercultural interactions and the various trajectories of the imagination needed to understand, theorize, and act responsibly in the global context.

Scenario one

In the hallway of a university in Southern California, three students – Immaculee who immigrated to the United States from Rwanda 17 years ago, Hamza, an international student from Morocco, Cathy, who came to the United States four years ago from France – spend the 15 minute break during their intercultural communication class talking with each other in French. They relish the comfort of speaking a language of "home," negotiating an intercultural relationship and alliance, however unlikely and transitory.

Scenario two

In 1989, laborers – primarily men – began traveling from the small town of Villachuato in Michoacán, Mexico to work in a meatpacking plant in Marshalltown, Iowa, United States. As economic conditions in Mexico worsened, larger numbers made the 3000 mile trek to *el norte* and by the late, 1990s, more than half of the employees at the third largest pork processing plant in the world were Latinos. Tensions between Anglos and Latinos flared when the plant was raided by the Immigration and Naturalization Service (INS) with the knowledge of plant supervisors and undocumented workers were deported. Efforts to build sustainable relations between the two communities improved when Marshalltown community leaders, the chief of police and others visited Villachuato (Grey and Woodrick, 2002).

Scenario three

Amitabh Bachchan, internationally revered Indian film star says, "When I first went to Moscow for the first time, I was received by Russian female fans, who were actually dressed in our Indian dress and wore the bindi and the jewelry and everything, and spoke Hindi … and said that they were going to university to study the language so they could follow our films. Remarkable" (Rose, 2005)

Scenario four

Environmentalists, human rights and labor activists, indigenous groups, students, religious groups, farmers, union workers, and teachers were among the 40 000 people from around the globe who converged on Seattle in November, 1999 to protest against the third meeting of the World Trade Organization (WTO). The *Washington Post* describes the protesters: "What they all seem to agree on is that giant corporations have gone too far in gaining control over their lives and defining the values of their culture" (as quoted in Maass, 2005, p. 111)

Scenario five

Filipina American, Grace Ebron recalls, "I arrive at the Rome Airport, thrilled at the notion of living in Italy. As I step out of the customs hall, I immediately see my boyfriend, waiting to meet me. His parents, whom I've never met, are with him and as I turn to them with my perfectly-rehearsed Italian greeting, they appear very confused. 'No- no' they stammer, a perplexed expression on their faces. They turn to Massimo: 'But where is your girlfriend – the American? Why did she send the maid?'" (Ebron, 2002)

The scenarios illustrate the dynamic, dis/placed, hybrid and contested nexus of peoples, cultures, markets, and relationships of power that are, on the one hand, deeply rooted in colonial histories and discourses and yet, are re-configured and re-articulated in the context of globalization. Cultural subjects – international students, immigrants, migrant workers, corporate managers, INS officers, residents, activists and tourists – and cultural objects – the dress, dance, language, and music from Indian Hindi films – coalesce and collide in unprecedented ways producing spaces of agency, resourcefulness, and alliance as well as tensions, contestations, and conflicts. These intercultural interactions are situated locally in particular spaces and are simultaneous closely linked to and yet dislocated from particular places globally; the interactions are enmeshed in contemporary circumstances while also inextricably coupled with historical conditions. Multiple contexts intersect, layer, clash, and inform each other as temporal and spatial dimensions are traversed and compressed in the context of globalization. The vignettes point to the ways people who are positioned very differently in terms of cultural, racial, national, economic, and linguistic power – material and symbolic forms of power within highly inequitable systems – are engaging with and consuming each others' cultural forms, ideologies and identities, developing relationships and struggling through conflicts, building alliances, as well as laboring with and for each other in the context of globalization.

Far from their "homes" of origin, Immaculee, Hamza and Cathy find themselves relating through a common language, connected and yet positioned quite differently in the United States and in the world today based on the politics of race and religious affiliation that link and yet reconfigure current geopolitics with colonial histories. Transmigrants cyclically cross borders of place, culture, status, and language, propelled by the forces of neoliberal globalization between their homes in Michoacán and Iowa. In postmodern moments of pleasure and power, women in Russia consume, appropriate, and perform an Indian "other." As fans around the world stay up to date on Amitabh Bachchan's latest public appearance through online websites, remarkably, very few people in the United States outside the India and Indian-American communities even know who Amitabh Bachchan is. Protests against the WTO in Seattle in, 1999, and later in Prague, Quebec City, Geneva, and Hong Kong highlight the structural inequities in global power and control as well as the unlikely yet increasingly common intercultural alliances forming in the context of globalization. Grace Ebron, excited to reconnect with her Italian boyfriend, benefits from her US citizenship, which affords her global mobility; yet, she is confronted with stereotypes and racialized assumptions that intertwine colonial histories with the current exportation of Filipina laborers to Italy as part of a development policy.

Clearly, our current context – the context of globalization – has dramatically altered the conditions that enable, constrain and constitute intercultural communication. As the scenarios above suggest, the context of globalization is characterized by an intensification of intercultural interaction and exchange in an increasingly dynamic, mobile world. Changes in economic and political policies, governance and institutions have escalated global intercultural interdependence ushering in an era of shared interests, needs and resources as well as tensions and conflicts. Intercultural and transnational alliances are occurring more frequently than ever before due to greater proximity and advanced technologies; yet, interdependence has also intensified intercultural, interethnic, interracial and international tensions and conflicts. The forces of globalization have magnified inequities within and across nationstates exacerbating already existing injustice that limit and exclude access to education, jobs, services, and opportunities. Increased disparities serve to structure and bind intercultural relationships in terms of power, privilege, and positionality, where, for example, the wealthy classes across national boundaries may have more in common with each other than they do with those who live in the same metropolitan area. Finally, injustice forged through colonization, Western domination, and US hegemony, while re-configured, continues to define and shape intercultural relations today. Yet, in the context of globalization, although dominant, the "West" and the United States are not by any means the only centers of economic, political and cultural production, and power (Ong, 1999; Shome and Hegde, 2002b). To make sense of, address and theorize about the complex, contradictory, and increasingly inequitable context of globalization, we need to utilize critical perspectives and activate our creative potential to re-imagine the study and practice of intercultural communication.

Re-imagining Intercultural Communication in the Context of Globalization

I propose four key areas for re-imagining intercultural communication in the context of globalization. First, we need to *revisit and expand our definitions of culture*. Second, we must *make visible the continuities as well as disjunctures between historical and contemporary patterns of interaction, institutional control and representational power*. Multifocal vision that attends to both the legacy of colonization, Western domination, and US hegemony as well as non-Western hegemonies and emerging centers of capital and cultural production is required. Third, the *links between the local and the global, forming interconnected yet fragmented and fractured webs in the global context, need to be drawn and underscored* with particular consideration to the interplay among micro, meso and macro levels of interaction. Finally, we need to *ground the study and practice of intercultural communication in critical engagement, democratic participation, and social justice*. While addressed separately in the discussion here, the four areas of focus are all inter-related and necessary to re-imagine intercultural communication in the context of globalization.

Redefining Culture

While traditional anthropological definitions used in intercultural communication define culture as a system of shared meanings, cultural studies perspectives, informed by Marxist theories of class struggle and exploitation, view culture as a site of contestation where meanings are constantly negotiated (Grossberg, Nelson and Treichler, 1992). This definition reveals how culture can function as a form of hegemony, or domination through consent, as articulated by Italian Marxist theorist Antonio Gramsci (1973). Hegemony operates when the goals, ideas, and interests of the ruling group or class are so thoroughly normalized, institutionalized, and accepted that people consent to their own domination, subordination, and exploitation. Cultural studies theorists argue that individuals and groups have the potential to challenge, resist, and transform meanings in their subjective, everyday lives. Fiske (1992) states, "The social order constrains and oppresses people, but at the same time offers them resources to fight against those constraints" (p. 157) noting that individuals and groups are consumers and producers of cultural meanings and can act in counter-hegemonic ways. Culture, then, is the "actual, grounded terrain" of everyday practices, representations, discourses, and institutions where meanings are produced, consumed, negotiated, and contested (Hall, 1997).

Given that culture today is inextricably linked to community, national, international and transnational economies and politics, American Studies scholar George Yúdice (2003) defines culture in the age of globalization as a resource. In the, twenty-first century, culture is a resource for economic and political exploitation, agency and power, which is mobilized and instrumentalized for a wide range of purposes and ends. Culture, in the form of symbolic goods such as movies, music and tourism as well as intellectual property, is increasingly a source of global trade and a resource for economic growth. Mass culture industries in the United States are the major contributor to the Gross National Product (Yúdice, 2003). Culture is also targeted for exploitation by capital in the media, consumerism, and tourism. As products are modified and marketed to cultural groups, cultural group differences are constituted and transnational identities constructed (Grewal, 2005). Cultural products, such Hindi and US films and hip hop culture, are commodified and appropriated functioning in complex and contradictory ways as sites of cultural remembrance, economic exploitation, and as locations of enunciation, empowerment, and opposition (Ram, 2004; Rose, 1994; Shome and Hegde, 2002a). While the commodification of culture is not new, the extent to which culture is "managed" as a resource for its capital generating potential and as a "critical sphere for investment" by global institutions such as the World Bank is new (Yúdice, 2003, p. 13).

In the context of globalization, culture is also utilized as a resource to address and solve social problems like illiteracy, addiction, crime, and conflict. Culture is used today discursively, socially, and politically as a resource for collective and individual empowerment, agency, and resistance. Diasporic groups and transmigrants engage and dispute collective cultural identities as they negotiate "homes" of familiarity, spaces of belonging and sites for the formation of resistance, agency, and political empowerment (Drzewiecka, 2002; Halualani, 2002; Mendoza, 2002; Shome and Hegde, 2002a). As illustrated in the scenarios, culture is a resource for Hamsa, Cathy and Immaculee in terms of their language use and their shared yet contested histories; culture is a negotiated site in their relational positionalities in the United States, their alliance building, and their linked yet asymmetrical colonial pasts. In the cultural media marketplace, culture is a resource for exploitation and potentially alliance in the performance of Indian identities by Russian women. As transmigrants from Michoacán, Mexico struggle for their right to survive, they draw on culture as a resource for collective economic and social agency and political mobilization. Today, in the context of globalization, "the understanding and practice of culture is quite complex, located at the intersection of economic and social justice agendas" (Yúdice, 2003, p. 17). Redefining culture from a cultural studies perspective and re-conceptualizing culture as a resource that is exploited, mobilized, engaged, and disputed enables us to grapple with the multifaceted economic, political, and social dis/junctures of intercultural communication in the context of globalization.

Role of History and Power

Martin and Nakayama (1999, 2000) and others have called attention to the importance of situating intercultural communication within historical contexts and relations of power. The broad historical context of the past 500 years of colonization, Western imperialism, and US hegemony, which includes the anti-colonial and independence struggles, the Civil Rights movements and the alter-globalization movements are critical for understanding intercultural communication today; yet, the conditions of globalization also require simultaneous attention to new and reconfigured sites of economic, political, and cultural power (Shome and Hegde, 2002a; Wallerstein, 2000). For example, we cannot make sense of the patterns of south to north migration today from former colonies to centers of imperial power without placing globalization within the broader context of colonization; yet, while migrants' experiences vary tremendously based on their differential access to capital, they serve global capitalist interests. We cannot understand the impact on intercultural relations of "free" trade policies and the outsourcing of jobs by more developed, powerful, and wealthier nations to less developed, less powerful, and poorer nations today without recognizing how these policies and practices re-articulate a twenty-first century version of the exploitation of labor that built and consolidated the economic wealth and political power of Europe and the United States during the colonial period (Shome and Hegde, 2002b); yet, we cannot ignore that elites in less politically powerful and economically strong countries promote and benefit from these practices. We cannot begin to grapple with the intercultural challenges faced by societies around the world today – racial and ethnic discrimination, tension and conflict, intensified economic inequity as well as disputes over immigrant rights and immigration policies – without recognizing how these struggles are embedded in and structured by racist, classist, white supremacist, patriarchal, heteronormative, and ethnocentric ideologies forged and institutionalized through the last 500 years of colonization, Western imperialism and US hegemony; yet, we also cannot disregard how these categories of difference are re-configured in the global context (Shome and Hegde, 2002a; Winant, 2001).

In each of the five scenarios presented earlier, history plays a foundational and yet nuanced role in shaping the assumptions, meaning-making processes and actions in the intercultural interactions. Relations of power established, negotiated, and historically contested continue to structure economic and political conditions in the current global context. Today, the notion of "race" as a biological concept has been thoroughly discredited (Graves, 2005); yet, sociologist Howard Winant (2001) notes:

> Race has been fundamental in global politics and culture for half a millennium. It continues to signify and structure social life not only experientially and locally, but national and globally. Race is present everywhere: it is evident in the distribution of resources and power, and in the desires and fears of individuals from Alberta to Zimbabwe. Race has shaped the modern economy and nationstate. It has permeated all available social identities, cultural forms, and systems of signification. Infinitely incarnated in institution and personality, etched on the human body, racial phenomena affect the thought, experience, and accomplishments of human individuals and collectives in many familiar ways, and in a host of unconscious patterns as well (p. xv).

The racial signification system that marks Grace Ebron's body as "non-white" and consequently, in the eyes of future mother-in-law, not American, is a legacy of colonization; Grace's family migratory history and experiences as a US citizens are only fully intelligible when the history of US imperialism and neocolonial relations of power with the Philippines are considered; her future mother-law's ascription of her identity as "the maid" can only be understood in the context of current economic labor agreements that echo colonial and imperial labor migration patterns; Grace's relationship with her fiancé, Massimo is enmeshed in gendered, racialized, and heteronormative matrices of colonial desire.

Contemporary intercultural encounters and relationships are deeply embedded in and framed by the symbolic and material conditions of neo/colonization, imperialism and globalization. Yet, the rhetoric of racelessness, claims of color-blindness, multiculturalism, and diversity that circulate in the context of globalization serve to erase or neutralize the centuries of historical injustice, exploitation, and asymmetrical relations of power that have produced current conditions of race, class, and gender-based inequity (Macedo and Gounari, 2006; Shome and Hegde, 2002b). Disowning the legacies of colonization, US imperialism and their links to current global conditions in the study of intercultural communication obfuscates and normalizes US/Western hegemony. Like European colonial cartographers who positioned the West as the geopolitical center of the world and misrepresented the sizes and shapes of continents, dehistoricizing and depoliticizing scholarship in the field of intercultural produces systematic distortions of the world (Munchi and McKie, 2001). Critiques from postcolonial and postmodern perspectives reveal how knowledge construction is an interpretive, invented, and value-laden representational process bound by relations of power (Collier, 2002; Nakayama and Martin, 1999; Mendoza, 2005). Thus, it is critical to contest concepts and frameworks that decontextualize intercultural interactions; we must re-imagine the study of intercultural communication to account for the ways historical and current conditions and relations of power are layered and stitched together in the context of globalization.

Local/Global Connection and Multilevel Analysis

Our current global context is characterized by a complex web of linkages between the local and the global, however fractured and disjointed. People, languages, identities, cultural forms, practices, and ideas are situated in particular local spaces and are simultaneously connected through phone, fax, email, text messaging, and media, by multiple modes of transportation, as well as through extensive social networks, memories and imaginations with particular and situated places around the globe (Drzewiecka, 2002; Goldring, 1996; Hegde, 2002; Mendoza *et al.*, 2003; Ong, 1999). The notion of the diaspora within, as discussed by Malhotra and Carrillo Rowe (2006), refers to populations that migrate in imaginative and culturally performative ways, such as employees at call centers, without ever actually crossing national boundaries. The processes and conditions of globalization require that we highlight the continuity and ties as well as the fissured and fragmented intersections of multiple global communities, positions and interpretations.

Each scenario illustrates interesting, complex, and provocative links and disjunctures between the local and the global and the need for a multilevel analysis to understand intercultural communication in the context of globalization. The globalization of capital, goods and labor has linked Villachuato, Michoacán, Mexico and Marshalltown, Iowa, United States to a global economy dominated by the United States. These communities are no longer marginal to the world economy; rather, they are part of an uneven global capitalist expansion (Grey and Woodrick, 2002). Like many towns across the United States and Mexico, the lives and livelihoods of people from Villachuato and Marshalltown are intertwined and interdependent in the global context. Drawing on world systems theory (Wallerstein, 2000) for a macrolevel analysis, colonization and military force were used historically to establish conditions for the accumulation of capital by European and US powers. Today, the conditions are established and maintained by "free" trade agreements negotiated through global bodies of governance such as the International Monetary Fund, the World Bank and World Trade Organization.

Yet, as "free" trade agreements, instituted by multilateral institutions at the global level, benefit elite classes and multinational corporations, at the local level, social networks of families and communities "actively pursue transnational social space, the 'trans-locality,' to sustain material and cultural resources in the face of the neoliberal storm (Smith and Guarnizo, 2006, p. 7). Mesolevel approaches to migration and intercultural adaptation suggest that migrant networks pass along knowledge and experience about safe migration routes, work, housing, and other services through interpersonal communication with friends, family relations, and community connections. The Villachuato-Marshalltown connection exemplifies transnational communities, which are characterized by intertwining familial relationships across locations, identification with multiple "homes," and the ability to mobilize collective material and symbolic resources (Goldring, 1996). Through remittances and fund drives organized by migrant networks that link several locations in the United States, wages made by workers are used to improve their Mexican community. Workers return to Villachuato frequently for annual religious events, weddings, and funerals often quitting their jobs and returning for re-hire. While these practices benefit the meatpacking plant in Marshalltown economically, White American managers view these practices as disruptive, criticizing Latinos for being "irresponsible," for not learning English and not wanting to settle permanently in the United States (Grey and Woodrick, 2002).

Interestingly, the characteristics that define transnational communities are often the source of intercultural misunderstanding and conflict on the microlevel. Transmigrants' social, cultural, economic, and political allegiance to and sustained contact with their community in Mexico disrupt and resist hegemonic assumptions of US superiority and the desirability of assimilating to and living in the United States, escalating tensions between the dominant group and transmigrants. The individual and collective agency of Villachuato transmigrants expressed through frequent travel between the two communities, remittances and fund drives to support the community in Mexico, and the ability to quit work are all strategies that challenge and subvert the assumed unidirectional power of US national and corporate interests. Yet, as community members from Marshalltown take an interest in the community in Villachuato, Mexico, a process of intercultural adaptation occurs not only for transmigrants but also for Marshalltown residents who are changed over time by forging as an intercultural transnational community.

As the analysis of the scenario suggests, we need to re-imagine pertinent themes in intercultural communication – identity construction, the use of language, cultural forms and cultural spaces, interpersonal relationships, as well as migration, adaptation and intercultural conflict – in ways that underscore the connections and disjunctures between the local and the global, that highlight parallel, asymmetrical and shifting positionalities in terms of power and that emphasize the interrelationship among micro, meso and macro levels of experience and analysis.

Social Justice

A central goal in critical approaches to intercultural communication includes challenging systems of domination, critiquing hierarchies of power and confronting discrimination to create a more equitable world. Redefining culture as a site of contestation where meaning-making is a struggle not a stable entity and where culture is understood as a resource, exploited for economic development and activated for empowerment, allows us to address the symbolic and material realities of inequality, difference, and marginalization. Situating intercultural communication within broad and specific historical, political, economic, and social contexts and drawing out the roles power, positionality, and privilege play also advance this goal. We challenge inequity and injustice on systemic and interpersonal levels by attending to the interconnected and yet fractured links between the local and the global and by engaging a multilevel (macro/meso/micro) analysis. Yet, as we re-imagine intercultural in the context of globalization, we also need to couple our critical analysis and theorizing with proactive engagement and collective action for social justice. "As a critical practice, pedagogy's role lies not only in changing how people think about themselves and their relationship to others and the world, but in energizing students and others to engage in those struggles that further possibilities for living in a more just society" (Giroux, 2004, pp. 63–64). In her book *Another World is Possible If...*, scholar and activist Susan George (2004) asserts:

> My answer is that another world is indeed possible – but only when the greatest pos-
> sible number of people with many backgrounds, viewpoints and skills join together to
> make it happen. Things change when enough people insist on it and work for it. No
> one should be left out and feel they cannot contribute. No one who wants to help
> build another world should, for lack of knowledge or connections, remain on the
> sideline (pp. xii–xiii).

The field of communication studies broadly and intercultural communication in particular are positioned well to provide processes and practices that engage multiple and diverse voices, build alliances and solidarity across various and shifting positionalities and imagine a world where equity and justice are the norm not the exception (Allen *et al.*, 2002; Broome *et al.*, 2005; Collier *et al.*, 2001; Swartz, 2008). As we confront the callous challenges and mobilize the creative potential of the context of globalization, we need to re-imagine the field of intercultural communication as a site of intervention, democratic participation and transformation. Amardo Rodriguez (2008) stresses that hierarchies of power that sustain inequities and injustices are not inevitable or natural but rather are created, reinforced, and justified through communication. Christina Pestana and Omar Swartz (2008) propose communicative imagination, an orientation that highlights the role communication plays in our lives and enables the actualization of human potential, the development of solidarity across difference and the promotion of participatory democracy. Gust Yep (2008) explicates the notion of intervention – forms of communication activism such as protests, boycotts, canvassing, sit-ins, teach-ins, street theater as well consciousness-raising in classrooms, churches and family gatherings, and emergent opportunities in informal settings – where pressure is exercised "on the fault lines of a network of power" (p. 196).

Along with Gordon Nakagawa, I introduce intercultural praxis, a process of engagement that joins critical, reflective, and engaged analysis with informed action for social justice (Sorrells and Nakagawa, 2008). Intercultural praxis provides a blueprint for integrating the four areas of focus discussed in this chapter in our scholarly, activist, and everyday lives as we re-imagine intercultural communication in the context of globalization. All moments in our day – when we make choices about what we consume from food to popular culture and from news to education, when we make decisions about when we intervene to challenge sexist, racist, homophobic, classist, and other discriminatory language, structures, and inequitable conditions, and when we develop relationships and build alliances with friends, coworkers, bosses, and strangers – provide opportunities to engage in intercultural praxis. Intercultural praxis operates as engaged communicative action informed by an understanding of the positionalities and standpoints of the communicators and is exercised within and is responsive to particular, concrete temporal and spatial contexts that produce historical and sociopolitical, as well as local and global conditions.

Through six inter-related points of entry – inquiry, framing, positioning, dialogue, reflection, and action – intercultural praxis utilizes our multifaceted identity positions and shifting access to privilege and power to develop allies, build solidarity, imagine alternatives and intervene in our struggles for social responsibility and social justice. From these points of entry, intercultural praxis may manifest in a range of forms such as simple or complex communication competency skills; oppositional tactics; and creative, improvisational, and transformational interventions. For example, as Immaculee, Hamsa and Cathy's friendship deepened, an understanding of their differing positionalities historically and as students at a US university in Southern California emerged, leading each to intervene on behalf of the other as allies against racism, sexism, and religious prejudice. As women in Moscow who are fans of Amitabh Bachchan choose to consume Indian films, their commitment to learn Hindi may shift the interactional dynamics from cultural appropriation to intercultural appreciation. "Acknowledging ways the desire for pleasure, and that includes erotic longings, informs our politics, our understanding of difference, we may know better how desire disrupts, subverts, and makes resistance possible" (hooks, 1992, p. 39). The alter-globalization movement and protests against the WTO like the one in Seattle in, 1999 produce alternative pedagogies that challenge hegemonic and undemocratic practices and provide spaces for learning about and creating intercultural alliances for collective resistance (cited in Giroux, 2004).

In the context of globalization, our choices and actions are always enabled, shaped, and constrained by history, relations of power, and material conditions that are inextricably linked to intercultural dimensions of culture, race, class, religion, sexual orientation, language, and nationality. Communicative imagination (Pestana and Swartz, 2008), dialogical intervention (Yep, 2008) and intercultural praxis (Sorrells and Nakagawa, 2008) each provide direction and insight to re-imagine intercultural communication as a site of democratic participation, intervention and transformation in the context of globalization.

Conclusion

People from different cultures have been engaging with each other for many millennia; however, the amount and intensity of intercultural interactions, the degree of interdependence, and the inequitable terms of engagement in the context of globalization are unprecedented. The manifest and latent challenges as well as the contestations and opportunities of globalization demand our full imagination and engaged creativity. Re-imagining intercultural communication in the context of globalization requires flexible, multidimensional focus and analysis; respect for (or the ability to look again at) the ways intercultural exchanges are deeply shaped by colonial, neocolonial, and imperial histories, discourses and relations of power and yet are re-articulated and re-configured today; recognition of how de/re-territorialized cultural subjects and objects are simultaneously situated in particular locals and yet are linked through travel, communication, and memory to specific geographic and cultural spaces around the globe; and a deep commitment to create counter-hegemonic spaces of agency, alliance, and activism among people who are positioned very differently.

In this chapter, I identified the theoretical foundations and assumptions of a critical perspective for re-imagining the study of intercultural communication in the context of globalization. Several scenarios provided the background for situating intercultural communication in the context of globalization. I elaborated four areas of focus for re-imagining the practice and study of intercultural communication including redefining culture, contextualizing intercultural communication in historical contexts and within relations of power, underscoring the links and disjunctures between the local and the global, and grounding the study and practice of intercultural communication in social justice. Intercultural praxis was briefly outlined as a way to integrate the four areas of focus as we theorize and practice intercultural communication in the context of globalization. When we understand communication as a "humanity-making, world-making practice," Rodriguez (2008) argues, "our humanity unfolds and the world becomes potent with possibilities" (p. 14). Dedicated to all 7 billion people who call our world "home," the normative conception at the heart of re-imagining intercultural communication in the context of globalization advances an ethic of critical engagement and democratic participation for justice and social responsibility.

Note

This chapter draws from and articulates the foundations for a larger body of work entitled *Globalizing Intercultural Communication*, forthcoming in 2011 with Sage Publications.

References

Alexander, J., and Mohanty, C. (2003) *Feminism without Borders: Decolonizing Theory, Practicing Solidarity*, Duke University, Durham, NC.

Allen, B.J., Broome, B.J., Jones, T.S. *et al.* (2002) Intercultural alliances: A cyberdialogue among scholar-practitioners, in *Intercultural Alliances, International and Intercultural Communication Annual, 25,* (ed. M.J. Collier), Sage, Thousand Oaks, CA, pp. 279–319.

Appadurai, A. (1996) *Modernity at Large: Cultural Dimensions of Globalization,* University of Minnesota, Minneapolis, MN.

Asante, M.K. (1987) *The Afrocentric Idea,* Temple University, Philadelphia.

Broome, B. Carey, C., De La Garza, S.A. *et al.* (2005) "In the thick of things": A dialogue about the activist turn in intercultural communication, Taking stock in intercultural communication: Where to now?, in *International and Intercultural Communication Annual, 26,* (eds W.J. Starosta and G.-M. Chen) Sage, Thousand Oaks, CA, pp. 145–175.

Butler, J. (1993) *Bodies That Matter,* Routledge, New York.

Collier, M.J. (2002) Transforming communication about culture: An introduction, in *Transforming Communication about Culture: Critical New Directions, International and Intercultural Communication Annual, 24,* (ed. M.J. Collier), Sage, Thousand Oaks, CA, pp. ix–xix.

Collier, M.J., Hegde, R.S., Lee, W.S. *et al.* (2001) Dialogue on the edges: Ferment in communication and culture, in *Transforming Communication about Culture: Critical New Directions, International and Intercultural Communication Annual, 24,* (ed. M.J. Collier), Sage, Thousand Oaks, CA, pp. 219–280.

Drzewiecka, J.A. (2002) Collective memory, media representation and barriers to intercultural dialogue, in *Intercultural Alliance: Critical Transformation, International and Intercultural Communication Annual, 25,* (ed. M.J. Collier), Sage, Thousand Oaks, CA, pp. 189–219.

Ebron, G. (2002) Not just the maid: Negotiating Filipina identity in Italy, *Intersections: Gender, History and Culture in the Asian Context,* 8, http://intersections.anu.edu.au/issue8/ebron.html (accessed May 19, 2010).

Fiske, J. (1992) *Introduction to Communication Studies: Studies in Culture and Communication,* Methuen & Co., London.

Freire. P. (1998) *Pedagogy of Freedom: Ethics, Democracy, and Civic Courage,* Rowman and Littlefield, Lanham, MD.

George, S. (2004) *Another World is Possible If...,* Verso, London.

Giroux, H.A. (2004) Cultural studies, public pedagogy, and the responsibility of intellectuals. *Communication and Critical/Cultural Studies,* 1 (1), 47–59.

Goldring, L. (1996) Blurring borders: Constructing transnational community in the process of Mexican-U.S. migration. *Research in Community Sociology VI,* 69–104.

Gramsci, A. (1973) *Selections from the Prison Notebooks,* Harper and Row, New York.

Graves, J.L. (2005) *The Myth of Race: Why We Pretend Race Exists in America,* Dutton, New York.

Grewal, I. (2005) *Transnational America: Feminisms, Diasporas, Neoliberalisms,* Duke University, Durham, NC.

Grey, M.A., and Woodrick, A.C. (2002) Unofficial sister cities: Meatpacking labor migration between Villachuato, Mexico, and Marshalltown, Iowa. *Human Organization,* 61 (4), 364–376.

Grossberg, L., Nelson, C. and Treichler, P. (eds) (1992) *Cultural Studies,* Routledge, New York.

Hall, S. (ed.) (1997) *Representation: Cultural Representations and Signifying Practices*, Sage, Thousand Oaks, CA.

Halualani, R.T. (2002) Connecting Hawaiians: The politics of authenticity in the Hawaiian diaspora, in *Intercultural Alliance: Critical Transformation, International and Intercultural Communication Annual*, 25, (ed. M.J. Collier), Sage, Thousand Oaks, CA, pp. 221–248.

Harvey, D. (2005) *A Brief History of Neoliberalism*, Oxford University Press, Oxford.

Hegde, R. (2002) Translated enactments: The relational configurations of the Asian Indian immigrant experience, in *Readings in Intercultural Communication. Experiences and Contexts*, 2nd edn, (eds J.N. Martin, T.K. Nakayama and L.A. Flores), McGraw-Hill, Boston, MA, pp. 259–266.

hooks, b. (1992) *Black Looks: Race and Representation*, South End, Boston, MA.

Inda, J.I., and Rosaldo, R. (eds) (2002) *The Anthropology of Globalization: A Reader*, Blackwell, Oxford.

Lui, M., Robles, B., Leondar-Wright, B. *et al.* (2006) *The Color of Wealth: The Story Behind the U. S. Racial Wealth Divide*, The New Press, New York.

Maass, A. (2005) *The Case of Socialism*, Haymarket, Chicago, IL.

Macedo, D., and Gounari, P. (eds) (2006) *The Globalization of Racism*, Paradigm, Boulder, CO.

Malhotra, S., and Carrillo Rowe, A. (2006) Diaspora within: Arrested subjectivities in Indian call centers. National Communication Association Convention, San Antonio, TX.

Martin, J.N., and Nakayama, T.K. (1999) Thinking about culture dialectically. *Communication Theory*, 9 (1), 1–25.

Martin, J.N., and Nakayama, T.K. (2000) *Intercultural Communication in Contexts*, Mayfield, Mountain View, CA.

McLaren, P., and Farahmandpur, R. (2004) *Teaching against Global Capitalism in the New Imperialism: A Critical Pedagogy*, Rowman and Littlefield, Lanham, MD.

Mendoza, S.L. (2002) Bridging theory and cultural politics. Revisiting the indigenization-poststructuralism debates in Filipino and Filipino American struggles for identity, in *Intercultural Alliance: Critical Transformation, International and Intercultural Communication Annual*, 25, (ed. M.J. Collier), Sage, Thousand Oaks, CA, pp. 249–277.

Mendoza, S.L. (2005) Bridging paradigms: How not to throw out the baby of collective representation with the functionalist bathwater in critical intercultural communication, in *Taking Stock in Intercultural Communication: Where to Now?*, (eds W.J. Starosta and G.-M. Chen), NCA, Washington, DC, pp. 237–256.

Mendoza, S.L., Halualani, R.T., and Drzewiecka, J.A. (2003) Moving the discourse on identities in intercultural communication: Structure, culture, and resignifications. *Communication Quarterly*, 50 (3/4), 312–327.

Miike, Y. (2003) Toward an alternative metatheory of human communication: An Asiacentric vision. *Intercultural Communication Studies, XII*, 4, 39–64.

Munchi, D., and McKie, D. (2001) Toward a new cartography of intercultural communication: Mapping bias, business and diversity. *Business Communication Quarterly*, 64 (3), 9–22.

Nakayama, T.K., and Martin, J.N. (eds) (1999) *Whiteness: The Communication of Social Identity*, Sage, Thousand Oaks, CA.

Nederveen Pieterse, J. (2004) *Globalization and Culture: Global Mélange*, Rowman and Littlefield, Lanham, MD.

Ong, A. (1999) *Flexible Citizenship: The Cultural Logics of Transnationality*, Duke University, Durham, NC.

Pestana, C., and Swartz, O. (2008) Communication, social justice and creative democracy, in *Transformative Communication Studies: Culture, Hierarchy and the Human Condition*, (ed. O. Swartz), Troubador, Leicester, UK, pp. 91–114.

Ram, A. (2004) Memory, cinema, and the reconstitution of cultural identities in the Asian Indian diaspora, in *Communicating Ethnic and Cultural Identity*, (eds M. Fong and R. Chuang), Rowman and Littlefield, Lanham, MD.

Rodriguez, A. (2008) Communication and the end of hierarch, in *Transformative Communication Studies: Culture, Hierarchy and the Human Condition*, (ed. O. Swartz), Trubador, Leicester, UK, pp. 1–15.

Rose, C. (2005) Amitabh Bachchan on Charlie Rose, April, http://twentyonwards.blogs. com/twenty_onwards/2005/04/amitabh_bachan__2.html (last accessed, August 22, 2005)

Rose, T. (1994) *Black Noise: Rap Music and Black Culture in Contemporary American Society*, Wesleyan, Hanover, NH.

Said, E.W. (1978) *Orientalism*, Pantheon Books, New York.

Shome, R., and Hegde, R.S. (2002a) Culture, communication and the challenge of globalization. *Critical Studies in Media Communication*, 19 (2), 172–189.

Shome, R., and Hegde, R.S. (2002b) Postcolonial approaches to communication: Charting the terrain, engaging the intersections. *Communication Theory*, 12 (3), 249–270.

Smith, M.P., and Guarnizo, L.E. (eds) (2006) *Comparative Urban and Community Research*, Vol. 6: *Transnationalism from Below*, Transaction, New Brunswick, NJ.

Sorrells, K., and Nakagawa, G. (2008) Intercultural communication praxis and the struggle for social responsibility and social justice, in *Transformative Communication Studies: Culture, Hierarchy and the Human Condition*, (ed. O. Swartz), Troubador, Leicester, UK, pp. 17–43.

Spivak, G.C. (1988) Can the subaltern speak?, in *Marxism and the Interpretation of Culture*, (eds, C. Nelson and L. Grossberg), University of Illinois, Chicago, pp. 271–313.

Stiglitz, J. (2002) *Globalization and its Discontents*, W.W. Norton, New York.

Swartz, O. (ed.) (2008) *Transformative Communication Studies: Culture, Hierarchy and the Human Condition*, Troubador, Leicester, UK.

Tomlinson, J. (1999) *Globalization and Culture*, Blackwell, Oxford.

Toro-Morn, M.I., and Alicea, M. (eds) (2004) *Migration and Immigration: A Global View*, Greenwood, Westwood, CT.

UNESCO (2006) EFA Global monitoring report – Literacy for Life, http://portal.unesco. org/education/en/ev.phpURL_ID=43283andURL_DO=DO_TOPICandURL_ SECTION=201.html (last accessed November 3, 2006).

United Nations (2004) *World Economic and Social Survey 2003: Trends in the World Economy*, United Nations, New York.

Wallerstein, I. (2000) *The Essential Wallerstein*, New Press, New York.

Wellman, B., and Haythornthwaite, C.A. (eds) (2002) *The Internet in Everyday Life*, Blackwell, Malden, MA.

Winant, H. (2001) *The World is a Ghetto: Race and Democracy since WW II*, Basic Books, New York.

Yep, G.A. (2008) The dialectics of intervention: Toward a reconceptualization of the theory/activism divide in communication scholarship and beyond, in *Transformative Communication Studies: Culture, Hierarchy and the Human Condition*, (ed. O. Swartz), Troubador, Leicester, UK, pp. 191–207.

Young, R.C. (2001) *Postcolonialism: An Historical Introduction*, Blackwell, Malden, MA.

Yúdice, G. (2003) *The Expediency of Culture: Uses of Culture in the Global Era*, Duke University, Durham, NC.

Further Reading

Chua, A. (2003) *World on Fire: How Exporting Free Market Democracy Breeds Ethnic Hatred and Global Instability*, First Anchor Books, New York.

Frey, L.R., and Carragee, K.M. (2007) *Communication Activism Vol 2: Communication for Social Change*, Hampton, Cresskill, NJ.

Giles, W., and Hyndman, J. (ed.) (2004) *Sites of Violence: Gender and Conflict Zones*, University of California, Berkeley, CA.

Gitlin, T. (2002) *Media Unlimited: How the Torrent of Images and Sounds Overwhelms Our Lives*, Henry Holt, New York.

Hannerz, U. (2001) Thinking about culture in a global ecumene, in *Culture in the Communication Age*, (ed. J. Lull), Routledge, London, pp. 54–71.

Hartsock, N.C.M. (1998) *The Feminist Standpoint Revisited and Other Essays*, Boulder, CO: Westview.

hooks, b. (1994) *Teaching to Transgress: Education as the Practice of Freedom*, Routledge, New York.

Sassen, S. (2002) *Global Networks, Linked Cities*, Routledge, New York.

12

Culture as Text and Culture as Theory
Asiacentricity and Its Raison D'être in Intercultural Communication Research

Yoshitaka Miike

The wealth of a common global culture [is] expressed in the particularities of our different languages and cultures very much like a universal garden of many-colored flowers. The "flowerness" of the different flowers is expressed in their very diversity. But there is cross-fertilization between them. And what is more they all contain in themselves the seeds of a new tomorrow.

Ngũgĩ wa Thiong'o (1993, p. 24)

Daisetsu Suzuki (1870–1966), who is perhaps the foremost interpreter of Zen Buddhism for the West, considered himself "a Japanese as a world citizen" and published one of his last books, *Toyoteki na Mikata* [The Eastern Viewpoint], at the age of 93. In this book (Suzuki, 1997), he ardently advocated something Eastern that must be preserved for a world culture. Yet Suzuki (1964) acknowledged the predicament of articulating what is Eastern: "The thing is there before our eyes, for it refuses to be ignored; but when we endeavor to grasp it in our own hands in order to examine it more closely or systematically, it eludes and we lose its track" (p. 35). Culture is deeply felt, but it is inherently elusive. Here lies the challenge of indigenous theorizing. Alternative theorizing today is further complicated by the seemingly excessive politics of representation. Any characterization would be put under close scrutiny and immediately prosecuted by postmodernists and poststructuralists for its essentialism. Moreover, sophisticated theorizing ought to evince global concerns such as feminist sensitivity, ecological consciousness, religious pluralism, and humanistic visions. Cultural re-theorizing, which entails historical collectivity and internal diversity, appears to be too controversial to be undertaken.

Nevertheless, the field of intercultural communication is entering a new phase of cultural re-interpretation, re-description, and re-vision. As we are increasingly aware that deconstruction alone cannot bridge differences, we come to the realization

The Handbook of Critical Intercultural Communication, edited by Thomas K. Nakayama and Rona Tamiko Halualani. © 2010 Blackwell Publishing Ltd.

that the reconstruction of cultural knowledge is an inescapable mission of interculturalists. It is in this intellectual milieu that centricity and centric paradigms will emerge as a vital metatheoretical notion and powerful metatheories. In recent years, intercultural communication scholars (e.g., Halualani, Mendoza, and Drzewiecka, 2009; Jackson, 2000, 2010; Kalscheuer, 2009; Martin and Butler, 2001; Mendoza, 2005; Mendoza, Halualani, and Drzewiecka, 2002; Nakayama and Martin, 2007; Tanno, 2007; Starosta and Chen, 2003a; Yoshitake, 2004) have formulated critical reflections on the field's knowledge production process. Some (e.g., Yoshitake, 2002) interrogated the dominant social scientific approach, while others (e.g., Martin and Nakayama, 2008) integrated traditional and nontraditional paradigms. Current metatheoretical debates, however, have not sufficiently addressed the role of culture in alternative theory building, which is a key to reconstructing new knowledge about culture and communication.

The objective of this chapter is, then, to make a plea for the centrality of culture in re-interpreting, re-describing, and re-envisioning indigenous communication in local and global contexts while elaborating specifically on Asiacentricity and its intellectual necessity in intercultural communication research. The essay first contextualizes the need of Afrocentric, Asiacentric, and other non-Western centric approaches by critiquing the hegemony of Eurocentrism in contemporary research on culture and communication. The essay then clarifies the idea of Asiacentricity by highlighting its major dimensions and dispelling its common misconceptions. The essay finally adumbrates three aspects of culture as a central resource for alternative theorizing and suggests possible Asiacentric innovations in the study of Asian cultures and communication. The underlying premise of the present chapter is that it is imperative for interculturalists to view cultures not merely as texts for knowledge deconstruction but also theories for knowledge reconstruction in the age of the "crisis" of representation.

Eurocentrism in Intercultural Communication Scholarship

Eurocentrism as intellectual imperialism has been problematized in communication studies as well as in other disciplines (e.g., Alatas, 2002, 2006; Asante, 1999, 2006b; Chu, 1988; Fals-Borda and Mora-Osejo, 2003; Jackson, 2000; Joseph, Reddy, and Searle-Chatterjee, 1990; Miike, 2003, 2004, 2007b; Wallerstein, 1997, 2006; Wong, Manvi, and Wong, 1995). According to Joseph, Reddy, and Searle-Chatterjee (1990), Eurocentrism has had three undesirable effects on academic pursuits: (1) it has made non-Western intellectuals unthink imitation of Western theory and research; (2) it has made Western intellectuals remain unaware of alternative sources of scholarship; and (3) it has functioned to legitimate and perpetuate unequal international systems of knowledge production, dissemination, and evaluation. Wallerstein (1997) succinctly summarized that Eurocentrism manifests itself in the social sciences in five respects: (1) its self-serving historiography, (2) its presumed universalism, (3) its idea of civilization, (4) its otherizing Orientalism, and (5) its ideology of progress.

Eurocentrism is a term that admits a plurality of definitions. Alatas (2002) defined Eurocentrism as "values, attitudes, ideas and ideological orientations that are informed by the notion of European uniqueness and superiority" (p. 761). Eurocentrism, he continued, involves "the tendency to understand non-European history and society in terms of the models, categories and concepts derived from European experiences" (p. 761). Eurocentrism should not be confused with Eurocentricity. *Eurocentrism as a universalist ideology refers to an ethnocentric approach to non-Western worlds and non-Westerners, whereas Eurocentricity as a particularist position refers to a legitimate culture-centric approach to Europe and Europeans* (Miike, 2008a). Eurocentricity, nonetheless, becomes Eurocentrism when the provincial masquerades as the universal. That is, as Asante (2006b) commented, Eurocentricity is "a normal expression of culture but could be abnormal if it imposed its cultural particularity as universal while denying and degrading other cultural, political, or economic views" (p. 145).

Because academic Eurocentrism is a complex phenomenon historically embedded in Western colonialist ideologies and political and economic dominance, Nakayama (2008) went so far as to say that "[t]here is no easy way to problematize Eurocentric approaches and there is no end to the need to do so " (p. 2). In this section, despite its conceptual complexities, I will specify three pillars of Eurocentrism in intercultural communication scholarship: (1) theoretical Eurocentrism, (2) methodological Eurocentrism, and (3) comparative Eurocentrism. In my view, these three pillars have shaped the Eurocentric structure of knowledge in the field of intercultural communication not in an independent way, but in an interactive manner (Miike, 2003).

Theoretical Eurocentrism

The first pillar of Eurocentrism in intercultural communication scholarship is theoretical Eurocentrism. In a plethora of books and articles in the intercultural field, theoretical frameworks grounded in Western intellectual traditions are employed to observe and describe, analyze and interpret, and evaluate and criticize non-Western cultures and communication. Shuter (2008) lamented that culture, the heart and soul of intercultural communication studies, had been neglected by social scientific cross-cultural investigators who published theory-validation research without exhibiting any passion for culture. In their published research, he cogently argued, culture has served as a "laboratory" for testing the generalizablility of US Eurocentric interpersonal and organizational communication theories. The same hierarchical arrangement of "Western theories" and "non-Western texts" has also been equally pervasive in interpretive and critical approaches to cultural communication and critique. With regard to a cultural approach to communication, Shuter (2000) postulated that "the approach is so linked to ethnography that it is more a methodological alternative than a new model for theorizing about communication in cross-cultural or intracultural contexts" (p. 3). Wong, Manvi, and Wong (1995) also posited that "the current fascination with postmodernism and post-structuralism is in continuity with the domination of Western perspectives in theory building" (pp. 138–139). Non-Western cultures, more often than not, remain peripheral targets of Eurocentric analysis and critique in intercultural communication research. They are treated as mere texts for deconstruction from Eurocentric theoretical viewpoints.

Bryant and Yang (2004), who conducted a content analysis of articles on Asia in nine "mainstream" communication journals, detected that all the theories adopted by the 65 articles in question were of Western origin. Bryant and Yang (2004) contended:

> With this seemingly wholesale adoption of theories from the West comes tacit accept-ance of the sorts of epistemological and metatheoretical intellectual infrastructure that has been derived from philosophers and theorists with Western mindsets. Implicit within any epistemological perspective are major assumptions that supposedly represent the essential elements of a culture, such as the foundational view of human beings that is represented, the nature of causality that is inherent in the model, the perception of the locus of control of the individual (i.e., determinism, free will, and the like), the essential nature of political reality, the relative importance of individuals versus community, the relationship between thought and action, and manifold other consid-erations that are part of the foundations of our ways of knowing. These assumptions creep, often unwittingly, into all of our theories.
>
> If you compare and contrast the essential philosophical and theological works, the arts and crafts, and the great literature of the East and the West, a substantial number of obtrusive differences routinely occur. This would seem to speak against wholesale adoption, without essential modification, of many communication theories.... [We should] routinely challenge the adoption of communication theories derived from Western mindsets without reconciliation of any parts of the theory or model that are not concordant with Eastern ways of knowing, thinking, symbol making, and action. We know that this is a "tall order," but this is the true challenge of multiculturalism, and nowhere is such diversity more acutely needed than in our essential theory construction (pp. 145–146).

Theoretical Eurocentrism in intercultural communication scholarship parallels the larger intellectual structure of "academic dependency" and the "global division of labor" in the human sciences. In an impressive and exhaustive treatment of Eurocentrism in the social sciences in Asia, Alatas (2006) voiced his perennial concern over such an academic climate where the West (primarily, the United States, the United Kingdom, and France) is perceived as producers of theoretical knowledge, and it is the mission of non-Western intellectuals as its consumers to do empirical research. This division of theoretical and empirical intellectual labor, according to Alatas, deters non-Western social scientists from learning and theorizing from their own intellectual legacies. Alatas' (2006) legitimate concern has been endorsed by a number of communication scholars in both Western and non-Western worlds includ-ing Chen (2006), Chu (1988), Gordon (2007a, 2007b), and Ishii (2007, 2008). When and how can intercultural communication specialists stop talking forever about certain Eurocentric theoretical constructs (e.g., individualism-collectivism,

independent-interdependent construals, and high-context and low-context communication) and move beyond these sweeping overgeneralizations that occlude
cultural and communicative complexities? Current theoretical Eurocentrism along
with English-language-based concepts, although possibly opening the first window
to new cultures, does not advance culturally situated and resonating knowledge.
The time is long overdue for the field of intercultural communication to disallow
Eurocentric theoretical concepts to totalize or "essentialize" all human beings as
people of European heritage and to reduce a wealth of human experiences to the
particular experiences of the West (Asante, 2006a).

Methodological Eurocentrism

The second pillar of Eurocentrism in intercultural communication scholarship is
methodological Eurocentrism. Three longstanding academic issues are germane to
this pillar: (1) the Eurocentric method-centered research; (2) the presumed universality of Eurocentric methodology; and (3) the neglect of non-Eurocentric indigenous literature. A heavy emphasis on methodology in the social sciences is a
representative of Eurocentrism. Implicit in methodological Eurocentrism is the
assumption that a researcher cannot explore a topic if she or he cannot find a
"correct" method. A method is correct, however, only when it complies with data
collection and analysis protocols established by European (American) scholars.
Hence, the problem with such a way of narrowing down research topics in terms
of the availability and feasibility of a certain Eurocentric method is that it has
encouraged academic dependence on mainstream Eurocentric theories that are
already congruent with Eurocentric methods.

For so long, in the intercultural communication field, and in the communication
discipline in general, the statistical method has been deemed the most "sophisticated" and "appropriate" mode of inquiry (Tanno, 2007). Widespread obsession
with quantification, objectivity, value freedom, replicability, generalizability, and
predictability is very much predicated on Western ontological, epistemological, and
axiological assumptions. As Gordon (2007b) attested, "The need to constantly
define our terms tightly, and numerically measure and manipulate our variables, has
stunted and dwarfed our thinking as to what 'communication' is and can be"
(p. 52). Such a functionalist methodological bias has tremendously disadvantaged
alternative theorizing about non-Western premises and practices of communication. Moreover, there is a measure of truth in the claim of the non-Western academy
that the dominance of quantitative (cross-cultural) communication research is primarily responsible for the proliferation of "safari scholars," "penny collaborators,"
"data exporters," and "instant experts" in the non-Western region (Chu, 1988).

Another issue with reference to methodological Eurocentrism is the deep-
seated belief that methods and ethics of research are universally applicable across
national borders and cultural boundaries. Even those non-Western cross-cultural
researchers who recognize that Western theories are biased may not question
whether Western *methods* are just as biased. Methods refer to appropriate

procedures of data collection and analysis and ethical guidelines for doing research. As such, they are necessarily culture-bound, if not context-bound. For it is the cultural context and the people that determine what is appropriate and what is ethical. In this respect, methodological recipes and regimens developed in Western contexts for Western participants cannot be equally appropriate and ethical for non-Western respondents in non-Western settings without modifications. Without being mindful of methodological Eurocentrism, more than a few intercultural investigators run the risk of providing woefully inaccurate empirical proof and trivialize alternative theoretical ideas for the reason that they are not in accord with their "hard data." After looking into Rogelia Pe-Pua's Filipino research method of *pagtatanong-tanong*, Linda Tuhiwai Smith's Maori research code of honor, and Joan E. Sieber's US Eurocentric norms of research, Tanno (2007) emphatically asserted:

> The important idea here is that in all these cases the good intercultural, multicultural, and international researcher – the ethical researcher – must have a very good under-standing of cultural assumptions (his/her own as well as those of the culture being studied) and also have an appreciation of the fact that one method cannot, should not, be used across cultures (p. 248).

Still another issue linked with methodological Eurocentrism is the neglect of indig-enous literature published outside the Western academy. By *indigenous literature*, of course, I do not mean mere translations or empirical replications of Eurocentric scholarship in non-Western local languages. What I have in mind is indigenous scholarship that contains original and creative theoretical ideas. Ishii (2004) casti-gated both Western and Asian intercultural communication professionals for their inclination to engage in research and education by referring exclusively to the English-language literature. He gathered that it is due to this inclination that "their customary research has inevitably become for the most part Westcentric, distorted, stereotyped, superficial, and duplicative" (p. 65). The advent of the age of multi-cultural scholarship impels us to rectify the methodological bias that academic literature in Western languages, particularly in English, is superior to that in non-European languages. The time is right for us to take advantage of indigenous scholarly literature for alternative theory construction and refinement.

Comparative Eurocentrism

The third pillar of Eurocentrism in intercultural communication scholarship is comparative Eurocentrism. There are countless cross-cultural communication research reports whose focus centers on US Eurocentric comparisons. Many intercultural communication researchers, albeit unwittingly or unintentionally, normalize and naturalize US European American cultural values and communica-tion styles and compare them with other dissimilar ones, notably East Asian coun-terparts. This comparative Eurocentrism hinders the intercultural field from

(1) demonstrating internal diversity and complexity within a non-Western region or nation; (2) exploring links and interconnections, and identifying collective identities and common values, among neighboring non-Western cultures; (3) examining similarities and differences from non-Eurocentric perspectives; and (4) projecting non-Western visions of the global village.

Alternative non-Eurocentric comparisons then will be able to change the cartography of intercultural knowledge in communication studies. They include (1) continent-diaspora comparisons (e.g., Japanese culture and communication in Japan and Brazil), (2) within-region comparisons (e.g., Indian and Sri Lankan cultures), (3) non-Western comparisons (e.g., Hispanic and Asian cultures), (4) diachronic comparisons (e.g., precolonial and postcolonial African cultures), and (5) cocultural domestic comparisons (e.g., Native American and Native Hawai'ian cultures). Yum's (2007) non-Western comparative study, for instance, focused on the Confucian notion of *jen* and the African notion of *ubuntu* in order to grasp what it means to be human in Asian and African communities. Yum's (2007) theoretical investigation is an innovative attempt to probe into the Asian and African concepts of humanity as they relate to cultural values, universal ethics, and communicative interactions. Non-Eurocentric comparisons of this kind will yield rich and refreshing insights into cultural similarities and differences and result in mutual referencing and learning in the global village (Tu, 2008).

Radhakrishnan (2003) advised cross-culturalists and interculturalists to direct their greater attention to whose images the comparison is initiated in, to who is honored by the comparison, and to whose values, standards, and criteria are deemed as universal, unmarked, and transcultural (e.g., Telugu as "the Italian of the East" instead of Italian as "the Telugu of the West"). He instructed them to be vigilant against hierarchical assumptions behind the comparison. Radhakrishnan (2003) posed a thought-provoking question relevant to comparative Eurocentrism in intercultural communication scholarship:

> In a world structured in dominance, clearly modern values seem more worthwhile than say communal or ethnic values. But this is the story of value as rendered by the victor. What about a multi-valent and multi-temporal valorization of the multiplicity of values and their historical development in different cultures, philosophies, and worldviews? These questions immediately land us in the problematic arena called "the politics of comparison." What kinds of comparisons are possible in a multicultural world that intends to honor difference without objectifying it or without resorting to a hierarchical calculus? (p. 72).

It should be stressed at the end of this section that the troubling Eurocentric regime of knowledge exists not only in cultural Western Europe but also in other non-Western territories of the world. Non-Westerners as well as Westerners have thoroughly participated in hegemonic Eurocentrism. If one counts the number of translations of Western books published in non-Western nations, it is abundantly clear that Eurocentrism thrives beyond cultural Western Europe. This debilitating problem with knowledge production and consumption compels us all to be critical of Eurocentrism in intercultural communication scholarship. Who is learning about whose culture from whose perspective? As Tanno (2007) lucidly stated, "The knowledges we pursue about intercultural communication have a variety of impacts. It affects how members of various cultures view themselves and how others view them" (p. 240). Theoretical, methodological, and comparative Eurocentrism has precluded us from seeing ourselves and others from truly diverse cultural locations. Ngũgĩ (1993) cautioned us about the real danger of internalized Eurocentrism in the non-Western mind:

> [T]he Eurocentric base of looking at the world is particularly manifest in the field of languages, literature, cultural studies.... The irony is that even that which is genuinely universal in the West is imprisoned by Eurocentrism. Western civilization itself becomes a prisoner, its jailors being its Eurocentric interpreters. But Eurocentrism is most dangerous to the self-confidence of Third World peoples when it becomes internalized in their intellectual conception of the universe (p. xvii).

Dimensions and Misconceptions of Asiacentricity

Alatas (2002) is right in saying that "recognition of the problem of Eurocentrism suggests the need for alternative discourses in the human sciences which should go beyond the critique of Eurocentrism towards the development of new concepts and categories, [and] new interpretations of history" (p. 765). Given the ascendancy of theoretical, methodological, and comparative Eurocentrism in the field of intercultural communication, I share Ngũgĩ's (1993) sentiment that the time is ripe for us to "discuss the possibility of moving the center from its location in Europe towards a pluralism of centers, themselves being equally legitimate locations of the human imagination" (p. 8). The purpose of this second section is twofold: (1) to explicate the notion of Asiacentricity as a metatheoretical concept by stipulating its major dimensions; and (2) to further clarify Asiacentricity a key to alternative knowledge by debunking its myths and misconceptions. Asiacentricity, as I have proposed and developed it in culture and communication studies (see Miike, 2003, 2004, 2006, 2008b), owes its intellectual debt to Molefi Kete Asante's (1998b, 2005, 2007a, 2008) enduring legacy of Afrocentricity. I will therefore make reference to the conceptual significance and paradigmatic development of Afrocentricity wherever appropriate and relevant.

Dimensions of Asiacentricity

Afrocentricity is, etymologically speaking, a simple combination of the two words, *Africa* and *center*. However, as a metatheoretical, methodological, and actionable concept, its meaning has evolved across disciplines for the past several decades. Afrocentricity is polysemic and multi-dimensional in the intellectual landscape today. Asante has proffered many definitions of Afrocentricity over the years. In one of his writings, for example, Asante (1998a) defined Afrocentricity with particular attention to subject-position, agency, and an orientation to data:

> Afrocentricity is the theoretical notion that insists on viewing African phenomena from the standpoint of Africans as subjects rather than objects. It is therefore a rather simple idea. The insistence on seeing African phenomena from the perspective of African people is neither novel nor extraordinary. What makes this view of reality so awesome for many people is the fact that it is stated in a way that suggests Africans have been viewed in the past as tangential to Europe, as peripheral to Eurocentric views, and as spectators to others. To theorize from the vantage point of Africans as centered is to provide a new vista on social, cultural, and economic facts. Thus, it is the orientation to data, not the data themselves, that matters (p. vii).

My close reading of Asante's numerous essays highlighted six major dimensions of Afrocentricity for the sake of conceptual clarification: (1) Africans as subjects and agents; (2) the centrality of the collective and humanistic interests of Africa and Africans; (3) the centrality of African indigenous values and ideals; (4) grounded-ness in African historical experiences; (5) an African contextual orientation to data; and (6) an African corrective and critique of dislocation (see Miike, 2008a). In accordance with these six interrelated constituents of Afrocentricity, then, I define *Asiacentricity* as (1) an assertion of Asians as subjects and agents, (2) placing Asian interests at the center of an approach to knowledge reconstruction about Asia, (3) placing Asian cultural values and ideals at the center of inquiry into Asian thought and action, (4) being grounded in Asian historical experiences, (5) an Asian con-textual orientation to data, and (6) an Asian ethical critique and corrective of the dislocation and displacement of Asian people and phenomena.

Asiacentricity hence demands that (1) Asian peoples or texts are viewed as subjects and agents in their narratives, (2) Asian interests, values, and ideals are prioritized in discussion and discourse on Asians and their experiences, and (3) an Asian person, document or phenomenon is located in the context of her/his or its own culture and history. When Asiacentricity is applied to theorizing activities of cultural re-interpretation, re-description, and re-vision, then, it invites us to view Asian cultures as central resources for Asiacentric insight and inspiration, not peripheral targets for non-Asiacentric analysis and critique. In other words, Asiacentricity insists that *Asian cultures should be viewed as theories for Asiacentric knowledge reconstruction, not as texts for non-Asiacentric knowledge deconstruction.* This idea of "culture as theory" has profound implications for intercultural communication research in the midst of Eurocentric intellectual imperialism. It urges us to locate a culture in its own context, recognize its collective subject-position and agency, approach the culture in a way to fully appreciate, not merely analyze, its unheard and silenced voices, and learn from their visions of humanity by centering its traditional values and ideals. It enjoins us to go beyond mere description of the culture, rediscover and recover positive elements of its heritage, and project its new future (Starosta and Chen, 2003b).

Asiacentricity pinpoints the pivotal role of Asian cultures in theorizing Asian thought and action. People in different cultures engage in communication activities in different linguistic, religious-philosophical, and historical contexts. Their thoughts and feelings in day-to-day life are expressed not through abstract universals but through concrete particulars. Accordingly, if we wish to understand and appreciate their cultural locations and communicative perspectives, we ought to theorize as they speak in particular languages, as they are impacted by particular religious-philosophical foundations, and as they struggle to live in particular historical experiences. Our theoretical accounts will be akin to their experiential perspectives when we theorize from their linguistic, religious-philosophical, and historical resources. This centrality of culture in theorizing endeavors is the overriding premise of Afrocentric, Asiacentric, and other non-Western centric scholarship.

It is noteworthy that centric scholarship strives to take into due consideration abiding traditions, collective memories, and primordial ties. In the age of postmodern, poststructural, and postcolonial thinking, ancient traditions of thought, classical texts, and concrete culture practices especially in the nonmetropolitan areas of the non-Western world are downplayed (Dissanayake, 2006b). But centrists are as discontent with such an intellectual orientation as Tu (1998) was:

> In fact, many of the postmodernists have informed us that boundary crossing, along with the continuous, restless, redefining of boundaries, and the ideal of the self, nation, or community have been deconstructed; if we try to essentialize any of them, we are merely modern and not postmodern. But if we focus our attention on some of the very powerful so-called macrotrends that have exerted a shaping influence on the global community since the end of the Second World War – science, technology, communication, trade, finance, entertainment, travel, tourism, migration, and, of course, disease – we may be misled into believing that the human condition itself has been structured by these newly emerging global forces without any reference to our inherited historical and cultural practices (p. 6).

As Ngũgĩ (1993) noted, "knowing oneself and one's environment was a correct basis of absorbing the world; there could never be the only center from which to view the world but that different people in the world had their culture and environment as the center" (p. 9). The idea of cultural "center" in Afrocentric and Asiacentric projects should not be misunderstood as the pure "essence" of an African or Asian culture or African and Asian cultures. Afrocentrists or Asiacentrists have no intention of creating *one* center in Africa or Asia. The terms, *subject* and *agency*, are also used in a specific manner in Afrocentric and Asiacentric discourse. They signify "self-definition," "self-determination," and "self-representation." The subject-object distinction concerns the question of how we approach a person, text, and document. Rather than scrutinizing the person, text, and document and treating them as if they were objects of analysis and critique, we must attend genuinely to them as subjects of voices as they tell their own stories about their cultural worlds. The concept of agency brings our attention to the activeness-passiveness distinction. It raises the question of uncovering the active-ness and actor-ness of a person or a person in a text and document instead of its passiveness and spectator-ness.

Perhaps it is suffice to say here that Asiacentricity is fundamentally about shared identities and collective representations. It does not subscribe to the Eurocentric view of the privileged that a totally "fluid" identity is, and will be, merely "performed" by "free will." As an Afrocentrist, Asante (2005) opposes "the notion of ruin," namely, "the idea that it is necessary to fragment the world in order to interrogate phenomena" (p. 11). He does not buy into the postmodern thinking of "unadulterated individualistic narcissism that under-mines the human capacity to feel solidarity with others" (p. 11). Asante (2005) proclaimed:

> Life as a random collage or free association of images may invoke an isolationist indi-viduality, but it is never cohesive enough to deal with the reality of community and communities, that is, groups of people who are bound together by similar historical experiences and who are developed by common phenomenological responses (p. 11).

From an Asiacentric standpoint, Dissanayake (2006a) also opined:

> The production of identities in the present world is often discussed in terms of axio-matics of postmodern theory, which valorize such phenomena as fragility, instability, and a multiplicity of identities. The very notion of identity has been characterized as illusory. It is argued that identities are constructed through role-playing and appro-priation of images; identity is matter of leisure and playacting. People are able to pick and choose their identities at will. Against this approach to identity, one has to coun-terpose the very real need that people, say, in Asia feel for a sense of collective belong-ing and group agency. Instead of the disappearance of identity, what one perceives is an attempt to recognize its centrality and to redefine and resituate it in newer social contexts. The need for identity is very real, and for most people living in Asia today, one important aspect of their identity is that they are victims of neocolonialism and global capitalism. (p. 43)

Misconceptions of Asiacentricity

Both Afrocentricity and Asiacentricity have been subjected to destructive criticisms. Some critics, whether intentionally or unintentionally, misread a growing body of Afrocentric and Asiacentric work and generated problematic discourse about cen-tricity. I have already responded to five major myths of Afrocentricity elsewhere: (1) Afrocentricity is a Black version of Eurocentrism; (2) Afrocentricity essential-izes Africanness and ignores the diversity of Africa; (3) Afrocentricity rejects hybrid-ity and ignores the dynamic nature of Africa; (4) Afrocentricity is always the opposite of Eurocentricity; and (5) Afrocentricity is still confined by Eurocentrism (see Miike, 2008a). I will herein address a few common misconceptions about Asiacentricity as a way of further clarifying this paradigmatic concept.

One widespread misconception about Asiacentricity is that to be Asiacentric is to be ethnocentric. Asiacentricity is neither a hegemonic Asiacentrism nor an Asian version of ethnocentric Eurocentrism. Asiacentricity is not a universalist position but a particuralist stance. Asiacentricity does not present the Asian worldview as the only universal frame of reference and impose it on non-Asians. It is the argument of Asiacentrists that to theorize from the vantage point of *Asians* as centered is the best way to capture the agency of *Asian* people and the cultural world of *Asia*. They do not deny the value of other non-Asiacentric perspectives on Asians. Nevertheless, they reject the hegemonic ideology that non-Asiacentric theoretical standpoints are superior to Asiacentric ones and therefore can grossly neglect the latter in the discussion and discourse surrounding Asian people and phenomena (Miike, 2008b).

It is often assumed that, if she or he is Asiacentric, one is against other centers. But one can be Asiacentric and also Afrocentric, for example. Afrocentricity and Eurocentricity (*not* Eurocentrism) can enrich each other's knowledge especially in intercultural studies. Afrocentric and Eurocentric theorizing about intercultural communication between Africans and Europeans can complement each other. As Ngũgĩ (1993) aptly pointed out, "The question was not that of mutual exclusion between Africa and Europe but the basis and the starting point of their interaction" (pp. 8–9). Asante (2007b) is of the opinion that centricity provides the basis of intercultural equality. He avowed that "recognition of one's cultural heritage and origin allowed a communicator on a level of respect that would not happen if one communicator was 'taken over' by another" (p. 73). If she or he is dependent on other cultures to define her or his own culture, Asante (2007b) asseverated, one will never have subject-subject intercultural relationships for mutual dialogue on an equal footing.

Another prevailing misconception about Asiacentricity is that to be an Asiacentrist is to be an essentialist. By implications, according to the critics, Asiacentricity also ignores the internal diversity, hybridity, and fluidity of Asian cultures. First of all, like Afrocentricity, Asiacentricity as a metatheory concerns itself more with *how* we theorize than with *what* we theorize. Karenga (2002) maintained that Afrocentricity is "a quality of thought and practice rather than thought and practice themselves" (p. 47). What he meant is that Afrocentrists can debate over the content of African values and ideals and yet remain committed to the metathereotical idea of the centrality of African values and ideals in their academic pursuits about African thinking and behavior. Asante (1998a) also made it explicit that "being Afrocentric in one's analysis does not mean conforming to the one 'doctrine' of Afrocentricity – there are many ways to discuss the centeredness of a text, document, or person" (p. ix). Likewise, to center Asian values and ideals in an Asiacentric inquiry is not the same as to essentialize Asianness.

Some Asiacentrists are often mistaken as essentialists because they take intense interest in commonalities among Asian cultures and continuities between Asians on the continent and in the diaspora. To be sure, Asiacentrists presuppose that some common aspects of Asian cultures exist due to their geographical closeness and subsequent intercultural exchanges. Asiacentrists and other centrists also believe that there are relatively stable aspects of a culture. However, this intellectual stance does not deny diversities among and within Asian cultures. As a matter of fact, following the principle of Asiacentricity, Asiacentric approaches can promote the most detailed and nuanced understanding of within-Asia cultural differences (Miike, 2006). Furthermore, taking a centric position does not lead to immutablism, which is "the belief that there can be no change, no influence, and no impact on cultures from outside" (Asante, pers. comm.). Being "Asiacentric does not mean that there is no possibility of influence from outside Asia, but simply that the Asiacentric perspective relates fundamentally to cultural, not racial, attitude, responses, and behaviors that have developed over time" (Asante, pers. comm.).

Still another pertinent misconception about Asiacentricity is that being Asian is equated with being Asiacentric. The underlying logic is that non-Asians cannot become Asiacentric. It is repeatedly made clear in Afrocentric and Asiacentric writings that being centric is a matter of consciousness. Non-Asians can be Asiacentric if they develop their Asiacentric consciousness by gaining a culturally centered location through culture learning. On the other hand, the fact that one was biologically born as a person of Asian decent does not guarantee that she or he is Asiacentric. No centrist presumes the direct link between biology and ideology. However, it may be the case that an Asian identity and cultural familiarity can foster the Asiacentric consciousness. Asian researchers, for example, may find it easier to be Asiacentric in scholarship because of their cultural familiarity with Asian languages, religious-philosophical traditions, and histories. Tanno (2007) mentioned that we cannot assume insider researchers are culturally sensitive while outsider researchers are culturally insensitive, but we can generally surmise that insider researchers have more "intimate" cultural knowledge and understand "sometimes double or triple meanings of words used in different contexts" (p. 242). Insiders in Asian communities thus may be more equipped to theorize and research culture and communication from Asiacentric perspectives.

I wish to emphasize once again before closing this section that neither Afrocentrists nor Asiacentrists are cultural chauvinists and separatists. They are indeed humanists. They are simply protesting that Eurocentric perspectives are too narrow to account for the richness and complexities of *human*, not European, experiences, and that there are different perspectives, expressed through different particularities, based on different cultural locations. Their thesis is that hearing all voices form all cultural locations is humane. Asante (1998b) eloquently remarked:

> We all possess the cultural capacity to see, explain, and interpret from the vantage point of our existential location. In the West and elsewhere, the European in the midst of other peoples, has often propounded an exclusive view of reality; the exclusivity of this view creates a fundamental human crisis. In some cases, it has created cultures arrayed against each other or even against themselves. Afrocentricity's response certainly is not to impose its own particularity as a universal, as Eurocentrism

has often done. But hearing the voice of African American culture with all of its attendant parts is one way of creating a more sane society and one model for a more humane world (p. 23).

Asian Cultures for Asiacentric Communication Theorizing

The first section of this chapter problematized theoretical, methodological, and comparative Eurocentrism. The second part of the chapter then clarified Asiacentricity by identifying its major dimensions and addressing its common misconceptions. This last segment of the chapter maps out three content dimensions of an Asiacentric metatheory that I have propounded (Miike, 2003, 2006, 2008b) and discusses the possibility of Asiacentric comparisons based on indigenous theorizing attempts from these dimensions. I have elsewhere delineated other components of the metatheory of Asiacentricity (i.e., metatheoretical assumptions, research objectives, and methodological considerations). I will thus focus mainly on the content dimensions because they constitute the core idea of "culture as theory." It must be kept in mind that I am not proposing *the* Asiacentric metatheory of communication. There may be other ways of metatheorizing based on the principle of Asiacentricity.

The linguistic dimension

The first dimension of culture as a resource for theory building is language. According to Ngũgĩ (1986), "Language, any language, has a dual character; it is both a means of communication and a carrier of culture" (p. 13). He held the view that "a specific culture is not transmitted through language in its universality but in its particularity as the language of a specific community with a specific history" (p. 15). Theorizing with key concepts in different languages is therefore one of the important steps toward diversifying analytical tools in intercultural communication research. Indigenous concepts inscribed in local languages open up different pathways to the nuanced understanding of cultural values and communication behaviors. As Mendoza (2006) tersely put it, language itself is "a powerful system of representation" (p. 169). Overviewing the Filipino practice of indigenous theory-building called *Pantayong Pananaw* (a "for-us" perspective), she contended that "the shift from English to Filipino is here viewed to be more than a mere formalistic gesture avowing (guaranteeing) national sentiment. Rather, it is seen as facilitating transformation of the very structure of knowing" (p. 169). Indeed, each language serves as an excellent theoretical window from which we can look at each cultural world (Miike, 2007b).

Theorizing from Asian linguistic resources will invigorate our thinking toward an Asiacentric terrain of intercultural communication research when we undertake three essential tasks: (1) to valorize and vitalize as many Asian concepts in Asian languages as possible as they relate to human interaction; (2) to locate those Asian concepts in relation to one another so that one can see how they intersect; and (3) to speculate on the deep structure of communication that is unfolding (Chen and Miike, 2006). Of prime importance is a thoroughgoing examination of indigenous communication-equivalent terms in Asian languages. There is a dire need to explore what "communication" means in an Asian sense by consolidating communication-equivalent terms in Asian languages. Chen (2002), for example, isolated eight communication concepts in traditional China:

1   *Chuan* means "to turn or to revolve," referring to delivering or forwarding a message, teaching knowledge and skills, recording a person's life, and orally distributing information.
2   *Bo* means "to sow seed," referring to spreading or disseminating messages.
3   *Yang* means "to rise up and flutter (as a flag), to flourish, to manifest," referring to consciously making a message or person flourishing or manifesting in public.
4   *Liu* means "to flow (like water)," referring to a process in which one's reputation or virtuous message is disseminated naturally and unintentionally.
5   *Bu* means "the woven cloth," referring to the downward process of announcing or disseminating organized information or government order to the public.
6   *Xuan* means "the emperor's room or the imperial decree or edict," referring to the dignified declaration or proclamation of the emperor's order.
7   *Tong* means "unobstructed," referring to the free flow of oral communication.
8   *Di* means "to deliver or exchange," referring to the exchange or delivery of materials via, for example, the courier system (pp. 256–257).

For another example, Nakazawa (2000) traced the history of the Japanese communication concept of *hanashiai* (mutual talk). This word, which is in everyday use in Japan today, connotes conversation, discussion, consultation, accommodation, negotiation, and resolution. According to Nakazawa (2000), *hanashiai* as a feeling-oriented mode of interaction was developed in farming villages during the Edo period (1603–1868). It was used in village meetings in order to resolve individual differences to reach a group consensus. Villagers needed to help one another for their survival but always had all sorts of conflict as any human community would. Thus, they had to develop a system of communication leading to mutual understanding and cooperation. *Hanashiai* aimed to avoid direct confrontation between villagers and required them to share a particular space and spend a certain amount of time, talking over things together. This practice helped them to develop a group identity. The role of the harmonizer in *hanashiai* was to listen very well, and very patiently, ask villagers to meet halfway, and propose to make a decision when the mood of consensus is beginning to emerge. Nakazawa's (2000) theoretical excursion reveals how Japanese *hanashiai* communication was, and still is, conceptualized in terms of its forms and functions.

The religious-philosophical dimension

The second dimension of culture as a resource for theory building is religion and philosophy. As Yum (2000) noticed, most US Eurocentric cross-cultural studies of communication simply discern and describe cultural patterns in other countries and then compare and contrast them to those of the United States, rarely going beneath the surface to explore the source of such differences. Such a tendency is particularly strong in a number of cross-cultural research reports on Asian communication. It must not be forgotten that, whether it is good or bad, religious-philosophical foundations have been institutionalized in Asia for centuries and have impacted the way Asian societies and communication systems are structured. Theorizing from religious-philosophical traditions as intellectual resources, therefore, will help us understand how the current presuppositions and postulates of Asian cultures and communication have come into shape and why. It will also demystify the broader socio-cultural contexts of communication in Asia. Chang (2008), who carefully read Confucian teachings about speaking in the *Analects*, concluded:

> To appropriately theorize about the Confucian view of language—and perhaps more importantly, how language is used in modern-day Confucianist cultures—one must appreciate the full scope of Confucian perspectives on human emotion, the role emotion plays in different orders of relationship, the cultivation of virtue and moral character, the coordination of form and substance, the establishment of society, and the overall view of the universe. It is only through such in-depth understanding of the philosophical roots and worldviews of Asian cultures that one can come to understand the meaning of Asian communication (p. 108).

Dissanayake (2003) elucidated the Buddhist teaching of *samma vaca* (right speech) and discussed its moral implications in Asian verbal communication. There are four primary guidelines for right speech: (1) it should be de-linked with falsehoods of any sort; (2) it discourages slander and calumny leading to friction and hostility among people; (3) it presupposes the absence of, and the refraining of use of, harsh language; and (4) it encourages speakers to desist from frivolous and idle chatter and to embrace purposeful and productive speech. In a nutshell, right speech addresses "all such precautions that should be taken for not hurting others by one's speech. On the other hand, speaking the truth cannot be compromised" (Verma, 1997, p. 31). It would be commendable to perform an Asiacentric rhetorical analysis to comprehend to what extent "good" speeches of contemporary Asian public speakers are compatible with the Buddhist ethics of right speech.

There have been not many theoretical investigations that draw out communicative ideas and insights from Asian classical literature in order to account for current patterns and practices of Asian communication (Miike, 2007b). This present paucity of theory construction from Asian canonized treatises leads us to prematurely conclude that Asian religions and philosophies are "past things" and "totally irrelevant" to contemporary research on Asian cultures and communication. If we do not know anything about Asian traditions of thought, then, how can we see its enduring influence on present-day Asian communication? For example, Bharat Muni's monumental book, *The Natyashastra*, is said to be the earliest work on communication philosophy in India and used an indigenous communication-equivalent term *Sadharanikaran* (Yadava, 1987). Informed scholars alluded to intriguing similarities and differences between Bharat's concept of *Sadharanikaran* and Aristotle's concept of rhetoric. To this date, however, *The Natyashastra* has not received the prominence it deserves among Asiacentric communication thinkers. Although Chen and Miike (2003), Dissanayake (1988), Kincaid (1987), Miike (2009a, 2009c), and Miike and Chen (2006, 2007) assembled many religious-philosophical inquiries into Asian communication, much remains to be done to theorize the nature and ideal of communication from Buddhism, Confucianism, Hinduism, Islam, Shinto, and Taoism as central resources of Asiacentric insight.

The historical dimension

The third dimension of culture as a resource for theory building is history. Traditional Eurocentric cross-cultural communication specialists, either social scientific or interpretive, have paid scant attention to Asian histories of domestic, within-regional, and cross-continental intercultural encounters. Eurocentric intercultural communication critics are predisposed to interrogate them only as targets of deconstruction through their Western theoretical lenses. Consequently, it is hardly surprising that there are few Asiacentric inquires in intercultural communication research that illuminate the rich histories of Asia as theoretical resources despite the fact that Asian historical struggles have much to offer in theorizing about intercultural communication problems, ethics, and competence. Throughout their long histories, Asians have had intercultural contacts with different peoples, ideas, and products from different neighboring communities. All Asian nations have extensively experienced the aggression and colonization of Western empires. Furthermore, Japan invaded other Asian nations under the highly politicized slogan of the "Greater East Asia Coprosperity Sphere." It behooves Asiacentric communication historians to hark back to historical events in Asia with the aim of theorizing about Asiacentric ethics and competence toward global and local harmonious communication (Miike, 2008b).

It would prove to be of immense value for Asiacentrists to tap into many biographies of outstanding Asian individuals who lived multicultural lives in order to theorize about the profile of an intercultural person from Asian perspectives. Gu Hongming (1857–1928) serves as an illustrative example. He was the first Chinese professor of English at the University of Peking. He was born in Malaysia, went to Europe to receive education, and married a Japanese woman by the name of Yoshida Sadako. He then settled in China – his cultural home. He called himself *Dongxi Nanbei* (East-West-South-North). He had an excellent command of English and was well versed in Western civilization. Nonetheless, he deployed neither his English competence nor his knowledge of Western intellectual tradi-tions for the Westernization of China. Instead, he was determined to expound on Chinese traditions of thought in English so as to further the understanding and resilience of Chinese ancient wisdom abroad (Hirakawa, 2005). His life was inter-cultural, but he chose to be rooted in Chinese cultural heritage. What kind of Asiacentric philosophy of multicultural life can we construct from biographical narratives of such Asian intercultural women and men as Gu?

Reading through cumulated voices of Asians who went to the West and returned to Asia would render it compelling to build an Asiacentric theory of identity trans-formation and intercultural competence. Even in a speculative estimate, four stages may be identifiable: (1) the yearning stage where one is so fascinated with Western languages, values, and lifestyles and tries to absorb everything Western; (2) the reflection stage where, after his or her certain exposure to the West, one is begin-ning to become reflexive and critical of the West and recognizes the limit of imita-tion; (3) the returning stage where one ruminates on her or his cultural roots and learns to embrace her or his heritage; and (4) the integration stage where in one's mind, there is neither a blind superiority complex nor a blind inferiority complex toward the West. Those Asians who reached the final stage know how to extend their own cultural heritage and what aspects of their culture should be changed. They can be critical of both their own and other cultures. They can assess strengths and weaknesses of their own cultures in local and global contexts. They demand that the West understand Asia more while they also tell other Asians that Asia needs to change for a better Asia. They are deeply rooted in their own cultures and yet have global visions.

Asiacentric assumptions and propositions

I have thus far sketched three content dimensions for Asiacentric theorizing in intercultural communication scholarship. One may be under the impression that they may still be very broad domains of theoretical inquiry. Through my extensive review of literature, I formulated philosophical assumptions and communication propositions from Asiacentric perspectives. These assumptions and propositions, along with other works such as Chen (2004, 2006), Chen and Starosta (2003), Dissanayake (2003, 2006b), Ishii, Kume and Toyama (2001), may be taken as points of departure for advancing Asiacentric theorizing from the above three dimensions. Miike (2003) spelled out three philosophical assumptions for an Asiacentric paradigm of communication. Ontologically, everyone and everything are interrelated across space and time. Epistemologically, everyone and everything become meaningful in relation to others. Axiologically, harmony is vital to the survival of everyone and everything. There are three implications for theorizing communication: (1) Communication takes place in contexts of multiple relation-ships across space and time; (2) The communicator is perceptually and behaviorally active and passive in a variety of contexts; and (3) Mutual adaptation is of central importance in harmonious communication processes.

Featuring the five main elements of an Asian worldview (i.e., circularity, harmony, other-directedness, reciprocity, and relationality), Miike (2004, 2007a, 2009b) also laid out five propositions on human communication from an Asiacentric perspective: (1) Communication is a process in which we remind ourselves of the interdependence and interrelatedness of the universe; (2) Communication is a process in which we reduce our selfishness and egocentrism; (3) Communication is a process in which we feel the joy and suffering of all sentient beings; (4) Communication is a process in which we receive and return our debts to all sentient beings; and (5) Communication is a process in which we moralize and harmonize the universe. In light of these aforementioned broad philosophical assumptions and communication propositions, Asiacentric communicologists may be able to embark on theorizing about deep and surface structures of communication in a specific Asian culture or coculture.

Asiacentric comparisons and visions

On the basis of indigenous theories from Asian linguistic, religious-philosophical, and historical cultural resources, Asiacentrists are prodded to engage in Asiacentric and non-Eurocentric comparisons so that they can overcome the foregoing theoretical, methodological, and comparative Eurocentrism in intercultural communication research. How do the Chinese concept of *keqi* and the Thai concept of *kreng jai* differ? How do the Korean concept of *nunchi* and the Filipino concept of *pakikiramdam* differ? How differently do Hinduism and Buddhism see silence? How differently do theories out of Sri Lankan and Indian colonial histories tell about the problems and ethics of intercultural communication? How were *gaman* and *shikata ga nai* used before World War II among Japanese Americans? How did their meanings change after World War II? Interestingly enough, for instance, both the Indian *rasa* theory of communication (see Kirkwood, 1990; Tewari, 1992; Yadava, 1987) and the Confucian ideas about communication (see Tu, 1984, 1991, 2002) recognized the primacy of emotion in human interaction and enunciated the sympathetic heart (*sahridaya*) and ego-detachment in order for communicators to share commonness and realize the undivided nature of the cosmic world. According to both theories, poetry is highly regarded as an important tool in understanding the true nature of the world around us. Curiously, the communication concept of *Sadharanikaran*, briefly touched on earlier, accentuates the simplification and exemplification of ideas, which parallels the Zen Buddhist view of communication.

By assessing which aspect of culture should be embraced as globally significant local knowledge, Asiacentric lines of communication inquiry hold great promise for presenting viable cultural visions for a new Asia. Furthermore, Asiacentric theories and comparisons make possible context-sensitive Asiacentric critiques of Asian cultures and communication. Hence, there is the possibility of Asiacentric *critical* intercultural communication studies. Conventional Asian communication scholarship is very much male-centered, heterosexual-oriented, urban-biased, and nationalistic (Chen and Miike, 2006). Past Asiacentric theoretical investigations have concentrated on East Asian cultures and communication. The Asiacentric scholarly enterprise must make concerted efforts to redress this imbalanced focus of theoretical exploration. Asiacentrists will widen their theoretical discourse by illuminating Asian female languages, Asian female interpretations of religious-philosophical traditions, and Asian female historical voices. In this regard, Yin's (2006, 2009) Asiacentric feminist theory of communication based on duty and responsibility is worthy of attention. Future Asiacentric theorizing activities will also benefit a great deal from South Asia, Southeast Asia, and West Asia input (Miike, 2006). There is no reason to conceive that the principle of Asiacentricity is only applicable to the East Asian region.

Critical intercultural communication scholarship focuses on issues of identity, power, privilege, and structural forces in reconceptualizing the nature and complexity of culture and in reconsidering the past and future of intercultural relations (Mendoza, Halualani, and Drzewiecka, 2002). The primary locus of its inquiry is macrocontexts (i.e., historical, institutional, economic, political, and ideological factors) that frame the conditions of (inter)cultural communication and the positions of (inter)cultural communicators. Critical studies of culture and communication aim to uncover and eliminate contextual constraints and hegemonic practices toward more equal and mutual relations within and across cultures. Critical interculturalists are, therefore, committed to more contextualized, historically situated, and politicized scholarship about culture and communication (Halualani, Mendoza, and Drzewiecka, 2009). The Asiacentric approach is in agreement with this general agenda of critical intercultural communication studies.

However, two important points can be made as to what it means to be a critical intercultural communication researcher, particularly in an Asiacentric sense. First, to be critical in theory and practice requires critical consciousness regarding the Eurocentric structure of cultural and comparative knowledge. We cannot be truly critical when we are blind imitators and perpetuators of Eurocentric theoretical knowledge and not original thinkers and theorists of our own communication realities. As the title of the present essay implicitly suggests, we cannot be critical, in the Asiacentric sense of the word, if we refuse to abandon the ideological structure of the hierarchical relationship between Western theories and visions (or ideas and ideals of humanity) and non-Western texts and realities, even when we are addressing social justice and global ethics in the postcolonial world.

Second, because knowledge reconstruction as well as knowledge deconstruction is an overriding goal of the Asiacentric project, the language of criticism, resistance, and prospect must be captured and theorized in Asian cultural specificities and particularities. The three content dimensions of the Asiacentric metatheory can not only describe and interpret Asian communication realities but also critique and transform them from the perspective of Asian communicators. From an Asiacentric vantage point, the role of critical interculturalists is to pluralize and localize theoretical lenses and political issues that are central to critical scholarship. The very notions of "power" and "equity," for example, should be conceptualized in multiple languages, within multiple national contexts, and between multiple international relationships. We ought to reevaluate and enrich the unitary and de-contextualized discourse on identity and hegemony in intracultural and intercultural interactions.

By Way of Conclusion: On Being Rooted and Open

Kumaravadivelu (2008) compared and contrasted the intercultural lives of two Indian historical figures, Jawaharlal Nehru and Mahatma Gandhi. They both encountered the colonizing West but dealt with its cultural impact in different ways. Nehru developed his peculiar hybrid identity and suffered from his feeling of belonging nowhere throughout his life. Gandhi, on the other hand, always remembered where his roots were and embraced the best of his own heritage without closing his windows to other cultures. Unlike Nehru, Gandhi felt neither culturally alienated nor psychologically ambivalent. Wherever appropriate, he was not reluctant to pronounce his debts to Western traditions and other non-Western philosophies in his own identity development. Kumaravadivelu (2008) observed that it is this "Gandhian view of cultural growth, with its twin pillars of rootedness and openness, that ... offers a strong foundation for the construction of global cultural consciousness in the contemporary world" (p. 169). Sparrow's (2008) recent research findings on multicultural identities seem to espouse Kumaravadivelu's (2008) observation that "Gandhi's thoughts on cultural consciousness have a greater relevance today than they had in his time" (p. 169).

The next phase of intercultural communication research exhorts us to face up to the challenge of finding a balanced way to re-describe culture and communication in context and re-interpret positive elements of all cultural traditions for both local and global communication in the contemporary world. It is self-evident that this task of theoretical re-articulation must rise above simple-minded cultural generalizations and cannot end in cultural criticism. It is the central contention of this chapter, as implied in Ngũgĩ's (1993) remark at the outset, that Asiacentricity, which views Asian cultures as central resources for theory building, is intellectually necessary not only to re-describe and re-articulate the contours and dynamics of Asian communication in concrete living, but also to re-interpret and re-envision the best of Asian cultural heritage. The Asiacentric idea is not an ethnocentric metatheoretical position, but a humanistic and humanizing stance. To be rooted in Asian cultures is not the same as to be against other non-Asian cultures.

Rootedness in the genuine sense requires a vision of pluralism (Tu, 1991). To be rooted is not to say that what is best for me is best for my neighbor. As Tu (2002) shrewdly pointed out, "The deeper you dig into our own ground of existence, the nearer we come to the common spring of humanity" (p. 88). We often presume that "universality is only attainable through abstraction, but ... it is through the 'lived concreteness' that we are in touch with the most universalized transcendence" (p. 88). Hence, abstract individualism and universalism will never work, and they will only damage human collectivity and diversity. We need to transform, not escape from, our embedded heritage to be a global citizen and have a cosmopolitan spirit (Tu, 2001). Both conventional and critical intercultural communication scholarship ought to take this point very seriously. Tu (2001) noted that equality and distinction are two complementary wheels of intercultural communication because "Without equality, there would be no common ground for communicating; without distinction, there would be no need to communicate" (pp. 69–70). Centricity provides a basis of equality and a mirror of distinction.

References

Alatas, S.F. (2002) Eurocentrism and the role of the human sciences in the dialogue among civilizations. *The European Legacy*, 7 (6), 759–770.

Alatas, S.F. (2006) *Alternative Discourses in Asian Social Science: Responses to Eurocentrism*, Sage, New Delhi, India.

Asante, M.K. (1998a) Foreword, in *Afrocentric Visions: Studies in Culture and Communication* (ed. J.D. Hamlet), Sage, Thousand Oaks, CA, pp. vii–ix.

Asante, M.K. (1998b) *The Afrocentric Idea*, rev. edn, Temple University Press, Philadelphia.

Asante, M.K. (1999) *The Painful Demise of Eurocentrism: An Afrocentric Response to Critics*, Africa World Press, Trenton, NJ.

Asante, M.K. (2005) *Race, Rhetoric, and Identity: The Architecton of Soul*, Humanity Books, Amherst, NY.

Asante, M.K. (2006a) The rhetoric of globalization: The Europeanization of human ideas. *Journal of Multicultural Discourses*, 1 (2), 152–158.

Asante, M.K. (2006b) Afrocentricity and the Eurocentric hegemony of knowledge: Contradictions of place, in *Race and Foundations of Knowledge: Cultural Amnesia in the Academy*, (eds J. Young and J.E. Braziel), University of Illinois Press, Urbana, IL, pp. 145–153.

Asante, M.K. (2007a) *An Afrocentric Manifesto: Toward an African Renaissance*, Polity Press, Cambridge, UK.

Asante, M.K. (2007b) Communicating Africa: Enabling centrity for intercultural engagement. *China Media Research*, 3 (3), 70–75.

Asante, M.K. (2008) The ideological significance of Afrocentricity in intercultural communication, in *The Global Intercultural Communication Reader* (eds M.K. Asante, Y. Miike, and J. Yin), Routledge, New York, pp. 47–55.

Bryant, J., and Yang, M.H. (2004) A blueprint for excellence for the *Asian Communication Research. Asian Communication Research*, 1 (1), 133–151.

Chang, H.-C. (2008) Language and words: Communication in the *Analects* of Confucius, in *The Global Intercultural Communication Reader*, (eds M.K. Asante, Y. Miike, and J. Yin), Routledge, New York, pp. 95–112.

Chen, G.-M. (2002) Problems and prospects of Chinese communication study, in *Chinese Communication Theory and Research: Reflections, New Frontiers, and New Directions*, (eds W. Jia, X. Lu, and D.R. Heisey), Ablex, Westport, CT, pp. 255–268.

Chen, G.-M. (ed.) (2004) *Theories and Principles of Chinese Communication* (in Chinese), Wunan, Taipei, Taiwan.

Chen, G.-M. (2006) Asian communication studies: What and where to now. *Review of Communication*, 6 (4), 295–311.

Chen, G.-M., and Miike, Y. (eds) (2003) Asian approaches to human communication (Special issue). *Intercultural Communication Studies*, 12 (4), 1–218.

Chen, G.-M., and Miike, Y. (2006) The ferment and future of communication studies in Asia: Chinese and Japanese perspectives. *China Media Research*, 2 (1), 1–12.

Chen, G.-M., and Starosta, W.J. (2003) Asian approaches to human communication: A dialogue. *Intercultural Communication Studies*, 12 (4), 1–15.

Chu, L.L. (1988) In search of an Oriental communication perspective, in *The World Community in Post-Industrial Society: Vol. 2. Continuity and Change in Communications in Post-Industrial Society*, (ed. Christian Academy), Wooseok, Seoul, South Korea, pp. 2–14.

Dissanayake, W. (ed.) (1988) *Communication Theory: The Asian Perspective*, Asian Mass Communication Research and Information Center, Singapore.

Dissanayake, W. (2003) Asian approaches to human communication: Retrospect and prospect. *Intercultural Communication Studies*, 12 (4), 17–37.

Dissanayake, W. (2006a) Globalization and the experience of culture: The resilience of nationhood, in *Globalization, Cultural Identities, and Media Representations*, (eds N. Gentz and S. Kramer), State University of New York Press, Albany, NY, pp. 24–55.

Dissanayake, W. (2006b) Postcolonial theory and Asian communication theory: Toward a creative dialogue. *China Media Research*, 2 (4), 1–8.

Fals-Borda, O., and Mora-Osejo, L.E. (2003) Context and diffusion of knowledge: A critique of Eurocentrism. *Action Research*, 1 (1), 29–37.

Gordon, R.D. (2007a) Beyond the failures of Western communication theory. *Journal of Multicultural Discourses*, 2 (2), 89–107.

Gordon, R.D. (2007b) The Asian communication scholar for the 21st century. *China Media Research*, 3 (4), 50–59.

Halualani, R.T., Mendoza, S.L., and Drzewiecka, J.A. (2009) "Critical" junctures in intercultural communication studies: A review. *Review of Communication*, 9 (1), 17–35.

Hirakawa, S. (2005) Yearning for the West and return to the East: Patterns of Japanese and Chinese intellectuals, in S. Hirakawa, *Japan's Love-Hate Relationship with the West*, Global Oriental, Kent, UK, pp. 191–209.

Ishii, S. (2004) Proposing a Buddhist consciousness-only epistemological model for intrapersonal communication research. *Journal of Intercultural Communication Research*, 33 (2), 63–76.

Ishii, S. (2007) A Western contention for Asia-centered communication scholarship paradigms: A commentary on Gordon's paper. *Journal of Multicultural Discourses*, 2 (2), 108–114.

Ishii, S. (2008) Human-to-human, human-to-nature, human-to-supernature intercultural communication: Toward developing new fields of scholarship (in Japanese). *Intercultural Communication Review*, 6, 9–17.

Ishii, S., Kume, T., and Toyama, J. (eds) (2001) *Theories of Intercultural Communication: In Search of a New Paradigm* (in Japanese), Yuhikaku, Tokyo, Japan.

Jackson, R.L. (2000) So real illusions of Black intellectualism: Exploring race, roles, and gender in the academy. *Communication Theory*, 10 (1), 48–63.

Jackson, R.L. (2010) Mapping cultural communication research: 1960s to the present, in *A Century of Transformation: Studies in Honor of the 100th Anniversary of the Eastern Communication Association*, (ed. J.W. Chesebro), Oxford University Press, New York, pp. 272–292.

Joseph, G.G., Reddy, V., and Searle-Chatterjee, M. (1990) Eurocentrism in the social sciences. *Race and Class*, 31 (4), 1–26.

Kalscheuer, B. (2009) Encounters in the third space: Links between intercultural communication theories and postcolonial approaches, in *Communicating in the Third Space*, (eds. K. Ikas and G. Wagner), Routledge, New York, pp. 26–46.

Karenga, M. (2002) *Introduction to Black Studies*, 3rd edn, University of Sankore Press, Los Angeles.

Kincaid, D.L. (ed.) (1987) *Communication Theory: Eastern and Western Perspectives*, Academic Press, San Diego, CA.

Kirkwood, W.G. (1990) Shiva's dance at sundown: Implications of Indian aesthetics for poetics and rhetoric. *Text and Performance Quarterly*, 10 (2), 93–110.

Kumaravadivelu, B. (2008) *Cultural Globalization and Language Education*, Yale University Press, New Haven, CT.

Martin, J.N., and Butler, R.L.W. (2001) Toward an ethic of intercultural communication research, in *Transcultural Realities: Interdisciplinary Perspectives on Cross-Cultural Relations*, (eds V.H. Milhouse, M.K. Asante, and P.O. Nwosu), Sage, Thousand Oaks, CA, pp. 283–298.

Martin, J.N., and Nakayama, T.K. (2008) Thinking dialectically about culture and communication, in *The Global Intercultural Communication Reader* (eds M.K. Asante, Y. Miike, and J. Yin), Routledge, New York, pp. 73–91.

Mendoza, S.L. (2005) Bridging paradigms: How not to throw out the baby of collective representation with the functionalist bathwater in critical intercultural communication, in *Taking Stock in Intercultural Communication: Where to Now?*, (eds W.J. Starosta and G.-M. Chen), National Communication Association, Washington, DC, pp. 237–256.

Mendoza, S.L. (2006) New frameworks in Philippine postcolonial historiography, in *Race and Foundations of Knowledge: Cultural Amnesia in the Academy*, (eds J. Young and J.E. Braziel), University of Illinois Press, Urbana, IL, pp. 145–153.

Mendoza, S.L., Halualani, R.T., and Drzewiecka, J.A. (2002) Moving the discourse on identities in intercultural communication: Structure, culture, and resignifications. *Communication Quarterly*, 50 (3/4), 312–327.

Miike, Y. (2003) Beyond Eurocentrism in the intercultural field: Searching for an Asiacentric paradigm, in *Ferment in the Intercultural Field: Axiology/Value/Praxis*, (eds W.J. Starosta and G.-M. Chen), Sage, Thousand Oaks, CA, pp. 243–276.

Miike, Y. (2004) Rethinking humanity, culture, and communication: Asiacentric critiques and contributions. *Human Communication: A Journal of the Pacific and Asian Communication Association*, 7 (1), 67–82.

Miike, Y. (2006) Non-Western theory in Western research? An Asiacentric agenda for Asian communication studies. *Review of Communication*, 6 (1/2), 4–31.

Miike, Y. (2007a) An Asiacentric reflection on Eurocentric bias in communication theory. *Communication Monographs*, 74 (2), 272–278.

Miike, Y. (2007b) Asian contributions to communication theory: An introduction. *China Media Research*, 3 (4), 1–6.

Miike, Y. (2008a) Advancing centricity for non-Western scholarship: Lessons from Molefi Kete Asante's legacy of Afrocentricity, in *Essays in Honor of an Intellectual Warrior, Molefi Kete Asante* (ed. A. Mazama), Editions Menaibuc, Paris, France, pp. 287–327.

Miike, Y. (2008b) Toward an alternative metatheory of human communication: An Asiacentric vision, in *The Global Intercultural Communication Reader*, (eds M.K. Asante, Y. Miike, and J. Yin), Routledge, New York, pp. 57–72.

Miike, Y. (2009a) "Cherishing the old to know the new": A bibliography of Asian communication studies. *China Media Research*, 5 (1), 95–103.

Miike, Y. (2009b) "Harmony without uniformity": An Asiacentric worldview and its communicative implications, in *Intercultural Communication: A Reader*, 12th edn, (eds L.A. Samovar, R.E. Porter, and E.R. McDaniel), Wadsworth, Cengage Learning, Boston, MA, pp. 36–48.

Miike, Y. (ed) (2009c) New frontiers in Asian communication theory (Special issue). *Journal of Multicultural Discourses*, 4 (1), 1–88.

Miike, Y., and Chen, G.-M. (2006) Perspectives on Asian cultures and communication: An updated bibliography. *China Media Research*, 2 (1), 98–106.

Miike, Y., and Chen, G.-M. (eds) (2007) Asian contributions to communication theory. *China Media Research*, 3 (4), 1–109.

Nakazawa, M. (2000) *Hanashiai* in village meetings: An archetype of Japanese communication (in Japanese). *Heian Jogakuin University Journal*, 1, 83–94.

Nakayama, T.K. (2008) Editor's statement: On (not) feeling rebellious. *Journal of International and Intercultural Communication*, 1 (1), 1–2.

Nakayama, T.K., and Martin, J.N. (2007) The "White problem" in intercultural communication research and pedagogy, in *Whiteness, Pedagogy, Performance: Dis/placing Race*, (eds L.M. Cooks and J.S. Simpson), Lexington Books, Lanham, MD, pp. 111–137.

Ngũgĩ, T. (1986) *Decolonizing the Mind: The Politics of Language in African Literature*, James Currey, Oxford.

Ngũgĩ, T. (1993) *Moving the Center: The Struggle for Cultural Freedoms*, James Currey, Oxford, UK.

Radhakrishnan, R. (2003) *Theory in an Uneven World*, Blackwell, Malden, MA.

Shuter, R. (2000) *Linking Theory to Practice in Intercultural Communication: Intracultural Theory and Research*, National Communication Association, Seattle, WA.

Shuter, R. (2008) The centrality of culture, in *The Global Intercultural Communication Reader*, (eds M.K. Asante, Y. Miike, and J. Yin), Routledge, New York, pp. 37–43.

Sparrow, L.M. (2008) Beyond multicultural man: Complexities of identity, in *The Global Intercultural Communication Reader*, (eds M.K. Asante, Y. Miike, and J. Yin), Routledge, New York, pp. 239–261.

Starosta, W.J., and Chen, G.-M. (2003a) "Ferment," an ethic of caring, and the corrective power of dialogue, in *Ferment in the Intercultural Field: Axiology/Value/Praxis*, (eds W.J. Starosta and G.-M. Chen), Sage, Thousand Oaks, CA, pp. 3–23.

Starosta, W.J., and Chen, G.-M. (2003b) On theorizing difference: Culture as centrism in *Ferment in the Intercultural Field: Axiology/Value/Praxis*, (eds W.J. Starosta and G.-M. Chen), Sage, Thousand Oaks, CA, pp. 277–287.

Suzuki, D.T. (1964) *An Introduction to Zen Buddhism*, Grove Press, New York.

Suzuki, D.T. (1997) *The Eastern viewpoint* (in Japanese), Iwanami Shoten, Tokyo.

Tanno, D.V. (2007) Intercultural communication: Its theories, its practices, its value, in *The Media and International Communication*, (eds B. Lewandowska-Tomaszczyk, T. Płudowski, and D.V. Tanno), Peter Lang, Frankfurt am Main, Germany, pp. 239–251.

Tewari, I.P. (1992) Indian theory of communication. *Communicator: Journal of the Indian Institute of Mass Communication*, 27 (1), 35–38.

Tu, W. (1984) Core values in Confucian thought, in *Confucian Ethics Today: The Singapore Challenge*, (ed. W. Tu), Federal Publications, Singapore, pp. 2–38.

Tu, W. (1991) A Confucian perspective on global consciousness and local awareness. *International House of Japan Bulletin*, 11 (1), 1–5.

Tu, W. (1998) Mustering the conceptual resources to grasp a world in flux, in *International Studies in the Next Millennium: Meeting the Challenge of Globalization*, (ed. J.A. Kushigian), Praeger, Westport, CT, pp. 3–15.

Tu, W. (2001) The context of dialogue: Globalization and diversity, in *Crossing the Divide: Dialogue among Civilizations* (ed. G. Picco), School of Diplomacy and International Relations, Seton Hall University, South Orange, NJ, pp. 49–96.

Tu, W. (2002) Confucianism and civilization, in *Dialogue of Civilizations: A New Peace Agenda for a New Millennium*, (eds M. Tehranian and D.W. Chappell), I.B. Tauris, London, pp. 83–89.

Tu, W. (2008) Mutual learning as an agenda for social development, in *The Global Intercultural Communication Reader*, (eds M.K. Asante, Y. Miike, and J. Yin), Routledge, New York, pp. 329–333.

Verma, J. (1997) Hinduism, Islam and Buddhism: The sources of Asian values, in *Progress in Asian Social Psychology*, vol. 1, (eds K. Leung, U. Kim, S. Yamaguchi, and Y. Kashima), John Wiley and Sons, Singapore, pp. 23–36.

Wallerstein, I. (1997) Eurocentrism and its avatars: The dilemmas of social science. *New Left Review*, 226, 93–107.

Wallerstein, I. (2006) *European Universalism: The Rhetoric of Power*, New Press, New York.

Wong, P., Manvi, M., and Wong, T.H. (1995) Asiacentrism and Asian American studies? *Amerasia Journal*, 21 (1/2), 137–147.

Yadava, J.S. (1987) Communication in India: The tenets of *Sadharanikaran*, in *Communication Theory: Eastern and Western Perspectives* (ed. D.L. Kincaid), Academic Press, San Diego, CA, pp. 161–171.

Yin, J. (2006) Toward a Confucian feminism: A critique of Eurocentric feminist discourse. *China Media Research*, 2 (3), 9–18.

Yin, J. (2009) Negotiating the center: Towards an Asiacentric feminist communication theory. *Journal of Multicultural Discourses*, 4 (1), 75–88.

Yoshitake, M. (2002) Anxiety/uncertainty management (AUM) theory: A critical examination of an intercultural communication theory. *Intercultural Communication Studies*, 11 (2), 177–193.

Yoshitake, M. (2004) Research paradigm for dialogue among diversities: Refinement of methodological pluralism, in *Dialogue among Diversities*, (eds G.-M. Chen and W.J. Starosta), National Communication Association, Washington, DC, pp. 16–42.

Yum, J.O. (2000) The impact of Confucianism on interpersonal relationships and communication patterns in East Asia, in *Intercultural Communication: A Reader*, 9th edn, (eds L.A. Samovar and R.E. Porter), Wadsworth, Belmont, CA pp. 63–73.

Yum, J.O. (2007) Confucianism and communication: *Jen, li*, and *ubuntu*. *China Media Research*, 3 (4), 15–22.

Further Reading

Asante, M.K., Miike, Y., and Yin, J. (eds) (2008) *The Global Intercultural Communication Reader*, Routledge, New York.

Gunaratne, S.A. (2008) Falsifying two Asian paradigms and de-Westernizing science. *Communication, Culture and Critique*, 1 (1), 72–85.

Miike, Y. (2010) An anatomy of Eurocentrism in communication scholarship: The role of Asiacentricity in de-Westernizing theory and research. *China Media Research*, 6 (1), 1–11.

13

Entering the Inter
Power Lines in Intercultural Communication

Aimee Carrillo Rowe

How are we to understand the "inter" within intercultural communication? What is at stake for the politics and possibilities within this rich field of study if we dwell in that in-between space toward which the *inter* gestures? This essay works the space of the inter to explore the transformative possibilities for theorizing subjectivity as a function of belonging. While the field of intercultural communication is often preoccupied with questions of identity, here I explore what might be gained from shifting our mode of inquiry from identity-based claims to being ("I am") to community-based reflections on our becoming ("I belong"). This is not to suggest that identity is not a salient category, but rather to explore the fluid spaces *between* categories as sites of potentiality for a new and more possible politics of accountability and love.

The inter of intercultural communication is a capacious site of unfolding interaction across lines of difference. It gestures toward the unknown and unknowable space between unevenly located subjects. The inter points to a process vexed with contradictions: a generative site of learning and yet one that can never be mastered; the specter of difference that haunts, even as it invites us to interrogate the privilege of alleged sameness; a space most productively approached with humility and a *yearning* for an/ other that inspires us to move to and through a space where we are not the expert. This is to say that the inter marks a process of becoming that is constituted *between* subjects, who, in engaging the inter are, in turn, reconstituted through their exchange.

To engage with an/other, to cross borders and communicate across categories of difference is also to move across and through *power lines.* Because the inter marks the process of exchange in which differently located subjects encounter an/ other, it is also a site enmeshed in power relations. We do not find each other on a level playing field. Rather, we find one an/other in uneven relations to power and privilege, marginality, and subordination. Yet the dominant discourse of race, class, gender, and transnational relations in the United States is organized through

The Handbook of Critical Intercultural Communication, edited by Thomas K. Nakayama and Rona Tamiko Halualani. © 2010 Blackwell Publishing Ltd.

disavowal of power: we do not see color; women and men are "equal"; gays are "included"; the poor are poor because they did not work hard enough; the immigrants broke the law; and so on. In spite of this investment in "power-evasive"[1] rhetoric, the boundaries of our becoming are organized to keep us safely aligned with "our own." "Despite intense and frequent disavowal that whiteness means anything at all to those designated," George Lipsitz observes (1998, p. viii), the insistence that race does not matter is belied by relational choices. Whites make virtually every major life decision around issues of race: whom they or their children may love, where they might work or go to school, which neighborhood they live in, who their friends and colleagues are. The power lines that connect us to others are not neutral; they are neither natural nor are they innocent.

Thus, in order to productively explore this space of the inter, we must attend to the power lines at stake in each encounter that constitutes the "intercultural." To do so, I draw upon my research on what I call "transracial"[2] alliances among academic feminists. Feminism is one of those sites of intercultural communication in which the potentials for truly engaging an/other are as vexed as they are productive. One challenge that unites "feminists" is a politics concerned with gaining gender equality for "women." However, when we look at feminism more closely, we realize that we cannot presume to know who "women" are, or that the *forms* of subordination that they experience are the same. Indeed, some women are subordinated by other women. Thus feminism, as a project that seeks to empower women, is saturated in power. So the encounters between feminists of difference are intercultural encounters. For feminists of difference to truly engage with one another, they must move across and mobilize power lines. These tensions make feminism a productive site to explore the inter of intercultural communication as each encounter between differently located feminists holds tremendous potential to transform *and* to reify power relations.

The communication process, then, is the site of our becoming. To remain bound within our own group is to naturalize categories of identity, and to risk the effort of crossing power lines is to transform those very categories. Yet the impulse to reify modes of belonging – particularly dominant modes of belonging like whiteness and heterosexuality – is so palpable as to seem "natural." We have little guidance in the practices that might empower us to form transracial belongings. To attend to the inter that constitutes all of our exchanges is to dwell within the possibilities and constraints of identity. It is to become mindful of the ways in which we conform to the weight of those constraints, the ways we rail against those constraints, and the stakes of our most intimate encounters in the larger landscape of intercultural communication. It is also to hold ourselves accountable for the identities we are creating: assimilating as "minorities," staking out a critical territory as "people of color," reifying whiteness as "whites," challenging hegemonic whiteness as "antiracist whites," "queers" moving in and out of the closet, "heterosexuals" remaining bound within the confines of heterosexuality or aligning their belongings with queers, and so forth. We also might pivot strategically among these modes of belonging.[3]

This is to suggest that to occupy a social location (e.g., as a working-class straight white male, as a queer Chicana, as a heterosexual African American woman, as a married Filipina) determines a range of possibilities through which we might engage the intercultural, but it does not bind us to any particular mode of belonging, set of assumptions, or communication practices that might animate our encounters. Identity is an *effect* of our belongings. Thus to dwell in the space of the inter is to gain awareness of, and by extension to hold ourselves accountable for, who we are becoming.

Bridgework, or Entering the Inter

To engage an/other is to reach across the power lines that would separate us; it is to place ourselves vulnerably in the hands of an/other and strive to acknowledge the position of an/other. Of course, such a placing will always elude us as we are constrained by the limitations of experience, empathy, and the sedimented histories of benevolence that might animate such a gesture. Thus, to engage in intercultural communication is to tread within the abyss of the inter; it is to place ourselves willingly in the "ability of (not) knowing."[4] As we do so, we are animated by a *yearning*[5] for an/other that gains its inspiration from the healing and political power at stake in building deep connections that span power lines.

To enter the inter, then, is to constitute ones-self as a bridge-worker. To bridge is to attempt community, Gloria Anzaldúa (2002) explains, and for that "we must risk being open to personal, political, and spiritual intimacy, to risk being wounded" (Anzaldúa, 2002, p. 5). Part of this work entails moving (in and) out of safe spaces, those which feel like "home," to allow ourselves to be "stripped of the illusion of safety" which accompanies belonging to that which feels familiar (Anzaldúa, 2002, p. 5). Bridging entails creating openings, passageways, connecting with others to transform power relations. Thus to engage the inter is to tread upon the often slippery ground of unknowing, of risk, and of yearning. It is to reach toward an/other with a yearning that has inspired us to take responsibility for educating ourselves about the power relations that constitute our location. It is also to hold ourselves responsible for grappling with our own oppression. "Without an emotional, heartfelt grappling with the source of our own oppression," Cherríe Moraga writes, "without naming the enemy within ourselves and outside us, no authentic, non-hierarchical connection among oppressed groups can take place" (Moraga, 1981, p. 29). This grappling circumvents the danger of "deal[ing] with oppression purely from a theoretical base" (Moraga, 1981, p. 29), opening us to "frightening questions: how have I internalized my own oppression? How have I oppressed?" (Moraga, 1981, p. 30).

These are frightening questions that are risked in order to more mindfully engage the power lines that shape the space between differently located subjects. These questions have guided my encounters with academic feminists. As I reflect on these questions, I consider the different ways I seem to be read. I am a mixed-race queer Chicana who passes, at times, for white and straight and at other times is read as a queer woman of color. How people read me seems to depend on who's reading me, their own investments in who they want me to be, and the modes of belonging, or intercultural communication, in which I engage. Let me share a few examples from my research. For my study on transracial feminist alliances, I interviewed white women and women of color to ask them how they thought about alliances, feminism, race, and identity. At the end of each interview I asked them how they were reading my identity. I was curious how they would identify me, and how my perceived location would shape our interaction.

Most of the white women and the black women I met felt, at least initially, pretty confident that I was a white woman. One white woman, Deborah, responded to my question, "How are you reading my identity?": "Um, OK, that's fun. I guess, I mean, I'm reading you as sincere, as sympathetic, thoughtful graduate student [laughs]." In spite of the fact that we'd spent the past two hours talking about issues of identity, power, and belonging, and that I'd asked Deborah about how she was reading my identity – she evaded the potentially challenging question of how she was reading my identity. To so do would be to comment on the dynamic racial difference and whiteness at stake *in the intercultural exchange*, and thus to transgress the power-evasive conditions of white belonging. Her response moves the discussion away from these more threatening topics by rearticulating "identity" as benign personality traits (sincere, thoughtful, sympathetic). This reading of "identity" elides the structural differences between identities and rewrites "identity" as a set of interpersonal qualities, especially ones that made Deborah feel comfortable in our difficult communication interaction.

However, I didn't want to let the conversation end there. I really wanted to know how she was reading my *identity*. "Do you read me as white?" I pressed.

"Oh sure," she replied quickly.

"And how does that affect what you say?" I continued.

"Um," she paused, gathering her thoughts. "I mean I was thinking about that when I was talking about the African American women, and I was real hesitant to talk about that stuff. Um, but I know that you know the literature through [she names a mentor of mine, who is a woman of color]. Um, I was asking myself, 'OK, would I say this to a black interviewer? And um, I'm gonna think about the fact of her being as critical as a black interviewer.' Um, because a black interviewer would be harder to say some of those things to, um, I think, um. God, I'm such a spill-your-guts person, you know?" She looked up at me, laughing and crying at the same time. "Because I know [your mentor]," she continued, "I'm gonna give both sides of the story … if it would have been a black person who I felt was similarly one-sided, I think I would have been more guarded." Another pause, "Your race is complicated too," she concluded.

This turn of the conversation moves *between* power-evasive and power-attentive modes of communication. Deborah had worked hard in our previous conversation to break with power-evasive communication when she discussed the pain she felt over her failure to build trusting alliances with the African American women in her department. Here she processes the difficulty of that move and the importance of my perceived whiteness as a condition that enabled her to "spill her guts" (i.e., to speak in power-attentive communication to get to the heart of the failed alliance).

Thus, she allowed herself to enter the "inter" by communicating with me in ways that departed from the white cultural norm of power evasion, which left her feeling vulnerable and emotionally charged. In retrospect she draws on my whiteness in order to distance herself from blackness, in order to recover some of the sameness that might cover over our frightening encounter in space of the inter. Ultimately, this reversion to sameness seems to unravel as she concludes that my "race is complicated." Certainly to transgress the boundaries of white belonging feels "complicated," especially to a white person, since whiteness functions within the space of the inter through "white solipsism."[6] A "white person," then, is someone who's been saturated in a culture and set of communication practices that constitute whiteness as a power-evasive mode of belonging.

An African American woman, Cheryl, also expresses confusion at the question of how she was reading my identity. "Well, I have to be honest that when you first emailed me, I thought, 'Aimee Rowe. Who is this white woman?'" she disclosed, laughing. "'What's she up to here?'"

"'What's going on?'" I encouraged, joining her power-attentive joke.

"And then I realized, there is a Latina identity there, so maybe she has some sense of what goes on for women of color," she paused, looking at me. "So I need to mentor this person by giving her some of my story." So while Deborah bridges to me across the inter of our power-attentive communication, Cheryl navigates the inter that arises between my whiteness and her blackness. She finds that bridge through our shared identity as women of color, which she uses as a resource to find the courage to trust me with her story. I, in turn, enter the inter by playfully affirming her suspicion of my whiteness in an effort to mutually engage the subtle critique of whiteness embedded in her initial disclosure. We meet in the inter enabled by power-attentive communication that allows her to bridge to me as someone who might treat her story and her experience with knowledge and respect – as a woman of color who shares similar experiences would.

Deborah and Cheryl and I found ways to bridge to one another across power lines within the often uncharted territory of intercultural communication. The excerpts suggest the tremendous amount of risk, vulnerability, and mindfulness with which one might enter the inter. But, we often don't know how to take such risks and the power-evasive quality of our national discourse tends to discourage us from doing so. To speak of "race" is to notice race is to risk being labeled "a racist."[7] The following section addresses some of the barriers between white women and women of color that undermine the formation of transracial feminist alliances.

The Power of Power Lines

Feminism has had a long history of racial division, based in a struggle to define the terms of power and oppression. For white feminists, who do experience and seek to remedy gender-based oppression, it is often challenging to face their privilege.

To acknowledge white, class-based, and/or heterosexual privilege, in fact, compli-cates any easy articulation of power and thus seems to undermine claims to margin-ality. Yet for women of color, who undergo quite different forms of oppression than white women, any simple gender-based notion of oppression is not only inadequate, but also covers over the very real experience of racism. Further, it elides the ways in which white women oppress women of color. For instance, because white women often serve as the privileged spokeswomen for "feminism," the theories, visions, and critiques of women of color are often marginalized. Such critiques, embedded in a feminist ethic of exposing power relations, are perceived as a threat to any unified feminism – in part because the challenge of taking respon-sibility for working against white/heterosexual privilege entails a risk on the part of white women that many would rather not take.

These power relations, in turn, shape the interpersonal and intercultural terrain of feminist alliances. With the exception of one white woman, none had significant alli-ances with women of color. Rather, they built their alliances exclusively with other whites because they recognize that in doing so, they can connect to institutional power. Carol defines alliances as "encouraging [you], letting you have positions, giving you responsibility," illustrating her point by recalling her close relationship with a dean who helped her move into administration. She concludes, "so in general, [allies are] putting me in positions where I would succeed." Heather defines an ally as "someone who listens to the problems and cares, who recommends me or says good things about me." Laura explains allies are "[p]eople who will help you. Not necessarily people you socialize with or friends, but more like mentors or alliances, people you ally yourself with to get things done … They're rooting for me to go through the process, get tenure, you know, become a full-time community member here." The purpose that alliances serve – as the gateway through which these women secure "positions" or "responsibility," a good recommendation or gain tenure – means that to be recognized as "allies" is to hold institutional power. The function of the alliance, then, is to help the individual woman gain institutional power, which comes to stand in for an individualized form of "feminism" in which each woman becomes empowered through her personal ability to connect to power.

This view of "alliances" tends to blind white women to the possibility that women of color might be considered allies. In spite of her account of an enduring "friendship" with her junior colleague, Carol does not consider Adela to be an ally. "She and I team-taught a class," Carol explained, "So we'd have lunch and we'd go over books, and it was really nice, and we've become real–," her voice trailed off. In spite of the fact that I'd been asking her if she had any allies who were women of color, she seemed to lack the word to describe what they were. "And we wrote a paper, and we've become, you know, we've remained friends for a long time," she concluded. Carol went on to explain that her relationship with Adela was "challenging," citing a situation in which Adela criticized the "exotica" in some of the readings Carol had selected. As we concluded our discussion of her relationship with Adela, Carol explained that part of the problem was that Adela was not interested in institutional power. "She could move up the ladder if she wanted to, but she doesn't want to," she asserted. So not only does Adela have less institutional power than Carol, she also challenges the political and intellectual ground of Carol's feminist work. Thus for Carol, who seeks allies who can help "[put her] in positions where [she] would succeed," building a deep alliance with Adela works *against* these investments. The resource that Adela brings to the alliance – perhaps in this case a critique of the white gaze – does not register with Carol as the kind of power she seeks to gain.

Alternatively, women of color tend to value honesty, mutual criticism, and "taking a risk" as qualities that are important in allies. An African American woman, Michele, explains that an ally "is a person who will tell you what you don't want to hear. But tell it to you anyway because they know it's right. An ally is someone who won't turn her back on you when the going gets rough. An ally is someone who has connected with you on some level, either professionally or personally, and believes in you, or if they have a higher position than you, in bringing you up. An ally is somebody who will take a risk on your behalf. They don't have to shout real loud. They don't have to say they're allies. They just have to do it." Michele sees allies as working together strategically within an uneven field of power. Unlike the white women who use alliances to connect to power, Michele seeks allies who "won't turn her back on you when the going gets rough," which presumes that the going may well get rough. Within this context of struggle, Michele seeks honest, loyal allies whom she can trust. Allies may or may not have more institutional power, and if they do, they use it to "bring you up." So for Michele, alliances function across differential power relations, foregrounding a diverse range of resources allies might bring to the alliance.

When women of color find white women whom they experience as honest and loyal, who value the critiques of white privilege, there is often ground for alliance building. However, when power-evasive communication permeates the encounter, women of color may find it difficult to connect across power lines. An African American woman, Donna explains that when she brings up racial difference with white women, she bumps up against the "perimeter" of the alliance. "You might think that you're close enough or that you've been through enough together, that you have this bond," she explains, "And you can say what's on your mind, but you don't have that bond." The "bond" becomes broken, she explains, when she feels the white woman's implicit remark to suggest, "Yes, I will support you, [but] don't cross over that border." She hits this "border," for instance, when she questions "whether or not the department might be acting in a racist way," and the response she hears is: "As a matter of fact, I don't want to discuss that racism with you at all. Or gender." For Donna, "That's the limit on the relationship. And if you can't, that to me, that perimeter, you can't discuss the things that are near and dear to your heart. You have a very superficial relationship." In this exchange of betrayal, Donna personifies both her own voice and that of her interlocutor. This suggests that the intercultural communication between white women and women of color may be quite subtle. A white woman may not realize that something she has said has broken a "bond," but by engaging in white, power-evasive modes of communication ("I don't want to discuss that racism with you at all") a "perimeter" is erected that cuts against the potential depth of the inter.

Robyn is a white woman who builds her primary alliances with women of color. Because her positionality is very much situated within the inter of an ongoing set of intercultural communication exchanges, her notion of alliances aligns not with those of white women, but with those of women of color. She describes the communication practices that enable her to connect across power lines. "When friends of color of mine have had one of those days when they've been shit on by white people and they want to bitch about white people," she reflects, "This is not the time for me to say, 'Well, you know, I'm white and I'm a nice person.'" Her voice becomes nasal as she pokes light fun at the confines imposed by white belonging. "It's not the time to do that kind of feed my ego stuff," she continues. "It's time to listen and to learn and to try to see myself in that and to see what I can, I mean, to provide support for the person, but also to use it as an opportunity to learn something about whiteness that I may very well not know." Unlike the white women in the above accounts, Robyn experiences her allies' critique of whiteness not as a detriment to belonging, but rather as an opportunity for her own growth and political edification. She views this critique, embedded in the intimate and daily experiences of racism her friends of color feel empowered to share with her, as a *resource* in her becoming. Her becoming eschews the power-evasive confines of white belonging in favor of a full-bodied immersion into the space of the inter.

Conclusion

Power lines are webs of heavy cable which criss-cross the globe. They serve to connect us to one another across time and space. They allow us to communicate with others, to build community, to shape the world within and against power relations. In their absence, no such communication/community would be possible. Power lines empower us by enabling our connectivity. Close attention to the webs of power we weave and into which we are woven renders visible the affective labor we invest into the lives of others, and how that labor is *constitutive* of the selves we are becoming. Perhaps too often such investigations produce a sense of loss or guilt or failure. The binds of whiteness, which would suppress our capacity to express and connect, often leave us feeling shallow and impotent in the face of legitimate criticism.

There is something of tremendous value, then, in becoming fluent in the histories of those who are different from us. Toni King *et al.* (2002) speaking as "African American Women in Higher Education," evoke the kitchen table as a "site of restoration and revolution" – a "black girl-to-woman rite of passage where earning a place at the table signals acceptance into womanhood. Like women before us, we sit around the kitchen table, talking deep – planning, strategizing, and healing each other's wounds" (King *et al.*, 2002, p. 405). This practice of "talking deep" prepares girls for womanhood by providing a context for them to become fluent in the politicization of their own lives.

Kitchen table talk is as strategic as it is healing, as restorative as it is revolutionary, and it need not be contained to the table talk of black women. Indeed, it might most productively be engaged by differently located subjects – men and women of color, white women and men, queers and straight folks – who seek to transform the power lines that would separate us. To sit at the table requires some effort to become fluent in the histories of those who are different from us and in the conditions of privilege and marginality that constitute our own. It entails "deep talking," vulnerable sharing, and honest, un-defensive listening.

Such engagements prepare us to encounter one another with both a more full awareness of the unevenness of our inter-relatedness and the affective investments which compel us to alter those conditions. They are one site in which we might become fluent in each other's histories as a function of coming to a more full awareness of our own. The space of the inter into which we must insert ourselves in order to engage an/other is fraught, frightening, even as it brims with transformative possibilities. It becomes vital to grapple with whatever forms of privilege we might have, because that privilege is an ongoing effect of a host of exclusions and often power-evasive communication practices that often unwittingly foreclose the space of the inter. We do our homework so we can more productively engage in bridge-work so we might vulnerably enter the inter. There, in the infinite space of un-knowingness, we stand to be transformed.

Notes

This essay was developed based on my work in *Power Lines: On the Subject of Feminist Alliances* (Carrillo Rowe, 2008). Some excerpts from that work appear in this writing.

1 In her interviews with white women Ruth Frankenberg (1993) deployed a "dialogic approach," offering information both about herself as a subject inscribed within racism and her analysis of systemic and interpersonal forms of racism as in an effort to break the "color- and power-evasive" silences that constitute white on white social relations. Frankenberg (1993) argues that white women tend to communicate in ways that evade addressing issues of power. Alternatively, women of color tend to communicate in ways that address power – what I call "power-attentive" communication.

2 Transracial is a term which strives to braid US third world (with its emphasis on the racial) and postcolonial feminist theory (with its emphasis on the trans) within a US academic context in an effort to mobilize the political insights that arise across geographical locations to rethink localized encounters from a differential theoretical framework. The trans draws upon the recent feminist work on transnational feminist alliances, which gestures toward the vitality of such alliances in transforming lives and building radical theory and praxis, but as of yet tell us little of the struggles that go on behind the scenes. Transnational feminist alliances are not automatic. Solidarity cannot be assumed, but must be fought for. But how do we fight? With whom? For whom? Against what?

3 Following Chela Sandoval (2000), I call this movement among modes of belonging "differential belonging." This concept allows us to strategically align our belongings in

ways that are flexible and self-reflexive. It calls us to be mindful of how, with whom, and for what political purposes we are engaging the intercultural.

4 Dawn Rae Davis (2002) warns, the politics of love becomes entwined with two interrelated projects of knowledge/power: knowing and its attendant extension, possessing the other as the "placeholder of marginality," while imagining this knowledge/possession through a sentimental frame of benevolence. To resuscitate feminist love, she calls for a "new commitment by which the ability of *not knowing* reconstitutes the *will to know* so that a feminist beholding of the Other woman is a witnessing of the *impossibility* of her appearance in the context of anything demarcated as knowability" (Davis, 2002, p. 155).

5 Jacqui Alexander's (2002) description of this relational labor exposes the alliance function of the heart-felt grappling which is a process of becoming "woman of color." She writes that "To *become* women of color we would need to become fluent in each other's histories ... to cultivate a way of knowing in which we direct our social, cultural, psychic, and spiritually-marked attention upon each other. We cannot afford to cease yearning for each other's company" (Alexander, 2002, p. 91). Our becoming is a *relational* process, an alliance-based inquiry. It arises neither from obligation nor fetishization, but from a *yearning* for one another that is expressed through holding ourselves accountable to our intersecting, divergent, and power laden histories. It is a labor of love that takes place in compassionate conversation, historical investigation, and relational excavation.

6 For a brief genealogy of this term, see how it has circulated in whiteness studies (see Hurtado, 1996; Moon, 1999; Rich 1979).

7 Eduardo Bonilla-Silva (2003) marks the emergence of this color blind rhetoric as emerging and gaining dominance in the late 1960s. While Jim Crowe racism worked through the assertion of the overt inferiority of people of color, color-blind racism compels "whites [to] rationalize minorities' contemporary status as the product of market dynamics, naturally occurring phenomena, and blacks' imputed cultural limitations" (Bonilla-Silva, 2003, p. 2). Ironic within this formulation is that it binds our communication into a power-evasive mode, abjecting those who speak the name of racial difference. It is based in the assumption that race did not exist until a person of color or outspoken white ally brought it into the room.

References

Alexander, J. (2002) Remembering *This Bridge*, remembering ourselves, in *This Bridge We Call Home: Radical Visions for Transformation*, (eds G. Anzaldúa and A.L. Keating), Routledge, New York, pp. 81–103.

Anzaldúa, G. (2002) Now let us shift ... the path of conocimiento ... inner work, public acts, in *This Bridge We Call Home: Radical Visions for Transformation*, (eds G. Anzaldúa and A.L. Keating), Routledge, New York, pp. 540–549.

Bonilla-Silva, E. (2003) *Racism without Racists: Color-Blind Racism and the Persistence of Racial Inequality in the United States*, Rowman and Littlefield, Lanham, MD.

Carrillo Rowe, A. (2008) *Power Lines: on the Subject of Feminist Alliances*, Duke University Press, Durham, NC.

Davis, D.R. (2002) (Love is) the ability of not knowing: Feminist experience of the impossible in ethical singularity. *Hypatia*, 17 (2), 145–161.

Frankenberg, R. (1993) *White Women, Race Matters: The Social Construction of Whiteness*, University of Minnesota Press, Minneapolis.

Hurtado, A. (1996) *The Color of Privilege: Three Blasphemies on Race and Feminism*, University of Michigan, Ann Arbor, MI.

King, T., Barnes-White, L., Gibson, N. *et al.* (2002) Andrea's third shift: The invisible work of African American women in higher education, in *This Bridge We Call Home: Radical Visions for Transformation*, (eds G. Anzaldúa and A.L. Keating), Routledge, New York, pp. 403–415.

Lipsitz, G. (1998) *Possessive Investments in Whiteness: How White People Benefit from Identity Politics*, Temple University Press, Philadelphia.

Moon, D. (1999) White enculturation and bourgeois ideology: The discursive production of "good (white) girls," in *Whiteness: The Communication of Social Identity*, (eds T.K. Nakayama and J. Martin), Sage, Thousand Oaks, London, New Delhi, pp. 177–197.

Moraga, C. (1981) La Güera, in *This Bridge Called my Back: Writing by Radical Women of Color*, (eds C. Moraga and G. Anzaldúa), New York: Kitchen Table Press, pp. 27–34.

Rich, A. (1979) *On Lies, Secrets and Silence*, W.W. Norton, New York.

Sandoval, C. (2000) *Methodology of the Oppressed*, University of Minnesota Press, Minneapolis.

14

Speaking of Difference
Language, Inequality and Interculturality

Crispin Thurlow

Identity is always a structured representation which only achieves its positive through the narrow eye of the negative.

(Stuart Hall, 1997)

Difference is the motor that produces texts.... Where there is no difference, no text comes into being.

(Gunther Kress, 1985)

I have had these two quotes on my website for a while. I like them, partly because they come from two scholars I greatly admire, but mainly because, together, they articulate the essential connection between language and identity: both are predicated on the perception, organization, and expression of difference. We make sense of ourselves by defining ourselves in relation to different people. We are impelled to speak in order to negotiate the meanings that differentiate us. Given the centrality – the unavoidability – of difference, it's all the more ironic that we struggle to handle the kinds of differences we encounter daily. Our handling of difference varies tremendously – the ways we react to difference, and the ways we speak of difference. Sometimes, we deliberately accentuate and exaggerate differences; at other times, we suppress them, either by trivializing them or by pretending that they are not there at all. Much of the time we seek to resolve or overcome differences in our yearning for commonality and solidarity. Too seldom are we willing or able to open up to differences, to recognize, accept and explore them.[1]

Difference is, of course, the bread-and-butter focus of intercultural communication – as both an academic field and as a human experience. The way in which scholars of intercultural communication engage with difference varies along much the same lines. In this regard, the work of Stuart Hall (1997) and Gunther Kress (1985; see also

The Handbook of Critical Intercultural Communication, edited by Thomas K. Nakayama and Rona Tamiko Halualani.   © 2010 Blackwell Publishing Ltd.

Kress and van Leeuwen, 1996) has helped me shape my own understanding of the links between culture and communication, and my work is accordingly framed by Critical Discourse Studies and by Critical (Inter)Cultural Studies. These are two scholarly perspectives which share a commitment to more problematized, broadly conceived views of culture and cultural identity, and both acknowledge the central role of language and communication in constituting social life. In keeping with their ritical (with a capital C – as in 'critical social theory') character, both perspectives also demand a focus on ideology, inequality, and power, as well as the interplay between microlevel textual (or discursive) practices and macrolevel economic/political processes. This is the general framework within which I situate my essay here, bringing Intercultural Communication "into dialogue" with language.[2]

Putting Language in the Picture: The Power of Words

> The deepest effect of power everywhere is inequality, as power *differentiates* and selects, includes and excludes. An analysis of such effects is also an analysis of the conditions of power – of what it takes to organize power regimes in society. The focus [should] be on how language is an *ingredient* of power processes resulting in, and sustained by, forms of inequality, and how discourse can be or become a justifiable object of analysis, crucial to an understanding of wider aspects of power relations. (Blommaert, 2005, p. 2, italics added)

Cultural mythologies are very conflictual about language. As children, many of us grow up with sayings like "Sticks and stones will break my bones but words can never harm me." At the same time, however, we are also constantly reminded that "The Pen is mightier than the sword." So, which is it to be? Does language matter or does it not? The answer is, needless to say, both a philosophical and a political one.

Most lay people and many scholars are often inclined to think of language as little more than a passive reflection of society; in other words, cultural identities, organizational hierarchies, and political structures find themselves neatly mirrored in the different ways people speak and write. Of course, to some extent this is true. However, it asks quite a lot of people to start thinking of language instead as an institution in its own right – one as powerful as any religious, state or educational system – which is also capable of creating and recreating social realities that feel so concrete and "natural". In fact, this is the ideology of language itself: persuading us that, like water and heterosexual sex, language too is somehow natural, neutral, and normal. Surely, people worry, not everything is socially constructed? Men are men, and girls are girls, right?

Well, yes and no. Just because something is *imagined* does not mean that it is *imaginary*, a fabrication without substance (cf. Gupta and Ferguson, 1992). Socially constructed identities, hierarchies, and structures certainly feel very real; they also have very real, material consequences for people. In addition to words, people really do throw sticks and stones (and worse) at those they find disturbing, threatening, or different. Nor are we at liberty to do our own thing with language, to create our own meanings. If we do there is again consequence – psychiatric or otherwise. For the most part, language is inherently *intersubjective*; we make meaning together, we learn meaning from each other, we share meaning. If we are to make sense to each other, we have to rely on the conventions of our language use, the traditions of our culture and the patterns of our relationships. When we speak, we therefore speak not with our own voice but with "social voices" – the words and worlds of meaning we inherit from others (Cameron, 2001). As Mikhail Bakhtin (1986, p. 69) famously put it: "Any utterance is a link in a very complexly organized chain of other utterances."

It is this endlessly inherited quality of language which can make it feel like a "given" or "fact" rather than an exchange or process. We are also constrained by this inheritance and, if we want to be creative, if we want to try to say something different, we have to work hard to resist the influence of these social voices which speak through us. It can be done, however. Usually, in small, one-at-a-time steps; but it can be done. In doing so, we also start to shift the conventions, traditions, and societal patterns. Feminist linguists are often ridiculed for their efforts to equalize language by, for example, challenging the use of the generic masculine pronoun (i.e. "he" or "man" for all humans/people). Do they really think they can bring about equality for women like this, ask detractors. No, says Deborah Cameron (2009), to suggest this would be either possible or sufficient is absurd. The political objective behind these linguistic moves, however, is rather to speak out against the social voices which condition us to believe that the generic masculine pronoun is the only choice we have, to help us gradually to shift our vocabulary, to rewrite the repertoire in a way which at the very least includes women and gives voice their perspectives and experiences. It's a start. It's a part of the much bigger process of social-political change.

Language really does matter. It is not simply a symbolic representation of the material; it *is* material. It is also bodily. When we speak, it is sound waves that beat against our eardrums; when we write, it is ink that is scratched, struck, or pressed onto paper. Language also has material consequence. It is with strings of words, bundles of texts, that we name and distinguish people so as to order and regulate them. We deploy our words and texts also to punish people, to harm them, to exterminate them, even. Understandably, we do not think – or like to think – of ourselves exercising language on this scale and to these ends in our everyday speech and writing. However, in using language we unavoidably amplify and augment the social voices with which we speak; and in doing so we unthinkingly privilege our own ways of speaking over that of others. On the one hand, it is the taken-for-grantedness of language which makes it so workable and so pleasurable. On the other hand, it is this same taken-for-grantedness which typically blinds us to the *significance* of our words – their meaning and their consequence.

There is a long lineage behind this way of thinking about language as a powerful social agent (or institution). Edward Sapir (1949), Benjamin Whorf (1956), Bronislaw Malinowski (2006/1946), J.L. Austin (1962), Erving Goffman (1967), Mikhail Bakhtin (1986), Michel Foucault (1981), Pierre Bourdieu (1991) and Judith Butler

What is the 'ideology'
construct um lague

(1990) – to name just a few of the better known scholars who have each demonstrated the complex, influential ways in which even the most mundane moments of
language work performatively to establish the relationships and meanings of social life
as well as many of the material realities by which our societies come to be organized.
In a nutshell, words *do* things – they make stuff happen. We do banal, well-intended
things with language, but language is never neutral. On the contrary.

There is ideology in even the most "innocent" utterances (cf. van Leeuwen,
1993) – or, rather, and to follow Jan Blommaert's advice, we can witness the *effects*
of power in all discourse. In fact, as Gunther Kress proposes, it is precisely the differential nature of power (or inequality) which also drives communication. As discourse analysts have shown for some time, the politics of language is expressed at
every level and in every domain of its use: for example, from the interactional
accomplishment of apartheid (Chick, 1985); to the gender politics of politeness
(e.g., Holmes, 1995); to the pragmatic double-bind of women saying "no" to rape
(Ehrlich, 1998); to inter-ethnic discrimination in the workplace (Gumperz, 1997)
and the classroom (Edwards, 1997). It is for this reason that most discourse analysis can be viewed as *critical* insofar as it questions "objectivity" and challenges
people's claims to "normality" and "factuality" (Jaworski and Coupland, 2006,
p. 27). Words provide us with powerful (or power-filled) resources for constructing the very differences which become the object of our study in Intercultural
Communication. There are also two additional reasons why language nowadays
warrants greater consideration in the field of Intercultural Communication, perhaps more so than ever before. I turn to these briefly as a backdrop to three case
studies which show the discursive production of cultural difference in practice.

Reason 1: Languages for Intercultural Communication

> The concept of intercultural communication can be used to gloss over the increas-
> ingly deep divide between the have and the have nots, between those who have access
> to Western discourse and power and those who don't, and the "discourses of colonial-
> ism" vehiculated by English as a global language (Kramsch, 2002, p. 282).

When we speak of language in the context of intercultural communication, it's
equally important that we speak also of *languages*. For many years, Intercultural
Communication scholarship has tended to assume that intercultural exchange only
ever happens in English, as Claire Kramsch notes in the quote above. Textbooks
and manuals devote pages and pages to helping students and practitioners "overcome" the "barriers" to "effective" intercultural communication: cultural norms,
values, and beliefs; prejudices and stereotypes; misaligned frames of reference; confusing nonverbal cues; and so forth. These are clearly important considerations but
they tend to gloss over the complexities of culture and the inequalities of life.
Surely any attempt to understand the ways of others requires that we first understand their ways of speaking?

Clearly, some people's ways of speaking are also more equal than others. Some people get to speak languages, others dialects and others "just" slang. Even then, some people's languages are considered prestigious, attractive, and cutting-edge, while others are dismissed as unimportant, insufficient, and backward. None of which are necessarily linguistic judgments. In fact, language scholars usually prefer to avoid evaluating and ranking people's ways of speaking like this, believing that labels like "language" and "dialect" are more matters of social, historical, economic, and political fact. That English is a "language" or "global language" and Ebonics or Estonian are not says more about colonial power and international political economy than it does about phonetics, syntax, and grammar. Similarly, people's attitudes towards other ways of speaking tells us lots about the material and cultural inequalities between the people who speak differently from each other.[3]

When it comes to intercultural communication, language is both everything and nothing. Speaking another person's language is no guarantee of mutual understanding and respect (native speakers consistently misunderstand and despise each other). Much can also be achieved in the way of communication outside language (see below). Nonetheless, there is often no intercultural encounter or engagement to be had in the first place, if someone has not made the effort – or been forced – to learn someone else's language. And English is far from being the *de facto* lingua franca that many English-speakers (and English-speaking Intercultural Communication scholars) seem to think it is. The same goes for our own academic discourse where the hegemonic "gold standard" continues to be publish in English or perish. With little apparent reflexivity, scholarly dialogues within (Critical) Intercultural Communication still profit from the neocolonial inheritance of English's symbolic capital.[4] Our scholarship is once again constrained by the tendency to think of language as merely (or neutrally) representational rather than as reproductive and politically invested.

In this regard, I have been working for nearly a decade with a community of (predominantly European) scholars committed to rethinking intercultural communication (the field and the practice) as a more multilingual affair, particularly in the context of modern language teaching and learning (see, for example, Jack, 2004; Glaser, 2005; Guilherme, 2007; Phipps, 2003; Wilson and Wilson, 2001).[5] These scholars are centrally concerned with promoting the communicative and transformative value of "foreign" language learning, as an end in itself, but also as a critique of the undue, taken-for-granted sway of World English. There is, it is suggested, a powerful expression and experience of interculturality to be hand first-hand in the language classroom, in language students' studies abroad, and in a sustained commitment to engaging with other people in their own terms – literally. This clearly means going beyond the already privileged languages of Europe (Glaser, 2005; Thurlow, 2004) and going beyond formulaic, "phrase-book" commodifications of local linguacultures (Phipps, 2003; Thurlow and Jaworski, 2010). Speaking of commodification ...

Reason 2: Language as a Technology for Global Capital

> In so far as the restructuring and re-scaling of capitalism is knowledge led, it is also
> discourse led, for knowledges are produced, circulated and consumed as discourses ...
> Moreover, discourses are dialectically materialized in the "hardware" and "software"
> of organizations, enacted as ways of acting and interacting, and inculcated ... as ways
> of being, as identities (Fairclough, 2002, p. 164).

Critical linguists like Norman Fairclough have become increasingly concerned with
the role of language in representing, promoting, organizing, and reproducing the
neoliberal discourses of global (or "advanced" or "postindustrial") capitalism. With
the shift from manufacture-based to service-based economics, language, and communication becomes more and more essential to contemporary life which is increasingly "textually mediated" (Fairclough, 1999) and *semioticized*. In economies
which rely on the selling and promotion of ideas, information, and lifestyles, it is
words, images and design – the look and sound of things – which become central.
If for no other reason, this should make language a major focus for (Critical)
Intercultural Communication. There are other reasons, however.

As language becomes more important to the (re)orderings of capital, it is subjected to even greater intervention and regulation – what Fairclough (1992, p. 3)
elsewhere describes as the *technologization* of discourse: "a calculated intervention
to shift discursive practices as part of the engineering of social change." Language
is therefore nowadays being used more than ever as an instrument for evaluating,
controlling and managing not just "products" but also the people who "make"
them. Along the same lines, Deborah Cameron (2000) has shown how workers
(e.g., in call centers) find themselves being policed into particular ways of speaking
according to scripts that are given to them. This kind of *stylization* is a form of
verbal hygiene (Cameron, 1995) which entails the imposition of a sanitized, "correct" way of speaking complete with its commodification as a work-related skill.
Furthermore, the kind of "have a nice day" MacDonaldization of language which
Cameron considers is also problematically gendered, rendering certain ways of
speaking both the province and the responsibility of women. Language is thus
politicized anew.

This strategic deployment of language as a technology of control is manifested
clearly in the nationalistic language testing of immigrant communities (Piller,
2001). However, what I would like to show, is how similar principles of commodification, technologization, and stylization sit at the heart of a range of banal,
everyday discursive practices. In particular, I offer three examples from my own
work of the ways language is more or less explicitly deployed as a resource for *producing* cultural differences.[6] The "hidden agenda" of these mediatized representations of language/s is to stylize a marked Other and, thus, an unmarked Self.
Cultural difference is thereby exaggerated for strategic gain, even if, on the surface,
speakers/writers appear to be celebrating "diversity" (cf. Jordan and Weedon,
1995). Ultimately, the effect is to reinscribe the unequal relation of power between

the speaker/writer and the othered community being spoken/written about, and to shore up the position of speaker/writer privilege.

Language and the Production of Difference: Three Case Studies

> Ideologies of language are significant for social as well as linguistic analysis because they are not only about language. Rather, such ideologies envision and enact links of language to group and personal identity, to aesthetics, to morality, and to epistemology (Woolard and Schieffelin, 1994, pp. 55–56).

In this section, I intend to put some of these broader ideas into practice – to make the politics of language (and languages) more concrete. In this regard, I will also draw on two language-related fields of scholarship which share an interest with Critical Discourse Studies in language and difference: Metalinguistics and Language Ideology.[7] In particular, these approaches are concerned with what people know and say about their own and other people's language practices. The focus is thus on the kinds of everyday talk about talk, language about language, or communication about communication as an integral component of social life. Everyday metalanguage not only reflects attitudes and beliefs about language itself, however; it is also powerful in constituting ideologies of difference and structures of social inequality (see, for example, Cameron, 1995; Fairclough, 2000; van Dijk, 1993). Furthermore, while metalanguage is surely instrumental in policing different ways of communicating (cf. Cameron, 2000), it is also – and often primarily – the speakers of different language/s who are being policed, as Kathryn Woolard and Bambi Schieffelin indicate in the quote above. Whether this policing appears to be done on linguistic grounds and for the sake of communicative transparency it inevitably reproduces hierarchies of symbolic and economic inequality (Bourdieu, 1991). This is particularly so in the case of mediatized discourse (e.g., newspapers, television shows) which, as major mechanisms of representation, act as tremendously influential, often elitist gatekeepers (cf. van Dijk, 1993). So, while scholars usually try to avoid judging everyday metalanguage as "incorrect" against their own professional standards of accuracy or "truth", mediatized commentary about language deserves more rigorous critique – especially when it claims merely to be presenting the facts, reporting a serious issue, or just having a bit of fun. I'll start with the "fun."[8]

Case 1 – Crazy foreigners: Tourist linguascaping and the exoticization of locals

One major site of intercultural exchange in contemporary life is tourism (Jack and Phipps, 2005). As the world's single largest international trade, and representing an enormous global movement of people, the infamous "tourist gaze" is powerful in shaping the way many people think about, and interact with, cultural difference.

Central to all tourism discourse are the communicative practices of brochures, posters, commercials, guidebooks, postcards, and, television vacation shows, each of which not only represents an image of the tourist destination but also produces a particular vision (or version) of tourism itself – what it means to be someone privileged enough to travel by choice.

It was this in mind that my colleagues and I examined the representation of local, non-English languages in British television vacation shows (see Thurlow and Jaworski, 2010). Although most local people featured in these shows were seen to use English with the tourist-presenters, occasionally presenters were depicted interacting with a local person speaking in a local language (e.g., Extract 1 below), or quoting foreign language phrases in their commentaries/narratives (e.g. Extract 2), or making metapragmatic comments about the local language or their own use of it (e.g., Extract 3). The extracts I'm presenting here are typical of the kinds of fleeting encounters we found from a dataset of nearly six months of programming: the first is an instance of "expert talk" in Italy, the second a greeting ritual in Fiji, and the third a service encounter in Spain.

Extract 1: Mary Nightingale (presenter) at a family-run hotel in Italy

```
 1   MN: (voiceover) I found all the hotels very comfortable and what's nice is
 2              they're all so individual and they feel so (.) Italian (1.0) this farmhouse
 3              has been in the family for generations (.) Vera is the boss (.) and the
 4              chief pasta maker
 5   Vera: (cut to Vera's kitchen where is making pasta) quest'e' la pasta queste
                                             this is the pasta these
 6              sono (.) l'impasto (.) mangiala cruda mangiala cruda
                are (.) the mixture (.) eat it raw eat it raw
 7   MN: (picks up a single strand of raw pasta, moves away from Vera, raises the
 8              piece of pasta to the camera) there's a piece of Vera's tagliatelle (.) isn't
 9              that absolutely beautiful (.) it's perfect
10   Vera:      (looks baffled at MN's interest in the piece of pasta)
```

Extract 2: John Savident (presenter) walking through a marketplace in Fiji
              (JS apparently wandering through a market place)

```
 1   JS:    away from the hotel the town of Nandi [sic.] is just ten minutes away (.)
 2          Fiji is such a friendly place and you're always greeted with a big smile
 3          (cut to a woman smiling) and a call of ((BULA)) the local greeting
 4          (to a street vendor) bula
 5   Vendor: bula bula John (JS continues walking past her stall, laughs to her) how
 6          are you bula bula la la la
```

Extract 3: Lisa Riley (presenter) in Spain

```
 1   LR: (voiceover) it's well worth taking a wander up the side streets off the
 2              square (camera on LR and friend) where you can find traditional tapas
 3              bars just like this one (points to bar) ((shall we take a look)) (LR walks to
 4              bar; to barman) hola me puedes dar la carta por favor?
               hello can you give me the menu please?
```

5   Barman: (hands over menu) ((unclear))
6   LR: gracias (to camera, cheerfully) been learning that all day (giggles)
         thank you

Much more detailed analyses of these three extracts are given in Thurlow and Jaworski (2010); for now, however, I mean only to highlight some of the main conclusions my colleagues and I draw from these types of mediatized intercultural encounters with specific reference to the linguistic production of difference.

What is immediately striking is how brief the encounters are and how tokenistic the depiction of the local language is. It is this which immediately gives lie to a core mythology in tourism discourse: that travel promises an engagement with – a chance to "get to know" – local people and local culture. Generally, the ethos of the TV shows positions English as a global language, with the local languages reduced to the status of a handful of fixed phrases found in guidebook glossaries. In this sense, English is presented as the "global language" while local people's ways of speaking are invariably deployed as little more than an exoticizing resource for *linguascaping* – that is, as a backdrop for added local flavor or authenticity. In keeping with the ideas of writers like Cameron and Fairclough, this is language being represented in only its most instrumental form rather than as a mode of relationship, of interpersonal or intercultural exchange.

In the first case, Vera, the "chief pasta maker", is cut off midstream – midsentence, even – as the presenter turns to camera to show the audience back home a strand of "exotic" pasta. In Fiji, meanwhile, the presenter performs his role of down-with-the-locals tourist in a highly staged (the vendor uses his name!) greeting with the appreciative, "friendly" local. In the last extract, the presenter reveals what's really at play in these moments: dipping into the local language is all about having a bit of fun. Using local languages constitutes just another form of 'fun' activity on a par with trying different local culinary specialties or learning new skills such as sailing, horse-riding, skiing, and so on.

The predominant pattern of local language use in these television shows takes the form of linguistic crossing, which allows the presenters to orient to their audiences (it's their job after all) through an interactional frame which remains firmly rooted in their Britishness. In other words, as influential, celebrity role models, the presenters invite (and encourage?) tourists to take up this performance – or script – of the cosmopolitan traveler: "Here's how to be a (British) tourist", "Here's an appropriate way to interact with local people", "Here's what intercultural exchange looks like". While it may be tempting to think of these staged, stylized exchanges as expressions of cultural hybridity or a resistant politics on the part of local people, the effect is largely to (re)establish a neocolonial vision/spectacle of Other and of intercultural exchange.

As such, local languages render Other in the service of Self. The ideological effect at play here is similar to the use of "mock Spanish" by Anglo-Americans in the United States. Jane Hill (2001) has shown how apparently jocular incorporations and ungrammatical approximations of languages other than English are employed by nonnative speakers. Hill argues that these playful, flippant snatches of Spanish-language materials serve to elevate the identities (or Whiteness) of Anglo-Americans. Much the same argument, we believe, can be made for the use of phrasebook expressions by presenter-tourists and the general linguascaping of the tourist landscape; in this case, however, it is the elevation and constitution of a *Britishness* which is at stake. What may appear to be little more than fun – the general participation frame of tourism, – unfolds as a kind of Orientalizing of local people even while appearing to celebrate them (cf. Jordan and Weedon, 1995; Said, 1978).

The point behind this type of discourse analysis is to demonstrate that even the smallest, quickest, most trivial moments of language use reveal the effects of power (recall Chick, Holmes, Ehrlich etc. cited above). The point of a critical analysis is, furthermore, that these banal enactments of ideology, when repeated over and over, establish particular regimes of truth (Foucault, 1980) about the world. As a regime of everyday *intercultural* truth, the language ideologies of television holiday shows are, for me, troubling.

Case 2 – Generation grunt: New-media language and the fabrication of youth

In a second study, I turned my interest in metalanguage to the way young people's new media language (e.g. text- and instant-messaging) is commonly depicted in the media (see Thurlow, 2007). Take a look at these two indicative extracts from a sample of over 100 international (English-language) newspaper reports all centrally focused on young people, new communication technologies, and language: "Fears are growing that today's teenagers are becoming 'Generation Grunt', a section of society that has effectively lost the ability to talk or express itself. We may well be raising the thickest, most incoherent and sub-literate generation for centuries."

As these examples show, adult-driven media commentary is often unapologetically exaggerated and remarkably hostile towards young people (cf. Giroux, 2000; Males, 1996). In fact, I find it hard to imagine it being appropriate nowadays to speak openly in the same way about any other community defined, say, by disability, race, age, or sex. Certainly, youth (as a period in the lifespan) is almost always represented as strange, exotic, or just different.

Central to any mythology of youth is its description in sweeping, homogenizing terms. Throughout my dataset, for example, I found young people being continually lumped together as "the keyboard generation," "Generation IM," "the gen-txt community," "Generation Text," "mobile generation," "the thumb generation," "gen.txtrs," and "GNR8N TXT." This entire of generation of wired whizzes was, on the other hand, just as likely to be caricatured as techno-slaves: their use of communication technologies depicted as a "craze," "mania," "youth obsession," or of having "cult status." Although true of all intergenerational complaining of this type, the issue of young people's literacy was key – or, more correctly, their illiteracy and their deleterious impact on "good" English. Instant messaging, emailing and especially text messaging were, for example, described throughout as "destroying," "harming," "limiting," "damaging," "ruining," "threatening," "massacring," "corrupting" or "eroding" Standard English. This apparent onslaught was epitomized with references to formal markers of received practice and canonical standards of literature, as with this comment: "The text messaging craze is … systematically destroying grammar, syntax and even spelling."

In spite of this "misrecognition" (Bourdieu, 1977) of language, it is the blatant misrepresentation of young people which warrants most concern. In particular, the way that this mediatized metalanguage is strategically deployed in the production – and exaggeration – of difference. Throughout the newspaper articles I looked at, young people's new media language was consistently depicted as being impenetrable and inaccessible to adults (e.g., "baffling," "causes confusion," "abbreviations and bizarre acronyms"). For "uninitiated" adults (i.e., journalists and parents), new media language is apparently seen in the following terms:

> a mysterious lexicon, hieroglyphics, technobabble, cryptic chat, a bizarre activity, hodgepodge communication, secret code, language soup, jumble, impenetrable, ramblings, cryptograms, garbled, encoded messages, gobbledegook, gibberish, arglebargle, cipher, exclusive, a secret language, code language, obscure, effective code against POS ['parent over shoulder']

On the surface, it appears that young people's new-media language is an artful hieroglyphic code which must be cracked. Beneath the surface, however, it is a prime resource by which adults are fetishizing the teen-ness of new-media language, young people's communication more generally, and young people themselves. Just as Rosina Lippi-Green (1997) sees the "burden of communication" being always forced onto ethnic minorities, it is young people who are evidently obliged to make themselves understood to adults. The powerful demand of the powerless that they speak their language and that they speak it clearly! As it is, there is something a little self-absorbed in adults' persistent implication that young people are somehow deliberately texting or messaging in order to exclude (or 'foil', as in the following example) them. "They have created their own words to foil teachers and other adults" and "The page was riddled with hieroglyphics, many of which I simply could not translate."

There are, I would suggest, several different ways in which this metalanguage is all about technology – not counting the communication technologies themselves. To start, youth (as a period in the lifespan) is itself a technology: a complex of mechanisms or a system of knowledges designed by adults with which to socialize people into citizenship and to discipline them into societal hierarchies (Lesko, 2003). Within this broader framework, the new media also fulfill their potential as "technologies of the self" (Foucault, 1988), for young people and also, in a second-hand, metalinguistic way, for adults who construct their own identities as adults by talking about young people's new media in this way. Finally, young people's language is technologized in the way Fairclough (above) uses the term.

This *stylization* of young people – as being wired whizzes and techno slaves – imposes or "scripts" certain ways of speaking as well as rendering language a matter solely of transactional, utilitarian value.

It is in this way that adult journalists and other media commentators create and promote a specific image (or style) of 'teentalk' and new-media language – one which often bears little resemblance to actual practice. Not only, therefore, does public metalanguage about young people's new-media language work to sustain the technology that is adolescence itself and to service the identificational needs of adults, this same metalanguage technologizes young people by rendering them as uniformly and universally wired or hooked. In more sinister terms, however, language, and new-media language in particular, are thereby also exploited as resources by which adults may not only demonize but also commodify youth (cf. Miles, 2000). We therefore find journalists and marketers working together to exaggerate the separateness – the difference – of youth in order to distinguish young people as a profitable market.

Case 3 – Wooly sluts and regular guys: Selective stylization and taboo language

My final case-study example comes from a recent study in which I've been looking at the way the print media represents – or supposedly tries *not* to represent – taboo language (see Thurlow and Moshin, in prep.). In this instance, Jamie Moshin and my interest lies in the curious typographic and discursive tactics journalists and their editors use to depicts swear words like 'shit' and 'fuck' or high-profile uses of these word (e.g., by George Bush or Dick Cheney), as well as the naming of sexualized body parts as in the notorious incidents of Janet Jackson's exposed breast/nipple at the 2004 Superbowl tournament and paparazzi snapshots of Britney Spears' exposed vulva/labia in 2006. What quickly becomes apparent is how this metalanguage is once again shot through with social (and moral) judgments of class, race/ethnicity, age, and gender. Put simply, taboo language is deployed by the media as a resource for stylizing Other and as an ideal resource for *producing* difference – and all in a way which is suitably newsworthy.

As it happens, taboo language generates a veritable "incitement to discourse" just as Foucault characterizes Victorian England's prudish prurience; a people so busy regulating sex that all they talk/write about is sex! In our data, we find dozens of semiotic tactics for *appearing* not to speak the naughty words; for example: institutionalized formats (e.g. "This is (expletive) awesome!"), deictic referencing (e.g., it, that word, the obscenity), typographic substitution (e.g. s**t, F#ck, SH!T), formulaic contextualization (e.g., I'm f----- seriously pissed, F**k you!, shut the f..k up), initialisms (e.g., WTF, they can F right O, FU), x-word formulae (e.g., f-word, f-bomb, the s-word), euphemisms/infantilisms (e.g., frikkin, No. 2s, fig, fudge) and orthophemisms (e.g., ordure, an angry obscene version of 'get lost'). The options seem to be endless. There also appears to be little reluctance in drawing attention to the taboo words; in fact, much time is spent, much copy space

expended, finding witty ways to mention the unmentionable, as in these circumlo-
cutious examples:

> the C word … not the one you think, the one no one is ever supposed to use … you'll
> be able to grasp it (deliberate choice of phrase) if I tell you the second and third syl-
> lables are "sucking"

> It closed with a reference to the constituent as a certain anatomical part. No, not that
> one. The one you sit on.

It is precisely in this way that the metalanguage is able subtly to conceal itself as
either humorous, clever, or just factual. What was more telling about the ideologies
of language which underpin this particular type of metalinguistic commentary were
the contexts of their use. For the most part, swear words only ever seem to appear –
either spelled out or "omitted" – when journalists write about an artist, a celebrity,
a rap musician, a gang member, or a criminal. It is a kind of "selective stylization"
in which taboo language is used as a metalinguistic resource for characterizing – or
caricaturing – some people but not others. This is dirty language for the supposedly "great unwashed".

In the rarer instances when "shit" and "fuck" were reportedly used by someone
outside these communities, the taboo was invariably marked as exceptional by
comments such as "I pause, shocked, thinking it is another expletive" or "using his
online posting moniker (that can't exactly be reproduced in a family newspaper)".
These words were also openly *othered* as "G-rated language," "adult language" or
"spicy language" in opposition to the ingroup characterizations of "clean language," "family-friendly language," and "civil discourse."

In this case, we also witness the production of difference working in two ways:
one indirect and one direct. The first of these is evident in the reporting of high-
profile swearers like George Bush and Dick Cheney. While these instances are often
met with criticism, figures like the President and Vice-President are typically given
the benefit of the doubt; their swearing is justified by metapragmatic accounts of
their original intention. For example, journalists are found interpreting (as fact)
George Bush's recorded use of the word "shit" at a G8 summit in 2006 as his
being "frustrated" or "impatient," or that it was said in "a moment of frustration
and passion" and that "at least Bush's words were honest".[9] Sure, this was "rough-
edged," "unvarnished," "unpolished" "blue prose" or "raw language," but it was
also, we are told, "plain-folk talk," "a refreshing blast of candor," "politics without
the spin," "earthy," "straight-talking" from a "regular guy." Here, the value judgment that is often left implicit is that these instances of taboo language are made
even remotely newsworthy by the fact that they were used by a political elite of
educated, professionalized White men. The taboo is thereby marked as Other by
condemning moments when it is used by Self. Having said which, the kind of selective stylization mentioned above is also evident in reverse here too when Bush and
his use of taboo language are characterized in otherwise ageist and racist terms:

barely comprehensible grunts you hear from teenage boys / frat-boy / ANIMAL HOUSE SUMMIT / insouciance and smart-alecky attitude / he can make even a global summit meeting seem like a kegger / demeanour of a petulant adolescent

Homey G-8 / Bush's gangsta rap summary of the crisis in Lebanon / they conversed not as statesmen but rather as semi-articulate homeboys / his rap with George Bush / with all the diplomatic – and eating habits – of a Cossack

At other times, this production of difference is done more directly. In fact, any doubt about the "hidden agendas" of metalinguistic commentary about taboo words in the media falls away when our analysis turns to the reporting of sexualized body parts. In the case of the paparazzi snapshots of Britney Spears' genitals, the tension between prurient delight and puritan distaste makes way for a more unapologetic moral condemnation. This type of overt "opinion-making" is all the more problematic given the value supposedly placed by journalists on impartiality and the reporting of facts. Once again, we find the same taste for knowing circumlocutions (e.g., "her naughty who-nose-what," "her aversion to underwear," "underwear is over-rated," "sans panties," "that's not all she's flashing around," "the art of not wearing underclothes") and other punning and word play (e.g. OOPS. JUST A LI'L BRIT MISSING, "flashionista", rock-bottomless, over-exposure, Undersecretary for Undergarments, PANTIES 911!, FLASH PHOTOGRAPHY). Very easily, however, the prejudicial edge reveals itself in a lurid attention for details such as when we are offered the following kind of information about Spears' body: "shaved," "well-groomed," "fresh caesarian scars," "gaudy c-section scar," "livid herpes sores," "deforested," "showing off her post-baby figure (a little too much)." The misogyny of this commentary is left in little doubt with the following types of overt evaluations of Spears which appeared in the main text or in headlines (capitals): *gross, rancid nudity, skank, wild and wooly slut, whore-level makeup, slagosphere, trampy, celebretard, vulgar exhibitionist displays, tragic flesh baring induced slight nausea, SLUTTY AS EVER*, and *SHRINKY, SLINKY AND STINKY.*

The naming of women's genitals is always fraught with ideology (Braun and Kitzinger, 2001) and language about sex is likewise always morally charged (Hall, 1995). All of it, however, works performatively to constitute identities and ideologies of difference. What taboo (meta)language in particular reveals is also the inherently repressive nature of discourse (see Billig, 1997) and its strategic use for demarcating people as good/bad, clean/unclean, acceptable/unacceptable (cf. Douglas, 1991, 1996). Ultimately, the effect is to reproduce the taboo around particular language (i.e., the words 'shit' and 'fuck') and particular speakers, as well reinscribing the notion of taboo itself (i.e., that things and some people *should* be marked out as unspeakable). Once again, we learn that there is "proper" language and there is "improper" language, just as there are useful languages and useless languages. Of particular note in this last case study is the slippage between talk about speakers' words and talk about their bodies, their lives and their status in society.

Putting Language in Perspective: Words Are Not Enough

in every society the production of discourse is at once controlled, selected, organised and redistributed by a certain number of procedures whose role is to ward off its powers and its dangers, ... to evade its ponderous, formidable materiality (Foucault, 1981, p. 52).

The kinds of defensive justifications one hears often – "they're just words" or "I'm only joking" – make important philosophical, epistemological, and political assumptions about the "nature" of language and about the role of language in social life. These kinds of comments can only be made if one believes that language does little more than merely represent a pre-existing reality – words are simply vessels of meaning, and language a conduit for reality. It is this same misrecognition of the powerful, constitutive role of language in society that plagues so much (conventional) Intercultural Communication scholarship. This, in turn, leads us to overlook the banal, seemingly innocuous communicative or representational *tactics* by which *strategies* of power and inequality are enacted daily (cf. de Certeau, 1988). Yet, as Foucault warns, these moments of frivolous textuality always conceal their "formidable materiality."

In presenting my case study examples, I have deliberately wanted to reconceive interculturality in its broadest terms – broader, at least, than Intercultural Communication scholarship would normally do (see Thurlow, 2004). Often, people think of cultural difference only with regards markers of difference such as race/ethnicity or nationality. Cultural others are seldom so quickly reduced; nor are they so easily identified. The representation and production of difference occurs in any number of everyday, banal enactments of otherness as a subjectively and socially constituted phenomenon. At the very least – and without meaning to fall into the trap of simply exaggerating the differences between people – *critical* intercultural scholars are more willing to recognize the cultural meanings and practices of people whose lives are also distinguished by their age, (dis)ability, class status, sexual identity, and so on. It is in this way, that interculturality comes to be more about material inequalities, power relations, and ideologies of difference, rather than simply skin color, geographical location, passport, clothing, food, nonverbal behavior, or, of course, languages. As Russell Ferguson (1990 quoted in Nakayama and Krizek, 1995, p. 291) reminds us:

The place from which power is exercised is often a hidden place. When we try to pin it down, the center always seems to be somewhere else. Yet we know that this phantom center, elusive as it is, exerts a real, undeniable power over the entire framework of our culture, and over the ways we think about it.

Nor can/should language be isolated from its own context of production. Language too is discursively constructed, its meanings constantly changing and being rethought. As Alastair Pennycook (2004, p. 17) puts it, language is "called into being" in the moments of its use. This is important to remember because it helps prevent us from falling into the trap of fetishizing and unduly privileging language. Language is, after all, only one of many semiotic systems; indeed, it is often far less useful for intercultural exchange than many other modes of communicating (see Aiello and Thurlow, 2006). Furthermore, semiotic modes never exist in isolation of other meaning-making practices. Language is only ever made truly meaningful and/or understandable in the context of paralinguistic and other nonverbal resources (cf. Kress and van Leeuwen, 1996). So much in the way of intercultural exchange also occurs outside language and our encounters with difference as much material, spatial, affective, and visual as they are linguistic.

Notwithstanding this, language *per se* should be an important consideration for Critical Intercultural Communication – and not in the way it typically gets glossed into the conventional textbooks as just another "barrier" to be overcome. Language is a key social institution in and of its own right (cf. Cameron, 1997); it is a field (or source) of negotiation, conflict, and oppression. As such, language is unavoidably implicated in the regulation not only of words, sentences, and texts but also of bodies, of speakers and writers. It is, as I have shown, a powerful technology– of both Self and Other – as well as a technology of control. Herein lie the materiality and the material consequence of language. In the symbolic marketplace in which language is a major currency, not all speakers are equal; some people's ways of speaking are always valued more highly than other people's ways of speaking. It is in this way that we see ethnic other, aged other, sexualized and classed other being disciplined through the way they (apparently) use language. At the same time, privileged speakers (and writers) are able to shore up their own capitals – symbolic, cultural, social and economic – at the expense of others. Just as those who control the means of production and the mechanisms of representation wield power, so too do those in the privileged position of being able to manage and manipulate language, those whose words matter when speaking of difference. A mastery of language is also a mastery of concealment – most notably, the concealment of the mastery itself.

Before I finish, there is one other important sense in which "words are not enough" and this has to do with the critical (and self-critical) of Critical Intercultural Communication. What each of the case-studies above also has in common is that it represents a site of privilege in which I myself am implicated – and not as the victimized but rather the victimizer. When I travel, I am invariably a tourist. When I interact with young people, I am nowadays always adult. When I talk about women, I am unavoidably man. What matters most to me, therefore, in thinking/writing *critically* about interculturality and cultural difference is that I address myself as the problem before presuming that I might also be/have part of the solution. By addressing the "absent center" – and my own absent- or self-centeredness – I therefore begin also to redress the "ethnocentric construction of radical alterity" (Bauman, 1996, p. 12) which characterizes so much conventional Intercultural Communication scholarship. In this regard, Russian cultural theorist Mikhail Epstein's (1995) use of Bakhtin's notion of *vnenakhodimost* – of being located outside any particular mode of existence – helps support a similar shift in focus from differences *without* to differences *within*.

A more fruitful approach [to interculturality] calls on each group to take account of its own insufficiency.... Perhaps the most effective way to feel difference is to embrace the feeling of one's own incompleteness (p. 13).

To be clear: this is not a disingenuous "poor me" tactic – an arch form of neocolonial narcissism – but rather a move towards *taking responsibility* (Thurlow, 2004), towards recognizing that my own acts of cultural identity, like all collective affiliations and actions, are inherently contrastive, hierarchical, and exploitative in the sense that they are (and have been) achieved at the expense of others. Words, especially academic ones, are seldom enough; being critical – with a capital C – also means putting ones words into (different) action. This means working towards both personal and social change. As Tom Nakayama and his colleagues (e.g. Nakayama and Krizek, 1995; Collier *et al.*, 2002) often argue, *Critical* Intercultural Communication demands a lived, followed-through commitment to social justice, the redistribution of privileged resources (material and symbolic), and a reflexivity about the knowledges we ourselves produce and the privileged places we inhabit. Using our work to "call out" power is important, but merely speaking of difference – or writing about it – will never be enough.

Notes

1 I'm grateful to Norman Fairclough (2003, pp. 41–42) for this schema for thinking about the ways people (and texts) commonly orient to difference – in his case, as a manifestation of the "dialogical" social relations which structure our lives (and our texts).

2 My talk of "language" here is heavily influenced by sociolinguistics and linguistically-oriented discourse analysis. There are, of course, other critical intercultural scholars who concern themselves with linguistic practices – most notably, in the US American tradition of rhetoric (e.g., Nakayama and Krizek, 1995; Flores, Moon and Nakayama, 2006).

3 For more information about these key sociolinguistic principles a number of good introductory texts are available; for example, Coupland and Jaworski (1997).

4 The journals recommended at the end of this essay are academic spaces committed in different ways to redressing the undue privilege of English speakers/scholars.

5 For information about the *International Association of Languages and Intercultural Communication* (IALIC) see http://www3.unileon.es/grupos/ialic/ (accessed June 10, 2010). The scholarship of IALIC is represented well in the affiliated journal *Language and Intercultural Communication*, http://www.informaworld.com/smpp/title~content=t794297827~db=all (accessed May 19, 2010).

6 My decision to look at these three specific examples is also motivated by wanting to offer some practical insight into the range of sites, topics, concepts, data, and analyses that can be used in a more language-oriented intercultural communication.

7 For good overviews on metalinguistics and language ideology see, respectively, the edited collections by Jaworski *et al.* (2004) and Schieffelin *et al.* (1998).

8 I am able to present only the bare essentials of the three studies here; more thorough theorizing, detailed analyses and nuanced interpretations are to be found in the original publications.

9   A BBC report of this incident can be found online at: www.youtube.com/
    watch?v=6Xq3DobSCKQ (accessed May 19, 2010)

References

Aiello, G., and Thurlow, C. (2006) Symbolic capitals: Visual discourse and intercultural
    exchange in the European capital of culture scheme. *Language and Intercultural
    Communication*, 6 (2), 148–162.
Austin, J.L. (1962) *How to Do Things with Words*, Clarendon Press, Oxford.
Bakhtin, M.M. (1986) *Speech Genres and Other Late Essays*, University of Texas Press, Austin, TX.
Bauman, G. (1996) *Contesting Culture: Discourses of Identity in Multi-ethnic London*,
    Cambridge University Press, Cambridge.
Billig, M. (1997) The dialogic unconscious: Psychoanalysis, discursive psychology and the
    nature of repression. *British Journal of Social Psychology*, 36, 139–159.
Blommaert, J. (2005) *Discourse: A Critical Introduction*, Cambridge University Press,
    Cambridge.
Bourdieu, P. (1977) *Outline of a Theory of Practice*, Cambridge University Press,
    Cambridge.
Bourdieu, P. (1991) *Language and Symbolic Power*, Polity Press, Cambridge.
Braun, V., and Kitzinger, C. (2001) Telling it straight? Dictionary definitions of women's
    genitals. *Journal of Sociolinguistics*, 5, 214–232.
Butler, J. (1990) *Gender Trouble: Feminism and the Subversion of Identity*, Routledge, New York.
Cameron, D. (1995) *Verbal Hygiene*, Routledge, London.
Cameron, D. (1997) Demythologizing sociolinguistics, in *Sociolinguistics: A Reader and
    Coursebook*, (ed. N. Coupland and A. Jaworski), Macmillan, Basingstoke, pp. 55–67.
Cameron, D. (2000) Styling the worker: Gender and the commodification of language in
    the globalized service economy. *Journal of Sociolinguistics*, 4 (3), 323–347.
Cameron, D. (2001) *Working with Spoken Discourse*, Sage, London.
Cameron, D. (2009) Demythologising sociolinguistics, in *The New Sociolinguistics Reader*,
    (eds N. Coupland and A. Jaworski), Palgrave Macmillan, Basingstoke, pp. 106–118.
Chick, J.K. (1985) The interactional accomplishment of discrimination in South Africa.
    Language in Society, 14 (3), 299–326.
Collier, M.J., Hegde, R.S., Wenshu, L. *et al.* (2002) Dialogue on the edges: Ferment in
    communication and culture, in *Transforming Communication about Culture: Critical
    New Directions*, (ed. M.J. Collier), Sage, Thousand Oaks, CA, pp. 219–280.
Coupland, N., and Jaworski, A., ed. (1997) *Sociolinguistics: A Reader and Coursebook*,
    Macmillan, London.
de Certeau, M. (1988) *The Practice of Everyday Life*, University of California Press,
    Berkeley, CA.
Douglas, M. (1991) *Purity and Danger: An Analysis of Concepts of Pollution and Taboo*,
    Routledge, London/ New York.
Douglas, M. (1996) *Purity and Danger: An Analysis of Concepts of Pollution and Taboo*, Ark,
    London.
Edwards, V. (1997) Patois and the politics of protest: Black English in British classrooms,
    in *Sociolinguistics: A Reader and Coursebook*, (ed. N. Coupland and A. Jaworski),
    Macmillan, Basingstoke, pp. 408–415.

Ehrlich, S. (1998) The discursive reconstruction of sexual consent. *Discourse and Society*, 9 (2), 149–171.

Epstein, M. (1995) *After the Future: The Paradoxes of Postmodernism and Contemporary Russian Culture*, University of Massachusetts Press, Amherst, MA.

Fairclough, N. (1992) *Discourse and Social Change*, Polity, Cambridge.

Fairclough, N. (1999) Global capitalism and critical awareness of language. *Language Awareness*, 8 (2), 71–83.

Fairclough, N. (2000) Discourse, social theory, and social research: The discourse of welfare reform. *Journal of Sociolinguistics*, 4 (2), 163–195.

Fairclough, N. (2002) Language in new capitalism. *Discourse and Society*, 3 (2), 163–166.

Fairclough, N. (2003) *Analysing Discourse: Textual Analysis for Social Research*, Routledge, London.

Ferguson, R. (1990) Introduction: Invisible center, in *Out There: Marginalization and Contemporary Cultures*, (eds R. Ferguson, M. Gever, T.T. Minh-Ha *et al.*), MIT Press, Cambridge, MA, pp. 9–14.

Flores, L.A., Moon, D.G., and Nakayama, T.K. (2006) Dynamic rhetorics of race: California's racial privacy initiative and the shifting grounds of racial politics. *Communication and Critical/Cultural Studies*, 3 (3), 181–201.

Foucault, M. (1980) *Power/Knowledge: selected Interviews and Other Writings, 1972–1977*, Pantheon, New York: Pantheon.

Foucault, M. (1981) The order of discourse, in *Untying the Text: A Poststructuralist Reader*, (ed. R. Young), Routledge and Keegan Paul, London, pp. 48–77.

Foucault, M. (1988) Technologies of the self, in *Technologies of the Self: A Seminar with Michael Foucault*, (eds L.H. Martin, H. Gutman and P.H. Hutton), University of Massachusetts Press, Amherst, MA, pp. 16–49.

Giroux, H.A. (2000) *Stealing Innocence: Youth, Corporate Power, and the Politics of Culture*, St. Martin's Press, New York.

Glaser, E. (2005) Plurilingualism in Europe: More than a means for communication. *Language and Intercultural Communication*, 5 (3&4), 195–208.

Goffman, E. (1967) *The Presentation of Self in Everyday Life*, Pantheon, New York.

Guilherme, M. (2007) English as a global language and education for cosmopolitan citizenship. *Language and Intercultural Communication*, 7 (1), 79–90.

Gumperz, J.J. (1997) Interethnic communication, in *Sociolinguistics: A Reader and Coursebook*, (eds N. Coupland and A. Jaworski), Macmillan, Basingstoke, pp. 395–407.

Gupta, A., and Ferguson, J. (1992) Beyond culture: Space, identity and the politics of difference. *Cultural Anthropology*, 7 (1), 6–23.

Hall, K. (1995) Lip service on the fantasy lines, in *Gender Articulated: Language and the Socially Constructed Self*, (eds K. Hall and M. Bucholtz), Routledge, New York, pp. 183–216.

Hall, S. (1997) The local and the global: Globalization and ethnicity, in *Culture, Globalization and the World-System: Contemporary Conditions for the Representation of Identity*, (ed. A.D. King), University of Minnesota Press, Minneapolis, pp. 20–39.

Hill, J.H. (2001) Language, race, and white public space, in *Linguistic Anthropology: A Reader*, (ed. A. Duranti), Blackwell, Malden, MA, pp. 450–464.

Holmes, J. (1995) *Women, Men and Politeness*, Longman, London.

Jack, G. (2004) Language(s), intercultural communication and the machinations of global capital: Towards a dialectical critique. *Language and Intercultural Communication*, 4(3), 121–133.

Jack, G., and Phipps, A. (2005) *Tourism and Intercultural Exchange: Why Tourism Matters*, Channel View, Clevedon.

Jaworski, A., and Coupland, N. (2006) *The Discourse Reader*, Routledge, London.

Jaworski, A., Coupland, N., and Galasinski, D. (eds) (2004) *Metalanguage: Social and Ideological Perspectives*, Mouton de Gruyter, Berlin.

Jordan, G., and Weedon, C. (1995) The celebration of difference and the cultural politics of racism, in *Theorizing Culture: An Interdisciplinary Critique after Postmodernism*, (eds B. Adam and S. Allan), UCI Press, pp. 149–164.

Kramsch, C. (2002) In search of the intercultural. *Journal of Sociolinguistics*, 6 (2), 275–285.

Kress, G. (1985) *Linguistic Processes in Sociocultural Practice*, Deakin University Press, Geelong.

Kress, G., and van Leeuwen, T. (1996) *Reading Images: The Grammar of Visual Design*, Routledge, London.

Lesko, N. (2003) *Act Your Age! A Cultural Construction of Adolescence*, Routledge, Falmer, New York.

Lippi-Green, R. (1997) *English with an Accent. Language, Ideology, and Discrimination in the United States*, Routledge, New York.

Males, M.A. (1996) *The Scapegoat Generation: America's War on Adolescents*, Common Courage Press, Monroe, ME.

Malinowski, B. (2006/1946) On phatic communion, in *The Discourse Reader*, (ed. A. Jaworski and N. Coupland), Routledge, London, pp. 296–298.

Miles, S. (2000) Consuming youth, in *Youth Lifestyles in a Changing World*, (ed. S. Miles), Open University Press, Buckingham, pp. 106–126.

Nakayama, T.K., and Krizek, R.L. (1995) Whiteness: A strategic rhetoric. *Quarterly Journal of Speech*, 81, 291–309.

Pennycook, A. (2004) Performativity and language studies. *Critical Inquiry in Language Studies*, 1 (1), 1–19.

Phipps, A. (2003) Languages, identities, agencies: Intercultural lessons from Harry Potter. *Language and Intercultural Communication*, 3 (1), 6–19.

Piller, I. (2001) Naturalization language testing and its basis in ideologies of national identity and citizenship. *International Journal of Bilingualism*, 5 (3), 259–277.

Said, E. (1978) *Orientalism*, Pantheon Books, New York.

Sapir, E., (1949) *Selected Writings in Language, Culture, and Personality*, University of California Press, Berkeley, CA.

Schieffelin, B.B., Woolard, K.A., and Kroskrity, P.V. (eds) (1998) *Language Ideologies: Practice and Theory*, Oxford University Press, New York and Oxford.

Thurlow, C. (2004) Relating to our work, accounting for ourselves: The autobiographical imperative in teaching about difference. *Language and Intercultural Communication*, 4 (4), 209–228.

Thurlow, C. (2007) Fabricating youth: New-media discourse and the technologization of young people, in *Language in the Media: Representations, Identities, Ideologies*, (eds S. Johnson and A. Ensslin), Continuum, pp. 213–233.

Thurlow, C., and Jaworski, A. (2010) *Tourism Discourse: Language and Global Mobility*, Palgrave Macmillan, Basingstoke and New York.

Thurlow, C., and Moshin, J. (in prep.) "What the f#@$!* Representing the unmentionable: Omission, repression and taboo language in the media".

van Dijk, T. (1993) *Elite Discourse and Racism*, Sage, Newbury Park, CA.

van Leeuwen, T. (1993) Genre and field in critical discourse analysis, in *Critical Discourse Analysis: Critical Concepts in Linguistics*, (ed. M. Toolan), Routledge, London, pp. 166-199.

Whorf, B.L., and Carroll, J.B. (eds) (1956) *Language, Thought, and Reality: Selected Writings of Benjamin Lee Whorf*, MIT Press, Cambridge, MA.

Wilson, S.-X., and Wilson, J. (2001) Will and power: Towards radical intercultural communication research and pedagogy. *Language and Intercultural Communication*, 1 (1), 76–93.

Woolard, K., and Schieffelin, B.B. (1994) Language ideology. *Annual Review of Anthropology*, 23, 55–82.

Further Reading

Blommaert, J. (2005) *Discourse: A Critical Introduction*, Cambridge University Press, Cambridge.

Cameron, D. (2001) *Working With Spoken Discourse*, Sage, London.

Corbett, J. (ed.) *Language and Intercultural Communication*, Routledge, London.

Fairclough, N. (1999) *Critical Discourse Analysis: The Critical Study of Language*, Longman, London.

Shi-Xu (ed.) *Journal of Multicultural Discourses*, London, Taylor and Francis.

Thurlow, C., and Mroczek, K. (eds) (in press) *New Media Discourse: Sociolinguistic Perspectives on Language and Technology*. Oxford University Press, Oxford.

van Dijk, T. (ed.) (2007) *Discourse and Society*, Sage, Thousand Oaks, CA.

15

Speaking Against the Hegemony of English
Problems, Ideologies, and Solutions

Yukio Tsuda

[handwritten: Western centric communication]

Introduction

English is widely used around the world and perceived as a lingua franca of international communication today. However, there is an increasing concern about the Hegemony of English which causes a number of problems of inequality and discrimination. In this essay, I shall critically focus on the problems caused by the Hegemony of English, examine some ideologies that support it and make some concrete proposals that may solve these problems.

The global spread and use of English is taken for granted today, and it is seldom addressed. Thus, it is very important to give it a critical examination so that the Hegemony of English will be acutely perceived and recognized as one of the sources of inequality, injustice, and discrimination in intercultural and international communication. In order for intercultural communication studies to be "critical" in the true sense of the word, it is essential to address the issue of inequality in communication such as the Hegemony of English.

Development of the Critique of the Hegemony of English

Before starting to discuss the problems of the Hegemony of English, I will briefly refer to the development of the critical studies of the Hegemony of English.

I published my dissertation *Language Inequality and Distortion* in 1986 (Tsuda, 1986) in which I pointed out that the dominance of English causes inequality between the English-speaking people and the non-English-speaking people.

Several years later, *Linguistic Imperialism* was published by Robert Phillipson, a linguist in Denmark (Phillipson, 1992). Phillipson argues that there is a structure

The Handbook of Critical Intercultural Communication, edited by Thomas K. Nakayama and Rona Tamiko Halualani. © 2010 Blackwell Publishing Ltd.

[handwritten: Summary of eg court]

of inequality between English and other languages, which is justified and reinforced by international power politics, exploiting development aid and worldwide
English language teaching.

Also in 1994, Alastair Pennycook published *Cultural Politics of English as an
International Language* in which he critiques the Hegemony of English by using the
notion of "discourse." He argues that it is the "discourse" of English as an international language that has primarily justified the present dominance of English. In 2001,
The Dominance of English as a Language of Science was published by Ulrich Ammon,
a German linguist. This book is a collection of international studies surveying how
much English is used in each country in academic activities. The results show that
there is a definite dominance of English in academic communication. More recently,
The Hegemony of English was published by Donald Macedo and his associates (Macedo,
Dendorinos and Gounari, 2003). They criticized the linguistic racism that exists in the
United States and Europe, especially referring to the "English-Only" ideology.

A brief history of the development of these critical studies of the Hegemony of
English shows that there is indeed a growing concern and interest in this serious
linguistic issue. When I first started research on the Hegemony of English in the
early 1980s, I found that there was almost no research being done on this issue in
the English-speaking academia except for Esperanto studies. Sociolinguistics in the
United States is so descriptive and objective that it has failed to recognize and criticize the Hegemony of English. This scientific apathy is accompanied by the Western-
centric consciousness that allows the American scholars to take it for granted that
the world will speak English and therefore there is no problem in it.

On the contrary, there are plenty of problems. Therefore, it is very important to
make a critical examination of the Hegemony of English, because it allows us to
understand that the Hegemony of English is not a purely linguistic matter, but it
is directly connected with "power," namely, "Who controls the world?"

Six Problems of the Hegemony of English

The Hegemony of English refers to the situation where English is so dominant that
inequality and discrimination take place in communication. As far as I have studied,
there are at least 6 problems of inequality and discrimination caused by the
Hegemony of English. They are: (1) Linguicism; (2) Linguicide; (3) Americanization
of Culture; (4) Information Control; (5) Mind Control; (6) English Divide. I shall
discuss them one by one.

Linguicism

What is linguicism? The word has been coined by Tove Skutnabb-Kangas, a Finnish
linguist, following racism and sexism. Linguicism is defined as follows: "Linguicism
refers to ideologies and structures where language is the means for effecting or maintaining an unequal allocation of power and resources" (Phillipson, 1992, p. 55).

Looking back in history, we discover a great number of cases of linguicism. Speakers of dialects were discriminated against because of the linguistic variety they spoke. In the process of building a modern state, the government established a standard language which served as a linguistic norm and became a basis of discriminating against the speakers of the nonstandard languages.

English functions and is widely recognized as a global standard language today. That very fact serves as an enormous power and becomes as a basis of discrimination, because it gives the speakers of English an enormous power and control in communication. The very fact that the use of English is taken for granted also gives an additional power to the English-speaking countries and people.

In most international conferences English is used as the only or one of the official languages. For example, the International Whaling Committee adopts English as its only official language. The non-English-speaking countries have to provide translations if they wish to use their own languages. In 1993 when the International Whaling Committee was held in Kyoto, Japan, I had a chance to observe one of the meetings. Most delegates spoke in English except for France, China, and Japan. I was surprised to find that when the delegates for these three countries spoke in their languages, the audience did not even pay attention to the speakers. Some people chatted among themselves. They started listening only when the translators provided the English translations.

This example shows that the Hegemony of English not only deprives the languages other than English of the chance to be used, but also marginalize them as meaningless "noises." In other words, the non-English-speaking people are not only deprived of their language rights, but their human dignity is also violated as they are ignored.

The Hegemony of English forces the non-English-speaking people to learn and use English. However, the English spoken by the non-English-speaking people is often labeled "Broken English," which is rather an unkind label to degrade the non-English-speakers. In addition, a new label has been created and used recently. The new label is BSE (Ammon, 2003). BSE stands for Bad, Simple English. The label ridicules and degrades the English spoken by nonnative speakers of English. Thus, the nonstandard English becomes the target of discrimination.

In international scientific journals, linguicism seems to be prevalent as scholars of the non-English-speaking countries have difficulty getting their papers accepted not necessarily because of the quality of their researches per se, but because of the quality of their English. In today's international academic community, the system is already organized in such a way that benefits the scholars who are native speakers of English, because English is now the language of sciences, and the ideas and voices of the non-English-speaking scholars are often ignored unless they are very proficient in English.

Donald Macedo, a critical sociolinguist at the University of Massachusetts, and his associates present a very interesting case of linguicism, which happened some years ago at the prestigious Massachusetts Institute of Technology.

They describe it as follows:

> A group of students petitioned the administration not to hire professors who spoke English with a foreign accent, under the pretext that they had difficulty understanding their lectures. By barring professors who spoke English with a foreign accent, these students would have kept Albert Einstein from teaching in U.S. universities (Macedo, Dendrinos and Gounari, 2003, p. 12)

Thus, linguicism, or inequality and discrimination because of the dominance of English is real. Non-English-speaking people are not only forced to learn and use English, but they are also discriminated against because of the variety of English they use.

Linguicide

There is a prediction among some linguists that in several hundred years from today, only one prestigious global language will prevail in the world. It will be English.

Linguicide refers to the killing of languages, especially weaker and smaller ones. The term linguicide derives the word, genocide (the deliberate killing of a people because of their difference). Daniel Nettle and Susanne Romaine, British linguists, have provided a detailed account of linguicide in their book *Vanishing Voices* (Nettle and Romaine, 2000). They attribute linguicide to the global spread of Western modernization which has destroyed the social environments of non-Western countries since the sixteenth century. Western modernization has transformed traditional societies into the so-called modern societies across the world that encourage the use of Western languages and degrade the indigenous languages. The creation of the modern societies has led to the establishment of societies that are centered on Western languages and indigenous languages have been marginalized. Nettle and Romaine (2000) report that there around 5000–6700 languages in the world today. The number of languages has decreased by 50% over the past five centuries, and the speed at which languages disappear is increasing, with, on average, one language disappearing every two weeks.

There have been a lot of voices raised and warnings given to the crisis of ecology, especially, in reference to the problems of endangered species, or the disappearance of animals and plants. Linguistic ecology is in crisis too. This planet is filled with endangered languages which may disappear at any moment. Along with the disappearance of these languages, related cultures, values, knowledge, philosophy, poetry, songs, memories, and linguistic souls also disappear. In a few hundred years from today, there will be only one language left on earth – English.

Living in the United States, many people often feel threatened by the rise of Spanish. It has brought about a linguistic movement called the 'Official English Movement' in the 1980s, trying to officially adopt English as the national language of the United States. English is not an officially national language by law in the United States.

However, this movement underestimates the enormous power and influence of English, especially in the international and global context. Many people of the world feel threatened by English, as it dominates as the global language for business, science, media, tourism, politics, diplomacy, education, and so on. In France and Brazil, the governments have passed a law that restricts the use of English in their countries. English dominates all the spheres of human life in many countries in the world. The majority of international organizations adopt English as a sole or official language. As the global economy spreads in the world, there will be no choice for most people of the world but to learn and use English. It is true that English is a lingua franca today, but because of that it threatens other languages. It deprives us of the opportunity to use other languages.

I suspect that the Hegemony of English is one of many factors causing global language shift. Language shift is a phenomenon in which a person changes his/her primary language. This happens to most immigrants. They gain a language of the host country, and they tend to lose their own in order to survive. So language shift is accompanied by language loss. Economically and politically strong languages often replace the weaker languages.

Some people argue that English Hegemony is not responsible for global linguicide by pointing out that it is the dominant languages in each country that cause the weaker languages to disappear. This is partially true. But, we are living in the age of globalization in which we are greatly influenced not by the forces in each country, but the global forces that come across the national borders. It is very difficult for any language to escape the enormous influence of English which dominates as the global standard language. For example, the dominant languages such as French, Spanish, and Arabic have been losing power in international communication in the face of the Hegemony of English. The percentage of speeches made in the United Nations in English during 1992–1999 increased from 45% to 50%, while the percentages of speeches made in French, Spanish, and Arabic all decreased: 19% to 13.8% for French, 12% to 10% for Spanish, and 10% to 9.5% for Arabic (Calvet, 1998). Even the very strong languages are under the influence of Hegemony of English.

English, being the language of globalization and the greatest economic and political power, makes people gravitate and shift to it and lose their own languages. Louis-Jean Calvet, a French linguist, names English a "hypercentral language" that makes many people around the world gravitate toward it. Calvet provides what he calls the gravitation model of linguistic hierarchy in which most people gravitate toward English, the hypercentral language, causing many people to shift to English (Calvet, 1998).

Indeed, many people all around the world are now living in a social environment that centers on English. In China, more than 500 million people are learning English. In Korea, unless you have good scores in the English test, you cannot have a job interview. In Japan, billions of money is spent every year on the learning of English. The teaching of English for small children is becoming a big industry. It is possible that in these countries many people will shift to English in the future.

Not only in Asia, but throughout the world, the "Englishmania" or obsession with English is taking place. Why? It is because the whole world has been organized in such a way that leaves no other choices but to choose English. Many people believe they have chosen English on their own free will, but actually they are made to choose English and are not allowed to choose other languages. We are now living in an age of "Speak English, or Perish." This may result, sooner or later, in a global language shift in which people throw away their own languages and shift to English. This would lead to global language loss and that is global linguicide.

Americanization of culture

The impact of English hegemony upon culture is another serious problem. You may have already heard the words and concepts such as Coca-colonization and McDonaldization of culture, both referring to an enormous influence of American consumer culture upon the local cultures of almost all parts of the world. The global spread of American products influences people's minds, values, and ways of life. In this influence, English plays an important role. The spread of American products goes hand in hand with the spread of English, thus buying and using American products facilitates the spread of English which in turn facilitates the global spread of American products, creating the cycle of reinforcing the hegemony of English and American materialistic culture.

Some people say that although Americanization of culture is happening, it is changing only the surface of the local cultures across the world. I suspect, however, that its effects are larger than we imagine. The impact of Americanization of culture penetrates the depth of human imagination and lifestyles. It has changed the value-systems and belief-systems of many cultures to American ones. The invasion of English and American culture is causing not only the replacement of languages, but also the replacement of mental structures.

I can give you two typical examples to illustrate this point. One is from China, the other is from the Ladakh, a minority tribe living in the Himalayan mountains.

First, China is now at the height of growing capitalism which promotes Americanization of its culture. As early as 1997, *Asiaweek*, a weekly magazine, featured an article on a rapid Americanization of China (*Asiaweek*, 1997). The article introduced the comments by some specialists on China. One commentator says: "The Chinese want the American lifestyle, a modern lifestyle, the way they think Americans live."

Another comment is as follows: "America represents an ideal for the Chinese. It's lifestyle that they aspire to, the spirit of America."

The article also reports that today Michael Jordan is now more popular than Mao Zedong, the late charismatic leader of China.

Another example that vividly illustrates the Americanization of culture has been provided by Helena Norberg-Hodge, a Swedish ecologist. She reports that the impact of American culture penetrates even the small ethnic tribal people living in the high mountains of the Himalayas. They are called Ladakh. She deplores the Westernization of Ladakh as follows:

The sudden influx of Western influence has caused some Ladakhis – the young men in particular – to develop feelings of inferiority complex. They reject their own culture wholesale, and at the same time eagerly embrace the new one. They rush after the symbols of modernity: sunglasses, Walkmans, and blue jeans several sizes too small – not because they find these jeans more attractive or comfortable, but because they are symbols of modern life (Norberg-Hodge, 1991, p. 98)

It is very sad to see that the young Ladakhis have lost confidence in their own culture and develop inferiority complex toward the Western culture. It will be very difficult for the Ladakh culture to be transmitted to the next and the following generations. (Also, I notice that Norberg-Hodge referred to the Japanese product, Walkman as a Western influence, which indicates that Japan has been highly Westernized.)

Helena Norberg-Hodge further argues that due to the influence of violent Hollywood movies, the young Ladakis show a tendency toward violent and emotionally unstable behaviors. She regrets to say that traditionally calm and considerate Ladakhis have transformed into a more aggressive people.

These two examples clearly demonstrate that the impact of Western culture, especially the American material and media culture is not superficial, but profound to the extent that is affecting the very nature of each local culture across the world and that the Hegemony of English plays an important role in its effects.

There is no doubt that English is the language of globalization and global economy. If any country wants to have a share of benefits of globalization, they have to incorporate English into their society. Rather, they are forced to choose English. However, doing so may jeopardize the independence and uniqueness of their traditional cultures as demonstrated above. The dominance of one language is now affecting the cultures and ways of life all over the world and homogenizing them into a Western and particularly American pattern of life. Indeed, Coca-colonization, McDonaldization, and Hollywoodization of the world is taking place.

Information control

The fourth problem I have discovered in the Hegemony of English is information control. Language and culture are inseparable, and so are language and information.

When English dominates, the information in English will dominate too. It is reported that about 80% of the international database is stored in English. On the Internet, about 70% of the web pages are in English.

Also, most international news is sent by way of international news agencies such as UPI, AP, and Reuters located in the United States and the United Kingdom. The flow of this international news is one-way: from the English-speaking countries, especially the United States, to the rest of the world.

Frustrated by this unequal flow of international information, some non-Western countries have been raising voices against "information inequality" and "imbalance in information flow." Since the 1970s, mainly the countries belonging to the non-aligned movement started a project which was later called "New World Information

Table 15.1 Seven global news media

Media	Countries
APTN	UK
Reuters TV	UK
CNN	USA
Fox News Channel	USA
MSNBC	USA
BBC	UK
Al Jazeera	Qatar

and Communication Order" (NWICO). In the 1976 "New Delhi Declaration" they pointed out how badly information inequality and imbalance affects developing countries. Here is an excerpt of the declaration:

> The present global information flows are marked by a serious inadequacy and imbalance. The means of communication of information are concentrated in a few countries. The great majority of countries are reduced to being passive recipients of information which is disseminated from a few centers.

However, instead of staying to discuss and tackle this issue, the United States and the United Kingdom withdrew from UNESCO where the debate on the New World Information and Communication Order was going on. The two countries obviously decided that the debate was against their national interests. Then, faced with financial difficulties, the debate in UNESCO quickly lost power, even though it still continues to exist. Since then information gap and imbalance have continued and even worsened.

The Japanese communication scholar, Yasuhiro Inoue, pointed out the structure of monopoly of the global news media by the United States and the United Kingdom in his recent research (Inoue, 2005). Table 15.1 shows that 6 out of the 7 global news media are located in the United States or the United Kingdom. Referring to this situation of monopoly and imbalance, Inoue comments as follows:

> The news and information provided will be biased and will not represent the diverse realities of the world. This is a serious issue, since such news and information will be accepted as "fact" and the images of the global media have a great impact on the formation of public opinions and international relations" (Inoue, 2005, p. 191).

From these examples we can say that global information is heavily concentrated in the English-speaking countries, especially the United States. The United States controls global information and the hegemony of English plays a large part in it.

Mind control

The next problem I have discovered in the Hegemony of English is mind control, or the colonization of the mind.

Language is not just a tool or a medium. It represents a way of thinking, a mental structure. Learning a language is not simply learning a tool. It affects people's emotions.

It influences their thoughts, beliefs, and values. Learning to speak English often means learning to become and behave like Americans or British. Through learning English many people in the world will possibly become mentally controlled by English. You become supporters and admirers of English, its culture and countries through the experience of learning it, while at the same time you devalue your own languages, cultures, and countries.

The Hegemony of English operates to reward the successful learners of English: they will be gain high-paid jobs, achieve higher social statuses, and individual accomplishments. They admire English and even become ardent advocates of the Hegemony of English. For example, Mauro E. Mujica, a successful immigrant from Chile to the United States, is now a chairman of the US English, Inc, (US English, Inc, 2008) an organization advocating making English the official language of the United States.

At the same time, however, successful learners of English tend to give up their own languages. In California, the Hispanic people decided (Matsubara, 2002) to oppose bilingual education for their children in 1998, because they wanted their children to be able to speak English. They seem to have chosen individual successes at the expense of maintaining their own linguistic heritage, Spanish. The economic rewards provided by the Hegemony of English, thus, make people believe that it would be better to choose English and throw away their own languages. The Hegemony of English controls people to the extent that they choose English and give up their own languages.

English divide

The last problem of the Hegemony of English is English Divide. English Divide takes place as a result of the formation of the English language based class system (see Figure 15.1).

As English is increasingly becoming a global standard language, ability in English will become a very important basis of evaluation. There will be a great divide between English-speaking people and non-English-speaking people. The Hegemony of English will create a global class society where native speakers of English who often possess the highest English abilities will compose the ruling class. As native speakers of the prestigious global language they monopolize the powers of communication and they can participate fully in global communication.

Next come the speakers of English as a second language. In the English-based class system, they constitute the middle class, and therefore they have the second

Figure 15.1 English language-based class system.
ESL: English as a Second Language; EFL: English as a Foreign Language.

strongest powers of communication. These people are speakers of different varieties of English such as Indian English, Singaporean English, and so on. Their participation in global communication is almost equal to that of native speakers of English.

Then come the speakers of English as a foreign language. They form the working class of the English-based class system because they suffer from the labor of learning English for many years, often for a lifetime. They do not have as much power of communication as native speakers or speakers of English as a second language. Their participation in global communication is very much restricted and easily become discriminated against or treated unfairly. The majority of the world's population belongs to this class.

At the bottom of the English language based class system exists what I call the silent class that has no or little contact with English. In any country where there is a severe restriction upon overseas influence, especially Western influence, there seems to be almost no contact with English. The people in such a country are the silent class. Their power of global communication is almost none existent and their participation in global communication will be very constrained.

As the Hegemony of English develops and becomes stronger, we will find ourselves living in the English language based class system which produces and reproduces English divide. In such a system, only the people who can speak English well will prosper at the expense of those who cannot or do not speak English. In fact, the English-speaking countries gain as much as about one third of the world's GDP (Gross Domestic Product), even though they represent only 8% of the total population of the world (Tsuda, 2006). In many non-English-speaking countries in Europe and Asia, the English divide is happening: people get jobs and promotions if they demonstrate English abilities. The Hegemony of English thus causes the practice of inequality, always operating to reward speakers of English and deprive the non-English-speaking people of the opportunities to participate in global society.

Ideologies of the Hegemony of English

We have seen that there are plenty of problems caused by the Hegemony of English. The underlying problem is that there has been almost no criticism of the Hegemony of English. Rather, the Hegemony of English has been unconsciously accepted; it has been perceived as inevitable. The notion of English as a Global Standard Language has become taken-for-granted knowledge: it has never been called into question.

Why has the Hegemony of English been unchallenged despite a great number of problems it creates? How has the Hegemony of English been legitimated? What ideologies prevent us from understanding the realities of the Hegemony of English?

In this section, I will discuss the three main ideologies that justify and reinforce the Hegemony of English. They are (1) Western-centered Universalism; (2) Monolingualism; (3) Selfish individualism. These three ideologies are combined to operate to reproduce and reinforce the Hegemony of English.

Western-centered universalism

Western-centered Universalism refers to the idea that the West creates and represents the universal values, and that therefore the rest of the world should follow the Western model. Western-centered Universalism believes that the Western culture and civilization is the model for all the countries and cultures to follow.

Especially during the times of Western imperialistic invasion of the whole world, Western-centered Universalism was employed to justify Western rule and control. Below is a speech by an Englishman who invaded Australia in the nineteenth century:

> Black men – Love White men. Love other tribes of black men. Do not quarrel together. Tell other tribes to love white men, and to build good huts and wear clothes. Learn to speak English. If any man injure you, tell the Protector and he will do you justice (Bailey, 1991:85).

Western-centered Universalism is evident in this speech: the whites are the absolute rulers whom the natives are supposed to obey. Whites' culture, religion, and language are directed toward the natives with an absolute authority, as a Universal Truth. The Englishman's order that the natives should modernize themselves just like the Westerners is based on the Western-centered Universalism. He ordered, "Learn to speak English" as he believed that English is a civilized, chosen, and universal language. He believed that the "savage" natives would be saved and modernized if they became like the Westerners. This is what is usually called "The Messiah Ideology" an idea that justifies the Western imperialistic invasion in the name of saving and modernizing the non-Western cultures.

Western-centered Universalism is still prevalent and serves as an idea that justifies the Hegemony of English. Many people, Western or non-Western, believe that English is the language that the world should speak because the West is equal to the World representing the universal model. This kind of belief seems to be consciously and unconsciously held by a great many people in the world.

Monolingualism

Monolingualism is an ideology that believes in the use of the only one dominant language in a society. Monolingualism is an ideology held by the dominant linguistic group who wishes to maintain their interests, power, and dominance. Monolingualism supports the Hegemony of English in that it encourages the use of the most dominant language.

The ideology of monolingualism is clearly reflected in the "US English" movement in the United States which seeks to legislate English as the official language of the United States. US English sees the growing use of languages other than English and the resultant multilingualism as a threat to the unity of the nation. They believe that the use of only one language, English, will realize a "unified America." They argue that multilingualism is too expensive and the use of the most dominant language, English, will help the immigrants to succeed in the United States.

US English expresses its opposition to multilingualism by presenting a number of statistics to show how expensive multilingualism is and monolingualism is therefore a wiser decision. Below is an example of the statistics presented on their homepage:

> It costs $1.86 million annually to prepare written translations for food stamp recipients nationwide. The cost for oral translations skyrocket to $21 million nationally per year (US Office of Management and Budget, 2002).

The statistics indeed shows how costly multilingualism is, which makes most people believe more in monolingualism, or the use of English. Nowadays most people are very economic-minded, so economical monolingualism has a great appeal.

Also, most people believe in the use of a common language because it is convenient. That makes them believe more in monolingualism. The value of being economical and convenient is so prevalent today that it makes most people accept the existing Hegemony of English in which the most dominant language is used as a common language.

Selfish individualism

Selfish individualism is a form of individualism that seeks only the self-interests. English is a passport to success today and most people want to learn it for their own interests and achievements. They need English for their own profits. They do not care about the problems caused by the Hegemony of English. Rather, they support and accept English as a global standard language and try to get rewards by learning it.

When I went to the United States in 2007 on a Fulbright grant and gave lectures on the Hegemony of English to the American professors and students, I received quite a lot of feedback to my lectures that was based on Selfish individualism.

At one of the lectures I gave, the following voice came out from the audience showing the feelings of discomfort to my lecture on the Hegemony of English: "I take pride in mastering English as a second language. What's wrong with that?"

The student was proud of his mastery of English and seemed to be doing well in the United States. He failed to understand that the Hegemony of English is a social and public issue and therefore it should be addressed beyond the scope of individual gain or loss. English enabled this student to become a successful immigrant and he benefits from the Hegemony of English. Instead of trying to understand the problems of the Hegemony of English, he confines himself in selfish individualism.

On another occasion, there was even more emotional response to my lecture coming from a professor: "The world has chosen English. And there is nothing wrong with it!" This emotional statement was made by a professor who I imagine had immigrated to the United States.

The reason that these successful immigrants to the United States strongly disagree to my arguments on the Hegemony of English is that they feel as though they were criticized because they had taken advantage of the Hegemony of English. They feel it is English that has made them what they are today. They have benefited from English and gained a lot of rewards from it.

These individual successes and achievements prevent them from recognizing the realities of the Hegemony of English. They have been deluded into the confines of selfish individualism and fail to recognize the significance of the Hegemony of English beyond the scope of individual success and achievement. The Hegemony of English is also a product of an achievement-oriented competitive society.

Ecology of Language Paradigm: An Alternative to the Hegemony of English Paradigm

Having discussed the problems and ideologies of the Hegemony of English, I will now discuss some ways to deal with and possibly fight against it.

First of all, we need to have a theory or a philosophy that will guide us and give us a new way of thinking in order to deal with and fight against the Hegemony of

English. For this purpose, I have proposed "The Ecology of Language Paradigm" (Tsuda, 1994, 1999) as an alternative paradigm to "The Hegemony of English Paradigm," the dominant ideology that supports the Hegemony of English. It is a part of the larger paradigm called "Western Modernization Paradigm" which advances Western-centered universalism, monolingualism, and selfish individualism as well as modernization, industrialization, capitalist economy and materialism. Western modernization paradigm, however, causes a number of serious problems such as environmental destruction, global warming, population explosion and concentration, urbanization problems, widening gaps between the rich and the poor, and so on. Western modernization paradigm assumes that there are no limits to growth and development, but that is where this Paradigm fails. It should be replaced by a more sensible paradigm that will allow for sustainable growth and development.

Therefore, I have proposed "The Ecology of Language Paradigm" which is based on ecology. A part of ecology pursues the preservation and maintenance of the environment. The Ecology of Language Paradigm thus aims to preserve and maintain languages all over the world. There are three goals in the Ecology of Language Paradigm. They are: (1) the establishment of language rights; (2) the establishment of linguistic equality; (3) the establishment of multilingualism and multiculturalism.

Language rights

Language is one of the most important components for human beings, therefore, it should be recognized and established as the essential part of human rights. In 1996 the "Universal Declaration of Linguistic Rights" (1996) was adopted at a meeting in Barcelona, Spain in order to internationally raise consciousness about the importance of language rights.

Skutnabb-Kangas and Phillipson name language rights "Linguistic Human Rights" and define them as follows:

> We will provisionally regard linguistic human rights in relation to the mother tongue(s) as consisting of the right to identify with it/them, and to education and public services through the medium of it/them. ... In relation to other languages we will regard linguistic human rights as consisting of the right to learn an official language in the country of residence, in its standard form (Skutnabb-Kangas and Phillipson, 1995, p. 71).

This definition stresses the social aspect of language which acknowledges and encourages social participation. Language is important not only for its social function, but also for what it is, because we are what we speak. Language, especially the mother tongue, is not merely an instrument, but it is a source of human pride and dignity. Therefore, language rights should be established as an essential part of the right to be oneself. Everyone is entitled to the right to use the language(s) s/he chooses to speak and this right should be honored in all forms of communication.

Linguistic equality

Linguistic equality is a necessary condition for social and communicative equality. There are a variety of reasons for social inequality, but linguistic inequality is the one that is the most serious and yet not recognized. In any country, the most dominant language often becomes the standard language, putting all other languages into a lower status. In international communication today, English has become the most dominant language, which has made all the other languages less prestigious. Thus, linguistic inequality is prevalent today, which justifies and reproduces social and communicative inequality. In order to overcome social and communicative inequality, linguistic equality should be realized.

Linguistic equality refers to the situation where all the languages are endowed with the equal statuses, so that they will be used equally in communication. Linguistic equality will be realized when language rights are established because then everyone can use the language they have chosen.

All the international declarations and agreements including the United Nations Charter, Universal Declaration of Human Rights (1948), and International Covenant on Civil and Political Rights prohibit us from having language as a ground for discrimination.

Linguistic equality together with language rights thus should be urgently established so that a more equal and democratic international communication will be made possible where voices of different languages will be heard and recognized.

Multilingualism and multiculturalism

Multilingualism and multiculturalism are a new set of ideas that are against Monolingualism and monoculturalism. Multilingualism and multiculturalism aim to preserve and promote linguistic and cultural diversity where different languages and cultures can coexist harmoniously without having a single dominant language and culture. Linguistic and cultural diversity are indispensable for the establishment of language rights and linguistic equality and vice versa.

Looking back upon human history, we discover that humankind has been advancing monolingualism and monoculturalism especially during modernization which required the establishment of a single standard national language. By origin, our languages and cultures are diverse. Modernization has suppressed linguistic and cultural diversity, marginalizing weaker languages and cultures.

It is time to acknowledge these weaker languages and cultures so that we will be able to restore linguistic and cultural diversity.

In 1953 UNESCO published a report titled, "The Use of Vernacular Languages in Education", stressing the importance of the use of mother tongues in education which has promoted multilingualism, especially in education. In its recent document titled, "Education in a multilingual world" 2003, UNESCO has provided a new set of principles to further encourage linguistic and cultural diversity in education around the world.

The following is the three basic principles proposed by UNESCO:

1 UNESCO supports mother tongue instruction as a means of improving educational quality by building upon the knowledge and experience of the learners and teachers.
2 UNESCO supports bilingual and/or multilingual education at all levels of education as a means of promoting both social and gender equality and as a key element of linguistically diverse societies.
3 UNESCO supports language as an essential component of inter-cultural education in order to encourage understanding between different population groups and ensure respect for fundamental rights (UNESCO, 2003, p. 30).

Multilingual education should be promoted and the practice and promotion of multilingualism and multiculturalism in education will serve as the foundation for the promotion of linguistic and cultural diversity in society.

In addition, UNESCO has recently issued declarations and conventions supporting the establishment of cultural diversity including the UNESCO Universal Declaration on Cultural Diversity (2001) and Convention on the Protection and Promotion of the Diversity of Cultural Expressions (2005).

Proposals to fight against the hegemony of English

In addition to the academic and theoretical explorations shown in the previous section, some concrete measures should be created and if possible, implemented, to solve the problems caused by the Hegemony of English.

There are 5 proposals I would like to make in order to deal with the problems of the Hegemony of English. They are:

1 Global language agreement
2 The English tax
3 Free English language learning
4 Obligatory use of foreign languages
5 Mother tongue-ism

I hope these proposals will be taken seriously and further discussed for improvement and consideration for actual implementation.

Global language agreement

This is an agreement among all the nations of the world which ensures linguistic and communicative equality. The fundamental spirit of this Agreement is: "Language should not be the reason for discrimination." The spirit has already been expressed in the important international declarations such as United Nations Charter, Universal Declaration of Human Rights, and the International Covenant on Civil and Political Rights. Global Language Agreement is based on this spirit and will operate as an international legal instrument to prevent discrimination on the basis of language.

Based on the important articles of the three major international declarations above, we will be able to devise three fundamental principles which express the core philosophy of global language agreement. The principles are as follows:

- 1st principle: No discrimination should be allowed on the grounds of language.
- 2nd principle: All people should be entitled to the right to their languages and right to their cultures.
- 3rd principle: All people should be entitled to the right of expression, opinion, and information.

The 1st principle could be called "The Principle of Linguistic Equality" as it stipulates against linguistic discrimination. The 2nd Principle could be called "The Principle of Cultural Equality" as it clearly expresses the need to preserve a person's own culture. The 3rd Principle could be called "The Principle of Equal Information Exchange," as it emphasizes a person's right of expression, opinion, and information.

In international communication where people of different languages and cultures interact, communication should be practiced according to the three principles above in order to ensure linguistic and communicative equality so that people can communicate with one another without interference, discrimination, or domination of a certain group of people who speaks a certain language with a certain culture.

We must make a proposal like a Global Language Agreement by incorporating the three principles above. So that people of the world will be able to communicate more equally without giving a special privilege to a certain language. In order to do that, it is urgently necessary to organize an international body to create Global Language Agreement and make it known to the world.

The English tax

The English tax has been inspired by the Tobin Tax, proposed by James Tobin, an American economist and Nobel Prize winner. The Tobin Tax is a taxation system which imposes tax on international banking transactions.

In foreign exchange market, a huge sum of money is transacted every day across the world, enabling some companies to use methods such as "Hedge Funds" and "Derivatives" to make billions of dollars. As aresult, the banking economy has become considerably lager than the real economy.

Also, the market for international banking transactions is exclusive, as most of the banking transactions are carried out in few large cities such as London, New York and Tokyo, implying that only a small number of people make millions of dollars.

Tobin, in his proposals, attempts to correct this situation by imposing a tax on international banking transactions in order to curtail speculative transactions. The money collected as "Tobin Tax," should then be redistributed to poor countries.

I was inspired by the "Tobin Tax" and decided to apply the idea to the problem of the hegemony of English. Then I came up with "The English Tax."

Like the Tobin Tax which proposes taxing international banking transactions to curtail speculative banking, The English Tax will tax the English language used in international communication, and the money collected will be used to the building of linguistic and communicative equality as well as the restoration and preservation of minority and endangered languages.

All the English words and sentences will be taxed. Not only the English documents, but also English e-mails, audio-visual materials, textbooks, and spoken words will be taxed. Hollywood movies will be taxed because of the English language used in them. Multinational corporations will be taxed for the English language for their business activities.

One of the objectives of the English Tax is the curtailment of the use of English. The users of English, whether they be native or nonnative, will hesitate to use English when the English Tax is practiced. They will think twice if they should use English or not, which I hope will somehow curtail the use of English, and thereby reducing the influence of the Hegemony of English. Tobin Tax has already been adopted in France and Belgium. It is being considered for implementation in the United Kingdom and Spain. Thus, it is very realistic and very urgently necessary to adopt an international taxation system such as the Tobin Tax as a counter-measure to excessive globalization which is creating poverty around the world. The same applies to the solution of the Hegemony of English.

In order to further justify "The English Tax," I shall bring up "Internet Tax" which was proposed by the United Nations Development Planning (UNDP) in its 1999 annual report.

The Internet Tax was proposed to reduce the Digital Divide that was caused by the global diffusion of information technologies and the spread of Internet. Namely, only the advanced nations enjoy the blessing of the IT revolution and the poor countries cannot afford it. The Internet Tax was proposed to correct this inequality.

According to UNDP report, 88% of the world's Internet user population is concentrated in the advanced nations which compose only 15% of the total of the world population. Also, North America, which composes only 4.7% of the world's total population, contains more than half of the whole Internet population.

The UNDP proposes that 1% should be taxed on each 100 e-mails. It is right that "the rich" are taxed and the money collected will be redistributed to "the poor." "Tobin Tax," "The English Tax," and "The Internet Tax" all share this position. That is why these ideas are all very realistic and should be seriously considered.

Free English language learning

My third proposal to battle against the Hegemony of English is Free English Language Learning, which means that English language learning all over the world should be free of charge.

Billions are spent by non-English-speaking people on learning English, but this should be stopped because it is not fair for the non-English-speaking people to spend so much money.

Who gains the most in the Hegemony of English? Undoubtedly, it is the English-speaking people and countries. There are about 500 to 1000 million English speakers around the world. These people benefit as English is a global standard language, while the most of the world, about 5 billion non-English-speaking people spend a lot of money and time on learning English, and there is no guarantee if they will really be able to become proficient in English. Rather, they become handicapped in international communication.

The English-speaking people and countries should help the non-English-speaking people and countries if they truly wish English to become a global standard language for everyone in the world.

That is why I propose that English Language Learning should be free. English is a common property for the entire world, it is wrong for the English-speaking people and countries to benefit from teaching English. English Language Learning should not be carried out as a business or an industry, because English may be a common good that should be equally shared by all, and not for a certain group of people to make money out of. English should be taught voluntarily and all resources produced and provided free of charge.

The English-speaking people and countries should be glad that the world is learning their language, and they should not demand any profit from it. They have already had enough benefit. English Language Learning should be free.

It is taken for granted that the non-English-speaking people should spend their money on learning English. If English is a global standard language that everyone in the world should learn, there should be some financial support for the learners so that they will not suffer from the financial burden.

Obligatory use of foreign languages

My fourth proposal is the practice of "Obligatory Use of Foreign Languages" in international communication. This proposal is made for the purpose of creating a new international custom of using a foreign language instead of the existing custom of using English.

If we make it a custom to use a foreign language in intercultural and international communication, it will help establish a more equal intercultural and international communication than the English-dominated communication. By having an equal foreign language handicap, we will be able to communicate more equally.

In intercultural and international communication in which English is a common language, English-speaking people often dominate, resulting in unequal communication. In contrast, in an international conference where the participants are obligated to speak a foreign language, no one can easily dominate communication because everybody has to speak a foreign language. Of course, the English-speaking people will have to speak a language other than English.

The objective of this proposal is to give an equal linguistic handicap to all the participants in intercultural and international communication. As it is now, the English-speaking people have the largest freedom of expression by speaking their own language, while the other people suffer from an enormous linguistic handicap. By obligating the participants in communication to speak a foreign language, linguistic equality in communication will be realized.

Some people may feel that if everybody speaks different language, it will be very difficult to understand one another. This problem will be solved with the use of translators. Also, in many cases, most non-English-speaking people may choose to speak English, I believe, and if the English-speaking people choose to speak French, then the communication will become bilingual and translation will not too complicated.

In addition, the practice of Obligatory Use of Foreign Languages will encourage the English-speaking people to learn foreign languages. By learning foreign languages, the English- speaking people will not only learn about foreign cultures, but also change their attitudes about languages. It is possible that they will change the imperialist consciousness and "English-Centrism" internalized in their minds. This change in their consciousness will be very important in terms of overcoming the Hegemony of English.

Mother tongue-ism

My final proposal is "Mother Tongue-ism." Using English is emphasized today, while using mother tongues is not. The emphasis on the use of English results in the neglect of mother tongues across the world.

In Japan, people are obsessed with speaking English. As a result, most Japanese speak English to foreigners even though they are in Japan. They never even try to speak Japanese. Japanese is thus neglected while English takes the center stage.

I suspect that this kind of neglect of mother tongues takes place all over the world in the face of the Hegemony of English. Minority languages that have little economic and political power are often neglected by their speakers. To deal with the neglect of mother tongues, the use of mother tongues should be encouraged.

Mother Tongue-ism, or the active use of mother tongues, is meaningful at least in two ways.

One is that Mother Tongue-ism promotes language rights. To use a mother tongue is to become aware of the right to one's own language. The active use of mother tongues is very instrumental in terms of enhancing and recognizing language rights. As a result, the importance of minority languages and endangered languages will be recognized.

The other significance of Mother tongue-ism is that it will promote the preservation of linguistic and cultural diversity. Mother Tongueism will help preserve a person's pride in his/her own language and culture, and these help enhance his/her cultural identity. Mother Tongue-ism makes us realize the importance of mother-tongue preservation which is necessary to preserve the wisdom stored in mother tongues and to restore and strengthen the pride in and identification with these languages.

Some critics may point out that in order for these 5 proposals to be successful, the structural transformations should be made simultaneously in the domains of politics, economics, and diplomacy as language and communication issues are closely intertwined with all of them. It is important to create social and international conditions that will help these proposals to be accepted and effectively implemented. At the same time, it is even more important to raise consciousness about the Hegemony of English so that more people will become aware of the problems.

Conclusion

As we have seen, the problems caused by the Hegemony of English are evident, and they should be addressed urgently.

Some people may feel some of my proposals are unrealistic, but all these proposals are the results of serious critical thinking and effort to create linguistic and communicative equality in the world.

The greatest obstacle to understanding and solving the Hegemony of English is the uncritical acceptance of it. This essay is an attempt to raise a critical awareness of the Hegemony of English. I hope that many English-speaking people as well as non-English-speaking people who are learning English for their own benefit will become aware of the Hegemony of English and begin to realize the importance of linguistic and communicative equality in intercultural and international communication.

Also there are very few linguists and communication scholars in the English-speaking countries who grapple with the Hegemony of English. I sincerely hope that many more English-speaking scholars and people will become aware of the Hegemony of English and begin to work for the establishment of a more equal global communication.

Note

Some portions of this chapter have been taken from my paper "English Hegemony and English Divide" (January 2008) published in *China Media Research*, 4 (1), 47–55.

References

Ammon, U. (2003) Global English and the non-native speaker: Overcoming disadvantage, in *Language in the 21st century*, (eds H. Tonkin and T. Reagans), John Benjamins, Amsterdam, pp. 23–34.

Asiaweek (1997) Americanization of China, July 4, 38–44.

Bailey, R. (1991) *Images of English*, Cambridge University Press, London.

Calvet, Louis-Jean (1998) Language wars: Language policies and globalization. http://nanovic.nd.edu/assets/8706/calvetpaper.pdf (accessed June 8, 2010).

Convention on the Protection and Promotion of the Diversity of Cultural Expressions (2005) UNESCO, http://portal.unesco.org/en/ev.php-URL_ID=31038&URL_DO=DO_TOPIC&URL_SECTION=201.html (accessed June 8, 2010).

Inoue, Y. (2005) Global media to news eizou no kokusai ryuutuu – beiei tsuushinshaniyoru kasen kouzouno mondaiten, in *News-no kokusai ryuutsuu to shimin ishiki*, Keio University Press, pp. 171–194.

Macedo, D, Dendorinos, B., and Gounari, P. (2003) *The Hegemony of English*, Paradigm Publishers, Boulder, CO.

Matsubara, K. (2002) America no kouyougowa Eigo?: Tagengoshakai America no gengo ronsou, in *Sekai no Gengo Seisaku*, (ed. T. Kawahara), Kuroshio Shuppan, Tokyo, p. 20.

Nettle, D., and Romaine, S. (2000) *Vanishing Voices: The Extinction of the World's Languages*, Oxford University Press, Oxford.

Norberg-Hodge, H. (1991) *Ancient Futures: Learning from Ladakh*, Rider, London.

Pennycook, A. (1994) *Cultural Politics of English as an International Language*, Longman, London.

Phillipson, R. (1992) *Linguistic Imperialism*, Oxford University Press, Oxford.

Skutnabb-Kangas, T., and Phillipson R. (1995) Linguistic human rights, past and present, in *Linguistic Human Rights: Overcoming Linguistic Discrimination*, (eds. T. Skutnabb-Kangas and R. Phillipson), Mouton de Gruyter, Berlin, pp. 71–100.

Tsuda, Y. (1986) *Language Inequality and Distortion*, John Benjamins, The Netherlands.

Tsuda, Y. (1994) The diffusion of English: Its impact on culture and communication. *Keio Communication Review*, 16, 49–61.

Tsuda, Y. (1999) The hegemony of English and strategies for linguistic pluralism: Proposing the ecology of language paradigm, in *Worlds Apart: Human Security and Global Governance*, (ed. M. Teheranian), I. B. Tauris, London, pp. 153–167.

Tsuda, Y. (2006) *Eigo shihai to kotoba no byoudou* (The Hegemony of English and Linguistic Equality), Keio University Press, Tokyo.

UNDP (1999) *Human Development Report: Globalization and Human Development*, Oxford University Press, Oxford.

UNESCO Universal Declaration on Cultural Diversity (2001) http://unesdoc.unesco.org/images/0012/001271/127160m.pdf (accessed May 20, 2010).

UNESCO (2003) Education in a multilingual world, UNESCO Education Position Paper, France.

Universal Declaration of Human Rights (1948) http://www.un.org/Overview/rights.html (accessed May 20, 2010).

Universal Declaration of Linguistic Rights (1996) http://www.linguistic-declaration.org/index-gb.htm (accessed May 20, 2010).

US English, Inc Homepage (2008) http://www. us-english.org/inc (accessed May 20, 2010).

US Office of Management and Budget (2002) Report to Congress: Assessment of the Total Benefits and Costs of Implementing Executive Order No. 13166: Improving Access to Services for Person with Limited English Proficiency, March 14.

16

Coculturation
Toward A Critical Theoretical Framework of Cultural Adjustment

Melissa L. Curtin

It has become almost trite to observe that we live in a highly globalized world with increasingly diverse communities and intensified transnational interaction. Nevertheless, these conditions are central to two issues that frequently arise in a wide range of discourses – intercultural sensitivity and cultural adjustment. Concerning immigrants within the US borders, for example, there is heavy news coverage regarding immigration policies as well as ongoing debates about how recent arrivals should adapt to their new "national culture." Perhaps embracing a more outward-looking mentality, many businesses and institutions of higher education in the United States have instituted programs to encourage domestic employees and undergraduate students to develop their "global competence." A number of scholars are engaged in deliberation about cultural adaptation, having developed a vast and varied research literature on the cultural adjustment of sojourner and migrant populations. It is quite clear, then, that investigations of cultural adjustment are highly relevant to current social issues. In fact, academics in the United States have been addressing this issue at least since the days of Richmond Mayo-Smith's (1894) and Sarah E. Simon's (1901–1902) writings on assimilation in "America" (Kivisto, 2004).

Theoretical frameworks are never impartial, however. For any particular framework, it is important to examine underlying metatheoretical assumptions and to ask whose interests are primarily being served. For example, theories about cultural adjustment inevitably entail certain ontological understandings about the nature of *identity, competence, nation* and *culture*. Axiological concerns include recognition of researchers' values and whether relations of power are incorporated into the theory. Overall, we should consider how both a researcher's positionality and theoretical assumptions might shape research findings, as well as how these findings reinforce or challenge existing relations of power and constructs of knowledge (e.g., Collier, 2001).

The Handbook of Critical Intercultural Communication, edited by Thomas K. Nakayama and Rona Tamiko Halualani. © 2010 Blackwell Publishing Ltd.

I begin with a brief consideration of dominant public discourse, noting common presumptions concerning cultural adjustment in the United States. I then turn to the historical development of assimilation and acculturation theories. Next, I review three frameworks commonly referenced in current research, highlighting particular contributions and limitations of each. To address these limitations, I then propose an initial framework toward a *critical theory of coculturation*. While I primarily draw on specifics in the US context, the theoretical framework is intended to be amenable to situated processes of coculturation among different cultural groups in any locale. My goal is in part to highlight the importance of structural forces (e.g., immigration policies and economic structures) and historical context, as well as to incorporate notions of the contested nature of culture. It is within this broader framework that I emphasize that discursively shaped processes of identification are highly situated and ideologically informed, as are perceptions and practices of cultural and communicative competencies. Overall, I underscore that members of all cocultural groups are faced with adjusting to an increasingly culturally and structurally pluralistic environment and to relations of power within any community (local, national, or transnational).

Discourses of Assimilation and Theories of Acculturation

In general, common private and public discussions on acculturation in the United States come together in an overall discursive formation that holds an idealized model of cultural adjustment that is unattainable and/or undesirable for many newcomers. Everyday conversations, letters to the editor, and news coverage of immigrants all commonly presume an imagined national host community of a white, monolingual English-speaking America to which immigrants should quickly assimilate. This cultural model is exemplified in a November 2002 letter to the editor in the *Wisconsin State Journal*:

> Learn more languages but put English first: This is America – the world's melting pot of nationalities. That is our greatest strength; it is also one of our greatest challenges. From the beginning, people who found their way to our shores learned our language, which is English. This tradition has done us well in the past and should continue. We should expect students to learn in English only.... If one wants to be an American – wants to share in the American dream – that person should learn English and learn in English ("Your Views", 2002).

The same kind of idealized model is also evidenced in news stories, such as the one by the Public Broadcasting Service (PBS) about "the rise of non-English media" in California wherein one viewer queried, "How do ethnic (i.e., non-English) media assist, or impede, the assimilation of immigrants into the greater 'American culture?'" The news story and the question both implied that (1) there exists some "greater 'American culture'," (2) immigrants can and should "assimilate" into this culture, and (3) non-English media might impede assimilation to (predominantly) monolingual

English-speaking "American" culture ("Changing Times", 2002). Rodríguez makes a similar point, noting that news stories may indicate a tolerance for the performance of "ethno-identities" in the private sphere, but the supposedly "inclusive model of 'Americaness'" is understood as being middle class, accepting the English language and identifying with European American values (2009, p. 167).

In general, cultural models are understood to be abstract notions that provide "scenarios or action plans for how to behave in some given situation or how to interpret the behavior of others" (Kronenfeld, 2008, p. 69); and they frequently involve exclusions (Gee, 1999). In this model, immigrants should "behave" by quickly becoming "American," including eagerly and rapidly shifting to English in most or all public contexts. Largely absent is any notion of how residents of the "host" community should themselves "behave" in adapting to increasingly diverse settings. Thus, despite counter discourse envisioning a multicultural, even multilingual, "American culture," the dominant model constructs a picture of current immigrants as outsiders who resist acculturation/assimilation and break with the (imagined) history of previous immigrants quickly assimilating into a "greater American culture" (a white, monolingual, English-speaking, middle class America) (cf. Takaki, 1993). This model is an important component of a highly naturalized *folk ideology of acculturation (assimilation)*.

The question arises, then, in what ways might academic theories of cultural adjustment support or challenge such folk ideologies in the United States and elsewhere? To address this question, I first review early theories of assimilation, noting that these echo long standing folk ideologies. I then examine whether current academic discourse on cultural adjustment has executed a discursive disjuncture with earlier scholarly theories of assimilation or with current folk ideologies of acculturation.

Theories of assimilation

A historical accounting of the ethnographic research in anthropology and sociology exposes a connection between theories of assimilation and those of acculturation/adaptation. Kivisto notes that for the past century, "assimilation has been the hegemonic theory of ethnic group relations in sociology" (2004, p. 149). Vidich and Lyman (1998) sketch an even broader picture in tracing the history of ethnographic research: from early ethnography beginning before the seventeenth century to studies of ethnicity and assimilation extending from the 1950s to the 1980s to postmodern era studies since 1990 where assumptions about the "other" are questioned. For each era, researchers' findings usually confirmed pre-existing beliefs (Denzin and Lincoln, 1998). Thus, early ethnographers worked to fit the racial and cultural diversity of different peoples into "a theory about the origin of history, the races, and civilizations" (p. 12). US ethnographers investigated Native Americans as a window into the prehistoric past. A colonialist gaze was also turned to US immigrants arriving with the industrialization of the United States; this research lens was then extended to studies of ethnic communities, with assimilationist studies proliferating until the 1960s.

However, the 1950s to 1970s research of many "minority" communities failed to support the common unidirectional model of assimilation, triggering a crisis in the field. Some decried the failure of "ethnic groups" to assimilate and called for a stricter adherence to dominant mainstream society, with greater cooperation from ethnic groups who purportedly resisted assimilation. Some called for social programs that would better facilitate the incorporation of "ethnic others" into American society. Others warned of inevitable race problems now that the (failed) assimilationist model no longer held out promise for an eventual resolution of difference. Others, however, argued that one should *expect* a wide range of responses to the complex interaction of different cultural groups, responses which would include assimilation, isolation, subordination, nativist movements, and even secession (Vidich and Lyman, 1998).

Two key points emerge: (1) similar reactions are found in public discourse today (calls for white hegemony, social programs, and/or greater willingness on the part of arrivals to assimilate; warnings of racial problems; and/or proclamations of pluralism); and (2) a unidirectional, teleological model of assimilation has been abandoned in most scholars' explicit discourse. Instead, assimilation is often considered as one of several options that newcomers may negotiate when interacting with host members.

Nevertheless, vestiges of assimilation remain in many theories of cultural adjustment. For example, Berry and associates' bidimensional model of acculturation was developed from Gordon's 1964 work which envisioned a continuum of change over the immigrants' life-span: a beginning point of maintaining one's immigrant culture, a transitional point of biculturalism, and a final state of assimilation into the dominant group (Bourhis *et al.*, 1997). Gordon's model is critiqued for implying a social hierarchy in which the host community is ranked above an immigrant group that is viewed as the *source of problems*. As a unidirectional model, it does not consider changes that the host community experiences via contact with immigrant communities. Despite these critiques, conflicting assimilationist and pluralist ideological positions toward cross-cultural adaptation still exist (Kim, 2005). And even more pluralist theories address these concerns only partially. This point leads us to a closer consideration of three commonly applied theories of acculturation.

Theories of acculturation

Scholars who present more pluralistic models of cross-cultural adaptation include Berry and associates' work on psychological acculturation, Bourhis and associates' more interactive modification of Berry's model, and Kim and associates' "integrative communication theory of adapting to a new culture" (Kim, 2005). I provide a brief review of work by these theorists, highlighting both their contributions to and limitations in conceptualizing cultural adjustment.

Berry (e.g., 1997) is well known for his model of the four acculturation strategies of integration, assimilation, separation/segregation, and marginalization. Integration, the most successful strategy, occurs when a person maintains a degree of (original) cultural integrity while also participating as an "integral part of the larger social network." This is possible only in multicultural host societies when the acculturating group as a whole wishes to maintain its cultural heritage. (Note that this concept of a stable bicultural adaptation is quite different from Gordon's notion of biculturalism as an unstable midpoint on the path to assimilation). The least successful adaptive strategy is marginalization, when there is little or no possibility and/or interest in maintaining one's original culture *or* in interacting with members of the host community, often because of issues of exclusion/discrimination. The two middle-ground strategies, assimilation and separation/segregation, involve voluntary or involuntary deculturation ("culture shedding"), and rejecting/being rejected by the culture of the host community, respectively.

Berry's decades-long work is to be credited for acknowledging the complexity of acculturation processes, including the active influence of host community attitudes and policies as well as the individual and cultural levels of adjustment involved. However, this model is still a mostly unidirectional one of newcomers adjusting to a vaguely monolithic host society via choosing one of the four strategies of acculturation. Further, as Ward notes, the process elements in the emergence of acculturation strategies have been largely overlooked in the work that uses Berry's model and acculturation "has most often been examined as a static outcome in itself or as a predictor of broader adaptation" (Ward, 2008, p. 107).

To present "a non-determinist, more dynamic account of immigrant *and* host community acculturation in multicultural settings," Bourhis *et al.* developed the Interactive Acculturation Model (IAM) (1997, p. 379). The IAM has two models of acculturation orientation. The first orientation adapts Berry's bidimensional model for immigrant orientations by dividing "marginalization" into "anomie" (cultural alienation, similar to marginalization) or "individualism" (a healthier dissociation from both cultures due to strong individualist identity). The other is a new bidimensional model for *host community orientations* which assesses hosts' views on issues such as cultural maintenance, intermarriage, employment and housing of immigrants. Host orientation is based upon two dimensions: "Do you find it acceptable that immigrants maintain their cultural heritage?" and "Do you accept that immigrants adopt the culture of your host community?" (p. 380). There are five acculturation orientations that host community members hold *for immigrants*: assimilation (become members of host community), integration (a stable biculturalism), segregation (maintain culture and live separately), exclusion (neither maintain original culture nor become incorporated into host culture), or individualism (all members are all seen as individuals).

In framing the IAM, Bourhis *et al.* (1997) provide a rich discussion of the complexities of cultural adjustment in a diverse society, noting the importance of public policy as well as socio-psychological issues of immigrant and host community group members. They also recognize that immigrants may need to define themselves in relation to indigenous host minorities and other established immigrant communities as well as in relation to the dominant majority. Unfortunately, the authors limit their "discussion to cases involving immigrant adaptation to a single host community that often constitutes the dominant majority of the host society" (p. 372). Additionally, the IAM looks primarily at what host community members claim to think about what immigrants should do and it does not consider what host community members themselves should or should not do. The IAM presents a mostly unidirectional model of change on the part of newcomers to a dominant homogeneous target culture; it thus falls quite short of the stated goal of presenting a nondeterminist, dynamic account of cultural adjustment for both immigrant *and* host community members in multicultural settings.

Kim's (2005) Stress-Adaptation-Growth model foregrounds the stress of intercultural adaptation (due to both acculturation and so-called deculturation), but positively frames the overall process as one of learning and growth. Emphasizing the role of communication, the dynamic process of adaptation is described as "a continual resolution of the dialectical relationship between ... engagement and disengagement" which results in "a greater personality integration and maturity" (Gudykunst and Kim, 2003, p. 381). While acknowledging the difficulty in researching the subtle process of "intercultural identity development," the authors presume an "upward-forward progression" with an "increased level of functional fitness (greater adaptation) and psychological health (less adaptive stress)" (p. 382) that hopefully culminates in "intercultural personhood."

Kim's configuration of the host culture's role in the adaptation process is similar to Bourhis *et al.*'s (1997) two dimensions of acculturation orientation for host members. *Host receptivity* is the degree to which "a given environment" (i.e., people and institutions of the host culture) "is structurally and psychologically accessible and open to strangers" (Kim, 2002, p. 241). *Host conformity pressure* concerns the degree of demand by the host culture for acculturation, and is "often reflected in the expectations the natives routinely have about how strangers should think and act" (Kim, 2002, p. 241). A third environmental condition involves *ethnic group strength*. Kim claims that if a group holds a strong ethnic group identity, they are less likely to participate in "host social communication activities that are necessary for their adaptation to the larger society" (2002, p. 241).

Kim's model is valuable in positively framing the processual nature of cultural adjustment and for noting that host attitudes are important. However, much of the specific language used tends to frame the process in terms of responsibility of members of the immigrant group developing "intercultural personhood." The expressions "host society" and "strangers" are problematic as they legitimize one group over the other. The expression "host environment" implies a politically and historically neutral environment in which the newcomers are sometimes "hostile and alienated" and in which they should learn to "manage themselves more effectively." Newcomers are thus advised to become less "culturally parochial" and more mature and complex in their "psychic patterns." Absent is a process of change for members of the *host* society, many of whom may be culturally parochial, lack complexity of psychic patterns, and/or fail to develop intercultural personhood.

Kim could also more fully explore the likelihood that degree of host receptivity and conformity pressure are important factors in ethnic group strength. Instead, she presents an overall unidirectional view of the acculturation process that apparently does not allow for the possibility of both having a strong ethnic group identity and adjusting well to a new culture. Furthermore, Kim's claim that those with a strong ethnic identity are less likely to participate in and adapt to the larger society may not be true. An immigrant group may have a strong identity and yet members may still integrate into the host society in some areas of life and less so in others. For example, Martin and Nakayama (2010) point out that some may *assimilate* economically in their jobs, *integrate* linguistically through bilingualism, and *remain separate* socially in their marriage or social circle.

Kim's language and model also hold vestiges of assimilationist theories. In fact, she states that the "ultimate theoretical directionality of adaptive change is toward *assimilation*, a state of the maximum possible convergence of strangers' internal and external conditions to those of natives.... assimilation remains a lifetime goal rather than an obtainable goal and often requires the efforts of multiple generations" (2005, p. 383, emphasis original). Thus, since her mid-1970s work on cultural adjustment of Korean immigrants in Chicago, much of Kim's discussion of cultural adjustment has presumed a model of an idealized, homogeneous host community to which individual newcomers and/or their descendents can and should assimilate.

Recently, however, Kim (2008) has extended the notion of "intercultural personhood" to a more general "way of being" in a globalized world (in earlier work, it pertained only to immigrants and refugees who were to attain this state via a psychological orientation that expanded beyond boundaries of nationality and ethnicity). This notion incorporates valuable insights such as the dynamic nature of identity and that "one no longer has to leave home to experience acculturation" (2008, p. 363). However, the construct borders on being overly prescriptive and idealistic, with a near-utopian ideal of "identity transformation" in which one can (and should) "evolve" to reach an "intercultural identity" which transcends "points of difference and contention" and recognizes the "common humanity among different cultures and ethnicities" by "locating points of consent and complementarity" (via the processes of individuation and universalization).

Another serious critique of Kim's recent work is that she wrongly charges that so-called pluralistically inclined social scientists, especially critical scholars, do not acknowledge "the 'dark side' of cultural identity – the tendencies of collective self-glorification and denigration of other groups" (p. 361) and that they tend to conceive of cultural identity in a monolithic, static manner which presumes that people belong exclusively to a particular, highly homogeneous category. She thus contends that these scholars' work is flawed by "positivity bias" and "oversimplification," but hers is a "constructive" theory built upon a view of identity that "conjoins and integrates, rather than separates and divides" (p. 360). In fact, as presented in the discussion below, many critical scholars do incorporate the highly complex processes of social group identification into their work. They are also aware of the struggles within and across boundaries of identification, recognizing that "difference is both necessary and dangerous" (Hall, 1997, p. 234).

The notion of "intercultural personhood," however, is not to be summarily discounted. It aligns somewhat with Bennett's (1998) notion of "integration," the sixth stage in the Developmental Model of Intercultural Sensitivity where a person has in-depth knowledge of at least two cultures and evaluates situations from multiple frames of reference. However, the DMIS is not prescriptive; only certain people have the life experience, motivation, and ability to attain integration. Additionally, by focusing on individual development and exaggerating the potential for individuals to build a "relatively simple civic consensus," the idea of intercultural personhood differs significantly from "intercultural alliance building" in which alliances must develop in highly situated contexts and are "constrained and enabled by institutions, ideologies, and histories" (Collier 2003, p. 2). In a world often filled with intergroup conflict, Kim's call for intercultural personhood is laudable; however, the theoretical formulation is itself open to charges of "oversimplication and positivity bias."

In sum, these theories of cultural adaptation make valuable contributions by revealing that acculturation is an extremely complex process that varies greatly on individual and cultural group levels. Yet they are presented in a mostly ahistorical and depoliticized socio-psychological frame. They generally favor the position of the privileged over that of the disadvantaged and focus primarily on the behavior, attitudes, and understandings of the newcomers while failing to fully incorporate these concerns for members of the host culture. There is a general strategy of presenting the "stranger" (as used by Gudykunst, Kim, and others) as a deficient "other" who is lacking in "cognitive, affective, and operational" categories of competence (e.g., Kim, 2005). Also, the "target culture" is generally abstracted as a single monolithic society.

Thus, these theoretical models do not adequately challenge the dominant cultural model of acculturation in which immigrants are expected to (and presumably allowed to) follow an imagined historical account of "willing and eager acculturation" into a greater American society which is naturalized as a white, English-speaking "America." Largely overlooked are the social complexity of modern societies, the realities of multilingualism, and the multiple, often contested, histories of a nationstate. With these concerns in mind, I now outline an initial conceptualization of a *theory of coculturation*, a critically based framework of cultural adjustment.

Proposing a Theory of Coculturation

"Assimilation, acculturation, accommodation, adaptation, adjustment, coping, deculturation, integration, alienation." A variety of terms is used to denote different aspects of cultural adjustment, and distinctions among the terms are not consistently applied in the field. At the risk of "just" adding one more term to the mix, I propose the construct of *coculturation* as a *distinct model* of cultural adjustment that works toward a discursive disjuncture with many folk and professional theorizations of assimilation and acculturation. The term is intended to underscore the complex and ongoing processes of identification for all members of a community; to challenge any notion of a static, monolithic target culture; and to foreground that macrolevel sociopolitical and sociohistorical contexts, as well as microlevel social interactional processes, are important in understanding cultural adjustment.

Identities

Notions of identity are central to understanding processes of cultural adjustment. More than a product of internal psychological processes, *identities* are social and cultural products of communicative practices that emerge in highly situated, interactional microcontexts. While they involve macrolevel demographic categories, identities are relational, multiple, negotiated – and often contested (e.g., Collier, 2001). Furthermore, processes of identification often involve a *politics of recognition* that entails a positioning in relation to others which is enacted via three main tactics: similarization/differentiation, authentication/denaturalization, and legitimation/delegitimation. Through these processes, perceptions of group boundaries are constructed, as well as notions of who belongs and who does not. Furthermore, boundaries of identities are historically, economically, politically, and ideologically situated. On the whole, then, identification is an ongoing social and political process for everyone (adapted from Bucholtz and Hall's 2005 five principle framework for the analysis of identity).

This is not to say that newcomers do not have particular challenges (and strengths) in orienting to a new locale, such as when recent Asian American immigrants have arrived in the United States and been faced with a complex interpenetration of class and racial dynamics shaped by multiple levels of newly framed local, national, and transnational contexts (e.g., Wong (Lau), 2002). Somewhat similarly, many immigrants and their children with a "black phenotype" manage highly complex social interactions where race and ethnicity, socioeconomic status, notions of homeland, languages and ways of speaking, and other forms of social semiotic expression (e.g., dress, hair) are intricately intertwined in establishing and challenging highly situated boundaries of group identities, as seen, for example, in De Andrade's (2000) study of a Cape Verdean American community in New England. Thus, in addition to acknowledging that newcomers must situate themselves in relation to indigenous host minorities, established immigrant communities, and the dominant majority, my goal is to *incorporate* this social reality into the theoretical framework of coculturation via a close consideration of micro- and macrolevel processes of identification for members of all social and cultural groups.

Culture and place

In proposing the framework of coculturation, I also want to underscore that cultural processes are not fully functionally integrated (e.g., Hannerz, 1996) and that cultural "consensus," where it is perceived to exist, does not spontaneously arise as some organic whole, but rather is the "result of a complex process of social construction and legitimation" that serves the "given dispositions of class, power and authority" (Hall, 1982, p. 63). "Culture," then, is often a contested zone (Martin and Nakayama, 2010). Furthermore, "territories cannot contain cultures" (Hannerz, 1996) and, for any particular geographical space, there are various "cultural realities" where "different groups struggle to define issues in their own interests" (Moon, 2002, pp. 15–16). Additionally, the very conceptualization of any geographic space, such as a nation or homeland is "imagined" (Anderson 1983) and, as such, discursive idealizations of a particular national culture *and* of who belongs are ideologically framed and contested (e.g., Moon, 2002, Ono, 1998).

Contestations of culture, then, are based on material practices and on relations of power and resistance; together these shape notions of belonging via disparate histories, competing politics of place making and differing legitimations of identities. In arguing for a different theoretical framework of cultural adjustment, I thus use the notion of *coculturation* to emphasize a particular "definition of the situation" (Hall, 1982, p. 64) in which, for all contexts, newcomers are entering (and coming from) highly situated and dynamic cultural processes that are not constrained by national or other borders; these processes are "organizations of diversity" (Hannerz, 1996). It is within *this* broader ideological and structural context, as well as within specific microcontextual interactions, that one's communicative and cultural competencies are enacted, judged, and challenged.

Communicative and cultural competencies

The conceptualization of negotiated/contested competencies therefore differs from the idea of "competence" as understanding and performing what is "appropriate and effective" (Koester, Wiseman and Sanders, 1993, p. 6). As Collier (1998) explains, competence is inherently based on privilege and needs to be problematized because all criteria of competence are situated within particular ideological frameworks and sociohistorical contexts. Bartlett (2001) likewise problematizes concepts of appropriateness, conventions, and cooperation which assume a relationship of equality and mutual assistance between speakers. Thus, assessments of competence are themselves a locus for contestation in which "more marginalized groups seek to resist, subvert and make use of dominant perceptions of competency" (Moon, 2000, p. 230). Therefore, any consideration of ways in which communicative competencies are performed and evaluated must take into account competing discourses of history, processes of identification/differentiation, as well as immediate interactional context.

Methodological considerations

Processes of coculturation must therefore be considered at multiple levels, from highly situated interpersonal interactions to broader structural and ideological contexts. In fact, these levels are coconstitutive; microlevel interactions are greatly shaped by ideological and structural contingencies and interpersonal enactments also shape (e.g., by reinforcing or challenging) "macrolevel sociopolitical and sociohistorical processes" (Bucholtz and Hall, 2008, p. 151). At the immediate level, communicative strategies are simultaneously responding to *and* creating microcontexts in which various social group identities are being bounded and claimed – and accepted or challenged. The interactions are simultaneously drawing upon broader community, national, and transnational levels of "imagination" which are perceived in relation to the dominant discursive formation (cf. Anderson's (1983) "imagined communities"). This is not to say "all exchanges are equal." That is, relations of power inhere both to microlevel interaction and to broader macrocontexts shaped by a host of institutional discourse and practices (e.g., immigration policies, housing policies, language policies, systems of education, news discourse, and, yes, scholarly discourse).

The call for a multilevel theoretical *and* methodological framing of coculturation aligns with other critical scholars' frameworks. Kraidy's (2005) "critical transcultural analysis" seeks to integrate (1) text, (2) discourse, and (3) material practice. Similarly, Fairclough's (1995) 3-dimensional framework of discourse examines: (1) text (linguistic analysis of text); (2) discursive practice (analysis of text in relation to other texts and discourses, i.e., intertextual and interdiscursive analysis); and (3) discourse as social practice (linking discourse to social and political structures). For both, the three dimensions inhere to every discursive event; discourse is at the same time text, discursive practice (including the production and interpretation of texts) and social-material practice. Silverstein's orders of indexicality (2003) also conceptualize text and discourse as social practice when analyzing the complex interplay between concrete texts of social interaction and broader ideological contexts.

These frameworks are useful in developing a methodology for the study of any particular context. For example, in examining the dynamic relationship between structural formations and cultural practices in diasporic identity formation (via case studies of Polish and Hawaiian diasporas), Drzewiecka and Halualani (2002) also argue for a multilevel analysis. Further examples are found in other critical intercultural studies research, such as that by Drzewiecka, Shome, Ribak, and Zupnik, in Collier (2001), where multiple identities (immigrant, ethnic and national) are explicitly situated within larger historical contexts and structural forces.

To summarize, a key point of *coculturation* is that whenever newcomers arrive at a new "place," they are entering a highly complex arena in which individuals from multiple social and cultural groups are already engaged in negotiating (perceived) boundaries of identities. Of course, newcomers are coming from their own complex arenas of social identifications. Thus, while newcomers do have particular experiences and insights, everyone in the locale is involved in ongoing processes of cultural adjustment, or, coculturation. In the never-ending process of "establishing one's place" (on individual and group levels), there are multiple, interpenetrated boundaries of identity that are negotiated on the basis of notions of ethnicity, race, religion, language, nationality, and homeland, as well as social class, gender, sexual orientation, and a multitude of other affiliations. The "negotiations" of these identities are discursive (via text and social practice) and they are highly situated in particular socio-historic and econo-political contexts that extend from very local to widely global framings. By understanding processes of cultural adjustment within this multilayered framework, we can gain deeper understanding into the complexities of processes of group identification (and differentiation) within any cultural-geographic space. The result is that we can break with many traditional models of assimilation/acculturation and avoid tendencies to pathologize the condition and temperament of relative newcomers. We can also directly challenge the broader ideological discourse of acculturation that naturalizes a cultural model of a white, monolingual English-speaking, middle class America to which all supposedly can and should aspire.

Coculturation and Orbe's theory of cocultural communication

The construct of coculturation aligns with several aspects of Orbe's cocultural communication theory. For example, in emphasizing that *everyone* in a nationstate is a member of one or more coculture groups, I too am embracing the "legitimacy of all co-cultural standpoints" (Orbe, 1998, p. 19). Orbe also notes that cocultural group status is "reinforced, augmented, and/or challenged through everyday discursive interaction" (Orbe and Spellers, 2005, p. 175). Also, similar to notions of situated communicative competencies, Orbe (1998) argues that cocultural group members strategically adopt a cocultural orientation and communication strategy for each specific situation, variously striving for interactional outcomes of assimilation, accommodation, *or* separation from dominant structures in society.

From cocultural communication theory, we note that long established members of US American culture are negotiating their social identities through highly contextualized acts of daily communication, and they are selectively exercising a range of communicative practices when doing so. Quite obviously, relative newcomers to the United States also position themselves in relation to various cocultural groups and are engaged in negotiating their identities in highly contextualized, daily communicative practices. A number of critical intercultural communication scholars have demonstrated these points very well in their empirically informed work, such as in Drzewiecka's study (e.g., 2000) on the discursive construction of differences among Polish immigrants in Phoenix, Wong (Lau)'s (2002) consideration of differing notions of "authenticity" among different generations Chinese immigrants, and Hegde's (1998) exploration of the emergence of identity among Asian Indian immigrant women in the United States as they "walk in and out of cultural frames" (1998, p. 35).

Some points of distinction between coculturation and cocultural communication are necessary, however. Various scholars have asked whether dominant group members also use cocultural communication practices (Orbe and Spellers, 2005). It should be clear that all people are by definition members of cocultures (as noted by Orbe, 1998); consequently everyone engages in highly situated cocultural communication practices (within particular relations of power and structural constraints). Otherwise, excluding white, middle/upper class, English-speaking, heterosexual, able-bodied males in the United States as members of coculture groups simply substitutes "coculture" for "subculture" and can further reify a center of whiteness (as well as heteronormativitity, able-bodiedness, monolingualism, etc).

Some applications of Orbe's theory also presume quite static cultural group identities (e.g., race, ethnicity, gender). Yes, researchers must consider the categories people use because these are experienced as "common sense identities" that "*feel* natural and essential" (Ang, 2001, p. 151). As critical scholars, however, we must investigate communication practices through which identities are invented and yet come to be fixed as naturalized categories that legitimate certain groups over others. Furthermore, heterogeneity and relations of power *within* cocultural groups must be considered, a point nicely demonstrated by Ramírez-Sánchez (2008) in a case study of Afro Punks who are marginalized within the already marginalized (mostly White) punk cocultural group.

A final point of distinction regards the metatheoretical positioning of both theories. Orbe and Spellers claim that cocultural theory can be applied in postpositivist research (e.g., using measurement tools), as well as more phenomenologically and critically oriented research. While recognizing that all paradigmatic research provides insights into human communication, I am soundly positioning coculturation in the cultural studies-critical theory camp. Coculturation theory incorporates, but reaches beyond, investigating communication styles. It is a critical interpretive theory (based on empirical studies) to serve as a sensitizing, analytical framework for investigating the social interactional processes of identification and cultural adjustment as these are positioned within more macrolevel sociopolitical and sociohistorical processes. The construct of *coculturation* is thus presented with the explicit goal of challenging naturalized hierarchies of power and working toward a discursive disjuncture with current folk and professional theorizations of assimilation and acculturation that often pathologize newcomers as "resistant others;" these are oppressive theorizations which predominantly guide public discourse and policy and which must be challenged.

Toward a Theory of Coculturation

No single theoretical framework can fully capture all of the complex intricacies of human interactions involved in the ongoing cultural adjustment of all members of contemporary US society in this highly globalized twenty-first century. Through the years, researchers in the areas of social psychology and communication science have refined a number of theoretical models that provide valuable insights into the complexities of cultural adjustment, particularly on the level of internal psychological processes of individuals. And in other work that is often ethnographically grounded and is informed by cultural theory, critical intercultural communication researchers have added a great deal of understanding to the complexities of cultural adjustment through examining processes of social and cultural group identification that are highly situated at micro- and macrolevels of context.

Drawing upon the insights from these works, as well as from recent empirical and theoretical research in sociocultural linguistics, I have worked to provide an outline of a more unified, critical theoretical framework of *co*culturation. While this framework is likely to be useful in examining cultural adjustment in many locations around the world, I have focused primarily on public and professional discourses of acculturation in the United States, as I am most familiar with these. Of course, I invite any and all interested scholars to examine this framework and offer corrections, clarifications, and any other refining insights.

In championing a framework of coculturation, I hope it is clear that I seek to deeply underscore that everyone is continually engaged in social and political processes of identification, and that these processes are highly situated and discursively based. Furthermore, they are an inextricable part of an ongoing politics of recognition regarding who "belongs" in a particular imagined community, whether that be a local site or an entire nation. In the US context, notions of assimilation and acculturation have often been conflated with Americanization. Yet, as Abrahamson noted some time ago, "American society… is revealed as a composite of not only many ethnic backgrounds but also of many different ethnic responses…. There is no single response or adaptation. The variety of styles in pluralism and assimilation suggest that ethnicity is as complex as life itself" (1980, p. 160; as quoted by Vidich and Lyman, 1998, p. 71). Perhaps this is what Sitting Bull had in mind when pronouncing, "It is not necessary that eagles should become crows" (Morris, 1997, p. 165).

References

Abramson, H.J. (1980) Assimilation and pluralism, in *Harvard Encyclopedia of American Ethnic* Groups, (ed. S. Thernstrom), Belknap Press of Harvard University, Cambridge, MA, pp. 150–160.

Anderson, B. (1983) *Imagined Communities*, Verso, London and New York.

Ang, I. (2001) *On Not Speaking Chinese: Living Between Asia and the West*, Routledge, London and New York.

Bartlett, T. (2001) Use the road: The appropriacy of appropriation. *Language and Intercultural Communication*, 1 (1), 21–39.

Bennett, M.J. (1998) *Basic Concepts in Intercultural Communication: Selected Readings*, Intercultural Press, Yarmouth, ME.

Berry, J.W. (1997) Immigration, acculturation, and adaptation. *Applied Psychology: An International Review*, 46 (1), 5–34.

Bourhis, R.Y., Moíse, L.C., Perreault, S. *et al.* (1997) Towards an interactive acculturation model: A social psychological approach. *International Journal of Psychology*, 32 (6), 369–386.

Bucholtz, M., and Hall, K. (2005) Identity and interaction: A sociocultural linguistic approach. *Discourse Studies*, 7 (405), 585–614.

Bucholtz, M., and Hall, K. (2008) Finding identity: theory and data. *Multilingua*, 27, 151–163.

Changing times (2002, October 14). *Online Newshour*. www.pbs.org/newshour/bb/media/july-dec02/ethnic_10-14.html (accessed May 20, 2010)

Collier, M.J. (1998) Researching cultural identity: Reconciling interpretive and postcolonial perspectives, in *Communication and Identity Across Cultures*, (eds D.V. Tanno and A. González), Sage Publications, Thousand Oaks, CA, pp. 122–147.

Collier, M.J. (ed.) (2001) *Constituting Cultural Difference through Discourse*, Sage Publications, Inc., Thousand Oaks, CA.

Collier, M.J. (2003) Negotiating intercultural alliance relationships: Toward transformation, in *Intercultural Alliances: Critical Transformation*, (ed. M.J. Collier), Sage Publications, Inc., Thousand Oaks, CA, pp. 1–16.

De Andrade, L.L. (2000) Negotiating from the inside: Constructing racial and ethnic identity in qualitative research. *Journal of Contemporary Ethnography*, 29 (3), 268–290.

Denzin, N.K., and Lincoln, Y.S. (1998) Introduction: Entering the field of qualitative research, in *The Landscape of Qualitative Research*, (eds N.K. Denzin and Y.S. Lincoln), Sage Publications, Thousand Oaks, CA, pp. 1–34.

Drzewiecka, J.A. (2000) Discursive construction of differences: Ethnic immigrant identities and distinctions, in *Intercultural Alliances: Critical Transformation*, (ed. M.J. Collier), Sage Publications, Inc., Thousand Oaks, CA, pp. 241–270.

Drzewiecka, J.A., and Halualani, R.T. (2002) The structural-cultural dialectic of diasporic politics. *Communication Theory*, 12 (3), 340–366.

Fairclough, N. (1995) *Critical Discourse Analysis: The Critical Study of Language*, Pearson Education Ltd, Harlow, England.

Gee, J.P. (1999) *An Introduction to Discourse Analysis: Theory and Method*, Routledge Press, New York.

Gudykunst, W.B., and Kim, Y.Y. (2003) *Communicating with Strangers*, 4th edn, McGraw Hill, New York.

Hall, S. (1982) The rediscovery of "ideology": Return of the repressed in media studies, in *Culture, Society and The Media*, (eds M. Gurevitch, T. Bennett, J. Curran, and J. Woollacott), Methuen, London, pp. 56–90.

Hall, S. (1997) The spectacle of the "other," in *Representation: Cultural Representations and Signifying Practices*, (ed. S. Hall), Sage Publications, London and Thousand Oaks, CA, pp. 223–279.

Hannerz, U. (1996) *Transnational Connections: Culture, People, Places*, Routledge, London.

Hegde, R.S. (1998) Swinging the trapeze: Negotiation of identity among Asian Indian women in the United States, in *Communication and Identity Across Cultures*, (eds. D.V. Tanno and A. González), Sage Publications, Inc., Thousand Oaks, CA, pp. 34–55.

Kim, Y.Y. (2002) Cross-cultural adaptation: An integrative theory, in *Readings in Intercultural Communication: Experiences and Contexts*, 2nd edn, (eds J.N. Martin, T.K. Nakayama and L.A. Flores), McGraw-Hill, New York, pp. 237–245.

Kim, Y.Y. (2005) Adapting to a new culture: An integrative communication theory, in *Theorizing about Intercultural Communication*, (ed. W.B. Gudykunst), Sage Publications, Thousand Oaks, CA, pp. 375–400.

Kim, Y.Y. (2008) Intercultural personhood: Globalization and a way of being. *International Journal of Intercultural Relations*, 32, 359–368.

Kivisto, P. (2004) What is the canonical theory of assimilation? Robert E. Park and his predecessors. *Journal of the History of Behavioral Sciences*, 40 (2), 149–163.

Koester, J., Wiseman, R.L., and Sanders, J.A. (1993) Multiple perspectives of intercultural communicative competence, in *Intercultural Communication Competence*, (eds R.L. Wiseman and J. Koester), Sage Publications, Newbury Park, CA, pp. 3–15.

Kraidy, M.W. (2005) *Hybridity: Or the Cultural Logic of Globalization*, Temple University Press, Philadelphia, PA.

Kronenfeld, D. (2008) Cultural models. *Intercultural Pragmatics*, 5 (1), 67–74.

Martin, J.N., and Nakayama, T.K. (2010) *Intercultural Communication in Contexts*, 5th edn, McGraw-Hill, New York.

Mayo-Smith, R. (1894) Assimilation of nationalities in the United States. *Political Science Quarterly*, 9 (3&4).

Moon, D.G. (2000) Interclass travel, cultural adaptation, and "passing" as a disjunctive inter/cultural practice, in *Constituting Cultural Difference Through Discourse*, (ed. M.J. Collier), Sage Publications, Thousand Oaks, CA, pp. 215–239.

Moon, D.G. (2002) Thinking about "culture" in intercultural communication, in *Readings in Intercultural Communication: Experiences and Contexts*, 2nd edn, (eds J.N. Martin, T.K. Nakayama and L.A. Flores), McGraw-Hill, New York, pp. 13–20.

Morris, R. (1997) Educating savages. *Quarterly Journal of Speech*, 83, 152–171.

Ono, K.A. (1998) Problematizing "nation" in intercultural communication research, in *Communication and Identity across Cultures*, (eds D.V. Tanno and A. González), Sage Publications, Thousand Oaks, CA, pp. 193–202.

Orbe, M. (1998) From the standpoint(s) of traditionally muted groups: Explicating a co-cultural communication theoretical model. *Communication Theory*, 8 (1), 1–26.

Orbe, M., and Spellers, R.E. (2005) From the margins to the center: Utilizing co-cultural theory in diverse contexts, in *Theorizing about Intercultural Communication*, (ed. W.B. Gudykunst), Sage Publications, Thousand Oaks, CA, pp. 173–191.

Ramírez-Sánchez, R. (2008) Marginalization from within: Expanding co-cultural theory through the experience of the Afro Punk. *Howard Journal of Communication*, 19 (2), 89–104.

Rodríguez, I. (2009) "Diversity writing" and the liberal discourse on multiculturalism in mainstream newspapers. *The Howard Journal of Communications*, 20, 167–188.

Silverstein, M. (2003) Indexical order and the dialectics of sociolinguistic life. *Language and Communication*, 23, 193–229.

Simons, S.E. (1901–1902) Social assimilation. *American Journal of Sociology*, 6 & 7.

Takaki, R. (1993) *A Different Mirror: A History of Multicultural America*, Little, Brown and Company, Boston.

Vidich, A.J., and Lyman, S.M. (1998) Qualitative methods: Their history in sociology and anthropology, in *The Landscape of Qualitative Research*, (eds N.K. Denzin and Y.S. Lincoln), Sage Publications, Thousand Oaks, CA, pp. 41–110.

Ward, C. (2008) Thinking outside the Berry boxes: New perspectives on identity, acculturation and intercultural relations. *International Journal of Intercultural Relations*, 32, 105–114.

Wong(Lau), K. (2002) Migration across generations: Whose identity is authentic?, in *Readings in Intercultural Communication: Experiences and Contexts*, 2nd edn, (eds. J.N. Martin, T.K. Nakayama and L.A. Flores), McGraw-Hill, Boston, MA, pp. 95–101.

"Your views": Bilingualism (2002) *Wisconsin State Journal*, November 17, pp. B1, B7.

17

Public Memories in the Shadow of the Other
Divided Memories and National Identity

Jolanta A. Drzewiecka

Revisions of official history and public affirmation of counter memories have been among the most significant processes following the collapse of the communist bloc in Poland. Historians, politicians, artists, and the media have been focusing on examining wrongs committed by and in the name of the communist regime against the Polish nation. This process of post-Communist nation construction continues as the media report newly uncovered facts, questions, and suspicions about the received versions of past events. Although memories are deployed strategically to advance interests of groups who hold them, memories cannot be controlled (Schudson, 1989). While the prevailing process of revision targeted the crumbling communist versions of history in the interest of ideological reformation, the collapse of the communist bloc also opened "Poland" to confrontation with its others holding stakes in its history, sites, and culture. Jewish (Polish) history and memory challenged Polish national myths of victimhood, survival, and valor most powerfully. A particularly intense challenge to Polish history and memory was posed by a book, *Neighbors; the destruction of the Jewish community in Jedwabne, Poland* (2001a) by Jan Tomasz Gross, which rendered a historical account of a pogrom of Jews by their gentile neighbors in a small Polish eastern town of Jedwabne during World War II.

Neighbors presented a devastating account of the brutality which was clearly a manifestation of the anti-Semitism of the Poles who killed their Jewish neighbors under an unclear degree of Nazi orchestration. According to Gross, Polish Jews were gathered up in the town square, pulled out of their homes, and chased around town and the surrounding fields; some were killed then, others were gathered and burned alive in a barn. The number of the victims claimed by Gross, 1600, was perhaps the most shocking. However, powerful and vivid testimonials of survivors and witnesses also grasped readers' imagination. The monument which stood in

The Handbook of Critical Intercultural Communication, edited by Thomas K. Nakayama and Rona Tamiko Halualani. © 2010 Blackwell Publishing Ltd.

town for 50 years ascribed the crime exclusively to the Nazis. The publication of *Neighbors* led to an investigation of the mass grave at the site of the pogrom by Instytut Pamieci Narodowej (IPN). The investigation confirmed the crime although lowered the number of victims from 1600 stated by Gross to "at least 300" who were burned in the barn, and "at least 40" who were killed in an undetermined way (IPN, 2003). The Polish President Aleksander Kwasniewski made a national apology; the monument attributing the crime to the Nazis was replaced by a new one which stated the crime but did not identify the perpetrators.

Jews have been, historically, the most significant Other shaping Polish identity, even in spite of the absence of Jewish minority structures in Poland since World War II. The state socialist system managed to temporarily suppress cultural and ethnic differences by its imposition of the socialist subject and thereby, more importantly, unifying Poles by focusing their resistance on Soviets and communists (Crowford, 1996). The systemic collapse dislocated signifying relations embedded, not in the least, in the official versions of Polish history. At that point, as economic and political restructuring began, regional and cultural groups started to renew their claims to specific identities. In contrast to regional groups such as Kaszubi or Slazacy who began to publically claim their distinct identities, Jews were no longer an internal minority even as they were historically internal to Polish identity. Polish Jewish/Polish voices are limited in Poland to a few public intellectuals, organizations situated outside Poland, and public engagement with Polish-Jewish issues involves individuals who had either migrated, were forced out, or descended from those who did. As a result, "the Jew" as the Polish Other is positioned both nationally and transnationally complicating the national identity logics which compete against diasporic logics in memory discourses.

The national and transnational dimensions intersect powerfully in *Neighbors* and its reception illustrating the complexities of national, group, and personal histories. The book was written by Jan Tomasz Gross, an NYU professor at the time, who had emigrated from Poland after he was imprisoned for participation in the political unrest of 1968 and then was permitted to leave because his mother was Jewish. By Gross' (2001b) own account, he began to study the Holocaust in the United States because Polish historiography separated out the Polish history of World War II and the Holocaust. His personal biography crossed multiple borders and made his challenge to Polish historiography and national myths particularly powerful. Likewise, the survivors and witnesses of the Jedwabne pogrom quoted in the book and in the Polish news coverage are part of the Jewish diaspora. The publication of the book in Poland did not receive much notice; however, when the date of its publication in the United States neared, intense and enduring media coverage of events, scholarly debates, and journalist investigations lasted for over a year. One of the predominant themes in the media was a concern about how Poland would be perceived internationally. The book and the response in the media demonstrated that Jewish Other was central to the negotiation of Polish memory and national identity. In her discussion of the importance of the significant others in the formation of national identity, Triandafyllidou (1998) makes a distinction between internal and external others who become significant because they are perceived to threaten the claims to purity and innocence of the nation. Jews had been a significant minority in Poland and had been cast in the role of the most enduring other whose significance continues to trump other historical others of Poland in its persistence and acuteness. However, although in the past Polish Jews were internal to Polish national identity construction as an internal minority group, "the Jew" as a conceptual Other (Bauman, 1989) continues to be internal to Polish national identity through erasure and invisibility, while most Jews of Polish background are materially situated outside the national polity. The Jewish/Polish positionalities are complex as demonstrated by Krajewski's (2005) claim that he is *a Polish Jew*. The internal/external position of the Jewish Other complicates the internal and external national identity negotiations in public discourses.

In my analysis, I take my cue from scholars who argue that political identity is constructed in part through memory (Anderson, 1991; Browne, 1999; Gordon, 2001; Zelizer, 1995). I argue that the negotiation of the Polish Jewish/Jewish Polish memory is an attempt to recuperate the Polish nation through the trans/national Jewish other as the entry point to negotiate Poland's position in the post-Communist geopolitical context. I view public memory as a discourse of exclusion which defines the imaginary horizon of the belonging of groups implicated in each others' history. I will also argue that sustained attention to history and memory is key to understanding negotiations of political identities and relations among groups from a critical intercultural communication perspective.

I will first chart a history-memory framework for critical intercultural studies. I will then analyze a commentary written by Adam Michnik, a Pole of Jewish background, an anti-Communist activist imprisoned several times by the Polish government during the communist regime, currently Editor in Chief of *Gazeta Wyborcza* (*GW*), the largest daily in Poland. His commentary was written at the invitation of the *New York Times* (*NYT*) and published simultaneously in GW. A few weeks later Leon Wieseltier, the Editor of the *New Republic* (*NR*) whose Jewish mother was saved by Poles during World War II, published a scathing response in NR which was translated and published in GW. Michnik and Wieseltier exchanged two more responses. I will limit myself here to the analysis of Michnik's commentary which encapsulated some of the most persistent themes playing out in the Polish media discourse and was "a Polish response" to *Neighbors* in the New York Times. In my analysis I will focus on the denial of anti-Semitism in and through memory discourse as a strategy of recuperating the Polish nation in the present. I will end with a discussion of the concept of border memories and the possibilities it offers for thinking about progressive and inclusive engagements with multiple and conflicting memories.

History as Intercultural Communication

Intercultural communication scholars have only relatively recently begun to consider history as a factor critical to understanding how groups communicate with each other (Asante, 1980; Gonzalez and Peterson, 1993). Lee *et al.* (1995)

provided a notable early example when they argued that a full understanding of interpersonal remarks and rituals has to be grounded in a historical account of power relations and social categorizing. A few other scholars demonstrated the power of the historical lens in capturing the complexities of communication processes such as cultural production in museums (Katriel, 1994), othering of Asian Americans (Nakayama, 1994), the Arab-Israeli conflict (Hasian, 1998), Filipino identities (Mendoza, 2001, 2002), the identity of the Hawaiian diaspora (Halualani, 2002), diasporic Polish-Jewish relations (Drzewiecka, 2002), and negotiations of white identity in postapartheid South Africa (Steyn, 2004), among others. In these works, history does not appear as a backdrop to communication processes but is examined as a constitutive process that produces groups and shapes communication practices. However, intercultural communication scholars have not explicitly theorized the role of history in intercultural processes. Hence, insights developed by rhetoricians about the relationships between history, language, political identity, and constitution of reality (Blair and Neil, 2000; Browne, 1999; Clark and McKerrow, 1998; Hasian, 2002, 2006) offer useful starting points for mapping out a critical intercultural approach to history.

History is crucial to the understanding of relations between groups not because it verifies facts beyond doubt, but rather because it offers sets of competing interpretations which are always partial, interested, and contested (Clark and McKerrow, 1998). Attention to the contested nature of historical accounts is crucial to understanding how groups come to be, the discursive possibilities of communication among them, and the nature of cultural contestation and circulations of meaning. What is needed in the intercultural communication field is not a simple recounting of a collection of facts – a linear story – but greater attention to how that story is being shaped in relationship to the ever changing relations, needs, and goals in the present. A critical approach towards history must enlarge the reservoir of interpretations by presenting alternative histories, and nurturing doubt against certitude of received interpretations. As Popular Memory Group authors argue, "there are real processes of domination in the historical field. Certain representations achieve centrality and luxuriate grandly; others are marginalized, excluded or reworked" (1982, p. 207). In other words, we must be attentive to how histories are rhetorically constructed.

The special significance of understanding the complexities of history and memory in communication was made clear to me by Gramsci (1971) who noted, that "the starting point of all critical elaboration is the consciousness of what one really is, and is 'knowing thyself' as a product of the historical processes to date which deposited in you an infinity of traces, without leaving an inventory" (p. 324). One can hardly get a firm grasp on infinity. However, my engagement with critical intercultural communication resonated personally only when I turned my attention to the historical traces of the Jewish Other and began to see the claims to Polish homogeneity as strategies of nation building and denials protecting myths of purity and valor. It took some time to understand the constitutive power of the memory of the other which functioned through denial and absence as it was nevertheless ubiquitous. The process required remembering stories I heard from my grandmother and others, taking note of casual comments in everyday conversations whose anti-Semitism is so banal its glare is invisible, remembering passing by a Jewish cemetery as a child in my home town and listening to the primary school teacher explain that the town was mainly Jewish before World War II but the cemetery was the only "visible" Jewish presence when I grew up. While daunting, Gramsci's observation presents an important challenge for critical intercultural communication scholars to engage with histories and memories as discourses which cannot be taken at face value but require careful analysis to provide insight about current relations. We must map the historical horizon and then question the exclusions and pry open the closures in historical representations to understand what is at stake in contestations. We must be constantly attentive to new forms of exclusions and silencing, reproduction and remaking. Since identity in the sense of knowing thyself necessarily involves knowing the Other, our task should be to search out those traces which intersect with traces of the multiple others as a beginning point of investigations of communication processes. Such projects are inherently political as they involve complex relations between groups and multiple layers of meaning. In this sense, and from a critical intercultural communication perspective, intercultural communication is always political. That means that as scholars we must be attentive to various viewpoints and what is at stake in contestations, but that we must not be bound or paralyzed by them. This will almost always mean that our interpretations will be at odds with group political agendas and perhaps not welcome – but that is a risk that we must take. In my work, I strategically chose to concentrate on my critique on the "Polish" side – the side I am more intimately connected with from a distance. The categories "Polish" and "Jewish" necessarily hide internal diversity of opinions and experiences which are masked by hegemonic pressures to unify within and dichotomize from each other.

Polish Jewish History Under Revision

Polish history, including its Jewish history, has been undergoing revision in both scholarly and public discourses. A plethora of different historical and literary investigations of Polish Jewish history have been published in recent years, often a result of collaborations among scholars in Poland, the United States, Israel, and elsewhere. Likewise, the popular press, documentaries, movies, and novels have been presenting forgotten aspects of Poland's Jewish history. I will highlight only a few historical "traces" (Gramsci, 1971) of Polish Jewish history and then focus on the recent shifts in the historical discourses.

Jews began their migration to Poland in the eleventh century escaping persecution in Spain, England, and France. By the sixteenth century, the Polish Jewish community was well established and over time became the largest in pre-World War II Europe (Bauman, 1989; Fisher, 1993; Irwin-Zarecka, 1990, Weinryb, 1973). Its relations with the gentile Christian majority ranged from separatist and separated to integrated, converted, and/or Polonized (Irwin-Zarecka, 1990).

Although Poland became a destination for Jews because it was religiously tolerant at the time – a fact that has become a stock claim of racist denials repeated whenever anti-Semitism in Poland is discussed – anti-Semitism played a significant role in the very complex relations between Jews and gentiles at both interpersonal and institutional levels. The separation between the two groups whose boundaries are not discrete and multiply transgressed on both sides on the ground, is manifested ideologically by a persistent and seemingly unbridgeable separation between the categories of "Jew" (applied universally with no distinctions and with seemingly no discursive possibility for other labels such as "Jewish Poles" in the Polish language) and "Pole" (implying almost always Catholic) in the Polish discourse. This discursive separation masks the complexities and cultural hybridities which resulted from centuries of interactions.

World War II and the Holocaust were critical for the construction of the Jewish identity and history of Poland. Poland was invaded by Nazi Germany in 1939 and occupied till 1945. Most of the concentration camps were established in Poland where most of Europe's Jews lived at the time. Auschwitz, the most well-known death camp, which became a crucial site of history and for memory making after World War II as a museum, was established in 1940, initially for Polish intellectuals and political prisoners, but later became a primary site of extermination of Jews. Of the 1.1 to 1.5 million victims of Auschwitz, 90% were Jews from all over Europe. The Holocaust reduced the 3 200 000 Polish Jews to between 240 000 to 300 000 which means that about 90% of Jewish Poles died during World War II (Hoffman, 1997). Nearly 3 million gentile Poles perished during World War II totaling 6 million Polish citizens. These numbers show tremendous losses shared by Polish Jews and gentiles, and they also acutely demonstrate differences between the two groups. The near total annihilation of Jews in Poland speaks to their different position and experiences which soon were also to be marginalized by Polish historiography.

Initially after World War II Jewish martyrdom was honored (Irwin-Zarecka, 1990) but the "Jewish" and "Polish" tragedies were not separated out (Hoffman, 1997). Gradually however, the specificity of Jewish World War II experience was erased by Polish historiography which reconstructed Polish Jews as "Poles" (Irwin-Zarecka, 1990). Various motives are suggested in the literature including a desire to avoid the repetition of the Holocaust tragedy by not singling out Jews yet again (Irwin-Zarecka, 1990). However, a more convincing argument faults the post-World War II nation building project which aimed to construct a homogenous socialist citizen subject within the narrow constraints of the socialist/communist ideology under the domination by the Soviet Union (Zubrzycki, 2006) as it must have been influenced by anti-Semitism.

Zimmerman (2003) argues that the isolation of Poland under "communism," an absence of Jewish community structures in Poland, and a lack of contacts between Poles and Jews in scholarly and public settings were important factors shaping perspectives on World War II. On the one hand, some historians, many of them situated in Poland, took an apologetic stance and emphasized factors which made it difficult for Poles to provide more help to Jews, interpreted accusations of anti-Semitism and insufficient action in response to the Holocaust as anti-Polish stereotypes, and emphasized the shared Polish-Jewish suffering. On the other hand, the condemnatory position developed by Israeli and other western historians emphasized anti-Semitism in Poland as the key factor determining the "success" of the Nazi genocidal policies and accused Polish historians of downplaying its importance and inflating Polish gentile help to Jews. Zimmerman (2003) explains that this division remained in place throughout the Cold War period highlighting the role of structural factors in the shaping of historical representations.

As the end of the communist bloc loomed, exchanges among scholars across borders increased and challenged long held positions, assumptions, and myths. Zimmerman (2003) describes three studies which particularly strongly challenged entrenched convictions. In a study published in 1987, Teresa Prekerowa found that between 1.0 to 2.5% of the adult Polish population provided shelter to Jews hiding from the Nazis. This record was typical for Europe and did not distinguish Poles. Nechama Tec found that there were two impediments to Christian aid to Jews: a threat of immediate death to self and family members from the Nazis and a fear of denunciation by neighbors. These findings demonstrated that anti-Semitism and betrayal of Polish Jews in hiding were not an aberration. Furthermore, Alina Cala found that in the 1970s and 1980s, several decades after World War II and largely in the absence of a Jewish community or contacts with Jewish individuals, peasants persistently maintained old fashioned stereotypes of Jews. Zimmerman argues that these studies challenged the persistent notions that: significant numbers of gentile Poles provided aid to Jews; the threat of death was the major impediment to providing more help; and that anti-Semitism was and continues to be marginal. These studies began a process of historical reinterpretation of "Polish-Jewish" relations in Poland. It is a deeply contested process where various national, transnational, and group interests compete and intersect. It demonstrates that history as a representation of the past is shaped by changing structural and political conditions, which call for new forms of identity and changes in memory.

Memory as intercultural discourse

Incisive investigations of historical representations enable a thorough understanding of how relations between groups have been structured. Nevertheless, while communication between groups is shaped in part by history, groups are often not fully aware of their complex histories or their implications in them, sometimes willfully so. Their memories are inaccurate, limited, self-serving, creative and perpetually in reconstruction in response to needs in the present. While intercultural communication scholars are beginning to account for the formative function of history, fewer yet have turned their attention to the twists and turns of memory. Again, crucial insights come mostly from rhetorical scholars informed by memory scholars. Nora's distinction between history and memory is perhaps most often cited in communication literature:

Memory is life, borne by living societies founded in its name. It remains in permanent evolution, open to the dialectic of remembering and forgetting, unconscious of its successive deformations, vulnerable to manipulation and appropriation, susceptible to being long dormant and periodically revived. History, on the other hand, is the reconstruction, always problematic and incomplete, of what is no longer. Memory is a perpetually actual phenomenon, a bond tying us to the eternal present; history is a representation of the past (as cited in Katriel, 1994, p. 2)

While both history and memory are subject to contestation and rhetorical interpretation, it is memory that tells us more about what ideas live on and how, and consequently, about how we conceive of ourselves and others. Katriel (1994) challenges any easy separations between the two and argues that the history-memory dialectic is a more powerful analytical category for understanding the role of ideology in the cultural production of the past. In rhetoric, the study of memory has already involved the understanding of its relationship to history as it focused on what aspects of history are engaged, towards what ends and interests, and through what erasures (Browne, 1999; Gronbeck, 1998, p. 58; Hasian and Carlson, 2000). The scholarship on memory developed in communication and other disciplines offers important insights to intercultural communication.

Memory involves collective, cultural, social, and public processes and all these labels are used in the literature, sometimes seemingly interchangeably, at other times denoting distinct foci. While there is no space here to examine the differences in implications of these terms, one of the thorniest issues in the literature has been the question of the extent to which memories are shared, how, when, where, and by whom. Group membership which has often been used both analytically and descriptively to define particular sets of memories as collectively national, religious, racial, and so forth, often proves to be both vivid and simultaneously inadequate as it homogenizes and erases internal differences. Zelizer contends that the term "collective memory" implies "multiple conflicting accounts of the past" rather than a unified shared version of it (1995, p. 217). Other scholars prefer the term and focus on "public memory" which implies a zone of cultural debate and contestation; "[public] connotes both the shared and the contested aspects of memory at the same time" and directs our attention to the public strategies through which "different groups and individuals in society promote their own versions of memory in order to serve their interests in the present" (Özyürek, 2007, p. 9). This means that memories are deeply localized as a result of "a cultural process in which a shared sense of the past is created from the symbolic resources of human community" (Browne, 2007, p. 3). Any localization entails borders and differences which have to be negotiated, no matter how strong the "desire to enshrine a singular, 'official' civic past" often through "unofficial channels" (Gordon, 2001, p. 6). Public memories are deeply communicative, "Memory has a texture that is both social and historic: it exists in the world rather than in people's heads, finding its basis in conversations, cultural forms, personal relations, the structure and appearance of places, and ... in relation to ideologies which work to establish a consensus view of both the past and the forms of personal experience which are significant and memorable" (Bommes and Wright, 1982, p, 256). These aspects make the notion of memory critical to intercultural communication and raise important questions. Can all memories be shared? What borders limit the sharing of memories? How do memories figure into social struggles around equality, justice, and social structures? I find the term public memories most appropriate for answering such questions but I will discuss useful insights from the literature on collective memory as applicable.

Public memory is a group process; the engagement with the common past is a means of inventing and investing in collective identities in relations to other groups (Bellah *et al.*, 1985; Irwin-Zarecka, 1994; Gordon, 2001; Sturken, 1997). Groups negotiate their shared sense of self in their relations to other groups through memory work, commemorations, and historical narratives and sites. However, how group's memories are created, and the group's access to the wider process of public memory construction in a national setting are delimited by the group's relations and interests in a particular social structure. These delimitations are also reflected in "the fabrication, rearrangement, elaboration, and omission of details about the past, often pushing aside accuracy and authenticity so as to accommodate broader issues of identity formation, power and authority, and political affiliation" (Zelizer, 1998, p. 3). When memories are labeled as "Polish" and "Jewish," these labels reflect not only differences in experience of the groups which choose to remember and forget, but also on-going processes of structural and hegemonic pressures towards discursive closures. From a communication perspective, it is critical to understand that groups struggle as much about the memories they hold, as about memories held by other groups about their common pasts. The categories "Polish" and "Jewish" necessarily hide internal diversity of opinions and experiences which are masked by hegemonic pressures to unify within and dichotomize from each other. A question then arises about the extent to which the notion of identity limits the understanding of the social processes of memory. Can the categories obscure more than they might reveal about which memories are created, circulated and challenged, and how? From a critical intercultural communication perspective, it is important not only to understand multiple differences between groups, but also to understand differences and points of contention within groups to challenge dichotomies as discursive effects.

A crucial aspect of memory is that it is strategically and selectively constructed to satisfy particular goals, needs, and emotions in the present (Hasian and Carlson, 2000; Zelizer, 1995). In this sense, the reconstruction of the past is likely to become "a resource for legitimation rather than as an avenue towards truth" (Schudson, 1989, p. 106). Absences resulting from the strategic shaping of memories are powerfully constitutive of public memories (Irwin-Zarecka, 1994), as they might be a result of willful and strategic erasures as well as discursive hegemonic closures. Public memory construction is a dynamic process and changes in political and cultural structures might dislocate the symbolic order, and open up spaces for multiple voices to attempt to fill in the rift (Howarth and Stavrakakis, 2000; Laclau and Mouffe, 1985). At such moments of dislocation, public memories become much more textured and complex, and cannot be easily molded to serve the interests of one particular polity because they are challenged and struggled over by implicated groups. Conflicts among groups about their memories provide insight into their relations in the present. In spite of powerful globalizing processes, the national imaginaries define a powerful discursive horizon shaping the symbolic possibilities for public memories, even as they might be challenged by diasporic imaginaries.

Memory of Nation/Nation in Memory

National logics play powerfully in the creation and negotiations of public memories, and, conversely, public memories play a crucial role in the construction of the "national symbolic" which "transforms individuals into subjects of a collectively held history. Its transitional icons, its metaphors, its heroes, its rituals, and its narratives provide an alphabet for a collective consciousness of national subjectivity" (Berlant, 1991, p. 20). National structures and institutions, including language, memorials and monuments, national media, judiciaries, and so on, generate and constrain public memories within the nation as a frame of intelligibility as they simultaneously reproduce it. That is, memories are discursive resources through which the meanings of nation are "simultaneously established, questioned, and refigured" revealing its identity, divisions, agendas, and complex political stakes (Sturken, 1997, p. 13). Public memories provide insight about who is included and who is excluded, as well as what is remembered and what is forgotten, and these are key processes of nation building. Some forgetting erases or diminishes differences and enables forging collective identities (Anderson, 1991; Gordon, 2001); but there is also forgetting which exacerbates differences and divisions as it tries to will some memories out of existence. We are reminded that "a nation that loses an awareness of its past, gradually loses its self" (Kundera, 1980, p. 235) which might suggest that erasures of Polish Jewish/Polish memories of Poland are a loss to the "Polish self" and that a struggle over how to remember is a struggle for a Polish national self.

Inclusion in public memories indicates inclusion in the imagined community (Browne, 1999). Public memory discourses are then a good barometer of cultural anxieties over the meanings of the nation (Browne, 1999), and heightened debates over the past might indicate a crisis of the meanings of the nation and a potential for transformations. Memories of World War II are for Polish gentiles inextricably tied up with the nation and its survival. However, while the Polish nation has been a home to Jewish Poles for centuries, it has also been a site and a frame of their exclusion – materially as well as discursively constitutive of the nation itself. Yet, because the nation provides a frame of intelligibility for history as well as public memories, Polish Jewish/Polish memories had been excluded and to some extent functioned outside the Polish national symbolic for some time. The collapse of the communist regime dislocated the national imaginary constructed after World War II, and exposed the crisis of meaning and the anxiety about what it means to be Polish without the restrictions, but also protection, of the Iron Curtain.

Polish Nation through the Jewish Other

The shifts in the conception of the Polish nation are a crucial context for the politics of exclusion of Jews in Polish national memory. The Polish state, in a pre-modern form, was recognized in 996 when Mieszko I converted to Christianity. However, Christianity and Polish nationhood were inextricably tied together only near the end of the nineteenth century (Zubrzycki, 2006). The early conceptions of the Polish nations which developed in the seventeenth and eighteenth centuries were surprisingly broad compared to those of other European nations and defined Polish nationality as a political relation between citizens and noblemen based on the loyalty to the territorial state. Polish nationality was not in principle limited to any one particular ethnic background or religion and included a possibility, however tenuous, of "natione Polonus, gente Ruthenus, origine Judaeus" (Zubrzycki, 2006, p. 37). Even when Poland was first partitioned by Russia, Prussia, and Austria in 1791, Polish nationalism struggling against the imperial powers did not narrow the concept of Polish nation in ethnic terms. Polish nationalism between 1830 and 1863, after the successive partitions, was most inclusive defining a small group of assimilated Jewish Poles who participated in the uprising against Russia as "Poles of the Faith of Moses" and brothers-in-arms (Potter, 2000). Potter (2000) and Zubrzycki (2006) carefully point out that anti-Semitism was certainly present in relations between gentiles and Jews in Poland, but the rhetoric of nationalism itself was not anti-Semitic during that time. The point here is not to argue that "Jews" found a safe haven in Poland during virulent religious persecution in other parts of Europe – a stock claim of anti-Semitism denials in Poland. Rather, this aspect of Polish history suggests that the present hegemonic mono-ethnic-religious constructions of what is "Polish" have only achieved such status relatively recently and the historical precedence for inclusivity should be reinserted in Polish national memory and reclaimed for the present.

When Poland regained its independence after World War I, one of the competing political conceptions of nation-building defined nationhood in exclusive ethno-linguistic terms, equated Polishness with Catholicism, and proclaimed a program of cultural Polonization in a "new" country where ethnic Poles constituted only 64% of the national population and the Polish territory included significant portions of Lithuania and Ukraine. During this time, Jews were conceived as culturally, racially, and religiously alien – an other (Walicki, 2000). "Jews" had already been cast as the alter ego of the Church, now they became the national other; that construction entailed emptying out the category "Jew" of its specific cultural content and references to real individuals and their social relations, making it ready to be filled with contradictory stereotypes as expedient on short notice

(Bauman, 1989). At various moments "Jews" were constructed as both capitalists and communists, and thus the enemies of the state and of the people. The category "Jew" was separated out from and juxtaposed to "Poles" coded as exclusively Catholic. At this time still, the Polish state was diverse, but, in Potter's words, Polish nationalism began to hate (Potter, 2000).

Poland's ethno-linguistic diversity was violently expunged by World War II and the following transition period. About 90% of Polish Jews perished in the Holocaust. Most of those who survived either migrated or were pushed out of the country in a series of anti-Semitic scapegoating campaigns in March 1968, December 1970, and 1975–1977 by the socialist government desperately trying to retain its hold on power (Checinski, 1982). The initial promise of communism to promote equality and inter-nationalization which attracted many Polish Jews (Irwin-Zarecka, 1994; Krajewski, 2005) was broken early on. Yalta Accords shifted Polish territory westward; Poland lost half of its pre-war territory to Lithuania, Belarus, and Ukraine, now part of the Soviet Union, and gained a third of its postwar territory from Germany. Resettlement and often bloody ethnic cleansing along the new eastern border further homogenized a population that had been mixed for centuries. As a result, when the socialist government set out to create a new socialist national symbolism and its subject, the socialist citizen, Poles were 96.6% Catholic, more homogenous than ever in the history of the Polish state (Walicki, 2000). Poles' popular opposition to the Soviet domination united them and, paradoxically, aided in the socialist nation-building project producing a monolithic national identity. Singular political ideology did not allow for a diversity of interrogations or open questioning of the official history which featured Soviets as long-term "friends" and "the West" as the enemy. The "Communist" period was understood by many Poles as a loss of national self-determination. During this time, the Catholic Church provided the only viable resistance to the regime continuing the close links between Polish nationalism and Catholicism.

The collapse of the communist regime, whose censorship and suppression of political issues provided an illusion of unity against a common enemy, dislocated imposed narratives of identity, history, and memory. Polish economic markets were opened to Western capital. International cultural and intellectual exchanges increased. Poland relatively quickly become a member of NATO and then was scheduled to join the European Union. Although they had been desired, political democratization and economic liberalization increased anxieties about Polish identity and its place in the new order. The monolithic national identity cracked as various groups begun to publicly assert their identities and needs, including gay, regional, and national minorities within Poland as well as groups situated outside of Poland such as the Jewish diaspora. Questions about Polish Jewish identity and historical memory of the Holocaust began to reemerge in popular, political, and scholarly discourses (Czajkowski *et al.*, 2000; Gutman, 2000; Hoffman, 1997; Irwin-Zarecka, 1990, 1994; Steinlauf, 1997). The repressed Jewish other returned and griped public discourses in a country with a very small Jewish population. Poland was re-creating its national identity through the Jewish Other in the predominant, but not complete, absence of Jewish Poles.

"Jewish" and "Polish" Memories Divided

The division between "Jewish" and "Polish" memories is a result of complex cultural and national processes. Immediately after World War II, the separation between "Polish" and "Jewish" perspectives was not strict and the Holocaust itself was not separated out as the singular greatest crime (Hoffman, 2004). Hoffman discusses a variety of different literary and popular culture texts which addressed Jewish martyrdom, Polish guilt and implication, and the relations between the two groups in the immediate post-World War II years. A child of two survivors sheltered by gentile Poles, Hoffman grew up in Krakow before her family immigrated to the United States. Nevertheless, she remembered a difference in how people talked about their war experiences,

> The neighbor in our building who had fought in the underground army [anti-Communist/Soviet resistance against Nazis] spoke about it in lowered tones and allusive phrases, but he spoke through gritted teeth with a fervor of fury and pride. I sensed, on the other hand, that what happened to my parents and their Jewish friends was a more obscure matter, the kind of secret one wraps in a cocoon of silence, or protects as one protects an injury (Hoffman, 2004, p. 25).

Overtime, Polish public memories focused on and defined all World War II suffering as "Polish" suffering. Huener (2003) demonstrates the effects of this process in his analysis of the Auschwitz museum which was coded as a site of primarily Polish suffering. Jews were listed among many other "nationalities" imprisoned and exterminated at the camp. Zubrzycki adds that:

> the diminution of Auschwitz's Jewish fact was also, if not primarily, a strategic ideological manipulation by the Communist state intended to create a Socialist shrine, replete with victims ("victims of Fascism," Poles at the head) and heroes (the liberating Red Army, the resistance movement, and so on) (2006, p. 105).

The institutional discourses parallel data on individual memories of gentile Poles. In 1992, 47% of Poles thought that Auschwitz was primarily a place of Polish martyrdom, in 1995, that declined to 32% (Zimmerman, 2003). Still, there are enduring myths and fallacies in historical conceptions. The notion of Jewish Communists who betrayed Poland to the Soviets and committed crimes against the nation, Zydokomuna, is particularly persistent (Irwin-Zarecka, 1990). Zimmerman points out that the predominant fallacy in the Jewish memory of World War II was that "Hitler built the death camps in Poland because of Polish anti-Semitism" (2003, p. 3). Myths on both sides have been undergoing revision but this is not to suggest symmetry in fallacies or past wrongs on both sides that is evoked in some current memory discourses.

History and memory are both contested representations, although history's claims to "factuality" may powerfully legitimate memories (Katriel, 1994). For example, the history of Jewish pogroms has been constructed in the past to serve the interests of Polish nationalism while disregarding contradictory, or lack of, evidence (Engel, 2003). In these representations, "Jews" played a role of the national other who in the imaginary of national memory has always committed more grave crimes and was blamed for causing the violence committed against Jews in Poland. In a startling account which exemplifies the wider processes contesting and revising Polish history, Engel (2003) demonstrates that a particular historical construction of the 1918 pogrom of Jews in Lviv not only fit within the cannon of memory of Polish-Jewish relations but, significantly, played a role in governmental level negotiations about the defense of Poland and the help to Jews during World War II. The consequences of these constructions are still acutely felt in the present. Hence, memory and history feed into each other as history legitimates memories, and memories authenticate history (Katriel, 1994). Nevertheless, memories can also disregard history.

Memories challenged

Myths always compete with other myths and cannot achieve a complete and permanent discursive closure. The first public challenge to Polish identity and its heroic myths was an article written by a literature professor Jan Blonski and published by the progressive Catholic weekly, *Tygodnik Powszechny*, in 1987. Blonski contended that Poles have in general been closed and defensive about gentile-Jewish relations, particularly during the Holocaust, and that critical self-examination was required. His assertion that "Yes, we are guilty" (1987/1990, p. 44) was met with many vehement objections expressed in the letters to the editor. Blonski further stated,

> Nobody can reasonably claim that Poles as a nation took part in the genocide of the Jews. … More significant is the fact that if only we had behaved more humanely in the past, had been wiser, more generous, then genocide would perhaps have been "less imaginable," would probably have been considerably more difficult to carry out, and almost certainly would have met with much greater resistance than it did. To put it differently, it would have not met with the indifference and moral turpitude of the society in whose view it took place (p. 46).

The article struck a nerve; the weekly received 200 letters and its long-time editor commented that the reaction to the article "was greater than anything known in the course of the 42 years during which I have edited the paper" (Turowicz cited in Zimmerman, 2003, p. 6). The responses were split indicating powerful emotions.

During this time, two significant events highlighted the centrality of Polish memory of its Jewish past to its negotiation of identity in the present. First, in the early 1980s, a Carmelite Convent was established right outside the grounds of the former Nazi concentration camp and now museum, Aushwitz. The convent was established in the building which served as a store house for Zyklon B used to asphyxiate camp prisoners. After strong objections and protests by Jewish groups, a brief occupation of the grounds led by Rabi Avraham Weiss from New York, Polish governments removal negotiations, and finally a personal intervention by John Paul II, the nuns relocated in 1993.

In 1988, as these events were unfolding, a tall cross which had commemorated a papal mass at Birkenau in 1979, and was later stored in a church basement, appeared on the grounds of the convent, in the area called the gravel pit, without ceremony or public acknowledgment. The cross became a point of contention between various international Jewish circles and Polish nationalist groups, in part, because although the gravel pit is outside the grounds of the museum, it was a site of the labor and execution of prisoners. When its possible removal was mentioned in a media interview with a Polish government official, a political storm started charging "religious profanation and national humiliation" (Zubrzycki, 2006, p. 8). A political mobilization in defense of the Cross developed into the *War of the Crosses* in the summer of 1998 when responding to a popular call by an ex-Solidarity activist different groups and individuals from all over Poland erected over 300 crosses in the gravel pit. The majority of the crosses bore plaques with a name of a person who had perished in Auschwitz and the name of the sponsor. Most of them included additional text which emphasized the Polishness of the victims of Auschwitz and indicated that Poland was under attack, this time by Jewish foreigners. Some plagues and additional banners were anti-Semitic and presented Jews as communists and atheists, and thus unPolish. Such use of the cross was opposed by many Poles. Zubrzycki (2006) argues that the War of the Crosses was a significant moment in the negotiation of the meanings of Polish national identity. After intense negotiations which lasted 14 months and involved US and Israeli based groups and Polish government representatives, and a passage of new legislation regarding the protection of the grounds of the museum, the crosses were removed by the Polish authorities. However, in what was seen as a victory by the ethno-religious nationalists, the papal cross remained. Soon however, Polish national identity was to be challenged again through the Jewish Other.

The shock of *Neighbors*

In 2000, the Polish media focused on the soon to be published in the US book, *Neighbors*, by Jan Tomasz Gross. The book was a result of Gross' historical investigation of the pogrom of the Jewish inhabitants of a small eastern Polish town Jedwabne by their gentile neighbors under an unclear degree of Nazi orchestration. That an extensive media debate erupted only when the book was about to be published in the United States, although it had already been published in Poland, suggests that Poland's identity, in its relationships to the United States and the western world where Poland desired admittance, was at stake. The issue was whether Poland would be perceived as anti-Semitic, *again*. This time, however, Poland was not an embattled communist country in the midst of the Cold War which made it possible to present accusations of anti-Semitism as part of the ideological warfare of the capitalist West against the communist East (Irwin-Zarecka, 1994). Poland was now a free and democratic country being integrated into western economic and political structures and an accusation of atavistic anti-Semitism would portray it as backward and not belonging with the "civic" nations of Western Europe. Hence, the question of its past anti-Semitism was a question about its current identity, and how the past was remembered was key in the negotiation of identity. Once again, Polish identity to the western world was mediated by its historical Jewish Other, but this time, the Jewish other was transnationally dispersed, complicating relational dynamics which could not be contained within the nation-state. The Jewish Other was returning, as it were, gazing at Poland expectantly from a distance.

When Adam Michnik was invited by the *New York Times* to write a commentary on *Neighbors*, he was in a position to respond to the devastating account that gentile Poles perpetrated violence on Jewish Poles targeted for extermination by the Nazis in a small Polish town. Michnik tried to present Poland in the best possible light and simultaneously account for *Neighbors*, and thus confined himself to parameters of national discourse. The anxiety about the meanings of the nation was palpable in his response addressing readers of *GW* and *NYT*. *Neighbors* delivered a very specific blow to Polish national myths in the larger context of the increasing anxiety about Poland's economic and political situation shaped by the impeding membership in the European Union and the effects of free market economy. Michnik's response attempted to recuperate the nation by denying anti-Semitism in memory and thus simultaneously demonstrating its constitutive presence and power in Polish national imagery. My analysis is informed by Wodak's (2002) and van Dijk's (2002) work on strategies of denial of charges of racism.

Who is shocked?

The title of Michnik's commentary, "The shock of *Neighbors*" claimed a total historical blank slate and innocence. Michnik then began by asking, "Do Poles, along with Germans, bear guilt for the Holocaust? It is hard to imagine a more absurd claim." Such a claim – a claim or a question? – however, was never posed by Gross, or any other serious historian, nor was it mentioned in the brief introduction by the *NYT*. To whom was then Michnik responding if he was not responding to Gross? While this question falls under a type of strategy which distorts criticism to then easily defeat it (Wodak, 2002), the question itself has complex reverberations in Polish memories. Blonski had asserted in 1987 that precisely that question had never been far below the collective consciousness of gentile Poles because of

> the fear that one might be counted among the helpers of death. It is so strong that we do everything possible not to let it out or to dismiss it.... the questions will have to be asked. Everybody who is concerned with the Polish-Jewish past must ask these

questions regardless of what the answer might be. But we – consciously or unconsciously – do not want to confront these questions. We tend to dismiss them as impossible and unacceptable (1987/1990, p. 42).

He continued, "The accusation is seldom articulated but is felt to hang in the air
"(p. 43). Blonski boldly wrestled with the past addressing readers of the progressive Catholic *Tygodnik Powszechny*. Michnik took a step back and a defensive posture in his statements addressed to a wider audience. He let the question out to
dismiss it and shift the focus away from the fact that some Poles killed their Jewish
neighbors during Nazi occupation in Jedwabne to proving that Poles are not
responsible for the Holocaust. His commentary did not address what the murder
of Polish Jews by their Polish gentile neighbors might mean for Polish people and
their conceptions of their history. Instead, seemingly in answer to the question that
has been haunting Poles since World War II, Michnik discussed Polish victimhood
under Hitler and Stalin, the glory of Polish resistance and the international recognition it received from the British and US leaders, and Poland's victimization by
the Yalta Accords. He then charged Stalinism for stymieing discussions about anti-
Semitism after the war. This, however, spoke neither to the issues presented by
Gross nor to the haunting question. A charge implicit in both the question and
Neighbors, a charge of anti-Semitism, was rejected through a national self-
glorification shifting the responsibility of anti-Semitism onto others.

Van Dijk explains that the strategy of nationalist self-glorification is used to deny
charges of racism in parliamentary discourse where "international norms and values, such as democracy, equal rights, and tolerance are involved. Accusations of
racism in such a context may easily be heard as a moral indictment of the nation as
a whole" (2002, p. 316–317). The impending publication of *Neighbors* in the
United States brought the issue of Polish anti-Semitism into the international
arena. However, it is Michnik's commentary that cast *Neighbors* "as a moral indictment of the nation as a whole" and thus distorted its claims. Van Dijk argues that
the strategy of national self-glorification is often accompanied by emphatic denials
of racism. Michnik's response differs in that he did admit anti-Semitism, albeit in
euphemistic terms, by referring to "deeply rooted" "anti-Semitic traditions" which
he further mitigated as a function of hostile neighbors, a besieged nation, and
Russian occupiers. He then conjured up an image of Poland as a safe haven for
Jews, although he did admit that when Jews began to "feel increasingly discriminated against and unsafe," they indeed were. The source of discrimination was
described as "noisy anti-Semitic groups," and thus marginalized and trivialized.
Michnik did not explicitly deny anti-Semitism. An emphatic denial would have
sounded suspect in the liberal context of *GW* and *NYT*. Instead Michnik engaged
in a dance of admission for the purposes of denial. Admission created an appearance of a reckoning and thus made more subtle forms of denial possible.

In the next move, Michnik pushed further to recuperate anti-Semitism by
stressing that the anti-Semitic nationalist right in Poland did not collaborate
with the Nazis like the right factions in other European countries. He then pre-

sented "a singularly Polish paradox: on occupied Polish soil, a person could be an anti-Semite, a hero of the resistance and a savior of Jews." This attempt at capturing historical and cultural complexities strived to exonerate the Polish nation by presenting anti-Semitism not only as benign but honorable in its service to the larger cause, the nation. To support his case, Michnik discussed at length the case of a Polish Catholic writer, Zofia Kossak-Szczucka, who had been imprisoned in Auschwitz and issued an appeal to condemn the genocide of Jews. Her rationalization is well-known through the following excerpt quoted by Michnik:

> Our feelings toward the Jews haven't changed. We still consider them the political, economic, and ideological enemies of Poland. Furthermore, we are aware that they hate us even more than they hate the Germans, that they hold us responsible for their misfortune. ... The knowledge of these feelings doesn't relieve us of the duty to condemn the crime. We don't want to be Pilates. We have no chance to act against the German crimes, we can't help or save anybody, but we protest from the depth of our hearts, filled with compassion, indignation and awe.

There is no doubt that Kossak-Szczucka's appeal was both "openly poisoned by anti-Semitic stereotypes" and commendable in some respects. However, when Michnik used the term paradox again to conclude that, "the anti-Semitic tradition compels the Poles to perceive the Jews as aliens while the Polish heroic tradition compels them to save them," he drew up a generalization that could not be sustained by references to any historical records. Anti-Semitic Poles were not massively helping Polish Jews, as more recent historical studies have argued (Zimmerman, 2003). The claim to the contrary is startling in response to a detailed account of a pogrom. The insistent public memory that Poles saved Jews has not been pierced the way history had already been. Saving Jews, here once again supported by worn out references to the trees planted at Yad Vashem to honor those who risked their lives to save Jews, excused anti-Semitism and more, it recuperated the nation in memory.

Michnik proceeded by making small admissions – concessions – and then immediately neutralizing them and shifting the blame to others. Yes, there was anti-Semitism, but anti-Semites saved Jews. In the following excerpt, he made a qualified admission that there were reasons for guilt.

> The lives of those Poles who felt the guilt of being helpless witnesses to the atrocity were marked by a deep trauma, which surfaces with each new debate about anti-Semitism, Polish–Jewish relations and the Holocaust. After all, people in Poland know deep inside that they were the ones who moved into the houses vacated by Jews herded into the ghetto. And there were other reasons for guilt. There were some Poles who turned Jews in and others who hid Jews for money.

This brief acknowledgement of "reasons for guilt" is, however, quickly rejected in a counter-attack (van Dijk, 2002) which reverses the charges, real and invented.

Polish public opinion is rarely united, but almost all Poles react very sharply when confronted with a charge that Poles get their anti-Semitism with their mothers' milk and with accusations of their complicity in the Shoa. For the anti-Semites, who are plentiful on the margins of Poland's political life, those attacks are proof of the international anti-Polish Jewish conspiracy. To normal people who came of age in the years of falsifications and silence about the Holocaust, these allegations seem unjust.

Michnik's counter-attack reduces Gross's account to anti-Polish prejudice which creates anti-Semitism by evoking a notorious statement by the Israeli Prime Minister Yitzhak Shamir, who said when he was in office in August 1989 during the height of the Carmelite convent controversy that, "Poles imbibe anti-Semitism with their mother's milk" (Perlez, 1993) While in the sequential flow, "normal people" are juxtaposed to anti-Semites, the phrase reinforces the common sense of historical amnesia which writes out anti-Semitism as formative of the Polish nation and insidious presence in its everyday life and everyday talk (Swida-Ziemba, 2000). The amnesia results from and reinforces the separation and devaluing of Jewish experience in Poland during World War II. It is in this discursive context, that Michnik then returns to the theme of innocence claimed in the title and asserts that "an average Polish reader couldn't believe that something like this could have happened. I must admit that I couldn't believe it either and I thought that my friend Jan Gross had fallen victim to a falsification." The average Polish reader is presupposed to know nothing about violence against Jews in Poland, and that it indeed might be the case is further evidence of how deep anti-Semitism and separation have been, rather than of innocence as Michnik would have it. His subsequent comparison of Polish reactions to *Neighbors* to "the Jewish community's reactions" to Hannah Arendt's "Eichmann in Jerusalem" which revealed that some Jewish official collaborated with the Nazis served to bring in negative information about Jews to discredit *Neighbors* and negated any further claim to innocence.

One of the most intriguing aspects of Michnik's commentary is how he framed his claim to Jewish identity. The Polish publication of Michnik's article highlighted the following excerpt:

> Writing these words, I feel a specific schizophrenia: I am a Pole, and my shame about the Jedwabne's murder is a Polish shame. At the same time, I know that if I had been there in Jedwabne, I would have been killed as a Jew.

The two sentences following "I am a Pole ..." are very powerful as they might have hinted at a possibility of seeing from a double perspective, crossing borders, and injecting complexity against the certainty of dichotomies. The power of the claim to both identities is undercut by the term schizophrenia. The term schizophrenia refers both in English and Polish to contradictory or antagonistic attitudes. Michnik describes a seeming conflict between his two identities which he portrays as separate and irreconcilable.

According to DuBois two irreconcilable identities create a double consciousness of two separate perspectives divided by a color line. The division is not easy or comfortable, it is a split inducing tension. Michnik continues,

> Thanks to my choice, I am a Pole, and I am responsible to the world for the evil inflicted by my countrymen. I do so out of my free will, by my own choice, and by the deep urging of my conscience. But I am also a Jew who feels a deep brotherhood with those who were murdered as Jews. From this perspective, I assert that whoever tries to remove the crime in Jedwabne from the context of its epoch, whoever uses this example to generalize that this is how only the Poles and all the Poles behaved, is lying. And this lie is as repulsive as the lie that was told for many years about the crime in Jedwabne.

In this case, the two perspectives do not create a double consciousness. Instead, one voice or perspective is silenced in favor of another, the "Jewish" voice in favor of the "Polish" one. Although the singular ethno-religious construction of "Pole" is relatively recent, the persistent separateness of the labels in discourse projects the separateness of the groups onto the past that had been a result of multiple, intensely mixed, sometimes separated and segregated, and lengthy entanglements. Although I have been purposefully using the term gentile earlier in this essay, the label does not resonate in Poland where "Polish Jews" is a rare alternative to "Poles" and "Jews," while "Jewish Poles" appears inconceivable. In Michnik's commentary, Jews are not us. The category of the Jew is firmly separated from the category of "Pole," even, and tellingly so, as he discussed his own Jewish identity. The labels "Poles" and "Jews" whose referents are multiple and not mutually exclusive, hide diversity in culture, nation, and religious dimensions. Michnik perpetuated this dichotomy which enacts exclusions in the present through memory of denial. Instead of a double positionality which might offer a potential for richer insight, he activated a dichotomy and an antagonism in which a Polish and a Jewish perspective can never productively engage each other.

Wieseltier rightly charges in his response:

> He appears to have experienced a contradiction, to have needed to experience a contradiction, where there should be no contradiction. "Writing these words…" But this is not a schizophrenia at all. Hybridity, a common fate, is not always morally rending. The multiple identity that Michnik describes means only that he has multiple reasons for anger, for tears, for the repudiation of every excuse and every extenuation. As a Pole and as a Jew, he should have come to the same obvious conclusion: that Poland has many glories, but its history with the Jews is not one of them; and that the interest in innocence always stands in the way of interest in goodness.

Wieseltier thus raises important questions about the possibilities of border memories which not so much reconcile different perspectives, but productively explore the tensions between them. Michnik's commentaries evade the tensions through a discourse of denial. As Wieseltier remarked in his final response,

Respect for the other is infirm and untrustworthy if it is forever an act of self-over-coming. Must we settle for so little? If you believe that anti-Semitism is an ineradicable feature of Polish life, then you should say so. But I have never known you to be a pessimist in affairs of conscience.

Could a discourse of border memory open up a broader space for examination of "Jewish" and Polish" memories and challenge some dichotomies?

Border memory

Browne (2007) argues that "remembrance is literally grounded by the material and symbolic locations in which that act takes places. To the extent that we often (always?) occupy several such locations at any given time, it follows that remembrance occurs at the liminal junctures of human experience (p. 1)." He further proposes a specific concept of border memory to describe "the curious and often profound experience of discovering oneself as between two worlds, situated, so to speak, in a poised simultaneity, in which one is made incessantly aware of the past even as it threatens to slip away, and of the future even as it threatens to overwhelm a precarious present" (p. 5). Browne turns to Du Bois' notion of double consciousness and argues that the concept of border memory attempts to understand the language of Du Bois' "unreconciled strivings." Browne understands the doubleness as an interplay between remembering and forgetting of the pre-immigration past in the process of negotiating the present identity as it is oriented towards the future. Du Bois' notion of double consciousness focuses on exclusion and difference by "race" as it irreconcilably fractures identity of African Americans. For Browne, ethnicity marks the immigrant as different and presents not easily reconciled strivings for identity in-between past-present-future, here and there, in the immigration context of the United States where assimilationist melting pot logic continues along other competing discourses of ethnic and immigrant identity. He thus brings together notions of identity and cultural location and explores how they are negotiated through memories. The notion of border memory and its dimensions are very helpful in addressing the negotiation of different memories by groups and individuals who share historical traces. It raises important questions about whether and how it might be possible to overcome the hegemonic closures which shape memories in the service of group, and especially national, interests. Can border memories be forged between groups on a wider scale? Can groups or nations develop border memories? What would discourses of border memories look like?

The dimensions of exclusion, connection and difference emphasized by Du Bois are crucial to these questions. Du Bois used the term double consciousness to refer to an internal conflict between African and American identities within African Americans.

It is a peculiar sensation, this double consciousness. This sense of looking at one's self through the eyes of others, of measuring one's soul by the tape of a world that looks on in amused contempt and pity. One ever feels this twoness, – an American, a Negro;

two souls, two thoughts, two unreconciled strivings; two warring ideals in one dark body, whose dogged strength alone keeps it from being torn asunder. The history of the American Negro is the history of this strife – this longing to attain self-conscious manhood, to merge his double self into a better and truer self. In this merging he wishes neither of the older selves to be lost (Du Bois, p. 102, 1903/1997).

In this passage, double consciousness is an effect of an internal fracture and conflict created by racism which powerfully obscures the sense of self. The term poses a problem of duality and alienation as one *is and is not seen* by others as well as by self. The self is distanced and displaced by racist perceptions. Hence, double consciousness has two meanings; it refers to a dialogic and conflicted relationship between two modes of thought giving African Americans a double perspective. It also describes a racist displacement from the category of "American."

The notions of double consciousness and border memory are highly relevant to rethinking of "Polish" and "Jewish" memories, undermining hegemonic discourses and encouraging engagement which capitalizes on multiplicities and fluidities of identities and perspectives. The notion of double consciousness suggests a doubleness in perspective and a displacement from any singular category. We need to displace gentile Poles from the hegemonic category of "Pole" to open it up to various positionalities such as Krajewski's (2005) Polish Polish Jew. Border memories are not memories which reconcile all differences and resolve all dilemmas. Instead, border memories work through a tension between different perspectives. Each perspective in the border zone rings with the echo and doubt of other perspectives, follows their traces, and explores their implications. Hence, debates over *Neighbors* and other historical accounts should aim to engage different voices and explore tensions rather than aim to arrive at a certain and singular version of "what happened."

References

Anderson, B. (1991) *Imagined Communities: Reflections on the Origin and Spread of Nationalism*, (Rev. edn), Verso, London.

Asante, M.K. (1980) Intercultural communication: An inquiry into research direction. *Communication Yearbook*, 4, 401–410.

Bauman, Z. (1989) *Modernity and the Holocaust*, Cornell University Press, Ithaca, NY.

Bellah, R., Madsen, R., Sullivan, W.M., Swindler, A., and Tipton, S. (1985) *Habits of the Heart: Individualism and Commitment in American Life*, University of California Press, Berkeley.

Berlant, L. (1991) *The Anatomy of National Fantasy: Hawthorne, Utopia, and Everyday Life*, University of Chicago Press, Chicago.

Blair, C., and Neil, M. (2000). Reproducing civil rights tactics: The rhetorical performances of the civil rights memorial. *Rhetoric Society Quarterly*, 30, 31–55.

Blonski, J. (1987/1990) The poor Poles look at the ghetto, in *"My Brother's Keeper?" Recent Polish Debates on the Holocaust*, (ed. A. Polonsky), London, Routledge, pp. 34–52.

Bommes, M., and Wright, P. (1982) The charms of residence: The public and the past, in *Making Histories: Studies in History-Writing and Politics*, (eds R. Johnson, G. McLennan, B. Schwartz and D. Sutton), The Centre for Contemporary Cultural Studies, University of Birmingham, London, (pp. 253–301).

Browne, S.H. (1999) Remembering Crispus Attucks: Race, rhetoric, and the politics of commemoration. *Quarterly Journal of Speech*, 85, 169–187.

Browne, S.H. (2007) On the borders of memory. Paper presented at the Ethnicity and Memory Conference, Lewis and Clark College, Portland, Oregon.

Checinski, M. (1982) *Poland: Communism, Nationalism, Anti-Semitism*, Karz-Cohl Publishing, New York.

Clark, C.E., and McKerrow, R.E. (1998) The rhetorical construction of history, in *Doing Rhetorical History*, (ed. K. J. Turner), University of Alabama Press, Tuscaloosa, AL, pp. 33–46.

Crowford, K. (1996) *East Central European Politics Today*, Manchester University Press, New York.

Czajkowski, M., Friszke, A., Krajewski, S., and Wilkanowicz, S. (2000). Polowanie na idée: Dzielic cudzy bol. *Znak*, 541, 67–82.

Drzewiecka, J.A. (2002) Reinventing and contesting identities through constitutive discourses: Between diaspora and its others. *Communication Quarterly*, 50, 1–23.

Du Bois, W.E.B. (1903/1997) *The Souls of Black Folk*, Bedford Books, Boston.

Engel, D. (2003) Lwów, 1918: The transmutation of a symbol and its legacy in the holocaust, in *Contested Memories: Poles and Jews during the Holocaust and its Aftermath*, (ed. J.D. Zimmerman), Rutgers University Press, New Brunswick, NJ, (pp. 32–46).

Fisher, M.M. (1993) Working through the Other: the Jewish, Spanish, Turkish, Iranian, Ukrainian, Lithuanian, and German unconscious of Polish culture; or one hand clapping: Dialogue, silences, and the mourning of Polish romanticism, in *World War II*, (ed. G.E. Marcus), University of Chicago Press, Chicago, pp. 187–234.

González, A., and Peterson, T.R. (1993) Enlarging conceptual boundaries: A critique of research in intercultural communication, in *Transforming Visions: Feminist Critiques in Communication Studies*, Hampton Press, New York, pp. 249–278.

Gordon, A. (2001) *Making Publics Past. The Contested Terrain of Montréal's Public Memories, 1891–1930*, McGill-Queen's University Press, Montréal and Kingston.

Gramsci, A. (1971) *Selections from the Prison Notebooks of Antonio Gramsci*, (eds and trans. Q. Hoare and G.N. Smith), Lawrence and Wishart, London.

Gronbeck, B. (1998) The rhetorics of the past: History, argument and collective memory, in *Doing Rhetorical History*, (ed. K. J. Turner), University of Alabama Press, Tuscaloosa, AL, pp. 47–60.

Gross, J.T. (2001a) *Neighbors: The Destruction of the Jewish Community in Jedwabne, Poland*, Princeton University Press, Princeton, NJ.

Gross, J.T. (2001b) *Upiorna dekada: Trzy esseje o stereotypach na temat Zydow, Polakow, Niemcow i komunistow*, TAiWPN Universitas Krakow, Poland.

Gutman, I. (2000) Uczmy sie byc razem. *Znak*, 541, 63–66.

Halualani, R.T. (2002) *In the Name of Hawaiians: Native Identities and Cultural Politics*, Minneapolis, MN, University of Minnesota Press.

Hasian, M.A. (1998) Intercultural histories and mass-mediated identities: The re-imagining of the Arab-Israeli conflict, in *Readings in Cultural Contexts*, (eds J. Martin, L. Flores, and T. Nakayama), Mayfield, Mountain View, CA, pp. 97–104.

Hasian, M.A. (2002) *Colonial Legacies in Postcolonial Contexts. A Critical Rhetorical Examination of Legal Histories*, New York, Peter Lang.

Hasian, M.A. (2006) *Rhetorical Vectors of Memory in National and International Holocaust Trials*. Michigan University Press, Ann Arbor.

Hasian, M.A., Jr., and Carlson, A.C. (2000) Revisionism and collective memory: The struggle for meaning in the *Amistad* affair. *Communication Monographs*, 67, 42–62.

Hoffman, E. (1993) *Exit in History: A Journey through New Eastern Europe*, New York, Viking Penguin.

Hoffman, E. (1997) *Shtetl: The Life and Death of a Small Town and the World of Polish Jews*, New York, Houghton Mifflin.

Hoffman, E. (2004) *After Such Knowledge: Memory, History, and the Legacy of the Holocaust*, Public Affairs, New York.

Howarth, D., and Stavrakakis, Y. (2000) Introducing Discourse theory and political analysis, in *Discourse Theory and Political Analysis* (eds D. Howarth, A.J. Norval, and Y. Stavrakakis), Manchester University Press, New York, pp. 1–23.

Huener, J. (2003) *Auschwitz, Poland, and Politics of Commemoration, 1945–1979*, Ohio University Press, Athens.

IPN (Instytut Pamieci Narodowej) (2003) Postanowienie o umorzeniu sledztwa *Bialystok*, July 30.

Irwin-Zarecka, I. (1990) *Neutralizing Memory: The Jew in Contemporary Poland*, Transaction, New Brunswick, NJ.

Irwin-Zarecka, I. (1994) *Frames of Remembrance: The Dynamics of Collective Memory*, Transaction, New Brunswick, NJ.

Katriel, T. (1994) Sites of memory: Discourses of the past in Israeli pioneering settlement museums. *Quarterly Journal of Speech*, 80, 1–20.

Krajewski, S. (2005) *Poland and the Jews: Reflections of a Polish Polish Jew*, Wydawnictwo Austeria, Krakow, Poland.

Kundera, M. (1980) *The Book of Laughter and Forgetting*, A.A. Knopf, New York.

Laclau, E., and Mouffe, C. (1985) *Hegemony and Socialist Strategy; Toward a Radical Democratic Politics*, Verso, New York.

Lee, W.S., Chung, J., Wang., J. *et al.* (1995) A sociohistorical approach to intercultural communication. *Howard Journal of Communications*, 6, 262–291.

Mendoza, S.L. (2001) Nuancing anti-essentialism: A critical genealogy of Philippine experiments in national identity formation, in *Between Law and Culture: Relocating Legal Studies*, (eds D.T. Goldberg, M. Musheno, and L.C. Bower), University of Minnesota Press, Minneapolis, pp. 224–245.

Mendoza, S.L. (2002) *Between the Homeland and the Diaspora: The Politics of Theorizing Filipino and Filipino American Identities*, Routledge, New York.

Nakayama, T. (1994) Dis/orienting identities: Asian Americans, history and intercultural communication, in *World War II: Essays in Culture, Ethnicity, and Communication*, (eds A. González, M. Houston, and V. Chen), Roxbury Publishing Company, Los Angeles, pp. 12–17.

Özyürek, E. (2007) *The Politics of Public Memory in Turkey*, Syracuse, NY, Syracuse University Press.

Perlez, J. (1993) At Warsaw ghetto, Poles and Jews bound by hope, available at: http://www.nytimes.com/1993/04/20/world/at-warsaw-ghetto-poles-and-jews-bound-by-hope.html (accessed June 7, 2010).

Popular Memory Group (1982) Popular memory: Theory, politics, method, in *Making Histories: Studies in History-Writing and Politics*, (eds R. Johnson, G. McLennan, B. Schwartz and D. Sutton), London: The Centre for Contemporary Cultural Studies, University of Birmingham, London, pp. 205–252.

Potter, B. (2000) *When Nationalism Began to Hate: Imagining Modern Politics in Nineteenth Century Poland*, Oxford University Press, New York.

Schudson, M. (1989) The present in the past versus the past in the present. *Communication*, 11, 105–113.

Steinlauf, M.C. (1997) *Bondage to the Dead: Poland and the Memory of the Holocaust*, Syracuse University Press, Syracuse, NY.

Steyn, M.E. (2004) Rehabilitating a whiteness disgraced: Afrikaner white talk in post-apartheid South Africa. *Communication Quarterly*, 52, 143–169.

Sturken, M. (1997) *Tangled Memories: The Vietnam War, the AIDS Epidemic, and the Politics of Remembering*, University of California Press, Berkeley.

Swida-Ziemba, H. (2000) *Rozbrajac wlasne mity* [Disarming our own myths]. *Znak*, 541, 41–48.

Triandafyllidou, A. (1998) National identity and the "other." *World War II*, 593–612.

van Dijk, T.A. (2002) Denying racism: Elite discourse and racism, in *Race Critical Theories*, (eds P. Essed and D. T. Goldberg), Blackwell, Malden, MA, pp. 307–324.

Walicki, A. (2000) The troubling legacy of roman Dmowski. *East European Politics and Societies*, 14, 12–46.

Weinryb, B.D. (1973). *The Jews of Poland: A Social and Economic History of the Jewish Community in Poland from 1100 to 1800*, Jewish Publication Society of America, Philadelphia.

Wodak, R. (2002) Turning the tables: Antisemitic discourse in post-war Austria, in *Race Critical Theories*, (eds P. Essed and D.T. Goldberg), Blackwell, Malden, MA, pp. 231–248.

Zelizer, B. (1995) Reading the past against the grain: The shape of memory studies. *Critical Studies in Mass Communication*, 12, 214–239.

Zelizer, B. (1998) *Remembering to Forget: Holocaust Memory through the Camera's Eye*, Chicago, University of Chicago Press.

Zimmerman, J.D. (2003) *Contested Memories: Poles and Jews during the Holocaust and its Aftermath*, Rutgers University Press, New Brunswick, NJ.

Zubrzycki, G. (2006) *The Crosses of Auschwitz; Nationalism and Religion in Post-Communist Poland*, Chicago, The University of Chicago Press.

18

Critical Intercultural Communication, Remembrances of George Washington Williams, and the Rediscovery of Léopold II's "Crimes Against Humanity"

Marouf Hasian

Every single stipulation of any importance in the Berlin Treaty … is daily broken … reports are coming [in] of terrible atrocities in these regions, as the natives are forced to bring in rubber, etc. … state authorities always flatly deny the existence of such outrages.

William M. Morrison, 1902[1]

As many critical intercultural scholars have observed, the study of both international and intercultural relations inevitable involves analyses of power, sedimented knowledges, and historical practices. In this particular essay, I want to provide a case study that illustrates how certain intercultural relations have influenced the ways that we remember and forget particular historical figures as we debate about how to recall traumatic colonial pasts. More specifically, I want to illustrate how historical and contemporary political and social needs often shade the way that we think about individual and collective social agencies in cultural disputes over the ontological existence of historical "holocausts."

If you ask international lawyers or students of the World War II Holocaust about the origins of the concept of "genocide" they will often mention the name of a Polish writer by the name of Raphael Lemkin who coined the term in the 1940s, but rarely will you hear any mention of the work of George Washington Williams, an African American critic of empire who for a time was viewed as one of the leading critics of what was once known as the "Congo Free State" (CFS) (1885–1908). It would be Williams who would raise the clarion call that "crimes against humanity"[2] were being committed by European interlopers. As I note below, observers today still debate about whether this CFS should be remembered as an independent state that helped with the missionary and mercantile development of large parts of Africa, or a nineteenth-century failed state that was accurately represented in Conrad's

The Handbook of Critical Intercultural Communication, edited by Thomas K. Nakayama and Rona Tamiko Halualani. © 2010 Blackwell Publishing Ltd.

Heart of Darkness. We now know from our studies of the World War II Holocaust that the communities that live within nation states do not-enjoy being tarred with the brush of having allowed or perpetrated genocide, but our postcolonial histories are also filled with recollections of many other administrative massacres that may have been forgotten. In this particular case, an American journalist by the name of Adam Hochschild has argued that many transatlantic communities have forgotten that many Congo Free State officials may have been involved in the perpetration of a Congolese "holocaust," that took the lives of between 8 to 10 million Africans.

From a critical intercultural perspective, no human can be dispassionate as they think about the power and politics of remembering these horrific types of events, and trying to search for a single apolitical history that will help us find the "truth" about this Congolese "holocaust" would be a fool's errand. The more that a critic or student studies any "history" that is filled with tangled ethnic relations, intercultural politics, and competitive postcolonial needs, the more that one realizes that choices have to be made about historiographic criteria, historical remembrances, and select histories. Given the fact that the Congo Free State was once viewed as the brainchild of a Belgian king by the name of Léopold II we should not be surprised to learn that for generations many European history books treated the CFS as the forerunner of the model "Belgian" colony, while other texts remind us of the tragedies that were once labeled the "red rubber" atrocities. One type of history monumentalizes the work of the CFS, while the counter-histories celebrate the importance of a social movement known as the Congo Reform Association, a group that was led by the English journalist E.D. Morel. From a critical cultural perspective, both of these histories have conveniently left out the work of George Washington Williams and other people of color who critiqued the CFS.[3]

If you look at any representative map of the world today you will not find the name of any "Congo Free State," and rarely will treatises about African colonization mention Williams' name. Entire library shelves are filled with research on Henry Morton Stanley – one of Léopold's employees who is remembered as a great African explorer – but only in recent years have researchers around the world demanded that we reconsider the role that Williams played in the critique of Congolese abuses.

Make no mistake, I am not trying to unduly magnify the social agency of George Williams or any "great" leader who might have been forgotten – I am arguing here that from a critical cultural vantage point this particular forgetting is tied to larger symbolic and material structures. Today we often assume that various generations will remember some of the genocides of the twentieth century or the importance of having selective international interventions, but there have been times when practical diplomatic considerations have influenced our reception of individual or idealistic matters of conscience. We now have several excellent analyses of the textual and visual rhetorics that have influenced the ways that various audiences have thought about modern genocidal campaigns,[4] but we are just beginning to engage in studies of historical critiques of what Mark Osiel has called the remembrance "storytelling" associated with "administrative massacre."[5]

In this essay I contextualize and historicize some of the earliest mediated debates about the Congo Free State that circulated in the early 1890s. Unlike more traditional analyses that try to present some single "truth" about a genocide or a monolithic "history," I try to complicate these matters by highlighting some of the colonial and postcolonial receptions of the work of George Washington Williams. He was a Cassandra-like figure who tried desperately to warn Americans about the dangers of the Belgian monarch's rapacious practices, and today he is sometimes credited with having presented some of the key strands of arguments that would be redeployed by the Congo Reform movements of the early twentieth century.[6] Sharon Sliwinski has recently credited Williams with having circulated some commentaries on crimes against humanity that appeared "some 50 years before Auschwitz."[7]

Sadly, part of my own critical contextualization of Williams' work must acknowledge that this was one African American who was lampooned, ignored, libeled, and marginalized. An analysis of extant texts reveals that his attacks on the CFS would be trivialized as the ruminations of a womanizer, a gadfly who knew nothing about American-Congolese relations, Léopold II, or European affairs. His "race" was considered to be variable that made him overly sympathetic in the ways that he characterized his African brothers and sisters. More than a hundred years had to pass before Williams' work would be remembered by journalists like Hochschild, who averred in *King Léopold's Ghost* that "Williams became the "first great dissenter" in the Congo reform campaigns.[8]

What accounts for this renascent interest in Williams' work and for this postcolonial remembrance of a Congolese "genocide"? Have our historiographic tools improved? Have we widened our lens to take into account oral histories of the times? Are postcolonial critics simply iconoclasts who search for any commentaries that help with the interrogation of dominant imperial practices? Have generational needs changed as younger audiences invite us to critique the colonial practices of their parents and grandparents' generations?

I hope to provide some tentative answers to some of these questions as I analyze some of Williams' work and the polysemic and polyvalent reception of his commentaries. Given page constraints, I want to concentrate on the alleged rhetorical power of Williams' "Open Letter" (1890), a document that he sent to Léopold II and several transatlantic presses. The first portion of the manuscript provides a brief contextualization of these Congolese controversies and explains just why so many fin de siècle audiences believed in Léopold's II beneficence. The second segment explains how George Washington Williams learned about Léopold's work, while the third part provides a textual analysis of the 1890 "Open Letter." The fourth portion supplements this analysis with a critique of some of the international reactions to this letter, while the conclusion explains how Williams' commentaries on "Crimes against Humanity" have been become a part of the intercultural histories of key modern day humanitarian movements.

The Beneficence of "New" Imperialisms and the Civilizing Mission of the Congo Free State

Hannah Arendt once argued that Léopold II of Belgium was "responsible for the blackest pages in the history of Africa"[9] but she had the benefit of witnessing how imperialism could be historically linked to the rise of totalitarian states. Interestingly enough, there was a time when this Belgian monarch was considered to be the next David Livingstone, an enlightened leader who would leave behind the "old" forms of imperial conquest and bring light to the "dark" continent. Henry Stanley and other Léopoldian employees were supposed to set up trading posts in the Congo Basin and obtain the lawful signatures of tribal "natives," and these efforts were believed to have helped establish what would be called "the *de facto* existence" of the "Congo State."[10] In other words, Léopold believed that the delegates who met in Berlin in 1884 were providing *de jure* legitimacy for *de facto* political relations. By posing as a neutral leader who would help missionaries and end the Arab slave trade, he appeared to be a progressive imperialist who would help end the messy "scramble" for African land. Given Belgium's relatively weak colonial status, Léopold was able to play the other European powers against each other as he became the private "protector" of what would be called the "Congo Free State." In theory, Léopold and his private companies would now be charged with developing regions that were 70 times the size of Belgium, and these colonizers were supposed to become the protectors of tens of millions of Congolese.

In his *Autobiography*, even W.E.B. Du Bois would acknowledge that he once believed that the establishment of this independent entity was "an act of civilization against the slave trade and liquor," and that there were times when he "did not question the interpretation which pictured this as the advance of civilization and the benevolent tutelage of barbarians."[11]

Yet within a matter of months, the Baptist Missionary Society was reporting that some "atrocities" were being committed by King Léopold's representatives in the Belgian Congo. Given the fact that many of these very same individuals wanted to stay in this region and spread the gospel, their complaints were often muted and contained, often addressed to private individuals. Imperial decorum and informal rules of empire provided the protocols that were needed when critics wanted to complain about particular colonial practices – they were supposed to start this type of process by seeking redress from Léopold's administrators who worked for the Congo Free State. Note, for example, how D.C. Rankin (a secretary of the Southern Presbyterian Board of Foreign Missions) once reacted when some members of the American press told their readers about potential abuses in faraway lands:

> From time to time rumors have reached this American Presbyterian mission at Luebo that atrocities were being perpetrated in the surrounding region by native solders in the employment of the Kongo Free State. As is well known, the affairs of this large territory are directly administered by a Governor General who resides at Boma, near the mouth of the Kongo. The State itself (as large as the United States east of the

Rocky Mountains) is divided into a dozen or more "Districts," in each of which a subordinate officer has charge of affairs. ... The members of this mission in the Kassai district have already sent their statement and protest to the authorities in Brussels, and doubtless proper steps will be taken by the Church which they represent in America to have the matter brought to the attention of the Belgian Government through our own Department of State. ... For twenty-five years he [King Léopold] has given evidence of a warm and philanthropic heart, and it can hardly be possible that such barbarous deeds as have been committed in the Kasai district will be approved by him.[12]

Later on a growing number of Anglo-American detractors would complain about these Congolese abuses, but before that period public criticism was often unorganized and sporadic. During the early years of the Congo Free State (1885–1900) various British and international news outlets occasionally commented on allegations that ivory collectors, porters, or other indigenous workers were suffering from coercive labor practices in the Congo, but there were few commentators who believed that this was systematic administrative abuse. All of this changed when the worldwide interest in the commercialization of rubber helped create massive markets for raw rubber goods. Now hundreds of thousands of Congolese "natives" were supposed to leave their villages and spend many hours harvesting this rubber, and this coercive work could be configured as "taxes" that were a part of the Congo Free State economy. Some of Léopold's troops looked for conscripts, crops in the field were left unattended, villages were depopulated, recalcitrant Congolese were shot, and some rubber workers lost their limbs as punishment for their transgressions.

American missionaries were some of the first Léopoldian critics who publicly commented on the magnitude of these abuses, and by the turn of the century there were a host of transatlantic newspapers that hinted at the possibility that the Belgian King's subalterns were violating their treaty obligations. William Morrison, one of the representatives of the American Presbyterian Congo Mission, worked in tandem with William Sheppard,[13] and the two of them started to collect first hand accounts of abuse that would be included in their missionary reports.[14] Yet, Morrison realized that he faced a situation where no one "save state officials," had been in "these districts."[15] He and some of his colleagues might have wanted to tell the world about the horrific nature of these alleged atrocities, but they would eventually have to deal with some of the harsh realities of a pragmatic world. Samuel Chester, a member of the Executive Committee for Foreign Missions, would send this typical note to the American Presbyterian Congo Mission in January of 1900:

The Executive Committee has received the report of the mission, together with several private letters concerning the difficulty as to securing concessions for our stations, and concerning the outrages being perpetrated by the Zappo Zap Tribe in your vicinity. We would first assure the Mission of our sympathy in its troubles, our approval and appreciation of the prompt action taken by the Mission in its investigation ... We can hardly think it necessary to remind the Mission as to the necessity of the utmost caution, in making representations regarding these matters to those in authority, or in publishing them to the world, to observe all proper deference to the "the powers that be," and to avoid anything that might given any color to a charge of doing or saying things inconsistent with its purely spiritual and non-political character.[16]

The Zappo Zap Tribe was supposed to be made up of cannibals who terrorized local communities, and yet many missionaries who wanted to avoid trouble hoped that Léopold's white soldiers could control these particular Africans. Cautious missionaries wanted to avoid making any public pronouncements that indicated that members of the Congo Free State were encouraging marauders like the Zappo Zap Tribe.

Undaunted, Morrison began sending some of the information that he had been collecting to the Aborigines Protection Society (APS) in London, and British reformers were able to get some of these commentaries into print.[17] In 1903 the Executive Committee of Foreign Missions finally had meetings where members admitted having "full knowledge of the whole sale violation" of pledges of freedom of trade and humane treatment of the natives,"[18] but by then Congolese reformation was in the air.

In 1890 George Washington Williams publicized his "Open Letter," and for a time Léopold II's administrators worried about a potential public relations crisis.

George Washington Williams and Early Colonial Idealism

John Hope Franklin averred in 1985 that "it took courage for Williams to write the *Open Letter* in 1890."[19] Williams would die prematurely from tuberculosis at the age of 41, but before that time he lived what looked like several lifetimes – at the age of fifteen he joined the Union forces fighting in the American Civil War,[20] and he rose to the rank of Lieutenant in the Mexican wars that were waged against Maximilian. He later graduated from the Newton Theological Seminary in 1874 and he temporarily served as a Boston minister. Williams then went back to school, got his law degree, and eventually served as the first African American senator in the Ohio legislature (1879).[21]

At one of his commencement exercises Williams delivered a class oration entitled "Early Christianity in Africa," and for a brief period it looked like President Chester Arthur was thinking about appointing him to be the US minister to Haiti.[22] In 1884 Williams would write a series of articles that disputed the Portuguese claims to the Congo, and he appeared before the Senate Committee on Foreign Relations so that he could comment on a resolution that would have the Americans recognize the International Association for the Congo (one of Léopold's first organizations) as a friendly government.[23] Like many other Americans, Williams apparently thought at one time that the American support of the Léopold's claims was a constructive course to take for the development of that part of Africa.[24]

During the fall of 1884 William went to Europe and met King Léopold II, and we have some evidence that they conversed about such topics as African labor and possible American involvement in the CFS. By the next year, he was hard at work writing a paper that effusively praised the efforts of those who had established the fledgling state, and he followed the lead of British authors who linked together imperial anti-slavery movements with some earlier European abolitionist campaigns. Williams left us some concrete illustrations of what he thought Americans should be doing if they seriously wished to help Léopold II and his economic battles with Arab slavers:

> They would not buy or use rice, sugar, coffee, cotton, or any other article they knew to be the product of slave labor. We can draw inspiration and instruction from the sublime action of the American colonies which passed the Non-Importation Act. We can refuse to send rum to the Arab with which to buy slaves and drug his hapless victims. We can talk against it, and pray God for light upon this dark subject which it is our duty to aid in settling.[25]

A textual analysis of this type of discourse indicates that during these early years Williams seemed to have viewed the activities of the CFS through idealistic prisms that assumed the paternal beneficence of a charitable monarch.

By 1889 Williams had attended a few anti-slavery meetings where he heard about some possible Congolese labor problems, and there is some historical evidence that he asked for another meeting with Léopold II. Williams wanted to visit the Congo, but Belgian administrators warned him that he needed to wait a few years because of the logistical difficulties of traveling in that region. In November of that year, *The New York Age* reported that:

> In the Boston *Herald* of last Sunday there was a copyrighted letter from Brussels by George W. Williams, purporting to give a talk had by him with the King of the Belgians about the Congo Free State. King Léopold is reported as saying among other things: "I have spent much in the Congo, and yet I not tired spending. What I do there is done as a Christian duty to the poor African: and I do not wish to have one franc back of all the money I have expended. God created Africa and the Africans as well as he did other countries and races of people; and we owe a duty to that country and people that should be discharged with cheerful willingness."[26]

John Franklin explains that when Léopold II learned that he could not dissuade Williams from going to the Congo region (after all, it was theoretically a "free trade" zone under international auspices) the Belgian monarch told Williams that he could not travel on the Congo Free State's steamer.[27]

At this point in his career there is little evidence that Williams knew anything about any specific Congolese atrocities, but perhaps it was his journalistic connections that worried Léopoldian officials. S.S. McClure, a leading magazine editor, had commissioned Williams to write a series of articles on Africa for Americans, so it may be inferred that some of the Belgians were worried about American sensationalism and muckraking.

In any event, Williams decided to cross the English Channel, and after purchasing his own supplies he sailed from Liverpool in early 1890. For seven months he traveled from the mouth of the river to Brazzaville and then back to Loango. We need to keep in mind that this was a 3000 mile roundtrip journey, and even this voyage would only take him to part of the vast Congo interior.[28]

Williams was no saint, and he occasionally wrote about how he threatened native villagers when they did not provide his caravan with food. He appeared to enjoy playing the part of the violent and yet fair explorer when he wrote about the possible execution of cowardly members of his own entourage. Yet he, like the Reverend William Sheppard, could clearly identify with the plight of the Congolese workers, and he refused to remain silent when he witnessed the perpetration of abusive practices. Several of our own libraries have copies of reports that he sent to the American president[29] and to Collis P. Huntington, the railway tycoon.[30] These texts outlined how millions of choice pieces of land were being wasted by the Compagnie du Congo Pour le Commerce et L'Industrie, and he characterized Henry Stanley (one of Léopold's employees) as an able correspondent who turned into a "romancer" when he took up the question of figures and trade.[31] These nationalistic tracts were written in ways that suggested that Americans needed to become more active interventionists, and Léopold II was caricatured as an absentee owner who had deceived the "friends of humanity and civilization."

These texts are interesting, but they are not the ones that captured the attention of many European and American audiences. William Parmenter once wrote that the "Williams' pamphlets had no effect" and that "later critics" did not "seem to be aware of their existence,"[32] but more recent studies have provided some evidence that the radical nature of his charges did worry at least some of Léopold's advisors. In this next section, I provide a textual analysis of Williams' most famous discursive fragment, his *Open Letter* (1890) – a text that did not "vanish."[33]

Williams' Open Letter to King Léopold and the Congolese "Crimes Against Humanity"

One of Williams' contemporaries characterized him as an eloquent "colored lawyer" whose "false pretensions" got him in hot water,[34] but more hagiographic remembrances portray him as a prescient critic of empire"[35] Williams' "Open Letter" to "His Serene Majesty, Léopold II" was sent from Stanley Falls to the Belgium monarch, and its public circulation outraged European readers who believed that it impugned the motives of a man of integrity. One of the first chroniclers of the Congo Reform movements, E.D. Morel, recalled how William's *Open Letter* was read out loud at some of the earliest gatherings of Congolese reformists.[36] Theoretically, this former soldier, lawyer, adventurer, and journalist wrote a scathing indictment of an entire regime, and his texts have left us some of the most graphic discursive materials that can be used in our own reconstructive documentations of the Congolese "atrocities."

In many ways the Williams' *Open Letter* is a story of betrayal, of a fall from grace, where a noble monarch's crown lost its imperial luster. The "Colonel" begins his letter with an open admission that for some six years he had worked alongside Léopold II. Williams crafts a narrative where he plays the role of a disenchanted journalist who must tell the public and the Belgian king about what he had seen with his own eyes, the "truth" that belongs to "*History, Humanity, Civilization,*" and the "*Supreme Being*" [emphasis in the original].[37]

Williams makes some preliminary remarks before he enumerates some specific indictments, and in this portion of his letter he questions the king's legal entitlements to the territories of the Congo. Here he publicly presents one of the first arguments that I can find in Anglo-American texts that specifically alleged that Léopold II's agents collected treaties that were signed by disempowered African leaders. Williams contends that the "Association International du Congo" was an organization that was profiting from illegal activities, and he attacks Henry Stanley and other Congolese agents who tricked the Congolese. A few years later, a supporter of the King sent a letter to an American Committee on Foreign Relations, averring that it was safe to "assert that no barbarous people have ever so readily adopted the fostering care of benevolent enterprise, as have the tribes of the Congo, and never was there a more honest and practical effort made to increase their knowledge and secure their welfare." Williams explained to the King that he saw this as a solemn pledge, and the rest of his letter is framed around the overarching question of whether his "brilliant programme" had actually accomplished these goals.[38]

Williams starts to comment on some of his own preconceptions, and he admits that at one time he had personally believed that this "rising Star of Hope" for the "Dark Continent" (alluding to the Congo Free State's flag] would help with the betterment of African conditions. In this idyllic world, King Léopold II would be the leader who would help with the building of established governments, tropical hospitals, and well-staffed churches. William argues that his hopes were dashed when he traveled to a region where he found buildings without hospitals, sheds that were not "fit to be occupied by a horse," sequestered land, burned towns, stolen property, and enslaved children. He asked his readers whether this was the type of "fostering care" that was mentioned in that 1884 letter to Congress.[39]

Williams crafts a narrative that assumes the contingent nature of American recognition of the Congo Free State, and he implies that this recognition could be revoked if the Belgian King was breaking his diplomatic promises. At this point in the letter Williams begins to question Léopold's motivations and his spending strategies, and readers are told that the Europeans in the Congo Free State did not have any "natives" working in the governmental capital at Boma. The Belgian King supposedly "never spent one franc for educational purposes," and many of these policies worked "against the natives in nearly every respect." Williams' indictment is filled with arguments about how foreign soldiers and laborers were imported from places such as Sierre Leone, Liberia, Zanzibar, and Lagos. Many of these employees were said to have died as they traveled to the CFS. Many of the young, white officers who supervised these men were "ignorant of native character," who lacked "wisdom, justice, fortitude, and patience." Some were configured as arsonists, murderers, and robbers.[40] Many of the courts in the region were viewed as "abortive, unjust, partial and delinquent."[41]

As if this was not damning enough, Williams begins to write about excessive cruelty to prisoners, the existence of chain gangs, and the discretionary use of the "chicote [sic]," an infamous whip that was made of dried pieces of hippo skin. Years later missionaries would circulate pictures of some of these whips, but Williams would provide one of the first textual commentaries on these practices. In this tale of human depravity, employees of his "Majesty's Government" were said to be importing women from the Portuguese coast for "immoral purposes," and the "State" was thought to be hiring these women out to the "highest bidder" – the "officers having the first choice and then the men."[42] These charges of immorality augmented the earlier claims that had been made about contractual violations of the 1880s Berlin Acts.

Thomas Pakenham has written about the importance of "commercial self-interest" in the Congolese reform debates,[43] and Williams certainly did not ignore many of these issues when he wrote his *Open Letter*. In the second half of that text, he complained that the Congo Free State was monopolizing trade and hurting the commerce of England, France, Portugal, and Holland. This was all taking place at time when the Congo Free State prohibited indigenous bartering with foreign traders. When obstinate Africans violated these Léopoldian rules, their villages were burned.

Perhaps one of the most potent arguments came in the section of the *Open Letter* that addressed the question of the slave trade. Williams averred that his "Majesty's Government" was "engaged in the slave trade, wholesale and retail." Léopoldians had prided themselves on having waged costly battles against heathen Arab slave-traders, but now Williams was scolding the Europeans for having officers who were overseeing slave-hunting raids. Here he named names as he talked about the State deployment of "bloodthirsty cannibalistic Bangals," the mutilation of bodies, and the steamship that fired on shoreline villages.

In recent years Adam Hochschild has credited Williams with having presented the "first comprehensive, systematic indictment of Léopold's colonial regime written by anyone,"[44] and in many sections of the *Open Letter* he implies that he was speaking for the silent African "other." The suturing together of economic, political, and ethnic arguments allows him to be a mouthpiece for silenced multitudes as he interrogates the actions of a deceptive monarch:

> against the deceit, fraud, robberies, arson, murder, slave-raiding, and general policy of cruelty of your Majesty's Government to the Natives, stands their record of unexampled patience, long-suffering and forgiving spirit, which put the boasted civilization and professed religion of your Majesty's Government to the blush.... All the crimes perpetrated in the Congo have been done in *your* name and *you* must answer at the bar of public opinion [emphasis in original].[45]

In sum, Williams may have hoped that the cataloguing of these specific charges would convince the other European powers that Léopold had broken his covenants, and he called for the creation of a new international commission that would look into the charges that he had brought in the name of "Humanity, Commerce, Constitutional Government and Christian Civilisation."[46] Williams concluding by asking that all of the philanthropists and statespersons throughout the world unite and hasten the end of this tyrannical reign.[47]

International Reactions to the *Open Letter*

Williams' *Open Letter* to Léopold II was considered by many imperialists to be a libelous piece of parchment, an inflammatory indictment that brought together a host of unsubstantiated assertions. Moreover, although some of his other letters focused on the need for American involvement in the Congo, this particular text was not calling for joint ventureship with Léopold, and it did not appear to be an unqualified defense of American expansionism. This attack on the Belgian monarch could also be viewed as anti-imperialist critique of all types of old and new colonial development plans.

The power of anti-Léopoldian diatribes could therefore be blunted, domesticated, and contained, and incredulous readers could take comfort in the fact that Williams could be vilified for a host of reasons – including his allegedly questionable character. In April of 1891 the *New York Times* ran an article that summarized many of the main charges that had been leveled against Léopold II, and it would be Henry M. Stanley who entered the lists and defended the Belgian crusader. Stanley told reporters that he knew that "colonel" Williams was a "colored man" who fought in the Civil War, and that at one time C. P. Huntington had paid for some of his African travels. The famous Welsh/American/English explorer explained that he once met Williams in London, and that Sir William McKinnon had shown him these charges before he left Liverpool. Stanley belittled the *Open Letter*, characterized it as a typical example of disreputable material. He elaborated by explaining that:

> These [blackmail] attempts … are liable to be made by anyone who has had a falling out with the promoters of any African explorations. I have discharged fifty men myself and laid myself liable to attacks of this sort. Other schemes are worked. Men come to me with the most piteous tales and want to be given big money to go on some expedition. They break my heart with their stories. If satisfactory arrangements cannot be made, some of them may bring me a story of abuses in my expedition and it is a question of how much it is worth to prevent publication. I presume Léopold has had his share of these and has paid all the money he cares to. He has seen these charges. He saw them before the public did, and I suppose refused to be bled. So the document is published.[48]

The very next day the same newspaper ran a long essay entitled "Developing the Congo," that invited American readers to read all of Stanley's writing so that they could see how "the problem of encouraging native labor" was "already solving itself" in the "rich and promising field" that had opened up for "the trade of nations."[49] Who were Anglo-American audiences going to believe – the white man who found David Livingstone, or the black man who defamed a Belgian monarch?

Given the symbolic power of these dominant colonial defenses, is it any wonder that at least on the American side of the Atlantic, Williams' *Open Letter* would pass into oblivion? For a short while he would be remembered as the "colored Massachusetts lawyer in England," an attendee of the Anti-Slavery Conference in Brussels who misrepresented himself as the official representative of the United States.[50]

By the time that Williams wrote his 1890 *Open Letter* he must have given up any lingering hope that Léopold II would become an active agent for constructive change, and he must have surmised that the radical nature of his critique might worry some potential allies.[51] One modern journalist notes that Williams was a "keen observer and experienced interviewer" who had that rare ability of being "uninfluenced by what others had already written."[52] This also meant that he risked censure and ostracism for advancing arguments that did not resonate with other witnesses (today we would perhaps call them bystanders) who must have seen similar abuses. For example, we have evidence that George Grenfell actually spoke to Williams when he stayed at one of the visitor's stations, and Grenfell wondered what Williams would say "if he saw, as we did, nine slaves chained neck to neck in the State Station at Upoto and waiting for a steamer to carry them down to Bangala." Yet as Pagan Kennedy notes, unlike Williams, Grenfell was "not willing to go public with what he knew."[53]

Williams was also one of the first writers who commented on what Africans had to say about Henry Stanley and the practices of other state officials, and this clearly violated some of the informal rules that were a part of the tenets of the "new" imperialism. Moreover, when Williams was writing about slavery, he was not just writing about the Christian war against the Muslim traders, but rather the conditions of porters and soldiers of the *Force Publique*, who "where, in effect, slaves."[54] The confrontational nature of these more radical claims meant that more moderate writers were worried about their public impact. For example, Guinness would write in a popular missionary circular (*Regions Beyond*) that "on the whole, the picture is not so black as a Colonial Williams would paint it."[55]

While many of Williams' Anglo-American critics refused to grapple with many of the specifics of the claims that surfaced in his *Open Letter*, this was not the typical reaction of many members of the Belgian press, who wanted to see official refutations. Victoria Brittain noted that while the Williams report was "published as a pamphlet by a trading company hostile to the King's trade monopoly in ivory, and taken up by the press" in New York and Paris, it would be in Belgium that it would be "subject to furious propaganda attacks by the King's associates."[56] David Lagergren explains that:

In spite of the reservations which were to be found among individual missionaries and which were occasionally expressed in the columns of mission periodicals, it must be said that the attitude of the Protestant missions towards the State was largely positive during the years 1885–1892. ... This was most noticeable when the extremely sharp criticism expressed by G. W. Williams ... which had aroused a lot of attention in the press and had led to a question being asked in the Belgian Parliament, either went unmentioned or was corrected in the mission publications.[57]

While the missionaries tried to argue that Williams was advancing exaggerated claims, the Belgians recognized that he was casting aspersions on the entire Léopoldian concessionary venture. This is part of the reason why Léopold's agents tried to counter each and every one of his major arguments.[58]

Léopold II's administrators tried to recontextualize some of Williams' activities,[59] and the pages of the *Journal de Bruxelles, La Réforme, La Nation,* and *Courrier* were filled with commentaries about the merits of his claims. Williams was lampooned for his soldiering under Juarez, his former illiteracy, and his transient labor habits. Other reporters tried to use their critiques of the *Open Letter* as a way of commenting on the rectitude of the administrators who worked for the Congo Free State, and eventually even members of the Belgian parliament had to answer some of these caustic attacks.

When the Belgian parliament met in June of 1891, several Belgians stood up and publicly condemned Williams for having written these libelous remarks. At least one official was convinced that all of this would have gone unnoticed if the Belgian press had simply ignored his *Open Letter.* Deputy Calier remarked that Williams had insulted the army, the lawyers, and the medical corps who worked in the Congo Free State. After Prime Minister Beernaert explained to the Belgian gallery that Léopold II had donated almost 2 million francs for his Congo ventures, Deputy Northomb closed the discussion by noting that Léopoldian trade had replaced cannons and swords.[60]

Sylvanus Cookey has astutely observed that George Williams' early death "saved the Congo government from what might have been an embarrassingly formidable opponent."[61] Decades later, one African critic told readers that they ought to remember the accomplishments of a person like Williams, who did denounce "the inhuman regime of Belgian King Léopold II," but that this recognition ought to be qualified with the acknowledgment that we "should not exaggerate their impact" on European policies at that time.[62] After all, the annexation of the Belgian Congo in 1908 did not end the colonial use of coercive labor or the expropriation of raw materials.

Interestingly enough, not everyone participated in the production of the collective amnesias that would be handed down as parts of some complex imperial legacies. We have been left some historical fragments that underscore the fact that at least some of his contemporaries appreciated his efforts. Williams would be buried in the Layton Cemetery in Blackpool.

Conclusion: Remembrances of the Williams Open Letter and Modern Humanitarian Movements

Trying to provide a fair assessment of Williams' influence is not an easy task for critical cultural critics, because we want to believe that we too understand the spirit that animated this dogmatic defiance of an authoritarian monarch. Ira Berlin, for example, would write that Williams

> denounced the Belgian King first in an "Open Letter" to Léopold himself and then in a series of reports to Huntington. Once again, Williams had bitten the hand that fed him. Léopold and his retainers publicly denounced Williams's charges and privately spread rumors that Williams was a blackmailer or worse. Huntington's patronage suddenly dried up. But Williams could not walk away from a fight; perhaps he did not know how. His willingness to follow his own lights sustained himself against denunciations by men more powerful than himself. While liberal missionaries and diplomats quietly watched Léopold's agents strip native peoples of their wealth and enslave them, Williams spoke out boldly. At last he had found a cause worthy of his talents.[63]

As far as I know Williams did not leave us much in the way of any photographic documentation of any alleged abuses, nor did he leave us records of any extrapolations of just how many victims were suffering in the Congo.

However, within a few years there would be no shortage of Léopoldian critics, armed with Kodaks and pens, and many of their narratives would be filled with arguments and allegations that looked a lot like some of the material that appeared in his *Open Letter*.[64] Note, for example, how William Morrison would write about the misgovernment of the Congo Free State in 1903:

> those of us who know, often from bitter experience, the adeptness of the native African at driving a trade and his [sic] cleverness in diplomacy can only laugh at Stanley for trying to be serious about his native treaties…[Léopold] is willing to descent to any depth in order to keep the world blinded as to the fact that he has been in these eighteen years metamorphosed from a philanthropist into a money-monger and task master … I have seen at least 50,000 people hiding for weeks in the forests without food or shelter, seeking refuges from the white Belgian officials and their native soldiers[65]

When Morrison wrote his essay, his text contained both discursive and iconic proof of the existence of Léopoldian abuses. The editors of *The Independent* who published Morrison's essay included a sketch that contained these words: "A victim of a rubber raid. The boy shown in the illustration is now cared for by a British missionary in the Upper Congo."[66]

George Washington Williams was dead, but the prefigurative templates and sedimented knowledges that he had tapped into were now being circulated by others. William Sheppard, for example, regaled audiences in Virginia with narratives that outlined how Léopold "assessed each tribe so much ivory or rubber which they had to deliver each year." Listeners did not have to guess about what would happen if they did not turn over the amount specified, because Sheppard elaborated by noting that "so many young children were taken and their hands cut off."[67] What Sheppard did not know was that some of his gatherings were attended by the Belgian ambassador and newspaper reformers, and his own story "received both national and international attention."[68]

By the fall of October of 1904, Booker T. Washington could tell readers about the collection of right hands by Congolese troops. Washington was convinced that regardless of whether the CFS was "directly or indirectly" responsible for this "hideous piece of savagery," it could not escape responsibility. He noted that:

> It is clear that the native is not the only victim of this system. What a comment on the whole situation is the single fact that only a few months ago an officer of the Government was condemned to fifteen years' imprisonment, after he had been convicted of killing one hundred and twenty-persons! If anything that I have said will serve to call the attention of civilized nations, and especially that of our own country, to the conditions existing in the Congo Free State, and will further serve to bring about such action as will in any way modify or improve the present state of affairs, I shall feel that I have not written in vain. Certainly the whole subject demands careful investigation and swift action.[69]

Williams' commentaries on Léopold and the "crimes against humanity" could be viewed as precursors for many of these anti-Léopoldian diatribes. We can trace some of the evolutionary effectivity of some of this rhetoric by looking at the concrete policies of decision-makers like the British Foreign Office, but even the optimistic E.D. Morel had to admit in 1909 that that department "made grave mistakes in its handling of the Congo problem," because "British diplomacy was not in earnest and would do nothing but talk."[70]

The passage of a hundred years has changed valences and epistemes, and now one modern critic contends that Williams' coinage of the phrase "Crimes Against Humanity," was the "first link in the chain that has ensnared Pinochet."[71] Victoria Brittain, who wrote about the Williams' *Open Letter* in 1999, thought that it seemed "surprising that Léopold had got away with his confident trick of the philanthropist for so long." She characterized the fragment as "the most scathing indictment" of Léopold's real "that was imaginable," and that "it threw the King into a fury." Yet she also remembered after reading Hochschild's *Léopold's Ghost* that:

> 1,000 Europeans and Americans, mostly missionaries and traders, had been in the King's territories by the time Williams saw it in 1890, but had chosen to take the conditions of exploitation for granted. A twentieth-century parallel would be the long complicity of the West with apartheid South Africa. In both cases, racism proved to be as strong a pillar of colonialism as was religion.[72]

Five years later, Emily Krasnor would write that she was sure that "Williams dreamed of a legal mechanism to practically address the situation" in the Congo, and that his efforts reminds "us today of the plight of the Jews in the 1930s and 40s."[73]

In spite of my clear epistemic skepticism, I emotively share some of these normative beliefs. Yet I wonder about the leap of faith that is needed to make these types of inferential claims, where we are forced to sift through the dustbins of history as we investigate the rhetorical power of even the most evocative of texts. Williams, after all, spent only a few months in the Congo and he did not witness the loss of millions of lives within a short span of time.

Does the muted response of many of his missionary contemporaries mean that these "abuses" did not reach the point of being fairly called a "holocaust"?[74] I have ambivalent feelings about that claim, and I think we need to keep in mind that many of the opinions that are circulating as demographic facts are based on plausible (but contestable) evidentiary claims. Yet some of Williams' partial representations may have helped revive interest in the investigation of complex colonial pasts.

Notes

1   William M. Morrison to the Aborigines Protection Society, October 7, 1902 (Morrison, 1996). For more on other American missionary efforts, see Williams (1982).
2   Hochschild argues that Williams used the phrase "crimes against humanity" to describe some of the Léopoldian activities, and that this phrase appeared in a letter that Williams wrote to the American secretary of state Hochschild (1998, pp. 111–112). This interpretation has in turn been used by scholars who now credit Williams with having coined that phrase. See, for example, Orentlicher (1998); Schabas (2005).
3   To give writers a sense of George Washington William's historical invisibility, see the work of Stanley Shaloff, considered one of the leading experts on the Presbyterian Church in America and Congolese reform. Shaloff spends an incredible amount of space writing about the work of William Morrison and William Sheppard, but he barely comments on Williams' contributions. Shaloff simply states that Williams visited the Congo region in February of 1890 and that he decided that it was not a suitable place for African-American settlement. Shaloff notes that Williams was "discouraged" by "what he observed of the administrative practices of the government" Shaloff (1970, p. 24, n.7). For a little more on Williams' work, see McStallworth (1954). For missionary work in general, see Johnston (2005).
4   Zelizer (1989) has provided us with one of the best examples of the heuristic value of this type of analysis of genocidal rhetorics. Note here the work of Mueller (2004) and Palczewski (2005).
5   Osiel (1997).
6   For an example of a more recent summary of Williams' work that appeared in America's mainstream press, see Berlin (1985).
7   Sliwinski (2006, p. 334).
8   Hochschild (1998, p. 102).
9   Arendt (1968, p. 64).
10   Reeves (1909, p. 100)
11   W.E.B. Du Bois, quoted in Shepperson (1985, p. 47).
12   Rankin (1900, pp. 304–306).
13   William Sheppard was generally regarded as one of the most influential missionaries working in the Congo during this period. See Phipps (1991); Tidewell (2000,

pp. 12–13); Kennedy (2002). In 1897, Sheppard would find evidence that some of Léopold's employees were involved in the slave trade, and in a report he argued that Congo Free State agents were committing atrocities on behalf of the private companies who were working in the region. Sheppard's report was then put in the hands of William Morrison, who in turn sent copies to international Congo reform organizations. See Slade (1959, p. 254) and Johnson (1979, p. 39). For textual examples of how Morrison publicized some of these materials, see Morrison (1902, pp. 1604–1608).

14   There were exceptional cases where a few white commentators where talking or writing about these atrocities before 1899. As Benedetto (1996) observes:

> Stories of Congo atrocities were periodically reported in the foreign press, were heard in the public criticisms of E.D. Morel, Charles Dilke, and Richard Fox Bourne of London, and were documented by a small number of eyewitnesses. These were the written account of British army doctor Sidney Hinde (atrocities by Free State soldiers), and the accounts of Swedish missionary E.V. Sjöblom, the American missionary J.B. Murphy, British explorer Edward Glave, and German Trader Leo Frobenius. (p. 8)

15   Benedetto (1996, p. 139). For some interesting examples of the types of arguments that were used by promoters of African American emigration projects, see *The New York Tribune* (1879).

16   Chester (1934), quoted in Benedetto (1996, p. 127). For more detailed discussions of Presbyterian mission policies in general, see Thompson Brown (1987, pp. 158–159).

17   See *The London Times* (1900, p. 6).

18   Chester (1934, p. 168).

19   Franklin (1985, p. 220).

20   Franklin (1977, pp. 65–66).

21   For a brief overview of the life of this forgotten "pioneer" (a term that was used to self identify many of the American missionaries), see Anon (1997–1998, p. 93).

22   This apparent political ploy failed. Grover Cleveland would not recognize Washington's Haiti assignment.

23   Franklin, (1977, p. 68).

24   Maier-Katkin and Maier-Katkin (2004) once noted that even though George Washington Williams would become one of the "leading contemporary critics" of Léopold's regime in the Congo, he still believed in the importance of bestowing "the blessings of civilization" on the Congo, and was considering bringing a number of educated blacks from the American South to that region, (p. 593).

25   George Washington Williams, quoted in Franklin (1977, p. 69).

26   *The New York Age* (1889, p. 2).

27   Franklin (1977, p. 69).

28   William took this arduous journey after already having met the vice president of the Boers' Transvaal Republic, the Sultan of Zanzibar, and the Khedive of Egypt. Hochschild (1998, p. 107).

29   Williams (1890a).

30   Williams (1890b).

31   Franklin (1977, p. 73).

32   Parmenter (1952, p. 149).

33   Franklin (1979, pp. 160–163).

34 See, for example, *The New York Times* (1891a). The anonymous contributor of this piece also claimed that Williams was ignoring the "resident colored people entirely" as he "sought admission into white society." Williams allegedly was "desirous of marrying a white woman with money" (p. 5).

35 One could of course argue that Williams was using several different terms that could be clustered together in ways that got at the spirit that is invoked when rhetors talk about "crimes against humanity." For example, in the (in)famous *Open Letter* that was sent to Léopold II, Williams mentions some of Léopold's transgressions that violated the norms of "humanity," while in another report he commented on breaches of the American "elevated sentiments of humanity." See the appendices in Franklin (1985, pp. 243–254, [Open letter to Léopold II], pp. 264–279 [Report to US President]) A copy of the original 16-page open letter to the Belgian King can be found in the archives at Brown University in Rhode Island. More accessible copies have also been reprinted in Conrad (1988, pp. 103–113).

36 See Morel (1902, p. 320; 1905, p. 104; 1919).

37 Franklin (1985, p. 244).

38 Franklin (1985, p. 245).

39 Franklin (1985, pp. 243, 246).

40 Franklin (1985, pp. 246–247).

41 Franklin (1985, pp. 248–249).

42 Franklin (1985, pp. 249–250).

43 Pakenham (1991, p. 592).

44 Hochschild (1998, p. 109). I share Hochschild's assessment. I have yet to find an earlier, more comprehensive fragment that lays out so many indictments in such a clear fashion at this early date. Some of my issues, of course, have to do with evidentiary considerations and the supporting proof for so many of his claims.

45 Hill and Kilson (1969, pp. 106–107).

46 Thirty years later many Europeans were still debating the merits of having other Conferences that would revise the Berlin Act. See, for example, Berriedale (1919, pp. 249–261).

47 Franklin, (1985, pp. 253–254).

48 *The New York Times*, (1981b, p. 1).

49 *The New York Times*, (1981c, p. 5).

50 *The New York Times*, (1981d, p. 1).

51 Hochschild (1998, p. 129).

52 Hochschild (1998, p. 108).

53 Kennedy (2002, p. 46).

54 Hochschild (1998, p. 129).

55 Guinness, H.G. (1891) quoted in Langergren (1970, p. 106).

56 Brittain (1999, p. 140).

57 Langergren, (1970, p. 106).

58 For a Belgian commentary on these responses, see Bontinck (1966, pp. 441–449).

59 Cookey (1968, p. 36).

60 Franklin, (1985, pp. 214–215).

61 Cookey (1968, p. 36).

62 Sithole (1986, p. 328).

63 Berlin, (1985, BR-12).

64 Slade (1959, p. 239).

65 Morrison (1902, pp. 1605, 1607). Morrison did not provide readers with any guidance regarding the methods or the evidence that he was using when he made these demographic assertions.. He estimated in 1903 that within the Congo domains, there lived "a native population variously estimated at from fifteen to forty millions" (p. 1604). Williams, in one of his reports that was sent to one of the American presidents, indicated that he believed that there were "not more than 15 000 000 people in the entire country." Franklin, (1985, p. 273). This last figure needs to be put in context, because Williams was arguing that H.M. Stanley or the State of the Congo were using inflated figures that gave population figures of between 49 000 000 and 50 000 000. He goes on to note that many towns had been moved or destroyed by war or smallpox epidemics.

66 Morrison (1902, p. 1604).

67 McKnight Wilson (1971, p. 144); Benedetto (1996, p. 13).

68 Benedetto (1996, p. 13).

69 Washington (1904, p. 377).

70 Morel (1909, p. 4)

71 *Toronto Star* (1999, para. 6). This unidentified author would go on to say that Williams' "redolent" phrase was not used again until the Nuremberg trials, and that today it has become a part of our everyday vocabulary. When the producers of a film entitled "Congo: White King, Red Rubber, Black Death," did not provide very much commentary on the role that African Americans like Williams or Sheppard played in the Congo Reform movement, they were criticized by some critics for leaving out important parts of what I would call the new reformist rescue or master narratives. See Brath (2004).

72 Brittain (1999, p. 139).

73 Krasnor (2004, p. 179).

74 We do know that Williams had a diary that has been lost, and that he probably used these materials as he wrote some of his letters and reports.

References

Anon (1997–1998) The forgotten pioneer of African-American history. *The Journal of Blacks in Higher Education*, 18 (Winter), 93.

Arendt, H. (1968) *Imperialism: Part Two of Origins of Totalitarianism*, Harcourt, Brace, and World, New York.

Benedetto, R. (1996) *Presbyterian Reformers in Central Africa*, (trans. Winifred K. Vass), E.J. Brill, New York.

Berlin, I. (1985) Soldier, scholar, statesman, trickster. *New York Times*, November 17.

Berriedale K.A. (1919) The revision of the Berlin Act. *Journal of the Royal African Society*, 17, 249–261.

Bontinck, F. (1966) *Aux Origines de l'État Indépendant du Congo: Documents tirès d'archives américaines*, Nauwelaerte, Louvain.

Brath, E. (2004) Review: Congo: White King, Red Rubber, Black Death, *WBAI*, December 8, http://wbai.org/index.php?option=com_content&task=view&id=4406&Itemid=2 (accessed June 7, 2010).

Brittain, V. (1999) Colonialism and the predatory state in the Congo. *New Left Review*, 236, 133.

Chester, S.H. (1934) *Memories of Four-Score Years: An Autobiography*, Presbyterian Committee of Publication, Richmond, VA.

Conrad, J. (1988) *Heart of Darkness*, 3rd edn, (ed. Robert Kimbrough), W.W. Norton and Company, New York.

Cookey, S.J. (1968) *Britain and the Congo Question, 1885–1913*, Humanities Press, New York.

Franklin, J.H. (1977) George Washington Williams and Africa, in *Africa and Afro-American Experience: Eight Essays*, (ed. Lorraine A. Williams), Howard University Press, Washington, DC, pp. 65–66.

Franklin, J.H. (1979) Afro-American biography: The case of George Washington Williams. *Proceedings of the American Philosophical Society*, 123, 160–163.

Franklin, J.H. (1985) *George Washington Williams: A Biography*, University of Chicago Press, Chicago.

Hill, A.C., and Kilson, M (eds) (1969) *Apropos of Africa*, Frank Cass, London.

Hochschild, A. (1998) *King Léopold's Ghost: A Story of Greed, Terror, and Heroism in Colonial Africa*, Houghton Mifflin, New York.

Johnson, W.R. (1979) The Afro-American presence in Central and Southern Africa, 1880–1905. *Journal of Southern African Affairs*, 4, 39.

Johnston, A. (2005) *Missionary Writings and Empire, 1800–1860*, Cambridge University Press, New York.

Kennedy, P. (2002) *Black Livingstone, A True Tale of Adventure in the Nineteenth-Century Congo*, Viking, New York.

Krasnor, E. (2004) American disengagement with the International Criminal Court: Undermining international justice and U.S. Foreign Policy goals. *OJPCR: The Online Journal of Peace and Conflict Resolution*, 6, www.trinsitute.org/ojpcr/6_1krasnor.pdf (last accessed May 12, 2010).

Langergren, D. (1970) *Mission and State in the Congo: A Study of the Relations Between Protest Missions and the Congo Independent State Authorities with Special Reference to the Equator District, 1885–1903*, (trans. O.N. Lee), Gleerup, Lund.

Maier-Katkin, B., and Maier-Katkin, D. (2004) At the heart of darkness: Crimes against humanity and the banality of evil. *Human Rights Quarterly*, 26 (3), 584–604.

McKnight Wilson, H. (1971) *The Lexington Presbytery Heritage*, McClure Press, Verona, VA.

McStallworth, P. (1954) The United States and the Congo question, 1884–1914. Dissertation, Ohio State University.

Morel, E.D. (1902) *Affairs of West Africa*, Heinemann, London.

Morel, E.D. (1905) *King Léopold's Rule in Africa*, Funk and Wagnalls Company, New York.

Morel, E.D. (1909) Congo reform, *The [London] Times*, October 5, p. 4.

Morel, E.D. (1919) *Red Rubber*, 4th edn, National Labour Press, Manchester.

Morrison, W.M. (1902) The misgovernment of the Congo Free State. *The Independent*, 55, 1604–1608.

Morrison, W.M. (1996) to the Aborigines Protection Society, October 7, 1902, reprinted in *Presbyterian Reformers in Central Africa* (R. Benedetto, trans. W.K. Vass), E.J. Brill, New York, pp. 138–139.

Mueller, A.G. (2004) Affirming denial through preemptive apologia: The case of the Armenian genocide resolution. *Western Journal of Communication*, 68, 24–44.

Orentlicher, D.F. (1998) *The Law of Universal Conscience: Genocide and Crimes Against Humanity*, Unites States Holocaust Museum Committee On Conscience, Washington, DC, http://www.ushmm.org/genocide/analysis/details/1998-12-09-01/orentlicher. pdf (accessed June 7, 2010).

Osiel, M. (1997) *Mass Atrocity, Collective Memory, and the Law*, Transaction Publishers, New Brunswick.

Pakenham, T. (1991) *The Scramble for Africa, 1876–1912*, Random House, New York.

Palczewski, C.H. (2005) When times collide: Ward Churchill's use of epideictic moment to ground forensic argument. *Argumentation and Advocacy*, 41, 123–138.

Parmenter, W.K. (1952) The Congo and its critics, 1880–1913. Dissertation, Harvard University, Boston, MA.

Phipps, W.E. (1991) *The Sheppards and Lapsley: Pioneer Presbyterians in the Congo*, Presbyterian Church, USA, Louisville.

Rankin, D.C. (1900) Atrocities in the Kongo Free State. *The Independent*, 52 (February), 304–306.

Reeves, J.S. (1909) The origin of the Congo Free State, considered from the standpoint of international law. *The American Journal of International Law*, 3 (1), 99–118.

Schabas, W.A. (2005) The "odious scourge": Evolving interpretations of the crime of genocide, http://www.armeniaforeignministry.com/conference/w_schabas.pdf (accessed June 7, 2010).

Shaloff, S. (1970) *Reform in Léopold's Congo*, John Knox Press, Richmond.

Shepperson, G. (1985) The Centennial of the West African Conference of Berlin, 1884–1885. *Phylon*, 46 (1), 37–48.

Sithole, M. (1986) Black Americans and United States Policy toward Africa, *African Affairs*, 85 (340), 325–350.

Slade, R. (1959) *English Speaking Missions in the Congo Independent State, 1878–1908*, Brussels Académie Royale des Sciences Colonials, Brussels.

Sliwinski, S. (2006) The childhood of human rights: The Kodak and the Congo. *Journal of Visual Culture*, 5 (3), 333–363.

The London Times (1900) The Congo Free State, February 23, p. 6.

The New York Age (1889) In the *Boston Herald*, November 23, p. 2.

The New York Times (1891a) Williams in Middletown: He prospered for a time, but his true character was learned, April 15, p. 5.

The New York Times, (1981b) Col. Williams's charges, April 14, p. 1.

The New York Times, (1981c) Developing the Congo, April 15, p. 5

The New York Times, (1981d) No friend to bury him, August 5, p. 1

The New York Tribune (1879) The colonization of Africa, December 15, p. 5.

Thompson Brown, G. (1987) Overseas mission program and policies of the Presbyterian Church in the U.S., 1861–1983. *American Presbyterians: Journal of Presbyterian History*, 65 (Summer), 158–159.

Tidewell, M. (2000) The missionary who fought a king. *American Legacy*, 5, 12–13.

Toronto Star (1999) African holocaust remembered. October 10, 1999, paragraph 6. http://ww/proquest.umi.com.

Washington, B.T. (1904) Cruelty in the Congo Country, *Outlook*, 78, 377.

Williams, G.W. (1890a) *A Report upon the Congo-State and Country to the President of the Republic of the United States of America*, Congo State.

Williams, G.W. (1890b) *A Report on the Proposed Congo Railway*, Congo State.

Williams, W.L. (1982) *Black Americans and the Evangelization of Africa, 1877–1900*, University of Wisconsin Press, Madison.

Zelizer, B. (1998) *Remembering to Forget: Holocaust Memory through the Camera's Eye*, University of Chicago Press, Chicago.

Part III

Critical Topics in Intercultural Communication Studies

Part III Introduction

Informed by and across multiple traditions, critical intercultural communication studies – as a perspective, approach, method, and or practice – enables the full engagement of a variety of topics of cultural (intra, inter, cross), communication, and sociopolitical discourses and phenomena. These topics can traverse a significant range of subjects that require a deeper re-reading from a critical perspective given its foci of attention such as the historical specificities and contexts involved, the shifting power dynamics, the larger global forces and economic/market conditions, interdependent and connected structures of power, historicized power forces, and the surrounding prevailing ideologies, hegemonies, struggles, and cultural politics. In the next major section of this handbook, several topics of culture are analyzed in terms of these foci and represent the scope and breadth of analysis and inquiry within critical intercultural communication scholarship.

Such vibrant and multilayered topics abound here. First, as a wonderful contribution to intercultural communication work, Laura Lengel and Scott Martin, trace for us the situated location of gender and the muddled power dilemmas and oppositions gender highlights in relation to culture. Next, a diverse set of scholars who bring varied expertise from critical communication pedagogy, critical race theory, performance theory, and media and feminist studies (Ronald L. Jackson II and Jamie Moshin, Bryant Keith Alexander; Jim Perkinson; Bernadette Marie Calafell and Shane Moreman; Lisa Flores, Karen Ashcraft, and Tracy Marafiote, and John T. Warren) fully interrogate the politics and communication practices of racialization (and the intersections this brings and or denies) that take hold of specific social roles we inhabit, discourses we consume, practices we witness and or participate in, performances within cultures that we may know, the hegemonies we navigate, and contexts of which we are a part. As a much needed contribution to a completed neglected area of culture, Deanna L. Fassett insightfully demonstrates how we are fully (materially, physically, and symbolically) embodied and invoked into a world based on "ability" and "ablebodiedness" and the ways in which disabilities become marked, muted, and further disempowered. Moreover, while gender, race, and ability are tackled by the previous contributors, Richard Morris uncovers key communicative strategies of exclusion, excision, and immorality for Othering individuals and groups in public and religious spheres.

With a focus on power, historical context, and cultural migration, several scholars (Victoria Chen, Etsuko Kinefuchi, Radhika Gajjala) concentrate on "diasporas" (as opposed to the traditional notion of immigrant groups) engage in rich analyses of the ever changing diasporic politics around the notions of belonging, home, space, and community in three separate contexts. From diasporic contexts to postcolonial ones, Melissa Steyn examines a discourse articulated by young White South Africans as they attempt to remake and recuperate their identity positions (and the public memory of those positions) in post apartheid South Africa. Taking critical scholarship to applied frameworks and contexts, Hsin-I Cheng and Sara DeTurk underscore the importance of a critical perspective in intercultural training and intergroup dialogue contexts, respectively. They both contend that the traditional staples of these contexts – a focus on intercultural competence and mutual understanding and structured and facilitated intergroup dialogue – can help to reinforce and reproduce existing (and historically persistent) power relations and hierarchies and thus, in so doing, call for critically infused trainings and dialogic frameworks to problematize and interrupt such relations. Lastly, as a segue to a discussion on the future of critical intercultural communication studies, Brenda Allen maps out the productive possibilities for collaboration, dialogue, and necessary work and organizing between the burgeoning areas of critical organizational communication and critical intercultural communication (as well as other areas such as critical communication pedagogy). This mapping points to a larger network of critical scholars who strive to engage in work that challenges what we have come to know, believe, and that with which we still do not take notice. Taken together, these essays represent the exciting work that is taking place in the field and in this designated area and the possibilities in insight, inquiry, analysis, and activism of what can be done and elucidated through critical intercultural communication scholarship.

19

Situating Gender in Critical Intercultural Communication Studies

Lara Lengel and Scott C. Martin

Intercultural communication, and the key concepts and contexts that are situated in the study of communication and culture, have undergone what Lily Mendoza (2005) suggests is an "irreversible process of destabilization, a kind of unhinging, as it were, from their presumed normative grounding in objective, unquestioned ontological fact" (p. 238). This "unhinging" has presented scholars important and urgent challenges in the critical turn in intercultural communication. One of the most vital challenges is to "understand the role of power and contextual constraints on communication in order ultimately to achieve a more equitable society" (Martin and Nakayama, 2000, p. 8). Situating and analyzing gender within the series of debates on power and culture in critical intercultural communication studies, we face several specific challenges. First, we cannot underestimate the many ways in which gender is understood. For our purposes in this essay, gender refers to socially constructed and culturally mediated ideas about the defining qualities of male and female, masculine and feminine. These ideas, which originate in and reflect the concerns of a variety of social formations – ethnic or "racial" groups, socio-economic classes, occupational organizations, religious associations – frequently coalesce into ideologies of gender that express in relatively coherent form norms for male and female behavior that are presented as natural and salutary rather than artificial and prescriptive.

When unpacking assumptions about gender it is impossible to examine gender without situating it as it intersects with other identity markers. We acknowledge that a careful investigation of identity markers such as "race" and nation requires a far more comprehensive interrogation beyond the scope of this particular essay. John T. Warren's work (2003) on whiteness and intercultural communication, for example, analyzes how gendered material bodies and gendered discourses or rhetorical strategies produce "race," through "the repetition of acts, verbal and

The Handbook of Critical Intercultural Communication, edited by Thomas K. Nakayama and Rona Tamiko Halualani. © 2010 Blackwell Publishing Ltd.

nonverbal, that continue to communicate differences" (p. 29). Fellow contributors also pursue questions of "race", nation, and communication elsewhere in this volume. In acknowledging our limitations, we affirm that the theoretical rigor and contextual range of critical intercultural communication studies makes engaging in this area of study a formidable task – and we cannot embark upon this endeavor alone. We present our inquiry here as members of "the cultural community that [we] seek to explore and examine ... as a way of reading between the lines of [our] own lived experience and the experience of cultural familiars – to come to a critical understanding of self and other and those places where we intersect and overlap (Alexander, 1999, pp. 309–310). This community of scholars includes, of course, those who have been at the forefront of critical intercultural communication studies. The community has welcomed voices from outside the communication discipline; the resulting new alliances, that have been formed, can interrogate the relationship of culture and power from a broader set of perspectives. Interdisciplinarity is also essential to address what Halualani and Nakayama in this volume's introduction, call the macrocontexts – historical, social, and political contexts as they implicate, reinforce, or disassemble power structures – the historical constructions of gender that inform and implicate the present. We, thus, draw from our own areas of experience (as scholars of transnational and intercultural communication and of nineteenth century cultural history respectively) and from the insights of other members of the cultural community who contribute to this volume, in order to fully engage our study of how the institutional, political, economic, and social forces of the past enlighten our understanding of contemporary (re)productions of gender.

Theorizing Gender

Throughout decades of foundational intercultural communication research, we see a multitude of studies of how women and men (usually from a specific nation) communicate, and male and female characteristics of intercultural communication. While some of this research has revealed important understandings of gendered communication, is tends to establish operational definitions of gender through inherently reductionist and essentializing theoretical and methodological strategies and practices. It has situated gender differences in a static bipolar opposition of "masculine" and "feminine." By contrast, scholars employing a critical perspective clearly articulate that gender is complex, multifarious, and changing. Critical intercultural communication scholars draw from an interdisciplinary body of scholarship (history, psychology, anthropology, cultural studies, as well as communication studies) that positions gender as an unfixed, fluid variable that (re) positions given varied circumstances, situations, and frameworks, and that considers what Judith Butler (1994) terms the "historical and anthropological positions that understand gender as a relation among socially constituted subjects in specifiable contexts" (p. 10).

Butler's contributions to gender theory highlight the difficulties and pitfalls with which any analysis of intercultural communication must grapple. Butler's work on gender and performativity approaches gender as a mere performance, a set of manipulated codes; in fact there is no gender identity (a phenomenon, a thing, as it were) at all. Rather, gender is what we *do*. Butler (1994) refers to what we do as "expressions of gender"; through these expressions or performances gender identity is "constituted by the very 'exceptions' that are said to be its results" (p. 25). Further, in *Gender Trouble* Butler (1990) asserts there can be no "authentic" female or male performance, only patterns of constructed identity with which we have become familiar because they have been repeated frequently enough to establish themselves as cultural norms.

Even as sophisticated an approach to gender as Butler's could not capture completely its complexity. Three years after *Gender Trouble* was published, Butler responded to some of the reactions and interpretations of the groundbreaking work. In an interview published in *Radical Philosophy* Butler (1994) revealed that she shifted her thinking about the gendered body, that she "overrode the category of sex too quickly":

> One of the interpretations that has been made of *Gender Trouble* is that there is no sex, there is only gender, and gender is performative. People then go on to think that if gender is performative it must be radically free. And it has seemed to many that the materiality of the body is vacated or ignored or negated here – disavowed, even (p. 32)

Butler (1994) subsequently wrote *Bodies that Matter* in order to bring debates about gender back "to the category of sex, and to the problem of materiality, and to ask how it is that sex itself might be construed as a norm" (1994, p. 33). One of the questions she wanted to work out, in her words, was "how a norm actually materialises a body, how we might understand the materiality of the body to be not only invested with a norm, but in some sense animated by a norm, or contoured by a norm" (1994, p. 33).

The issues raised by Butler point to another dimension of analytical and theoretical complexity for intercultural communication scholarship: the question of power. Clearly, both women and men may, and usually do, contribute to the promulgation of a relatively coherent ideology of gender within a given group or society. This does not imply, however, that both participate under conditions of equality, or that power relations that privilege men and disadvantage women do not shape the contours of gender ideologies. Moreover, though different, and even conflicting, ideologies of gender may coexist within a given society, it is often the case that the predilections and values of one group gain ascendancy, resulting in that group's approach to gender gaining what could be termed hegemonic status. Such hegemony is never absolute, and does not necessarily eliminate dissent or determine individual behavior. It does, however, exert a powerful influence on social relations and inter-group communication on a host of issues related to gender.

When gender is situated and problematized within a myriad of identity dimensions, additional challenges emerge. As we learned in the previous section of this volume, identity is a complex, fluid, and ever-changing sense of self. Clearly, gender is a central component of identity, that may be constituted as "more or less central to self-identity by each individual, or might be made significant by external social circumstances" (Gauntlett, 2002, p. 13). Gender cannot be analyzed alone, however, and must be situated with other aspects of identity, creating another challenge for critical intercultural communication studies. Gender is a complex phenomenon in and of itself, let alone when it intersects with sexuality, "race," nation, "class" and other identity markers that correlate and intersect to provide the essence of communicative practices in intercultural contexts. Until recently, intercultural communication scholarship largely ignored this complexity, relying on the reductive understanding of gender noted above. According to Nakayama and Martin (2007), the foundations of the field of intercultural communication "lack resources to challenge or grapple with these constructions" p. 128).[1] Perhaps it is the need to examine "collective representation or what can be more crassly terms as 'cultural profiling'" (Mendoza, 2005, p. 239) that has situated gender as a largely unproblematized, operationalized concept in intercultural communication, and why there have been so few insightful studies on gender outside the body of scholarship of critical intercultural communication studies. Recently, critical scholars have begun to employ a more complex understanding of gender and power in their work on intercultural communication. In particular, they have taken account of the historical and structural forces that shape the relations of gender, culture, and power, and influence intercultural communication contexts, encounters, and relationships.

Historicizing Gender and Intercultural Communication

Understanding gendered historical contexts and the gendered relationship of culture and power, we argue, is crucial for a critical consciousness of intercultural communication. The mere recognition that gender is not natural, but constructed, does not further the critical study of intercultural communication unless scholars can analyze the characteristics and impact of that construction on the exchange of information between divergent individuals and groups. We suggest that a primary means of understanding gender for this purpose is to examine it in specific historical contexts. Inevitably gender reflects prevailing relations of power that are also more fruitfully examined in historical and structural contexts. One example would be Westerners encountering veiled Muslim women. British and French colonial sojourners to Muslim regions, such as North Africa, would have had different reactions to gender divisions in the eighteenth, nineteenth and even the early-twentieth centuries, when even in the West there were established cultural and institutional structures that forbade women's and girls' immodesty in the public sphere. During that timeframe, the colonial self would most likely have approved of Muslim societies' emphasis on such female modesty. Even though the practice of *hijab*[2] has not changed much in the past century, Western political and cultural views of *hijab* have changed dramatically. In fact, the Western gaze has practically fetishized this concept of modesty in popular media and academic research alike.

Our appeal for recognizing the importance of historical forces draws upon the work of Pierre Bourdieu, who argues for the importance of historical contexts in the construction and interpretation of meaning. For our discussion of gender and communication, attention to historical contexts emphasizes that the negotiation and interplay of male and female attributes are not fixed or unchanging, but variable depending upon the specific time and place in which they occur. Bourdieu's point about the historical contexts surrounding sexual division, for instance, applies just as well to gender. "One has to ask," Bourdieu (2001) notes, "what are the historical mechanisms responsible for the relative dehistoricization and eternalization of the structure of the sexual division and the corresponding principles of division" (p. vii). To demonstrate, he continues, that

> what appears, in history, as being eternal is merely the product of a labour of eternalization performed by interconnected institutions ... is to reinsert into history, and therefore to restore to historical action, the relationship between the sexes that the naturalistic and essentialist vision removes from them (p. vii).

Through analyzing the past, critical intercultural communication scholars can attend to current institutions of power as an Otherizing force. Otherness, as Nakayama (1994) notes, "is neither simplistic, nor monolithic", rather it is "coalitional" and requires we bring cultural codes, norms, and contexts into question as we analyze intercultural interaction (p. 162). Power is always and in all ways inherent in culture and intercultural encounters, however, analyses of power have largely been absent in intercultural communication research prior to the critical turn. Accounting for the complexity of power and privilege is, Asante, Miike and Yin (2008) argue "one of the formidable challenges that interculturalists are facing today" (p. 4). The challenge involves the complexity of the concept of power. Here we return to Bourdieu who distinguishes several types of power – economic, political, and ideological/symbolic. Bourdieu's (2001) idea of symbolic power (which, he argues, is "*worldmaking* power" – the power to define one's lifeworld) is useful as a frame of analysis for critical intercultural communication. Symbolic power can be used a rhetorical tool for dominating others, and maintaining a status quo that serves the interest of those in power. Bourdieu and Passeron (1977) argue:

> Every power to exert symbolic violence, i.e., every power which manages to impose meanings and to impose them as legitimate by concealing the power relations which are the basis of its force, adds its own specifically symbolic force to those power relations (p. 4).

When viewed in historical cultural contexts, symbolic power (for a millennium at least) has socially constructed feminine gender roles. Those in power to shape their lifeworlds have drawn on a continuum of putatively "natural" female qualities ranging from morality, religiosity, and physical weakness at one end to lasciviousness, vanity, and insatiability at the other. Changing historical conditions may alter which part (or parts) of this continuum a society considers the most relevant and true account of female nature. During times of war, conflict, or revolution, for example, notions of female physical incapacity may be deemphasized in the interests of furthering a political entity's war through the recruitment of women as workers for the production of war material. This was certainly the case in the United States during World War II, when the bulging bicep of Rosie the Riveter became a familiar symbol of women's necessary and effective contributions to Allied victory. The exigencies of wartime have even allowed the exceptional women, from Joan of Arc to Molly Pitcher, to serve in various capacities on the battlefield without overt violation of gender norms.[3] That female gender roles have frequently returned to their antebellum pattern after the cessation of hostilities – Rosie, after all, was displaced from the factory to the home to make room for returning male veterans – does not minimize the extent to which historical developments can influence gender roles.

Historicity and Gender Hegemonies

Historicizing the imagined timelessness and naturalness of male and female attributes reveals the power relations that underpin ideologies of gender. Attention to historical forces and contexts also facilitates the analysis of how some ideologies of gender assume hegemonic proportions in a given society. Whether embodying, in the Gramscian sense, the interests of a socio-economic class or those of some other social formation, it is undeniable that gender hegemonies have, during various periods of history, coalesced from ideologies of gender and ramified beyond their points of origin. In so doing, they impacted intercultural communication in a wide range of geographic and temporal contexts. This point is well illustrated by the hegemony of middle-class morality in the Anglo-American world since the nineteenth century. In Britain, the emergence of Victorian sexual mores reflected the ability of an increasingly preeminent middle class to impose its beliefs about proper sexual behavior on the rest of society. Emphasizing female chastity until marriage and fidelity thereafter as hallmarks of "natural" feminine modesty, Victorian morality also tolerated male promiscuity and infidelity as reflections of innate vigor and appetite. In this schema, inherent female virtue and love of home served society by ensuring that English families would transmit effective moral values and private property to succeeding generations. Male appetite and energy, on the other hand, proved useful in economic and political struggles, as well as in expanding Britain's imperial reach across the globe. With these inestimable benefits to be gained, the occasional male lapse in sexual propriety – what we have come to call the sexual double standard – was a small price to pay. Though middle-class English women gained some benefits from this ideology of gender, and had some role in creating it, the disadvantaged position in which it placed them reflects the obvious imbalance in sexual power characteristic of Western society. The resulting gender norms, which contrasted female emotion to male rationality and woman's genius for nurturing family to man's capacity for economic and political competition, ramified beyond the middle class to influence a variety of activities ranging from reform movements to foreign policy, articulating both class and patriarchal power.

The hegemonic status of gender norms shaped social relations and intercultural communications in Britain and around the world. Attention to the poverty, class conflict, crime, and other social problems that accompanied nineteenth-century English industrialization was frequently informed by Victorian gender norms. The provision of poor relief and other services to the working class, often administered by middle-class men and women, for instance, made distinctions between the worthy poor and their dangerous, unworthy counterparts. This categorization rested, in part, on the gender norms promulgated by the Victorian middle class, rather than on an analysis of the impact of social and economic circumstances on disadvantaged groups. Thus personal failings, as measured against putatively natural gender roles, rather than structural conditions, defined worthiness. Energetic, industrious workers who fulfilled their inherent male responsibilities to wife, family and employer were worthy recipients of aid and charity; the drunken, dissolute, or lazy were not (Martin, 2008). Conversely, working class women who kept a tidy home, protected their children, obeyed their husbands, and remained sexually virtuous merited sympathy and support; those who violated these gender norms did not. If laboring men and women could bridge the divide of class culture and communicate worthiness by embodying (or at least convincingly performing) Victorian gender roles for their would-be middle-class benefactors, they stood a much better chance of receiving help. Similar points could be made for the United States, where middle class gender hegemony developed along lines related to its Victorian counterpart, and influenced reform and cross-class relations in similar ways.

Victorian mores also shaped intercultural communication in Britain's global empire. As Edward Said (1978), Gayatri Spivak (1988), and others have shown, gender ideology inflected Western, and particularly British, perceptions of the East, in effect constructing Others whose gender attributes seemed at odds with those that held sway in the West. Indolent, effeminate men and voracious, hypersexual women contrasted sharply with Victorian gender norms. The disparity could be explained by reference to racial and ethnic hierarchies: "natural" gender roles only found their true expression at the (Western) pinnacle of human evolution and development, and provided a model to which Others should aspire. As the British Empire expanded through Asia and the Middle East, imperial policymakers justified repression, conquest, and dominance with gendered metaphors of civilization and progress. Here, as with the English working class, gender ideology complicated intercultural communication. Colonial subjects who could, through deference or calculation, convey admiration for and allegiance to Victorian gender ideology stood a much better chance of finding favor with their imperial governors.

History, Gender Ideology, and Intercultural Communication: An Extended Example

Proximity in time and space to intercultural processes often makes them difficult to analyze and understand; our very positionality within the intercultural nexus biases perception. We provide an extended example here from a relatively familiar historical episode in the hopes that it will illustrate at a distance the interplay of the forces that shape power relations and intercultural communication, and thus provide an entrée to more contemporary issues. For this purpose, we use incidents from the history of contact between English settlers in North America and the indigenous people they encountered in what would later be called New England. Beginning in the early-seventeenth century, English religious dissenters established settlement colonies in the future colony of Massachusetts Bay and surrounding areas. Immediately upon arrival the English encountered the Mashpee Wampanoag, Narragansett, and Nipmuc Peoples, whose indulgence and aid the settlers at first required. To maintain peace, gain land, gather information about the terrain and its resources, and secure an adequate food supply, the settlers had to communicate with Native American Indians.[4] In the process of communicating, the indigenous Americans were situated as the Other, an "'Otherness'", notes Homi Bhabha (1994), which "is at once an object of desire and derision" (p. 96).

The communicative acts and intercultural interactions occurring in this historical moment posed many obstacles, not the least of which was the dramatic difference in language. Even when this difficulty could be diminished through the use of bilingual interpreters – frequently American Indians or English who had been involved in sporadic commerce and learned some of their trading partner's language – pitfalls remained. indigenous Americans and settlers viewed the world in different, sometimes diametrically opposed, ways and these differences expressed themselves in problematic intercultural communication. Notions of human relations to the land, for instance, became a point of contention. To the Mashpee Wampanoag, Narragansett, and Nipmuc Peoples, the English concept of ownership as sole and exclusive possession of an area or region proved difficult to translate or understand. They thought in terms of usufruct, or use value. "Selling" land to the English did not necessarily mean that they would abandon it, but rather, that they would allow the newcomers to partake of and share in the resources – game, fish, plants, wood, fruit – on land the Mashpee Wampanoag, Narragansett, and Nipmuc controlled (Cronon, 1983). The potential for conflict between these culturally divergent understandings of land ownership, essentially the contrast between usufruct rights and private property, would have been great, even without the additional complication of vastly different languages.

Over time, the English established themselves in Massachusetts, and became less dependent on aid and cooperation of the Mashpee Wampanoag, Narragansett, and Nipmuc Peoples. With greater security and confidence, English negotiators, representing individuals, towns, and the colonial government itself, sought to secure more land from indigenous groups. They also meant to ensure their sole possession of the land, and acceptance of English governmental authority. Experience and persistence in New England, the establishment of effective social and political entities to support a growing population, and the increasing importance of English military technology had changed the power relations between the two cultures. Not surprisingly, many indigenous peoples in New England resented the newcomers' aggressive expansion and presumptuous quest for control of the land, and resisted. As conflict over land and resources intensified, the English attempted not only to gain land, but to justify to themselves their right to wrest it from its original inhabitants, now conceptualized as the Other.

A potent source of intercultural misunderstanding, and of justification for land seizure, was the differing understanding of gender roles between English and indigenous Americans. The English believed that men should do the heavy physical labor of clearing the land, farming, and constructing shelter. Women, by contrast, should tend the fireside, prepare food, and raise children. The American Indian division of labor shocked and dismayed them. Though men pursued hunting and warfare with energy and exuberance, they spent much time in any given day lounging around their villages, eating, smoking, and discussing their martial exploits. Women planted crops, tended the fields, and brought in the harvest, in addition to other duties necessary to the maintenance of the village. This arrangement seemed barbaric and unnatural to the English, whose notions of female delicacy prohibited women laboring while men lazed about. In addition, indigenous men's seemingly excessive fascination with the hunt and chase struck the English as an obstacle to the permanent settlements and regimented agriculture they valued as the hallmark of civilization. The settlers constituted Mashpee Wampanoag, Narragansett, and Nipmuc gender roles as improper and unproductive, in an identity constructing process that replicated itself through centuries of colonization and produced legacies of colonization that remain in contemporary disempowered peoples, American Indians included.[5] The settlers considered the Mashpee Wampanoag, Narragansett, and Nipmuc sexual division of labor a violation of divinely ordained male and female roles that constituted an intolerable tyrannization of women by men. Completely lost on the English was the political role that American Indian women played in many tribal groups, or the authority accorded by matrilineal social organization. Viewing gender roles from across an intercultural divide, and with increasing confidence in their ability to impose their will on the Other, English settlers judged what they saw and found it wanting.

At the same time, English mores made little sense to the Mashpee Wampanoag, Narragansett, and Nipmuc Peoples. In their view, men were intended to be warriors and hunters; agriculture was women's work. Any attempts to bridge this gap, notably English efforts to convince indigenous Americans of the error of their ways, or to impose English gender roles on the indigenous people who came under their authority and control, met with resistance and failure. Soon, the land-hungry English concluded that an Other so wedded to unnatural relations between men and women could not use the land efficiently, or as they knew God intended. Many Mashpee Wampanoag, Narragansett, and Nipmuc Peoples, after all, did not erect permanent settlements or plant orderly fields, bordered by fences. Some abandoned their habitations altogether for parts of the year to pursue migratory game. From this failure of intercultural communication, it was easy for the English to decide that they were justified in taking land that Mashpee Wampanoag, Narragansett, and Nipmuc men failed to use properly. Their addiction to the hunt, and their willingness to purchase their own ease at the cost of woman's unnatural labor bespoke an unmanly selfishness and immaturity. When war and European epidemic diseases such as influenza and smallpox devastated the indigenous populations without immunity to them, the English concluded that this was God's way of clearing the land for their possession and occupancy.

The case of the settlers and the Mashpee Wampanoag, Narragansett, and Nipmuc Peoples exhibits intercultural misunderstanding, and the processes of establishing structures of power and privilege over the Other. In the early meetings of the settlers and indigenous Americans, both could view each other mutually as the Other through an "exchange of looks between native and settler that structures their psychic relation in the paranoid fantasy of boundless possession and its familiar language of reversal" (Bhabha, 1994, p. 63). As power shifted in favor of the English, through the acquisition of land, their ability to establish a foothold and develop their political, social, and military institutions, it was they who were established as the powerful norm in contention with the Other.

As the foregoing example demonstrates, attention to historical factors can illuminate the complexities of gender in intercultural communication, and to the power relationships that underpin it. Clearly, historical investigations are not themselves unproblematic, nor can they supplant other modes of analysis. Historians themselves, as well as scholars in other disciplines, have written widely on the limitations of historical scholarship to provide an unmediated view of a "real" past (see for instance, Barthes, 1981; Foucault, 1969/1972; Stanford Friedman, 1995).[6] Though contextual, historical analysis provides no panacea for the many problems encountered by communications scholars, we have emphasized it as a useful tool for addressing some of the difficulties encountered in traditional intercultural communication scholarship, and for supplementing the theoretical approaches favored by feminist and critical communication scholars. In the former case, historical analysis addresses many of the shortcomings of traditional intercultural communication scholarship by transcending a simplistic, timeless gender binary by revealing the numerous permutations of gender and their chronological development. In the latter, it supplements theoretical insights by providing more nuanced and historically grounded descriptions of masculinity, femininity, and other gender identities (intersexuality, bisexuality, among others) in specific temporal and geographic circumstances.

Notes

1   See, also, Asante, Miike, and Yin (2008); Collier *et al.* (2002); Lengel and Warren (2005), and others in this volume.
2   The literal meaning of the term *hijab* in the Arabic language is "covering." The term also carries a broader connotation of "modesty." *Hijab* as a social practice embraces not only clothing/bodily covering but also values and behavior that define modesty. The term *hijab* is more often than not mistranslated as embodied in a distinct object – the "veil" or headscarf. For more details on feminine modesty in Islamic cultures and its contrary, a concept known as *tabarruj*, see Lengel (2004).
3   Mary Ludwig Hays McCauley (1754–1832) (a.k.a. Molly Pitcher), is recognized as a US Revolutionary War hero for her efforts during the Battle of Monmouth on June 28, 1778. The July heat and intensity of battle left soldiers exhausted and many wounded. Hays McCauley, the spouse of private John Hays, was granted the name Molly Pitcher after she spent the day carrying water in a pitcher back and forth from a well to Hays and his fellow artillery gunners. After John Hays was wounded in the battle and could not continue, Hays McCauley knew her spouse's job well enough to pick up his gun and keep it firing. Once the fighters noticed her bravery, she was asked to serve at the cannon for the remainder of the battle.
4   Although Native People identify by the name of their Nation, they also prefer certain inclusive group names. Many Indians in the West and the Northeast prefer Native American; American Indians in the Midwest and South prefer American Indian and as an inclusive name Native People of Alaska. Many current cultural studies scholars of the First Nations prefer the inclusive group name American Indian. For more on the Mashpee Wampanoag, Narragansett, and Nipmuc Peoples, and other indigenous peoples of present day New England see, for instance, Strong (1999) and Thee (2006).
5   For more on the gendered and emasculating processes of colonialization and postcolonial structures of power see, for instance, Bacigalupo (2004), Sinha (1995), and Tengan (2008). Consult Krishnaswamy (2002) for an explication of *effeminism* which refers to a "racialized construction of 'femininity-in-masculinity'" in colonial contexts (p. 295).
6   Kearns (1997) provides more details on the "obligation of the real." For a discussion on the problems of "objective" historical analysis, see Scott (1992, 2002).

References

Alexander, B. (1999) Performing culture in the classroom: An instructional (auto)ethnography. *Text and Performance Quarterly*, 19, 307–331.

Asante, M.K., Miike, Y., and Yin, J. (2008) Issues and challenges in intercultural communication scholarship, in *The Global Intercultural Communication Reader*, (eds M.K. Asante, Y. Miike, and J. Yin), Routledge, New York, pp. 1–8.

Bacigalupo, A.M. (2004) The struggle for Mapuche Shamans' masculinity: Colonial politics of gender, sexuality, and power in Southern Chile. *Ethnohistory*, 51, 3, 489–533.

Barthes, R. (1981) The discourse of history, (trans. S. Bann). *Comparative Criticism*, 3, 7–20.

Bhabha, H.K. (1994) *The Location of Culture*, Routledge, London.

Bourdieu, P. (2001/1998) *Masculine Domination*, (originally published as *La Domination Masculine*, Editions du Seuil, Paris, 1998), (trans. R. Nice), Stanford University Press, Stanford.

Bourdieu, P., and Passeron, J.-C. (1977) *Reproduction in Education, Society and Culture*, (trans. R. Nice), Sage, Beverly Hills, CA.

Butler, J. (1990) *Gender Trouble: Feminism and the Subversion of Identity*, Routledge, New York.

Butler, J. (1994) Interview, in *Radical Philosophy*, (eds P. Osborne and L. Segal), 67 (summer), pp. 32–39.

Collier, M.J., Hegde, R.S., Lee, W. *et al.* (2002) Dialogue on the edges: Ferment in communication and culture, in *Transforming Communication about Culture: International and Intercultural Communication Annual*, 24, (ed. M.J. Collier), Sage, Thousand Oaks, pp. 219–280.

Cronon, W. (1983) *Changes in the Land: Indians, Colonists and the Ecology of New England*, Hill and Wang, New York.

Foucault, M. (1969/1972) *The Archaeology of Knowledge*, (originally published as *L'Archéologie du Savoir*, Éditions Gallimard, Paris), (trans. A.M. Sheridan Smith), Tavistock, London.

Gauntlett, D. (2002) *Media, Gender and Identity*, Routledge, London.

Kearns, K. (1997) *Psychoanalysis, Historiography, and Feminist Theory: The Search for Critical Method*, Cambridge University Press, Cambridge.

Krishnaswamy, R. (2002) The economy of colonial desire, in *Masculinity Studies Reader*, (eds. R. Adama and D. Savran), Blackwell, Oxford, pp. 292–317.

Lengel, L. (2004) Performing in/outside Islam: Music and gendered cultural politics in the Middle East and North Africa. *Text and Performance Quarterly*, 24 (3/4), 212–232.

Lengel, L., and Warren, J.T. (2005) Casting gender, in *Casting Gender: Women and Performance in Intercultural Contexts*, (eds L. Lengel and J.T. Warren), Peter Lang, New York, pp. 1–17.

Martin, N. (2008) *Devil of the Domestic Sphere: Gender, Temperance and Middle Class Ideology, 1800–1860*, Northern Illinois University Press, DeKalb.

Martin, J., and Nakayama, T.K. (2000) Thinking dialectically about communication and culture. *Communication Theory*, 9, 1–25.

Mendoza, S.L. (2005) Bridging paradigms: How not to throw out the baby of collective representation with the functionalist bathwater in critical intercultural communication, in *International and Intercultural Communication Annual, Vol. 28: Taking Stock in Intercultural Communication: Where to Now?* (eds W.J. Starosta and G.-M. Chen), National Communication Association, Washington, DC, pp. 237–256.

Nakayama, T. (1994) Show/down time: "Race," gender, sexuality, and popular culture. *Critical Studies in Mass Communication*, 11, 162–179.

Nakayama, T.K., and Martin, J.N. (2007) The "white problem" in intercultural communication research and pedagogy, in *Whiteness, Pedagogy, Performance*, (eds L. Cooks and J.S. Simpson), University of Kentucky Press, Lexington, pp. 111–123.

Said, E. (1978) *Orientalism*, Penguin, London.

Scott, J.W. (1992) Experience, in *Feminists Theorize the Political*, (eds J. Butler and J.W. Scott), Routledge, London, pp. 22–40.

Scott, J.W. (2002) Feminist reverberations. *Differences: A Journal of Feminist Cultural Studies*, 13 (3), 1–23.

Sinha, M. (1995) *Colonial Masculinity: The "Manly Englishman" and the "'Effeminate Bengali'" in the Late Nineteenth Century*, Manchester University Press, Manchester.

Spivak, G. (1988) Can the subaltern speak?, in *Marxism and the Interpretation of Culture*, (eds C. Nelson and L. Grossberg), University of Illinois Press, Chicago, IL, pp. 271–313.

Stanford Friedman, S. (1995) Making history: Reflections on feminism, narrative, and desire, in *Feminism Beside Itself*, (eds. D. Elam and R. Wiegman), Routledge, London, pp. 11–54.

Strong, P.T. (1999) *Captive Selves, Captivating Others: The Politics and Poetics of Colonial American Captivity Narratives*, Westview, Boulder.

Tengan, T. (2008) *Native Men Remade: Gender and Nation in Contemporary Hawaii*, Duke University Press, Durham, NC.

Thee, C.J. (2006) Massachusetts Nipmucs and the long shadow of John Milton Earle. *The New England Quarterly, 79* (4), 636–654.

Warren, J.T. (2003) *Performing Purity: Pedagogy, Whiteness, and the Reconstitution of Power*, Peter Lang, New York.

20

Identity and Difference
Race and the Necessity
of the Discriminating Subject

Ronald L. Jackson II and Jamie Moshin

For many years social science researchers have been keenly aware that the body is the primary medium through which we experience the world. It is also the site and surface of identity, difference, and representation (cf. Bourdieu, 1991). Identities, as Stuart Hall (1997a) implies, are the names given to locate broad social histories, critical personal antecedents, and subjective interpretations of others that encase our realities. No matter how hard we try we are incapable of accessing or defining our identities outside these three contextual cues. We can no more eat without our mouths than we can comprehend identities without a context for what "identity" means.

Any understanding of identity is predicated on the notion of the subject (Grosz, 1994). There must be something on which we must focus that distinguishes itself from something else. This very small interstitial dynamic is what catalyzes difference. At the moment we are compelled to designate a name for some person, place, thing, or experience we are beginning the practice of discrimination. This sounds horrible because of the complex connotative baggage that comes along with that word. However, the fact is that discrimination is nothing more than acting upon something with which we are confronted by noticing its particularity, differentiating its characteristics, assigning meaning to its novelty, and treating it differently than we would something else with which we are more familiar. Discrimination is innate, it is unavoidable.

Naming the Other

The naming process, Fanon (1967) explains, promotes an ontological fixity that complicates discursive relations because those who belong to a speech community are then forced to coalesce around shared meanings in order to communicate.

The Handbook of Critical Intercultural Communication, edited by Thomas K. Nakayama and Rona Tamiko Halualani. © 2010 Blackwell Publishing Ltd.

They are unified by their approach to difference. The problem with this becomes apparent when we explore how North Americans have been unified around their approach to social differences such as those related to race, gender, class, sexuality, disability, and so forth. For example, when words like urban become the synecdoche for Black, when phrases like "cheated me out of money" are replaced with "Jewed," when students refer to things that they do not like or find to be uncool as "gay" or "retarded," we are let in on the potential vulgarity and epistemic violence of naming acts that lead to discrimination. Following Burke (1984), the process of naming immediately positions us for or against the Other. In the United States, therefore, our social approach to difference is inherently discriminatory.

Naming is inherently an iterative discursive process. As Fanon puts it, echoing Sartre's famous assertion that it is the anti-Semite who makes the Jew, "It is the racist who creates his inferior" (1967, p. 93). This is similar to Foucault's notion that subjects are created within discourse, and by regimes of truth – the Other is "created" by those in power (Hall, 2001). Naming is a part of the larger discursive/ ideological act of creating the Other, of maintaining difference. But, just because it is a discursive act – using the terms "urban," "Jewed," "gay," and "retarded" is surely different than physically attacking those whom we ascribe to be members of those categories – it does not mean that this derogatory language, intentional or otherwise, does not have any real, felt ramifications. As Thurlow (this volume) puts it, "Language really does matter. It is not simply a symbolic representation of the material; it is material." It is the process of naming *itself* that allows us to see and act upon difference, in a myriad of ways. However, it is a mistake to say that these sociolinguistic processes are inherently bad or damaging; naming also gives us something to belong to. The ethnicity/race to which we avow is also a process of naming – ethnic/racial groups are discursively constructed, and are therefore permeable. Names change, races change, and races even change to ethnicities. These naming processes therefore implicate not just the Other, they affect us as well. There is therefore a constant tension between the naming of the self and Other – it is always both inclusionary and exclusionary, comforting and hurtful, ideological and mundane. But to not implicate ourselves or others in this naming process, to let people off the hook because "it's just words," "words will never hurt me," and "it's just a joke" is what Jean Paul Sartre might label a self-deceptive move.

In his 1941 treatise *Being and Nothingness*, Sartre maintains that self-deception is the business of those who refuse to acknowledge how they participate in their own predicament; they are unable or unwilling to transcend the boundaries of their oblivion (Cumming, 2001). As a result, their sense of being and nothingness can be easily misconstrued. Being is established in relation to the material body and its location or place at any given moment. Nothingness is more about negation. When a newscaster reports a crime perpetrated by a Black person, for example, that person's race is more often noted than if the perpetrator was White (Dixon and Linz, 2000; Entman and Rojecki, 2000; Jackson, 2006). One explanation for this is that the newscaster's consciousness is trained to be directed toward race and nonrace, that is, non-White and White, respectively.

It is only by negation that we think of Whites and Whiteness as being raced. When set alone in an independent text or news story, "White" appears translucent, clear, normal, average, and nonraced. With this flash logic the reflex suggests that the White perpetrator does not deserve the kind of linguistic marking and concomitant pathological ascriptions assigned to the Black perpetrator. Even in this simple routine act we have uncovered a systemic microbe that eats away at the American social structure. We have identified a principal ideological interest in consistently sustaining and protecting the White subject by marking racial difference for non-Whites and disengaging such a process for Whites. As Brown (2009) points out, this becomes awfully real when we take a moment's glance at websites like www.rahowa.com (acronym for racial holy war), which conspicuously spew racial hatred and offer their own propaganda for advancing the White race. Brown (2009) is only one among a growing legion of critical intercultural communication scholars who have steadied their scholarly lens on Whiteness.

Others whose work resonates with the idea of race and the necessity of the discriminating subject are Dreama Moon, Tom Nakayama, Jennifer Simpson, Murali Balaji, Leda Cooks, Sean Tierney, Kathleen Glenister Roberts, and Mark Orbe, all noted here because of what they teach us about the means by which rhetoric can facilitate habits of racist perception, behavior, and in some cases physical, emotional, and epistemic violence. While this chapter can be situated in the context of these scholars and their works, perhaps the way in which we most advance this body of work is in conceptualizing discrimination as an act of articulation and negotiation. Stuart Hall's (1997a, 1997b, 2001) body of work suggests that articulation is at any given point merely the naming of a set of positions and oppositions in an intricately tangled web of self-defining discourse. Human beings are always at work trying to define and redefine themselves. It is this struggle to negotiate the self in varying contexts and encounters that intensifies extant critical cultural communication scholarship while holding liable both the individual and the society that have coconstructed racial identities, and hence racial meaning.

Within this essay, we will attend to a few contemporary dialectical naming acts in order to highlight how the power of naming is interwoven with identity politics that continually marginalize Others and sustain the hegemonic power of White subjectivity in the United States. In contemplating the ideas of identity and difference, there are several significant issues that come to mind. This essay will explore the following: (1) the I–Other dialectic; (2) naming the other; (3) sustaining the White subject; and conclude with a few recommendations for what we must do next as researchers to address this problem.

I–Other Dialectic

The clearest way to explain the I–Other dialectic is to point to its most explicit analog – the sentence. Sentences are structured so that there is a subject, verb, and object. The subject is the predicate nominative; it is what controls the sentential arrangement. The object is either controlled by the subject or is indicated by the subject as the "what" in the sentence. The verb signifies the character of the relationship or situation. If I say, "I love her," the "I" occupies the subject position, as always. "Love" is the verb that carries action and shows what is done to something or someone else; and "her" is the object. In the English language "her" does not get to be "she." "She" would signify autonomy and perhaps even control over the encounter. When "her" is placed in the object position it is an object waiting to be acted upon.

Marginalized groups in the United States are too frequently positioned in the object space. The interjected questions tend to be "Who puts them there" and "Don't they put themselves in that position?" Later in this essay we will explore how White subjectivity is protected. For now, it is important to recognize that what makes the I–Other dialectic useful as an ontological and epistemological construct is that it demonstrates the etiology of race relations. It helps to unravel the otherwise entangled dynamics of a discursive system that reinforces negative difference. It acknowledges Whiteness as the perpetual subject and non-Whiteness or otherness as the perpetual object. Attempts to contravene this dialectic tend to be squelched. That is why in 1997 when President Clinton appointed the taskforce on race relations headed by Duke University distinguished professor John Hope Franklin there was a glimmer of hope that this would be the rallying call for the beginning of the end of racism. Their series of town hall meetings were interesting, but overwhelmed by the sheer force of America's social history and its embraced legacy of racism. In 2001, just before 9/11, the United Nations sent out a call for a world conference on racism. This, too, was a monumental moment despite the White House's resistance to accepting the invitation to actively participate. At a time when the United States was being politically pressured to accept the invitation as a world leader, 9/11 dashed our memories of anything else besides this horrific event. The world conference on racism went on without us, as we had hoped.

The stain of racism remains and citizens of the United States are stifled when conversations about it arise, especially when that conversation includes those who usually occupy the subject position – Whites, because they tend not to construct their realities as the Other. This was clearly the case when distinguished Harvard University African American Studies professor Henry Louis Gates was falsely arrested at his home in July 2009: after Gates' neighbor called the Cambridge police to report that two Black males were breaking into his home, the police mistook Gates to be one of the burglars of his own home. After indicating the home was his, he was asked to step outside and was immediately handcuffed, placed under arrest, booked, and charged with burglary. Although the charges were dropped, Professor Gates was incensed and took his story to the national news and demanded an apology. Even President Barack Obama went on record, denouncing the police for having "acted stupidly," a statement that was later retracted after public officials pressured him to recalibrate his words. Part of Professor Gates' frustration was that he thought he had earned enough respect in his career to not be treated like other Black males in the United States who periodically report having been racially profiled or mistreated by police. He learned he was not exempt from this mistreatment despite his outstanding record of achievement. Professor Gates' experience also teaches us something about the mix of race and class dynamics. Professor Gates is a wealthy Black man. He may not be a millionaire, but he is clearly among the 3% of those in the United States who make over $250,000 per year. He was born and raised in the small coal-producing river town of Piedmont, West Virginia. His family was not wealthy; they were working class folk. He left there for school at Yale and subsequently at the University of Cambridge. After receiving his PhD he took positions at Yale, Cornell, Duke, then Harvard. He has had a storied career, one that has placed him among the elite. While he teaches Black Studies, the complexity of his subject position is such that he inhabits a space that is predominately White. This has created a schism for him as it relates to how he identifies with Blacks. He is removed from the common everyday experiences of Blacks. This became evident in his arrest when he proclaimed during a news conference that this is the first time he had recognized that Black men like him were subject to acts of capriciousness. He thought this was relegated to Black males from lower-income neighborhoods, surely not him. This statement illustrated just how out of touch he had become. It also suggested a certain separation from non-upper class Blacks. It suggested that it is possible that even though someone is non-White he or she may gain access to White space and White privilege, and may even begin to identify with Whiteness until such time that he or she is reminded of his or her otherness.

This is what Peggy McIntosh is talking about, in her list of ways that she experiences White privilege daily. She tries to explain that many Whites rarely get it when racial Others explain to them the travails of being in an othered space. It is confusing to them because it is not their reality and they live in the same country, same town, and sometimes the same neighborhoods as Others. So, they frequently wonder how it is that their experience is so vastly differently than that of Others? The answer is clear. They cannot know what it is like until they are the Other. That is why so many college courses on race and/or culture tend to have students (usually mostly White students) visit an unfamiliar cultural environment such as a Chinese new year celebration, Indian Pow Wow, or Black church, and then report back to the class what it felt like to be different.

One thing we would like to argue here, then, is that there is a vast space between recognition and action. It seems that many critical scholars champion the advancement of knowledge – getting others to see how subjectivities are constructed and ascribed – as the way to an egalitarian society. We do not deny that this is true, or that this work is important – quite the contrary. However, there is an ambivalence and quiescence that accompanies this gain – the idea that acknowledging and seeing one's privilege is enough. However, as we have seen firsthand through sharing these concepts with students, friends and family, shedding a light on the privileges that come with certain subjectivities does not in and of itself lead to change. Showing White students that their Whiteness is an invisible backpack (Dyer, 1997) that has all the tools to diminish obstacles that loom large in the lives of Others is not enough to change the fact that Others will still *see* them as White, and to ascribe them with power. It is not enough to motivate them to action and it is not easy to convince those who share the privileges that Whiteness lends to disavow those very privileges (Jacobson, 1998). Knowledge, therefore, is but a first step; as hooks (2003) argues, we also need action, and activism.

It is fascinating what US citizens have come to understand about difference. It is illustrated in words like "ethnic." When we ask our students to tell us the first thing that comes to mind when they hear the word "ethnic," they tend to refer to food, religion, clothing, artifacts, and sometimes nationality. Then, as the conversation progresses we come to realize that "ethnic" signifies something exotic, foreign, strange, or unfamiliar. In fact that is its etymological root. Even as we consider what it means to be different, difference is capitulated by its distance from what is typical or normal. That is, what makes something different is not how similar it is, but how it is distinguished from the average, which begs the question, "What is average, typical, or normal?"

As you will read in the next section, "naming the other," normalcy is the primary possession of Whites in the United States. In fact, many Whiteness researchers have discovered that Whites see no separation between what it means to be White and what it means to be American. Their reflex is to consider the two as synonyms (Jackson, 1999; McIntosh, 1994; Nakayama and Krizek, 1995). On the other hand, Blacks, Latinos, Asians, Jewish Americans and even Native Americans do not think of their cultures as synonymous with what it means to be American. How could they? If we can agree that media are the most potent visual and auditory stimuli available to us that assist in our socialization from childhood through adulthood, then it is obvious that the manner and frequency with which the media represents our cultures steadily impacts how we see ourselves and how others see us. The near absence of Native Americans in the media is symptomatic of a larger effort to prevent First Nations people from claiming America as primarily their own. The sparse positive representations of Blacks, except when presented by Black filmmakers, is another indication of White normalcy and non-White otherness.

Otherness has proven useful to xenophobes. It permits the kind of interplay between groups where the Other rarely gets to be in the subject position. So, it makes sense that when a subject is juxtaposed to an object, or an "I" is contraindicated by an "Other," a dialectic emerges that privileges the subject by resisting the rotation of hegemony (Wise, 2008). The I–Other dialectic is a priority in the mindsets of American citizens. It is not so much that we consciously embrace the kind of neoliberal, capitalist politic that embodies our racial predicament, but that we have been trained to think this way. Institutional forms of systemic oppression remain uninterrogated in the minds of the average citizen. We would rather enjoy a latte while browsing a home-improvement magazine than have a vibrant intellectual conversation about the political struggles in Myanmar. This is a result of our well-developed capitalist instinct. Capitalism does not promote critical examination of the human condition except as a means to secure more capital. Capitalism is not immoral; it is amoral; it has no regard for morality (Kelley, 1997).

This mindset can easily lend itself to a corrupt social system that spills over into politics, education, media, and every sphere of national life. It gets ingrained in the culture.

Grossberg (1997) calls culture "the struggle over meaning ... Culture is never merely a set of practices, technologies or messages, objects whose meaning and identity can be guaranteed by their origin or their essences" (p. 157). If culture is the systematic means by which groups make sense of and interact with the world, it becomes clear why intercultural communication can be so problematic. It is not so much the differences of the cultures as it is the conflict over meanings those differences engender. Cultures survive by providing meaning, and when those meanings are called into question, there is an impulsive need to establish the primacy of one meaning as right and others as wrong. Therefore, as we will touch upon in further detail later, it is not enough to demonstrate lacunae around the theorization of certain groups, the ways in which various subjectivities are implicated in discourses, and so forth. While this work is essential, and is most often driven by the identities of researchers themselves, we cannot forget the larger critical intercultural goal of exposing the sociolinguistic practices and ideological discourses which make these smaller inequalities and hierarchies possible.

So, as Kim (1991) suggests, intercultural conflict is the location of the struggle over meaning, of deciding what is appropriate and inappropriate and who is competent and/or incompetent. What is perceived to be at stake is cultural solidity, often articulated as "our way of life." Too often, however, members of certain cultures have a very limited or distorted understanding of how to relate within and between cultures, and this is only exacerbated when race becomes a marked facet of intercultural discourse.

When discussing race, it has become ordinary to talk about the I-versus-Other dialectic, but it is also possible to be Self and Other, though Homi Bhabha (1986) rearticulates this equation as follows: "[it is] not Self and Other, but the Otherness of the self inscribed in the perverse palimpsest of colonial identity" (p. xv). That is, the sickly nature of hegemonic inscriptions may influence an individual to begin to view the self as a stranger, as an obscure Otherized corporeal object rather than a familiar subject. So then, it is both the Other and the Other's formulated inscription that is at work in Bhabha's "Self and Other" equation. This is exemplified in Bill Cosby's recent commentary about Blacks.

Referencing the astounding 50% drop-out rate among Black youth in inner cities in his 2004 speech in Washington DC at the 50th Anniversary commemoration of the Brown vs. Topeka Board of Education Supreme Court Decision, Bill Cosby remarked:

> 50 percent drop out. Look, we're raising our own ingrown immigrants. These people are fighting hard to be ignorant. There's no English being spoken, and they're walking and they're angry. Brown v. Board of Education, these people who marched and were hit in the face with rocks and punched in the face to get an education and we got these knuckleheads walking around who don't want to learn English (clapping).

I know that you all know it. I just want to get you as angry as you ought to be. When you walk around the neighborhood and you see this stuff, that stuff's not funny. These people are not funny anymore. And that's not my brother. And that's not my sister. They're faking and they're dragging me way down because the state, the city, and all these people have to pick up the tab on them because they don't want to accept that they have to study to get an education.

His comments clearly revealed his own sense of separation from lower-income Black families who he summarily dismisses as folks with "names like Shaniqua, Shaligua, Mohammed and all that crap and all of them are in jail." Although his incendiary remarks drew criticism and applause alike, few have argued the overall truth-value of his claims. It is his outright dismissal of lower-income inner-city Black family experiences that yields skepticism and lacks context. After hearing the speech or reading the transcript it is easy to presume that lower-income Blacks are all or mostly uneducated, angry, slang-speaking, unemployed, baby-making, gun-toting, $500 sneaker-buying, criminal misfits who are undeservingly draining the state of its tax-based resources.

In fortifying his claims, Cosby suggests that the civil rights era was a utopic environ for the Black family where everyone coparented other kids in the neighborhood, and drugs, crime, incarceration, criminality, and skipping school were virtually nonexistent. Besides this idealization of the 1950s and 1960s, we are shown through his comments that Bhabha was right. One can be both Self and Other at the same time. Upon reading his speech, it is clear when he uses phrases like "we have to begin to build" and "we have got to take the neighborhood back" that he is expressing an affinity with the people who he chastises. He recognizes that he is a part of the same culture, but that he is disappointed with what that culture has come to mean to some people. His remedy is sort of a shock treatment. Rather than having independent, private kitchen-table conversations about Black folk, Cosby prefers to violate the unspoken rule forbidding the "airing of dirty laundry," and shared openly among a multiracial crowd the kinds of shared, private concerns many Blacks have had about other Blacks for years.

This implicit rule is significant because it permits a certain authenticity and essentialism. It suggests that if you are truly Black you will hold any such communal rules as inviolable. When you step over the line and betray your race by abetting White people's perceptions about Black inferiority you should be denounced as a traitor. Randall Kennedy (2008) tries to grapple with this in his best-selling book *Sellout*, where he discusses the identity politics at work within the conversation about racial disloyalty. To the question, "when can Black community members talk outside of these prescribed identifications, constructions, and rules," the answer is both never and any time. It is never permissible as long as White supremacy is viable enough to affect the everyday lives of marginalized Others, because it has the great potential to do much more harm than good. However, another answer may be "any time," because there are always exceptions to the rule. There are always unforeseen circumstances that emerge that can serve as teachable moments. Also, if there is ever to be a break in the cycle and if there is ever an interest in trying another strategy toward racial progress, this may be a possible option. Nonetheless it is important to remind ourselves that intentionality is critical here. If the intent is to move toward racial progress that is one thing; however if the intent is to provide evidence of racial inferiority that is another. In either case, there are political consequences of each action.

In distancing himself from "these people" Cosby positions his own subjectivity in such a way that "these people" become othered. They are different to him. He explicitly states, "that's not my brother" and "that's not my sister." They are the negation of his experience and identity. When Sartre talks about nothingness in his aptly titled book *Being and Nothingness* he is talking about how we know what something is by what it is not. Borrowing from Sartre and Heidegger, Foucault calls this the principle of exteriority. Nothingness is characterized by the lack of something rather than anything. In other words, something is what it is not. In this case, Cosby no longer occupies a space among the underclass. He belongs to an upper class, bourgeoisie elite. He is not the underclass; and that is how we know who he is. He is also letting us know that he is not part of a cultural community that condones or accepts undereducation and delinquency. He disavows any such affiliation.

So, the I–Other dialectic works as a distancing device. It is also a mirror that forces us to reflect on the image in front of us. Without the dialectic there is no comparative text that allows us to demonstrate difference, to know how we are distinctive from others. It can be useful as a way for us to innocently understand how something as simple as colors, tastes, or shades are distinguished, but it can be dangerous when used to marginalize others. Knowing how the I–Other dialectic operates is important; but to move toward radical progressive change we must also recognize when Others are being marked or named.

Naming the Other in Ghetto Films

In the same way that thug or gangsta hip hop music, as hooks (2003) explains "lets us know Black life is worth nothing, that love does not exist among us, that no education for critical consciousness can save us if we are marked for death, that women's bodies are objects, to be used and discarded," (p. 222) ghetto films commit equally egregious epistemic violence upon Black communities. One particular genre of ghetto films usually involves a White teacher who decides to work in an urban community in order to save the savage inhabitants from themselves. A few examples of these include "Dangerous Minds," "Lean on Me," "Half Nelson," "Freedom Writers," "Take the Lead," and "Music from the Heart."

While these films are feel-good films for White audiences who experience themselves as good, well-meaning, liberal Americans, the films often have an opposite effect for minority audiences who get to see themselves otherized once again. They get to witness another narrative where the disprivileged, uninformed, wild, uncontrollable, incompetent, and delinquent nobodies in the film represent their racial and cultural groups. They get to see how the only missing ingredient to the success of this derelict character is either having the privilege of being or behaving White, or striving to be like normal, average, civilized, and of course intellectually inclined Whites.

We rarely if ever get to see a Black, Latino, Native American, or Asian teacher enter a predominately White school and save the misguided youth from themselves. The implied racist message inherent in this conspicuously absent storyline is not only Whites do not experience this, but also that it is only when they intermingle, cohabitate, or attend school alongside minorities that they become less intellectually astute and to go wayward.

Another debilitating lesson audiences learn is that poor people are the bane of American culture. They represent the true underclass. Gans (1995) reminds us that when Gunnar Myrdal invented the term "underclass" in 1962, he was referring to an economic condition exacerbated by a combination of factors – chronic unemployment, underemployment, and underemployability. So, while they remain unemployed, underemployed and/or underemployable the rest of us hardworking Americans pay taxes to fix the many problems their individual irresponsibility leaves us. None of this invites us to explore the state or institutional responsibility to rehabilitate an infrastructure that includes quality schools, homes, and businesses in lower-income communities. Moreover, we are shown via these narratives that all these other people need is to take hold of their lives, take responsibility for their actions, and lift themselves out of their socioeconomic conditions. This solution demonstrates little to no regard for how they began to experience these material conditions in the first place.

Meanwhile, the feel-good narratives continue, and the underlying conversations about racial difference and racialized bodies persist. The epistemic violence referred to earlier ensues. These repeated storylines get lodged into the subconscious of media consumers to the extent that the mere racial physiognomy of a Black or Latino person cues negative reactions and stereotypes. A mere interaction with a dark-skinned, deep-voiced man now instigates fear and anxiety, not because he has done anything, but because the media have trained viewers and listeners to pay attention to the scripts about racial bodies – the complacent Indian male, the harmless affluent Jew, the hardworking Korean grocer, the lamenting Native American, the uneducated, violent and angry Black male, and so on. Movies like "Dangerous Minds," "Lean on Me," "Half Nelson," "Freedom Writers," "Take the Lead," and "Music from the Heart" set up that dynamic and it spills over into the everyday lives of the moviegoers as their trained consciousness guides their interactions with others.

The visual field has enormous potential for radical progressive pedagogy. All media have this potential, but there is something special about the visual. Evans and Hall (1999) remind us that visual culture is not merely about images, but it is also about cultural representations and racial memory; hence it has the potential to further complicate race relations or further enhance racial progress. The visual immediately resonates with everyday experiences and it offers a different dimension to truth. When we listen to a radio show or hear music we can enjoy the sounds only, but when you see a film you access the text visually and aurally. This, of course, is unlike print magazines, journals, or newspapers. Watching the images can offer more lasting impact. This is why positive, progressive visual representations have such powerful potential to provide significant advancements in racial reconciliation and toward social transformation. When racial memory shifts, so also will the discourse followed by daily behavior and perceptions about the Other.

Presently, the Other has been named, and now all one must do is remember to match the mediated discourses with the actual interactions. It is only shocking when the two do not align, when they find that most Black males they meet are intelligent and noncriminal, for example (Johnson, 1994). The flip side occurs when the stereotypes hold true enough times that the stereotype becomes the rule. hooks (2003) asserts, "The tragedy is ... that there is no countercultural message that is equally powerful" (p. 222).

Unfortunately, marginalized, racialized bodies in popular culture too rarely transcend the surfaces of their imposed inscriptions (Smith, 1998; Watkins, 1998) and ghetto movies continue to do damage. It is not so much that those stories should not be told, because they do represent one dimension of American life, but rather these stories should be accompanied by additional narratives that show that no one culture is perfect, ideal, or normal. If it is true that we are all human, and therefore inherently equal, then the messages should reflect that.

Sustaining the White Subject or Protecting White Subjectivity

We maintain that the reason messages do not often reflect an equitable range of cultural personalities and experiences is that it is important to sustain the White subject and protect White subjectivity. Hence, we bear witness to marginalized racial Others whose identities remain seemingly inescapably constituted, defined, and dominated by the perennial White subject. This dialectic is an apparent relationship that cannot be assumed, overlooked, or underestimated because we all apprehend our histories at different moments with varying levels of interpretation and experience that not only guide our sense of who we are but also our subjectivity. Everyone, at some point occupies the position of subject in their own experience. West (1999) argues, "To be American is to give ethical significance to the future by viewing the present as terrain capable of transcending any past and thereby arriving at a new identity and community" (p. xix). While being American theoretically allows individuals to uninhibitedly pursue their dreams and reinvent themselves, these dreams and reinventions for many marginalized group persons are slowed down by sociocultural conditions that define difference in ways that are stifling.

So, when you say "identity," it does not mean the same exact thing to me despite us sharing the same dictionary simply because it is subject-oriented. It is personal, social, and subjective all at once. It does not mean we cannot have a conversation about it, but that that conversation is constricted by the boundaries of our own imagination and experience, or what we call interpretation. The subject is never singular in the sense that individuated experience counts as the entire subject. One's own individual experience is merely a reflection of a composite set of dialectical interactions, all of which are constituted and defined by histories. That is why the notion of difference matters. This is even more crystallized and understood when we think about race and culture because those are notions clearly confined by the body. That is, it is the physical body that serves as an instrument to jog the personal and institutional memories, which drive and indeed motivate racial proscriptions about the body. The thick lips, dark skin, and nappy hair texture are all corporeal zones that serve as preverbal cues about Black bodies (Jackson, 2006). Every social group is marked by the physical bodies of their members. As human beings we tend to memorize these zones and cues in order to reduce uncertainty of unfamiliar others. We do this for Queer, Lower-income, Disabled, Racial, and Gendered communities. So, identity, difference, and the body are inextricably entwined and implicated, especially when discussing race and culture in the United States.

White subjectivity has been protected in the media industries. Dixon and Linz (2000) found that Blacks and Latinos receive differential news coverage than Whites when they are perpetrators rather than victims of a crime. Entman and Rojecki (2000) discovered something similar about how racial images are constructed in the media for Blacks and Whites. Their study compelled Oliver *et al.* (2004) to conduct an experimental study where participants were placed in groups to get a sense of how they would recall articles from an invented newspaper stimulus that showed a mixture of successful Blacks and delinquent Whites. When asked to recall which faces appeared next to each article, participants more often than not identified the Black male as the perpetrator of a crime rather than his true identity as an award recipient for some community action. In short, these participants like so many others have memorized corporeal ones and preverbal cues so well that they need not even think of the story content before they have subconsciously assigned minorities into stereotypical categories. This study signifies the success of media enculturation. Inundated by racial ideologies, images, representations, and storylines, media audiences gradually learn to protect White subjectivity (Tierney and Jackson, 2002). They learn that there is a purity to Whiteness that they can trust. They do not have to fear or put up defenses in White neighborhoods, but they must be on guard in minority neighborhoods, especially in lower-income neighborhoods. This is what we have been taught about racial bodies and White subjectivity.

Where Do We Go From Here?

The body is not inherently political; it is socially constructed and disciplined as such. Much of what extant studies tell us about race and racialized bodies tries to convincingly suggest human beings are innately endowed with a set of encoded messages. Furthermore, we are informed that men and women behave in certain ways, because it is their nature. We are told heterosexuality is predetermined and homosexuality is an abominable aberration of the natural order. These are all myths enwrapped in ideologies, which preserve a norm centering White Anglo-Saxon, Christian, heterosexual males and marginalizing everyone else. Some of these myths fail to survive public scrutiny, while others are so believable that they merge with social norms and practices; hence, they become camouflaged as a natural part of everyday life and are said to be "just the way it is."

Even as we acknowledge the multidisciplinary, multidimensional investigations of identity as being related to self-concept, status, self-construal, face-saving, self-verification, behavioral confirmation, management, self-presentation, social constructivism, and so on, the conversation goes nowhere until the researcher disciplines the subject by characterizing its essence. Subjectivity, then, is about interiority and consciousness as much as it is about exteriority or the social world. The subject is not satisfied or complete without a dialectical mirror.

Paul Gilroy (1992) recommends rethinking the I–Other dialectic as flows rather than fixities. That is, rather than concentrate on cultural ancestry and heritage, cultural citizens should allow their selves to reside in the moment, in the location most relevant to now. By doing so, he argues, there will be less historical strain, and our inquisitions will be newer, fresher, and less bound by historical baggage. His offering is enchanting, titillating actually. As we escape into this Gilroy utopia, it seems liberating to think of ourselves of coauthors of all history henceforth, not just the most immediate history that is signified by a fleeting set of moments with which we did nothing really productive. At the same time, this utopic instant seems anachronistic, like we have visited this temporal space previously, but we have no historical reference point, conjunctural protocol, or discursive strategies for managing the social crises in which we find ourselves. The point is by erasing history and its consequences, we simultaneously affect the outcomes, the now. Even if we purge ourselves of the emotional baggage that sometimes promotes nihilism, we still are left with the contemptuous objectifications, scripted irregularities, and materialist practices that inhabit our capitalist milieu. The solution must be more profound than a prescribed historical amnesia.

Many cultural critics and popular writers are addicted to quick fixes and half-baked solutions. They are also bound together in this conceptual mode of forgetting, which frees up psychic space to reconsider ontological options, but leaves us void and in a space that only re-manufactures the current social conditions. Instead, solutions must include remembering: we must remember the past perils so they can later be avoided; we must remember that when we unravel privilege, we have a colonialist subject standing there; we must remember epistemic violence is attached to power/knowledge matrix, which includes its own body politic; we must remember that forgetting is ignoring symptoms of a disease that is deteriorating our social bodies. We must also remember that identity and difference are predicated on subjectivity and it is our responsibility to critically interrogate how we consume messages that affect our consumption of difference.

For us, then, as critical intercultural scholars of communication, we find our-selves constantly negotiating between the "Scylla" and "Charybdis" (Omi and Winant, 1994) of thinking of "race" as mere ideology on one hand, and as fixed and naturalized on the other. Even though we know, write, and teach that race/gender/ethnicity/sexuality and the like are simulacra, we are constantly faced with real-world situations that belie this knowledge, and therefore we must pay these fictions scholarly attention because of their implications. The name "critical inter-cultural scholars" points to this very conundrum: on one hand, it is our goal and duty to expose and alter extant ideologies, and on the other it is to examine how cultural differences are enacted and maintained, and the ramifications this has. This is what Lisa Flores and Dreama Moon call the racial paradox, in which "we see how the tensions between exposing the social construction of race while living in a world in which race is as real as our physically different bodies complicate both the theory and practice of race" (2002, p. 182). Being a critical intercultural scholar is thus inherently political, because it is ideology and hegemony that create these dif-ferences which we are trying to expose, these injustices that we are trying to change. The notion of difference itself is ideologically laden, and it is a political boon to construct and maintain that very difference: "Identity is always a structured repre-sentation which only achieves its positive through the narrow eye of the negative" (Hall, 1997b, p. 21).

Being critical intercultural scholars – or indeed, perhaps, any type of critical scholar – is therefore a dual-pronged undertaking. We must both expose and thwart the extant discourses of power (cf. McKerrow, 1989). Being a critical intercultural scholar means first exposing that race, culture, ethnicity and the like are social con-structions, and that differences of status, power, class, and rights are not necessary or natural differences, but ones in which we ourselves are implicated: "Even while apprehending the world in reified terms, man [sic] continues to produce it. That is, man is capable paradoxically of producing a reality that denies him" (Berger and Luckmann, 1966, p. 82). Second, it means that we are also, hopefully just for the time-being, citizens of a nation and a world in which bodily differences result in dramatically uneven amounts of symbolic capital (cf. Bourdieu, 1991). Therefore we must point out the illusion of differences, but we must also act and speak out for those who suffer because of them.

References

Berger, P.L., and Luckmann, T. (1966) *The Social Construction of Reality: A Treatise in the Sociology of Knowledge*, Anchor Books, Garden City, New York.

Bhabha, H. (1986) Signs taken for wonders: Questions of ambivalence and authority under a tree outside Delhi, May 1817, in *"Race," Writing, and Difference*, (ed. Henry Louis Gates, Jr), Chicago University Press, Chicago, pp. 145–174.

Bourdieu, P. (1991) *Language and Symbolic Power*, (ed. J.B Thompson; trans. G. Raymond and M. Adamson), Harvard University Press, Cambridge, MA.

Brown, C. (2009) WWW.HATE.COM: The White supremacist discourse on the Internet and the construction of Whiteness ideology. *Howard Journal of Communications*, 20 (2), 189–208.

Burke, K. (1984) *Attitudes toward History*, 3rd edn, University of California Press, Berkeley.

Cumming, R. D. (2001) *Phenomenology and Deconstruction*, University of Chicago Press, Chicago.

Dixon, T., and Linz, D. (2000) Overrepresentation and underrepresentation of African Americans and Latinos as lawbreakers on television news. *Journal of Communication*, 50 (2), 131–154.

Dyer, R. (1997) *White*, Routledge, London.

Entman, R.M., and Rojecki, A. (2000) *The Black Image in the White Mind: Media and Race in America*, University of Chicago, Chicago.

Evans, J., and Hall, S. (eds) (1999) *Visual Culture: The Reader*, Sage, Thousand Oaks, CA.

Fanon, F. (1967) *Black Skin, White Masks*, Grove, New York.

Flores, L., and Moon, D. (2002) Rethinking race, revealing dilemmas: Imagining a new racial subject in race traitor. *Western Journal of Communication*, 66, 181–207.

Gans, H. (1995) Deconstucting the underclass, in *Race, Class, and Gender in the United States: An Integrated Study*, (ed. P. Rothenberg), St. Martin's Press, New York, pp. 51–57.

Gilroy, P. (1992) It's a family affair, in *Black Popular Culture*, (ed. G. Dent), Bay Press, Seattle, pp. 302–316).

Grossberg, D. (1997) *Dancing in Spite of Myself: Essays on Popular Culture*, Duke University Press, Durham.

Grosz, E. (1994) *Volatile Bodies: Toward a Corporeal Feminism*, Indiana University Press, Bloomington.

Hall, S. (1997a) *Representation : Cultural Representations and Signifying Practices (Culture, Media and Identities)*, Sage, Thousand Oaks, CA.

Hall, S. (1997b) The local and the global: Globalization and ethnicity, in *Culture, Globalization and the World-System: Contemporary Conditions for the Representation of Identity*, (ed. A.D. King), University of Minnesota Press, Minneapolis, pp. 20–39.

Hall, S. (2001) Foucault: Power; knowledge and discourse, in *Discourse Theory and Practice: A Reader*, (eds M. Wetherell, S. Taylor and S.J. Yates), Sage, London, pp. 72–81.

hooks, b. (2003) *Rock My Soul: Black People and Self-Esteem*, Atria Books, New York.

Jackson, R.L. (1999) White space, white privilege: Mapping discursive inquiry into the self. *Quarterly Journal of Speech*, 55 (1), 1–17.

Jackson, R.L. (2006) *Scripting the Black Masculine Body: Identity, Discourse and Racial Politics in Popular Media*, SUNY Press, Albany, NY.

Jacobson, M.F. (1998) *Whiteness of a Different Color: European Immigrants and the Alchemy of Race*, Harvard University Press, Cambridge.

Johnson, C. (1994) A phenomenology of the Black body, in *The Male Body*, (ed. L. Goldstein), University of Michigan Press, Ann Arbor, MI, pp. 121–136.

Kelley, R.D.G. (1997) Playing for keeps: Pleasure and profit on the post-industrial playground, in *The House that Race Built: Black Americans, U.S. Terrain* (ed. W. Lubiano), Pantheon, New York.

Kennedy, R. (2008) *Sellout*, Pantheon, New York.

Kim, Y.Y. (1991) Intercultural communication competence: A systems-theoretic view, in *International and Intercultural Communication Annual* (eds S. Ting-Toomey and F. Kerzenny), Sage, Newbury Park, CA, pp. 259–275.

McIntosh, P. (1994) White privilege and male privilege: A personal account of coming to see correspondences through work in women's studies, in *Race, Class, and Gender: An Anthology*, (eds. M. Andersen and P. Hill-Collins), Wadsworth, Belmont, CA, pp. 76–87.

McKerrow, R.E. (1989) Critical rhetoric: Theory and praxis. *Communication Monographs*, 56, 91–111.

Nakayama, T., and Krizek, R. (1995) Whiteness: A strategic rhetoric. *Quarterly Journal of Speech*, 81, 291–309.

Oliver, M.B., Jackson II, R.L., Moses, N., and Dangerfield, C. (2004) The face of crime: Viewer's memory of race-related features of individuals pictured in the news. *Journal of Communication*, 55 (1), 88–104.

Omi, M., and Winant, H. (1994) *Racial Formation in the United States: From the 1960s to the 1990s*, Routledge, New York.

Smith, F. (1998) *American Body Politics*, University of Georgia Press, Athens, GA.

Tierney, S., and Jackson, R.L. (2002) Deconstructing whiteness ideology as a set of rhetorical fantasy themes: Implications for intercultural alliance building in the United States, in *Intercultural Alliances International and Intercultural Communication Annual, 25*, (ed. M.J. Collier), Sage, Thousand Oaks, CA, pp. 81–106.

Watkins, S.C. (1998) *Representing: Hip Hop Culture and the Production of Black Cinema*. University of Chicago Press, Chicago.

West, C. (1999) *The Cornel West Reader*, Basic Civitas Books, New York.

Wise, T. (2008) *White Like Me: Reflections on Race from a Privileged Son*, Soft Skull Press, Brooklyn.

21

Br(other) in the Classroom
Testimony, Reflection, and Cultural Negotiation

Bryant Keith Alexander

I am standing in class supervising an engagement that deals with cultural stereo-types. I have encouraged my students to brainstorm for lived experiences of stere-otyping; times when they have felt *marked*, *minimized*, and *marginalized* due to some specific quality or characteristic they possess. As I stand in front of the room looking at my students, I see for the first time a mock family portrait. The back wall of the class is lined with five young Black men who, in many ways, are my "cul-tural" brothers and who reflect a near replica of my four "biological" brothers and myself. Their attitudes and postures are shockingly familiar and resonate with my lived experience as the fourth of five boys, the fifth of seven children born into a social experiment that my parents called a family.

In the far corner is "Jamale." Like my big brother Joseph, he is a bear of a man, a gentle giant who does not know his own strength. He is a football player who enters the room like a tank, yet sits sheepishly in the corner avoiding participation. He is wonderfully intelligent and personally charming, but academically apprehen-sive. He uncomfortably fits his man-sized body into a child-sized chair. Like my brother, he often looks out the corner of his eyes to see if someone is watching him. I am not sure if he thinks his largeness is now somehow camouflaged in the small desk, or if it is some self-defense mechanism. He seems prepared, yet resist-ant. I think of my own brother, Joseph, six years older, who would strangle me in hugs and suffocate me with love. He was always shocked and amused by my screams of pain and suffering. Yet, he would shy away from overt violence and often sit on the outside of discussions. He, too, had to be pushed into participation.

Three seats down is "Darnel," poised and strident in his manner. He is scath-ingly articulate in his critique of the course content and my interpretation of it. His performative display of critical thinking and pedagogical challenge fills me with the memory of my now deceased brother Nathaniel, four years my senior. In my every

The Handbook of Critical Intercultural Communication, edited by Thomas K. Nakayama and Rona Tamiko Halualani. © 2010 Blackwell Publishing Ltd.

interaction with Darnel I find myself measuring my words and weighing thoughts. His display of confidence is a performative mirroring and sometimes playful mocking of my own behaviors. It is also a challenge to the content and integrity of the course. I rejoice in the necessary effort that clarity demands. My brother, Nathaniel and I had a lovingly antagonistic relationship based in reflected appraisal. We saw both our best and worse qualities reflected in each other. Our perceptions of these qualities often led us to both embrace and reject each other.

"Tyron" *is* my brother Vincent. With dark skin, white teeth, and shining eyes he poses in the desk wearing a hat in defiance of class policy. His silence screams of attitude and position. His eyes are fixed on me in a piercing Black masculine gaze that seems to look right through me. Often I sense that in his silence, and later in his questioning, there is a challenge of me as Black man, not as the teacher. It is within our relationship that I struggle against the conflation – "this (Black man) but not that (teacher)" – or visa versa: "teacher, but not Black man." Our discussions become struggles, with him often increasing his volume and me counter performing a super "cool" response to his impassioned pleas. This negotiation is one that I am slightly afraid of because it pits us against each other as Black men struggling for power and control in the classroom, rather than working together toward knowledge and understanding. In many ways my brother Vincent (two years older) and I were flip sides of this same coin. He was the rugged, rough and tumbled boy, the highly sexualized teenage boy who would talk about girls and grab his crouch as if the action signified the person. By many, he was constructed as the "masculine" one – as communities often construct highly sexualized heterosexual performances of Black masculinity. On the other hand, I was thin, nonaggressive, nonathletic, a bookworm, and particularly uninterested in sexualizing girls. Hence, by many, I was the "effeminate" one. Throughout our childhood we negotiated differences in Black masculinity in a battle of wills. In the process we both engaged our strengths, a quite calm versus a raging storm. Like my brother Vincent, Tyron and I seem to be defining our identity against each other.

In the far right corner is "David," very much like my own brother Daniel – present today, but often absent. Wonderfully charming and creative, he is most alive when we do engagements or conduct open class discussions. During lectures he is listless. He does poorly on exams and his writing skills need improvement. My own brother, nine years younger is also wonderfully creative. He excelled in sports. His joy was in carpentry and welding. He inevitably dropped out of high school after years of struggling in remedial classes and battling an "at-risk" label. As I did with Daniel, I stay up late at night thinking up engagements, mnemonic devices, and narratives in which to embed or exemplify certain concepts and terms that would be meaningful to David. Like Daniel, David is a student who is interested in learning but needs additional attention and alternative approaches to the curriculum.

Nestled between Tyron and David is "Jonathan." Slight in build and soft spoken, he wears glasses and seems uncomfortable between these two guys. Before speaking, he checks himself by looking quickly from side to side. He is a conscientious and always prepared, yet he is an apprehensive student. He participates only when necessary. Uncomfortably, I see myself in him. After years of struggling with my own personal identity in which I compared myself against my brothers – the athletic brother, the talented brother, the handsome brother and the younger brother – I often found myself negotiating what and how I should be. This was positioned against the broader social and cultural prescriptions of being a Black male. As a student, I found myself wanting to excel, but not wanting to seem more than I was supposed to be and thereby risk being admonished by the "brothas," my Black cultural brothers. The exception to this circumspection was in classes where the teacher seemed interested in what I had to say.

My students engage the assignment by openly sharing personal examples of stereotyping. The young Black men tell stories of when they have walked into department stores and were followed. They talk about when people expected them to be good athletes, singers, or dancers and conversely poor students, and young men who are physically and sexually aggressive. While they tell their stories, I wonder how in our thoughts, and possibly in our actions, we have *marked, minimized,* and *marginalized* each other by virtue of our shared public-racial-cultural-identity and experiences as Black men. I wonder how many of these stereotypes we unknowingly have accepted and adopted as forms of an internalized racism. This internal racism functions as a false yardstick on which we measure and punish each other. In my own reflections, as I see my biological brothers reflected in these young men, I wonder if I have reduced or raised my expectations for them as students. Have they changed their expectations of me as a teacher in their orientation to me as a Black man? Do they see me as a *brotha*?

In making the analogy between my real brothers and my Black cultural brothers I seek to draw upon common images of Black masculine identity. I seek to figuratively play within the space that lies between the culturally connotative and the biological denotative meanings of "brother," to draw upon common features linked by bloodlines of a biological and a racial nature and move beyond the biological genesis that link male children to the same parents. Yet also in the process of making this allusion and concretizing this discussion in the relational dynamics of Black male teachers and Black male students, I am in fact engaging in an act of both testimony and confession; the tensive process of revealing privatized thoughts that effect our social orientation and perception of the world. In this moment I clearly admit, though I suspect that most teachers probably would not, that my subjective perception of my students might effect my objectivity

The fact that we are Black men *marks* our racialized and gendered presence in the classroom. Our Blackness signals ancestral ties that for me, demand recognition as a struggle against invisibility. I see Black males in my class not only as students but as the *racially familiar*. By envisioning my biological brothers and myself in them (through their specified performances), I also claim them as the *culturally familiar*. Yet, like my own biological brothers, differences are present and they demand negotiation. These differences are no less paralyzing in a classroom context than they are in a familial context, for we all exist within the broader cultural realm that influences our performances of Black masculinity.

In this essay I explore multiple approaches to defining, constructing and orienting to the notion of "brother" in various disparate but interconnected ways. The essay situates the definition into four relational orientations that speak to the multiple and varied components that undergird the notion of "brother." First, I explore Black male teachers as "cultural brothers," in terms of establishing a "brotherhood." Within this approach I offer a theoretical frame that describes the cultural origins of the referent "brother," as pedagogical constructions of affinity seeking.

Second, the essay explores the notion of "br(other)" and the construction of "otherness." There is a strong dialectic of power that creates difference within the population of Black men, especially based in alternative masculinities. Under the rubric of "Big Brother," the third relational approach focuses on *mentoring and caring* as a form of sociocultural identification and responsibility. This approach looks at the Black male teacher's use of racial commonality as a bridge to the curriculum, and as a tool in teaching. The fourth relational approach uses the notion of "Big Brother" in the Orwellian sense of *surveillance*. It explores multiple configurations of power that are practiced within the classroom between teachers and students. This approach also notes that even though cultural affinity may serve as a bridge in the classroom between Black male teachers and Black male students, there is also a form of cultural power that mediates that relationship. This cultural power is based in the lived experiences and shared racial communities of the Black male teacher and the Black male student.

These four relational orientations are voiced, practiced, and concretized within the classroom. They are intricately interwoven with each other, but have been isolated here to focus on their individual features. Although the essay is focused on the broad notion of "brother," the term itself is relational in nature and refers to the dialectic between the Black men who would claim that status. Thus, my exploration positions the Black male teacher and Black male students in a constantly shifting negotiation of brother status and the residual effects of that relational assessment. Karamcheti (1995) argues that "[t]he minority teacher performs a generic ethnicity in which the personal is simultaneously a symptom of powerlessness within academia and a strategy for gaining power (as is identity politics in general)" (p. 146). Within each "brother" orientation I foreground primary issues of race and masculinity, the construction of "otherness," support, and power. In many ways, this project also teases at the staid constructions of intercultural communication that looks at communication between members of different cultures (from different racial and ethnic groups), foregrounding issues of people marked by difference, without looking at the particularity of cultural difference within racial communities. This project explores a form of intracultural variability as intercultural difference within a shared racial category through the particular frame of the cultural construction of "brother" between Black male teachers and Black male students in the classroom.

Cultural Brother: Notions on "Brotherhood"

In their anthology entitled *Brotherman*, Boyd and Allen (1996) offer a representative definition of "brother" invoked in the greeting of "brotherman":

> "Brotherman!" is a special greeting among Black men. With that single word [and acknowledgment] a bloodline is invoked, a gender proclaimed ... The coded exchange

of 'brotherman' signals immediate recognition and rapport. It conveys a message that is at once an affirmation, an affectionate embrace, and a battle cry. It proclaims: *Our bloodlines and soulforce are the same and we have a common fate – what happens to one happens to all.* [Original emphasis] (p. xxi)

The cultural reference of "brotherman" emerged as a result of the civil rights movement of the 1960s. At this time a spirit of unity forced Black men and women to collectivize their efforts and come to an understanding of common oppressions and the intricate racial strife that links as family, all peoples of African descent. Yet, the political move of claiming "brother/sister" status based on racial identification and common political ideology does not completely explain the notion of "brotherhood." Commonly, it manifests itself within the lived location of Black male identity formation. The status of being a "brother" often invokes a culturally specific performative criterion of a Black masculine ideal.

I know that I buy into a cultural "brother" connection with my Black male students. This is not through some political ideology or some false essentializing – but through an empathic, if not specifically somatic experience of felt significance. I see the performative choices that my Black male students are using to foreground self. I see them as myriad performances that I myself have given, both privately and publicly. These choices are concretized in my performance of Black male teacher: proud and strong, direct and challenging, sometimes strident, but flexible in considering the personal as political, and strategically engaging the political as personal. Surely my performance of Black male teacher is a means of recuperating some degree of power over the conditions of powerlessness and dependency in relation to the White master subject that is integral to the traditional educational system. In my classroom presence (especially to the limited experience of my Black male students in the White university), I assume a power and authority that has often been relegated to the White teacher.

When looking at my students I experience a kind of reflected appraisal, seeing myself in them as they sit in the classroom in the predominantly White university. In this site they (we) are reduced to numbers, literal "minorities." We are alike in that we rarely see ourselves represented in the curriculum, much less in the classroom or the university structure, as teachers or administrators. Our connection as teacher and student is forged not only in our shared Blackness but in the shared and collectively felt oppression that comes from isolation.

In claiming "brother" status I participate, as do most teachers, in an active process of "affinity-seeking" as a means of gaining power and influence in the classroom. Bell and Daly (1984) define affinity seeking as "the active social-communication process by which individuals attempt to get others to like and feel positive about them" (p. 91). Although most of the research regarding teacher affinity-seeking focuses on the White teacher, the definition suggests two performative strategies that can be applied to the Black teacher/Black student dynamic. First, affinity-seeking is an "active rather than passive activity" which negates racial identification as a guaranteed factor of affinity (Daly and Kreiser, 1992, p. 122). Second, the definition also suggests that affinity is "centrally a communication construct" (Daly and Kreiser, 1992, p. 123). Hence, through performative practices – what people do and how they do it concretized as performance and presentation of self in everyday life – affinity is sought, granted or denied.

While I claim a cultural affinity (i.e., brother status) with my Black students, I know well that in my role as teacher I am associated with a White patriarchal structure that immediately marks me as "other" in spite of my racial commonality. Though I may hold cultural membership as a Black man, my performative role as teacher may be incongruent with the "expected" performance of Black masculinity. In some ways, my brother status is obscured, complicated, and compromised, if not rendered invisible. Like Ellison's (1947) invisible man: "That invisibility to which I refer occurs because of a peculiar disposition of the eyes of those with whom I come in contact. A matter of the construction of their inner eyes, those eyes with which they look through their physical eyes upon reality" (p. 3). Black male students see Black male teachers through their *inner eyes* or what McLaren (1993) calls the "street state," their culturally lived experience and the accompanying codes of etiquette and behavior. Their physical eyes directed in the "school state" must focus on the disparity between the two performances of Black man (p. 87).

The dilemma lies not in racial identification, but in the culturally specific performative criteria for Black masculinity and the competing ways in which that notion is perpetuated, rejected, and reconfigured, outside as well as within the classroom. In essence, the classroom becomes a kind of fish bowl where differences in racial and gender performances are magnified.

The presence of Black male students in my class is meaningful to me, just as it is meaningful in every walk of life. Black men have a way of acknowledging each other that has always brought me a comfort. It is a visual recognition of seeing and being seen. The recognition of a Black male presence signals a historical connection that demands recognition against invisibility, even if there are contested performances of gender. Certainly that recognition occurs in the traditional handshakes, "giving some skin" or "the dap," that occurs between acquaintances or during introductions.

The recognition also takes place within the subtle moments of a visual acknowledgment. Those passing moments when the eyes of Black men connect and the head moves downward in a quick motion, saying hello. That is a moment of recognition, a moment of validation, which might be accompanied with: "Whass hapnin?" or "Whassup?," but can stand alone as a moment of contact. Those moments can cut through the politics and the continuum of performing man, manly, and masculine. Maybe it is the historical legacy of slavery. Maybe it is an empathic sense of wanting to be acknowledged. Maybe it is the fear of invisibility that causes the lens to focus, to see, to acknowledge. The notion of brotherhood signifies community, but even in community there are constructions of difference that must be negotiated.

Br(other): The Construction of Otherness

In her article "Performative Acts and Gender Constitution" Judith Butler (1990) offers a prophetic statement that crosses gender and racial lines of performance and identity construction. Alluding to Beauvoir, Butler notes, "to be a woman is to have become a woman, to compel the body to conform to an historical idea of 'woman,' to induce the body to become a cultural sign, to materialize oneself in obedience to an historically delimited possibility, and to do this as a sustained and repeated corporeal project" (1990, p. 273). The Black man is similarly a historical idea. Through intracultural socializing and the mandate of specified performance strategies, the Black community sustains the historical idea of Black masculinity as a "repeated corporeal project."

In *Oneself as Another*, Ricoeur (1992) develops a concept of constructing other that I am loosely applying to the Black community. Ricoeur suggests that self is based on the dialectic between selfhood and otherness. Identity involves meanings of sameness shared within a specified community, which help to constitute character and selfhood. A collective, often cultural, narrative identity mediates character and selfhood, so that the individual is responsible to a community-based repertoire of performance expectations. A community such as the Black community develops a primary narrative description that identifies or sanctions specified behaviors, specifically in terms of Black masculinity. Through a form of narrative fidelity, those who participate in the cultural community by performing the specified behaviors maintain what Ricoeur might call "narrative identity" (pp. 114–115). Those who break the fidelity of the narrative description are then considered "other."

This notion of constructing a cultural member is explored by Butler (1990). She emphasizes that the "body suffers a certain cultural construction, not only through conventions that sanction and proscribe how one acts one's body, the 'act' or performance that one's body is, but also in the tacit conventions that structure the way the body is culturally perceived" (p. 274). The implication of what I am calling "intracultural performative otherizing" in the Black community is centered in such cultural sanctions and constraints. Tacit patriarchal and phallocentric structures are created within the community that govern how the Black male body is perceived. These identifying markers of Black masculine identity may confirm or disconfirm individual expression in relation to a collective identity.

In the classroom, the notion of embracing a kind of "brotherhood" with my Black male students in both a political and cultural sense becomes a contested act. If we are to believe McLaren (1993) that resistance is a form of self-protection, then the resistance performed with and against the Black male teacher – who visibly (may) represent shared racial identification, if not specific cultural practices – becomes a double resistance. It is a resistance to educational or classroom practices that deny their experiences, as well as a resistance to the Black teacher who may not display the specified standards of Black masculine performance that they deem appropriate. As a Black-gay-man, I realize that my body is a contested site. I realize that my Black male students may sense my difference and immediately cast me as other, "[s]ince so much of the quest for phallocentric manhood ... rests on a demand for compulsory heterosexuality" (hooks, 1992, p. 112). In this case my racial/ cultural affiliation as a Black male is *e-raced* if not reconfigured. I become subject to a critique based on what hooks (1994b) called dick-thing masculinity. My perform- ance of Black masculinity may ultimately be perceived as being counter intuitive to the Black masculine ideal that they have constructed and which they maintain.

In *Testimony: Young African-Americans on Self-Discovery and Black Identity*, (1995) Natasha Tarpley suggests that "in the classroom, Black students often find themselves fighting battles similar to those being waged against Black people on the streets. The same forces that work to silence and render invisible Black people outside of the classroom are also represented in our educational system"(p. 3). Whereas Tarpley speaks of an *intercultural racism* that intersects the educational experience of Black students, I speak of an *intracultural performative otherizing* that intervenes in the Black male teacher/Black male student relationship. This otherizing intervenes at the nexus of Black masculinity and sexuality with all of the accompanying performative displays.

As I write about my experiences as a Black male teacher (and consequently as a Black-gay-male-teacher) I once again become a tentative border crosser. These borders mark the territories of Blackness, masculinity, sexuality, and pedagogy. The necessary bridge is to forge a new Black masculine mystique that in its very exist- ence and persistence is a critique of sexism, patriarchy, phallocentrism, and misog- yny. There is a need to establish a brotherhood that can embrace a rich racial and cultural heritage not constrained by hyper-masculinity. This is the project for all Black men, gay or straight, for the legislation of desire has nothing to do with being a man and it should not mediate pedagogy. This is the challenge, for as West (1994) says, "our truncated public discussion on race [and masculinity] suppresses the best of who and what we are as a people, because we fail to confront the com- plexity of the issues in a candid and critical manner" (p. 4).

I echo Adrienne Rich (1986) in "If Not With Others, How?" when she says: "My hope is that the movement we are building can further the conscious work of turning Otherness into a keen lens of empathy, that we can bring into being a politics based on concrete, heartfelt understanding of what it means to be Other" (p. 787). Ultimately, I am interested in working with my Black male students to embrace the "other" in br*other*. Within that embrasure is a development of men- toring relationships that facilitate the growth of the student by capitalizing on ele- ments of racial affinity.

Big Brother: Mentoring and Caring

The notion of enjoining the Black teacher and Black student in a relationship of acknowledgment and mutual support is analogous to the national support organization for Big Brothers and Big Sisters. The organization promotes a positive self-image in the child by matching them with an adult volunteer. The notion of Big Brother as applied to the relational dynamic between the Black male teacher and Black male students is similar in that it fulfills the representational needs of an adult, as well as the cultural affiliation needs of students in the form of mentoring.

Blackwell (1989) defines mentoring as "a process by which a person of superior rank or special achievements and prestige instructs, counsels, guides and facilitates the intellectual and/or career development of a person identified as a protégé (p. 9). Within the academic setting the student becomes the protégé, or the one whose welfare, training, and academic career is promoted and supported by the teacher. In *Involving African American Students*, Greer (1993) constructed a definition of mentoring:

> The student (mentee) is drawn to the other (mentor) initially by physical attraction developed through language and nonverbal behavior. Interactive management leads to bonding between both participants. The encounter is helped by the authenticity of both individuals while exemplifying mutual respect for the other. The mentor is perceived to exemplify availability and immediacy giving the mentee a sense of comfortability and manufacturing psychological closeness. It is a relationship that produces self enhancement and humility leading to an enhanced perception of the university community through persuasion offering a positive university experience (p. iii).

Greer grounds mentoring in "connectedness where lived experiences becomes the connectedness with the university system." Students see within the mentor aspects of their lived experience accompanied with a genuine desire to connect in ways that enhance the student's educational experience. Greer argues that mentoring includes an element of caring, and further, that mentoring relationships between Black teachers and Black students take on special meaning in the predominately White university where students may feel a sense of isolation and cultural deprivation.

Mentoring in my classes has always been based on consistency of caring which has led to bonding with some Black male students, particularly those for whom differences in personalities and masculine performative displays were not problematic variables. The mentoring occurred when they felt comfortable in asking questions that extended beyond the scope of their experience in the classroom to include aspects of their personal life and their full participation as students within the university.

The mentoring relationship helps the Black student to tap into and recognize the significance and value of his or her own lived experience as well as alternate ways of knowing. Speaking in terms of a shared passion, hooks (1994b) suggests that this approach "can provide an epistemological grounding informing how we know what we know which enables both professors and students to use such energy in a classroom setting in ways that invigorate discussion and excite the critical imagination" of all students present (p. 195). McLaren (1993) speaks of this process in terms of "enfleshed knowledge." McLaren suggests that students often resist educational settings, inclusive of teachers and curriculum, because they see schooling as denying their lived experience. Their resistance is a form of assertion and a method of recovering and validating a form of "enfleshed knowledge" and self-expression that is being repressed and oppressed. He suggests:

> Enfleshment is that meeting place of both the unthought social norms in which meaning is always already in place and the ongoing production of knowledge through particular social, institutional and disciplinary procedures. Enfleshed knowledge is not the matching of information to external reality but rather the building of discursive positionalities and economics of affect from the discourses and material practices available and the histories and regulatory practices of their operations (p. 275).

Enfleshment speaks to the lived and somatic experiences of students that serve as filters and frames for their learning. Using "enfleshed knowledge" as a facilitative part of the educational experience is not an exclusive project of Black teachers. Yet, the practice offers a point of entry into understanding the relational dynamics between Black male teachers and Black male students.

The Black teacher augments standardized methods of teaching and engaging Black students, acknowledging the limitations of such processes to getting at enfleshed knowledge. The Black teacher attempts to engage a form of critical pedagogy that acknowledges and critiques the inadequacies of the schooling process for Black students. Mncwabe (1988), in *The Black Teacher's Dilemma*, suggests that the Black teacher must "become accustomed to unconventional presentations of situations around him, to ways of talking with which textbooks cannot deal. Only if [s/]he breaks with fixed, customary modes of seeing can [s/]he remove the blinder of complacency" (p. 122).

Big Brother as mentor moves towards establishing what Darder (1991) calls a "cultural democracy" in which educators even-out the field of play, if only in the specific site in which the Black (or racialized) teacher and student encounter each other.

The term cultural democracy reflects the perspective and philosophy of Ramiréz and Castañeda (1974):

> Specifically, it pertains to an educational philosophy that affirms the right of individuals to be educated in their own language and learning style and the right to maintain a bicultural identity – that is, to retain an identification with their culture of origin while integrating, in a constructive manner, the institutional values of the dominant culture. Further, this view argues for the necessity of institutional milieus, curricular materials, and educational approaches that are sensitive to the student's history, sociopolitical reality, and cultural orientation (p. xvi–xvii).

A cultural democracy supports and acknowledges student characteristics, specifically race and culture that are often ignored if not maligned. Its intent is to facilitate the educational and personal development of Black and bicultural students. White students are not reduced in the process, as much as Black and bicultural students are encouraged and supported to join their voices in dialogue with others.

The goal is to begin reversing or reducing the ill effects of "those dominant cultural values and practices that function in the schooling process to marginalize and silence the voices of Black, Latino, Asian, Native American and other bicultural students in the United States" (Ramiréz and Castañeda, 1974, p. xv).

When I think about mentoring and caring for Black male students, I see its connection to "reflected appraisal," the practice of evaluating or orienting to others based on perceived similarities. Greer (1993) suggested that the mentoring relationship begins as a moment of attraction in which the mentee "is drawn to the mentor." The attraction is based in a physical attraction, but also the sensed feeling of comfort and a psychological closeness akin to caring. The concept of "reflected appraisal" undergirds a lot of the research on affinity seeking under the notion of "similarity" (Bell and Daly, 1984; McCroskey and McCroskey, 1986; Tolhuizen, 1989). The concept specifically focuses on attraction, both social and intimate, based upon resemblance and similarities in attitudes, "nationality, race, ethnicity, ability, physical characteristic. We are often attracted to mirror images of ourselves" (Devito, 1992, p. 312).

When encountering young Black men in the classroom I see a part of myself reflected in them. I am not trying to essentialize all Black men, but to rather note a shared lived experience that positions me also as Black male student in predominately White educational institutions. I saw myself then, as I see myself now, struggling in isolation and difference. I want to offer them assistance, yet I do not make the gross assumption that our common racial heritage signifies a common struggle on the academic terrain. I have often had Black male students resist any special attention because it is incongruent with their way of being. Some do not want to call attention to themselves and actually prefer "the pleasure of coming independently to their own conclusions with the Black teacher simply as the facilitator of their meeting or deliberation" (Mncwabe, 1988, p. 72). I can understand this because for years my own identity as Black male student was based in the same logic – a sort of *rugged individualist*, which is very much a "cool pose."

The mentoring of Black male students by Black male teachers is an act of projection and reflection. If in fact a mentor helps the mentee to come to an understanding of his/her own potential, then mentoring is an act of projecting possibility and moving towards that goal. "The possibilities may be physically or psychologically perceived. Mentoring becomes the source for presenting possibilities not previously exposed to students" (Greer, 1993, p. 87). If, in fact, mentoring relationships begin with an attraction to sameness, whether in the field of study or cultural affinity, then it also is an act of reflecting embodied possibility. The Black male teacher may engage in a mentoring relationship with a Black male student that operates on both of these levels. Greer (1993) says that mentoring leads to "self enhancement and humility" (p. 89), the enhancement of the student and humility as act of submission in which the mentor gives freely of his/her knowledge, academic, and cultural to meet the needs of students.

I agree with Thomas Merton in "Learning to Live" (cited in hooks, 1994b) when he says, "the purpose of education is to show students how to define themselves 'authentically and spontaneously in relation' to the world" (p. 199). Greer (1993) specifies this as an act of mentoring when he says:

> Mentoring as a tool of persuasion is able to provide African American students with a positive university experience. The relationship shared between mentor and mentee establishes for the student a central focal point for maintaining cultural idiosyncrasies [sic] and receiving alternative beliefs, values, and attitudes prevalent within the university community (p. 20).

I have found myself addressing the changing needs of Black male students throughout the course of any given semester, fielding questions relating to financial services, religious services, and the presence of other Black teachers on campus. I also serve as a sympathetic ear for problems that Black students in general may be experiencing with White teachers. While acknowledging our common racial heritage, the performative variations in Black masculinity, and other differences marked by being teacher and students, together we navigate the landscape of the academic terrain within the predominately White university.

Within the mentoring relationship the mentor in essence "watches out" for the mentee, providing a kind of close observation and direction of their educational progress. Such close observation facilitates the overall growth of the student. Yet, this form of surveillance may become suspect when linked to assertions of power and control.

Big Brother: Surveillance in the Classroom

In George Orwell's (1949) anti-utopian novel *1984*, Big Brother is the central object of contemplation in the province of Oceania. According to Tucker (1983), "Big Brother ... is the guise in which the Party chooses to exhibit itself to the world. His function is to act as a focusing point of love, fear and reverence, emotions which are more easily felt towards an individual than towards an organization" (p. 99). Inevitably while the citizens of Oceania are looking to Big Brother for guidance, Big Brother is Watching them in a form of socio-political surveillance.

The practice of surveillance is clearly present in the classroom given the unequal power and authority between teachers and students. For young Black men this feeling of being under surveillance is not unlike entering public spaces such as malls and department stores, only to be followed by store managers and security. The eyes of Big Brother watch them (us), waiting, expecting, suspecting them (us) to steal. The act of surveillance then becomes a safeguard in which cultural markers become evidence for suspicion and alarm, ultimately a cultural assessment of difference. It happens reciprocally in the predominately White university where race becomes a cultural marker as distinction and risk. Black male teachers and Black male students maintain a form of surveillance of each other. The managing and wielding of power become a reciprocal act of measuring cultural membership – for the classroom and the Black community.

Orwell's Big Brother is constructed in a society whose purpose is solely that of power over its citizenry. Re-situated in the classroom, Big Brother takes the form of the authoritarian teacher. Power in the classroom is a form of control and surveillance that becomes relevant to the Black teacher/student dynamic. Richmond and McCroskey (1992), in *Power in the Classroom: Communication, Control, and Concern*, outline five basic types of power which are useful touchstones for the power negotiated between Black male teachers and Black male students: (1) Reward power, based on the ability to mediate rewards; (2) Coercive power, based on ability to punish; (3) Legitimate power, grounded in position and status; (4) Referent power, based on allocated authority through identification; and (5) Expert power, based on perceived knowledge or expertness (pp. 4–5). These varying forms of power are often associated with authority and status, a set of practices that teachers exert over students. The *power of the grade*, though an assessment of student performance, can be perceived as "reward power" for work well done. This becomes indicative when students say things such as: "The brother *gave* me an A." Conversely students might view grading as a "coercive power," a form of punishment for not meeting specified standards, as in the case of the Black male student who says, "I can't believe you *gave* a brotha a C." Yet, in the role of authority, the teacher is given a "legitimate power" in the classroom to make decisions and control content and form. In the process, the teacher is authorized to expect certain levels of performance or informed communication from students, as reflected in tests, reports, and presentations. This is both the legitimated power to test and demand accountability, as well as to reward acceptable behavior. With the status of teacher there is also an assumed "expert power" based in knowledge of the subject or the ability to disseminate information and follow prescribed methods.

Although the teacher-student roles are formally defined in academia, and the teacher assumes the aforementioned powers, these powers are always socially negotiated. They are not innate so much as they are assigned and assumed. Thus, the teacher is also granted, by students, a form of "referent power" as a confirmation of their designated roles. Students grant the teacher authority to practice power over them or to assume a certain position in relation to them. The power dynamic between the Black male teacher and Black male students is further complicated by the negotiation of cultural power.

If as a teacher I stand as a model for students, then as a Black male teacher I stand as an alternative model to Black male identity, which is problematized cultural politics. I literally become Big Brother. Tucker (1983) responds to the question in "Does Big Brother Really Exist?"

> He exists in every instance of the nightmare state, and it is his needs – above all the colossal grandiosity, the need to be adored, worshipped by millions of subjects, and to gain never-ending vindictive triumphs over hated enemies ... They motivate its repression of every fact that contradicts a Big Brother's monstrously inflated image of

himself as one who could never err; its insistence on some form of culture of anti-sex so that all erotic emotion can focus on the single object at the center of it all; its projection of violent hatred upon the collective and individual enemy demands of Big Brother's demented self (p. 100).

I do not assume that critique to apply to my own intention as a teacher. Yet, I can see how a form of tension might exist with the Black male teacher who places himself in the position as a model; model as standard. This teacher might advocate a "Be Like Me" rhetoric that truly engages the role of Big Brother. This stance would suggest that Black male students should act like the Black male teacher and alter their indigenous way of being, which may be a part of their natural resistance to schooling anyway.

In Orwell's novel, *1984*, the reader is led to favor the Brotherhood only because it opposes the party. Yet, neither the Party nor the Brotherhood have any clear politics other than the destruction of the other group (Bloom, 1987). If Black masculinity (or the Brotherhood) has been forged out of resistance to the White power structure (or the Party), then the perceived difference of a Black male teacher by Black male students may be reflective of both a variation of Black masculinity, as well the power laden position of teacher-student.

Power in the classroom is a conflicted construct and a mediated practice. It refers to a teacher's ability or capacity to act or perform effectively in executing the demands of the class and meeting the needs of students. In this sense power is not something that is practiced *over* students, but something that is negotiated *with* students to facilitate the educational process. It also can be the ability or official capacity to exercise control, in which the ultimate authority that resides with the teacher and students is *acted upon* in the process of schooling. In *Empowering Education*, Shor (1992) suggests that "the teacher directs the process [of learning] but not as a unilateral authority. The themes, thoughts, and diverse cultures of students come first; into this material the teacher integrates expert knowledge and social issues" (p. 144). With Black male students I am inevitably called to reflect on how multiple and varied forms of power come into play and mediate the nature of our relationships within the classroom. In many ways the cultural power that Black male teachers and Black male students negotiate is ultimately based in "brother status."

I am often oddly positioned in situations where Black male students suggestively ask for favors. These favors are real or imagined. They either are sincere attempts at some form of accommodation or a test of my "brother status." They may approach me by saying, "Say Bryant, brotha I was wondering if … " The request is made in relation to an extension on an assignment, a special consideration for absences or a host of other "favors." In these instances I know that they are capitalizing on my "brother-teacher" status – and maybe my graduate student status as a means of getting what they want. Often they transform the generic and standardized "brother" into the ebonetic "brotha" accompanied by a three moved clasped handshake, somehow establishing or suggesting a cultural link. When the consideration is not granted they respond by saying, "Thanks for nothing "brotha!" The emphasis in this phrase is placed on the *brotha*, as if to call attention to, or call into question "brother status."

In many ways I have come to understand that the cultural power that students exert in those instances is ultimately the power to name someone as brother – and thus to claim or disclaim their identity. I am actually aware that my brother status can be achieved through a specified performative response, in this case agreement to the request. It is a variable positionality that is based in a social orientation to the other and which can be revoked or suspended on command.

In some ways I feel that they are testing me, as if my brother status is based in my willingness to give them consideration beyond the constraints of classroom policy, as if a "real brotha" would make concessions. I wonder at what point does being a "real brotha" become just another form of an enabling victimage when sameness is validated and difference is surpressed. Would I victimize myself if I engaged their validated brothering performances? Do they realize that the form of power that I am choosing to practice in the classroom is highly sensitive to our shared racial and cultural ties? I want to create a space where they can practice their voice and way of being, but not silence my own. The classroom becomes a place where we can capitalize on common ties without using them as an ideological noose.

The power dynamic between the Black male teacher and Black male student is situated within cultural performances of Black masculinity that also must be negotiated within the classroom. Black male students inevitably exert what they have come to know as "cultural truths" using these assumptions about Black masculinity to mark difference in the classroom. The truth is based in their enculturated experience, especially if they themselves have been marginalized, or more importantly if they have been valorized for particular performative displays.

The dialectic between culture and power is central to critical social theory in general and critical pedagogy in particular. McLaren (1994) offers three logics that inform the relationship between culture and power:

> First, culture is intimately connected with the structure of social relations within class, gender, and age formations that produce forms of oppression and dependency. Second, culture is analyzed not simply as a way of life, but as a form of production through which different groups in either their dominant or subordinate social relations define and realize their aspirations through unequal relations of power. Third, culture is viewed as a field of struggle in which the production, legitimation, and circulation of particular forms of knowledge and experience are central areas of conflict (p. 180).

The relationship between culture and power is dialectical in that cultural communities assert power over the artifacts and ritualized performances that mark membership and signify difference. Power in this sense is reconfigured as a functional component of cultural maintenance; it asserts the truth of a cultural group. Foucault (1977) suggests that truth within a specific culture is "the ensemble of rules according to which the true and the false are separated and specific effects of power attached to the true" (p. 132). In this study the "truth" I will be exploring is the students' and teachers' construction and experience of a particular Black masculinity, and the "ensemble of rules" that reference the specific performance through which that masculinity is enacted.

Hence, previous encounters and negotiations with other Black men impact the relational orientation that the Black male teacher has with Black male students. Conversely, the cultural performative expectations that Black male students have of other Black males are placed against their expectations of the Black male teacher. Experiences in the classroom are mediated by forms of knowledge that speak to and against lived cultural experiences and a specified academic discourse. When the Black male teacher asserts the varying forms of "power" that are traditionally granted to the teacher, it is enacted in contradistinction to the cultural power that is negotiated within the community of Black men. Hence, the Black male teacher is often depicted as "The Man," the patriarchal White man who oppresses Black male students in the classroom. Inevitably, "The Man" and "Big Brother" are one in the same.

I end this final reflection where I began, standing in front of my class reflecting on my orientation to my Black male students. In exploring the notion of "brother" I realize that our relationship as Black men is mediated by a wide variety of variables. These variables are grounded in shifting performative criteria of Black male identity. First, I come to understand that the conflicted theorizing on Black masculinity is not just an intellectual activity, it is rooted in the lived performative displays of Black men. The phallocentric and heterosexist bias that serves as a measuring stick of Black masculinity comes to play regularly in my classes in the form of personal and pedagogical challenge.

Second, I come to understand that *pedagogy is personal* and that the Black male teacher and the Black male student do not operate in a cultural void; the classroom is not a cultural void. I agree with hooks (1994b) that there is no "even emotional ground we stand on that enables us to treat everyone equally, dispassionately" (p. 198). The racial and cultural affinity that I have with my Black male students demands a recognition of worth. This may be a means for me to recuperate from my own lived experience as a Black male student in the White university. It also reflects my desire to help them succeed. Their orientation to me is going to be refracted through whatever lens they use to see other Black men and the accompanying ideology that governs their behavior. Within the classroom we must negotiate the difference between where we meet and where we diverge. We must negotiate the difference between what it means to be a brother and what it means to be other. To do this, we must acknowledge the "other" in br(other).

Third, I know that I enter our relationship with a cultural dialect. I address my Black male students periodically as "brotha." I call upon them, often forcing them to talk, to engage. I ask them their opinions – as a form of pedagogy, as a form of respect. I use our common racial and cultural heritage as a point of entry to the curriculum. I desire to be their cultural Big Brother, their Brother-mentor-teacher-friend. Yet, I know that as the teacher, the accompanying power deferential may stand in the presence of how we negotiate those roles. At the same time, I realize that they wield a cultural power that in some ways is more potent than any referent or legitimate power that I might have as the teacher.

The approval or disapproval of me as a brother by my Black male students is intricately interwoven in my identity as a Black man. Whether or not I choose to engage the cultural performance descriptions that historically dictate the lives of Black men, the narrative has been written into my lifescript. The tensions that exist between my Black gay performative masculinity and what can be referred to as a "Black normative masculinity" is still sensitive to cultural scrutiny. I address their cultural critique in ways that affirm my own performative displays. Yet, the resonant trace of their critique impacts my sense of self and my performative role as the teacher. Their positionality is one that I can painfully rebuke, but I cannot easily dismiss it. It is interwoven into the larger cultural fabric of a community that I claim and embrace.

Fourth, standing in class supervising an engagement that deals with cultural stereotypes, I realize that as a Black male teacher with Black male students, we are all stereotypes. We are "standardized conceptions or images invested with special meaning and held in common by members of a [specified] group" (Stewart and Logan, 1993, p. 86). Perhaps we are not stereotypes, with that delimiting possibility, but archetypes in which we represent reoccuring patterns of Black masculinity. As I draw references between my biological brothers and my cultural brothers, I realize that I am drawing on character types that I both celebrate and critique within my family as well as the larger Black cultural community.

In Boyd and Allen's (1996) representational definition of "brotherman" they suggest that when Black men encounter each other a "bloodline is invoked, a gender proclaimed" (p. xxi). When Black men encounter each other in the classroom these racial and gendered variables intervene in the process of teaching and learning. Consequently, to be a "brother" in the classroom is to realize that border identities *always* bleed. A shared race and culture reconfigures the line that seemingly divides our roles as teachers and students. The confluence of these multiple variables makes the classroom a baptismal of truth and knowledge about self and other, and self as other.

References

Bell, R.A., and Daly, J.A. (1984) The affinity-seeking function of communication. *Communication Monographs*, 49, 91–115.

Blackwell, J.E. (1989) Mentoring: An action strategy for increasing minority faculty. *Academe*, 75 (5), 8–14.

Bloom, H. (1987) *George Orwell's 1984: Modern Critical Interpretations*, Chelsea House Publications, New York.

Boyd, H., and Allen, R.L. (eds) (1996) *Brotherman: The Odyssey of Black Men in America – An Anthology*, Ballantine Books, New York.

Butler, J. (1990) Performative acts and gender constitution: An essay in phenomenology and feminist theory, in *Performing Feminism*, (ed. S. Case) Johns Hopkins University Press, Baltimore, MD, pp. 270–282.

Daly, R.A., and Kreiser, P.O. (1992) Affinity in the classroom, in *Power in the Classroom: Communication, Control, and Concern*, (eds V.R. Richmond and J.C. McCroskey), Lawrence Erlbaum, Mahwah, NJ.

Darder, A. (1991) *Culture and Power in the Classroom: A Critical Foundation for Bicultural Education*, Bergin and Garvey, New York.

Devito, J.A. (1992) *The Interpersonal Communication Book*, Harper Collins, New York.

Ellison, R. (1947) *Invisible Man*, Vintage Books, New York.

Foucault, M. (1977) *Power/Knowledge: Selected Interviews and Other Writings*, Pantheon Books, New York.

Greer, N. (1993) A phenomenological explication of mentoring relationships involving African American students. Dissertation. Southern Illinois University at Carbondale.

hooks, b. (1992) Reconstructing black masculinity, in *Black Looks: Race and Representation*, (ed. b. hooks), South End Press, Boston, MA, pp. 87–113.

hooks, b. (1994a) *Outlaw Culture: Resisting Representations*, Routledge, New York.

hooks, b. (1994b) *Teaching to Transgress: Education as the Practice of Freedom*, Routledge, New York.

Karamcheti, I. (1995) Caliban in the classroom, in *Pedagogy: The Question of Impersonation*, (ed. J. Gallop), Indiana University Press, Bloomington, pp. 138–146.

McCroskey, J.C., and McCroskey, L.L. (1986) The affinity-seeking of classroom teachers. *Communication Research Reports*, 3, 158–167.

McLaren, P. (1993) *Schooling as a Ritual Performance: Towards a Political Economy of Educational Symbols and Gestures*, Routledge, New York.

McLaren, P. (1994) Life in schools: An introduction to critical pedagogy in the foundations of education. Longman, New York.

Mncwabe, M.P. (1988) *Teacher Neutrality and Education in Crisis: The Black Teacher's Dilemma in South Africa*, Skotaville Publishers, Johannesburg.

Orwell, G. (1949) *Nineteen Eighty-Four, A Novel*, Harcourt and Brace, New York.

Ramiréz, M., and Castañeda, A. (1974). *Cultural Democracy, Bicognitive Development and Education*, Academic Press, New York.

Rich, A. (1986) If not with others, how? In *Blood, Bread, and Poetry*, in *New World of Literature*, 2nd edn, (eds J. Beaty and J.P. Hunter), W.W. Norton & Company, New York, pp. 786–791.

Richmond, V.R., and McCroskey, J.C. (1992) (eds) *Power in the Classroom: Communication, Control, and Concern*, Lawrence Erlbaum, Mahwah, NJ.

Ricoeur, P. (1992) *Oneself as Another*, (trans. K. Blamey), University of Chicago Press, Chicago.

Shor, I. (1992) *Empowering Education*, Chicago, University of Chicago Press.

Stewart, J., and Logan, C. (1993) *Together: Communicating Interpersonally*, McGraw-Hill, New York.

Tarpley, N. (ed.) (1995) *Testimony: Young African-American on Self-Discovery and Black Identity*, Beacon Press, Boston, MA.

Tolhuizen, J.H. (1989) Affinity-seeking in developing relationships. *Communication Reports*, 2, 83–91.

Tucker, R.C. (1983) Does big brother really exist?, in *1984 Revisited: Totalitarianism in our Century*, (ed. I. Howe), Harper and Row, New York, pp. 89–102.

West, C. (1994) *Race Matters*, Vintage Books, New York.

22

When Frankness Goes Funky
Afro-Proxemics Meets Western Polemics at the Border of the Suburb

Jim Perkinson

we be young   virile   sweaty with passions
you gotta

    understand to experience

and tonight we don't care or give a damn
why our parents don't seem to understand

why sweat   be friend of ours
and together we gots to get real real
                          friendly
Regie Gibson (2001)

This chapter will probe the crossover phenomena represented by the popularity of hip-hop culture among white suburban youth to pose a challenge about cultural encounter in the new millennium. That rap rhyme, b-boy and girl rhythm, "phat" beats, and "dope" tags on urban walls have gone global and virtual in the past 20 years offers a living text of profound cross cultural communication. What is it that communicates? Why the white fascination with black "funk," enabling a "paralinguistic conquest" of the suburb by the city that at the same time constitutes the most profoundly paradoxical proxemics of our times. Here the black body begins to "possess" white subjectivity in the form of tone and gesture, rhythmic cadence of speech and kinesic mode of movement, in a commodified form of appropriation that ironically reinforces rather than overcomes suburban/ghetto distance in actual social congress, economic exchange, or intellectual understanding. The chapter will explore these racialized pulses of attraction and repudiation that operate below the level of

The Handbook of Critical Intercultural Communication, edited by Thomas K. Nakayama and Rona Tamiko Halualani. © 2010 Blackwell Publishing Ltd.

conscious intentionality to offer commentary on the most labyrinthine communication conundrum of the modern era. Race remains in our time the great huge unspoken that ever defies all of the speaking it generates even as it ever "morphs" into new forms of communicative knottiness and power slippages. The goal of the work is to expose the continuing asymmetries of power and access that race has always organized and policed historically while exhibiting the complexities and complicities of the nonverbal exchanges in this hierarchical ordering of social interaction.

Introduction

The piece is offered under the rubric of intercultural communication as a study in paradox. Clearly the kinesics and proxemics, the chronemics and paralanguage, encoding "ghetto" struggle and black pleasure, are potent. The suburb is indeed "penetrated," in the words of Jon Michael Spencer, by a black cultural code that simultaneously excites imitation and reinforces segregation (Spencer, 1995, pp. 136, 142, 145, 149). In asking the question (above) "what communicates?" the intimation is that hip-hop stages a certain kind of encounter. Yet it is a strange meeting. The argument pursued here will exhibit something other than "understanding." The efflorescence of the culture is not through heightened engagement, but through an intensification of experience whose intention in the suburb is hybrid: gaining access to "black" forms of power while remaining comfortable in white middle class privilege and protection. The traffic here is two-way, but not symmetrical. *Economics* (in the quite limited sense of large incomes for a few mega-stars) and *respect* (quite widely disseminated and enjoyed)[1] flow from the white suburb to the black inner city; while *black intensity* in modes at once *erotic* and *militant* are sought and claimed (though largely by way of posturing) by white youth, even as corporate profits swell coffers largely Anglo and elite. Certainly break-dance arenas, DJ battles, ciphers and slam contests, and some tag teams do afford a cross-racial mixing that does involve mutual exchange. But most of the communication in question in American (and now global) youth culture is digital rather than corporeal, a matter of commodified sound and video-taped image, not actual intermixture under conditions of shared vulnerability and risk. In what follows, the question of what communicates from black to white (black appropriation of white substance is a different question) will focus on both history and the body, divining meaning below the level of express intentionality or conscious reception. Under the indices of "frankness" and "funk," the hip-hop body will be read as an artifact of the culture at large, condensing an overdetermined sign of the racial congress of the country. In its eloquence of gesture and velocity of tongue and base-beat repeat of the hardness and heat of the street, this is a sign that admits of no easy comprehension or simple resolution for the continued operation of the supremacy wreaking havoc across the globe. It rather enjoins self-confrontation and hard work in decoding the history of racialized violence sedimented in all of our forms of embodiment and a slowly assembled savvy in groping towards a different kind of future.

It is also important to say that my interest in this chapter is not definitive inter-pretation, as much as suggestive "sounding." "Sounding out" reality is both a Nietzschean methodology for exposing "idols" and an African American form of vernacular virtuosity (Nietzsche, 1990, pp. 31–32; Baker, 1993, pp. 46, 48). Somewhat analogously to the way seismographers use sonar to probe physical mor-phology or search for oil, black culture has often projected rhythm as a medium for exploration of community identity and individual singularity. What is articulated here is in some sense a reflection of that methodology – both the result of my own experience of having been so probed and of learning to use language to pursue a similar effect in my own writing.[2] So I offer here a kind of "sonic reading" – of my own body, of other bodies in the country, of black bodies on streets, in clubs, in the inner cities of Detroit and Chicago, where I have lived and worked, played and partied, for more than two decades, but also of white bodies in suburbs, and white bodies in proximity to black bodies in clubs and on basketball courts, in malls and offices, in schools.

The probe is a membrane of rhythm, articulated in popular culture idiom, through TV and theater, radio and arena, club and court, around the country – a sonority of polyphony, crafted in anonymity in the city, articulating pathos and anger, bombast and pleasure, elaborated communally, pirated commercially, pen-etrating the farthest corners of the culture at large, with a frequency like a stealth bomber, dropping grenades of vitality and protest, lighting up the night with color and defiance. Its bomb is the body "on" sound – not just the body in the medium of movement, but in the community of "funk" – the form it takes and the signifi-cance it signals when it gets sweaty with others getting sweaty, on a mission of motion, in fear and fascination, probing, collectively and "conjuristically," if I can put it that way, the density of existential absurdity in postindustrial America. As pop culture critic Nelson George (1999) has said of the "elemental nihilism" found in "the most controversial crack-era hip-hop that wasn't concocted by the rappers" but rather reflected "the mentality and fears of young Americans of every color and class living an exhausting, edgy existence, in and out of big cities": this is an absurd-ity that does not disappear, because its social conditions have not disappeared and because, "deep in the American soul, it speaks to us and we like the sound of its voice" (George, 1999, p. 49). So I confess both drive and delirium in this project: a two-decade-long affair of love and hate with the opacity of American history, experienced in the city, undulating with meaning like a renegade "code of the real" under the trickster surface of Americanized skin-color.

The Frankness

The title of the piece fronts "frankness" as a central figure of American history. This is in specific reference to the mid-1960s alteration in the public face of racialized blackness that leapt – full-blown with weapons drawn, like some postmodern Athena – straight from the head of the southern freedom struggle of the late-1950s and early-1960s. The Civil Rights movement of that time and place had given profound political expression to the collective self-exorcism begun by the black community in its 1955 bus boycott in Montgomery, Alabama, that also began a revelation of America to America, a kind of return of the repressed inside the mirror of the Same (Bloom, 1987, pp. 46–66). The clamor of the movement up through its Voting Rights success of 1965 was for inclusion; its vision, integration; the victory realized emblematically by the boycott, an assertion of black public agency, unbowed and laughing on black porches, before white-sheeted red-necks, riding through "negro" neighborhoods, trying to re-project the demon of terror back inside the southern black body as a primary lever of supremacist control. The defiance dared on the porches halted the march after only a few blocks. The movement that resulted, in its decade-long deliverance, left black progeny forever changed and Jim Crow dismantled. In response, the national mirror only managed to reflect a more determined narcissism. White gain – in whatever color it came – remained the reigning game.

Black Power, on the other hand, stepping into the public space opened by civil rights struggle in 1966, consolidated the profile, looked into the mirror and looked back at what looked out without looking away.[3] Indeed, it looked deeper – naïve, vitriolic, patriarchal, homophobic – but clear (as in fact, King was also becoming clear) that the entire structure of the country, from the factory to the White House, from the mud of the Mississippi to the delta of the Mekong, was at issue, and not just a lunch counter or bus seat. It cracked the mirror with a definitive line of difference – a clenched fist, a thunder-cloud 'fro, and a body like a panther, unrepentant, proud, loud, beautiful, serving food to hungry kids and alternative histories to hungry minds, demanding a new world.[4] This was the moment race became frank in America – a public performance of "black" difference from white dominance, that was unapologetically eloquent in its defiance and alterity. Of course, the reaction was state repression; liberal compassion disgorged its fascism; the church went home to the suburb; the school and the municipality bought off the braggadocio, the police killed or jailed whatever remained un-buyable (Omi and Winant, 1994, pp. 113–136). And, music one more time[5] became the medium of black refuge and retooling as real political power and economic leverage retreated north of Eight Mile Road in Detroit and around the country from the late-1960s, onward.

It is no mystery that the 1970s birthed a new genre – syncopated like a machine-gun flow in its lyric mode, innovative in its scratch-code and re-loading of old technology with a new virtuosity of dexterity, miming the factory in a robotic body, defying gravity in the levity of a head-spinning boogie, tagging turf with the mirth and self-assertion of youth, claiming pride of birth-place in the struggle's rubble.[6] Despite being impoverished in its Old School genesis, party-happy in its early vision, cynical and criminal-stupid in New School collisions with crack and collateral damage, gangsta-hyped and booty-dumb in its 1990s version, bought-off in the commercial and chump-chunked in the contract-game, hip-hop, arguably, became the new sign of the continuing grind for freedom and justice. Though not always conscious of its possibility or its responsibility, hip-hop's creativity carries the charge of the history of resistance. It continues the legacy of the irrepressibility. Within its multiple manners, "reality" or "gangsta" rap could be said to be the moment when black power itself goes frank, in unmasking the entire country as predatory. Although with different levels of ironic self-reference and sardonic poignancy, the OG (Original Gangsta)-romance spits out a rendition of the entire nation as gang-banging in history and fantasy. Not merely Brando and Dean in filmic fame, but the real historical profile of the polity – from native genocide to African slave trade, from foreign policy bellicosity to prison-industry brutality – reveals a gangland glam operating with impunity behind the Invisible Hand of the business clan, eviscerating inner city and Third World country alike in its rapacious drive to accumulate. Gangsta rap in the mouth of a Tupac Shakur – before he became martyr to his own code – gives a complex report of the fact (Dyson, 2001, pp. 157, 208, 228). Not only the ghetto but the grotto of imperial decision-making in Washington and transnational fortune-raking on Wall Street are gangsta on the final balance sheet.

The Funk

Finally, I am arguing also that the frankness is not merely or even primarily straight up communication about race, but begins to engender a complex crossover of beat and gesture, attitude, and posture, whose future remains as undetermined in disclosure as its profile is stereotypic in dismissal by the dominant culture. The frankness goes funky in a manner underground and ineluctable for the country, when "the krunk"[7] rides a beat straight out of the Bronx and into the feet – and heart – of America's teenagers. Funk[8] is the living ferment of the claim here: an afroferocity and fecundity of spirituality; indeed, a conjuration of divinity; incarnating, in the communal body gathered in ceremony, as *perspiration:* summoned from the below, on a spirit-pole, historically in a ritual garden in Haiti or Brazil, now in the strobe-light effect of a club in Detroit or Miami, Queens or Compton, a shamanic intensification, a constructed crossroads,[9] where past and future, death and life, sex and loss, meet, under a rhythm, cut with a beat, beggared with a low frequency probe of base, rhythm-upon-rhythm, beat-on-beat, piled up, birthing melodic froth, driving the pelvis to remember, lathering the hearer in dread or laughter, grabbing the feet, grabbing the thigh, arcing the back … until the sweat comes. The funk – literally the sweat, the odor, the excreta of sex or religion, or of unwashed poverty, or of the terror of a midnight knock on the door in a Georgia alight with cross-burning perdition – is an alternative and active "text" for knowing compared to the Western privileging of "the written" as definitive for epistemology. Funk! itself a modality of divinity, a medium of meeting, a demand for reciprocation, never commodified on MTV, though representable there as sheen, as glisten. Funk! as funk-smell, as a skin lived in intimate communion with other skin, as lubrication climbing towards climax with unction, bearing its work on its surface, in its hair, exuding its orifices as already occupied by the god-become-the-devil, Saturday-night-secretion-in-Sunday-morning-summons, heaven-and-hell in cross-dressing embrace, spirit really become matter. Funk! as the body in motion, under duress of fear and pleasure, in drench of ecstasy or terror, in labor that is not only work or shaking that is not merely mimesis.

Listen for a moment to W.E.B. Du Bois from the beginning of the twentieth-century, but paradigmatically not different than the slave quarters a century before or the hip-hop club of today:

> It was out in the country, far from my foster home, on a dark Sunday night. The road wandered from our rambling log-house up the stormy bed of a creek, past wheat and corn until we could hear dimly across the fields a rhythmic cadence of song – soft, thrilling, powerful, that swelled and died sorrowfully in our ears. I was a country school-teacher then, fresh from the East, and had never seen a Southern Negro revival ... And so most striking to me as I approached the village and the little plain church perched aloft, was the air of intense excitement that possessed that mass of black folk. A sort of suppressed terror hung in the air and seemed to seize us, – a pythian madness, a demonic possession, that lent terrible reality to song and word. The black and massive form of the preacher swayed and quivered as the words crowded to his lips and flew at us in singular eloquence ... the people moaned and fluttered ... the gaunt-cheeked brown woman next to me suddenly leaped into the air and shrieked like a lost soul ... round about came wail and groan and outcry, and a scene of human passion such as I had never conceived before (Du Bois, 1961, pp. 140–141).

Funk is not merely "of," but "between," bodies. It is climate and medium – specifically, mediation and effect of the spirit made flesh. That spirit admits of a "making" is African in genesis (Murphy, 1994, pp. 6–7). Not exclusively; not exhaustively. Africa is both geography *and* metaphor. It is also, in genetic and anthropological claim alike, the ultimate "home from which," the ancestor of us all. But Africa is also the home of a ritualized "work-up" of "the ghost" into grammar. "Possession," "occupation" of a body by an energy from elsewhere – whether erupting from within or irrupting from without is a question begging Western notions of an individualized body that is itself a mere ideology and not a fact[10] – "animation" of a corpus by a compulsion of motion, articulated in a kinesics of proliferation, is "Africa" in one of its gifts to the world (Reed, 1983, p. xi; Bynum, 1999, pp. 81–84, 87–88, 92–100). Just ask the Frenchman watching Alvin Ailey or the white girl watching Lauryn Hill. Possession is also, however, both anciently and lately, simply the condition of being human, indeed, of modern and postmodern "human being" alike – the invasion of organic muscle by engineered chemical, of the naked body by the cyborg machine, of desire by the green of capital and adver-tising, of the eye by an entire menagerie of fabricated need, and the brain by ideas from Kellogg's. Possession is the condition of all of us (Kroker, 1992, pp. 2–3). It is "primitive" only in the mistake of a projection – a colonizer afraid of the mirror.

However, possession crafted communally into artistry and relativity is another thing.[11] Genealogically in this country, the " 'getting' down ugly" work-up of terror into beauty – now encountered existentially in gospel, in the blues, in jazz, in hip-hop – was a historical product of black spiritual alchemy under the whip and shackle of slavery (Long, 1986, pp. 123–125, 165, 178, 196; Gilroy, 1993, pp. 37, 77, 217). Possession in the bush arbor at night or on the picnic grounds on Sunday afternoon in 1832 was jujitsu without a guru, a deflection of the dread, a re-possession, in ecstatic mime, of the great crime – the rape, the hanging, the burning – in a body now syncopated into many. This was what Du Bois realized in his backwoods visit. Possession was communalization of the terror that cannot be contained in just one, a surfeit of energy, a dismembering explosion and re-assemblage of the psyche under a multiple regime of identity, given theatricalization for the sake of survival. Here, in black church ritual, Jesus and the Devil became flesh together[12] in a great carnival of "knowing," a probing, in every capillary of motion, in spasm and groaning, the inner wave, the tsunami of violence visited on the community without reason or announcement, in an episteme of improvisation that actually amplified and re-distributed the energies of calamity across a vast metonymy of personality. Pain and pleasure, abreaction and overcoming, wounding and healing were emblematized together in the collectively improvised body,[13] offering a "thick" gestalt for re-negotiating identity and agony. Not least among the archetypes enlivened in the exchange, transvaluing Death into Life across a complex code of mutation, was Eros. Numerous scholars of these arts of resistance – Toni Morrison and Amiri Baraka, Paul Gilroy and bell hooks among them – have remarked the phenomenon.[14] Black ritual dramaturgy reworked fear into furor and pleasure, canalized murder into an intimacy of succor, repossessed the collective possession of the community, in modes at once picaresque and bathetic, ironically sharp and grotesquely blunt. Funk, in such a context, was then (and remains now) the evidence of having treated, bodily, with such a transforming numinosity.

Also it is critical to recognize, in such an experience, that there is no capacity for "prevenient grace," for knowing, before embodiment, the character of the energy to be channeled. In such a cultural ethic, under such conditions, the body *is* the means of knowing the Force that animates, and indeed, of knowing oneself – inside the community that interprets and protects.[15] Even though, from outside, such a ritual "acculturation" of the incursions of terror can be evaluated in opposite ways: as a reproduction of the very fear that enslaves, in the body that remembers; or as its transfiguration, making the demon yield life in spite of itself. But funk, in any case, references a communal episteme, an articulation of an entire world in the void between the undulating surfaces of skin, a charging up of the air itself with intimations of memory and visitation, embodying excess as a mode of divination. In the mix, the energy of the terror is broken apart and distributed like a host, made to animate an entire puppet theater of desire and repulsion, engulfed in a code of time[16] and assembled like an ensemble of haints: there, not there, present "between." This is ancestry in the key of mimesis, of somatic syntax, of odor and sheen, grounded in a recognized vocabulary of dance and scream. The communal "text" licenses both pain and pleasure, hosts both God and the Devil, and cannot yield discernment *a priori*. The meaning is made and apprehended "in process," in a ritual proxemics of synchronized muscle, a syncopated chronemics of the "lower bodily strata," an improvisational augury of possibility in so slight a declivity as a faint, a head cock, a pop and lock, performed on the damage of existence! The entire sensorium is made a corporeal palette for portrayal – and probe – of the hardness of reality.

The Polemic

Strangely, this black "work up" of the terroristic spirit of modernity is also one of the "prison-houses"[17] the European peasant body – celebrated by Bakhtin in its pre-modern "Feast of Fools" freedom and scatology[18] – was forced into, when the West went white and "American" in its historical migration. And here race complicates every possible meaning.

Richard Dyer has traced the way the United States, historically, has parsed its paradigm of embodiment along the divide of color, especially in late-nineteenth and early-twentieth century disciplines of industry and scriptings of citizenry (Dyer, 1988, pp. 55–58). In filmic exhibitions of lived social relations (the early twentieth-century classic, *Jezebel*, in this instance), whiteness becomes coterminus with a "talking head" representation – everywhere speaking, nowhere listening, "contained" in a vaunted rationality, floating above the fray of the economy, and indeed above its own body. Blackness, on the other hand, in projections illusory and harsh, enforced by rope in the south and wallet in the north, is made the new topography of emotion and expression (for both races), depicted (and "pornographically" enjoyed by whites[19]) as dancing in buffoonery, grinning in eclipse of pain, writhing, like a symptom of the social dismemberment it is made to refract. The result is a kind of white somatic ventriloquism – a profound economy of hysteria inside the interdictions of race that historically has required black ardor to go bail for white experience.

Extremes of both pain and pleasure found increasingly narrowed registers of acceptable expression in middle class social order, as tacitly elaborated "rules" of white propriety gained social traction and colonized the white body (Dyer, 1988, pp. 56, 58; cf. also, Elias, 1978, pp. 140, 257; 1983, p. 243). Certainly this proscriptive occupation of the white body selected quite differently for class and gender positioning; Marx had already in the nineteenth century vividly pilloried factory discipline as a "Frankenstein" operation, reorganizing the working body into a fraction of itself – a single monstrous appendage repeating the same motion hundreds of times a day, while the rest of the flesh atrophied (or drank itself to death in the bar after hours) (Marx, 1967, p. 360). Whether hand or head – or in female domestication, a smiling face or a swooning limpness – physical whiteness was made subject to social seemliness and industrial order. A separation of brain from brawn was enforced across an entire culture-scape of meaning and the emergent nation, living a Protestant truncation of middle-class expression and a capitalist de-capitation of industrial effort, alienated its intimate energies into commodity fetishes inside the bourgeois gate, while sublimating its wilder animations onto communities of labor outside, darkened in various fantasies of race and terror.

This peculiar racial bifurcation was part and parcel of Western processes of sub-jectification. The vaunted "individuality" that emerges out of the growing rejec-tion of soil and community in early modern Europe – and the grotesque body of Bakhtin which was its corporeal artifact – was deeply "colored" by white Western projections of "black" physicality and subhumanity all across the European theat-ers of colonization.[20] "Enlightenment" did not only refer to the mind. The "modern bourgeois individual" that was finally made to stand on the horizon of the entire Western world as an impossible[21] iconography of order and rights, was normed in hollowed gesture and tightly buttoned dress, corporealized in a terror of odor or spilled "excess." It was a body made to reflect its genesis in social spaces never volatilized in improvisational dance (indeed, only stoically reinforced in the "scrip-torium" of the waltz), never theatricalized in antiphonal modalities of possession or multiplied in a kinesics of mimetic humor. It was rather the Body-Contained – quintessence of the enshrinement of the visual as the modern hegemony of knowl-edge, a body haunted by the internalized eye of discipline, taken in like a Foucaultian panopticon, institutionalized first in European court and salon as Norbert Elias has tracked, then racialized in its inner and outer gaze as David Roediger has traced in relationship to American industrialization and bourgeois urbanization, possessing entire classes and countries, incessantly and nearly unconsciously watching every least move, every nuance of gesture, policing the palavers of genitalia and aggres-sion alike, monitoring, finally, in the late twentieth-century, both the mall and the mansion (Foucault, 1979, pp. 200–205; 1980, pp. 92–100; Elias, 1978, pp. 140, 235, 257; 1982, pp. 238-243; 1983, pp. 35, 55, 243; Roediger, 1991, pp. 14, 21, 60, 151). Forged in a strait-jacket of skin and propriety, bourgeois in taste for mediocrity and similarity, heterosexual in relationality and exchange of fluids, male in power and white in culture – this modern hegemonic body is precisely *not* the body of funk. But neither is it, arguably, continuing its reign uncontested in post-modernity.

The Border

Hip-hop has emerged out of the postindustrial American city as a crossover medium vastly more potent than any other cultural influence that has emerged from the African American community yet in history. Under its protocols, black forms of gesture and posture, black modes of ritualizing space and articulating time, black codes of greeting and verifying or disavowing recognition, have taken over white adolescent behavior.[22] While adaptation of the ever-shifting argot of the street is certainly one way white youth appropriate black style, the argument here is that the deeper levels of communication take place inside the body, in scriptings of corpo-real movement that are much less accessible to conscious intention or univocal interpretation. Appropriation of the black body – observable in as subtle a motion as a stiff-necked head bob signaling proud defiance by both male and female white kids, for instance – is now simply a fact of popular culture (and is not limited only to adolescence, but percolates up through middle-aged populations as well, as can be observed in the "high-five" congratulatory-gesture typically following a good shot on any golf course in the country).

Here intercultural communication has gone *intra*-cultural in a peculiar mode of internalization and possession – taken in from without in studied imitation, but also, unleashed from within in a corporeal elaboration of rhythm that begins in inchoate depths and finds satisfaction in tentatively offered motion. As indicated earlier – this is a body "on" sound, in motion, giving flesh to beat, articulating meaning from the inside-out. But the beat here is not merely entertainment. It carries a code of survival struggle. In black negotiations of history as agony, it has functioned as a form of augury, a probe of the hardness of American constraint on black existence that has conscripted that hardness into service as an internal code of attitude.[23] That attitude has been explored in a sonic vocabulary of percussion,[24] ramified in communal celebrations that push participants to deepen their familiarity with reality by exploring and using their body as a tool of knowing and a "text" of representing. Funk is simply the "oil" of participation, the evidence of having given oneself over to such communal work, a mode of somatic "confession."

What happens when the confession is adopted by a white suburban body, subject to the history of containment and propriety outlined above, schooled in modesty, coiffured in safety, living a Disney-fantasy of delight and triviality in a life-world constructed from the trasnationalized piracy of other peoples' goods and labor? Certainly erotics is one of the body-codes at work – a probe of white desire by a frank aspiration to "get it on." In one sense, this is merely an unapologetic "outing" of the capitalist occulting of desire in which sex is pervasively ramified as the subtext of the market, while middle-class etiquette and imagery dissembles the logic (Spencer, 1991, p. 5). Modern Western culture is sexualized through-and-through in the in-satiety of an advertised arousal, attached, one way or another, to almost every commodity marketed.[25] Hip-hop simply speaks, unapologetically and frankly, straight from the capitalist groin, exactly what everyone else is fantasizing and hiding.

At another level, hip-hop is also the frank conjuration of the violence of the country – also capitalist in character, even as, post-World War II, it has become imperial in vision and practice. Here the deeply gendered subtext of American politics finds profoundly paradoxical representation. At the beginning of the invasion of Iraq, George W. Bush epitomized the imperative of the masculine archetype whose appeal had surreptitiously won him the Presidency: "for a long time our culture has said, 'if it feels good, do it;' now America is embracing a new ethic and a new creed: 'let's roll.'" Norbert Elias' genealogy of the "civilized body" referenced above has underscored the way the aggressive orientation of the older warrior classes of Europe was gradually contained and tamed in the courtly protocols of a modernizing social order (Elias, 1982, pp. 238–243). The bourgeois body profiled in the previous section is the result. The undercurrent of testosterone left untapped in middle class pedagogies of masculine expression found release largely in sports or one form or another of abuse (spousal, familial, workaholic, or corporate – often coupled with the use of substance). Neither factory nor office opens a space demanding collective competence in articulating aggression or trans-figuring fear with aplomb and creativity. The kinesics of the corporate world – at either end (office or factory) – is highly structured in an instrumentalized, nonde-monstrative protocol; the proxemics are equally rigidified and "white." And edu-cational institutions for more than a century have routinized the body in a sedentary pedagogy that only imposes itself with greater rigor the higher one aspires for cre-dentialing. In such a context, the promulgation of war realizes a legitimation of male aggression that is at least subliminal and "spectacular"[26] for the culture at large (even while it also becomes actual and awful for many of those farther down the socioeconomic ladder). The hip-hop body, in such a milieu, gives confusing signals and offers contradictory possibilities.

Clearly, in giving somatic texture to a percussive mixture of sounds, hip-hop edges towards a kinesics of conflict and war, a training of motor-memory in a cer-tain belligerence of posture and gesture.[27] This is unquestionably part of its potency for young white male wanna-bes. But the militancy thus given bodily definition in white imitation is so much somatic "bluster and pontification" to the degree its social ecology remains in the white suburb. Certainly it offers ready alchemy for teenage angst and rebellion against parental authority. But the sound begging mimetic expression also encodes bellicosity of another kind. Both racial oppug-nancy and class antipathy resonate within its edginess. This is the case at a much more inchoate and subtextual level than any merely lyrical elaboration would indi-cate.[28] The percussive structure of the aesthetic (evident not only in the music, but in the visual imagery of the graffiti, the digital dexterity of the turntablism, the robotics of the boogie and swipes of the breaking, and the boomboxing or rhyme-spitting of the MC) is not absent its historical genealogy or contemporary inten-tionality (as argued above). The history goes back to West Africa; the intensity is related to the duress of slavery and anti-black supremacy which has been slavery's contemporary social legacy; the contemporary impulse, a protest against the urban dereliction and abandonment resulting from white flight to the suburbs (eliminat-ing jobs and eroding the tax base).[29]

In a white body, the percussive grammar growing out of such a pedigree gener-ally over-weights the actual experience of struggle. Yes, Eminem can gain a modi-cum of black respect in foregrounding his "trailer-trash" pathology and anguish (rather than pretending to some kind of gangsta theme). Underground rappers using the idiom to query the structure of oppression can find a note of authenticity to the degree they put their own bodies at risk in their politics. But absent a share in the jeopardy created by white supremacy, white participation in hip-hop rhythm only continues the transgression. Like a University of Denver student I once had who gave a class presentation on a Poor Righteous Teachers song he liked for its beats without understanding its lyric riposte of all things white (including himself), the result is both rip off and buffoonery. The student gravitated to the song because of its rhythmic potency, but in his comments and the discussion that followed, exhibited no understanding of either the lyrical polemics or the historical *gravitas* of the sound. The result of his discussion was bathetic. The sonic vitality offered a resonant template for experience that was nowhere within his somatic ken. Elias's discussion of the body gives expression to a structure that can help focus the simultaneous fascination and failure and is discussed in the next section.

The Proxemics

In his history of the civilized body, Elias outlines the modern emergence of a particular mode of self-control that intrudes as "discipline" and "boundary," interrupting the relationship between emotional impulse and skeletal or muscular response (Elias, 1978, p. 257; 1983, p. 243). This self-control he notes as "bourgeois morals" or "rational thought." But this history can just as appropriately be denoted as a social genealogy and morphology of violence – in modernity, increasingly the province of a state monopoly – in which the male body is no longer routinized in an economy of feud or war, but of money-acquisition and prestige. In consequence, the explosive force of insecurity and threat now appears as a "continuous uniform pressure … exerted on individual life by the physical violence stored behind the scenes of everyday life, a pressure totally familiar and hardly perceived, conduct and drive economy having been adjusted from earliest youth to this social structure" (Elias, 1982, p. 238). The monopolization of violence by the modern state produces in unarmed men in pacified social spaces, an intertwining of restraint and calculation, reducing danger to an experience of symbolic threat and emotional behavior to moderation. This is in sharp contrast to medieval society in which everyday life was much more subject to sudden reversals of fortune and affect much less stabilized under reflection; in such a context, passion was not interdicted by reflective consideration, but rather deployed in sudden outbursts of combat or indulgence of pleasure, or just as violently subdued in self-renunciation and extreme asceticism (Elias, 1982, p. 239).

However, here hip-hop culture gains illumination as a kind of postmodern correlate of the state in its economizing of violence – an alternative affective economy of masculine force, trained in a social space subject to brutalizing police practices, penetrated continuously by the gratuitous denigrations and violations of white society, in-grained in an immediacy of response that either survives by the sheer velocity and savvy of its repartee or pays in the coin of scar-tissue, incarceration, or violent death. Juxtaposing such an economy of masculinity to white middle class modalities is not a matter of likening black affect to European medieval "peacockery" and readiness to retaliate or perpetrate. Black male habituation is modern through-and-through. Only, in the formation and "schooling" of the relationship between affective impulse and motor-behavior typical of "ghetto" experience, it is not bourgeois "morality" that intrudes, but black history and collective performance. The pressure of violence on everyday life even in black middle class experience is not generally uniform as it is in Elias' description of the "civilized body," but episodic, cataclysmic, and interruptive, in addition to being continual. What is brought to bear "between" affect and action is not merely "rational thought" but "rational sensation," a hyper-attentive register of emotion, elaborated over a long communal history, giving sharp nuance to physical gesture, piercing inference to gaze and posture, and layered significance to the kinesis of memory. It is animated by life-long memorializations of pain in polymorphic economies of rhythm, mobilized in the moment at hand in an improvisational heuristic of entrainment and mimesis. Whatever bodies can be gathered in whatever *fora* – black church or family meal, backyard party or basement posse – the characteristic communicative style will likely "work up" the intrusive episode in a repetitive kinesics of funk.

In contrast white middle class "biting" (imitation) of this form of embodiment generally lacks any capacity to grasp the physical terrors or psychic desperation its artistry encodes. It sees genius and experiences arousal and senses danger in the communication ethic encountered in hip-hop culture, but cannot fathom, by means of its own somatic (im)motility, the absurdity so caricatured and transformed. It may imitate the affect, but until it can decipher the intimate connection between its own formation under pressure of merely background violence (as Elias outlines), and the unprotected and too often foreground experience of the same in black social formation, the imitation will only reinforce misperception. The primary social structure interrelating white male and black male experiences of embodiment is a racialized mediation of violence that has had everything to do historically with suburban affluence and inner city effluence, middle class upward mobility and ghetto poverty.[30] The violence is not entirely definitive of either form of experience, but also never outside the economies shaping the kinesics of each.

Inside the mobius strip of fascination and ignorance that characterizes white male appropriation of black male gesture in hip-hop culture is the convoluted history of race. At work there are both the continuing economic effects of an unpaid slave labor bill of more than US$ 2 trillion and the deep psychic confusions resulting from the history of rape of black women perpetrated by white males on southern plantations. That an uncanny reversal of this economy of rape has been accomplished in the spread of hip-hop "fashion," in which black maleness now "penetrates" white vulnerability, is profoundly evocative and densely significant. Only now the equation involves a double displacement: the violent licentiousness predicated of black males in white fear and fantasy (the reverse image of *actual* white male *practice* in relationship to slave women) becomes the source of a convoluted proxemics. Commodified black male aggression is internalized by white males in an intimacy of appropriation that makes of the crossover idiom a postmodern equivalent of the possession cult. Although interestingly, here it is the white male body that invites "penetration" by black maleness! At the same time, the historic white terror projected onto actual black male bodies, when encountered "up close and personal," continues its social traction in maintaining and policing the distance between suburb and city. Everything from employment practices to arrest priorities, real estate manipulations of the housing market to remedial tracking in educational institutions, profiling in the mall and gating in the community,[31] conspires inchoately but really to reinforce the difference so that it continues to make a difference.

In a word, whites may well choose to sweat under the strobe light and grimace like *Funkdoobiest* in a search for erotic "bombastics" capable of conferring virility on an otherwise compromised masculinity. However, the kinesics are empty of ancestry and the funk not exactly a modality of God. The frankness remains unfaced and the proxemics, however closely the bodies may wriggle, a cipher of continuing terror, not its undoing. The distance between white and black is unbridged.

Notes

1 So much so, Harvard sociologist Orlando Patterson can lament that black males now boast the highest levels of self-esteem of any ethnic group while also giving evidence of the highest rates of dropping out of school (Patterson, 2006, p. 26).

2 Cf. my two books working out this methodology in different interdisciplinary frameworks Perkinson 2004, 2005.

3 Omi and Winant describe it as the moment of emerge of a paradigm shift in race relations (Omi and Winant, 1994, pp. 95–96).

4 Cf. James Cone's characterization of the difference in the public profiles and polemical tactics of Martin King and Malcolm X in his book, *Martin and Malcolm and America: A Dream or a Nightmare* (Cone, 1991, pp. 304–305, 310–311).

5 Cf. the way African American beat poet Robert Kaufman speaks of the earlier genre of jazz (Kaufman, 1961, pp. 225–228).

6 Tricia Rose details and analyses the basic elements of hip-hop in her classic work *Black Noise: Rap Music and Black Culture in Contemporary America* (Rose, 1994, pp. 38–39).

7 Krunk (also "crunk") references an emphasis in hip-hop culture on the "hype," "fun," and "excitement" especially associated with party-time and "booty-rap" (lyrics and beats oriented towards celebrating/exploiting erotic encounter).

8 Robert Farris Thompson traces the derivation of the term in his art-historical work, *Flash of the Spirit: African and Afro-American Art and Philosophy* as referencing strong body odor attendant, in Bakongo culture, on the exertion necessary to achieve integrity in art and life-aims (Thompson, 1983, pp. 104–105).

9 Again, Thompson gives the genealogy of the complex Afro-diasporic worldview behind the term (Thompson, 1983, p. 109).

10 Cf. for instance, Arthur Kroker's *The Possessed Individual: Technology and the French Postmodern*, exhibiting, among other things, postmodern subjectivity as a kind of "possession effect" of information technologies (Kroker, 1992, pp. 1–3, 21, 69).

11 Cf. A. David Napier's *Foreign Bodies: Performance, Art, and Symbolic Anthropology* for a wide-ranging and provocative re-evaluation of trance and dissociation as perhaps necessary counter-parts to "self-consciousness" in human maturation (Napier, 1992, pp. 160, 198).

12 While this might seem a bit of hyperbole, the idea of hosting and working through contradictory spiritual and ethical impulses is characteristic of possession cult activities that, again and again, historically, have relativized irresistibly incursive forces that violate the community by internalizing them in the cult and making them yield meaning and beauty in spite of themselves (McCarthy Brown, 1984, pp. 197–199; Long, 1986, p. 165; Kramer, 1993, pp. 127–128, 131–132). Cf. Michel Mafesoli's *The Shadow of*

Dionysius: A Contribution to the Sociology of Orgy for an attempt to theorize the ineluctable demands of contradictoriness in broadly sociological terms that also translate into a certain necessity in wedding ideas like "prostitution" and "deity" (Mafesoli, 1993, pp. xxv, 4–5, 11, 35, 41, 50–51).

13 Cf. the work of Amanda Porterfield on black preaching as a combination of shamanic therapy and prophetic challenge and Theophus Smith's adaptation of her work to argue that black appropriation of the bible generally amounts to a form of "collective shamanism" (Porterfield, 1987, pp. 728–729; Smith, 1994, pp. 384–385). Cf. also my own work building on Smith arguing that black ways of re-working "blackness" itself is similarly shamanistic (Perkinson, 2005, pp. 62–65).

14 Cf. Gilroy for a sample of the way sexuality becomes a site of complex negotiation of broader social stakes (Gilroy, 1993, pp. 201–204).

15 Cf., for instance, George Brandon's *Santeria from Africa to the New World* for an account of how such works in Santeria (Brandon, 1993, pp. 142, 148, 158).

16 That is to say, the energies of oppression are transmuted and changed in part by subjecting them to the dance vocabulary of the possession cult, in which the past and ancestral memory (ancestral spirits) are mobilized to help decode and recode the present trauma.

17 One of the metaphors that Du Bois offers for the effect of racialization in black experience of being "American" (Du Bois, 1961, p. 17).

18 Bakhtin traces the modern demise of the "grotesque body" – the body in intimate intercourse with its environment and its ancestry and offspring, celebrated with cyclic regularity in various "pagan" feasts of the otherwise inquisitorial Catholic Church, notorious for all manner of inversions of order and exchanges of foods and fluids, odors and erotic desires, in great "send-ups" of disciplinary control and social propriety (Bakhtin, 1984, pp. 11, 27, 32, 84).

19 David Roediger argues that the emergence of black-face minstrelsy in the early nineteenth century (in which whites "blacked" up and acted "Negro" and "wild" on stage for other whites and then often went out and beat up actual blacks to re-secure their identity as "white") actually enacted a kind of pornography of the losses suffered by immigrant whites, in moving from the rural freedoms of the body enjoyed as peasantry back in Europe to the industrial disciplines of the factory in America (Roediger, 1991, pp. 95–97, 106, 108, 119, 124).

20 Cf. Charles Mills' theory of the "the racial contract" as more accurately descriptive of the functioning of "the social contract" giving rise to Western notions of individuality (Mills, 1997, pp. 17, 25–27, 46).

21 Cf. Mafesoli's accounting of how the Promethean impulse to orchestrate the social in a totalitarianism of productivity generates its own Dionysian subversion and return of the repressed "shadow economy" of orgy and excess, re-animating the entropy of the "one" with a dynamism of plurality and contradiction (Mafesoli, 1993, pp. 82, 85, 95).

22 Here again, see Rose's (1994) elaboration of the four elements of hip-hop which tattoo space, time, and the body with an identifiable code of differentiation and recognition.

23 Long gives potent historical delineation to this transvaluation as a peculiar form of "lithic consciousness"; Adam Krims teases out of the street code of "hardness" a compelling characterization of the aesthetics as yielding a unique form of sublimity (Long, 1986, pp. 178, 197; Krims, 2000, p. 73; 2002, p. 71).

24 Thompson identifies percussion as a major mark of Afro-diasporic style that is not mere surface texture, but revelatory of a profound life orientation and philosophy, having as a primary value the intensification of energy to enhance vitality (Thompson, 1983, pp. xiii–xiv). Cf. Kochman for a description of the way this orientation can translate into conflict between whites and blacks sharing the same classroom (Kochman, 1981, pp. 108–115).

25 Cf. the comments of Jeanne Kilbourne and Bernard McGrane in the study guide for the video, *The Ad and the Ego,* for a clear exposé of the work advertising is intended to accomplish inside the body (Kilbourne, 1996, p. 3; McGrane, 1996, p. 4).

26 Cf. the discussion by the Bay Area's Retort collective of Guy Debord's notions of "spectacular power" in relationship to 9/11 and the invasion of Iraq (Retort Collective, 2004, pp. 1, 3).

27 Public Enemy's Chuck D, for instance, offered in an interview in 1992, that "what always gave rap a leg up on other music was the anger in it" even though he also lamented that the anger was usually misdirected towards other rappers than towards "the government and people responsible for what was happening in society" (Perkins, 1996, p. 21).

28 R.A.T. Judy has given trenchant expression to an ontology of what he calls "n … a authenticity" as embodied particularly in hard-core gangsta rap that transcends any simple calculus of morality, but rather poses the existential question of what it means to be human in the midst of a globalized culture of hyper-commodificiation (Judy, 2004, pp. 114–115).

29 Rose's (1994) second chapter in her book is a layered analysis of hip-hop's rise in relationship to the economic malaise of New York city in the early 1970s.

30 I have also written about this in some depth elsewhere (Perkinson, 2005, 189–201).

31 Cf. for instance, Thomas Dumm's analysis of the way new monitoring technologies have re-constituted spatiality of the gated enclave around a norm of white maleness, while surveillance remains the tactic in policing dark skin in the inner city (Dumm, 1993, pp. 1–187).

References

Baker, H. (1993) Scene … not heard, in *Reading Rodney King, Reading Urban Uprising,* (ed. R. Gooding-Williams), Routledge, New York, pp. 38–50.

Bakhtin, M. (1984) *Rabelais and His World,* (trans. H. Iswolsky), Indiana University Press, Bloomington.

Bloom, J.M. (1987) *Class, Race, & the Civil Rights Movement,* Indiana University Press, Bloomington.

Brandon, G. (1993) *Santeria from Africa to the New World: The Dead Sell Memories,* Indiana University Press, Bloomington.

Bynum, E.B. (1999) *The African Unconscious: Roots of Ancient Mysticism and Modern Psychology,* Teachers College Press, New York.

Cone, J. (1991) *Martin and Malcolm and America: A Dream or A Nightmare,* Orbis Books, Maryknoll, NY.

Du Bois, W.E.B. (1961/1903) *The Souls of Black Folk,* Fawcett Publications, Greenwich, CN.

Dumm, T. (1993) The new enclosures: Racism in the normalized community, in *Reading Rodney King, Reading Urban Uprising*, (ed. R. Gooding-Williams), Routledge, New York, pp. 178–195.

Dyer, R. (1988) White. *Screen*, 29 (4), 44–64.

Dyson, M.E. (2001) *Holler if You Hear Me: Searching for Tupac Shakur*, Basic Civitas Books, New York.

Elias, N. (1978) Review of the civilizing process: The history of manners. *The Wilson Quarterly*, Autumn, 2 (4), 158.

Elias, N. (1982/1939) *The Civilizing Process, Vol. 2: State Formation and Civilization*, Blackwell, Oxford.

Elias, N. (1983) *The Court Society*, Blackwell, Oxford.

Foucault, M. (1979) *Discipline and Punish: The Birth of the Prison*, (trans. A. Sheridan), Vintage, New York.

Foucault, M. (1980) *Power/Knowledge: Selected Interviews and Other Writings, 1972–1977*, (ed. C. Gordon, trans. by C. Gordon *et al.*), Pantheon Books, Brighton, UK.

George, N. (1999) *Hip Hop America*, Penguin Books, New York: Penguin Books.

Gibson, R. (2001) *Storms Beneath the Skin*, EM Press, LLC Joliet, IL.

Gilroy, P. (1993) *The Black Atlantic: Modernity and Double Consciousness*, Harvard, University Press Cambridge.

Judy, R.A.T. (2004) On the question of N***A authenticity, in *That's the Joint!: The Hip-Hop Studies Reader*, (eds M. Forman and M.A. Neal), Routledge, New York, pp. 105–117.

Kaufman, R. (1961) Hawk Lawler: Chorus. *New Directions*, 17, 225–228.

Kilbourne, J. (1996) Quoted in *The Ad and the Ego: Curriculum Guide*, California Newsreel, San Francisco.

Kochman, T. (1981) *Black and White Styles in Conflict*. University of Chicago Press, Chicago.

Kramer, F. (1993) *The Red Fez: Art and Spirit Possession in Africa*, (trans. Malcolm Green), Verso, New York.

Krims, A. (2000) *Rap Music and the Poetics of Identity*, Cambridge University Press, Cambridge.

Krims, A. (2002) The hip-hop sublime as a form of commodification, in *Music and Marx: Ideas, Practice, Politics*, (ed. R.B. Qureshi), Routledge New York, pp. 63–78.

Kroker, A. (1992) *The Possessed Individual: Technology and the French Postmodern*, St. Martin's Press, New York.

Long, C. (1986) *Significations: Signs, Symbols, and Images in the Interpretation of Religion*, Fortress Press, Philadelphia.

Mafesoli, M. (1993) *The Shadow of Dionysius: A Contribution to the Sociology of the Orgy*, (trans. C. Linse and M.K. Palmquist), SUNY Press, New York.

Marx, K. (1967) *Capital: A Critique of Political Economy*, vol 1, (ed. F. Engles, trans. S. Moore and E. Aveling), International Publishers, New York.

McCarthy Brown, K. (1984) Why women need the war god, in *Women's Spirit Bonding*, (eds. J. Kalven and M. Buckley), Pilgrim Press, New York, pp. 190–201.

McGrane, B. (1996) Quoted in *The Ad and the Ego: Curriculum Guide*, California Newsreel San Francisco.

Mills, C. (1997) *The Racial Contract*, Cornell University Press, Ithaca and London.

Murphy, J. (1994) *Working the Spirit: Ceremonies of the African Diaspora*, Beacon Press, Boston.

Napier, A.D. (1992) *Foreign Bodies: Performance, Art, and Symbolic Anthropology*, University of California Press, Berkeley, CA.

Nietzsche, F. (1990) *Twilight of the Idols*, Penguin Books, New York.

Omi, M., and Winant, H. (1994) *Racial Formation in the United States From the 1960s to the 1990s*, 2nd edn, Routledge, New York.

Patterson, O. (2006) *New York Times*, March 26, p. 26.

Perkins, W.E. (1996) The rap attack: An introduction, in *Droppin' Science: Critical Essays on Rap Music and Hip-Hop Culture*, (ed. William E. Perkins), Temple University Press, Philadelphia, pp. 1–45.

Perkinson, J.W. (2004) *White Theology: Outing Supremacy in Modernity*, Palgrave Macmillan, New York.

Perkinson, J.W. (2005) *Shamanism, Racism and Hip-Hop Culture: Essays on White Supremacy and Black Subversion.* Palgrave Macmillan, New York.

Porterfield, A. (1987) Shamanism: A psychosocial definition. *Journal of the American Academy of Religion*, 55, 728–729.

Reed, I. (1983) Foreword, in *Tell My Horse: Voodoo and Life in Haiti and Jamaica*, (ed. Z.N. Hurston), Turtle Island, Berkeley, CA, pp. xi–xv.

Retort Collective (2004) Afflicted powers: The state, the spectacle and September 11. *New Left Review*, May–June, 1–13.

Roediger, D. (1991) *The Wages of Whiteness: Race and the Making of the American Working Class*, Verso, London.

Rose, T. (1994) *Black Noise: Rap Music and Black Culture in Contemporary America*, Wesleyan University Press/University Press of New England, Hanover, NH.

Smith, T. (1994) *Conjuring Culture: Biblical Formations of Black America*, Oxford University Press, New York.

Spencer, J.M. (1991) Introduction, *The Emergency of Black and the Emergence of Rap*, (ed. J.M. Spencer) (A special issue *of Black Sacred Music: A Journal of Theomusicology*). Duke University Press, Durham, NC, pp. 1–11.

Spencer, J.M. (1995) *The Rhythms of Black Folk: Race, Religion and Pan-Africanism*, Africa World Press, Inc., Trenton, N.J.

Thompson, R.F. (1983) *Flash of the Spirit: African and Afro-American Art and Philosophy*, Vintage Books, New York.

23

Iterative Hesitancies and Latinidad
The Reverberances of Raciality

Bernadette Marie Calafell
and Shane T. Moreman

The murals adorning the interior courtyard of El Palacio Nacional in México City tell the story of México's history spanning from the Spanish Conquest to the 1930s. Bernadette and Shane, during their two week stay in México City, excitedly venture out to read the murals' historical representation of their own latinidad as it is understood through their Mexican heritage. While in México they have visited, either separately or together, many sites of the icons of latinidad: La Virgen de Guadalupe, La Malinche, Frida Kahlo, Montezuma, Tonatzin. Now they are heading to where the muralist, Diego Rivera, documented a history that both Bernadette and Shane understand to be their own.

Walking at a brisk clip, they pass through the Zócalo, through the doors of El Palacio Nacional, into the palace courtyard and up to its second floor. While there are machine gun armed guards at the front door to the palace, nobody chaperones Bernadette and Shane around the grounds and no one seems to be monitoring their moves. In Foucaltian fashion, they self-monitor and act the part of the well-behaved guest. Part of the reason for their manners is that they are mesmerized by the murals. Arranged like Mayan hieroglyphs, the visual history linearly evolves from optimism, purity, and naivety to pessimism, pollution, and suspicion.

Moving through the faces and forms of their sacred history, Bernadette and Shane absorb this story, their story. Occasionally they interject with quiet exclamations, but mostly it is only their footsteps that can be heard echoing off the red tile floor throughout the grey stone archways. According to Rivera's visual rhetoric, both Hernán Cortés and Malintzin Tenépal irrevocably damage the New World. Toward the conclusion of the conquest tale, Hernán does business with a thug and Malintzin hangs her head. In this final scene, both Hernán and Malintzin stand in side-profile. The only one daring to stare directly out to an on-looking audience is a quiet baby with blue eyes – Martín Cortés – their son, one of the first mestizos

The Handbook of Critical Intercultural Communication, edited by Thomas K. Nakayama and Rona Tamiko Halualani. © 2010 Blackwell Publishing Ltd.

and arguably one of the first Latinas/os. Guilelessly he dangles in a papoose on his mother's back. Like the bag carrying his father's gold, the papoose carries him. Like the gold that is exchanged by his father, both he and his mother will eventually be traded-off too ... separately. At the conclusion of this story, their story, Bernadette and Shane meet the stare of Martín's blue eyes and then mark the occasion with photographic evidence. Alternating digital camera-poses under his mural locale, they position their bodies near him and stake their connection to him.

After our travels to México City we both separately wrote of our Mexican pilgrimages (Calafell, 2005; Moreman, 2008). However, much remains unsaid, particularly concerning the son of Hernán Cortés and Malintzin Tenépal. For us, Martín Cortés and our experience with him is not a story's ending but rather a beginning. After all, it is the cry of this mestizo boy as he is birthed into the New World that begins the Chicana/o iteration. Though Martín's story is specifically tied to Chicana/o and Mexicana/o colonialism; the reverberations and implications of mestiza/o identity performances have significance for all others who lay claim to being Latina/o such as Puerto Ricans, Dominicans, and Cubans. Thus, we use the story of Martín and our own mestiza/o existences to speak to the possibilities and impossibilities of Latina/o performance.

It is not our intent to use Chicana/o histories to generalize to all Latinas/os; however, we consider how our Chicana/o performances are also Latina/o performances. Likewise, Hill Collins (2009) makes clear that a core theme of Black feminist thought is the relationship between the individual and the collective in that African American women share histories of oppression; however, the ways the reverberations of those racial histories are experienced is different for individual women. We see a similar relationship as the story of Martín, a story of colonialism, is a story that has not just Chicana/o reverberations, but also Latina/o reverberations. In this essay, we come together with Martín as our muse to theorize how Martín's story can be understand as part of a larger understanding of latinidad.

In order to accomplish this goal, we use the metatheory of performativity as a theoretical framework. In drawing upon our experiences and making Martín our muse, we take up Moon's (1996) call that intercultural communication scholars shift perspectives from the position of the dominant culture defining Others and towards Nakayama's (1994) notion of being "Other/wise." Moon asks, "What would intercultural communication look like when viewed from these 'Other' places?" (p. 77). Chuang (2003) compliments Moon's call through her observation that, "A very large problem exists in the fact that mainstream intercultural communication literature is saddled with a stance that does not allow for the Others to speak for themselves.... The traditional research paradigm's attempt to examine 'groups of cultural Others' unwittingly reveals overt and covert 'academic imperialism'" (p. 31). Additionally, traditional intercultural research based in a positivist paradigm reifies essentialisms (Chuang) and the nationstate (Moon) which in current times are no longer viable lenses through which to view culture.

Furthermore, we recognize, as does Moon, that the positionality of the researcher is of central concern as it is implicit, thus making research an explicitly political act. We follow in the direction of aforementioned scholars, and Chicana feminists Moraga and Anzaldúa (2002) who call us to draw upon our theories of the flesh or sub-jugated knowledges as we articulate a space in critical intercultural communication that attends to the importance of researcher positionality and experience via per-sonal narrative. In a similar vein as Moraga and Anzaldúa, Calafell (2007) examines Latinas/os through the areas of critical intercultural communication, performance studies, and rhetoric. We connect to this work as we embrace and integrate our positionalities as Latina/o scholars synthesizing the reverberations of Martín's story onto and through our bodies.

Racial Performativity and Latinidad

While Butler (2006) may not have originated the term "performativity," her use of the term caught on as a popular way to explain identity in contemporary times. As scholars within the Communication field who are either Performance Studies-trained or who utilize the performance paradigm for their communica-tion work know, performativity has most frequently been employed to explain gen-der and sexuality. However, more and more, performativity has also been used within the Communication field as a way to explain cultural identity. Akin to Madison's (1999) statement that "Performance has become too popular," (p. 107) an argument might be made that the concept of performativity may have become too popular as well. Indeed, Hall (1996) called for caution against too-easily grafting an understanding of race and ethnicity onto Butler's gender-focused arguments.

This essay then, heeding Hall, explores the performativity of the authors' latini-dad within the current US discourse of race and ethnicity. We do this by combining the story of Martín with our own – reading him through us and us through him. We use the phrase "iterative hesitancies" to describe the awkwardnesses and com-plexities of the racial discursive iterations of being Latina/o by marking our racially performative moments and then attending to performativity's over-reliance on the ocular, grammatical correctness, and identity singularity. To accomplish our goal we will first explain performativity and latinidad. Then we will provide an overview of the history of Martín Cortés and how reading ourselves through him is a Latina/o performance. Next we will explicate the complications of our Latina/o identities through the three iterative hesitancies: the ocular, the grammatical, and the singu-lar. Finally we will summarize how we understand latinidad to advance current usages of performativity and current articulations of racial identity. In the end we find that despite the welcoming of Latina/o into the lexicon of the US imaginary, being Latina/o is still difficult to iterate due to its relationship to Whiteness – a relationship that is both germane to latinidad as well as inapplicable.

Butler's (2006) work on performativity primarily focuses on the gendered body. Inda (2000) follows her work on performativity by applying the concept to under-standings of the Latina/o body. As both Butler and Inda express, language plays tricks on the eyes and the rest of our senses. The readily apparent somatic differences in contrasting racial bodies is a sleight of the discursive tongue in that these very material differences are brought into naturalization through the effect of their naming. As attested by Inda,

> [R]acial difference is an issue of material difference to the extent that "race" is a difference inscribed on the body. However, racial difference is never simply a function of material differences that are not in some way marked and formed by discursive practices (2000, pp. 91–92).

Our cultural identity is a successful achievement per the correct performance of the discursive practice by which we are called forth. As we repetitively answer the discursive call, our racial identity becomes naturalized for ourselves and for others.

Just as language unstably morphs and changes throughout time, so do our discursive racial constitutions. Inda admits that the resignification possibilities of pushing through discursive determinates is precarious but possible. Future enunciations of ourselves are limited by the historical citations of the words we are given but these future enunciations are also limitless due to the burgeoning meanings that we might assign. Optimistically, for Inda (2000), racial performativity "calls attention to the ways in which 'race' is always actively constructed, to how its referents are inherently unstable, thus making it open to multiple rearticulations" (p. 97). The process of harnessing the power of discursive constitution is not formulaic nor is it a process that is formalized. For example, Moreman (2009) found examples of racial rearticulations among the literary memoirs of hybrid Latina/o-White individuals. These memoirs explained the complexities of a hybrid ethnic identity but more importantly, through their self-tellings, they also challenged the naturalizing effects of racial discourse.

In recent years scholars have begun theorizing latinidad to understand pan-Latina/o connections and also to consider a formulation of cultural identity that is not based in essentialisms. Aparicio (2003) defines latinidad as a way to "explore moments of convergences and divergences in the formation of Latino/a (post) colonial subjectivities and in hybrid cultural expressions among various Latino national groups" (p. 93). Latinidad, as manifested in cultural texts, "evokes in its audience, and perhaps to its interpreter, an analogous structure of feeling having to do with the pain of exile and of geocultural displacements" (Aparicio, 2003, p. 93). Similarly, Muñoz (2000) sees latinidad as "an anti-normative affect" that creates a sense of group identity not based in static notions of identity (p. 100). Muñoz (2000) elaborates on this idea when he writes of "feeling brown" as a way to describe a feeling of Otherness shared by Latinas/os whose identities are often seen as inappropriate or excessive in comparison to what is constructed as normative national affect (based on White middle class subjectivities). More recently, Calafell (2007) locates performances of latinidad across Latina/o identities through music, pointing to spaces of possibility and contradiction. At the heart of the intersection of performance and latinidad is a desire to find spaces of possibility, instability, and coalition across difference which are not static, sentimental, or overly utopian. Valdivia (2004) cautions against the uncritical embracement of latinidad as it has the potential to ignore or erase Blackness while reprivileging Whiteness.

For the purposes of this essay, the performatives that underlie latinidad complicate our understandings of performativity leaving us with the question of what happens when performativity is utilized to explain a mestiza/o or Latina/o body in everyday interactions. Butler's (2006) work addresses repetition, performance, and the disciplining of flawed or wrong performances of gender; Inda's work postulates about the Brown body in its changing historical vernacular manifestations. In our work we bring the concept of performativity into our everyday racial identity expressions by examining the racial constitutions we are called through and against. In references to the multiplicity associated with our Latina/o identities (i.e., hybridity) we mark the moments when the Latina/o body is subsumed by or resumed through racial discourse. How does Latina/o performativity elude the ocular, grammatical, and the singular themes found in understandings of performativity? Moreman (2008) began a conversation questioning the possibilities and impossibilities of cultural identity as it is understood through performativity – we continue that conversation here with a focus on the Latina/o body.

Martín Cortés and Latina/o Performance

Scholars have written generally about how mestiza/o identity in Mexico was birthed, both discursively and literally, out of Spanish colonialism (Anzaldúa, 1999; Del Castillo, 1997; Moraga, 2000; Tafolla, 1993); however, much more remains to be said specifically about Martín Cortés. In these re-imaginings and rearticulations of the narrative of Malintzin Tenépal, Chicana feminist writers have included allusions to Malintzin's feelings about being the symbolic mother of mestizas/os. For example, Esquivel (2007) writes that when Malintzin was pregnant, she knew her child would "unite two worlds. The blood of Moors and Christians with that of the Indians, that pure, unmixed race" (p. 146). In this and other reimaginings of Malintzin's voice, her unborn mestizo child signals possibility in that the child's mixed racial presence could challenge ideologies that serve to stigmatize mestiza/o identities (see Anzaldúa, 1999; Tafolla, 1993). Other such as Gaspar de Alba's retelling signal potential rejection by the Spanish father;

> When [Martín] was born, his eyes opened Aztec black, his skin shone café-con-leche.
> His mother wet his fine curls with her saliva to make them straight. His father cursed
> the native seed in that first mixed son. (Gaspar de Alba, 2005, p. 4)

Each of these narratives of Martín's birth theorizes the complicated articulations of Martín as a symbol of mestizaje.

Of direct importance to our essay is the understanding that Martín's narrative is often occluded by the story of his native mother. Adding to the reclamation work by Chicana feminists of Malintzin's narrative (i.e., Anzaldúa, 1999; Tafolla, 1993), Calafell (2007) attempts to link this project of reclamation to performance looking by grounding Chicana identities within a space of reclaimed absence and stigmatization. Calafell asserts that through Malintzin and her narrative, we as Chicanas/os are able to performatively understand or locate our own possibilities in a history in which we are implicated. More recently, this essay's authors have examined contemporary mediated representations of La Llorona (Anaya, 1984) as a way to understand current meanings around Latina/o identities (see Moreman and Calafell, 2008). In the same way, we read Martín's story against our own in order to understand and performatively feel the reverberances of his and our mestizaje.

In examining the narrative of the male Martín Cortés it is important to note that it is not our desire to re-center patriarchy or a potentially patriarchal symbol of "national genesis" (Alcalá, 2001, p. 33). Alcalá has argued persuasively for the examination of not Martín, but instead Maria Jaramillo, his sister and the daughter of Malintzin Tenépal and Juan Jaramillo. Additionally, scholars have questioned the legitimacy of the positioning of Martín as the first mestiza/o, arguing that there were other children born before from relationships in which Spanish men accepted an indigenous way of life (Messinger Cypus, 2005). As a way to explain the prominence of Martín as the first mestiza/o despite potential historical incongruencies, Messinger Cypus asserts that social class and standing make Cortés a more desirable patriarchal figure than some of the other men who fathered mestiza/o children before him. Additionally, Alcalá connecting to Paz (1991) explains that Martín is a representative symbol of violation for Chicano and Mexicano writers because he is born from a mother understood as passive and violated by colonialism. While we are attentive to these critiques of potentially re-centering patriarchy, we maintain that the prominence of the relationship of Malintzin Tenépal and Hernán Cortés in histories of colonialism and the ensuing birth of Martín Cortés as the symbol of a new people make him important for examination.

Moreman (2009) uses Anzaldúa as a way to argue that writing and reading are types of performances. Anzaldúa (1999) importantly characterized her written work as performance when it is written and when it is read. She says,

> My "stories" are acts encapsulated in time, "enacted" every time they are spoken aloud or read silently. I like to think of them as performances and not as inert "dead" objects (as the aesthetics of Western culture think of art works) (p. 89).

Gil-Gómez (2000) says of Anzaldúa, "[She] feels that the writing itself is a mode of performing identity – both directly and indirectly" (p. 142). Adopting Anzaldúa's views, as this essay's coauthors are writing, we are performing our identity for and through you, the reader. As we smooth out sentences trying to provide clarity of concepts (e.g., Latina/o and Chicana/o) and consistency in references (e.g., Malinche, Matinzin, and Malinalli), we hope to convey the potentialities of latinidad without promising false or naïve utopias. In reviewing a range of Latina/o staged performance, Román (1997) drew some similarities in the works that this essay's authors embrace in our own performative work. Of Latina/o performers Román says that they "insist on the visibility and coherence of Latino identity even as they refuse to stabilize the identity as any one image, role, stereotype or convention" (pp. 163–164). Holling and Calafell (2007) point to the stage as a place for Chicana/o performers to work through or exorcise post-colonial ills. We look to the page as a stage for our lives as they are lived performatively through mestizaje.

In the next section, we describe the three iterations (the ocular, the grammatical, and the singular) and follow each with narratives that connect these iterations to Martín's life as the symbolic first mestizo. Running alongside of these narratives we include our stories of these iterations in our mestiza/o existences. Finally, we conclude with some thoughts about the implications of this work for current understandings of racial performativity.

The Three Iterative Hesitancies: The Ocular, the Grammatical and the Singular

Reinelt (2002) expresses the relationship between the quotidian and the theatrical for performance theorists. While respecting the history of theater and the manifestations of its cultural contributions, performance theorists are pushing past the doors of the theatre to explore performativity in a range of cultural performances and in everyday, mundane performances. Reinelt states that these theorists are:

> committed to articulating an acute awareness of cultural differences and historical specificities, producing work on race, gender, and sexuality as they are asserted and inscribed in performance: as they become performative (p. 202)

In work on performativity, race has more recently been addressed. Previous to performativity's application, race was consistently considered within the realm of the visible. Using the invisibility of sexual orientation as juxtaposition to race, Reinelt writes:

> In the United States, race and sexual preference have been constituted as binary opposites in a visual economy of readable identity. Race, understood as the manifest truth of melanin, forms the polar opposite of the "hidden truth" of sexual preference (2002, p. 226).

However, the metatheory of performativity, when understood through race, can be expanded for understanding race outside the ocular rather than just limiting understandings of race to the visible. Even though denotatively the terms race and ethnicity are distinct, connotatively they are more similar than different.

Chow (2002) explains that the terms "race" and "ethnicity" are often conflated and this conflation is overly critiqued by scholars. Thus, the very circumstances that bring about talk and understandings of race and ethnicity are so similar that the terms themselves can be used in very similar ways. Popularly, however, ethnicity is still not seen as something everyone has, but rather as something that is "not White." In fact, Chow notes, "for the ideal American, ethnicity is seen as something to be overcome and left in the past" (2002, p. 30) – to be read as White. Understanding the contemporary articulations of race to include Latina/o identity, we critically comment upon the ways that the contemporary racial discourse in the United States either is interrupted by us or interrupts us in our everyday lives. We refer to these moments as iterative hesitancies and have divided them into three distinct areas: the ocular, the grammatical and the singular.

The Ocular

"So who is White, your mom or your dad?" I am taken aback for a moment asking myself if I actually just heard what I thought I heard. We have been talking about research and courses I teach and then out of nowhere the question emerged. What is it that makes her ask the question and lets her think she can? Is it because I do not match whatever racial logics she uses to make sense of identity? Is it because within these logics my skin is too white to signal difference? Is it because of my performance of White middle-class norms? She stands there waiting for an answer, blissfully unaware of the level of pain and offense her words have just given me. She is not the first to make this assumption. She is just the first to so boldly ask the question. I cannot help but wonder about her motivations. I scan the room wondering if anyone else sees my anger and embarrassment. I see other faculty engaged in conversations with prospective students. None of them look as uncomfortable as I feel. I attempt to recoup, as my presence at this function is not pleasure, this is work and I am performing my role as the faculty of color, potential mentor, and recruiter at an academic conference. Does she see the hurt in my blue eyes? The disappointment on my face? The anger?

I began a recitation I have learned well from years of practice. This is a recitation, an iteration that allows others to somehow place me into a racial logic that makes sense to them, but not to me. As flawed as they may be, it is easier than giving a history lesson about mestizaje. Like many Chicanas before me, I am a translator. This time unfortunately I try to translate my identity into a sense-making frame without losing myself in the process. The explanation of my family history and the look of disbelief it causes when I disappoint the listener by sharing that indeed both my parents are Mexican American are occurrences I am used to. Some listeners have even been so bold as to say, "No. You're lying. Really?!" I want to fight with them and let them know exactly how much they have offended me, but I dismiss their ignorance particularly because more often than not we both call ourselves Chicanas/os.

My offense lies not in the fact that I am assumed to be mixed, but it is the offense of misrecognition and essentialism. It is the offense that caused so many to feel isolated from a Chicano movement that in many cases held the visibility of heterosexuality, patriarchy, and brownness at its heart. It seems that many of us internalize the politics of visibility. For someone like me the politics of misrecognition continue to be painful every time they are performed. In talking about my Whiteness and the pain of misrecognition I want to be clear in stating that I understand the unearned privileges that come along with my white skin. I do not pretend to be marginalized in the same way as other Chicanas/os who have darker skin colors. As Cherríe Moraga (2000) writes, "I don't really understand first-hand what it feels like being shitted on for being brown" (p. 45). However, I want to layer our experiences of the essentialisms that we internalize and how they play out in our interactions with one another.

Of course, the name Calafell does not help. Often explaining this as well, this is when the Spanish relatives enter the picture and just a bit of the disbelief goes away. These relatives often bring Whiteness to the forefront both in terms of making sense of my visible identity and through a name that is somehow more discursively tied to Whiteness than say Muñoz, Salinas, or Pérez within US centered understandings of Latina/o identities. Despite my explanations, the questions remain. For a long time I looked for voices that might help me make sense of my experience. A few, such as Gloria Anzaldúa (1999) or Cherríe Moraga (2000), talked about their Whiteness; however, each of them had a non-Latina/o parent – something I do not share. I look for my story. After explaining my family history; thus, justifying my Whiteness, I proceed to finish my pitch for my department. I have done my duty and I need to get out of the room as it is becoming extremely claustrophobic. Quickly I excuse myself hoping to be done with the questions. At least for tonight.

It was Martín's vivid blue eyes that punctuated our experience of Diego's murals. Gaspar de Alba's (2005) imagines his eyes to be black. Lanyon (2003) envisions Martín's somatic appearance,

> What did he look like at seventeen? I think of him as a boy like any boy one might see in Mexico City today: slightly built, with coal-black hair, an aquiline nose, copper skin and almond eyes. (p. 77)

Does everyone have the same desire to see Martín, the symbolic first mestizo? In our journeys we had to see what Martín looked like in Diego Rivera's murals. But, what does our desire mean? Does this image somehow mark him as original and thus serve as a visual pronouncement for mestiza/o identity?

The stability of the visual is a myth which we certainly know from all the Spaniards' elaborate charts of racial makeup and color caste. Martín as a figure is a site to point to mestiza/o origin; however, within him we cannot ground ourselves to a specific visual referent for our identities, even if we so desire. Arteaga (1997) argues that "At each reproduction of the Chicano body, the racial characteristics of European and indigenous American compete for presence" (p. 10). Mestizaje Arteaga continues, "is the confluence of different races, in the sense of descending from an original hybrid begetting, of continually procreating mestizo offspring, and of simply being, in the present incarnation, multiracial" (1997, p. 11). Seeking legalistic legitimacy for his son, Hernán Cortés sought and secured a papal decree so that Martín "could not be burdened with the stain of illegitimacy for the rest of his life" (Lanyon, p. 64). This formalized legitimization signifies the intersections of race, nationality, and class and in many ways the desire for permanency or stability. The complexity of this hybridity is not lost on us in our desire to see Martín and perhaps locate ourselves within him. Very often, this desire is inflected by a larger racial discursive logic that is dictated by the ocular.

The Grammatical

One December, a friend calls with a last minute invitation to see the production of "La Virgen del Tepeyac" staged by El Teatro Campesino. Ear to the phone, I stand in my apartment shaking my head, readying to say "no." I am reluctant to give up an evening of writing to see the production of a story I have known since childhood. The story of La Virgen de Guadalupe can be considered a Christmas season tradition for Catholic Mexican-Americans, much like "The Nutcracker" for White people. Stressed from writing and rewriting, I decide to escape into the holiday season and my "no" becomes "yes."

Arriving a bit late, my friend and I skulk through a side door of the church-turned-theatre. We scoot into a pew behind a young Latina/o couple. The young mother holds her toddler who stares over her shoulder at us with wide eyes. No one, except the curious child, seems to notice our late arrival as everyone is focused on the cast, dressed in Aztec plumage, singing "Buenos Días Paloma Blanca." Hearing the song takes me back to my own youth. As they sing, I harmonize in a low tone ("Buenos Días Paloma Blanca, Hoy te vengo a saludar"), remembering a childhood of South Texas Christmases ("Saludando tu belleza, en tu trono celestial"), seasonal visits to the Catholic Church, ("Eres Madre del Creador, que a mi corazón encantas), and a lifetime of contemplation of Virgin Mary apparitions (Gracias te doy con amor, Buenos Días Paloma Blanca). The baby gazes at me throughout the song occasionally blinking with long, dark eyelashes.

Discussing the relationship between race and performativity, Butler (2006) calls for a reading of "multiple lenses" when examining the enactments of racial identity. Since the ocular is not reliable for the mestiza/o individual, this essay's authors try to always use lenses outside the visual. Stretching the metaphor of lens, we attend to details beyond the visual and into the aural (e.g., language) and affect (e.g., emotion). Not only in our self-enactments but in our readings of the world, a multiplicity of meaning and interpretation is inherent in the understandings of the mestiza/o as we theorize the multiplicities of latinidad as it is attached to issues of class, gender, and sexuality. Indeed, understanding the mestiza/o requires pushing past the limits of performativity. Butler argues that self-expression is still dressed in language and the linguistic politics therein. Thus she is warning that expression is not without its politics. She writes, "I am not outside the language that structures me, but neither am I determined by the language that makes this 'I' possible"

(p. xxiv). Therefore, we are delivered to others within the "grammar that establishes my availability to you" (p. xxiv).

The mestiza/o is not grammatically correct. We confuse subject/verb agreement – sometimes we are one, sometimes we are two. We pollute a sentence with more than one language – sometimes Spanish, sometimes English, sometimes Spanglish. We switch up vocabulary as we go along. In English, "My name is Shane." In Spanish, "Me llamo Chango." I move from subject to predicate while still in the same body. Our words' etiology branches and borrows as do our complex family trees. We move between the linguistic and the theatrical, between the languaged and the enacted, between thrust upon and the strategy. In these moments of grammatical adjustment, we meet the demands of dominant discourse and sometimes we only approximate those demands. In these moments, there is agentic enterprise.

Our situation is not unique, however. Heterosexuality, masculinity, middle classness – these identities are just as unsettled and offer just as many possibilities for ranges of performativity as the mestiza/o. The difference between these status quo identities and us is that the grammar of these status quotidian identities has been well-established and promulgated. The mestiza/o is still within various facets of novelty. "Hispanic" has been relatively recently coined and understood. Whiteness is very recently under intellectual scrutiny. Hybridity as an identity is most recently being considered and weighed. Latinidad has only come to the academic fore as of late. Therefore, the imaginative possibilities of our mestizaje lie in its grammatical awkwardness. This identity draws upon various identities that have different relationships to privilege. For the Latina/o, cultural capital has been lost or has never been accessible. For the White, cultural capital has been unfairly gained as entitlement or is threatened to be redistributed. For the mestiza/o cultural capital is in abundance – and this is the default. For the mestiza/o, our grammar is more optimistic. Our grammar is consistently in the subjunctive mood.

Our excess of cultural capital allows us to understand the fictions of reality as desirable foundations for our "selves." Our excess of cultural capital allows us to understand performativity as composed of materiality, history, and agency – and all three of these elements are in excess, not in short supply or finite qualities. Performativity is productive in that it offers "the possibility of a different sort of repeating, in the breaking or subversive repetition of style" (Butler 2006, p. 520). Inherent in iterations of latinidad are also the possibilities of a different sort of repeating and subversions of repetition. While our identity is not outside the grammar of performativity, it is outside the correct grammar of racial identity and therefore within the racial identity's clumsy yet creative grammatical structures.

That night at the play, I notice the "incorrections" of the play, and wonder if they are intentionally subversive spins. Aztec dancers are played by blonde haired, blued eyed actors. Spanish church clergy are all played by black haired, brown skinned actors. And most noticeably, the Virgin de Guadalupe, the paragon of chastity, is a bit sexy. These creative reiterations of the cultural, sexual, and historical meanings are instabilities that I cannot label as definite subversions. However,

I am hopeful. Just as the latinidad exists and resists within the performativity of race – it is the instability of that performativity that leaves the performance of ourselves and all others open for a multitude of possibilities.

For our muse, Martín, the story of his parents and historical archetypes based on their relationship with one another persists. However, much remains unknown about the illegitimate son. Lanyon seeks to piece together a coherent narrative through historical documents and thus provide a fuller story of Martín. Of the historical records she scoured for Martín's story, Lanyon writes,

> I knew they could not capture the multiplicity of the man who was Malinche's son. I never saw him smile or dance or fall in love, laugh or yawn, or act ignobly. I had no impression of him as a husband and a father, except that like any European or Amerindian noble he had tried to negotiate a good marriage for his son. Did he carry a sense of loss about him? Did he walk through the great plaza of the city of Mexico with the air of someone who knew he was in danger? The documents I had found offered glimpses of him as he passed, nothing more (2003, pp. 246–247)

Like our opening story, her narrative is both punctuated with desire and absence. What would it mean to really know Martín's story? What possibilities would this fixity foreclose?

The lack of clarity, stability, and knowledge about Martín allows him to be for a sign of and for possibility. Corey (2006) writes about ethnography and the desire to uncover possibility. Our search for Martín's story mirrors this desire as we seek to not only articulate Martín's history, but also to harmonize that articulation with our own. His existence as a symbol of possibility lies not only in the ability to write oneself into his story or to re-imagine the story in new ways (a story in which we are historically and materially implicated), but also in the possibility signaled by the ambiguity of latinidad. As performance scholars we understand the value of the personal narrative and the possibility of it to re-write and disrupt history (Corey, 1998); thus, Martín's openness operates as a possible real (Pollock, 1999) that allows us to re-compose a history in which we are implicated. The instability of Martín's story is symbolic of the ways that Latina/o identities defy the grammatical logics of identities. Nothing is ever certain in a history and a body of latinidad.

The Singular

In popular histories of Martín, his younger brother of the same name is not always present. His existence is not well known. However, Lanyon (2003) sheds light on this history by filling in some of the story about Hernán Cortés' second son of the same name by a mother who was not Malintzin, but instead a Spanish noblewoman. Though Cortés gave his son the same name as Martín, he intimated in letters that his love for the first Martín was just as great as his love for the second. In his will Cortés left the majority of his inheritance to the second Martín, while agreeing to give the first "one thousand gold ducados every year for the rest of their lives" (Lanyon, 2003, p. 90). However, this was contingent upon the fact that he would recognize and serve his younger brother as the head of the family. Contextualizing Cortés' choice, Lanyon observes that it would be unheard of for him to make Martín, his mestizo son, the head of the family. Later in his life Martín was made to pay for the sins of his brother; however, his legacy was also tied to the second Martín who could be cruel and vindictive. Martín suffered physical torture because of his Spanish brother and is often assumed to be the one who committed many acts of violence that his brother initiated. His legacy is forever marred by his brother's actions.

Martín occupies a complex space of both privilege and disempowerment. As a child he was brought to Spain and lived among the aristocracy; however, he was never really a legitimate part of it. His slightly off-legitimization granted him entry but also marked him as Other. Furthermore, his servitude to the his younger brother in many ways reified racial castes of colonialism;

> the fact that the mestizo son suffered for his half-brother of "pure" Spanish blood, and was exiled from his mother's land – all this seems to resound with forlorn meta-phorical meaning for our postcolonial times. (Lanyon, 2003, p. 239)

The relationship between the brothers points to our own tenuous relationship with Whiteness – the ability for some of us to grab brief moments of privilege; however, overwhelmingly we must come to terms with its history of oppression and that articulation of it on our bodies.

Even if commonly denied, the academy is a space that is governed by White male heterosexual middle class norms. Norms we do not and cannot meet. That is not to say that each of does not have access to some of these privileges, but in an inter-sectional way we are cognizant of how some of our identities can at times negate the privilege of other parts of our identities. The excesses of our brown, feminist, queer, and untenured bodies often seep into our everyday interactions in the acad-emy in ways that make others uncomfortable when we are unable to perform the White male heterosexual middle class standard. These excesses mark us as impolite and angry. They also mark our relationship to Whiteness. We have access to the space and we are invited to perform in ways complicit with the space; but it is clear that the academy is not our space and in many ways it continues to work against us. No more is this feeling apparent than at an academic conference where the "excesses" of our brown, feminist, queer, and untenured bodies are often at the service of ideologies of Whiteness that ask us for White, heterosexual, middle class performances.

The academic conference holds promise for the exchange of ideas and scholarly expertise; that is the best possible scenario. However, we know that some ideas are more welcome than others as are some bodies. Imagine you are the brown, femi-nist, queer, and untenured body formally responding to papers that directly go against, contradict, and in many ways negate your queer, brown, feminist, and untenured politics. Can you tame your "excesses" so they are at the service of White male heterosexual middle class standards? Do you even want to? Martín's Otherness/his mestizaje was literally at the service of the Spanish brother who represented legitimacy and privilege. Years and iterations later, this relationship to Whiteness both symbolically and literally persists. The queer, brown, feminist, untenured body must reconcile the tenuous relationship with White male heterosexual middle class academic politeness in considering the appropriate performance.

Identity is often understood through a singular model. This is most clearly evident in social movements. Women are White, queerness is White, and Black signals male. A similar uni-dimensionality governs racial logics in the academy. Latinas/os occupy a space that is out of place in these logics. Our presences are often misunderstood ("Do we call them Latino? Hispanic? Mexican? Chicano?") and our allegiances are questioned as we become suspect for occupying a bridge position ("As a woman of color do you side with the White women in the department or the man of color?"). Often read as the "diversity hire" the visibility or lack of Whiteness manifested on our bodies governs the assumptions our colleagues make about our ideological standings. For example, one cannot be both white skinned and Chicana/o as the racial logics about the singularity of identity negate this possibility.

Whiteness is further complicated by our performances, lack thereof, or accessibility to Whiteness. Furthermore, as mestizas/os, we negotiate our Whiteness through the materiality of our bodies. What happens when you disrupt the racial logics at an academic conference? What happens when your "excesses" spill over in ways that not only disrupt the White male heterosexual middle class norms of the conference, but also go against your assumed ideologies position because of your Whiteness, ambiguity, or bridge position? In a false continuum that governs understandings of race, Latinas/os are located somewhere between Black and White, rather than understood as being inclusive of both. This middle space causes anxiety, distrust, and fear as our bodies are "read" in ways that seek to locate us in dominant logics and assign an assumed ideological underpinning. Martín was bound to his brother of the same name by finances, but perhaps also because of some allegiance to a long dead conquistador father. We are bound to Whiteness through our history as a colonized people and through our relationship to an academy that is governed by White middle class norms. We are drawn to the academy with the hope of social intervention, but we often end up playing a game that contravenes our own survival.

Conclusion Beginnings

In this chapter we have used Martín Cortés as our muse. Both Martín's and our stories demonstrate how the current logics of performativity must be complicated through the lens of race. Performativity becomes further problematized as attempts are made to ground it on a mestiza/o body, a body that challenges through the ocular, the grammatical, and the singular. It is our hope that the discussion we begin here can be a starting point for not only theoretically extending performativity, but finding ways to locate Latina/o identities and experiences within a performance paradigm that is largely governed by essentializing racial logics. This work further adds to scholarship within critical intercultural communication studies that privilege the body as a site of knowledge, extending the relationship between performance studies and intercultural communication. This privileging of the body and our acknowledgement of ourselves as researchers who are "positioned and embodied beings – gendered, racial, sexual, and social class" (Moon, 1996, p. 77) makes not only our subject matter political, but also our methodological contribution to critical intercultural communication.

Furthermore, we have seriously engaged an intersectional perspective seeking to be attentive to the ways our intersecting identities position us in a matrix of domination that is informed by history, power, and cultural memory. Taking up performativity and mestizaje within the realm of the everyday we are forced to be accountable to the intersections of our embodied experiences. Furthermore, we wonder how the theoretical and methodological choices made in this essay might implicate readers in ways that enable a "performance of possibilities" (Madison, 1998) that previous scholarship in intercultural communication has not.

Additionally, we see this work as an invitation to ground Latina/o identities in sites of historical re-imaginings and possibilities rather than on racial essences and essentialisms. Within national and international changes, Latina/o research is emerging simultaneous to a time when intercultural communication scholars are re-assessing our new global situation and assessing our next steps. Through publishing about somatics, borders, ethnic and racial categorizing, and invisibility – we are hopeful that our Latina/o focused research contribution to intercultural communication not only brings Latina/o culture into theoretical relevance but also brings the wisdom of Latina/o culture into a much needed pragmatic application. Martín's story is our story and the iterations of it are felt in our lives every day. However, it is our hope that these iterations challenge understandings of performativity thus offering possibilities for the articulations of the complex performances of a mestizaje and latinidad.

References

Alcalá, R.C. (2001) From chingada to chingona: La Malinche redefined or, a long line of hermanas. *Aztlán, A Journal of Chicano Studies*, 26, 2, 31–61.

Anaya, R.A. (1984) *The Legend of La Llorona: A Short Novel*, Tonatiuh-Quinto Sol International, Berkeley, CA.

Anzaldúa, G. (1999) *Borderlands: La Frontera*, (2nd edn), Aunt Lute Books, San Francisco.

Aparicio, F.R. (2003) Jennifer as Selena: Rethinking *Latinidad* in media and popular culture. *Latino Studies*, 1 (1), 90–105.

Arteaga, A. (1997) *Chicano Poetics: Heterotexts and Hybridities*, Cambridge University Press, Cambridge.

Butler, J. (2006) *Gender Trouble: Feminism and the Subversion of Identity*, Routledge, New York.

Calafell, B.M. (2005) Pro(re)claiming loss: A performance pilgrimage in search of Malintzin Tenépal. *Text and Performance Quarterly*, 25 (1), 43–56.

Calafell, B.M. (2007) *Latina/o Communication Studies: Theorizing Performance*, Peter Lang, New York.

Chow, R. (2002) *The Protestant Ethnic and the Spirit of Capitalism*, Columbia University Press, New York.

Chuang, R. (2003) A postmodern critique of cross-cultural and intercultural research: Contesting essentialism, positivist dualism, and Eurocentricity, in *International and Intercultural Communication Annual Volume, 26: Ferment in the Field: Axiology/ Value, and Praxis*, (eds W.J. Starosta and G.-M. Chen), Sage, Thousand Oaks, CA, pp. 24–53.

Corey, F.C. (1998) The personal: Against the master narrative, in *The Future of Performance Studies: Visions and Revisions*, (ed S.J. Dailey), National Communication Association, Annandale, VA, pp. 249–253.

Corey, F.C. (2006) On possibility. *Text and Performance Quarterly*, 26 (4), 330–332.

Del Castillo, A. (1997) Malintzin Tenépal: A preliminary look into a new perspective, in *Chicana Feminist Thought: The Basic Historical Writings*, (ed. A.M. García), Routledge, New York, pp. 122–126.

Esquivel, L. (2007) *Malinche*, (trans. E. Mestre-Reed), Washington Square Press, New York.

Gaspar de Alba, A. (2005) Malinchista: A myth revisited, in *Feminism, Nation and Myth: La Malinche*, (eds R. Romero and A. Nolacea Harris), Arte Público Press, Houston, TX, pp. 4–5.

Gil-Gómez, E.M. (2000) *Performing La Mestiza: Textual Representations of Lesbians of Color and the Negotiation of Identities*, Garland, New York.

Hall, S. (1996) Introduction: Who needs "identity?," in *Questions of Cultural Identity*, (eds S. Hall and P. duGay), Sage, Thousand Oaks, CA, pp. 1–17.

Hill Collins, P. (2009) *Black Feminist Thought: Knowledge, Consciousness, and the Politics of Empowerment* (3rd edn), Routledge, New York.

Holling, M.A., and Calafell, B.M. (2007) Identities on stage and staging identities: ChicanoBrujo performances as emancipatory practices. *Text and Performance Quarterly*, 27, 1, 58–83.

Inda, J.X. (2000) Performativity, materiality, and the racial body. *Latino Studies Journal*, 11 (3), 74–99.

Lanyon, A. (2003) *The New World of Martín Cortes*, Da Capo Press, Cambridge, MA.

Madison, D.S. (1998) Performance, personal narratives, and the politics of possibility, in *The Future of Performance Studies: Visions and Revisions*, (ed. S.J. Dailey), National Communication Association, Annandale, VA, pp. 276–286.

Madison, D.S. (1999) Performing theory/Embodied writing. *Text and Performance Quarterly*, 19 (2), 107–124.

Messinger Cypus, S. (2005) "Mother" Malinche and allegories of gender, ethnicity, and national identity in Mexico, in *Feminism, Nation and Myth: La Malinche*, (eds. R. Romero and A. Nolacea Harris), Arte Público Press, Houston, TX, pp. 14–27.

Moon, D.G. (1996) Concepts of "culture": Implications for intercultural communication research. *Communication Quarterly*, 44, 1, 70–84.

Moraga, C. (2000) *Loving in the War Years: Lo que nunco pasó por sus labios*, (2nd edn), South End Press, Boston, MA.

Moraga, C., and Anzaldúa, G. (eds) (2002) *This Bridge Called my Back: Writings by Radical Women of Color* (3rd edn), Third Woman Press, Berkeley, CA.

Moreman, S.T. (2008) Hybrid performativity, south and north of the border: Entre la teoría y la materialidad de hibridación, in *Latina/o Communication Studies Today*, (ed. A.N. Valdivia), Peter Lang, New York, pp. 91–111.

Moreman, S.T. (2009) Memoir as performance: Strategies of hybrid ethnic identity. *Text and Performance Quarterly*, 29 (4), 346–366.

Moreman, S.T., and Calafell, B.M. (2008) *Buscando para nuestra latinidad:* Utilizing *La Llorona* for the cultural critique of *Chasing Papi. Journal of International and Intercultural Communication*, 1 (4), 309–326.

Muñoz, J.E. (2000) Feeling brown: Ethnicity and affect in Richard Bracho's *The Sweetest Hangover (and Other STDs). Theatre Journal*, 52, 67–79.

Nakayama, T.K. (1994) Show/down time: "Race," gender, sexuality, and popular culture. *Critical Studies in Media Communication*, 11 (2), 162–179.

Paz, O. (1991) *The Labyrinth of Solitude: The Other Mexico, Return to the Labyrinth of Solitude, Mexico and the United States, The Philanthropic Ogre*, Grove Press, New York.

Pollock, D. (1999) *Telling Bodies, Performing Birth: Everyday Narratives of Childbirth*, Columbia University Press, New York.

Reinelt, J. (2002) The politics of discourse: Performativity meets theatricality. *SubStance* #98/99, 31 (2 & 3), 201–215.

Román, D. (1997) Latino performance and identity. *Aztlán, A Journal of Chicano Studies*, 22 (2), 151–167.

Tafolla, C. (1993) La Malinche, in *Infinite Divisions: An Anthology of Chicana Literature*, (eds T.D. Rebolledo and E.S. Rivero), University of Arizona Press, Tucson, AZ, pp. 198–199.

Valdivia, A. (2004) Latinas as radical hybrid: Transnationally gendered traces in mainstream media. *Global Media Journal*, 3, 1–21.

24

We Got Game
Race, Masculinity, and Civilization in Professional Team Sport

Lisa A. Flores, Karen Lee Ashcraft and Tracy Marafiote

People say, I'm what's wrong with sports. I say, I'm a three-time NBA All-Star.
People say, I'm America's worst nightmare. I say, I'm the American Dream.
Latrell Sprewell, cited in Lefton, 1999, para. 4

For many players, fans, and spectators the event seemed almost unreal. Simultaneously sudden and yet a long time coming, the brawl that broke out at the Detroit Pistons/Indiana Pacers game in November of, 2004 "tore at the nation" (Brown, 2004, para. 10). That "madness" – fans throwing beer-filled cups at players, players rushing into the stands, and both ultimately tossing fists and bodies – indicated to some "a breach of sportsmanship extraordinary … in the present day" (Sappenfield, 2004, para. 2). The fight was depicted as the latest, perhaps most egregious, sign of the allegedly declining times. Media coverage both prior to and immediately following the fight traced what many describe as a sports culture in trouble (See, for instance, Nichols, 2002; Downey, 2003; Cohen, 2004). Sports fans are probably familiar with the various questionable acts associated with high profile athletes – arrests for drug use, domestic violence, and sexual assault; tensions between athletes, coaches, and referees; and fights between players. Athletes, media reports argue, seem increasingly surrounded by trouble (Araton, 2003).

According to commentators, these incidents, though extreme, reflect a troublesome trend in many US professional sports today (Slambrouck, 1998). Namely, the civilized aura of morality, teamwork, and passion for sport that once dominated the industry is decaying into a childish game among greedy, defiant, brutish stars. Typically, the NBA is touted as the archetype of decline, with Michael Jordan as the prized relic of a dying breed and Latrell Sprewell, Allen Iverson, and Ron Artest as the poster children of a sorry new lot. According to one report, basketball season means "another N.B.A. summer soap opera, the Young and the Felonious" (Araton, 2003, para. 6). Commentators

The Handbook of Critical Intercultural Communication, edited by Thomas K. Nakayama and Rona Tamiko Halualani. © 2010 Blackwell Publishing Ltd.

of various ilk call to reverse the trend. Arguing that "unnecessary violence and fight-ing" have got out of hand and that "changes must be instituted," reporters highlight what they depict as an alarming pattern (Denver Post, 2004, para. 2).

Long-time basketball and sports enthusiasts remind readers that such misbehav-ior is not new: "Over the last 15 years, fans have hurled bottles, batteries, snowballs and racial slurs at players, who have responded with fists, chairs, baseballs, and even spit" (Brown, 2004, para. 8). However, these writers also mark the current moment as unique: "It's a different era and a different violence" (Saraceno, 2003, para. 3). That difference is linked to larger issues, primarily the overall decline it allegedly represents. Moreover, concern revolves not just around the potential moral impli-cations, but adds a nostalgic cry for a past era in which players, coaches, and fans were ostensibly committed to the sport, not to the individual stars or the celebrity culture that surrounds them. Significantly, what emerges consistently in the con-temporary discourse is the argument that *this* moment is new, that this violence, this culture, this behavior is markedly different from previous times: "we're defi-nitely in the final days" (Zin, 1999, para. 4).

Such apocalyptic cries merge with another notable development. The new era is marked by the increasing dominance of African American men and more impor-tantly the related "hip-hop" culture commonly associated with urban Blackness in professional sport. Though evident across several sports, the trend is especially vivid in the NBA, where Black players comprise the overwhelming majority of stars. Today, the NBA sells its players in a strategic package of gritty, hip-hop Black masculinity. As one sports writer explains,

> The NBA's marketing machinery has sold a league that is 80% African-American (sic) to White fans and corporate America by embracing the culture – urban, inner-city, whatever code words for black [sic] you prefer – in which many of its players grew up. Listen to the rap music that is played in the arenas, watch the hip-hop dance moves of the cheerleaders and the edgy sneaker commercials that add to the celebrity of NBA stars. It has all given the league a street credibility, a cachet, that no other league enjoys. (Taylor, 1997, para. 3)

That marketing, commentators fear, had unanticipated consequences: "they've dis-covered the dark side of hip-hop has also infiltrated their game, with its 'bling-bling' ostentation, its unrepentant I-gotta-get-paid ruthlessness, its unregulated culture of possess, and the constant underlying threat of violence" (Wilbon, 2004, para. 2).

With some exceptions (For example, see Taylor, 1997; George, 1999), most pundits take care to sever race from their claims of civil decline of the NBA and professional sports more generally (Harris, 1997). For instance, Black icons like Michael Jordan and Tim Duncan are invoked to deny the role of race in the fall of civilized sport (Taylor, 1995; McCallum, 1997). Skeptical of such persistent disa-vowal, this essay places the discourse of decline and the surge of that "cool pose" of Black masculinity alongside one another to explore the gender and race subtext of the alleged degeneration of the NBA (Beavers, 1997). We take a closer look at public discourse to see if and how the narrative of decline in professional sport is racialized and with what theoretical and practical consequences for gender and race relations. We argue that the narrative of decline provides a discursive managing of civilized/primitive tensions in masculinity. More specifically, we maintain that the discourse of decline is but one contemporary manifestation of a racial, even racist, tale that serves to demonize Black masculinity.

We pursue this contention through a critical intercultural lens so as to underscore the centrality of historical, social, material, economic, and other cultural contexts on interactions across and within cultural groups. In doing so, we highlight the situatedness, the particularity – to a culture, nation, region, era, decade, year, moment – of any communicative feat, and we demonstrate the significance of intersections of subjectivities, with particular attention to race, ethnicity, and gender, but also to class and sexual orientation. From a critical intercultural viewpoint, then, the examination of intercultural tensions in the NBA can never be only about Blackness or Whiteness or about masculinity or, especially, only about basketball – it must necessarily take into account the axes of multiple cultural markers (Black masculinity and White masculinity) and their positioning in relation to other social events (histories of racial tensions and oppressions), institutions (the NBA and various genres of media), and processes (the framing of particular players, such as Latrell Sprewell, and coaches, like Bobby Knight).

As critical intercultural scholars, our goals extend beyond a focus on only the written word, the disseminated image, or even the embodiment of gender, race, or sexuality. Rather, immersion in critical work entails identifying both patterns of communication and inequities that span cultural borders and thereby reify difference and distance between members of colliding cultural units (See, for instance, Moon and Nakayama, 2005). Still, critical intercultural communication assumes a haziness in these cultural boundaries, noting differences within cultures as well as similarities between them, refusing to reduce identity to *one* style of Black masculinity or *the* manifestation of White masculinity as, for instance, these subjectivities mix on and off the court (Nakayama, 2000). Our analysis is informed by and seeks to contribute to the argument within critical intercultural communication that race and gender are ideological constructions that pervade and shape cultural encounters. More specifically, logics of dominance such as masculinity and Whiteness are, critical intercultural communication scholars argue, foundational structures within US history and culture, and as such these logics operate throughout all intercultural encounters, whether interpersonal or mediated (See, for instance, Butterworth, 2007; Dickinson and Anderson, 2004; Fassett and Warren, 2004; Hasian, 2003; Oates, 2007; Rogers, 2007; Warren, 2001; Watts, 2005; Willink, 2008).

Engaging this approach to scholarship demands integrating principles that go beyond the page and spill over into the lived experience; it is making daily choices that shore up and model the ideals so easily laid down in ink. A critical intercultural lens requires engagement with the political and social processes that subtly and sometimes imperceptibly shape popular cultural, political, educational, militaristic – and on and on – discourses, and in these ways construct partitions and paths that channel internal perceptions and external interrelations into narrow, extant possibilities (see Watts and Orbe, 2002).

This essay is an example of a critical intercultural analysis of seemingly mundane, naturalized practices, places in which popular cultural practices (e.g., recreational pastimes like basketball) draw on, salvage, and recycle familiar historical themes. In the United States, traditional racial relations have hinged upon assumed difference between (primitive) Blackness and (civilized) Whiteness in particular, as these racial markers have coincided with embodiments/enactments of masculinity. Below, we offer a conceptual context for the importance of civility to professional sport. Specifically, we theorize professional team sport – especially that which emphasizes aggressive physicality – as an ongoing cultural performance that manages White masculinity's problematic relation to mind and body, "civilization" and "primitivity" through reliance on what we call a racial contract. Turning to an in-depth analysis of press coverage, we demonstrate how the discourse of decline is a distinctively gendered and raced tale, which mourns the passing rule of a civilized White masculinity and loathes the rising reign of a primitive Black masculinity. We conclude with arguments for critical and social attention to this tale, both for its repetition of long-standing racial assumptions and for attendant possibilities to contest those assumptions.

Professional Team Sport and the Trade in Civilized and Primitive Masculinities

Civilized imperatives, primal longings: An enduring tension in white masculine subjectivity

Of course, the very notion of White masculinity is problematic. Like all identities, White masculinity is multiple and variable, shifting in relation to time (history and age), space (material and symbolic location), structure (formal and informal arrangements like institutionalized class systems), and so forth. Despite such important fluctuations, White masculinity – in most, if not all, of its forms – tends to dominate masculinities of color. Recognizing this point, critical studies of gender and race often depict White masculinity as a monolithic and stable hegemonic identity (Mumby, 1997, 1998). Yet, while predictable, dominance is never guaranteed, for identity discourse is fraught with tensions that require ongoing maintenance (Hall, 1985). It is the process of discursive maintenance, of navigating such tensions, that interests us here. In particular, we are concerned with the relationship between White masculinity and social constructions of the "civilized" and "primitive." Our primary aim is to theorize broader racial struggles embedded in this relationship by scrutinizing it through the lens of a tacit social racial contract.

In the United States, at least, civilization has come to connote the triumph of mind, will, and rationality over body, impulse, and nature. The term summons images of morality, sophisticated organization, technological and scientific progress, intellectual labor, and a general ethos of self-restraint. In contrast, primitive is symbolically linked to the corporeal, associated with unmediated nature and raw physicality – things bodied, impulsive, passionate, sexual, indulgent, and savage (Torgovnick, 1990, 1998). Especially in the United States, the civilized-primitive binary is imbued with gendered and raced meaning. In a compelling historical account of "manliness and civilization" in the United States, Bederman traces how the notion of civilization became aligned with White masculinity through alternating contrast and affiliation with the discourse of essential femininity and the discourse of the primal rapist (Bederman, 1995). One strand of discourse depicted White men and women joining hands to advance and protect civilization from the dark savage. A second strand of discourse proposed that White men save civilization from feminization by reclaiming the suppressed savage within; the words of popular public figures like Teddy Roosevelt and G. Stanley Hall illustrate this logic. Whereas the former discourse cast civilization as an exclusively White terrain, the latter entrusted men only with civilization's defense. Together, these discourses at once invited and refused the participation of gendered and raced figures, who embody the respective vulnerabilities of excessive civilized or primitive influence. Namely, civilized masculinities risk feminization, while primitive masculinities are perilously subject to bodily whim.

Although US White masculinities vary in relation to the civilized-primitive binary (e.g., blue- vs. White-collar identities), discourses of Whiteness today remain generally aligned with those of civilization. As hinted above, however, Whiteness, in particular White masculinity, also remains prone to the primitive. In such narratives, the primitive is often depicted as a dark, crude, and dangerously irresistible manliness, desired, deflected, consumed, feared, obeyed, and subjugated (Bederman, 1995; see also Torgovnick, 1990, 1998). Given this complex of raced and gendered meaning, White masculinity can be said to straddle the civilized-primitive binary; to "overdo" one pole is to deny the other and thereby render racial or gender identity suspect. Yet it is no simple feat to perform both poles, considering their depiction as unequal opposites. Bederman describes this chronic tension in White masculinity as "the neurasthenic paradox," referring to its materialization in a so-called nervous disorder that neared epidemic proportions in the United States between 1880 and, 1910. Neurasthenia was attributed to over-civilization, and at greatest risk "were middle-and upper-class businessmen and professionals whose highly evolved bodies had been physically weakened by advances in civilization" (1995, p. 87). The discursive formation of this "disease" flagged a persistent ideological contradiction: "Only White male bodies had the capacity to be truly civilized. Yet, at the same time, civilization destroyed White male bodies. How could powerful, civilized manhood be saved?" (p. 88).

Possible discursive "solutions" to the neurasthenic paradox abound. One option can be found in cultural alternation between ideal forms of White masculinity, from tough guy to sensitive man and back again. In response to the neurasthenia "outbreak" of the late-nineteenth century, for example, public discourse of the time embraced "fantasies of recovering an unspoiled, primitive masculinity," which "drew on the images and ideology of the savage Other" to articulate a "passionate manhood" (Bordo, 1999, p. 249). Several scholars note striking parallels with contemporary discourses that depict hyper-civilized and emasculated White, middle-class men craving primitive encounters (Ashcraft and Flores, 2003; Bordo and Robinson, 2000; Rotundo, 1993). Rarely does such identity discourse reject civilization altogether. Rather, in Tarzan-like fashion, conflicted subjectivities merge to support " 'civilization's larger narrative of millennial advancement toward a higher race and perfect manhood" (Bederman, 1995, p. 218).

Another option entails flirtation, rather than consummation, with the primitive. Such discourse might encourage White men to "sow wild oats" in youth or to seek periodic primal inoculations throughout life. For instance, G. Stanley Hall pre-scribed savage behavior as a crucial developmental boyhood rite (and *right* – in today's terms, "boys will be boys" (Bederman, 1995). Likewise, many organized sports are discursively cast as ritualized outlets for boyish primal development and manly savage expression. In some contrast to discourses of alternation and consum-mation, flirtation discourse proposes access to the primitive in controlled doses – a temporary and measured primal high to counteract civilized repression.

Binding these and other discursive options is a tricky relation between civilized and primitive, wherein both can rouse trust and suspicion, but one primitivity pre-dictably services the other (civilization), in what we identify elsewhere as a "con-stant juggling act" (Ashcraft and Flores, 2003, p. 8). For White masculine subjectivities in particular, primitive symbolism appears to provide relief, stimula-tion, pain, comfort, conquest, and endless pangs of insecurity; hence, it is an indis-pensable force to be monitored and tamed by narratives of civilization. Extending current research on gender and sport, we argue that professional team sports sup-ply a crucial arena for the discursive negotiation of this enduring tension in White masculinity.

Navigating the neurasthenic paradox: Professional team sport and the civilized-primitive binary

Research on sport has only recently turned from studies of men's sport to those that explicitly examine male players as men, marking the centrality of gender in sport (See, for instance, McKay, Messner and Sabo, 2000). Much of this work demonstrates that men dominate on court while women remain on the sidelines, often as sexualized objects of an implicitly male gaze.[1] The research also calls atten-tion to multiple forms of masculinity at play, noting that all men are not equally dominant (see Boyd, 1997; Hoberman, 1997). For example, the gender coding of sport, in which hard bodies are lauded and soft demeaned, often demands and rewards a kind of primitive masculinity (Miller, 1998). We develop this branch of the literature by theorizing how professional sport – at least, those forms that emphasize a kind of raw physicality and/or tribal warfare constrained by rules of order – engages the civilized-primitive binary.

Central to much professional sport is its larger frame of competition. Often depicted as battles, team sports in particular tend to summon war imagery. Such discourse – in which enemies are slaughtered, massacred, crushed, buried, stuffed, walloped, wiped out, and defeated – facilitates a primitive masculinity. Moreover, games entail grueling bodily contests of virile strength, in which athletes, coaches, and audiences alike expect that "every guy out there should be a killer" (NBA commentator cited in Messner *et al.*, p. 386). These narratives of combat and conquest suggest a masculine subject made potent through group solidarity and triumph amid physical violence (Jeffords, 1994).

Importantly, the characters in this play are deeply raced, for this battle – between teams, between civilized/primitive tensions – engages a historically situated struggle of race and gender and more precisely, of masculine superiority and White supremacy. Historically, the primal body has invigorated White masculinity with the awesome threat of its physicality, but primal worship only works if the savage body ultimately succumbs to the superior strength of the White rational mind. Herein lies the latent struggle enabled in sport – what we, drawing on Mills (1997) identify as a racial contract, or an implicit set of social rules and mores, both descriptive and normative, used to explain public relations and embedded in racial logics. A fundamental assumption of the racial contract is that "race is in no way an 'afterthought,' a 'deviation' from ostensibly raceless Western ideals, but rather a central shaping constituent of those ideals" (p. 14). Moreover, this racial contract creates and maintains a moral hierarchy where Whiteness reigns and through which it establishes economic relations that ensure its ideological and material dominance. We emphasize here the notion of "contract," which refers to implicit, preferred relationships of exchange among relevant parties (for example, players, coaches, audience, NBA, specific team organizations).

The archetypal racial contract of professional sport is illustrated poignantly by Bederman's analysis of the classic boxing match between Jack Johnson and Jim Jeffries, which at once embodied fear of, desire, and disgust for the "dark savage rapist" body (1995, p. 1–5). In brief, Bederman maintains that (White) uproar against, and discipline of, Black boxer Jack Johnson was triggered by his success against White boxers and with White women. That is, Johnson's refusal to defer to Whiteness, in and outside the arena of sport, violated social expectations of White masculine supremacy, reneging on a time-honored treaty. We argue that this enduring racial contract assumes a contemporary face in the discourse of decline surrounding the NBA. More specifically, we maintain that expectations about roles, rules, and relations, particularly as manifest in professional team sport, are laden with gendered and racial, as well as understood heteronormative, assumptions. If/when those expectations are not met, it is as if some players, notably Black players, have broken a tacit agreement. Here, we explore the concept of the racial contract.

As Mills (1997) explains, the racial contract presumes that spaces and the bodies at play within them are regulated by norms and ideals of race/mind/body. Spaces and the bodies within those spaces are socially delineated as civilized or savage, rational or emotional. Drawing on familiar tropes of race and biology, for example, professional team sports have long demarcated participants by brain vs. brawn (Banet-Weiser, 1999). Consider the typical divide between coach and player, or the common look of quarterbacks in contrast with that of team "workhorses." In part, this means that professional sport becomes a site in which Black men can and perhaps should defeat White men, for, per racial thinking, this space – the court – is about the body, the physically strong racialized body of Blackness. NBA superstar Dennis Rodman explains that, "When you talk about race in basketball, the whole thing is simple: a black [sic] player knows he can go out on the court and kick a White player's ass" (quoted in Carrington, 1998, p. 279). Such victories are permissible, within the racial contract, only when they remain ideologically confined, when they occur on court.

Further, the space and ideology of sport (e.g., the court) expects and encourages primitive play so long as that play respects the rules of civility. In other words, primal figures do not run free in sport; they are regulated and channeled through familiar methods of civilization. Particularly in the case of professional team sports, they are deeply bureaucratized. For example, the NBA's specialized roles, strict hierarchy of authority, and exhaustive system of technical rules – which mirror many corporate, educational, and militaristic enterprises – illustrate the point. Referees function as representatives of order and restraint, armed with the legitimate power (and the props to prove it, like uniforms and whistles) to discipline those who threaten "civilized" play with "savage" expressions. Coaches, often donning the suit-and-tie symbolism of corporate hierarchy, stand as visual reminders that the "killers" on court answer to the wisdom and command of experienced elders. These (White) bosses control the organization of sport. They oversee and manage, and their space is one in which rationality prevails. In this sense, a player's untamed strength *and* controlled aggression, his rage *and* submission, become uneasy teammates, as the primitive "requirements" of sport, at least per social expectations of racial relations, are entwined with expectations that players channel their primal natures as directed. As Rose and Friedman explain, "The star athlete must be tough, determined, and unstoppable, indifferent to opposition, and yet respectful of the rules of the game" (Rose and Friedman, 1997, p. 8). After all, a primary condition of the contract is respect for the principal hierarchy, which requires White domination and Black submission.

The contract, and its assumption of controlled violence, also expects Black male complicity in a gladiator-like fantasy made contemporary by commerce, wherein "civilized" (White) men can vicariously participate in performances of primitive (Black) masculinity. Put another way, it is in the spectacle of sport that racial narratives contrasting Black bodies against White minds team up with those that normalize Blacks in submissive service, willingly entertaining White society. Historically, Whites have attempted to consume Blackness, wearing and then discarding it, often with appreciation (see Roediger, 1991). Similarly, the commodification of an edgy urban Blackness that now dominates NBA discourse (Banet-Weiser, 1999) taps abiding interest in consumption of the ethnic and exotic (Lipsitz, 1998). Crucial to the contract, however, things ethnic are to be appreciated, appropriated, and diminished by Whiteness; they are not to pose a challenge. These "dressing-room" relations, wherein Blackness can be held at arms length and worn or removed at will, allow Whites a safe and comfortable way to negotiate racial affiliations. It is perhaps that "the very representations of race that generate terror in all of us at the sight of young black men ... compels most of America to want to wear their shoes" (Kelley, cited in Harrison, 2000, p. 35–39).

The public promotion and commodification of professional team sports facilitates civilized and primitive tensions. For instance, through the purchase of team or player paraphernalia, spectators who feel over-civilized in their mundane lives might affiliate with the primal ethos of masculine rivalry (Messner, Dunbar and Hunt, 2000). In this sense, the commerce of professional team sport may indirectly assist other economic endeavors (e.g., the emasculated corporate subject invigorated by temporary immersion in NBA narratives of gender, race, and warfare). Here, we go so far as to suggest not only that professional team sports involve a literal trade in discourses of masculinity, race, and civilization, but also that the trade can have material impact. As audiences consume professional team sports, they vicariously participate in cultural performances that may affect their own lived subjectivities, as well as larger social systems (Rose and Friedman, 1997).

In sum, we argue that professional team sports like US basketball provide a vital cultural arena for the discursive negotiation of White masculinity's problematic relation to the civilized-primitive binary. By releasing "the primitive" in the confines of a familiar "civilized" structure, professional team sports systematically allow the former to be exercised and enjoyed in the service of the latter. In this profoundly raced and gendered game, civilized masters direct, and (over)civilized spectators devour, the labor of primal players. Next, we apply this theoretical lens to explore the race and gender subtext of recent NBA discourse, which mourns the decline of civilization in professional basketball.

A Dark Day for the NBA: Civilized and Primitive Masculinities Face Off in the Discourse of Decline

In this section, we examine the discourse of professional basketball's decline for the ways in which that discourse engages the civilized-primitive binary. We turn to popular press accounts of the sport; specifically, we analyze 80 articles appearing in magazines such as *Sports Illustrated* and the *Village Voice*. Ultimately, we argue that the discourse of decline casts Black masculinity as boyish, impulsive, and immoral, painting White masculinity as mature, refined, and moral. What's more, the discourse longs for a time when White disciplinarians civilized professional sport and Black boy-savages knew their rightful place. We begin with a general narrative that constructs a problematic boyish masculinity and its attendant violent implications. We then compare coverage of two strikingly similar moments of violence, one surrounding Black "bad boy" Latrell Sprewell and his choking of his coach and the other involving the notoriously volatile White coach Bobby Knight and his choking of his player.

Men to boyz: What's wrong with the new generation

Central to the discourse of decline is the claim that a generational shift is underway in the NBA. Generally, the shift is characterized as something new – as a break between a venerable old guard and a sorry new lot of players, *not* as a gradual intensification of patterns long present. Neither is the shift set up as a necessary pass of the torch, with pros and cons of old and new; rather, the new is marked as an indisputable problem. Some liken the changing of the guard to a virus or epidemic ravaging the league. Others treat it as a contagious "attitude problem" or even mental illness (e.g., a "lunacy," "madness" that requires Freudian talents) (Taylor,, 1995, para. 1). A few depict the trend as a problem of organizational culture and the development of destructive group norms (e.g., NBA climate) (see Benedict, 1997). Whatever the diagnosis, the discourse of decline resoundingly vilifies the new generation based on the charges to follow.

It appears to be virtual consensus among critics that the youngest stars pose the biggest problem. As used here, "young" carries a dual meaning. First, it refers to literal youth: Young men in "their early, 20s … several are teenagers" (Harris, 1997, para. 20). It also connotes a childish immaturity: "prima donnas" with no clue what "growing up has [sic] to do with basketball … The NBA has more whiny youngsters than a day-care center at nap time" (Taylor, 1995, paras. 1, 4, 8). The juvenile theme is backed by a complementary image of NBA management as hapless guardians: "Like well-intentioned but weak-willed parents, the league has consistently doled out tepid justice" (Benedict, 1997, para. 6). Descriptions of NBA youth call to mind a particular kind of boy: the typecast of a privileged teen who fancies himself entitled to the world. One writer put it plainly, "The biggest issue currently facing the NBA is the growing perception that its players, particularly its youngest stars, are spoiled, arrogant brats" (Taylor, para. 11).

What commentators find most disconcerting about the juvenile new hoopster is that he is not simply "sowing wild oats," or releasing youthful steam on the path to responsible manhood. The discourse of decline suggests that, for him, boyhood is a chronic affliction – that childish rebellion *is* his definition of manhood. For example, Seattle guard Gary Payton[2] insists that:

> The players all have to stand up for themselves. Maybe it's more that way than it used to be, but it should be that way. A coach shouldn't just talk to you as if you're something less than who you are … This is about manhood. The respect of one man to another. If the coach doesn't respect you as a man, or treat you like a man, then you have to stand up for it (Taylor, 1995, para. 30).

It is likely, some writers lament, that this tendency to mistake boyish resistance for manhood was planted early, during the "unfortunate" background of these players who, we learn, have not actually enjoyed the life of privilege implied by the profile thus far.

In this narrative, the new NBA "boys" are "superbly talented athletes raised in neighborhoods saddled with poverty and crime," who catch a first glimpse of escape:

> when a slick-talking, highly paid coach with national prominence pays them a home visit in hopes of recruiting. The recruiter, who, more often than not, is White and affluent, stresses all the right concepts: academics, social life, support systems. He panders to the player, coddling him if that's what it takes to sign him (Benedict, 1997, paras. 3–4).

Harris explains that:

> The majority of the recipients of lucrative $100 million pacts, particularly in basketball, are African-American (sic) males barely in their early 20s. Several are teenagers who identify with rap stars such as Busta Rhymes and Puff Daddy, and they proudly maintain strong ties to their urban brethren. Often, this assemblage includes young men with gang affiliations from ... innercity areas. Sporting cornrow hairstyles and wearing baggy shorts below their knee (1997, paras. 20–22)

Invoking tacit articulations of race with class, such common depictions invite a kind of sympathy for the young player. They serve to make sensible, but nonetheless regrettable, his regressive rendition of manhood. The tacit message suggests that, due to fateful circumstance, today's hoopster has not been schooled in the games of civilization. Consequently, he is an immature boy caught up in the surface trappings of success yet unprepared – or unwilling – to shoulder the substantive obligations of "real" manhood.

Awarded instant fame and fortune but lacking a sense of their role in a larger system, today's NBA generation is described as approaching the game differently than their predecessors. The new generation, according to public coverage, manifests a superficial "me" attitude. Devoid of team spirit or a real love of the game, they are more concerned with "fancy passing and celebratory dancing" than with team success (George, 1999, para. 14). According to the discourse, the new generation is comprised of individualistic stars. College coach Bobby Knight complains that, these days, he rarely finds the "clean-cut kids in letter sweaters who would rather set a pick than see themselves on Sports Center" (Callahan, 1997, para. 18). Other observers note the institutional encouragement of player selfishness and entitlement. For example, older players reminisce of a time when fans came to watch games, not to emphasize particular jersey numbers and their latest video game or movie (Taylor, 1995). As Magic Johnson noted, "The league has promoted superstars, not teams, and the play reflects it" (quoted in Lopez, 1999, para. 5).

In the discourse of decline, the young NBA star is defined as engaging a brash, entitled, selfish boyhood as the ultimate manliness, thus rejecting the more civilized manhood of days gone by, based on professional dignity, restraint, teamwork, and responsibility. Many commentators complain that today's NBA player finds "new and creative ways to act unprofessionally" (Taylor, 1995, para. 1). Generally, this gripe refers to the new generation's lack of discipline and order. For instance, disregarding formal authority, players allegedly scoff at the notion that coaches, management, and other authorities inherently deserve respect. Taylor wonders how the young hoopsters can "demand respect from their coaches and team management while showing none in return" (para. 11). He cites specific sins of boyish insolence: forcing a trade by persistent pouting or refusing to cooperate, expressing public anger or disagreement with a coach, and engaging in rebellious acts of revenge for decisions about play/bench time.

Beyond basic respect for authority, today's player allegedly dismisses other fundamentals of hierarchy, such as the "understood rule" that one commands esteem only when he has earned it through "grunt" time served, experience, and performance history. Charles Barkley, a "hothead" from the older generation, distinguished old from new bad boys in this way: "A lot of the (younger players) haven't earned the right to walk around like they own the league. They feel they don't have to respect anyone. They act like they've accomplished so much when they haven't done a damn thing" (quoted in Harris, 1997, para. 22). Lacking a sense of place, the new breed is depicted as standing up for themselves and demanding respect before their time. Some commentators attribute such behavior to a selfish preoccupation with cash, enabled by the NBA: "Respect for the old establishment was clearly fading as huge salaries boosted egos and brash wannabe superstars began to elbow their way toward the inevitable post-Michael Jordan era" (Stein and Fulton, 1997, para. 8).

Exacerbating a greedy disrespect for hierarchy is an alleged trend among the new generation to exhibit a weak work ethic. Several articles criticize the tendency of young players to skip practice or arrive late. For instance, one writer credited the Nets' Derrick Coleman with this remark: "Well, whoop-de-damn-do. I miss practice ... It's no big deal. Some players are just practice players. They step on the court and don't do —. I come out and bust my butt every night" (quoted in Taylor, 1995, para. 21). According to the discourse of decline, the new NBA hoopster oozes raw, unrefined, almost natural talent, which he refuses to perfect through hard work. His casual disregard for the systematic cultivation of skill is contrasted against old-school players and coaches, who understood the demanding prerequisites of success. According to the discourse, players once knew that grueling physical routines and verbal abuse from coaches was meant to build excellence, not to demean, since "pat-on-the-butt" coaches did not win championships (Huber, 2000, para. 3).

Finally, the discourse of decline suggests that today's players lack professionalism not only in their game, but also in their self-presentation. Benedict comments, "An obvious chasm exists between the men wearing stylish suits and barking out instructions on the sidelines and the boys running up and down the hardwood in too-long shorts" (Benedict, 1997, para. 2). Those "boys" are commonly cited for balking at the idea of wearing jacket and tie, for refusing such reasonable demands as tying one's shoelaces before entering court (Taylor, 1995). Sporting cornrows and low-hanging shorts, today's hoopsters are credited with the rise of a new, flamboyant NBA style deserving of concern and ridicule (see, for instance, McCallum, 1997; Powell, 1999; Scott, 1998).

In sum, the discourse of decline paints the new generation of NBA players as an immature, impetuous, selfish, showy, and unprofessional band of boy-stars, spoiled with unrefined physical talent and sudden heaps of cash. The discourse suggests that the circumstances of their upbringing can explain their juvenile vision of manliness, but the discourse also holds that their version of masculinity should prompt social concern for several reasons. Among them, today's player does not aspire to civilized manhood; instead, his behavior implies that permanent boyhood is a viable stance. Moreover, that boyish stance rejects the substantive obligations of civilized manhood accepted by the former generation of players, such as a sense of professionalism entailing commitment to team, respect for hierarchy, a strong work ethic, and conservative self-presentation. Importantly, the discourse of decline depicts the masculinity of the new generation as more than socially *un*productive; it is also potentially *de*structive, fraught with volatile anti-sociability, "on-court thuggishness and off-court criminal conduct" (Benedict, 1997, para. 6). The "cuddly" Jordan "model" has been replaced with an "in-your-face" attitude; stars like Allen Iverson, Rasheed Wallace, and Latrell Sprewell are said to bring an unsavory, even dangerous aggression to the league (McCallum, 2000). Our reading of relevant texts suggests, first, that similar forms of aggression are coded differently depending on their agents and, second, that attending to how violence emerges as a destructive or constructive force can clarify the role of race in the discourse of decline. Next, we develop these claims by comparing press coverage of two specific and physically analogous instances of aggression in basketball.

Racial images in parallel cases of violence: the primitive present against a civilized past

In, 1997, basketball fans witnessed two strikingly parallel and noteworthy incidents: a choking attack by Black NBA player Latrell Sprewell on his White coach P.J. Carlesimo and a choking attack by White college basketball coach Bobby Knight on White player Neil Reed. At the time, the discourse of NBA decline was already gaining momentum, and commentators soon named Sprewell (or "Spree") the poster child of decline. Meanwhile, Knight was frequently depicted as an (over)enthusiastic defender of "the good old days" of basketball. The former incident met with a flurry of media indignation and the harshest non-drug-related penalty imposed by the NBA at that time (Starr and Samuels, 1997). The latter, in contrast, raised some eyebrows at excessive authority and resulted in what amounted to a warning.[3] Why such divergent responses, and what can they tell us about racial dimensions of the discourse of decline in civilized masculinity?

A violent spree

When Latrell Sprewell threatened and throttled his coach, P.J. Carlesimo, the Golden State Warriors terminated his lucrative four-year contract, and the NBA suspended him for a year without pay. In the surge of press coverage following the incident, a narrative of danger emerged around Sprewell as the embodiment of a rising, unpredictable, uncontrollable aggression in the NBA. Commentators noted that the "wild, pulsating, fearless" efforts that generated his on-court success also cast suspicion on his character (D'Alessandro, 1999, para. 20). They compared Spree to such social and political villains as Saddam Hussein and Oklahoma bomber Timothy McVeigh (Lefton, 2000; Stein an Fulton, 1997). They marked him as a "thug" (Leo, 1998, para. 2) and a "heinous" (*Sprewell rebounds*, 1998, para. 84) one at that for the "Bay Area Strangler" – as he was dubbed – was not only depicted as violent, but viciously, arrogantly so (D'Alessandro, 1998, para. 2; *Golden State*, 1999, para. 1).

Accounts of the choking episode stressed his inability to cool off in the locker room and his initial impenitence thereafter (See, for instance, Freidman, 1997; Harris, 1997; Lambert and Baker, 1997; Stein and Fulton, 1997). The choking was couched not as an isolated incident but as part of a long history of "on-court misbehavior," including threatening a teammate with a 2-by-4 (Freidman, 1997, para. 2). Players concerns over Spree's "intensity" were invoked; as Warriors' Adonal Foyle observed, "I had never seen anyone so hyper" (quoted in Lambert and Baker, 1997, para. 2). Several reporters depicted Spree as an off-court hoodlum as well: "[Sprewell] accumulated a number of driving-related offenses, and in September, 1995 he was charged with threatening Oakland police officer ... 'I make more money than you would ever see, and I'm from the ghetto ... You can be shot real easy'" (quoted in Lambert and Baker, para. 6). His reckless driving charge was detailed as further proof of volatility (*Latrell Sprewell*, 1998; O'Brien and Hersch, 1998). Allegedly attesting to his lack of civilized human feelings was his oft-quoted response to a pit bull's attack on his daughter: "These things happen" (quoted in Reilly, 1999, para. 2).

Despite arguable similarities to a long history of "bad boy" behavior in professional sport (e.g., Dennis Rodman, Charles Barkley), most commentators set the Sprewell incident apart as a new and different form of violence.[4] Former boxer and sports sociologist George Eisen put it this way: "Sport is ritualized aggression. In a sociological sense, it's tribal behavior, and when Dennis Rodman kicks a photographer, it's against another tribe. But this was against Sprewell's own tribe. That's something new" (quoted in Slambrouck, 1998, para. 12). And Carlesimo was not simply any member of "Sprewell's own tribe" but, to extend the somewhat problematic metaphor, its "Chief." The collective vehemence of reactions to the incident hints that it tapped into deep, racial and masculine insecurities: a trepidation of aging, physically deteriorating White "tribal" leaders who see him as a young, hard-bodied, brazen outsider whose hyper-masculine, primitive Blackness challenges their decaying, conventional White manhood and authority. Other observers underscore the unpredictability, if not irrationality, of Sprewell's aggression. As one explained, "So the animal trainer cracks the whip too close to the whiskers once too often, the beast swipes back, and now everyone wants to shoot the tiger"(Stravinsky, 1999, para. 5). Even this more sympathetic account portrays Spree's violence as wild, primal, instinctual self-defense, not as that of a civilized adult actor defending his manhood against challenge.

Certainly, responses to the choking episode ranged, but across much press coverage, Sprewell came to epitomize what was wrong with the new NBA generation. Even Spree's contrite return to basketball one year later evoked public concern. One NBA fan mourned, "I thought we all got away from [Sprewell's] primordial impulse" (quoted in Lee, 1999, para. 7). Indeed, that "primordial impulse" was raised to sound an alarm "all over the civilized universe" (Bing, 1998, para. 2). Critics feared a larger threat, namely that the impulsively defiant NBA hoopster is irresistible, particularly to a younger audience. Some commentators reported, for example, that high school athletes have internalized expectations of entitlement to special treatment (see, for instance, Jackson, 1997). As one high school coach lamented, "Today's athlete ... wants to be pampered" (quoted in Slambrouck, 1998, para. 9). Others worried about the message sent to young boys when violence and disregard for superiors carries minimal punishment (see *Sprewell rebounds*, 1998; Stravinsky, 1998). One imagined the following scenario:

> There will be a replay of Latrell Sprewell blowing by an opponent on the way to the rack. The kid will turn to his pops and say, "I want a Sprewell jersey." "I don't know," Pops will respond. "He did choke his coach, you know." The kid will listen and reply, "I know he did, Pops, but I like his cornrows" (George, 1999, paras. 1–2).

While some commentators expressed hope for role models in such figures as Grant Hill and Tim Duncan, most concurred that the post-Jordan era is beset by the "urban rhythms" and "street credibility" of players like Latrell Sprewell (George, 1999).

Hence, the discourse of decline – particularly as developed around Spree's violence – holds that, because of the growing social influence of the new "urban" player, the NBA is "becoming too dangerous," or – as few confess outright – "'too black'" (Taylor, 1997, para. 5). Indeed, many balked when Sprewell appeared in a commercial hailing him as a modern rendition of "the American Dream."

Overzealous high priest ... or white knight?
It seems that, 1997 was a year of poor anger management. Indiana University head coach Bobby Knight went on his own violent spree, choking player Neil Reed during practice and later, in, 1999, allegedly choking a man outside a local restaurant (Huber, 2000). Although it occurred in, 1997, the Reed choking was brought to light in April, 2000 with the release of a videotape. Like the Sprewell incident, this choking episode elicited much media attention. Yet, while few condoned or

dismissed Knight's actions, most responses did not reflect the demonizing rhetoric that dominated reactions to Spree.

As in the case of Sprewell, most commentators noted Knight's history of aggression. In fact, he was renowned for displays of temper entailing kicking, yelling, and throwing – chairs, punches, racial epithets, and so on (DeCourcy, 2000; see also Callahan, 1997; Huber, 2000). Simultaneously, however, he was described as a hugely successful coach and a consistent man of principle. Much commentary stressed Knight's successes and his refusal to adopt "softer" methods that might make him more popular but less effective as a coach (Huber, 2000). Observers emphasized Knight's insistence that "what was right twenty-five years ago is still right. I'm not going to change – it's up to them to change. The best teachers I've known are intolerant people. They don't tolerate mistakes" (quoted in Huber, 2000, para. 29). Defending his actions in the aftermath of the choking revelation, Knight explained, "I've always been confrontational, especially when I know I'm right" (quoted in Tresniowski *et al.*, 2000, para. 4). As with Spree, then, Knight's history of aggression took center court, as did his refusal to back down and repent. Also like Spree, Knight exerted violence against his own team. Yet whereas Spree's violent past served up evidence of reckless thuggery, Knight's history supplied proof of reliability. Whereas Spree's initial defense of his actions met with social outrage, which persisted even after he performed contrition, Knight's self-defense met with relative understanding of this man of consistent – albeit at times questionable – principle. In other words, Knight's actions against his own team, however regrettable, were framed not as disregard for the collective but as designed for its ultimate good. How was this striking contrast achieved amid such similar circumstances?

First, press coverage of Knight's behavior converged on two common themes: discipline and hierarchy. Characterized as a "demanding father figure" with a love of the game, Knight was – at least in some eyes – "the greatest teacher I have ever seen" (Tresniowski *et al.*, 2000, para. 5; Kindred, 2000, para. 17). Reacting to the choking video, some players portrayed Knight's violent instruction as serving their own best interests. IU forward Jarrod Odle explained, "I don't want him to change completely. I knew what I was getting into when I got here" (quoted in DeCourcy, 2000, para. 3). In short, Spree was a subordinate and Knight, a superior; while Spree thus appeared to lack all sense of discipline, Knight was configured as an instrument thereof.

Furthermore, Knight's aggression was contextualized as part of a more balanced personality. For instance, reports of his tantrums were tempered with attention to his "soft side." Accounts of Knight's selflessness as embodying the "old" spirit of basketball illustrate the point. Commentators described his concern for player discipline beyond court performance; we learn, for instance, of his high graduation rates and his "clean program" (Huber, 2000; Tresniowski *et al.*, 2000, para. 17). Other observers noted Knight's willingness to put his own professional success on hold to help others. From promoting former players to mentoring younger coaches, Knight often appeared as "doing the right thing" (Huber, 2000, para. 57). Evidence of generosity also emerged in attention to his efforts at fund-raising and his community-mindedness (Tresniowski *et al.*, 2000). The resulting image is of a gifted, caring, and admittedly demanding coach who strives to meet multiple professional and social obligations, such as cultivating his players and giving back to his community. In contrast, Spree was depicted as a self-centered animal devoid of caring and community. Consider, for example, the depiction of Spree as a threatened beast or the report of the pit-bull attack on his daughter.

Knight's violence was also contextualized in terms of temporal changes. Few accounts of his tenure as Indiana head coach failed to mention his outbursts, but most situated growing intolerance for his temper in terms of team struggles and era shifts. For example, some wondered if Knight's methods came under fire when his team lost (Callahan, 1997). Others suggested that Knight's temper becomes troublesome in a contemporary environment, where "it doesn't play well anymore" (Huber, 2000, para. 85). Former Hoosier Todd Lindeman explained, "Coach Knight hasn't changed; I just don't think kids want to go through the demands of his program anymore" (quoted in Callahan, 1997, para. 33). Knight's greatest flaw, it seems, is not so much his penchant for throwing chairs or screaming obscenities but his inability to keep up with the times (Geraci, 1998; Stravinsky, 1999). He is cast as out of touch with today's players, who resist his archaic demands for perfection (Callahan, 1997; Jenkins, 1999).

Seen through this lens, Knight comes to represent the fading glory of an old regime, which – for all its unfortunate excesses – is described as far more socially productive than the reckless aggression that's killing it. In this narrative, the increasingly outdated *appearance* of Knight's coaching methods (*not* the methods themselves) signals a great loss: the end of the civilized pursuit of relentless hierarchy, discipline, hard work, and high standards. In sharp contrast, Sprewell embodies the dangers of the new regime, largely represented as one-dimensional characters, socially irresponsible "thugs" on and off the court.

Boyz or Men? The Tacit Racial Contract of Professional Sport

Thus far in our analysis, we have demonstrated how contemporary discourse surrounding the NBA indicts a "new" generation of players as a sure sign of moral decline in civilized sport – different from past strains of bad boys, infinitely more destructive and dangerous, and therefore necessitating urgent discipline for their own and the greater social good. As the new generation's breed of aggression is generally marked as their most disturbing feature, we honed in on representations of violence and, specifically, the variable construction of physical aggression as a destructive or constructive force. Our comparison of Spree and Knight demonstrated divergent public responses to ostensibly similar cases of violence – the former deemed unpredictable, reckless, and without purpose, boyish if not bestial; the latter coded as cultured, methodical, and disciplinary, manly sophistication to a regrettable extreme.

Moreover, as suggested toward the end of our analysis, these disparate constructions appear deeply entwined, in that the selfish violence of the primal boy-brute seems to require heavy-handed taming from civilized fathers. In the discourse we traced, prevalent nostalgia for the "real men" of a bygone era hits up against the new generation. As "the General," Bobby Knight serves in tandem with other (less extreme) men of basketball to remind readers of what authentic adult manhood is supposed to look like (Wertheim, 1997). Masculinity, readers learn, is not about the arrogant "urban" flash of Spree, but about the discipline of the White Knight. Sports writer Taylor makes the point most explicitly:

> The thing about manhood is that it can't be guaranteed in a contract, it can't be bestowed by Nike or Reebok, and it's not a function of playing time. If the NBA's defiant ones want their manhood acknowledged, they would dispense with the childish displays of pique. They would make their complaints known to coaches and management, but they would not let those gripes keep them from conducting themselves as professionals, from showing up to practice and games, every day, without fail. The best way to earn respect as a man, they would surely discover, is to act like one. (1995, para. 31)

The disparity between the selfish insubordination of the new and the refined discipline of the old comes through undeniably, and in this narrative, harsh coaching – "a yeasty mix of screaming, jabbing fingers, up-close facial menacing, public humiliation, and use of four-syllable words pertaining to a subordinate's lineage" – is what turns boys into men (Bing, 1998). Knight and his cohort thus emerge as disciplined, devoted, educated, even ethical men. Even when Knight purportedly crossed the line, his violence was coded as surplus firmness, nonetheless oriented toward the right goal. After all, he was trying to transform boys into men, and that lesson demands willingness to learn from one's elders, to accept one's place, to mature and contribute to civilization (Kindred, 2000).

In closing, we wish to develop our broader argument: that today's discourse of waning moral civilization in the NBA is significant, first, because it recycles a racist historical pattern on a magnified scale and, second, because evident possibilities for using that growth in scale to disrupt the pattern appear to be minimizing. In an effort to sharpen the critical edge of our analysis along these lines, we read the contemporary discourse of decline in light of larger realities, particularly the historical formations of race and gender theorized earlier, as well as emerging trends in the relevant institutional and political economies surrounding the NBA. We conclude by suggesting possible avenues for productive discursive intervention that stem from our analysis.

At the outset of the essay, we conceptualized professional sport – specifically, those forms stressing physical aggression and rule-bound tribal competition – as a contemporary arena for the enactment of an abiding racial contract. We began by tracing historical threads of a chronic tension in White masculinity between constructions of the civilized and primitive: namely, the "neurasthenic paradox" fed by deeply entrenched and opposing notions that only White men can achieve true civilization, yet excessive civilization threatens to destroy White men's bodies (Bederman, 1995). Over time, one recurring means of managing this persistent ideological contradiction has entailed discursive flirtation with images of the civilized White feminine and the primal dark savage rapist. To effectively balance the tension and stave off associated vulnerabilities, discursive flirtation necessitates boundaries, such that White masculinity can be invigorated by the competing energies of White femininities and dark masculinities without succumbing to the dangers associated with either. Instead, White masculinity can continually rise above both by casting itself as a necessary taming force against excess, alternately affiliating and contrasting with gendered and raced "others," and ultimately, playing them off (and pitting them against) one another (see Ashcraft and Flores, 2003).

Professional sports can be understood to supply a modern arena – literally, as well as a coherent site of practices metaphorically – for safely exercising and consuming the mythic primal physicality of dark masculinities within the confines of civilized rules and management. Bederman (1995) acknowledged as much in her analysis of the Johnson-Jeffries boxing match in, 1910. In this tacit exchange, White civilized masculinity becomes revitalized by facing off with primal savagery, provided dark masculinities respect the limits of their challenge. Should primitive masculinity flex too much muscle, discipline typically follows to restore its terms (as when Jack Johnson was criminalized and ostracized from the United States). Several scholars have observed other arenas and instances in which this racial contract, as well as its violation and prompt restoration, became manifest over time (See, for instance, Bordo, 1999; Robinson, 2000; Rotundo, 1993; Torgovnick, 1990, 1998). In this essay, we situate the discourse of decline surrounding professional basketball as a contemporary moment that replays the basic plot lines of an old script and so, revives a historical racial (and racist) contract even as it also declares the unfettered advancement of Black professional athletes.

It is our claim, then, that the NBA puts a modern institutional face on an enduring set of race relations, ideologies, and practices. Indeed, we situate the NBA among the strongest contemporary institutional arms of the racial contract theorized here. Several key features of the NBA (like similar sports organizations, such as the NFL) distinguish it as a potent arena for negotiating cultural tensions, especially in comparison with other popular arenas, like literature, film, television programming, public education and government, and so forth. Consider first the incredible scope of the NBA's market, with an estimated national and global audience of 3.1 billion (Messner, Dunbar and Hunt, 2000; Jones, 2005). It is difficult to imagine a popular institution with wider appeal across walks of life, especially in terms of class, age, race, and increasingly, even gender. Arguably, the cultural influence of the NBA is intensified by its apolitical status. In other words, NBA "products" are consumed as acts of entertainment and leisure, not as matters of civic participation and policy; and in this sense, they are not regarded seriously or with suspicion. Of course, this is *not* to say that participants fail to take them seriously (generations of sports fans, pundits, and players would rightfully object), but that their coding as pastime generally frees them from close political inspection. Similarly, the products of the NBA are not contained within its explicit arena; rather, its civilized-primitive tensions are extended into derivative media territories such as sport channels, talk shows, columns, and so on. Such media genres, like the NBA itself, profit from the uproar evoked by the drama of young Black athletes contesting the status quo of White normativity, all the while energizing, reaffirming, and further disseminating the tacit rules of the racial contract by publicly castigating those who would refuse its terms (Hughes, 2004). The NBA – and the racial contract – therefore are components of an industrial complex that survives/thrives at least in part on the promise both of the exploitation and of the (struggle over?) control of primitivized Black male bodies. The consequences of such public discourses is, of course, not limited to the arena of sport, but echoes through social, organizational, educational, political, and other spheres. We see popular culture examples, for instance, in the din following the King Kong-like posing of all-star player LeBron James in a wide-stanced, open-mouthed roar with his thick, dark arm encircling the waste of White supermodel Gisele Bündchen on the March, 2008 cover of *Vogue* (Marikar, 2008; Associated Press, 2008). And, far from the sports arena, such racial politics reverberate in the literal political arena in coded references by angry White Republicans to bi-racial (marked Black) Democratic presidential candidate Barack Obama that link him with terrorists and Muslims – other dangerous foreign others. This was a historic competition that was, as this essay goes to press, momentously decided in favor of Obama as the first Black President in US history. Although far removed from the likes of Latrell Sprewell or Bobby Knight, the challenge of the self-assured young Black man to the once-predictable authority of aging White males was cause, for many, for outrage, and certain evidence of the reach of cultural decline.

Importantly, professional sports like basketball provide entertainment of a certain sort. Unlike the overtly fictitious character of much literature, film, and television, aggressive professional team sports carry a "real" quality for most participants. These events are generally taken as two teams competing against one other in real time (think: "head-to-head," "man-to-man"), with minimal behind-the-scenes orchestration (in contrast with complaints about much "reality TV," for example), and without a predetermined outcome. This sort of pure contest – raw physical skills and strategies confronting one another until a winner and a loser emerge – gets associated with a thoroughly embodied experience, not only for the players, but also for the viewers who feel vicarious adrenalin (and potato chips) rushing through their veins. The cultural influence of the NBA and similar organizations is further enhanced by its many outlets. Consumers can participate in the ongoing contest in any number of ways – through physically attending games or viewing them on television, following endless media coverage, purchasing and displaying related paraphernalia, playing NBA video games, mimicking professional dynamics in street basketball, and so on. In short, the NBA is available for mass consumption of enormous scale.

Mindful of these conditions, we treat the NBA as a leading ringmaster of the racial contract between White-civilized and dark-primitive masculine subjectivities. There is no doubt, as even the sports commentators cited in this essay observed, that the NBA has gone to great lengths – with the aid of countless commercial allies, of course (like ESPN TV, radio, and .com; athletic apparel and video game companies; the hip-hop music industry; and Hollywood) – to sell the particular form of Black masculinity analyzed in this essay: physically potent, brash, defiant, thuggish hipsters. Wherever this masculinity is widely promoted *and* mourned, it is typically called by other names – "urban," "gang," and "hip-hop," clad in "street cred," "corn rows," and "low-hanging shorts" – rendering the racial implications dubious. Our analysis, for instance, found explicit denial of race as the factor of decline, even as the discourse invoked code terms that are unmistakable allusions to a kind of Black identity.

A key part of our argument is that the commodification of this form of Black masculinity has proven too successful (i.e., effective in unintended ways), in that it has generated ironic consequences that threaten the tacit racial contract. For example, many NBA players appear to have internalized the discourse such that they publicly flaunt aggressive and entitled personas, rejecting both the celebrated Jordan-esque role model and the notorious old-school bad boy who acted out within limits in favor of a more impenitent, in-your-face style. Moreover, if fashion trends and sales volumes are any measure, their performances are finding eager reception, particularly among youthful audiences, and most conspicuously among White boys who appear to romanticize their anti-social dimensions. Consider, for instance, the magnitude with which youth, both across the United States and in other countries, consume basketball (Maguire and Falcous, 2005). McLaughlin powerfully argues this point: "as a commodity in that global market, basketball ... provid[es] global youth culture with a predictable and safe taste of ghetto cool" (2008, p. 108). These, of course, are chief among the complaints of the decline discourse analyzed in this essay. Our point here is *not* to concur with the evaluation of demise, but to suggest that there are some material grounds for such claims. The pervasive commodification of one kind of Black masculinity, as if it represents all of Black masculinity, has yielded conditions of massive opportunity, wherein Black athletes in the NBA and elsewhere can wield immense collective economic and cultural power. Put simply, scale matters. We are talking not of a token rebel here and there, but of a collective capacity for Black athlete influence at a national and even global scale, the likes of which have arguably not been seen before.

This is where we, as critics, grow especially concerned. As we read the current situation, the opportunity for *collective* influence is not being exercised, and we see signs that the window is closing. First, aside from a vast difference in scale, the NBA tale appears to reproduce the historical racial contract in another way not yet mentioned: namely, most Black players seem to understand possibilities for resistance in individualized terms (e.g., isolated acts of aggression and displays of personal prowess; salary negotiations, endorsement contracts, and other measures of celebrity status) that ultimately pit one against the other, failing to challenge the institutionalized racial contract itself. Crucially, we see this as a product of the particular discourse of Black masculinity at play here; that is, the subjectivity of Black NBA athletes is configured in a manner that encourages egoistic stars and discourages collective consciousness, thereby ensuring the perpetuation of a historical cycle.[5] Indeed, as we understand it, the primary danger of Black players internalizing the NBA's discourse of Black masculinity is *not* excessive and destructive cultural influence, as mourned by the pundit voices analyzed here. Rather, it is the failure to use that cultural influence collectively – to exercise the potential of collaborative awareness and action to expose, if not disrupt, the racial contract.

Our concern is amplified because, during the time we have written this essay, we have witnessed rising signs that the racial contract may already be under restoration. If history is any indicator, the birth of a popular discourse of moral decline – of manly civilization in ruin – is in itself a forceful first step that tends to galvanize popular momentum toward tangible action. And, since the time of our initial analysis, that discourse has exploded in intensity and circulation, moving, for instance, from claims that "a message does need to be sent" (Jackson, 1997, para. 6) to cries that current behavior is "shocking, repulsive, and inexcusable" (Vennochi, 2004, para. 1). Not surprisingly, substantial forms of discipline have already followed, including the institution of a strict league dress code designed to enforce player "professionalism." This dress code, for instances, forbids players who are on team or league business from wearing such racially/class coded accessories as chains and medallions over their clothing, sunglasses while indoors, and headphones (National Basketball Association, 2006). The length of players' shorts is also monitored. Recent changes in play rules, such as those that encourage so-called "smart" basketball over "athletic" basketball, can also be read as part of a move toward restoration of a racial treaty privileging White masculinity. And in a decision that claims to be in the best interests of the young players themselves – boys who, at the legal age of adulthood, are not mature enough to make rational choices – the NBA in, 2006 implemented the rule that players must be at least, 19 years of age. In search of cheaper talent and ever-expanding markets, the NBA has begun to recruit labor from around the world; the rise of White players, particularly from Eastern Europe, may be read as acutely noteworthy in this regard. The numbers of foreign players drafted in the first round has been up over the last few years, and future drafts are likely to also feature European players (Ford, 2008). These changes have led some African Americans to argue that the game is deliberately being Whitened: "From our perspective, the NBA is getting Whiter, and not too many brothers like it" (Robert "Scoop" Jackson, editor for *Slam,* cited in McGraw, 2003, para. 8–9).

The terms of a renewed racial contract, then, clearly promote new methods of Whitewashing an old stain. The racial discourses that demarcate intercultural relations have far-reaching implications both for White and for Black audiences – in particular, young Black men – for ways that they can perpetuate particular styles of and options for masculinity, while limiting others. These limitations then frame our intercultural communication and cross-cultural encounters, shaping perceptions and rationales for engagement with or retreat from an other. By interrogating historic racial conventions that are embedded within the relatively ordinary yet ubiquitous discourses of recreational sport, we enhance intercultural communication research that seeks to underscore ways that racial, gendered, and other discourses transcend evident social or political formats. Following Ono and Sloop's argument for critical prescription and social action, we find immediate utility in the strategic development and circulation of a more collective response to the discourse of decline (Ono and Sloop, 2002). Moreover, our analysis demonstrates the centrality of what Nakayama and Krizek (1995) name as the "strategic" workings of Whiteness (see also Moon and Nakayama, 2005).

Drawing on our analysis, we identify five related points on which a response might be fruitfully formulated: First, we propose refusal of the current suppression of race in the discourse of decline. NBA players and invested allies of various sorts could underscore the role of race, as well as eerie similarities between this moment in the NBA and other historical instances prone to arouse at least some public shame. At minimum, such talk could bring the possibility of another explanation – an institutionalized racial contract – to an audience that sees only brash boys (who "happen" to be Black) in need of regulation. Second, we suggest undermining the NBA's current dualistic configuration of Black masculinity into dutiful role models or treacherous thugs. By articulating multiple forms of Black masculinity, a collective response could promote public consciousness of racial complexity within and beyond the league, rather than lean on a forced, essentializing solidarity that denies current tensions among player identities and sows the seeds of future hegemony. Third, we believe that a viable response must call into question the reigning tale of (White) civilized fathers rebuking (dark) primal boys. Dismantling the notion that maturity and responsibility are the province of White masculinity could occur on at least two fronts: (1) by articulating alternative models of ethical community (e.g., "standpoint" stories that reveal how the lived circumstances of various Black men can engender concerns and contributions not visible to many White eyes) and (2) by exposing the contradictions and excesses of White masculinity, particularly those coded as civilized management (e.g., how the NBA-promoted model of Black masculinity induces a double-bind for players, how the NBA and other corporations profit on the backs of so-called thugs and then turn around and profit from their discipline). Elaborating the latter point, our fourth proposal invites a concentrated exposure and critique of racial functions served by disparate media constructions of similar behavior (e.g., the Spree–Knight comparison). Finally, we suggest redirecting the current focus on censuring negative role models and reversing the gaze toward White communities, for example, by pushing the question of why throngs of White boys find this brand of Black masculinity so compelling.

Of course, no discursive intervention is without complications, and short-term gain can till fertile ground for long-term loss. We concur with Ono and Sloop that understanding this rhetorical reality is not reason to sit idle. It is our contention that the short-term tactic currently at play – chiefly, individualistic resistance among Black players – will incur more long-term loss than our proposals here, for it follows the script of a predictable yet never certain historical plot. The moment is ripe, though fleeting, for improvisation. Like never before, Black NBA athletes are collectively situated to exert significant material and symbolic influence, but opportunity is waning. Will today's Jack Johnson maneuver a different role, and with whose support in his corner? Or does he face another round of domestication?

Notes

1   For a discussion of men's performances in sport, see Messner (1992) and Wheaton and Tomlinson (1998). Parameters on women's involvement in sport are discussed in Messner, Dunbar and Hunt (2000).
2   All indications of players' team affiliations reflect the affiliations of the time of the reference.
3   Having apologized for his outburst and "reformed," Sprewell now plays for the New York Knicks. Indiana University imposed on Knight a "zero-tolerance" policy, which stated that the next violation of the policy would cause him to lose his job. In the early fall of 2000, Knight was accused of grabbing and shaking an IU student. He was then fired (Tresniowski *et al.* 2000). He now serves as head coach at Texas Tech University.
4   For discussions of bad boys, in both the NBA and other professional sports, see, for instance, George 1999. Also see Reilly (1998, 1999).
5   For an interesting parallel with individualized resistance among women of color factory workers, see Hossfeld (1993).

References

Araton, H. (2003) Another N.B.A summer soap opera, *New York Times*, July 9, http://proquest.umi.com/pqdweb?did=356348931&sid=12&Fmt=3&clientId=9456&RQT=309&VName=PQD (accessed May 12, 2006).

Ashcraft, K.L., and Flores, L.A. (2003) Slaves with White collars: Persistent performances of masculinity in crisis. *Text and Performance Quarterly*, 23, 1–29

Associated Press (2008) LeBron James' *Vogue* cover called racially insensitive, *USA Today*, March 24, www.usatoday.com/life/people/2008-03-24-vogue-controversy_N.htm (accessed May 25, 2010).

Banet-Weiser, S. (1999) Hoop dreams: Professional basketball and the politics of race and gender. *Journal of Sport & Social Issues*, [Database] 23 (1999), Available at: http://ehostvgw9.epnet.com (accessed May 15, 2006).

Beavers, H. (1997) "The cool pose": Intersectionality, masculinity and the quiescence in the comedy and films of Richard Pryor and Eddie Murphy, in *Race and the Subject of Masculinities*, (ed. H. Stecopoulos and M. Uebel), Duke University Press, Durham, NC, pp. 253–285.

Bederman, G. (1995) *Manliness & Civilization: A Cultural History of Gender and Race in the United States*, University of Chicago Press, Chicago.

Benedict, J. (1997) Suspension tension: Sprewell vs. Carlesimo shows up NBA. *Village Voice*, December 16, http://ehostvgw11.epnet.com/ehost (accessed May 12, 2006).

Bing, S. (1998) Oh, sure, now you want to talk about it: Before you actually begin squeezing the windpipe of an abusive manager, there are many positive steps you can take. Really. *Fortune*, 137, January 12, http://ehostvgw11.epnet.com/ehost (accessed May 14, 2006).

Bordo, S. (1999) *The Male Body: A New Look at Men in Public and in Private*, Farrar, Straus, and Giroux, New York.

Boyd, T. (1997) The day the niggaz took over: basketball, commodity culture, and black masculinity, in *Out of Bounds: Sports, Media, and the Politics of Identity*, (eds A. Baker and T. Boyd), Indiana University Press, Bloomington, pp. 123–142.

Brown, T. (2004) Things don't sit well in the stands: fans respect the games but not a lot of athletes, and answers to violence issue aren't obvious. *Los Angeles Times*, December 19, http://proquest.umi.com/pqdweb?did=768235201&sid=6&Fmt=3&clientId=9456&RQT=309&Vname=PQD (accessed May 12, 2006).

Butterworth, M. (2007) Race in "the race": Mark McGuire, Sammy Sosa, and heroic constructions of Whiteness. *Critical Studies in Media Communication*, 24, 228–244.

Callahan, G. (1997) Knight errant. *Sports Illustrated*, May 12, http://ehostvgw11.epnet.com/ehost (accessed May 14, 2006).

Carrington, B. (1998) Sport, masculinity, and the black cultural resistance. *Journal of Sport & Social Issues*, 22, http://ehostvgw9.epnet.com (accessed May 12, 2006).

Cohen, R. (2004) Idiots itching for a fight. *The Washington Post*, December 1, http://proquest.umi.com/pqdweb?did=750113091&sid=7&Fmt=3&clientId=9456&RQT=309&VName=PQD (accessed May 12, 2006).

D'Alessandro, D. (1998) Despite choking his coach, Sprewell will be in demand. *Sporting News*, November 30, http://ehostvgw11.epnet.com/ehost (accessed May 12, 2006).

D'Alessandro, D. (1999) Step aside, Patrick: The Knicks are Spree's team. *Sporting News*, June 14, http://ehostvgw11.epnet.com/ehost (accessed May 14, 2006).

DeCourcy, M. (2000) For the sake of the program, Knight needed to return. *Sporting News*, May 29, http://ehostvgw11.epnet.com/ehost (accessed May 12, 2006).

Denver Post (2004) NBA melee rings an alarm bell. *Denver Post*, November 23, http://proquest.umi.com/pqdweb?did=743546381&sid=8&Fmt=3&clientId=9456&RQT=309&VName=PQD (accessed May 14, 2006).

Dickinson, G, and Anderson, K.V. (2004) Fallen: O. J. Simpson, Hillary Clinton, and the re-centering of White patriarchy. *Communication & Critical/Cultural Studies*, 1, 271–296.

Downey, M. (2003) Roll call of abusers. *Chicago Tribune*, July 20, http://proquest.umi.com/pqdweb?did=371874371&sid=12&Fmt=3&clientId=9456&RQT=309&VName=PQD (accessed May 12, 2006).

Fassett, D.L., and Warren, J.T. (2004) "You get pushed back": The strategic rhetoric of educational success and failure in higher education. *Communication Education*, 53, 21–39.

Ford, C. (2008) NBA draft prospects: Top 100, ESPN.com. October, http://insider.espn.go.com/nbadraft/draft/tracker/rank?draftyear=2009&action=login&appRedirect=http%3a%2f%2finsider.espn.go.com%2fnbadraft%2fdraft%2ftracker%2frank%3fdraftyear%3d2009 (accessed May 25, 2010).

Freidman, D. (1997) Not playing nice. *U.S. News & World Report*, December 15, http://ehostvgw11.epnet.com/ehost (accessed May 13, 2006).

George, N. (1999) All eyez on Spree: Latrell Sprewell brings his raw aesthetic to the New York Knicks. *Village Voice*, February 9, http://ehostvgw11.epnet.com/ehost (accessed May 12, 2006).

Geraci, R. (1998) Guys who need our help. *Men's Health*, 13 (March) http://ehostvgw11. epnet.com/ehost (accessed May 12, 2006).

Golden State Warriors (1999) *Sporting News*, January 18, http://ehostvgw11.epnet.com/ehost (accessed May 12, 2006).

Hall, S. (1985) Signification, representation, ideology: Althusser and the post-structuralist debates. *Critical Studies in Mass Communication*, 2, 91–114.

Harris, J.C. (1997) Sprewell incident raises sensitive issues of sports in America. *New York Amsterdam News*, December 11, http://ehostvgw11.epnet.com/ehost (accessed May 14, 2006).

Harrison, C.K. (2000) Black athletes at the millennium. *Society*, 37 (March/April), 35–39.

Hasian, M., Jr. (2003) Performative law and the maintenance of interracial social boundaries: Assuaging antebellum fears of "White slavery" and the case of Sally Miller/Salome Müller. *Text & Performance Quarterly*, 23, 55–86.

Hoberman, J.N. (1997) *Darwin's Athletes: How Sport has Damaged Black America and Preserved the Myth of Race*, Houghton Mifflin, Boston, MA.

Hossfeld, K.J. (1993) "Their logic against them": Contradictions in sex, race, and class in Silicon Valley, in *Feminist Frameworks: Alternative Theoretical Accounts of the Relations between Women and Men*, (ed. P.S. Rothenberg), McGraw-Hill, New York, pp. 346–358.

Huber, R. (2000) Bobby Knight needs a hug: the world is changing. He refuses to. *Esquire*, 133, (January), http://ehostvgw11.epnet.com/ehost (accessed May 12, 2006).

Hughes, G. (2004) Managing Black guys: Representation, corporate culture, and the NBA. *Sociology of Sport Journal*, 21, 163–184.

Jackson, J. (1997) The real lesson of Latrell Sprewell: This incident isn't about race but about athletes who are allowed to play by different rules. *Sports Illustrated*, December 22, http://ehostvgw11.epnet.com/ehost (accessed May 12, 2006).

Jeffords, S. (1994) *Hard Bodies: Hollywood Masculinity in the Reagan Era*, Rutgers University Press, New Brunswick, NJ.

Jenkins, C. (1999) Slingin' it '90's style. *Sporting News*, March 1, http://ehostvgw11. epnet.com/ehost (accessed May 12, 2006).

Jones, T. (2005) NBA's success on world stage leaves out U.S. fans. *The Columbus Dispatch*, June 17, http://web.lexis-nexis.com.tproxy01.lib.utah.edu/universe/document?_m= 6734e0eb7360150285597a72c65b907c&_docnum=1&wchp=dGLzVzz-zSkVA&_ md5= 33fb266d4d10058bd657f0b5864020dd (accessed May 14, 2006).

Kindred, D. (2000) Knight acts out a classic tragedy. *Sporting News*, May 22, http:// ehostvgw11.epnet.com/ehost (accessed May 12, 2006).

Lambert, P., and Baker, K. (1997) Dee-fense: A basketball star tries to undo the damage from his assault on a coach. *People*, December 22, http://ehostvgw11.epnet.com/ehost (accessed May 12, 2006).

Latrell Sprewell charged with reckless driving (1998) *Jet*, April 6, http://ehostvgw11.epnet. com/ehost (accessed May 12, 2006).

Lee, E. (1999) Don't choke. *Village Voice*, February 2 http://ehostvgw11.epnet.com/ehost (accessed May 14, 2006).

Lefton, T. (1999) Sprewell in And 1 Ad: "I'm not what's wrong." *Brandweek*, May 10, 1 http://ehostvgw11.epnet.com/ehost (accessed May 12, 2006).

Lefton, T. (2000) Feet on the street: To retain street cred, And 1 eschews NBA stars for playground heroes. Except, of course, for Latrell. *Brandweek*, March 27. http://ehostvgw11.epnet.com/ehost (accessed May 14, 2006).

Leo, J. (1998) The lawyers are at it again. *U.S. News & World Report*, March 16, http://ehostvgw11.epnet.com/ehost (accessed May 12, 2006).

Lipsitz, G. (1998) *The Possessive Investment in Whiteness: How White People Profit from Identity Politics*, Temple University Press, Philadelphia, PA.

Lopez, S. (1999). The new (and old) NBA. *Time*, February 15. http://ehostgvw11.epnet.com/ehost (accessed May 12, 2006).

Maguire, J., and Falcous, M. (2005) Making touchdowns and hoop dreams: the NFL and the NBA in England, in *Power and Global Sport: Zones of Prestige, Emulation and Resistance*, (ed. J. Maguire), Routledge, New York, pp. 23-40.

Marikar, S. (2008) Is Vogue's LeBron cover offensive? *ABC News*, March 19, http://blogs.abcnews.com/screenshots/2008/03/is-vogues-lebro.html (accessed May 25, 2010).

McCallum, J. (1997) Foul trouble. *Sports Illustrated*, December 15, http://ehostvgw11.epnet.com/ehost (accessed May 12, 2006).

McCallum, J. (2000) Spree for all. *Sports Illustrated*, May 15, http://ehostvgw11.epnet.com/ehost (accessed May 12, 2006).

McGraw, D (2003) The foreign invasion of the American game. *Village Voice*, May 28, http://www.villagevoice.com/news/0322,mcgraw,44409,1.html (accessed May 25, 2010).

McKay, J., Messner, M.A., and Sabo, D. (2000) Studying sport, men, and masculinities from feminist standpoints, in *Masculinities, Gender Relations, and Sport*, (eds J. McKay, M.A. Messner, and D. Sabo), Sage, Thousand Oaks, CA, pp. 1–12.

McLaughlin, T. (2008) *Give and Go: Basketball as a Cultural Practice*, SUNY Press, New York.

Messner, M.A. (1992), *Power at Play: Sports and the Problem of Masculinity*, Beacon, Boston, MA.

Messner, M.A., Dunbar, M., and Hunt, D. (2000) The televised sports manhood formula. *Journal of Sport & Social Issues*, 24, 380–394.

Miller, T. (1998) Commodifying the male body, problematizing "hegemonic masculinity"? *Journal of Sport & Social Issues*, 22, http://ehostvgw9.epnet.com (accessed May 15, 2006).

Mills, C.W. (1997) *The Racial Contract*, Cornell University Press, Ithaca, NY.

Moon D.G., and Nakayama, T.K. (2005) Strategic social identities and judgments: A murder in Appalachia. *Howard Journal of Communication*, 16, 87–107.

Mumby, D.K. (1997) The problem of hegemony: Rereading gramsci for organizational communication studies. *Western Journal of Communications*, 61, 343–375.

Mumby, D.K. (1998) Organizing men: power, discourse, and the social construction of masculinity(s) in the workplace. *Communication Theory*, 8, 164–183.

Nakayama, T.K. (2000) The significance of "race" and masculinities. *Critical Studies in Media Communication*, 17, 111–113.

Nakayama, T.K., and Krizek, R.L. (1995) Whiteness: A strategic rhetoric. *Quarterly Journal of Speech*, 81, 291–309.

National Basketball Association (2006), *NBA Player Dress Code*, http://www.nba.com/news/player_dress_code_051017.html (accessed May 25, 2010).

Nichols, R. (2002) In Portland, fans are blazing mad; players find trouble, team finds discontent. *The Washington Post*, December 10, http://proquest.umi.com/pqdweb? did=259542611&sid=8&Fmt=3&clientId=9456&RQT=309&VName=PQD (accessed May 12, 2006).

Oates, T.P. (2007) The erotic gaze in the NFL draft. *Communication & Critical/Cultural Studies*, 4, 74–90.

O'Brien, R., and Hersch, H. (1998) His daze in court. *Sports Illustrated*, June 1, http:// ehostvgw11.epnet.com/ehost (accessed May 12, 2006).

Ono, K.A., and Sloop, J.M. (2002) *Shifting Borders: Rhetoric, Immigration, and California's Proposition 187*, Temple University Press, Philadelphia, PA.

Powell, S. (1999) Being a player is the thing. *Sporting News*, 223, February 22, http:// ehostvgw11.epnet.com/ehost (accessed May 12, 2006).

Reilly, R. (1998) We feel their pane. *Sports Illustrated*, December 28, http://ehostvgw11. epnet.com/ehost (accessed May 12, 2006).

Reilly, R. (1999) Get the message? *Sports Illustrated*, June 21, http://ehostvgw11.epnet. com/ehost (accessed May 12, 2006).

Robinson, S. (2000) *Marked Men: White Masculinity in Crisis*, Columbia University Press, New York.

Roediger, D.R. (1991) *The Wages of Whiteness: Race and the Making of the American Working Class*, Verso, London: Verso.

Rogers, R.A. (2007) Deciphering Kokopelli: Masculinity in commodified appropriations of Native American imagery. *Communication & Critical/Cultural Studies*, 4, 233–255.

Rose, A., and Friedman, J. (1997) Television sports as mas(s)culine cult of distraction, in *Out of Bounds: Sports, Media, and the Politics of Identity*, (eds A. Baker and T. Boyd), Indiana University Press, Bloomington, pp. 1–15.

Rotundo, E.A. (1993) *American Manhood: Transformations in Masculinity from the Revolution to the Modern Era*, Basic Books, New York.

Sappenfield, M. (2004) Sports violence fed by both fans, athletes; Incidents throw harsh light on a culture fed by talk radio and disrespect for authority. *Christian Science Monitor*, November 24, www.csmonitor.com/2004/1124/p03s01-ussc.html (accessed May 27, 2010).

Saraceno, J. (2003) Permissiveness biting NBA now. *USA Today*, January 31, http:// proquest.umi.com/pqdweb?did=282238761&sid=1&Fmt=3&clientId=9456&RQT= 309&VName=PQD (accessed May 27, 2010).

Scott, D. (1998) Braidy Bunch: The sequel. *Sport*, 89, September, http://ehostvgw11. epnet.com/ehost (accessed May 12, 2006).

Slambrouck, P.V. (1998) The price of leniency in sports. *Christian Science Monitor*, March 6, http://ehostvgw11.epnet.com/ehost (accessed May 12, 2006).

Sprewell rebounds into the game (1998) *Newsweek*, March 16, http://ehostvgw11.epnet. com/ehost (accessed May 12, 2006).

Starr, M., and Samuels, A. (1997) Hoop nightmare. *Newsweek*, December 15, http:// ehostvgw11.epnet.com/ehost (accessed May 14, 2006).

Stein, J., and Fulton, G. (1997) Tall men behaving badly: An NBA star is stripped of his livelihood after throttling his head coach. Was justice served? *Time*, December 15, http://ehostvgw11.epnet.com/ehost (accessed May 12, 2006).

Stravinsky, J. (1998) The $6.4 Million question. *Village Voice*, March 17, http://ehostvgw11. epnet.com/ehost (accessed May 12, 2006).

Stravinsky, J. (1999) Spoilsports of the century: Bobby Knight, basketball coach, 1996-present. *Village Voice*, December 21, http://ehostvgw11.epnet.com/ehost (accessed May 12, 2006).

Taylor, P. (1995) Bad actors: The growing number of selfish and spoiled players are hurting their teams and marring the NBA's image. *Sports Illustrated*, January 30, http://ehostvgw11.epnet.com/ehost (May 12, 2006).

Taylor, P. (1997) The race card. *Sports Illustrated*, December 15, http://ehostvgw11.epnet.com/ehost (accessed May 12, 2006).

Torgovnick, M. (1990) *Gone Primitive: Savage Intellects, Modern Lives*, University of Chicago Press, Chicago.

Torgovnick, M. (1998) *Primitive Passions: Men, Women, and the Quest for Ecstasy*, University of Chicago Press, Chicago.

Tresniowski, A., Sandler, B., Clark, C. *et al.* (2000) Flaming out. *People*, September 25, http://ehostvgw11.epnet.com/ehost (accessed May 14, 2006).

Vennochi, J. (2004) Big bucks for bad conduct. *The Boston Globe*, November 23, http://proquest.umi.com/pqdweb?index=0&did=741707051&SrchMode=1&sid=2&Fmt=3&VInst=PROD&VType=PQD&RQT=309&VName=PQD&TS=1274984832&clientId=18938 (accessed May 27, 2010).

Warren, J.T. (2001) Doing Whiteness: On the performative dimensions of race in the classroom. *Communication Education*, 50, 91–108.

Watts, E.K. (2005) Border patrolling and "passing" in Eminem's 8 Mile. *Critical Studies in Media Communication*, 22, 187–206.

Watts, E.K., and Orbe, M.P. (2002) The spectacular consumption of "true" African American culture: "Whassup" with the Budweiser Guys. *Critical Studies in Media Communication*, 19, 1–20.

Wertheim, L.J. (1997) He doesn't throw chairs: Bob Knight's son Pat treads lightly as an assistant coach in the CBA. *Sports Illustrated*, February 10, http://ehostvgw11.epnet.com/ehost (accessed May 12, 2006).

Wheaton, B., and Tomlinson, A. (1998) The changing gender order in sport? *Journal of Sport & Social Issues*, 22, http://ehostvgw9.epnet.com (accessed May 14, 2006).

Wilbon, M. (2004) Courting hip-hop led to NBA's bad rap. *The Ottawa Citizen*, November 27, http://proquest.umi.com/pqdweb?did=752110131&sid=8&Fmt=3&clientId=9456&RQT=309&Vname=PQD (accessed May 12, 2006).

Willink, K. (2008) Economy & pedagogy: Laboring to learn in Camden County, North Carolina. *Communication & Critical/Cultural Studies*, 5, 64–86.

Zin, D.L. (1999) "Maybe the coach deserved choking": Latrell Sprewell and the politics of violence in America. *Peace & Change*, April, http://ehostvgw11.epnet.com/ehost (accessed May 12, 2006).

25

It Really Isn't About You
Whiteness and the Dangers of Thinking You Got It

John T. Warren

The first time I read something about whiteness, it was like a light had been turned on – as if, for the first time, I had been brought into a conversation that, with a complex and important history before me, I could now begin to engage. That first book, Ruth Frankenberg's *White Women, Race Matters: The Social Construction of Whiteness*,[1] had been assigned in a feminist theory course. I read it on a plane, heading on my way to a conference in San Antonio, Texas. I was struck by Frankenberg's engaging tone, her nonaccusatory nature, and the clarity of the issues involved. The stories of the women, the narratives of their experience often met my own, in good and bad ways alike. While I never actually met Frankenberg in person and am sad at her recent passing that will make such a meeting impossible, I credit her and that book with not only my research agenda in critical intercultural communication studies, but also with my own entrance into what has become a journey into my own whiteness. While it has been almost two decades since reading her book, my journey is still in its infancy.

Frankenberg, R. (1993) *White Women, Race Matters: The Social Construction of Whiteness,* University of Minnesota, Minneapolis.

Frankenberg's research centered on a series of interviews in which she sought to understand how white women narrated, understood, and, through their voicing of these experiences, participate in the making of whiteness as a racialized identity. Her book traces white identity along a continuum from race evasiveness (color-blindness) to race cognizance (awareness and action). For Frankenberg, there are morally/politically tolerable ways of doing whiteness, of living a raced life that

The Handbook of Critical Intercultural Communication, edited by Thomas K. Nakayama and Rona Tamiko Halualani. © 2010 Blackwell Publishing Ltd.

inflicts less violence upon others. Here, politically tolerable is not lip-service, but an engagement with others that is politically relevant and socially just. To be color-blind, argues Frankenberg, is to "dodge difference."[2] That is, to claim not to see color, you are choosing to not see race and the underlying power structure that continues to make race a difference that matters to people. To be race cognizant, on the other hand, is when the women were concerned with "white people's personal responsibility for and complicity with racism."[3] Here, one holds themselves accountable for their actions and seeks ways of being that are more ethically sound. Thus, whiteness, for Frankenberg, is "a location of structural advantage, of race privilege ... from which white people look at ourselves, at others, and at society ... [in ways] that are usually unmarked and unnamed."[4]

In graduate school, I began to read and process as much of this literature as possible, sketching out the various component parts of race and whiteness. I was curious how my being white – of having white-appearing skin – might have effects beyond my surface-level awareness. I was to learn that the stakes were much more complex than skin. To this end, my goal was to know everything, to begin to trace all the lines of thought on the topic so that when I was done, I'd finally be able to escape the guilt, the overwhelming sense of responsibility that being white had created for me. This was problematic on two levels: first, it assumed that I could read and process all that had been written. The past century is littered with research on the topic from multiple points of view. One need only to read Roediger's collection of literature on whiteness written by Black writers to see the state of affairs, to begin to understand the vast amount of work out there on this topic.[5] The literature, especially in the past decade, has exploded on the scene and taken us all quite by storm. Second, this assumption that by reading the literature on whiteness, I might be able to escape my own cultural positionality only created a dangerous illusion – it provided me the luxury of imagining that by studying whiteness, I might be able to avoid it. This was not a move toward being accountable, but a move toward denial.

I decided my dissertation, that final project that, once completed, would grant me access to my new name, my new title "Dr. Warren," would be a study of a classroom context that sought to examine how race was constructed, made, produced in/through student's on-going communication. For me, whiteness was communicatively constructed identity – a positionality that was produced through communication and, as such, was then a place from which one speaks and, even without being aware of how or in what ways, one levies power. Students in four consecutive semesters allowed me to witness their classrooms, generating two years worth of fascinating data on race and power within introductory communication courses. I began by setting up my theoretical context and then moved to analyzing their cultural performances, their enactments of self within this classroom space. I became exceptionally good at calling students out on their enactments of whiteness, claiming that whiteness is remade in and though their actions. I found that, in my careful analysis of their voices, I was missing the same critique of my own observing eye/I. The final chapter was my effort to return the gaze upon myself.

When I published the work as a book several years later, I was unsure how to feel about it.[6] It was the most exciting thing I've ever done, seeing my name in print; yet, it was also terribly troubling to know that my book, written by a white guy on whiteness, was going to re-center the conversation back on to my (and others like my) cultural location. Whiteness was going to benefit, even if under the pressure of my own critique.

In the book as a whole, my basic premise is that whiteness is a repetition, a reformulation of a pattern that works to reproduce the very idea of race. Thus, my body has a substance that is white-appearing (and that is powerful cultural capital in this environment to be sure), but to just look at that materiality, that body, outside a historical context is to forget the process that has made this white body possible. Biological reproduction certainly made this body, but the players in my past are no accident – they are subjects of a history, a social situation, a contextualized formation of individuals that got together within norms and regulations of the established social order. This is to say, my whiteness is strategic, a reproduction of an idea that, in the end, made me possible. The fact that my parents (necessarily products of their time) chose to mate is the ground from which I came (and their whiteness was certainly a factor). The point of my book is simple: we are a product of our communicative histories and, because this is so, we continue to reproduce these norms in and through our everyday communication. In this sense, our communication is performative, a generative making (again) of a historical idea, a social pattern.

Johnson, A.G. (2006) *Privilege, Power, and Difference*, 2nd edn, McGraw-Hill, Boston, MA.

In Johnson's remarkable book on privilege and power, he establishes a way of understanding white privilege, contextualizing it within discourses of difference. His argument circles around how well-meaning and kind individuals reproduce normative patterns that work to sustain and keep secure privilege systems. In particular, he considers gender, sexuality, race, class, and nondisability privilege to demonstrate how and why systems of power persist. From considering how capitalism, an economic system that requires more interest in making money and establishing differences than in sustaining equality, to tracing the mechanisms of power's production, he creates a wonderful narrative that puts privilege in context, asking for folks to be accountable without feeling solely responsible. White privilege, as Johnson might argue, is certainly a system beyond just our own self, but that does not mean we are forever destined to repeat the problems of the past.

I first began teaching the topic of whiteness and racial privilege in my classroom in 1996. I incorporated Peggy McIntosh's classic essay on white privilege that lists specific and material benefits she gets just by being white.[7] I began to discuss the ideas that Nakayama and Krizek offered in their now pivotal *Quarterly Journal of Speech* essay in which they importantly located whiteness as a rhetorical force that is sustained in and through our strategic use of language.[8] In my classroom moments, I asked students to engage in whiteness, to begin their own journey in recovering the past and seeing their actions in light of what has preceded them. It was my effort to make this literature matter. However, my lack of understanding and my limited exposure to this work made my efforts tough – I was less successful than I thought I would be, reproducing more privilege than I was undermining. My effort to sustain critique was coopted with an inability to articulate the current political/social implications of what I was saying. I was green, new to the ideas, and not yet capable of addressing them in a way that made an impact. Critical questions from students flowed like water and I was unable to hold back the tide, unsure, and unconfident of my own strength.

Additionally, I was unable to know what was within my power as an activist teacher. First, as a graduate student, I lacked the institutional support and authority to be "too radical" in the classroom; further, once I was an assistant professor, I struggled with earning tenure and proving myself a worthy colleague in the classroom, often relying on student evaluations for evidence of my effectiveness. While it is inappropriate to blame the institution of academy with one's lack of political activity, I did notice that I tempered my voice and actions during tenuous moments in my career. So I had to find my footing, seeking support with those others in the department, the university, and discipline that could feed my eagerness to do right by what I was studying.

I kept at it, determined to make these issues matter – I felt certain that in courses like introduction to public speaking, communication theory, intercultural communication, and introduction to performance studies, these issues were paramount. How can we understand the power of oratory, of literature, of communication without understanding that our subject locations are loaded with significance? That when we speak, we do not speak singularly; rather, we speak within a communicative context, as signifiers embedded in history. It is this lens, this effort to see context and history and power as significant that makes critical intercultural communication such a unique location to theorize culture, identity, and discourse.

McIntosh, P. (1997) White privilege and male privilege: A personal account of coming to see correspondences through work in Women's Studies, in *Critical White Studies: Looking Behind the Mirror*, (eds R. Delgado and J. Stefancic), Temple University Press, Philadelphia, PA, pp. 291–299. Nakayama, T.K., and Krizek, R.L. (1995) Whiteness: A strategic rhetoric. *Quarterly Journal of Speech*, 81, 291–309.

In Peggy McIntosh's essay, first printed in 1988 through the Wellesley College Center for Research on Women, stands as, I would guess, the most cited of all research articles on whiteness and privilege. In a sense, it was so powerful not only because McIntosh speaks in and through a language of privilege, considering racism through the white body, but because in a rare move of honesty, McIntosh names her privilege directly. In this sense, she acknowledges that she is privileged, she has benefits (most of them built on others), and she is willing to name them. In a list of 46 privileges, she shows what whiteness does to/for her own social power. Each time readers encounter this list, different elements of her privilege rise up as significant. From not having to be a spokesperson for her racial group to living in a mediated world where people with her own skin color are readily available to her on TV, print, or (now) online. Such privileges work to make her social position taken for granted, expected, and normal. Of course such privilege is not natural, but made to seem as if it were. Here lies the power behind McIntosh's theorizing of whiteness in and through her own experience.

In Nakayama and Krizek's essay "Whiteness: A Strategic Rhetoric," the authors established the communicative link to theorizing and writing about whiteness and social power. In the first major article in intercultural communication studies on whiteness, Nakayama and Krizek lay out the ways whiteness might be seen not in the seemingly concrete ways theorized through folks like McIntosh and others who link whiteness to white people, but rather within our every talk, our everyday communicative practices. The move here is to unlink whiteness as a system of power from the body – that is, many argue that we make a big mistake to assume that whiteness and white people are the same. To help clarify, the authors here begin to establish careful distinctions, outlining small codes in talk that work to re-establish power within those who are white. For instance, in a self description of racial identity, several students in their study noted that their race was "American," leaving this marker as their major identifier. Common sense might suggest that this is a progressive idea, promoting less divisiveness. So, while this may seem open-minded, Nakayama and Krizek note that this only works to recenter whiteness within the logic of America – they argue that nonwhite folks do not get the same credit for such claims, reminding us that policing of borders of national identity are common. One need only look to the aftermath of 9/11 to see the question mark that surrounds some claims to the ideal of "American" – citizens with Middle-Eastern/North African Arab background are often singled out. American is not an identity without racial implications. Such work has been followed by a number of intercultural researchers working along similar trajectories.[9]

My first graduate course, as a teacher, was entitled "Communication, Race, and Power," a complicated name for a course that examines whiteness in/through performative theories of communication. It was a remarkable experience, not only for the new found joys of teaching a graduate seminar, but more so for the quality of people with whom I had the pleasure of working and learning. Indeed, the course was filled with people who genuinely cared about their growth and the growth of their colleagues. We read scholarship from communication, education, cultural studies, and philosophy, each advancing critical arguments about the nature of whiteness and race as identities inscribed on our collective bodies.

The problem, almost inherent in this kind of class, is the mixture of folks and the diverse set of exposure to work of this kind. One student, an international student from Taiwan, wrote a complicated and intricate analysis of race and identity at play within the ESL program she was enduring. Her claim was that such programs often treat students as damaged entries into the university, as diseased participants that require correction. This, she argued, continues to mark and systemically marginalize students with different backgrounds, promoting the taken-for-granted whiteness upon which these Others were measured. For her, the singling out of students of color via language was less about helping them translate their experiences and more about reinscribing difference upon the lived bodies of students. Her remedial status, in effect, was a required part of her educational training.

Such students were common in this course, making the joy of working and thinking with them so worthwhile. However, this class also housed some folks who were, perhaps, not quite ready to enter this conversation. One particular student left each class with an exit line: "I guess I'm just a racist." This, of course, missed the point entirely. It was not that she was not a racist: she was, just as I am and the other students were. The nature of racism is that it is beyond the individual control of any one student, any particular person. Surely, if racism is a system that builds upon and maintains racism as an ideological ideal, then as members of this system, we are all implicated. This student may feel implicated by the research on whiteness to be sure – the reason for her feelings is because she is part of this machine, this system of racial privilege and power. Of course, the flip side is that she is not solely responsible for racism either. As a system that is beyond her individual control, she is caught up in the machine – she is swept up in the flow. The point is that as part of the machine, she gets benefits. In the end, whiteness is both about her and not about her – it is the both/and that makes this tough.

Hartigan, J. (1999) *Racial Situations: Class Predicaments of Whiteness in Detroit*, Princeton University Press, Princeton.

Sometimes a book captures the imagination and forces (allows) one to forget the basic components that make the book possible. In Hartigan's book, it is easy to get pulled into his ethnographic descriptions, his images, and the people who live in the pages of his tale. The book is colorful and presents a world of privilege juxtaposed to abject poverty. One is reminded in these pages that classed people – the wealthy and the poor and the in-between – are slammed together in Detroit, postwhite flight. Detroit, like so many other Midwestern industrial cities, suffers from the pains of dis/location and decaying infrastructure. Parts of these once magnificent cities look like the third world images on TV, gutted and collapsed buildings, broken down cars, and empty streets. Getting lost in his descriptions of these places juxtaposed to some of the wealthiest suburbs and the gentrification of certain "historic" districts can make one forget the powerful ways whiteness is at play in the making of Detroit. In his introduction, Hartigan notes: "Whiteness effectively names practices pursued by whites in the course of maintaining a position of social privilege and political dominance in this country."[10] Hartigan continues to explain that whiteness links white folks collectively to a legacy of racism – they are named as benefactors of racism as a productive system of power. What has happened in Detroit (or the flooded and drowned streets of New Orleans, as one might extend from Hartigan's work) is not without its links to racism as a system of decay in which we are all collectively linked. The bodies of those under the weight of whiteness's touch lift up the bodies of white folks, making a bed of comfort for them to rest upon.

Detroit is actually a powerful metaphor for what happens in my classroom. Like any member of the Detroit community, the students in my classroom are not individually responsible for racism, nor are they completely free from blame – indeed, to believe otherwise is to reduce the problem from a large systemic issue of social/political power to individual intent. Such moves are about protecting power from real critique.

This kind of analysis is not easy. Very quickly in conversations about racism we spin to the level of the individual as students become obsessed with their own intentions and mark the conversation as being about their own actions. In a recent semester, Ted, a white, traditional aged student, spoke of his unease with the conversation about whiteness and racism. As we talked about racism, he noted that too many classes are centered around culture, noting "it's not like I had slaves or anything." This line of thought is so common in my classrooms, the appeal to the extremes of racism and power. It is easy to call upon slavery (or any other overt kind of racial violence like the KKK, burning crosses, Japanese internment/concentration camps or Native American displacement practices) – to do so, is to mark one's behavior as a comparison. I am not as bad that those others, the logic goes. However, such modes of thinking only work to secure the more subtle ways power moves in and through us. Racism is surely reproduced when Rodney King is beaten in the streets of Los Angeles (1991), James Byrd Jr. is dragged to death in Texas (1999) or Amadou Diallo is shot to death by police in New York City (2000), not to mention the deaths of poor citizens (mostly African American) who died in the streets of New Orleans when governmental support was lacking or absent (2005). Indeed, the recent election of President Obama brought about its own brand of reinvented racism, including Tennessee Republican Chip Saltsman, a one time candidate for the Republic National Committee chairmanship, who mailed Christmas CDs to RNC members with the song "Barack the Magic Negro" (2009). These moments of overt action are relatively rare (though any such acts are too many). What is much more common are the small things, small moments in which what we say, what we do, how we gesture or look, reproduce racism. For instance, shifting conversation away from the structural elements of racism (as embedded in our talk or in our daily actions) toward overt acts of violence is exactly the way racism gets reproduced in and through our everyday logics. To shift the conversation from structure to intention is to shift the conversation from our participation to our witnessing – as if witnessing erases our culpability in the situation. As if our disapproving eye is somehow a way of letting us off the hook for what we (do not?) do.

These moments of relying on extremes[11] work a certain kind of magic – it is like a spell that affects the classroom. In McIntosh's early essay on white privilege, she discussed the notion of meritocracy, calling it a myth. The myth of meritocracy, an illusion that assumes that what we get in life we get because we earn it, is like magic, spinning a tale that works to reproduce the status of power, rather than remark on how we actually get to where we are in life. One need only look to local, regional, or federal political officers to see that power is embedded in these "achievements." In the state of Ohio where I lived for 5 years, our governor was Bob Taft (1999–2007). While no longer Governor, he was convicted of felony charges for accepting gifts and not reporting them while in office. Bob Taft is part of the Taft family – a political family that includes many powerful figures, including William Howard Taft, the 27th President of the United States and the 10th Chief Justice of the Supreme Court. Certainly, Bob Taft's position in the state of Ohio was not *only* because of his own efforts – having *this* family in *this* state helped him achieve that office. The myth of meritocracy, however, is powerful – it has a charm to it, a kind of "that's the way I want things to be" and, because we are so seduced, we tend to allow what is to be what should be. It is easier to assume that the relative of President Taft (or, for that matter, President George H.W. Bush) had just earned his position rather than to assume that the presence of his family made his road to power easier. We want to believe. It is a better story. It also makes us feel better for having voted for him. This is why the myth is so powerful – because we wish it to be so, and when you want something that badly, you can begin to make it so, even when the evidence speaks otherwise.

Keating, A. (1995) Interrogating "whiteness," (De)constructing "race," *College English*, 57, 901–918. Moon, D. (1999) White enculturation and bourgeois ideology: The discursive production of "good (white) girls," in *Whiteness: The Communication of Social Identity*, (eds. T.K. Nakayama and J.N. Martin), Sage, Thousand Oaks, CA, pp. 177–197.

Consider Keating's claim that an individual's skin color and his/her actions and thoughts are not causally connected: "The fact that a person is born with 'white' skin does not necessarily mean that s/he will think, act, and write in the 'white' ways."[12] To this end, Keating suggests that white skin does not necessarily cause individuals to levy whiteness in such oppressive ways. Keating tries to make clear distinctions between white people and whiteness, focusing her energies on the actor – that individual in culture – while then examining separately the circulation of power that whiteness grants to some over others. This is a useful correction – to assume all actors do whiteness in the same way (that is, embodied whiteness) is certainly a caution worth keeping at the forefront of our conversations.

Yet, Dreama Moon articulates the problem of denying the materiality of race: "While I agree that it is important not to conflate [whiteness and white people], I would argue that it is politically unwise to pretend that white people somehow are not implicated in the everyday production and reproduction of 'whiteness'."[13] What Moon reminds us of, ultimately, is the very real material benefit of whiteness – that is, whiteness may not be the same as white people but that distinction does not erase the real connections between the two. One may certainly (and wisely) ask for a more careful theorizing of the differences between whiteness and the members of our society that are produced as white, but such work should keep whiteness and white people in tension. To divorce them completely is to let white folks off the hook for their complicity in the perpetuation of whiteness.

This dialogue is one to remember; it points us, as caring and thoughtful members of society, to recognize how power is working through us, even as we resist the conflation of power and people. One needs to see their implication in racism, even as they seek to more sophisticatedly work out the language we use to talk about it.

In a class this summer, a student boldly stated that she was tired of reading all this whiteness stuff, claiming that we had "talked the issue to death" and that she was "done with it." The dynamics of my classroom permit this kind of dialogue – I ask students to tell me if they are bored as it is part of our community obligations to make ourselves committed to academic climates that are engaging and dynamic. Yet, I was, nonetheless, more than a little surprised, especially since this was early in a semester in which we would be reading much more about this subject. Indeed, my first concern was that she had not yet done the work that would enable one to make such a statement, to be so flippant about her ability to dismiss racism and her role within it.

Sandy was a white-identified student who, if looks could tell, was of a middle- to upper-class background. Between Sandy's laptop, cell phone, and PDA, she was well equipped and suggested an ease with material goods. Anyway, Sandy made this statement during our discussion of Harris's essay on whiteness as property.[14] I love this essay as it discusses how whiteness, legally conceived of as a possession, can be owned and counted on as a form of property. It is original and effective. In the midst of this conversation, Sandy announces that she has had enough. Since she offers this as a point of entry, I engage – her willingness to announce publicly her concern means a public issue is now on the table.

> We have talked the issue to death. I'm done with it.
> *Well, what about the topic are you done with?*
> This whole whiteness thing. I get that I'm the problem – I'm white, I'm the devil, I'm the cause and reason for racism, my life is great so I'm the reason everyone is miserable.
> *Is that what you are getting out of these readings?*
> Well, the readings tell me I'm privileged, I'm racist, I'm hording power, I'm doing things that hurt others. And because I'm white, I can't say anything about it – I can't disagree because then I'm being racist again. It is a trap, so I'm done. I accept my racism, recognize I'm a bad person, and now I want to stop talking about it.

You're a bad person? I'm not sure I follow.

I'm a racist – all these readings tell me so, so I must be so. I'm the reason for racism – it's my fault. Fine.

You know Sandy, I guess I'm not in agreement here. Yes the readings are discussing white folks' privilege and their contribution to racism as a system. I see where you might be feeling like you are the object of their critique, but remember that ideology – the notion that what is, should be – is built through logics embedded in our everyday talk. That

That makes me the big racist. I know. It's my fault, I get it.

Sandy, do you know what?

What.

It really isn't about you.

I look at her, waiting for it to hit her – to see where she takes it. She shrugs and sits back down. I realize in the moment that I've failed to follow though and before I can get it back, the moment moves on and the point I'm making, that symptom I am struggling to name, has flown by and we are now in a different place. I can't back up.

Richardson, T., and Villenas, S. (2000) "Other" encounters: Dances with whiteness in multicultural education. *Educational Theory*, 50, 255–273.
Warren, J.T., and Hytten, K. (2004) The faces of whiteness: Pitfalls and the critical democrat. *Communication Education*, 53, 321–339.

From educational foundations, Richardson and Villenas warn against white solutions to whiteness. That is, they remind us that "one of the many paradoxes here is that the underlying political culture, commitments, and habits of mind are a master narrative rooted in whiteness and yet proposed as multicultural education."[15] In other words, often what counters whiteness in dominant research on whiteness are solutions or responses embedded in whiteness. What does it mean to have your solution enforce power rather than work against it? For instance, how does the logic of democracy, inclusion, and integration work to benefit whiteness more than undermine it? How do these ways of constructing our social order work to benefit the dominant culture? What if being one big happy community is not what everyone wants? What if there were other ways of organizing ourselves toward some other, potentially better, end? Can we imagine that? The charge in Richardson and Villenas is to question the underlying nature of research before we assume there is not a negative effect of what we say.

In response, my friend and I wrote a response, a way of recovering elements of democracy within the logic of whiteness. Advocating a critical stance we called the "Critical Democrat," we claim that to occupy the space of democracy, to live in the space of liminality and humility that democracy might make possible, is to chart out innovative ways of imagining our futures in ways that breed less violence and a greater ability to hear others.[16] In the end, before white constituted folks can imagine the possibilities that Richardson and Villenas advocate, we must first learn to listen, understanding the Critical Democrat is a paradoxical, ever-changing, temporary space of possibility. In this moment, we might find new ways to see our futures.

In the moment with Sandy, what I wish I could have said in a more meaningful way was that whiteness is not an individual matter, regardless of how much we desire it to be. Sandy was trapped in class to be sure, but not, I would argue, by the readings. Rather, the readings were trying to create a complex matrix for her to see herself within. That is, whether she likes the idea or not, she is implicated in conversations of racism and power because she is a member of this social system. She did not sign up anywhere, she was never given her free pass, never joined any country club that provided freedom and luxury at the expense of others. Yet, she is implicated – the moment her body enters this social system and becomes part of our social machine, she became wrapped up in this system of power and privilege. This happens because we live in a social system that remakes skin and race meaningful – we talk about it, think about it, and thus produce it as meaningful. So, of course she is trapped, as we all are as members of this communicative context. Indeed, regardless of where we fall in terms of race, we are always already part of a system of power. She did not sign up to be sure, but she also cannot sign out simply because that is what she desires. It is the nature of her (and our) location within systems of power.

However, the thing I was trying (and probably failed to do) was to tell Sandy that only a white person, cloaked within the glory of privilege, could assume that this conversation was about her – that racism was about her, as an individual. It is a trap to make racism about her individual intent, her value as a person, her desire or effort to participate in racism. Racism, as it is propagated through everyday life, is not a T-shirt we wear on purpose, marginalizing those others we come in contact with; rather, it is embedded in our talk, in our assumptions, and in our everyday logics. It is invisible, guiding our interactions without our direct control, nor our consent. It is, as Nakayama and Krizek made clear, an unnoticeable logic, a communicative construct that promotes and secures racism without any direct effort on her/our part/s. It is truly a trap for Sandy to believe that she was responsible, for it is so much bigger than Sandy, bigger than me, bigger than any one individual. So while we, Sandy and I, are surely benefactors of whiteness, we are not the cause. To assume we are (or could be) is to make ourselves much more important than we really are. Racism is a process of power, shared power that functions as a social machine. The more we remember this, the better armed we are at speaking back to it.

The struggle with defining whiteness, naming whiteness, and locating our place within whiteness (and the critical intercultural communication scholarship analyzing whiteness) is the assumption that we can get to the root of whiteness that we can get the "it" of whiteness. Sandy is only an example of someone who sought, perhaps desperately, to know the monster that is whiteness and come to terms with it. Indeed, this essay is my attempt to talk about how one person makes sense of whiteness and his (my) role in the system. This essay may very well also participate in the doing of whiteness, the reproduction of power; yet, such fear does not let me off the hook from making my case, drawing my line, and standing a ground toward some better way of imagining my relationship to others. Whiteness is slippery. As varied as the different voices critiquing racism and whiteness become when placed next to each other, it shows how whiteness shifts over time (both our understanding of it and our ways of imagining our response). And because whiteness resists our efforts to speak back, we continue, even without trying, to remake whiteness and cultural power. That is its power, of course. To shift once one names it, to take on different clothes, to grow more powerful with critique, to manipulate around critique is the nature of whiteness. Our ongoing struggle is to be well read, well versed, humble and willing to be accountable for things we did not know we were doing. It is about taking a stance of grace in this conversation, being active without assuming we know how it will (or through what efforts it might) end.

From the Library of the Future

One can only imagine the future. A close of the eyes, a reaching forward to those texts and authors that change our lives by a detail, an insight, a critical argument that forever alters how we see our situated-ness in systems of power. I imagine the library has a promising future, filled with the innovations of my students, my friends, my colleagues who struggle to name hope in the face of injustice. Perhaps it is the final paper in a class or a presentation I witness at a conference – the moment of seeing something that is just different enough to raise the bar and complicate that which I have not yet seen. Sometimes it is a student question – an undergraduate who, perhaps unaware of the richness of the query, drives home a level of complication that makes me pause. The future is imagination, but if I were to lay down a bet, I might rely on three ruptures in fabric of academia that I see as hopeful.

First, I recently read George Yancy's new book *Black Bodies, White Gazes*[17] and have been raving about it to all my closest friends, even if they are not "academics." Quite frankly, the book is too good for it not to appear on more bookshelves than it currently is. In Yancy's book, he creates an "embodied philosophy of race" that incorporates philosophy, political theory, cultural studies, and critical intercultural communication to argue that the study of whiteness is still a productive and important venture.[18] Standing against those who argue that Whiteness Studies is passé, Yancy makes clear that such work is still developing that we all, as a community of scholars, need to invest. As a prominent African-American philosopher, Yancy argues that race and whiteness continues to affect us in meaningful ways and that we need to recommit to the work of social justice. In his final chapter, he offers a powerful insight on why whiteness needs to be examined by scholars of color as well as white folks, noting that white subjects can be ambushed by whiteness: "racism is embedded within one's embodied habitual engagement with the social world and how it is weaved within the unconscious, impacting everyday mundane transactions."[19] In other words, because white subjects have been constituted through a racist culture, we/they are not always able to foresee the ways whiteness can arise. It is a useful reminder for me, as a scholar in this area of research, that more work is needed in order to fully understand the role of racial power in maintaining dominance.

Second, a colleague and I recently published *Critical Communication Pedagogy*,[20] a book that attempts to capture a moment in time where, like intercultural communication, scholars are in the process of transforming toward a more critical and social justice oriented research trajectory. While I have great hope that the book will make a difference in the field, I am more inspired by what I have witnessed in the field since the publication of the book. From conference panels to graduate seminars, there has been rich conversation about the field and where pedagogical research should go in the future. The work I have witnessed has been humbling and I imagine a generation of scholarship that breeds more possibility and more innovation in (and outside) the classroom. Such new ways of seeing the relationship between critical communication pedagogy and critical intercultural communication might foster new and innovative ways of addressing the complicated ways citations of whiteness are offered by white and nonwhite bodies, suggesting a need to see how identity and discourse are not the same, but mutually inform each other.

Third (and finally), I see quite a bit of hope in critical intercultural communication as a field of inquiry. Perhaps one need only study the history of intercultural communication to see the ways that our scholarship has not always lived up to its potential. Yet, new scholarship is being written on diaspora,[21] gender and race,[22] transnationalism,[23] difference,[24] Latina/o studies,[25] and whiteness[26] (to name but a few areas of research) that pushes borders and challenges how and to what end we do our writing. What is significant about research conducted and published under critical intercultural communication is the extent to which communication – as both a vehicle for, as well as a producer of, power – plays a central role in the theorizing. While other critical avenues of research are important, it is this new movement in the field that locates theorizes power and difference within and through communication. It is for this reason that I am a critical intercultural communication scholar – because within this politically inflected, activist oriented, and hopeful body of work I find my theoretical and methodological home. In that movement, production and sustainment of power replaces the raw fact of its presence and, in the end, a much more complicated picture of intercultural exchange is painted.

With starts like this, one can only imagine the future.

Notes

The structure of this essay is inspired, in part, by Pacanowski (1988).

1   Frankenberg (1993).
2   Frankenberg (1993, p. 142).
3   Frankenberg (1993, p. 176).
4   Frankenberg (1993, p. 1).
5   Roediger (1998).

6　Warren (2003).
7　McIntosh (1997).
8　Nakayama and Krizek (1995).
9　See Crenshaw (1997); Hytten and Warren (2003); Johnson, Rich and Cargile (2008); Moon and Flores (2000); Shome (1999).
10　Hartigan (1999, p. 16).
11　See Hytten and Warren (2003).
12　Keating (1995, p. 907).
13　Moon, (1999, p. 179).
14　Harris (1998), pp. 103–118.
15　Richardson and Villenas (2000, p. 264).
16　Warren and Hytten (2004, p. 330).
17　Yancy (2008).
18　Warren (2009).
19　Yancy (2008, p. 230).
20　Fassett and Warren (2007).
21　Halualani (2002).
22　Alexander (2006); Jackson (2006).
23　Cheng (2008).
24　Warren (2008, pp. 290–308).
25　Calafell (2007).
26　Cooks and Simpson (2007).

References

Alexander, B.K. (2006) *Performing Black Masculinity: Race, Culture, and Queer Identity*, AltaMira Press, Lanham MD.

Calafell, B.M. (2007) *Latina/o Communication Studies: Theorizing Performance*, Peter Lang, New York.

Cheng, H-I. (2008) *Culturing Interface: Identity, Communication, and Chinese Transnationalism*, Peter Lang, New York.

Cooks, L.M., and Simpson, J.S. (eds) (2007) *Whiteness, Pedagogy, Performance: Dis/Placing Race*, Lexington Books, Lanham MD.

Crenshaw, C. (1997) Resisting whiteness' rhetorical silence. *Western Journal of Communication*, 61, 253–278.

Fassett, D.L., and Warren, J.T. (2007) *Critical Communication Pedagogy*, Sage, Thousand Oaks, CA.

Frankenberg, R. (1993) *White Women, Race Matters: The Social Construction of Whiteness*, University of Minnesota Press, Minneapolis.

Halualani, R.T. (2002) *In the Name of Hawaiians: Native Identities & Cultural Politics*, University of Minnesota Press, Minneapolis.

Harris, C. (1998) Whiteness as property, in *Black on White: Black Writers on What it Means to be White*, (ed. D. Roediger), Schocken Books, New York, pp. 103–118.

Hartigan J. (1999) *Racial Situations: Class Predicaments of Whiteness in Detroit*, Princeton University Press, Princeton, NJ.

Hytten, K., and Warren, J.T. (2003) Engaging whiteness: How racial power gets reified in education, *International Journal of Qualitative Studies in Education*, 16, 65–89.

Jackson, R.L. II (2006) *Scripting the Black Masculine Body: Identity, Discourse, and Racial Politics in Popular Media*, SUNY Press, Albany, NY.

Johnson, J., Rich, M., and Cargile, A.C. (2008) Why are you shoving this stuff down our throats? Preparing intercultural educators to challenge performances of white racism. *Journal of International and Intercultural Communication*, 1, 113–135.

Keating, A. (1995) Interrogating "whiteness," (De)constructing "race." *College English*, 57, 907

McIntosh, P. (1997) White privilege and male privilege: A personal account of coming to see correspondences through work in women's studies, in *Critical White Studies: Looking Behind the Mirror*, (eds. R. Delgado and J. Stefancic), Temple University Press, Philadelphia, PA, pp. 291–299.

Moon, D. (1999) White enculturation and bourgeois ideology: The discursive production of "good (white) girls," in *Whiteness: The Communication of Social Identity*, (eds T. K. Nakayama and J.N. Martin), Sage, Thousand Oaks, CA, p. 179.

Moon, D., and Flores, L.A. (2000) Antiracism and the abolition of whiteness: Rhetorical strategies of domination among "race traitors." *Communication Studies*, 5, 97–115.

Nakayama, T.K., and Krizek, R.L. (1995) Whiteness: A strategic rhetoric. *Quarterly Journal of Speech*, 81, 291–309.

Pacanowski, M. (1988) Slouching towards Chicago. *Quarterly Journal of Speech*, 74, 453–467.

Richardson, T., and Villenas, S. (2000) "Other" encounters: Dances with whiteness in multicultural education. *Educational Theory*, 50, 264.

Roediger, D. (ed.) (1998) *Black on White: Black Writers on what it Means to be White*, Schocken Books, New York.

Shome, R. (1999) Whiteness and the politics of location: Postcolonial reflections, in *Whiteness: The Communication of Social Identity*, (eds. T.K. Nakayama and J.N. Martin), Sage, Thousand Oaks, pp. 107–128.

Warren, J.T. (2003) *Performing Purity: Pedagogy, Whiteness, and the Reconstitution of Power*, Peter Lang, New York.

Warren, J.T. (2008) Performing difference: Repetition in context. *Journal of International and Intercultural Communication*, 1, 290–308.

Warren, J.T. (2009) *White gazes* as an embodied philosophy of race. *Review of Communication*, 9, 280–282.

Warren, J.T., and Hytten, K. (2004) The faces of whiteness: Pitfalls and the critical democrat. *Communication Education*, 53, 330.

Yancy, G. (2008) *Black Bodies, White Gazes: The Continuing Significance of Race*, Rowman & Littlefield, Lanham, MD.

26

Critical Reflections on a Pedagogy of Ability

Deanna L. Fassett

To know how to hide one's ability is great skill.

François Duc de La Rochefoucauld, *Maxims*[1]

I am very good at hiding my ability, especially from myself.

There are many different ways to take this, I know. What I mean to write is that when I do anything – even writing – I do not think about the fact that I can do it. I just *do*. I pick up a book, and I read. I sit down to the computer, and I type. I lace up my running shoes, and I run. I make a sandwich, and I eat. I do not have to think about how I do any of these things unless someone is watching me, causing me to reflect on how my own ways might be unique or unusual, or if I am trying something new (such as writing a poem instead of an academic essay or running a sprint instead of a long distance event), or if I am not able to perform the action in the way I ordinarily would (for example, healing from and accommodating a recent surgery). I have hidden my abilities in plain sight; I take them for granted. I have learned how to do this my entire life.

We have also learned this lesson as a discipline. Though our work is rich and nuanced, critical intercultural communication scholars have left questions of ability and disability largely overlooked and undertheorized. What exists in relation to identity and power, the structural and the personal, the cultural and the individual, is substantive and rich,[2] yet we do not extend this analysis to ability. While disability studies exists as a field in its own right, and while communication scholars may certainly benefit from these researchers' insights,[3] critical intercultural communication scholars are, by their commitment to interrogating and better understanding the intersections of identity, power and culture as constituted in communication, well-positioned to engage in analysis of how we become (and come to see ourselves as) ability-privileged or disabled.

The Handbook of Critical Intercultural Communication, edited by Thomas K. Nakayama and Rona Tamiko Halualani. © 2010 Blackwell Publishing Ltd.

Critical intercultural scholars are already engaged in analysis of privilege and power; further, we are working toward, in our writing and our teaching, greater reflexivity. By this I mean that we are diligent and probing about the role of communication in sustaining and challenging oppressive circumstances; whether this is with respect to whiteness and white privilege, heteronormativity, nationalism, or classism, we are increasingly able to understand how we each play a role in shoring up social structures that support and constrain, hinder and damage our relationships with one another and with ourselves. However, it is crucial that we continue, as a field, to examine culture as not only constituted in communication, not only as ideological and contested, but as constituted in communication by people who have, in every possible sense, material bodies – as variously and meaningfully raced, gendered, sexualized, classed and able (cf. Collier, Hegde, Lee *et al.* 2001).[4]

In what follows, I explore what it might mean for us, collectively and individually, to be steeped in a pedagogy of ability.

A Pedagogy of Ability: Exercises in Cartesian Dualism

Sit in a small, defined space for long periods of time, such as a desk. Face the front of the room, and focus on the person located there. Tell yourself that you are most interested in what s/he has to say; anything that interferes with that (such as an accent or unusual clothing) is a distraction. Do not look out the windows; do not pay attention to any extraneous sensory information, such as hunger. You are there to learn, and for that, you only need to pay attention.

Participate in workshops and classes that overemphasize a grand tour approach to culture, where the textbook and the instructor treat ethnicity separate from sexuality and sexuality separate from ability. Allow simulations to stand in for nuanced and thorny intercultural encounters; when you have the opportunity to imagine you are deaf or to role play someone who is "wheelchair bound," feel confident that this experience has helped you understand what that is like. Feel outraged at how people with disabilities get treated.

Carefully write all your observations about the world in third person, passive voice. Instead of saying "I observed this or that situation," make sure you remove all traces of yourself: "Participants were observed to." Better still, write your opinions as though they are fact. Assiduously ignore the ways in which your presence invariably changes whatever it is you observe. Be sure to point out when you can see how someone's body – her/his race or ethnicity, socioeconomic status, disability, age, faith, and so forth – influences how s/he understands something; do not hesitate to identify her/him as "biased" and her/his ideas as "opinions."

Mark other people's bodies only when their performance differs from your expectations of their performance. For example, you might say that someone has a remarkable ability to capture an audience's attention. In this way, an ability is a possession, something a person either does or does not own. Another option is to point out when someone is, for whatever reason, unable to do something; this helps establish that they lack a given ability (or possess a disability).

Though there are more precise and historically rooted definitions of "pedagogy," generally speaking, we can take it to be a way of teaching and learning. For example, communication studies professors are, by and large, interested in better understanding communication pedagogy – that is, how we go about teaching communication and how we might do that more effectively. Communication studies professors interested in critical communication pedagogy are committed to understanding better not only how best to teach communication, but also how that the teaching and learning process empowers some and disempowers others; they are committed to understanding better how the teaching and learning of communication gives rise to racism, sexism, heterosexism, ableism, monotheism, and other forms of oppression, as well how an analysis of classroom communication can challenge social injustice and inspire compassion, accountability and growth.[5] Particularly, critical communication pedagogy scholars are committed to illuminating how teaching and learning are not neutral processes of knowledge transmission and acquisition, but rather part and parcel of ideologies, in ways many people fail to realize or would prefer not to consider.

For these reasons, scholars of critical intercultural communication and critical communication pedagogy may forge productive alliances in investigation, analysis and social justice. Historically, research at the intersections of communication and instruction has been dominated by undertheorized, psycho-behavioral understandings of identity, where culture is more or less a trait to be manipulated or controlled; historically, research in intercultural communication has been shaped by a general lack of attention to ability and disability as cultural. Given that our classrooms are, in effect, a microcosm of the social, cultural, political forces we experience in our daily lives, drawing the two fields of study together engenders a more incisive reading of teaching and learning (i.e., the classroom as a site of cultural contact) and a more inclusive, less-disciplinarily rooted understanding of culture (i.e., as emergent and intersectional).

Each of us has been learning a pedagogy of ability, in most educational contexts and beyond, throughout our lives. From the time we are very small, we learn to control and mask our bodies – our desires and needs – from the contamination they might have on our learning. We learn the scientific method, we learn to remove the first-person pronoun from our writing, and we learn to live, to greater and greater degrees, a life of the mind. By contrast, in our physical education classes, we learn to value certain kinds of physical achievement over others; we learn to define our bodies in terms of what they can and cannot do, not by how our bodies inevitably affect what we can and cannot know.

The body as epistemic

While most of us would not claim to be philosophers, we each spend a fair bit of our lives embroiled in epistemological considerations: We worry about what is true, what is real, what matters. Whether or not we are prepared to acknowledge their influence, we have been influenced by a whole host of philosophers over the ages, from Plato and his dismissive attitude toward rhetoric (believing that rhetoric was deceptive because it masked a real, verifiable reality that the average person's perceptions could never quite apprehend) to Descartes' "cogito ergo sum" (or "I think, therefore I am," which suggested that our minds were of far greater importance – were more real, in this sense – than our bodies). We inwardly struggle with whether we understand our worlds best through our bodies or our minds, as though these are separable, as though we might contain one in pursuit of the other. We play these concerns out in questions of bias, in whether or not a researcher (e.g., a journalist, a teacher or a scientist) has achieved a certain degree of objectivity.

This emphasis on mind and rationality, however, masks the ways in which our bodies are epistemic: Our bodies are our way, maybe our only way, to understand our world. We see this process around us all the time; those of us who are parents, or who have cared for or spent time with children, witness how those children learn through their bodies – through sight, touch, smell, taste, and sound. As adults, we continue to learn through our bodies; however, we have learned how to mask that process better, especially when we engage in or write research. As I move through the world, if I am tired, hungry, worried, happy or angry, that will, however subtlely, influence my perception. My body, whether tall or short, large or small, muscular or slight, standing or sitting, injured or healthy, will influence what I may perceive about a given situation, what I can see, hear, or otherwise engage. Further, my ethnicity, gender, sexuality, and age will shape not only my access to a given situation, but also my interpretations of it. Also, while, as a researcher, I may try different approaches to minimizing my influence on the "facts" of a situation, I am still the instrument of analysis. It is through my body – its particular strengths and limitations – that I am able to understand a given phenomenon at all, through my senses and my emotional and intellectual capacities. (This is why it is so important to share your insights and observations with others, so that you might compare your understandings for where they are similar and where they are different.)

In schools, we have many different processes that help to produce docile or disciplined bodies.[6] As Fassett and Warren (2007) observe,

> Foucault (1977) reminds us that power ... is never housed easily in one site; rather, power is fluid, flowing through all of us ... As Foucault's work so carefully illuminates, power's greatest effect on bodies is to make them conform even when no one is watching; power works not because we are being watched – but because even when the powerful aren't watching, we, as educational subjects, perform on cue. Foucault calls this effect of power a disciplining of the body – a type of social control whereby, over time, we craft ourselves in the image of the oppressor (2007, p. 65).

We line up for recess, we sit in rows, we wear uniforms; in short, we engage in many behaviors that order and regulate – and ultimately background or minimize – our bodies. Our bodies become docile in that they are no longer even readily apparent to us, except for perhaps as a source of embarrassment (or, still more rare, pride). Reflect for a moment on your body in the classroom: Of all the times your body was made apparent to you, were any of them pleasurable or positive? You may have had the experience of enjoying your body in the classroom, perhaps in theatre or physical education, but generally speaking, we only notice our bodies when they do not conform, when they do not fit in the classroom desk, when other people point out our differences, or when they are injured or cause us pain. That we often have to discuss whether or not to "mainstream" students enrolled in special education tells us that they are already on the margins. As students, we see their (different) bodies and hear their (different) voices in isolated areas of our schools, and we learn that they are different from us in ways that matter, in ways that we should mark. Their bodies are obvious in ways that ours are not; their bodies, their differences, are obvious in ways we have learned they should not be.

Our language is significant to this process as well. We mark differences with labels; sometimes these are specific like "attention deficit hyperactivity disorder" and sometimes these are general, like "disabled student." Nevertheless, this mark, while making possible perhaps better resources or opportunities for access, shapes this person in an indelible way. In effect, the language of disability alters not only communication about students who have different needs (for example, students who might need mobility accommodations, temporal or technological accommodations, access to medications), but also relationships between educators and students, people of varying abilities, and so forth. If disability is, most often, in our talk with one another, a lack, then our communication – our language – carries forward a series of subtle and pernicious understandings of power. So-called "able-bodied" people fail to recognize the ways in which we are all limited in our abilities and bodies.

Marking Ability

We all have a range of abilities. For example, while I can complete a marathon, I am a slow runner. While I can write, I often find myself starting at a blank screen for hours on end, hoping I will think of something interesting to say. You might find it easy to read, but hard to focus; or, you might find it easy to learn, but difficult to negotiate the physical environment of the campus or classroom (for example, using crutches or wheelchair, or walking with a service animal).

Yet we – culturally, legally – only mark disability. For example, most universities require faculty to discuss their campus's ADA policy on the first day of class; to the extent that this statement or discussion underscores the importance of students registering their disability with an office on campus, we shore up the pervasive culture of disbelief and suspicion surrounding disability in general, and nonvisible disability (e.g., brain chemistry disorders like depression or schizophrenia, autoimmune disorders like lupus or arthritis, chronic pain conditions like fibromyalgia, and other disabilities that are not easily read on someone's body) in particular.[7] This marking process extends into many different aspects of the educational experience. Fassett and Morella (2008) offer an example to clarify:

the student with dyslexia doesn't just cross the stage and receive her diploma; she has to undertake diagnostic testing, register with the campus disability resource center, identify herself as dyslexic to each of her faculty and many of her coauthors and group members, ask for accommodations for testing at midterms and finals (leaving her to account for her absence from class), ask for her syllabi, textbooks and course readers well before many of her professors are willing to make them available to students, maintain constant contact with the media center on campus as her instructional materials become available, and purchase/remove/install particular hardware and software, in addition to the tasks ability-privileged students and professors take for granted, like completing the reading or revising written work (p. 146).[8]

This is but one example of the many ways in which we mark students (or employees or community members) with disabilities.

All of these steps are valuable and help to ensure educational access for students with disabilities, yet they come at a cost, both to the student who has a disability and to the ability-privileged student as well. The student we mark as disabled learns to mark her/his body as such for others; the ability-privileged student never learns the ways in which her/his body is always already functioning with limitations of its own, nor does s/he learn how these differences give rise to meaningful cultural differences in experience and understanding beyond legal distinctions. This reiterative process "functions to school the student who has a disability in the nature of her/his disability and how it is perceived by her/his peers, faculty, staff and institution … Because ability is not marked, we continue to teach students who are not required to out themselves as disabled that they are natural, normal, average, unproblematic, and otherwise unremarkable in a taken-for-grantedly positive way" (Fassett and Morella, 2008, p. 147).

Rather than articulating ability as a possession, as something we either have or we lack, it may be helpful to think of our ability in terms of what critical educator Paulo Freire (2000/1970, p. 99) refers to as "limit-situations," those situations or circumstances in our lives that limit or constrain us. We all experience limitations; for example, each of our bodies has a different experience of flexibility, range of motion, speed, precision, and so forth.[9] Our matter, our flesh and bones, our chemistry, makes possible some insights and makes difficult others. In his reading of Alvaro Vieira Pinto, Freire explains that we must reflect on and act in relation to these limit-situations; "as critical perception is embodied in action, a climate of hope and confidence develops which leads men [and women] to attempt to overcome the limit-situations" (p. 99). This process of reflection and action on the world, in order to transform it, is, according to Freire, our most human and humane responsibility and achievement. However, to engage in this praxis, we must regard our differences, our strengths and limitations – our range of abilities, for our purposes here, with unflinching compassion and efforts to engage in dialogue across those differences.

I do not mean to suggest, in noting that we may all perceive our own limitations, our own particular ranges of ability, that everyone has different abilities, and so distinctions of ability and disability are meaningless; such a move is like saying racism is unimportant because we are all raced, or heterosexism (and homophobia) is not an issue because we are all sexual and sexualized beings. We have, in the United States, historically and systematically disenfranchised people of color, women, people with disabilities, members of gay/lesbian/bisexual/transgendered communities, along with other marginalized groups; the consequences for variance from our collective assumed cultural norm have been severe. What I mean to suggest is that our differences matter, and we must explore both what we choose to mark and what we choose to normalize and naturalize.

It is worth considering here, as McIntosh (1988) observed regarding white privilege and male privilege, the many unearned privileges people whose ability is otherwise unmarked (i.e., people who are apparently able-bodied) receive, for example:[10] I can typically move through my world assuming most people are "like me," whether or not they are.

My differences in ability are not amplified or stigmatized by mass mediated representations. So, for example, I can get angry about the (in)action of government officials without people assuming I am paranoid or dangerous and worthy of observation, medication or hospitalization. Similarly, when I appear tired or frustrated, people do not typically assume my health is failing.

My safety does not depend on whether a group of people who do not share my experiences can effectively anticipate my needs (for example, whether campus culture is sufficiently welcoming to me, or whether sandwich sign boards are chained yards away from the poles to which they are attached, creating a hazard for me if I am partially sighted or use mobility aids).

I can be relatively certain that, wherever I go, I can negotiate pretty much all buildings, bathrooms, modes of public transportation, elevators, and furniture. Others will assume this of me, too. The standard issue classroom desk fits me well, and I can sit in it comfortably for hours at a time.

Others assume I can ignore my body without it adversely affecting my thinking or learning. They assume that I perceive the world pretty much as they do, without considering whether my different understandings of pain, for example, shape my worldview.

My success in school has not depended on whether my supervisors (whether professors, colleagues or students) understand my physiological (time, space, technology, environment) needs. For example, as a professor, my ability to respond to and grade students' work is not dependent on whether my university has the budget resources to purchase an expensive screen reading program and computing equipment for me. I am not asked to explain myself and my qualifications to fulfill my teaching assignment if I require students to submit their work electronically for my review (which would be necessary if I needed to use a screen reading program).

When I coauthor, people do not typically assume I had to do so in order to finish the task. People assume I have read all the sources I cite, and they do not question whether I had a lot of "help" with my writing.

People can hand me a piece of writing or ask me to undertake a task on the spur of the moment, and I can generally do it. People will assume that an absence of expressed anxiety or observed planning on my part means that my work is better.

People do not express surprise that I hold a BA, MS, and PhD. They do not express surprise that I hold full-time employment or that I am tenured.

No one has ever told me that I should be satisfied with my achievements because most people like me never made it this far.

I have never gone without health benefits, and I have never had to alter my career plans because I felt caught or stuck by needing Social Security or Medicare benefits and not being able to work full-time.

When people challenge my abilities, whether or not I can do something, they do so respectfully, and often with an eye toward encouraging me to see that I can, in fact, do it. I do not need to repeatedly document my range of abilities to other offices on campus, whether Human Resources or a Disability Resource Center.

When I identify my strengths or limitations in ability, people do not assume that I am dangerous, incompetent, untrustworthy, or a burden to my family, colleagues, culture, or society.

No doubt there are other advantages, other unearned privileges you experience along some axes of your abilities. Perhaps you are already considering the ways in which the above list seems incomplete or inaccurate. My own experiences of ability in the world lead me to some observations and not others; I hope you will add to this list. Or, you might be thinking, for instance, that your differences in ability make you just as subject to discipline (e.g., being fired for not being able to perform some function in the workplace), but because your difference in ability is not a disability in the formal sense, you do not receive any federal protection from the Americans with Disabilities Act. It is important to explore our own range of abilities, how we discuss these across a variety of contexts, and what the implications of our actions are and have been.

That said, it is also important to consider the nature of unearned privilege. Often when we think of privilege, we imagine spoiled millionaire children who, when busted for driving under the influence, only serve short sentences in relatively posh jails or other exceptional examples of abuse; in other words, thinking of privilege usually has us thinking of individuals and individual behaviors. McIntosh (1988) addresses this in her accounting of White and male privilege, pausing to remind her readers that exploring privilege is not so much about particular individuals, but rather our collective and unreflective investment in social systems (such as the legal system, the health care system, or the educational system) that continue to privilege, or lift up, some at the expense of others. Warren (2003) clarifies further by distinguishing racism, as a "system of domination ... enacted by everyone but not localized in any individual," and prejudice as "individual acts based on some arbitrary, though historically significant, characteristic" (p. 65). While each of us experiences a unique range of abilities, and while each of us attempts to engage others who are different from us in meaningful and respectful ways, we all participate in ableism – in a pedagogy of ability – in a social system that, by articulating ability as a possession we either own or lack, perpetuates the normalizing and privileging of apparently able-bodied individuals. Interrogating our participation in this process makes possible the praxis, the reflection, and action on the world in order to transform it, that is our responsibility and challenge.

Critical Intercultural Communication as Praxis

As students of critical intercultural communication, as people seeking to understand better the role of culture, and the interaction between cultures in our lives, we must work toward cultivating certain skills:

1   We must learn to situate the structural (or social systemic) in relation to the personal (or individual). In other words, how does each of us participate in oppressive social systems?
2   We must understand identities as complex and fluid – as situational, rather than static. Our own language complicates this: While it is certainly more respectful to say, when relevant, that a person has a given disability (as opposed to older, less sensitive language that defined the person as the disability – for example, "she's a schizophrenic" or "the learning disabled kid over there"), this language invites us to see qualities of our bodies, our broad range of abilities, as possessions or lacks. This is to say, how does the language we use move in and through us in ways we do not readily appreciate or wish? How does our language use alter our understandings of others and ourselves?
3   We must learn to perceive how we are products and producers of cultures across a nexus of complex and often contradictory lines of privilege and oppression. In this sense, culture is not something we simply inherit at birth, nor is it a group into which we can be thrust because of a sudden change in our circumstances. We enact cultures, and we do not enact them in their purest, textbook forms but instead as amalgamations that are both meaningful and puzzling to us. It is worth asking: How do the cultures we enact interact with one another or come into conflict with one another in ways that are painful, confusing, rewarding, or uplifting? In what ways is this intersectional, intercultural experience similar to/ different for others?
4   We must reflect on our actions and inactions, to understand how they may be empowering for some and disempowering for others, and to effect change. This means learning to recognize not only the similarities that exist across cultures, but also the meaningful differences, and to hold these both in dialectical tension (rather than as either/or positions we must accept or reject). For example, while it is true that we all experience varying degrees of ability, across the many different facets of our lives, it is also true that people with disabilities do experience meaningful differences – in the degree of stigma they experience, in the ways in which their experiences of the world lead them to different lessons and insights about it, and so forth. Each of us must, therefore, explore: How is

it that our bodies enable and constrain our abilities to learn, to understand, and to articulate our experiences? Further, how might the ways we mark (or fail to mark) ability in our lives shape our understandings of ourselves and our interactions with others? What are the consequences of these mundane markings, and for whom?

Critical intercultural communication scholars take seriously the ways communication creates, sustains, alters, and challenges not only culture, but also our experiences of power, privilege and oppression. Their praxis is to reflect on their own roles in these processes, and to engage others in action across difference. For some, our praxis has been to explore the classroom, the ways in which our hidden curricula may teach oppression, whether ableism or some other form. In your own investigations of culture and power, what have you learned? What have you hidden from yourself, and how has it shaped you? How will you act?

Notes

1 La Rochefoucauld (2006).
2 See, for example, work by: Delgado (1998); Halualani, Fassett, Morrison *et al.* (2006); Mendoza, Halualani and Drzewiecka (2002); Ono (1998).
3 In addition to the recommended readings see: Linton (1998); Longmore (2003); Mitchell and Snyder (2001); Siebers (2008).
4 Collier, Hegde, Lee *et al.* (2001).
5 Fassett and Warren (2007).
6 Foucault (1977).
7 Fraser (2007).
8 Fassett and Morella (2008).
9 Freire (2000 [1970]).
10 McIntosh (1988).

References

Collier, M.J., Hegde, R.S., Lee, W. *et al.* (2001) Dialogue on the edges: Ferment in communication and culture, in *Transforming Communication about Culture: Critical New Directions, International and Intercultural Annual* 24, (ed. M.J. Collier), Sage, Thousand Oaks, CA, pp. 219–280.
Delgado, F.P. (1998) When the silenced speak: The textualization and complications of Latino/Latina identity. *Western Journal of Communication*, 62, 420–438.
Fassett, D.L., and Morella, D.L. (2008) Remaking (the) discipline: Marking the performative accomplishment of (dis)ability. *Text and Performance Quarterly*, 28, 139–156.
Fassett, D.L., and Warren, J.T. (2007) *Critical Communication Pedagogy*, Sage, Thousand Oaks.
Foucault, M. (1977) *Discipline and Punish: The Birth of the Prison*, Vintage, New York.
Fraser, M.L. (2007) A literate dyslexic (LD). *Hastings Women's Law Journal*, 18, 223–228.

Freire, P. (2000) *Pedagogía del* oprimido (*Pedagogy of the Oppressed*), 30th edn, (trans. M.B. Ramos), Continuum, New York, originally published 1970.

Halualani, R.T., Fassett, D.L., Morrison, J.H.T.A. *et al.* (2006) Between the structural and the personal: Situated sense-makings of "race." *Communication and Critical/Cultural Studies*, 3, 70–93.

La Rochefoucauld, F. Duc de (2006) *Maxims* (trans. J. Heard, Jr.) Dover Publications, Minneola, NY, (Originally published 1665).

Longmore, P.K. (2003) *Why I Burned my Book and other Essays on Disability*, Temple University Press, Philadelphia.

McIntosh, P. (1988) White privilege and male privilege: A personal account of coming to see correspondences through work in women's studies. Working Paper no. 189, Wellesley College Center for Research on Women, Wellesley.

Mendoza, S.L., Halualani, R.T., and Drzewiecka, J.A. (2002) Moving the discourse on identities in intercultural communication: Structure, culture and resignifications. *Communication Quarterly*, 50, 312–327.

Mitchell, D.T., and Snyder, S.L., (2001) *Narrative Prosthesis: Disability and the Dependencies of Discourse*, University of Michigan Press, Ann Arbor.

Ono, K.A. (1998) Problematizing "nation" in intercultural communication research, in *Communication and Identity across Cultures*, (ed. D. Tanno and A. González), Sage, Thousand Oaks, CA, pp. 34–55.

Linton, S. (1998) *Claiming Disability: Knowledge and Identity*, New York University Press, New York.

Siebers, T.A. (2008) *Disability Theory*, University of Michigan Press, Ann Arbor.

Further Reading

Davis, L.J. (1995) *Enforcing Normalcy: Disability, Deafness and the Body*, Verso, New York.

Davis, L.J. (2002) *Bending Over Backwards: Essays on Disability and the Body*, New York University Press, New York.

Davis, L.J. (ed) (2006) *The Disability Studies Reader*, Routledge, New York.

Goffman, E. (1986) *Stigma: Notes on the Management of Spoiled Identity*, Touchstone, New York.

Sandahl, C., and Auslander, P. (ed.) *Bodies in Commotion: Disability and Performance*, University of Michigan, Ann Arbor.

Wilson, J.C., and Lewiecki-Wilson, C. (eds) (2001) *Embodied Rhetorics: Disability in Language and Culture*, Southern Illinois University Press, Carbondale.

27

The Scarlet Letter, Vigilantism, and the Politics of Sadism

Richard Morris

If it is asked what makes the sadism of a person so intense, one must not think only of constitutional, biological factors, but of the psychic atmosphere that is largely responsible not only for the generation of social sadism but also for the vicissitudes of individually generated, idiosyncratic sadism.

Erich Fromm (1973, p. 333)

In the opening scenes of Nathaniel Hawthorne's *The Scarlet Letter* the story's feature character, Hester Prynne, is brought from the darkness of the town's jail into the morning sun where she will be ridiculed, humiliated, and sent on her way to serve a life-long sentence for having committed adultery. This revealing scene works realistically and dramatically by placing the "criminal" in "the light of nature" and the light of the community, suggesting, albeit momentarily, that we are witnessing a clear, unmistakable act of revelation wherein Nature and community coincide. The force of that powerful collision is immediately called into question when one of the matrons in the crowd exclaims, " 'This woman has brought shame upon all of us, and ought to die. Is there not law for it? Truly there is, both in the Scripture and the statute-book. Then let the magistrates, who have made it of no effect, thank themselves if their own wives and daughters go astray' " (Hawthorne, 2003, p. 45). Neither Nature nor community has called for a supreme sacrifice, but the lack of an explicit horizon for community participants proves itself boundless.

In this very brief moment Hawthorne reveals the outline of a master trope for what we might term "communicative sadism" – the image of rage bursting through a social fabric in the guise of restoring a community to law and order, of saving and serving justice, of protecting the innocent and innocence. The lack of juridical horizon implied in these actions insinuate harsher penalties and grants to all members in good standing the right to punish the guilty – not merely more, not merely

The Handbook of Critical Intercultural Communication, edited by Thomas K. Nakayama and Rona Tamiko Halualani. © 2010 Blackwell Publishing Ltd.

longer, but as much and as long as one judges fit. More, the right to go on punishing the culprit continues to exert itself through the person of anyone with whom Ms. Prynne comes into contact for the rest of her life.[1] Even small children who cannot begin to conceptualize the "wrong" for which Ms. Prynne is being punished clearly exercise the right later in the book to levy punishment on her and her child *ad infinitum*.

Herein resides a formula that serves not only to justify vigilantism but also to enact marginalization via what we might term *rhetorica arcēre* for which there are two equally disturbing roles: an internalizing role that seeks "to shut in, to shut up"; and an externalizing role that seeks "to keep at a distance, to hinder, to prevent."[2] In its internalizing role *rhetorica arcēre* operates largely as a set of in-house strategies and tactics designed to keep the order orderly; it identifies limits and boundaries of inclusion; it announces that reprisals await members who disturb the order. In its externalizing role *rhetorica arcēre* not only sets the boundaries of exclusion (that point beyond which the excluded must not go), but also commands the rules of engagement at the borders, the consequences to outsiders for failing to observe said rules, the penalties to be visited on Others for breaching (or even attempting to breach) the borders between inside and out, and the severity of punishment for Otherness.

Although both internalizing and externalizing roles undoubtedly merit careful consideration, I focus attention exclusively on the latter here because its continued presence stands directly in the path of creating and sustaining sustainable societies. Having acknowledged that boundary, my main thesis is that strategies of the kind under consideration constitute specific types of destructive behavior that disallow the possibility of inclusion and unity between speaker and audience. I take as my starting point a set of remarks offered in response to the September 11, 2001 tragedies in New York City, Washington, DC, and Pennsylvania.[3] My examination pierces its subject in various places representative of points along twin axes of morality and motive, which serve to define our subject.

In the Name of an Angry God

For many people, it is very difficult to accept the sad truth that cruelty is usually inflicted upon the innocent (Alice Miller, 1990, p. 158).

During the September 13, 2001 broadcast of *The 700 Club*, Pat Robertson and Jerry Falwell explained to viewers that the September 11th tragedies were messages from God designed to remind believers that straying from the righteous path has devastating consequences. The broadcast materialized in two parts: (1) Pat Robertson's initial comments; and (2) Pat Robertson's interview with Jerry Falwell. Both sets of remarks leave no room for doubt that God sent this punishment for sins committed and that both sins and sinners are explicitly identifiable – all of which creates an inquisitive set of relationships.

First, there is the relationship between God and people. When people behave incorrectly, God punishes not only those who committed wrongful actions, but also those who have nothing to do with the actions taken. God in this representation becomes a prototypical sadist. A sadist, Erich Fromm (1973) has observed, is "a person with an intense desire to control, hurt, humiliate another person" (p. 282). This is precisely the image that Robertson and Falwell provide – a being who deliberately inflicts pain and humiliation on Others, including innocents, as a means of achieving control over those Others. Such a God immediately and boundlessly constructs a singular audience – one that can later be dissected into factions, but these will be human, not divine, distinctions.

As devoted believers, Falwell and Robertson mirror God's sadism in a number of notable modes. Most obviously, they are interpreters who gladly deliver God's message to other believers. They congratulate one another on having reached the same interpretation (which others will echo again and again in the months following this broadcast); they fortify one another's positions; they deepen one another's specific claims; and they do so with exultation. Theirs is not the kind of direct, catastrophic sadism manifested in their representation of God, of course; but their more insidious, rhetorical variety has an important place in the conduct and construction of the sadism that is yet to come.

In its rhetorical figure sadism is "[m]ental cruelty, the wish to humiliate and hurt another's feelings," which "is probably even more widespread than physical sadism. This type of sadistic attack is much safer for the sadist; after all, no physical force but 'only' words have been used. ... Parents inflict it upon their children, professors on their students, superiors on their inferiors – in other words it is employed in any situation where there is someone who cannot defend [themselves] against the sadist." Such rhetorical action "may be disguised in many seemingly harmless ways: a question, a smile, a confusing remark. Who does not know an 'artist' in this kind of sadism, the one who finds just the right word or the right gesture to embarrass or humiliate another in this innocent way" (Fromm 1973, p. 284)?

Whether one considers Falwell and Robertson "artists" in this sense, their sadistic assaults combine well with the mode they use to identify the culprits, who are clearly members of the "universal audience" called into being through God's judgment but who are so "fallen" that their presence (for purpose of self-defense, perhaps) is unnecessary, unseemly. The primary culprits are "these Islamic fundamentalists, these radical terrorists, these Middle Eastern monsters" who "are committed to destroying the Jewish nation, driving her into the Mediterranean, conquering the world." The secondary culprits include anyone who has "been so concerned about money" or "material things," who has focused on "their health and their finances, and on their pleasures and on their sexuality," who has been "self-absorbed," who has "allowed rampant pornography on the internet," who has "allowed rampant secularism and occult, etc. to be broadcast on television," "who has attempted to legislate" God "out of the schools," who has argued that religion and state must remain separate, "the federal court system," "the pagans, and the abortionists, and the feminists, and the gays and the lesbians who are actively trying to make that an alternative lifestyle, the ACLU, People for the American Way, all of them who have tried to secularize America."

Not only is the scope of duplicity enormous given these parameters, but the assault on the humanity of those identified as miscreants is devastating. Few people, including those in the program's immediate audience, can escape being pulled into the offending groups; and those who thus qualify become monsters. Even those who are guilty by association lose their humanity, which makes the assault licit and implicitly justifies additional action. If these monsters are truly responsible for calling God's wrath down upon all of us, then would not action against them be mere self-defense? Would not audience members be justified in ridding the world of these monsters to appease an angry God and insure a more tranquil future for themselves and their children?

Yet, actions alone are not the solitary concern here; for Falwell and Robertson also explicitly identify entire groups of "fallen" people as being responsible for God's anger simply because they exist. Feminists, homosexuals, Islamic fundamentalists, and others are responsible not because we "know" they have done anything conspicuously foul, but because they are what they are. That existential status encourages auditors to adopt a similar sadistic attitude toward Others and to act in ways that will promote the group's harmony and happiness.

All of this occurs within an epistemological stance of absolute certitude. God has left no doubt, and the speakers have left no room for doubt. Those who are directly responsible, those who are indirectly responsible, and those who are guilty by association have caused God to render such devastation. "We" have been punished because of "them" – because of who they are as well as what some of them have done. Their identities are exposed, leaving only courses of action open to members of the audience who "rightly" understand the situation.

As certitude at the axiological level temporally and logically precedes identity (no investigation of the facts and circumstances being required), the praxeological level is equally determined. One need not sort out the "good" lesbians from the "bad" lesbians, for instance, because their mere existence is the agency of their inhumanity and sufficient cause for God's anger and wrath. One need not identify with or even relate to pagans as if they had an inkling of human decency because they are always already guilty. Praxeologically, there can be no sympathy or empathy for these Others, and any notion of equality between these Others and true believers is quite literally out of the question. The Spaniards and English knew this well in their dealings with the Indians of the Americas, which allowed them to assume guardianship of the Indians and their resources. Germans in the Third Reich knew this when they ordered the extermination of millions of Others. Falwell and Robertson also know this as they broadcast their message to the world. They make no direct appeal for members of the audience to engage in physical or emotional sadism because such actions are innately justified through God's anger-as-judgment. Cruelty begets cruelty.

In her recent book, *For Your Own Good* (1990), psychologist Alice Miller presents a robust case for viewing much of human cruelty as having its ultimate source in childhood experiences. One of her crucial insights is that forbidden, unexpressed childhood anger "does not disappear, but transforms with time into a more or less conscious hatred directed against either the self or substitute persons" (p. 61). On the broader sociological level, "the ideology of child beating and the belief that beating is not harmful serve the function of covering up the consequences of the act and making them unrecognizable" (p. 78). In the present case the possibility of human cruelty receives vibrancy and specific being through God's response to wrong-doing and wrong-being and through Falwell and Robertson's sadistic rhetoric. To complete the pattern, the speakers cover over and make unrecognizable the consequences of their acts by presenting a united front of absolute certitude, by excluding the possibilities of empathy or sympathy or investigating the facts and circumstances, and by placing God between themselves and the audience. This is not their doing but God's doing, and subsequent actions will not be their doings but God's doings.

The parent–child relationship between God and humans transforms into a parent–child relationship between speakers and auditors. The kind of relationship that the speakers envision, as we have already noticed, mirrors the relationship between God and humans. One immediate implication is that other kinds of relationships, which is to say nonsadistic relationships, are impermissible. Treating Others with respect, imagining that context plays any role in the lives of Others, embracing the possibility that something is wrong systemically, seeking to bring an end to alienation and hatred and other factors that may have contributed to these actions is unjustifiable at any possible level not only because of what the speakers "know," but also because of what believers now know given God's actions *cum* judgment. We also know, as Miller (1990) points out, that "all advice that pertains to raising children betrays more or less clearly the numerous, variously clothed needs of the *adult*" (p. 97).

The needs of God, the adult, and of the speakers, as adults, come to us only through the latter, who tell us unequivocally that their need is for power, control, vengeance, and the dispersion of pain and humiliation. God, the father, has dispensed "justice," to be sure; but the possibility of future "justice" justifies actions of parents, who would bring errant children back into the fold. This equation is dreadfully amiss since children, however imperfect, are human beings, and Others in this formula are inhuman. Still, the parent–child relationship, which is to say the sadist–victim relationship, enables the speakers and other true believers who would assume the role of dutiful child of God *qua* parent to assume their rightful role as executioner, knowing full well that God's judgment eliminates any need for judge or jury.

Ideological Rape

Morality and performance of duty are artificial measures that become necessary when something essential is lacking (Alice Miller 1990, p. 85).

In the film *The Contender* (Dreamworks 2001) neoconservative Sheldon "Shelly" B. Runyon (Gary Oldman) relentlessly attempts to derail Senator Laine Hanson's

(Joan Allen) vice presidential confirmation hearings. The underlying reason, which we learn early in the story's development, is that Senator Hanson was once a Republican (Runyon's party) but switched to the Democratic party, which in Shelly Runyon's eyes makes her "the cancer of virtuous decay." The strategy, then, is to find as much dirt as possible to sling in Senator Hanson's direction. The principal vehicle for this strategy turns out to be a sexual escapade in which Hanson allegedly had participated during her first year in college.

Throughout the confirmation hearings, Shelly Runyon continually insinuates that Senator Hanson is not morally fit for the position of vice president, proclaiming at one point that Senator Hanson's status as an atheist necessarily means that she "has shown a disdain for religion and those practicing it." Shortly thereafter, Shelly "innocently" discloses the web address where the public might find photographs of the alleged sexual escapade. Then, after Senator Hanson is duped into appearing on a television talk show ("America Live") in which she is baited and badgered concerning her alleged moral deviancy, we come to a pivotal moment in which Shelly Runyon's wife, sitting on the Hanson's home porch, tells Laine Hanson that the confirmation hearings have turned into "an ideological rape."[4]

Ideological rape in the context of a more general exploration of *rhetorica arcēre* is the brutal imposition of one person's morality on an Other in such a way that the consequences for that Other are psychologically, spiritually, and/or emotionally damaging. Justification for such imposition is remarkably simple. Operating from a position of moral superiority, the sadist "knows" that truth, truth-telling, fairness, and all other matters pertaining to rules of civility and ethicality are irrelevant when dealing with inferiors and doubly so when dealing with the devil and Others who are "fallen." Ideological rape is not only self-justifying, it is also self-sanctifying.

Just so, Falwell and Robertson levy their morality violently, apodictically, sadistically; they do not simply indict, they execute. The first order of the execution is to assume the universality of their perspective, which defines membership and exclusion, life and death. Those who do not believe are not simply part of the problem, they are the problem and must be exterminated before peace, tranquility, righteousness, harmony, and God's favor can be restored. The second order of execution is to identify all those who are nonbelievers *qua* nonhumans so that "appropriate" action can be taken. The final order of execution is to ensure that no safe harbor remains. All tasks having been accomplished, the ideological rape is complete.

Conclusion

Sadism is not an infectious disease that strikes a person all of a sudden. It has a long prehistory in childhood and *always* originates in the desperate fantasies of a child who is searching for a way out of a hopeless situation (Alice Miller, 1990, p. 265).

That everyday life is distended with strategies for creating protected zones of communicative engagement in which Others face distinct and often permanent social and cultural disadvantage and estrangement is hardly news. Yet, we continue to find ourselves in places where we have little understanding of cultural and social rehearsals that individuals belonging to identifiable networks pride themselves on mastering at the expense of others. Clearly, such rehearsals are positively sanctioned behaviors belonging to an order of human destructiveness that stands apart from other actions precisely because they are not and cannot be phylogenetically programmed responses, defensively benign forms of aggression. On the contrary, their defining feature on the whole is that they are nonadaptive forms of human destructiveness: they occur as a matter of conscious choice. Insofar as they serve "to keep at a distance, hinder, to prevent," they also constitute identifiable forms of sadism.

What is striking about *rhetorica arcēre* from this point of view is not simply that human beings create strategies designed to inflict pain, but also that such strategies grow directly from morality as mode and from sadism as motive. Whatever their guise, such strategies emerge through the agency of moral action. In some cases, that moral action often is itself the sole justification for the sadist's behaviors. In other cases, sadists often appeal to some conceivably shared principle or, barring that, some principle that *ought* to be shared. In all cases, it is imperative that one judge the person and not simply the person's particular action because the conjunction of mode and motive valorizes the social quality of sadism.

At this moment in this society (and elsewhere, of course), *rhetorica arcēre* retains the status of fully accepted, even laudable behavior. Think of comedians who earn their living and build their career from the infliction of pain and humiliation on others; of colleagues who delight in the sadism they can dispense from their positions of power; of administrators and others in positions of authority who revel in their capacity to render the unfortunate helpless or place obstacles in the paths of those who are already disadvantaged; of legislators who pass laws designed to protect one group at the expense of others; of friends and neighbors who casually render moral judgments designed to damage an Other, of rumor mongers and gossips who savor the pain they inflict. Think of the countless instances where moral judgment issues a call for action. The strategies of *rhetorica arcēre* are not confined to the ramblings of bullies and maniacs; they typify and continually threaten everyday life.

When such practices are out in the open, they are undeniably to be lamented, challenged, and called by their rightful names. When they ooze from behind masks of equality, fraternity, sorority, duty, unity – often in the name of "diversity" – the magnitude of their destructive force increases in precisely the same proportion as their ethicality decreases. Within the context of communication theory and practice, what makes these forms of human destructiveness of such moment is that they promise to preclude even the possibility of unity and cohesion between and among us at every possible level.

Notes

1   In this particular story, Hester Prynne's subsequent behavior across many years earns her small reprieve from the constant harassment by the town-folk; yet, there can be no doubt that the right of the town-folk to reinvoke their right to punish her at any moment for any reason (or no reason at all) continues at the will of anyone at any time. Sadism is self-justifying.

2   This is, of course, an artificial distinction. Strategies that typically appear through internalizing or externalizing can just as readily appear in their opposite. Yet, the distinction holds to the extent that one imagines a more humane attitude on the part of members of the order toward other members of the order. Once that motive is abandoned, the distinction fails. The point here, as explained later in the essay, is that internalizing and externalizing instances locate along two axes, the moral axis, which serves as mode, and the destructive or sadistic axis, which serves as motive.

3   A complete transcript of this broadcast appears in the Appendix.

4   This is a harsh term that I wish to use advisedly and cautiously, as its physical and psychological applications refer to a brutal, despicable act; and I have no desire whatsoever to diminish its meaning or significance by applying it to a nonphysical act that can be and often is, in the present usage, just as brutal and despicable.

Appendix

Robertson's initial comments

And we have thought that we're invulnerable. And we have been so concerned about money. We have been so concerned about material things. The interests of people are on their health and their finances, and on their pleasures and on their sexuality, and while this is going on while we're self-absorbed and the churches as well as in the population, we have allowed rampant pornography on the Internet. We have allowed rampant secularism and occult, etc. to be broadcast on television. We have permitted somewhere in the neighborhood of 35 to 40 million unborn babies to be slaughtered in our society. We have a court that has essentially stuck its finger in God's eye and said we're going to legislate you out of the schools. We're going to take your commandments from off the courthouse steps in various states. We're not going to let little children read the commandments of God. We're not going to let the Bible be read, no prayer in our schools. We have insulted God at the highest levels of our government. And, then we say "why does this happen?"

Well, why it's happening is that God Almighty is lifting his protection from us. And once that protection is gone, we all are vulnerable because we're a free society, and we're vulnerable. We lay naked before these terrorists who have infiltrated our country. There's probably tens of thousands of them in America right now. They've been raising money. They've been preaching their hate and overseas they have been spewing out venom against the United States for years. All over the

Arab world, there is venom being poured out into people's ears and minds against America. And, the only thing that's going to sustain us is the umbrella power of the Almighty God.

Interview with Jerry Falwell

PAT ROBERTSON: Well after Tuesday's attacks, many Americans are struggling with grief, fear, and unanswered questions. How should Christians respond to this crisis? Well joining us now with some answers is a dear friend of ours, the Pastor of the Thomas Road Baptist Church and Liberty University, the head and founder of that, Dr. Jerry Falwell. Jerry, it's a delight to have you with us today.

JERRY FALWELL: Thanks, Pat.

PAT ROBERTSON: Listen. What are you telling the Church? You called your Church together. What was your response at Thomas Road to this tragedy?

JERRY FALWELL: Well, as the world knows, the tragedy hit on Tuesday morning, and at 2:00 in the afternoon, we gathered 7000 Liberty University students, faculty, local people together, and we used the verse that I heard you use a moment ago, Chronicles II, 7:14, that God wanted us to humble ourselves and seek his face. And there's not much we can do in the Church but what we're supposed to do, and that is pray. Pray for the President that God will give him wisdom, keep bad advisors from him, bring good ones to him, praying for the families of the victims, praying for America. And, you know this thing is not a great deal different than what I remember and you Pat. We're about the same age. December 7, 1941, when we entered the war against Japan, Germany, Italy Hitler's goal was to destroy the Jews among other things, and conquer the world. And, these Islamic fundamentalists, these radical terrorists, these Middle Eastern monsters are committed to destroying the Jewish nation, driving her into the Mediterranean, conquering the world. And, we are the great Satan. We are the ultimate goal. I talked this morning with Tom Rose publisher of the Jerusalem Post, and orthodox Jew, and he said, "Now America knows in a horrible way what Israel's been facing for 53 years at the hand of Arafat and other terrorists and radicals and barbarians."

PAT ROBERTSON: Jerry, I know that you shared several 40 day fasts for revival in America. We here at CBN had a couple of 40 day fasts during the Lenten season, and Bill Bright, I don't know, eight or nine. Do you think that this is going to be the trigger of revival, a real revival in the Church where we truly turn back to God with all our heart?

JERRY FALWELL: It could be. I've never sensed a togetherness, a burden, a broken heart as I do in the Church today, and just 48 hours, I gave away a booklet I wrote 10 years ago. I gave it away last night on the Biblical position on fasting and prayer because I do believe that that is what we've got to do now– fast and pray. And I agree totally with you that the Lord has protected us so wonderfully these 225 years. And since 1812, this is the first time that we've been attacked on our soil, first time, and by far the worst results. And I fear, as Donald Rumsfeld, the Secretary of Defense said yesterday, that this is only the beginning. And with biological warfare available to these monsters; the Husseins, the Bin Ladens, the Arafats, what we saw on Tuesday, as terrible as it is, could be miniscule if, in fact, if in fact God continues to lift the curtain and allow the enemies of America to give us probably what we deserve.

PAT ROBERTSON: Jerry, that's my feeling. I think we've just seen the antechamber to terror. We haven't even begun to see what they can do to the major population.

JERRY FALWELL: The ACLU's got to take a lot of blame for this.

PAT ROBERTSON: Well, yes.

JERRY FALWELL: And, I know that I'll hear from them for this. But, throwing God out successfully with the help of the federal court system, throwing God out of the public square, out of the schools. The abortionists have got to bear some burden for this because God will not be mocked. And when we destroy 40 million little innocent babies, we make God mad. I really believe that the pagans, and the abortionists, and the feminists, and the gays and the lesbians who are actively trying to make that an alternative lifestyle, the ACLU, People For the American Way, all of them who have tried to secularize America. I point the finger in their face and say "you helped this happen."

PAT ROBERTSON: Well, I totally concur, and the problem is we have adopted that agenda at the highest levels of our government. And so we're responsible as a free society for what the top people do. And, the top people, of course, is the court system.

JERRY FALWELL: Amen. Pat, did you notice yesterday? The ACLU, and all the Christ-haters, the People For the American Way, NOW, etc. were totally disregarded by the Democrats and the Republicans in both houses of Congress as they went out on the steps and called out on to God in prayer and sang 'God Bless America' and said 'let the ACLU be hanged'. In other words, when the nation is on its knees, the only normal and natural and spiritual thing to do is what we ought to be doing all the time- calling upon God.

PAT ROBERTSON: *Amen.* I wanted to ask you the reaction. I know that you had a major prayer meeting last night, and I know your people assembled, just a large gathering at your Church. What was the mood of the people? What did they say and what did you sense with your congregation?

JERRY FALWELL: A brokenness that I have not seen. I've been there pastor 45 years, 30 years Chancellor at Liberty. We had 7000 gather yesterday in the Vines Center and filled the Church last night. I sensed a brokenness, tears. People were sobbing at the altar. And, they have no shame about it. It was the kind of brokenness that no one could conjure, only God could bring upon us. And, that is to me the most optimistic thing that I see today as I look across America. And every city, I called a friend in Springfield yesterday. He said at least a hundred churches, Springfield, MO, at least a hundred churches have special prayer meetings for America today and tonight. And, that's happening by the thousands all over America. This could be, if we will fast and pray, this could be God's call to revival.

PAT ROBERTSON: Well, I believe it. And I think the people, the Bible says render your hearts and not your garments, and people begin to render their hearts and they weep before the Lord, and they really get serious with God, God will hear and answer. We'll see revival. I am thrilled to hear that about your Church because it's happening all over.

JERRY FALWELL: It's everywhere.

PAT ROBERTSON: Yes.

JERRY FALWELL: In the most unlikely of places. The general manager at the ABC affili- ate in our area called me this morning and said "we're going to ask for all the churches, all the people of faith to join us at the D-Day Memorial over in Bedford at 2:00, Sunday." And, Randy Smith is his name, the general manager, and he is calling central Virginia to healing through prayer and I suspect there will be thou- sands there.

PAT ROBERTSON: Jerry, this is so encouraging, and I thank God for your stand. We just love you and praise God for you. Liberty is a great institution and I congratulate you for that wonderful student body, and your Church. And, thank-you my dear friend for being with us.

JERRY FALWELL: God bless you brother. Let's stand together.

PAT ROBERTSON: Amen

References

Fromm, E. (1973) *The Anatomy of Human Destructiveness*, Rinehart & Winston, New York.
Hawthorne, N. (2003) *The Scarlet Letter*, Barnes and Noble, New York.
Miller, A. (1990) *For Your Own Good*, Farrar, Strauss & Giroux, New York.

28

Authenticity and Identity in the Portable Homeland

Victoria Chen

More than three decades ago Berger, Berger, and Kellner (1973) in *The Homeless Mind* provided an insightful description of modernity and a form of consciousness that developed out of the cultural and historical process. As posited by the authors, what characterizes the human condition in this development is the pluralization of social lifeworlds. Presented with multiple options and yet often compromised by incoherently bound identities, one can become anchorless or intellectually, mentally, and emotionally homeless in an emerging culture where established traditional practices are challenged and new trends cultivated and celebrated.

Whereas the homeless mind referred to a contemporary place of mentally belonging (or not belonging) and an uncertain space for ideas in transition to develop and be contested, the construction of "home" is certainly related to location, community, identity, and politics. bell hooks in her latest book *Belonging: A Culture of Place* (2009) writes, "Like many of my contemporaries I have yearned to find my place in this world, to have a sense of homecoming, a sense of being wedded to a place" (p. 2). She also points out that "naturally it would be impossible to contemplate these issues without thinking of the politics of race and class" (2009, p. 3). Issues related to finding a home, belonging to a community, positioning oneself politically, and having a legitimate public space and personal voice in society are intrinsically connected to the politics of identity. In this essay I explore the ideas of home in conjunction with the construction of cultural identity from a critical perspective. I propose that the indeterminate process of creating both home and identity can paradoxically lead to displacement and homeless.

There has been a proliferation of writing on the meaning of home across disciplines in anthropology, sociology, philosophy, and architecture. Travelers' tales also inform us that the search for a place one can call home is an ongoing quest for many who traverse across borders (Robertson *et al.*, 1994). Despite an array of diverse

The Handbook of Critical Intercultural Communication, edited by Thomas K. Nakayama and Rona Tamiko Halualani.   © 2010 Blackwell Publishing Ltd.

and sometimes contradictory views offered by scholars, home is generally understood as a multidimensional concept. It is not the purpose of this essay to examine whether home can be defined by a location, a territory, a feeling, or a state of being in the world. Rather, I offer a selective discussion of the construction of meanings of home as a reflexive context to understand the construction of identity.

Sarup (1994) in a discussion of home and identity acknowledges that the notion of home is not the same in every culture, and that the meaning of home as a metaphor changes throughout the decades. "Nevertheless, I want to suggest that the concept of home seems to be tied in some way with the notion of identity – the story we tell of ourselves and which is also the story others tell of us. But identities are not free-floating, they are limited by borders and boundaries" (p. 95).

In her discussion of Turkish identity across generations, Haydari (2006) poses several related questions:

> Where is "home"? Is it a piece of the geographic landscape to which we feel attached? Is it the sense of a history we share with a group of people with whom we used to live? What does it mean to visit Turkey once a year for a month, yet still call it home? Why does speaking Turkish, my mother tongue, become a symbolic connection to home?.. What are the politics of being a part of the majority in Turkey while being a minority and "other" in the United States? (p. 100).

While teaching her daughter the Turkish language, religion, and cultural practices, Haydari also wonders how the home where her family settled in the United States has different meanings for her American born daughter in a cultural and political climate that is changing.

Home can be conceptualized as a place of belonging that offers a sense of comfort and relational connections. It is a geographical construction and a spatial metaphor. To study the symbolic significance of home, it is useful to pose a question that explores what home means to a particular individual and how the dwellers construct meanings of their home within a historical, cultural, sociopolitical, and economic context. From a critical perspective, home can also be understood as a web of complex relationships and a site to struggle for coherence, coordination, and power. The process of creating a home thus involves ideological positioning of identity within a structure of affordances and constraints.

In a global context what we call home can be problematic where geographic and national boundaries are elastic. The location and significance of what one can claim as home as well as one's connection with a homeland can shift due to the changing national and international politics. Citizens in different parts of the world lose their home, build a new home, and become displaced in the process of political and cultural domination, border disputes, economic exploitation, and foreign invasion. Various refugee groups provide an example of how the idea of home changes with shifting cultural identities and political alliances. Ambiguous ideological positioning occurs as a result of individuals' experience of uprooting and disruption.

Witteborn (2008) in her study of Iraqi refugees in the United Stated explored the construction of their diasporic imaginations, which are characterized by "resistance and survival and transcended national, social, and political spaces" (p. 216). Through analysis of the Iraqi refugees' narration, Witteborn argued that they were able to create links between "being Iraqi, a displaced person, and a member of US society" (p. 202). The study suggested three locations that were imagined as the Iraqi refugees constructed their multiple identities as members of transnational communities: Iraqis in Iraq, Iraqis in refugee camps, and Iraqis in the United States. The personal accounts that are provided by the participants in Witteborn's study portray an array of cultural and political experiences that transcend geographic and national boundaries. Where is home for these Iraqi refugees, and how do we understand the complexity of their newly emerging personal, cultural, and political identity?

Tenzin Dorjee (2006), writing from a scholar's perspective in the United States. offers an in-depth analysis of cultural identity in the Tibetan diaspora. Growing up in Bylakuppe, one of the oldest Tibetan settlements in India, he came to the United States in 1993. Tenzin Dorjee in his personal narrative emphasized that "Tibetan cultural identity is essentially Buddhist identity" (p. 243). Living in a Western culture where Christianity is the most popular religion, Tenzin Dorjee struggled in his everyday life between different forms of social relationship and personhood, between spirituality and materialism (p. 245). In his essay he celebrates the Tibetan language and Buddhist views and practices. He laments the inability of the younger generation Tibetans in diasporic communities to speak the Tibetan language and appreciate the culture and religion. Tenzin Dorjee cannot go back to Tibet, and even if he could, he would find a Tibet under the control of China where Tibetans cannot freely practice Buddhism and honor His Holiness the Dalai Lama. In his essay we can sense his devotion to the Tibetan culture and religion through his teaching and translations. His Tibetan identity is reconstructed from a diasporic lens in the political context of US-China-Tibet relationship. Where is home for Tenzin Dorjee?

Mortland (1994) explores identity construction among Cambodian refugees. In her study she described a situation where a Cambodian refugee must determine "how to be Cambodian in America": "Part of identity construction for refugees takes the form of 'likeness' to other refugees of the same ethnicity and 'difference,' creating a back and forth movement between Americanization and re-establishment of their ethnic background" (p. 5). In their newly adopted country, these refugees tried to create a new place of belonging based on a process of Americanization and differentiation. If indeed "refugeeness" signifies "homelessness" (p. 8), how do we understand the Cambodian refugees' creation of a home in the United States where they can retain their culture, language, traditional Cambodian behavior, and Buddhism so they would not lose their "natural" identity as Cambodians?

"Refugeeism" may be said to be produced by political and economic conditions that make continued residence intolerable (Trinh, 1994). "The irreversible sense of 'losing ground' and losing contact is, however, often suppressed by the immediate urge to 'settle in' or to assimilate in order to overcome the humiliation of bearing the too-many-too-needy status of the homeless-stateless alien" (p. 12). In the examples of a Vietnamese refugee in Australia and a Cambodian refugee in France that Trinh offered, the prevailing tension in identity construction involves the problem of how "to be accepted rather than to accept." Chronicling the immigrant history of this country, Takaki (2008) retells American history through the lives and contributions of many minority groups who played a major role shaping the way this culture accepted and rejected new immigrants. The history of retaining and changing one's ethnic and cultural identity in this immigrant society is a messy one. The striving for a sense of belonging and local legitimacy takes place in a context where national, cultural, and international politics inevitably intertwine.

Given the history and cultural politics of multicultural America, the challenge for refugees to find a home can be extended to the experience of American citizens whose identity is often brought into question in a society that privileges white as the taken-for-granted norm. Nakayama (2004) remarks in his essay that there is an ongoing struggle with those who wish to deny his American identity. "Asian American identities cannot be understood outside of the context of international politics and histories, and Asian American history and politics *are* a part of US history and politics" (p. 30). How does one begin to establish a meaningful sense of home while being treated like a perpetual foreigner in his own country? In a series of conversations with Maxing Hong Kingston, she said, "No, we're not outsiders, we belong here, this is our country, this is our history, and we are a part of America … If it weren't for us, America would be a different place" (Skenazy and Martin, 1998, p. 109). Even the woman warrior has to fight off the suspicion and insists that this is the homeland where she belongs.

Kristeva in discussing the notion of becoming a stranger to one's own country, language, sex and identity, said that perhaps "a person of the twentieth century can exist honestly only as a foreigner" (cited in Trinh, 1994, p. 13). Almost a decade into the twenty-first century, the quest for acceptance and agency in one's home continues for individuals whose existence is characterized by migration and displacement. "The predicament of crossing boundaries cannot be merely rejected or accepted. Again, if it is problematic to be a stranger, it is even more so to stop being one" (Trinh, 1994, p. 16). Perhaps being a stranger is a multilayered construct. The betrayal of one's identity can take place in different contexts, just as the construction of one's home can paradoxically destroy a sense of belonging. "The best metaphor of America remains the dreadful metaphor – the Melting Pot. Fall into the Melting Pot, ease into the Melting Pot, or jump into the Melting Pot – it makes no difference – you find yourself a stranger to your parents, a stranger to your own memory of yourself" (Rodriguez, 1992, p.161).

In *Hunger of Memory* Richard Rodriguez (1982) writes with great pathos about growing up in Sacramento as a son of working class Mexican immigrants. Along the journey towards becoming a middle class professional and a very successful American writer, Rodriguez paid the price of separating from his parents' cultural identity and feeling alienated in his parents' home. Spanish language is like a private language that belongs to the intimate immigrant experience of his Mexican family. His English education legitimates him as a public citizen, a voice of American success. Home was not a comfort for Rodriguez; it reminded him how long he had traveled on his academic road and how far he had left behind his Spanish speaking parents. "The day I raised my hand in class and spoke loudly to an entire roomful of faces, my childhood started to end" (Rodriguez, 1982, p. 28). For Rodriguez home is a memory of loneliness and silence. His identity as a writer was puzzling to his parents and constantly aroused suspicion and disapproval. In the larger home of America, Rodriguez's race was also highlighted against his will and scrutinized for political purposes. Indeed race and class are an essential part in one's ongoing struggle for an identity and a place that one can call home.

The ubiquitous idea of an imagined community discussed by Anderson (1983) suggests that the nation is a political entity that derives its significance from forming a community as imagined by the citizens. "It is imagined because the members of even the smallest nation will never know most of their fellow-members, meet them, or even hear of them, yet in the minds of each lives the image of their communion" (p. 5). Home can be understood as an imagined construct that serves communal purposes and political functions. How do travelers, refugees, immigrants, and citizens imagine their communities? Who has the right to belong to this community and who has the power to deprive others the right to do so? Do citizens in a community have equal opportunity to claim it as home? Who defines what constitutes home, who benefits from this construction, and what purpose does it serve? Perhaps a key to the politics of identity lies in these issues.

In her personal reflection on the culture of place, bell hooks (2009) describes her relationship with her hometown in Kentucky and with other places where she has lived. As in her other writings, politics of race and class figure prominently in hooks' understanding of her sense of belonging and where she calls home. "Leaving Kentucky, I believed I would leave the terror of whiteness behind but that fear followed me" (p. 12). At Stanford University she did not feel a sense of belonging but constantly felt like an unwanted outsider: "I felt for the first time the way in which geographical origins could separate citizens of the same nation" (p. 12). This experience of distance and otherness is echoed by Rodriguez (1992): "When far from home, Americans easily recognize one another in a crowd. It is only when we return home, when we live and work next to one another, that Americans choose to believe anew in the fact of our separateness" (p. 164). For many individuals the desire of wanting to connect with their personal home and the country they call home is accompanied by a sense of uneasiness, if not marginalization, living in a place where justice and equality have not prevailed.

Scholars in various disciplines have addressed and written about the concept of diaspora. The idea of diaspora can illustrate the complex connections between identity (e.g., cultural, ethnic, and religious identity) and home. The ancient Greek etymology of diaspora means to "scatter over multiple sites from a particular place, as well as social condition and consciousness" (cited in Peteet, 2007, p. 629). Safran (2005) discussed the criteria of diaspora that are based on the Jewish exile as a paradigmatic case: "The Jews are the oldest diaspora; they lacked a 'homeland' for two millennia but thought about it constantly and the idea of a return to it ...

remained part of their collective consciousness" (p. 37). In exile the construction of a Jewish identity for many is explicitly tied to what they consider their homeland – Israel. Although the meaning of Jewish identity may vary between individuals and groups, it is important to understand how diasporic identity takes root and become significant in the cultural and political context wherever Jewish people settled. "The displaced have a deep and everyday connection to past time, place, and social relationships" (Peteet, p. 633). For individuals in exile, connections with their homeland are always ambiguous, and multiple meanings of their indeterminate identity can be constructed from a variety of viewpoints.

In a study of Tibetan diasporic identities in different communities in the world, Houston and Wright (2003) discussed how choosing different identities in exile gave different means of access to political power for Tibetan refugees. Whether to maintain refugee identity or to attain citizenship "creates a space for benefits and restrictions associated with different axes of power locally and globally" (p. 230). Examining how exiles weigh these and other options can provide insights into how diasporic Tibetans negotiate their lives. Drzewiecka and Halualani (2002) in their study of diasporic politics argued for a reflexive relationship between the structural forces and situated cultural practices. These two ideas are not separate entities but are simultaneously made meaningful through an individual's social activities. To understand how homes and identities are invented and reconstructed in diasporic communities' identity through communication requires an investigation of the imbricated power discourse in multiple contexts and on multiple levels (Chen, 2004).

Challenging the often uncritical prominence of place in diaspora studies, Clifford (1994), among other scholars, argued that "decentered, lateral connections may be as important as those formed around a teleology of origin/return" (p.306). Diaspora thus can be seen as a type of "identity discourse" more than a "type of population dispersal" (cited in Peteet, p. 630). What these scholars suggest is that a useful way to study identity should not focus primarily on one's ancestral homeland or "root" but on how one traverses the "route" to accomplish a complex array of identities. Identity always has to do with a continuous relationship with a place, as well as its history, ancestry, and geography (see Clifford, 1997). The practices of colonization, occupation of territory, purchase of land, and redrawing of boundaries all point to the contingent emergence of what we call identity.

Perhaps we can think of home as a fluid context that holds one's changing identity. As context shifts, one's identity takes on new dimensions and different meanings. Reflexively, the ongoing construction of identity shapes the location and significance of one's home. All these activities take place within a historical, cultural, sociopolitical, and relational context where power and privilege matter. In Hall's discussion of the politics of location and positionality (1990, 1996), identity is not only a process of becoming but something that is always being restructured and contested. Fluidity in identity, however, is not random. One not only needs to question identity but also must be mindful of the constraints placed by history on the shaping of an individual's or a group's place in the world. Clifford (2001) critiques postsixties "postmodern" identity politics as appealing to "ethnicity and 'heritage' by fragmented groups functioning as 'invented traditions' within a late-capitalist, commodified multiculturalism" (p. 472). The fabric of identity always consists of a long historical process of land ownership, (dis)placement of local inhabitants, and an ongoing struggle to gain a legitimate voice in the place where social groups and political institutions are formed.

Identity is inexorably bound up with what we do, how we make sense of what we do, and how we make choices of what we do. Just like we depart from home to encounter the outside world, identity is a specific point of orientation from which we experience and participate in communication. It has to do with how we enter a conversation and how we silence ourselves and others. It involves a particular form of consciousness in practice, constructed from a specific time and place, in a specific cultural and historical context. Just as our relationships are always based in location, our identity is constructed through a contingent process of self presentation, relational negotiation, cultural articulation, and global transformation. Rodriguez (1992) describes a sense of dislocation that is familiar to immigrant experience: "Cities, rivers, mountains retain Spanish names. California was once Mexico ... There is confluence of history" (p. 49).

Eva Hoffman (1991) in her biography *Lost in Translation* questioned the perspective that this is a society in which "you are who you think you are. Nobody gives you your identity here, you have to reinvent yourself everyday." She asked "But how do I choose from identity options available all round me?" (p. 160). Chow (1990) argues that ethnicity in America is not "voluntary" in character, and that "the consciousness of ethnicity for Asian and other nonwhite groups is inevitably a matter of history rather than of choice" (p. 45). In his trilogy, Rodriguez (1982, 1992, 2002) consistently insists that one cannot and does not choose one's identity. "Our parents came to America for the choices America offers. What the child of immigrant parents knows is that here is inevitability" (Rodriguez, 1992, p. 158). Hall's (1992) notion of articulation maintains that not everything is possible at any moment when it comes to cultural change; rather, possible (dis)connections are always constrained at any historical moment. This realization can be applied to identity construction as well. Possibilities of identity are always politically produced and pose a potential challenge in the process of creation.

The development of home and identity involves layers of reconstruction. Clifford's (1997) writing on travel refers to the "transcultural predicaments" in the making of homes away from home. Anzaldua's *Borderlands* (1987) further asserts the ambiguity, uncertainty, and paradoxical multiplicity of her Chicana identity in a changing historical cultural context where one is not always granted a legitimate voice or does not voice the language spoken by the powerful. The borderline is always ambivalent. Insiders and outsiders can easily switch sides and become allies or detractors. Family and strangers sometimes are interchangeable. Is it possible that different voices in one's identity work against each other? As Trinh (1994) insists, "identity is largely constituted through the process of othering" (p. 18). Travelers' tales inform us that identity is framed between "home" and "strange land," and these imagined boundaries are constantly shifting and dissolving through narration, representation, and questioning.

Critical anthropologists have long problematized the politics of representation and investigated the reflexive constitution between self and other (e.g., Clifford and Marcus, 1986; Marcus and Fischer, 1986; Rabinow, 1977; Rosaldo, 1989; Tyler, 1987; Trinh, 1989). Trinh's documentary of 1989 "Surname Viet Given Name Nam" intentionally blurred the boundaries between "real natives" and enacted "native identity." It invites the viewers to consider the possibility of multi-layered plural identity and poignantly questions the politics of representation of the "other." The cover of *Writing Culture* (Clifford and Marcus, 1986) captures an amusing paradox visually, featuring Stephen Tyler in the field writing notes while a local participant observes him from behind. Just like the problem with authenticity in cultural representation, one can problematize the idea of authenticity in identity. In fact, Spivak when discussing her concerns about the practice of speaking for and about the other points out the "unauthenticities that this process entails" (Spivak and Gunew, 1993, p. 193).

Hall's (1992) articulation theory allows us to see the breakdown of rigid categories – self and other, real and false, black and white, West and third world, civilized and primitive, dwellers and travelers, root and route. Authenticity is always secondary in the politics of articulation. As Clifford (2001) wrote, "One sees continuing struggles across a terrain, portions of which are captured by changing alliances, hooking and unhooking particular elements. There's a lot of middle ground; and crucial political and cultural positions are not firmly anchored on one side or the other but are contested and up for grabs" (p. 477). Perhaps seeking a true home or an authentic identity is only metaphorically meaningful. Is it a worthwhile activity to pursue only for academic purposes, or just to amuse ourselves? Is it ultimately an impossible quest? Perhaps home is where the heart resides. Maybe such things as identity and home can only be found in the adventure and the quest.

Borrowing from Clifford's arguments on an articulated tradition, an articulated identity can be seen as a kind of collective "voice," always an embodied, contingent construction at a specific place and time. It is a choice, whether intentional or not, from a vast repertoire of semiotic possibilities in our discourse across a wide spectrum of social practices. Thus not only is identity not singular, the creation of it is like forming a political coalition. We align part of our identity with a particular language in some relationships, and we join a different form of life in other situations when contextual demands call for a certain enactment or invention of our identity. Aspects of identity can be highlighted or dismissed in different communication contexts. In the language of the theory of coordinated management of meaning (CMM), structural affordances and constraints in a social system engender meaning and action in the process of becoming. If articulation "offers a nonreductive way to think about cultural transformation and the apparent coming and going of 'traditional' forms" (Clifford, 2001, p. 478), it also inspires us to think of identity construction as an ongoing process where *you make it up as you go along*, weighing possibilities in an emerging and changing sociopolitical context. In the process of reinventing ourselves, Clifford has called this newer view of ethnic authenticity a "local present-becoming-future" (cited in Smith, 1992, p. 513).

Travel, border crossing, diaspora, self-location, immigration, and displacement can all make the construction of home and identity ambiguous, indeterminate, and paradoxical. Questions such as "where is home" and "what is identity" thus become a living space for exploration, innovation, and contestation. In a global context living in a liminal space becomes a practiced ritual in the twenty-first century. Coping with the transitional betwixt-and-between condition can also be a virtue with possibilities of transformation. As Said (1988) pointed out, colonized and marginalized people are socialized to always see more than their own points of view; "the essential privilege of exile is to have, not just one set of eyes but half a dozen, each of them corresponding to the places you have been. There is always a kind of doubleness to that experience" (p. 48). A traditional conceptualization of the sense of belonging is challenged in the process of globalization. Cheng (2005) studied Chinese immigrants' constructions of belonging to multiple places in Vancouver, Canada. Through an analysis of the use of Chinese newspaper, Cheng proposed multiple homelands as a global context for multiple constructions of immigrants' identities across national borders. If this pluralization of social life-worlds creates contradictions and paradoxes, Maxine Hong Kingston (1976) tells us in *The Woman Warrior*, "I learned to make my mind large, as the universe is large, so that there is room for paradoxes. If one lives long enough with contradictions, they will form a larger vision" (p. 35).

Drzewiecka's (2001) study of Polish immigrants' different lived experiences of roots and routes presented a diverse range of constructed meanings of the immigrants' ethnicity and identity. She argues that it is "no longer the same habitus immigrants had in Poland, and it changes differently from the habitus of those who stayed in Poland" (p. 249). Similarly, Wong (Lau)'s (2002) account of the difficulty in calling a place "home" for older generation of Chinese immigrants also problematized the notion of "returning home," an understandable but also questionable nostalgic practice that can be pursued but never fulfilled. If immigration indeed is characterized by home on the move and ethnic categories are marked by heterogeneity, hybridity, and multiplicity as Drzewiecka suggested, the politics of home and identity can best be understood as a perpetual quest for stability, legitimacy, power, and a sense of belonging and connectedness. Culture makes itself at home in motion. It is a moving picture of a changing world that does not stand still. Cultural identity reveals itself en route. Home is never a place where one "just lives." Identity can never be reduced to a simple label or category for political convenience or expediency. Just like territorial boundaries are constantly challenged and disputed, boundaries between identities are elastic, negotiated, contested, and reconstructed in communication.

To explore the connections between home and identity is to investigate the relationship between edge and center in a power structure. Through a critical lens we see home not so much as a nostalgic place for comfort but as a moving site for relational and political struggle. Both home and identity are inventions in time and place that involve a political process of continuity, rupture, and transformation.

Houston and Wright (2003) urged us not to invoke a physical return to a home-land when studying diasporic identities or lived refugee experiences but to think of "re-turn" as "a repeated revisiting to the concept of homeland via texts, imagery and social and religious rituals" (p. 230).

Cited in Clifford (2001), Black Elk, the sage of the Sioux, said something like "Harney Peak [in the North Dakota Badlands] is the center of the world. And wherever you are can be the center of the world." Clifford then posed the questions "How do moving people take their roots with them" and "are there specifi-cally indigenous kinds of homes away from home?" (p.470). Clifford wrote that Black Elk somehow took Harney Peak along when he went to Paris. Perhaps a sound construction of identity is never a choice between self or other, center or margin, tradition or modernity. It is a matter of "sustaining a livable interaction as part of an ongoing struggle for power" (p. 471).

In response to her maternal grandmother's question "How can you live so far away from your people?" as bell hooks travels and lives in different parts of the country, she wrote, "When she posed this question I always felt it carried with it a rebuke, the slight insistence that I had been disloyal, betrayed the ancestral legacy by leaving home" (hooks, 2009, p. 17). Nothing in the politics of identity illustrates more poignantly the socially constructed assumptions and expectations in our cul-tural discourse and racial politics. As hooks reminds us here, race and class are his-torically significant; these constructs structure societal interaction and the formation of personal identity. Individuals who are historically and traditionally marginalized can always travel in a space of the homeless mind. Perhaps it is impossible to com-plete the search for a home conducted with all the cultural baggage of the place from which we have come. "Life is a journey, even for the stay-at-homes, and we are all exiles whose return is always deferred" (Robertson *et al.*, 1994, p. 6).

Anthropologist Carol Stack in researching return migration explained: "No one is seeking timeless paradise; and no one, however nostalgic, is really seeking to turn back the clock ... What people are seeking is not so much the home they left behind as a place that they feel they can change, a place in which their lives and strivings will make a difference – a place in which to create a home" (cited in hooks, 2009, p. 221). This drive to create a new communal center where one can simultaneously be and become parallels the spirit in travelers' tales where hope and possibility of a better place can be imagined, where new homes and identities can be forged.

Stack continued, "Ultimately, I want to return to the place where I had felt myself to be part of a culture of belonging – to a place where I could feel at home, a landscape of memory, thought, and imagination." As bell hooks put it, a place where the soul can rest.

References

Anderson, B. (1983) *Imagined Communities: Reflections on the Origin and Spread of Nationalism*, Verso, London.

Anzaldúa, G. (1987) *Borderlands/La Frontera*, Aunt Lute Books, San Francisco.

Berger, P., Berger, B., and Kellner, H. (1973) *The Homeless Mind: Modernization and Consciousness*, Vintage Books, New York.

Chen, V. (2004) The possibility of critical dialogue in the theory of coordinated management of meaning. *Human Systems*, 15, 179–192.

Cheng, H.L. (2005) Constructing a transnational, multilocal sense of belonging: An analysis of Ming Pao. *Journal of Communication Inquiry*, 29, 141–159.

Chow, R. (1990) Politics and pedagogy of Asian literatures in American universities. *Differences*, 2 (3), 29–51.

Clifford, J. (1994) Diasporas. *Cultural Anthropology*, 9 (3), 302–338.

Clifford, J. (1997) *Routes: Travel and Translation in the Late Twentieth Century*, Harvard University Press, Cambridge, MA.

Clifford, J. (2001) Indigenous articulations. *The Contemporary Pacific*, 13 (2), 468–490.

Clifford, J., and Marcus, G.E. (eds) (1986) *Writing Culture: The Poetics and Politics of Ethnography*, University of California Press, Berkeley, CA.

Dorjee, T. (2006) Transmitting cultural identity from generation to generation in Tibetan diaspora, in *From Generation to Generation: Maintaining Cultural Identity Over Time*, (ed. W. Leeds-Hurwitz), Hampton Press, Cresskill, NJ, pp. 227–253.

Drzewiecka, J.A. (2001) Discursive construction of differences: Ethnic immigrant identities and distinctions. *International and Intercultural Communication Annual*, 23, 241–270.

Drzewiecka, J.A., and Halualani, R.T. (2002) The structural-cultural dialetic of diasporic politics. *Communication Theory*, 12 (3), 340–366.

Hall, S. (1990) Cultural identity and diaspora, in *Identity, Community, Culture, Difference*, (ed. J. Rutherford), Wishart, London, pp. 222–237.

Hall, S. (1992) Cultural studies and its theoretical legacies, in *Cultural Studies*, (eds L. Grossberg, C. Nelson and P. Treichler), Routledge, New York, pp. 277–294.

Hall, S. (1996) Introduction: Who needs "identity"?, in *Questions of Cultural Identity* (eds S. Hall and P. du Gay), Sage, London, pp. 1–17.

Haydari, N. (2006) (Re)defining Turkish identity across generations: Politics of home, nation, and identity, in *From Generation to Generation: Maintaining Cultural Identity Over Time*, (ed. W. Leeds-Hurwitz), Hampton Press, Cresskill, NJ, pp. 99–119.

Hoffman, E. (1991) *Lost in Translation: Life in a New Language*, Minerva, London.

hooks, b. (2009) *Belonging: A Culture of Place*, Routledge, New York.

Houston, S., and Wright, R. (2003) Making and remaking Tibetan diasporic identities. *Social and Cultural Geography*, 4 (2), 217–232.

Kingston, M.H. (1976) *The Woman Warrior: Memoirs of a Girlhood Among Ghosts*, Vintage, New York.

Marcus, G.E., and Fischer, M.J. (1986) *Anthropology as Cultural Critique*, University of Chicago Press, Chicago.

Mortland, C.A. (1994) Cambodian refugees and identity in the United States, in *Reconstructing Lives, Recapturing Meaning: Refugee Identity, Gender, and Culture Change*, (eds L.A. Camina and R.M. Krulfeld), Gordon and Breach Publishing Group, Amsterdam, pp 5–27.

Nakayama, T. (2004) Dis/orienting identities: Asian Americans, history, and intercultural communication, in *Our Voices: Essays in Culture, Ethnicity, and Communication*, (eds A. González, M. Houston, and V. Chen), 4th edn, Roxbury Publishing, Los Angeles, pp. 26–31.

Peteet, J. (2007) Problematizing a Palestinian diaspora. *International Journal of Middle East Studies*, 39, 627–646.

Rabinow, P. (1977) *Reflections on Fieldwork in Morocco*, University of California Press, Berkeley, CA.

Robertson, G., Mash, M., Tickner, L., *et al.* (eds) (1994) *Travellers' Tales: Narratives of Home and Displacement*, Routledge, London.

Rodriguez, R. (1982) *Hunger of Memory: The Education of Richard Rodriguez*, Bantam, New York.

Rodriguez, R. (1992) *Days of Obligation: An Argument with my Mexican Father*, Penguin Books, New York.

Rodriguez, R. (2002) *Brown: The Last Discovery of America*, Viking, New York.

Rosaldo, R. (1989) *Culture and Truth: The Remaking of Social Analysis*. Beacon Press, Boston, MA.

Safran, W. (2005) The Jewish diaspora in a comparative and theoretical perspective. *Israel Studies*, 10 (1), 36–60.

Said, E. (1988) The voice of a Palestinian in exile. *Third Text*, 3/4, Spring-Summer, 48.

Sarup, M. (1994) Home and identity, in *Travellers' Tales: Narratives of Home and Displacement*, (eds G. Robertson, M. Mash, L. Tickner, *et al.*), Routledge, London, pp. 93–104.

Skenazy, P., and Martin, T. (1998) *Conversations with Maxine Hong Kingston*, University Press of Mississippi, Jackson, MS.

Smith, M.P. (1992) Postmodernism, urban ethnography, and the new social space of ethnic identity. *Theory and Society*, 21, 493–531.

Spivak, G.C., and Gunew, S. (1993) Questions of multiculturalism, in *The Cultural Studies Reader*, (ed. S. During), Routledge, London, pp. 193–202.

Takaki, R. (2008) *A Different Mirror: A History of Multicultural America*, (rev. edn.), Back Bay Books, New York.

Trinh, T.M-h. (1989) *Woman, Native, Other*. Indiana University Press, Bloomington, IN.

Trinh, T.M-h. (1994) Other than myself/my other self, in *Travellers' Tales: Narratives of Home and Displacement*, (eds G. Robertson, M. Mash, L. Tickner *et al.*), Routledge, London, pp. 9–26.

Tyler. S.A. (1987) *The Unspeakable: Discourse, Dialogue, and Rhetoric in the Postmodern World*, The University of Wisconsin Press, Madison.

Witteborn, S. (2008) Identity mobilization practices of refugees: The case of Iraqis in the United States and the war in Iraq. *Journal of International and Intercultural Communication*, 1 (3), 202–220.

Wong(Lau), K. (2002) Migration across generations: Whose identity is authentic? in *Readings in Intercultural Communication*, (eds J. Martin, T. Nakayama, and L. Flores), McGraw-Hill, Boston, MA, pp. 95–101.

29

Layers of Nikkei
Japanese Diaspora and World War II

Etsuko Kinefuchi

The year 2008 marked the 100th year anniversary of Japanese immigration to Brazil, a home to the largest number of Japanese descendants outside Japan. However, Brazil was not the first destination for the Japanese; immigration occurred as early as 1868, and Hawaii, Guam, California, Mexico, and Peru, among others, have already observed their centennial. Today, there are about 3 million Nikkei, or Japanese immigrants and their descendants, spread all over the world. I joined this group several years ago when I became a permanent resident of the United States. Having left my homeland myself, I was naturally gravitated toward intercultural communication as my academic home, and how immigrants and minorities navigate their identities became my research interest over the years. It is easy to imagine that transnational migration affects identity, but how does identity trans/formation occur? This essay addresses this question in the context of Japanese immigrants and their descendants.

There are at least two ways by which the above question can be approached. First, it can be examined from a cross-cultural adaptation perspective. In the field of intercultural communication, immigrant identity processes have been predominantly understood through this perspective (Kim, 1988, 1995, 2001; Gudykunst and Kim, 1992). Cross-cultural adaptation literature has theorized that migrants move through a predictable, upward linear path toward adoption of the host culture, known as acculturation, while leaving their home culture behind. This "progress" thus requires that migrants unlearn or "deculturate" from their home culture. Acquiring the new comes with the cost of losing the old (Kim, 1995). At a group level, the changes brought by acculturation may include complete or partial changes in political, economic, linguistic, religious and social institutions, and, at an individual level, acculturation changes a person's behavior, values, attitudes and identity (Berry, Kim and Boski, 1987). Successful cross-cultural adaptation

The Handbook of Critical Intercultural Communication, edited by Thomas K. Nakayama and Rona Tamiko Halualani. © 2010 Blackwell Publishing Ltd.

requires migrants to maximize their communication with the dominant society, while limiting (if not terminating) their intracultural socialization that hinders one's adaptation to the host culture (Kim, 1988, 2001). In the end, the theories suggest that, while the host society plays an important role in aiding migrants' adaptation, the ultimate power and responsibility of successful adaptation reside in migrants (Kim, 2001).

As a prescriptive theory, the cross-cultural adaptation model offers insights into immigrants' psychological, behavioral, and communicative practices that would help them or prevent them from assimilating to the dominant norms of the host society. However, many stories of Japanese immigrants (and other immigrants) I heard and read did not quite fit with the model. The assumptions of individual autonomy, linear transformation toward assimilation, and the place-bound identity limit the applicability of the theories to a variety of migrant experiences, for it fails to account for complex power relations and web of relationships in which immigrants are simultaneously situated (Halualani, 2008; Hegde, 1998).

Alternatively, then, as I unfold below, we may adopt a critical intercultural perspective and examine Japanese immigrants as diasporic subjects. Diasporic theorizing recognizes transnationality and double relationships immigrants have with their current residence and their homelands, thus challenging the pervasive views of nationstate as the predominant framework of culture and identity (Gupta and Ferguson, 1997; Lavie and Swedenburg, 1996). When seen as a diasporic cultural group, therefore, Japanese immigrants are approached with at least two important ontological and epistemological assumptions. First, for people who migrated across geopolitical borders, their identities can be as much tied voluntarily and involuntarily to the places and people they left behind as to the host society; it may be imagined, mobilized, or forced based on common origin, history, memories, and struggles. Second, the choices available to immigrants and the decisions they make occur within or at least in negotiation with structural constraints of laws, policies, institutions, ideologies, and thus existing power relations. In this regard, diasporic theorizing also urges us to see the host society not as a culture waiting to be adopted by immigrants but as a network of power relations that immigrants must negotiate.

Through the lens of diasporas, then, I discuss ways in which the identities of Nikkei, or Japanese immigrants and their descendants, are constructed and articulated in the nexus of dialectics between homeland and country of settlement and between structural forces and diasporic subjects. Japanese diaspora is vast and diverse due to many differences, including, but not limited to, geography, generation, gender, class, age, politics, historical, and economic circumstances. Obviously, I am unable to cover the scope and depth of this complex subject. For the purpose of this essay, I decided to limit my attention to the time period around World War II for two reasons. First, World War II was the most significant historical event for people of Japanese descent. Although the war and subsequent internment of Japanese Americans are well known, the war's influence on Nikkei in other countries has been given little attention. Second, the construction of Nikkei identity during this period gives much insight into diaspora. The articulations of Nikkei identity in response to the devastating war evocatively illustrate diasporic experience, reflecting the transnationality and dialectics of diasporic identity. In the following sections, I first offer a theoretical framework for examining diaspora and identity. Then, after a brief overview of Japanese dispersions, I discuss articulations of identity in Japanese diaspora during the World War II period.

Theoretical Framework

Defining diaspora, defined by diaspora

Diaspora initially referred to the forced dispersal and displacement of the Jewish, Armenian, and Greek people from their homelands, but has been extended to any ethnic group's forced transnational movements and experiences (Agnew, 2005; Tölölyan, 1996). Later, it has also come to include more than forced dispersal. As border-crossing became more widespread in the 1980s due to technological development and global economy, a variety of transnational migrations came to be subsumed under this term, raising the question, "what exactly is diaspora?" The term has been defined differently depending on the scholars' disciplinary affiliations, their given foci, and, most of all, the specific condition of the diaspora under study. Some have proposed a set of criteria to be met (Anthias, 1998; Safran, 1991), while other definitions focus on specific scope such as consciousness (Cohen, 1997) or postmigration cultural production (Agnew, 2005). Diaspora scholars agree that "diaspora" begins with dispersal of a group to at least two places in the world, but what else should be fundamental elements of the concept is much debated. In this study, I have adopted a combination of Drzewiecka and Halualani's (2002) dialectical approach and Vertovec's (1997) thematization to examine Japanese diasporic identity.

Drzewiecka and Halualani (2002) observed that often diaspora studies fall into one of two theoretical pitfalls. On one hand, some argued that diasporas' double consciousness allows them to necessarily resist oppressive ideologies of nationstates, both their homeland and place of settlement. In contrast, others deny diasporic agency and argued for ever powerful nationstates. To fill the shortcomings of these two opposing tendencies, Drzewiecka and Halualani (2002) proposed the structural–cultural dialectic of diasporic politics. Diasporic identities here are considered as a product of the tensions between diasporic resistance of being confined to a single nationstate on one hand and nationstates' seeming ever-presence in diaspora formation (e.g., claim for diasporas as their representatives and resources). Vertovec's (1997) thematization is one way to gain insights into the working of this dialectic; his three themes of diaspora serve as sites for examining dialectical tensions.

Vertovec (1997) presented three general groups of meanings that emerged from diaspora literature: diaspora as social form, type of consciousness, or mode of cultural production. As a social form, diaspora refers to the transnational relationships (e.g., social, cultural, economic, and political) that dispersed groups have with their homeland and/or other transnational groups of the same origin. Diasporic identity, therefore, collectively exists; its formation requires interaction with its communal institutions (Tölölyan, 1996). It also refers to their relationships with the host nationstate that are often characterized by their inability or unwillingness to assimilate due to the divided loyalty. As a type of consciousness, diaspora is a sense of identity characterized by paradoxical duality, multilocality, and potentially active engagement with politics that has sprung from their precarious conditions. Central to diasporic consciousness is the sense of doubleness; identification as part of the host country and identification with others who share the same route and root (Gilroy, 1993). Produced by discrimination and exclusion in the host nation on one hand and by identification with homeland on the other, the consciousness is marked by maintaining "identifications outside the national time/space in order to live inside" (Clifford, 1997, p. 251). The consciousness is thus derived from the "double relationship" that diaspora has with places (Lavie and Swedenburg, 1996) which historically includes the experiences of discrimination and exclusion in their host countries and identification with their "homes" (Clifford, 1997). Finally, diaspora is understood as a mode of cultural production and reproduction of cultural meanings and images. Agnew (2005), for example, argues that diasporas are defined by their "ability to recreate a culture in diverse locations (p. 4). However, the culture that is "recreated" is not a mirror image of the culture of their homeland. It is necessarily translated (Hegde, 1998).

In the end, Vertovec (1997) concludes, and I concur, that "diaspora" encompasses all three meanings. I further argue that the three meanings are interrelated, interdependent forces. The (re)produced cultural meanings, for example, largely, if not entirely, stem from a particular kind of consciousness that emerges from a specific kind of (trans)national relationship that diasporas experience. (Re)production of culture, moreover, is not entirely in the hand of the diaspora, for as much as diasporic consciousness may stand outside the constraint of the nationstate, the materialization of the consciousness is not. Thus, the study of diaspora must pay attention to both structure and agency (Drzewiecka and Halualani, 2002; Vertovec, 1997; Mendoza, Halualani and Drzewiecka, 2002). This study examines how three meanings of diaspora appear in Japanese diasporic identity and how negotiation between structural forces and agency construct and articulate the identity.

Articulation

Every social practice is ... articulatory (Laclau and Mouffe (2001, p. 113).

In order to examine communicative production of Nikkei within the interplay of structural forces and agency, I have adopted articulation theory as the analytical tool for this paper. Articulation is a communicative act that connects two different phenomena to establish social significance. The two phenomena have "no necessary correspondence" (Hall, 1985, p. 94). That is, for instance, a certain meaning gets attached to a particular concept where there is no inherent relationship between the meaning and the concept. The hitch that connects the two is ideology. Ideologies are most often promoted by institutions or what Althusser (1971/2001) called "ideological state apparatuses" such as media, laws, religious organizations, and political and law enforcement offices. However, whether the ideologies succeed as a hitch depends on whether social actors acknowledge them and act upon them. Articulation is thus a relational achievement (Laclau and Mouffe, 2001).

Articulation is constitutive of identity. In its simplest explanation, identity *is* an articulation. It is a social positioning or a point of suture, a representation (Hall, 1996) that discourse constructs for individuals. Considered as an articulation, identity is never complete or constant because discourse is always partial, leaving out other possibilities that exist in the "field of discursivity." Articulation of identity, therefore, creates meeting points that "partially fix meaning; and the partial character of this fixation proceeds from the openness of the social, a result, in its turn, of the constant overflowing of every discourse by the infinitude of the field of discursivity" (Laclau and Mouffe, 2001, p. 113). Due to this precariousness of identity, articulation plays a central role in power relations. In order to maintain hegemony, the ruling class or the dominant society must rely on articulations that link positive meanings to the existing structure (Artz and Murphy, 2000). On the other hand, if nondominant or marginalized groups succeed in attaching a different meaning to the existing practice, hegemony can be subverted. No articulation, even the most powerful, seemingly unshakable one, therefore, *possesses* a permanent status. Articulation must be "*constructed* through practice precisely because it is not guaranteed by how those [social or economic] forces are constituted in the first place" (Hall, 1985, p. 95). Articulation, in short, plays a central role in identity construction and the production of hegemonic and subversive powers that are negotiated in the construction. An analysis into Japanese diaspora requires attention to the dynamic, relational, and often contradictory or unpredictable construction of identity. Articulation theory is particularly useful for examining such complexity, for it provides analytical insights into how identity is produced and situated in the negotiation between structural forces and agency.

Japanese Diaspora

Japanese diaspora began in the late-nineteenth century. Though some groups of Japanese migrated as early as 1868 when Japan entered the modern era with the establishment of Meiji government, the first systematic overseas migration of Japanese was realized as a result of the 1885 Immigration Convention between Japan and Hawaii (Azuma, 2002). In the Convention, the governments agreed to implement *kanyaku imin* (contract laborers) program that allowed Japanese to work in the sugar plantations in Hawaii on a three-year contract. Between 1886 and 1894, approximately 29 000 migrated to Hawaii under this program (Azuma, 2002; Nikkei Net Association). Under similar contract work, some thousands of Japanese also migrated to other parts of South Pacific such as Australia and Fiji. The majority of Japanese migrants during this earliest period were sojourners who intended to return to Japan upon the expiration of their contract.

The first permanent Japanese migration was attempted at the end of the nineteenth century. In 1893, a group of Japanese foreign affair government officials, politicians, intellectuals, and journalists met to establish *shokumin kyokai* or the Colonization Society (Azuma, 2002; Nikkei Net Association, 2006). The group argued that, following the modern nationstates in the West, Japan must begin overseas expansion in order to solve its surplus population problem and develop its overseas market. The Society's first colonization project of 1897 aimed to establish a Japanese agricultural colony in Mexico. Though this project did not succeed due to financial and other reasons, the attempt marked the beginning of Japanese diaspora to Latin America. After 790 Japanese migrated to Peru as contract laborers in 1899, Latin America became a popular destination for Japanese seeking work. At the turn of the twentieth century and the following decades, Japanese migrated to various Latin American countries, including Mexico, Peru, Chile, Cuba, Argentina, Brazil, Panama, Bolivia, Columbia, Uruguay, Paraguay, and Venezuela (Konno and Fujisaki, 1994).

The popularity of Japanese migration to Latin America was accelerated by North America's policies against Japanese immigration at the beginning of the twentieth century. The rapid increase of the Japanese population in the United States and western Canada provoked xenophobia among the local whites, and the sentiment developed into political movements against Japanese presence in their countries. The federal governments responded to the public concerns by first prompting the Gentlemen's Agreement of 1908; in compliance with the Agreement, the Japanese government restricted Japanese migration to North America. Eventually, Canada prohibited Japanese immigration in 1923, followed by the US execution of a similar law in 1924 (Azuma, 2002; Nikkei Net Association, 2006; Yanagida, 2002). In response, Japan turned to Latin America as the main destination for migrants. By 1945, approximately 244 000 Japanese migrated to Latin America (Konno and Fujisaki, 1994), mostly to Brazil.[1] As compared to other parts of Latin America that were neither systemic or fully subsidized, migration to Brazil was large in scale and realized with great success due to the substantial financial support by both Brazilian and Japanese investors (Masterson, 2004).

Immigration to Latin America, particularly to Brazil, exploded after World War II. From the turn of the twentieth century to 1945, Japan expanded its territories in Asian and the Pacific and sent millions of its citizen to their colonies with the aim of agricultural development for the colonies and as a solution to the excessive population and poor resources in Japan. On Japan's defeat in the World War II, all Japanese in those colonies were ordered to repatriate, and over 6 million people returned to Japan (Befu, 2002).[2] The large repatriated population added a serious strain to the already trampled country. The Japanese government responded to this challenge by establishing treaties with Latin American countries to send Japanese, not as sojourners as in the previous years, but as permanent settlers in those countries. The first postwar group of Japanese left for Brazil in 1952, followed by many others who dispersed all over Latin America in 1950s and 1960s. Today, several generations later, there are at least 3 million Nikkei overseas, and over a half of them live in Latin

America (The Association of Nikkei and Japanese Abroad, 2004).[3] Though it comes as a surprise to many, Brazil has the largest concentration (1.4 million) of Japanese descendants outside Japan followed by the United States (1 million).

Multiple Layers of Nikkei

The word "Nikkei" refers to Japanese emigrants and their descendants. In *New World, New Lives*, a ground-breaking collection of research examining the impact of globalization on the people of Japanese descent living outside Japan, the editors noted that the word can also include those who are part-Japanese descent because "Nikkei" has "primarily, but not exclusively, to do with ethnic identity" (Hirabayashi, Kikumura-Yano and Hirabayashi, 2002, p. 19). While this may sound simple enough, Nikkei as diasporic identity is more than the ethnic origin; it spans many similarities and differences that are manifested in multiple sometimes unpredictable ways in which Nikkei-ness is articulated. In this section, I examine how Nikkei encompass transnational connections, doubleness of identity, and (re)production of culture during the World War II time period. I focus on a selected few sites of articulation to demonstrate that the tie that binds Nikkei to their homeland (imagined or otherwise) was, on one hand, oppressive and divisive, on the other, a source of collaboration and empowerment. I will first discuss the anti-Japanese campaign that led to the deportation of Nikkei Peruvians to the US internment camps. Second, I will present two contrasting Brazilian Nikkei responses to the anti-Japanese movement. Finally, using two examples, I will illustrate the connection that Nikkei communities cultivated with their ethnic homeland.

Violence of articulations: World War II and Nikkei Peruvians

I got a letter from Office of Redress saying that I was denied because I wasn't a citizen or a permanent resident at the time of internment. So then I appealed it. I appealed and then they came back saying that I didn't get my permanent residency until 1956. So I was denied again. And then there was another one that said that I went to Canada voluntarily. Now, I mean, the immigration office said the only way I can get my permanent residency is by leaving the country and re-enter. So, how can that be voluntarily? Just like when I got classified illegal alien. How can I be illegal when we didn't want to come here in the first place and the government brings us, brings us here, force us, force us to come here, and they bring us at gunpoint, and then they classify – and not only that, there were, some of the Peruvians were businessmen, so some people had passports. And those passports were confiscated when we boarded the ship. And then when we come, when we got off the ship they said we didn't have any papers so we were illegal. (Art Shibayama, Nisei Peruvian 2003)

It is well known that nearly 120 000 Japanese immigrants and their descendants in the United States were incarcerated between 1942 and 1945 without due process after Japan attacked Pearl Harbor. The mass incarceration was justified as military necessity. Nikkei were deemed to be threats to the United States solely due to their ethnic origin regardless of their emotional attachment to or identification with their ethnic homeland; indeed, two-thirds of the incarcerated Nikkei were American citizens. In the eyes of the US government, the ethnic origin became synonymous to Nikkei, and the constitution no more than a piece of paper. The Commission on Wartime Relocation and Internment of Civilians (1997) reported that the mass incarceration based on military necessity was not justifiable because it was not based on military considerations. Instead, the Commission concluded that the decisions were shaped on the basis of "race prejudice, war hysteria and a failure of political leadership" (p. 459). While redress was achieved in 1988, and the incarceration of Nikkei Americans is now public knowledge, it still largely remains hidden from the general public that Latin Americans of Japanese descent were among the incarcerated population. Though the Commission (1997) included a brief report on "Latin Americans" as an appendix, little attention has been paid to this important historical event. I want to focus my discussion here on how a series of social practices served as articulations that collectively influenced incarceration of Nikkei Peruvians. While much diaspora literature suggests a rather voluntary nature of transnational kinship that diasporic groups maintain, I will argue that the tie can be violently forced on them.

Roughly 2300 Nikkei Latin Americans were stripped of their passports and sent to various internment camps in the United States in 1942. About 80% of them were Japanese Peruvians (The Commission, 1997). The incarceration of Nikkei Peruvians was not due to military threat but was motivated by the corresponding needs of the federal governments. The United States wanted to secure a sufficient number of "Japanese" that they could use as hostages to be exchanged for Americans held by Japan, and Peru wanted to get rid of Japanese who were "taking over" the country by dominating businesses (The Commission, 1997). The majority of the deportees were Japanese nationals who immigrated to Peru, but the list also included many Peruvian-born Nikkei like Shibayama in the above quote. Later, over 800 of the Nikkei Latin Americans were indeed exchanged for Americans held by Japan as prisoners of war. When the war was over, many of the Nikkei Latin Americans were deported to Japan or, as Shibayama did, remained in the United States and struggled to acquire residency in the country. Since they did not have their passports and were considered "illegal aliens" in the United States, they were not eligible for redress, though many of them became US citizens after the war (Adachi, 2007).[4]

Shikataganai (it can't be helped). These things happen in war – Masterson (2004) wrote that these were general sentiments shared by Japanese Peruvian internees a half century later. To be sure, as the Commission (1997) concluded, war hysteria played a major role in the internment of people of Japanese descent. However, the deportation and internment of Nikkei from Latin America had its roots deep in racism and economic rivalries (Gardiner, 1981). In his renowned book, *Strangers from a Different Shore,* historian Ronald Takaki (1998) described the anti-Asian climate of the early-twentieth century that led to a series of laws restricting and prohibiting immigration and landownership by Asian immigrants.

A parallel history characterizes the experience of Japanese immigrants and their descendants in Peru.

Unlike their counterparts in other Latin American countries, many Japanese immigrants in Peru did not settle on plantation agriculture and moved to cities to seek commerce opportunities. By 1930s, 45% of Japanese immigrants owned businesses in Lima (Adachi, 2007). Some Japanese immigrants remained in agriculture and became prominent in cotton production (Masterson, 2004). Against the backdrop of the Great Depression, these successes were resented by the locals, and the anti-Japanese movement burgeoned. To start, a series of anti-Asian and anti-immigrant laws were passed. The Eighty Percent Law of 1932 required business owners to ensure that 80% or more of their employees be non-Asian (Adachi, 2007). The Immigration Act of 1936 restricted the population of foreign nationals to 16 000. Additional legislation in the next few years severely limited Nikkei's legal and economic status: Prohibition of foreign-nationals' travels to their homeland; denial of citizenship to newborns who were born to alien parents; stripping of citizenship from the native-born Peruvians who had never resided in their parents' homeland; and prohibition of the transfer of land from the foreign-born parents to their native-born children (Masterson, 2004). Though these laws did not outwardly name Nikkei as their target, it was clearly aimed at them; Nikkei comprised the largest immigrant group in the country, already exceeded the cap of 16 000, were economically most successful, and were the group that customarily sent their children to Japan for part of their education. Without naming its villain, the series of laws successfully articulated Nikkei as a threat to the nation's integrity and an untrustworthy alien and thus unsuitable to be considered Peruvian. In acting on behalf of the dominant society, the laws effectively stripped Nikkei of legal and economic status thereby legalizing racism.

In addition to the laws, the dominant media and intellectuals played critical roles in shaping the anti-Japanese climate. Major newspapers such as *La Prensa* and *El Comerico* spread rumors that Nikkei engaged in illegal businesses and that Nikkei males were really soldiers who were in Peru to take over the country (Gardiner, 1975). One critic in the Lima press commented that "No Peruvian can prosper as an artisan, merchant or professional; the Japanese reserve everything for their fellow nationals; the Peruvian is systematically excluded" (quoted in Gardiner, 1975, p. 70). Power elites organized an anti-Japanese campaign in 1937 and published in *La Prensa* a report called "Inflitracion Japonesa" ("Japanese Inflitration") to demonstrate the threat Japanese were causing to the Peruvian economy and the security of the country (Nikkei Net Association, 2006). Similarly, *La Tribuna*, the newspaper of the leftist underground party, Alianza Popular Revolucionaria Americana (APRA), promoted anti-Japanese campaign with slogans such as "We do not want to be Japanese" and spread a rumor that all Issei (immigrant generation) males were army veterans and were ready to overthrow the government on a signal from Tokyo (Masterson, 2004). At the same time, all but one (*Lima Nippo*) Japanese language newspapers that played a critical role in maintaining the Nikkei Peruvian community were terminated and Japanese schools were closed (Masterson, 2004). If the Peruvian laws did not explicitly name Nikkei as the nation's enemy, the dominant media did not hesitate to do so. The media campaigns constructed Nikkei's identity by articulating it as a representative of Japan and thus incommensurable with Peruvianness.

In the field of discursivity (Laclau and Mouffe, 2001), there are many possible ways to represent the agricultural and commercial successes of Japanese immigrants. However, in the context of the Great Depression and racism, Nikkei as menace, villain, and enemy emerged as the dominant theme of articulations in Peru. Ideological state apparatuses (Althusser, 1971/2001) such as laws and media not only productively drew public attention to the connection between Nikkei and Japan but constructed them to be synonymous. Laws and the mainstream media together helped to shape anti-Japanese hegemony by suturing Nikkei to Peru's economic deterioration and articulated them as an extension of Japan. The hostility then led to the 1940 riot that killed 10 Nikkei, injured hundreds, and destroyed nearly 600 Nikkei houses and businesses (Gardiner, 1975) and eventually to the incarceration of Nikkei Peruvians in the United States in 1942 as "enemy aliens" and their deportation to Japan as "prisoners of war" (Gardiner, 1981) although Peru was not at war against Japan then.[5]

As Art Shibayama's story at the beginning of this section illustrates, Nikkei's experiences cannot be simply understood as residing within a nationstate or a deculturation from the past toward an adaptation to the new home society. Diasporas' transnational relationships (Vertovec, 1997) with their ethnic homeland and their fellow diasporas in the United States were belligerently sutured to Peruvian Nikkei. The nations forced Nikkei's identification with Japan to satisfy their multiply vested interests; Peru wanted to jettison "Japanese," the United States needed "Japanese" prisoners of war to be exchanged for the US Americans held by the Japanese, and Japan, in turn, accepted their emigrants for the exchange.

Drzewiecka and Halualani (2002) argued that diasporic identity is not a complete move away from the essentialist notions of nationstate and identity but rather an articulation of the dialectics of "fluidity and fixity" because "diasporic identities are often built on claims to 'natural' or 'original' identities with the homeland" (p. 144). This essentialist view of the tie to the homeland may be strategically deployed by diasporas to carve out their positions in the transnational space. However, as seen in the case of Nikkei Peruvians, the tie has been and can be forced by nationstates on diasporas as a very tool for rejecting immigrants' ability and agency to adapt to and adopt the host nation as their home. Nationstates, then, are ever-present in diasporas' identity formations as they flexibly extend or tighten their boundaries to meet their political and economic needs of the time.

Nikkei articulations in Brazil: Integration and turning Japanese

Like their counterparts in the United States, Canada, and Peru, Japanese immigrants in Brazil in the years before World War II were met with resentment and fear as the immigrant community grew in size and established stable and quite successful lives through farming major Brazilian export items such as cotton, silk, and tea

(Yanagida, 2002). The immigrants tried to convince the natives that their loyalty was to Brazil through various means including publications that asserted their Brazilianness. A prominent Nikkei leader, for example, wrote in the preface of *Aclimação de emigrantes japones* that the Japanese immigrants are very willing to integrate themselves into the mainstream population not only for themselves but for their children (Lesser, 2001). There were also natives who favored Japanese immigration because of their hardworking ethics and cheap, docile labor. Nonetheless, the anti-Japanese movement grew. As in the case of Peru, laws and the mainstream media served as the mediums for articulating Japanese Brazilians as an extension of Japan and a national security threat. In 1934, Brazil passed a Constitutional amendment to severely limit immigration. Magazines and newspapers published anti-Japanese articles under the headlines such as "Japanese infiltration in Brazil" and "Japan invades Brazil" (Lesser, 1999). Rumors spread that Japan was plotting to turn the Amazon into a Japanese base and South America into their colony.

In response, President Getúlio Vargas launched the "brazilidade" (Brazilianization) campaign in 1939 to homogenize the country by restricting non-Brazilian influences. Vargas was known for his effort to centralize the country and his support of "the image of racial democracy" and "ideology of tolerance" (Marx, 1998, p. 170). According to Lesser (1999, 2001), however, his brasilidade campaign effectively marginalized the country's increasing nonwhite immigrant population. The campaign included prohibition of non-Brazilian congregations and ethnic neighborhoods, prohibition of non-Portuguese materials without permission, and enforcement of Brazilian education by requiring schools to be run by native-born Brazilians, in Portuguese, and on Brazilian topics. These policies led to the closure of over 600 schools (Lesser, 1999).

The law of 1934 and brazilidade, in short, legalized and legitimized xenophobia. If identity exists through discourse and ideology survives through institutions, the legislation and policies were aimed at annihilating diasporic identities. If diasporas are characterized by transnational relationships, double consciousness, and (re) production of ethnic culture in the land of settlement (Vertovec, 1997), the law and brazilidade that restricted social and cultural activities of nonwhite immigrants were articulatory practices to obliterate all that constitute Nikkei Brazilians as diasporas. On the other hand, the dominant media's articulation of Nikkei as an extension of Japan underscored the essential tie of Nikkei to their ethnic homeland, thus making contradictory demands on Nikkei identity.

The Nikkei community responded to the anti-Japanese prejudices and contradiction in at least two distinct ways. Some Nikkei, particularly Nisei, emphasized their biculturality and biraciality. For example, according to Lesser (1999), law students in São Paulo founded Nipo-Brazilian Student League (Liga Estudantina Nippo-Brasiliera) with an aim of advocating the position that ethnicity and nationality are different but are interrelated and coexist. This League's position is reflected in its hyphenated name, but their monthly newspaper, *Gakusei,* clearly articulated the goal by predominantly publishing expressions of Brazilianness and cultural and ethnic integration. The editor in chief, José Yamashiro, for example, wrote the following story to emphasize how hybrid identity can be beneficial to Brazil:

> The younger asked about the concept of "Yamato damashii," which the elder interpreted as a "Japanese soul" that led to an undying loyalty to the emperor. The younger man responded with shock, wondering why he, born in Brazil had to be loyal to the emperor. The elder's response, however, was pure Nikkei: "[You] should defend the Brazilian flag with the same ardor, with same dedication, as the Japanese soldiers defend their sovereign. What you should not do is interpret 'Yamato damashii' as only linked to the Mikado. ... If you promise to defend the integrity of the Brazilian fatherland, its institutions and order ... this is the essence of 'Yamato damashii'" (Lesser, 1999, p. 124).

The story illustrates a complex, dynamic, creative construction of diasporic identity. The diasporic double consciousness (Gilroy, 1993) here takes a form of cultural identity production that is not a recreation of the cultural meaning from the homeland but a re-interpretation of it (Drzewiecka and Halualani, 2002). Something that is considered a core of the Japanese character is underscored as also a central trait of Brazilianness. In the backdrop of the anti-Japanese climate that fostered the ideology of incommensurability between Japaneseness and Brazilianness, Brazilian Nikkei took the very contradiction and re-articulated the two identities as not only commensurable but fundamentally harmonious.

While there were many who emphasized the hyphenated position, there were also many others who responded to the anti-Japanese movement by strengthening their identification as Japanese. These "ultranationalist" Nikkei, many of whom were immigrants, harshly criticized other Nikkei as enemies when they did not show their loyalty to Japan (Lesser, 1999). The tensions developed into the emergence of several secret societies within the Nikkei communities in Brazil and other Latin American countries. The largest and most powerful of these groups was the Shindo Renmei (Way of the Subjects of the Emperor's League) in Brazil. The group aimed to maintain a Japanese space in Brazil by preserving culture, language, and religion and restoring Japanese schools (Reichl, 1995). By the end of 1945, Shindo Renmei had 50 000 members who were convinced that the news of Japan's surrender was US propaganda. The erroneous conviction was made possible because the Japanese language newspapers were demised, and few members had access to Brazilian newspapers. Soon after Japan's surrender, Shindo Renmei released a statement of the Allies' unconditional surrender and Japan's victory after Japan's "High Frequency Bomb" killed more than 100 000 American soldiers in Okinawa and circulated photos of President Truman bowing to Emperor Hirohito (Lesser, 1999). The statement was circulated quickly and widely, and more than 130 000 Nikkei had joined the group by 1946. There were of course those Nikkei who, having had direct access to Brazilian media and newsreels, circulated the actual surrender documents, but Shindo Remmei quickly dismissed them as fabrications by the traitors. This conflict came to divide the Nikkei community into two groups – Kaichigumi (one believing Japan's victory) and Makegumi (one accepting

Japan's defeat) (DiscoverNikkei, 2008). It was not until 1954 that the conflict between the two groups waned and a new chapter of Nikkei Brazilian history began with the influx of postwar immigrants between 1953 and 1973.

While the "ultranationalist" response seems incredulous today, it should not be dismissed as a peculiar occurrence of a war period. It illustrates the tie to the homeland, a diasporic consciousness (Vertovec, 1997), that Nikkei, particularly the immigrant generation, maintained after years of physically leaving Japan. The tie may be kept unarticulated when it is not necessary but can be hailed and utilized as an anchor for identity when immigrants' relationship to the nation of settlement becomes precarious. The contrasting responses – hybridity and ultranationalism – to the ethnic and racial prejudices illustrate heterogeneity and unity of diasporic Nikkei identity during war time Brazil in a few important ways. First, to a large extent, the divergent responses reflected the generational differences; the immigrant generation naturally kept more emotional ties to Japan, while the Brazilian-born Nisei were more Brazilianized in their culture, ideology, and language.

Second, the division, however, was not entirely along the generation line, either. There were many Issei who were eager to be part of the dominant Brazilian society, and, likewise, there were many Nisei who associated themselves with the ultranationalist groups. In this regard, whether one emphasized integration or ethnic heritage and loyalty, they were both ways to live in Brazil with difference (Clifford, 1997; Gilroy, 1993). Both diasporic articulations served to unify the dispersed diasporic members albeit very differently. The hybrid approach, as shown in the example above, articulated the commonalties that Issei and Nisei share among themselves as well as with Brazilianness. The ultranationalist movement utilized loyalty to the Emperor and refusal to believe Japan's defeat as a way to bring together Nikkei across generations. Third and importantly, the conflicts that existed in the community were not simply the internal dissonance; the Brazilian Nikkei example show that cultural politics within a community must be understood as a reflection of larger structural forces (Lowe, 1991). Rather than following a predictable path toward Brazilianization, the diasporic identities of immigrants and their descendants are constructed and expressed in negotiation with the political, economic, and social conditions that surround them.

Nikkei Articulations: Nurturing the Tie to the Ethnic Homeland

Japan's defeat in the war meant a number of things for Nikkei in the Americas. It of course meant starting from nothing for those who were incarcerated because their assets were taken away upon incarceration. Emotionally, many felt torn about their homeland's surrender. Many also suffered humiliation of being the target of discrimination and were ashamed of being of Japanese descent (Iino, 2002). One Nisei internee who started an annual pilgrimage to the Manzanar camp compared the feeling of shame and the difficulty of speaking about their internment to the experience of rape (Iino, 2002). This feeling of shame combined with the experience of being the victim of racism led many Nikkei to distance themselves from Japan. There were, however, also many who continued or even renewed their tie to Japan after the war by various forms of articulation. Among those were Nikkei and Nikkei organizations that engaged in the war relief efforts.

Nikkei communities in the North and South Americas found that they could help their ethnic homeland through a civilian organization called Licensed Agencies for Relief in Asia (LARA) that consisted of religious, labor, and social organizations. According to Iino (2002), it was in fact Nikkei who brought Japan's acute shortage of supplies to the attention of the US Americans and Canadians who would otherwise only be interested in helping European countries. LARA's relief efforts that lasted from 1946 to 1952 produced over 16 000 tons of food, clothing, medicine, and other goods in addition to livestock (Iino, 2002) that provided help to 14 million people in Japan (The Ministry of Foreign Affairs, 2008). The Japanese government estimated the value of the aid to be over ¥40 billion or US$400 million, with 20% of the total aid coming from 36 Nikkei organizations (The Association of Nikkei and Japanese Abroad, 2004).[6]

Nikkei's involvement with LARA sent substantial quantities of supplies to Japan, materially connecting them to Japan. What is equally important, however, is the symbolic significance of their effort. If the war and racism constructed Nikkei's tie to Japan as shameful and a root to be forgotten, those involved in the relief mission articulated an opposing meaning of what it means to be Nikkei. By helping the poverty-stricken country, Nikkei affirmed their tie to their ethnic homeland and people. The words of a Nikkei who returned to California from an internment camp are illustrative of this sentiment:

> Although we experienced isolated lives in the camps, deprived of our freedom, we never experienced lack of food and clothes. War victims in our homeland, Japan, on the other hand, have lost their houses and are unable to obtain even bread, we hear. We, their blood relatives, cannot bear to see their difficulties. We gathered together and looked for ways to save them from such a situation (cited in Iino, 2002, p. 68).

Their emotional investment can be seen not only in the amount of goods Nikkei collected but also in the velocity by which they came together as a community. In many cities of the United States, existing groups came together, and organizations were newly formed to realize relief within a month or so. In New York, the relief effort began only three days after Japan's surrender. Not only did Nikkei in these organizations affirm their ties to their homeland, the act of engaging in the relief effort became a source of strength and unity for many of the Nikkei organizations. While ethnic origin was used as a tool for dehumanization and domination before, during, and after the war, it was also this kinship that mobilized diasporic communities after the war.

Another interesting articulation of Nikkei surrounding the World War II time period comes from Canada. Before the eve of Pearl Harbor, there were 23 000

Nikkei in Canada, mostly concentrated in British Colombia, and three quarters of the Nikkei population were either naturalized or Canadian-born (Di Biase, 2000). The history of the relationship between Nikkei and the dominant Canadian society closely resembles that of the United States and Peruvian counterparts. The increasing number of Asian immigrants made the local whites uncomfortable, and, by the turn of the twentieth century, "yellow peril" became the dominant narrative of Asian presence in Canada. Racism and immigration restrictions continued, and, during the early months of 1942, nearly 22 000 Nikkei Canadians were interned (Ward, 1990). The climate after the war was still hostile, and it was not until 1949, four years after the end of the war, that Nikkei Canadians were permitted to travel freely.

In this postwar climate, Nikkei in Toronto built a Buddhist church in 1946. As in the case of the United States, this was the period when many of Japanese ancestry were ashamed of their ethnic origin and tried to divorce themselves from anything Japanese in order to minimize hostility directed to them. Building a Buddhist church does not seem a wise or even logical decision. Iino (2005), however, found from her interviews with the church members in the 1970s that most of the members were Nisei (second generation) whose parents were also Buddhists in Vancouver and that they built the church to represent their very willingness to become good Canadians. Iino (2005) shared the following thoughts in her interview with DiscoverNikkei:

> many people were shaken during the war, you know, because they had this feeling that that they'd face discrimination just because they were Nikkei, or had a relation to Japan. Their self-esteem was shaken. Very much a source for an identity crisis ... But these Canadian Nikkei, on the other hand, held on to their Japanese consciousness stronger than ever and built the Buddhist church, believing that it would serve as a path to becoming respected Canadians.

Though Buddhism, a prominent symbol of Japanese cultural heritage, seems at odds with Canadianness, they went perfectly together in the Nisei members' mind; in order to become Canadians who can make positive contributions to the country, one must first become a good Nikkei, and being a good Nikkei and being proud of the identity means cherishing their ancestor's important cultural heritage.

These sites of Nikkei Canadian identity – war relief and construction of a Buddhist church – represent articulations unique to diaspora. Nikkei's "relationship-despite-dispersal" (Vertovec, 1997) was maintained through renewing and strengthening their material and symbolic connections with Japan as well as other diasporic Nikkei. The two examples share in common doubleness or identification with both the society of their residence and their ethnic homeland. Despite (or perhaps because of) the dominant social climate that instigated them to be ashamed of their ethnic origin, the Canadian Nikkei's public actions and symbolic expressions defied this dominant articulation and instead connected their ethnic origin to pride, solidarity, and Canadianness. By renewing and reinforcing transnational kinships and re-producing cultural symbols in new ways, diasporic Japanese carved out their identities in the betwixt and between.

The articulations of Nikkei identity examined above illustrate that diasporas as social form, type of consciousness, and mode of cultural production are foremost communicatively produced through negotiation between structural forces and agency. More specifically, some common threads exist across the articulations. First, the experiences of Nikkei in the United States, Canada, Peru, and Brazil were all significantly affected by their respective nationstates' persistent nativism and racial politics that were expressed through dominant institutions such as media and laws. Within the hegemonic discourse of the institutions, the common ethnic origin, the tie that binds, were used as a tool of repression and marginalization. Second, the historical examples show that these forces could not entirely contain diaspora within the mold they had prepared. Though the hegemonic states marginalized and humiliated the diasporic subjects, they creatively and defiantly fashioned their own articulations that reflected their transnational relationships, double consciousness, and cultural meanings.

Conclusion

Using examples from Peru, Brazil, the United States, and Canada, this paper examined the construction and manifestation of Nikkei diasporic identity as negotiated between structural forces and agency. In this last part of the essay, I will situate this work in other critical intercultural communication scholarship. While subject matters and approaches may vary vastly, critical intercultural communication scholarship seeks to create through communication more just intercultural relations. To this end, by paying close attention to the role of macrocontexts such as history, politics, and economy and power (Martin and Nakayama, 1999) in the production of social realities, critical studies in intercultural communication have problematized much taken-for-granted concepts. The scholarship, for example, has challenged "nation" as the most powerful, relevant unit of analysis (Ono, 1998), emphasized the contested nature of "culture" (Collier *et al.*, 2002; Moon, 1996) and "identity" (Hegde, 1998; Yep, 2002). Rather than regarding these concepts as constant, unified, geographically tied variables that are thought to affect communicative behaviors, critical studies have contextually examined the discursively manifested power struggles through which certain definitions of these concepts become normalized, maintained, silenced, marginalized, challenged, or subverted. In the study of immigration and identity, and of diasporas in particular, critical scholarship in the field also scrutinized traditional theorizing of culture and identity and has shown the imperative of examining structural forces in identity formations through and after transnational migration (Drzewiecka and Halualani, 2002; Mendoza, Halualani, and Drzewiecka, 2002; Shome, 2003).

This essay builds on these works. By focusing on still largely hidden stories of Japanese diaspora, I sought to illustrate how the identities of Japanese immigrants and their descendants were constructed and articulated by state apparatuses and Nikkei themselves vis-à-vis Japan. In communication studies, such constructs as "Japanese culture," "Japanese identity," and "Japanese behavior" have been extensively studied, but most research presumes these concepts to be a priori, constant, coherent, and homogeneous. Moreover, in the received notion of Japaneseness, ethnicity, nationality, and culture are conflated and are often used interchangeably, which in turn continues to perpetuate the conflation. One corollary of the conflation is to see immigrant identity only through cross-cultural adaptation perspectives where Japaneseness is bound to the old home and something to be left behind or minimized upon migration. Examining Japaneseness in diaspora encourages us to see that this collective identity can be larger than nationstate and more complex, dynamic, and contested than it has been predominantly represented; it may be imagined, mobilized, or forced based on common origin, history, memories, and struggles.

To see these layers requires historicization. Though the sites of Nikkei identity I examine in this paper are six decades old, this history is very much relevant to our lives today. Historicization, I believe, is one of the significant contributions that critical intercultural studies can make to the understanding of cultural identity. Identity comes from somewhere, and, without knowing the path it takes, we are left with decontextualized representations. Historicization engages the issues of power and voice; it is about asking what stories are told, whose points of view the stories privilege or silence, how the silence contributes to marginalization, what prevent the telling of other stories, what stories are yet to be told, and how new stories may help to disrupt or transform the existing power relations. If, as Hall (1996) argued, identity is about how history, language, and culture are used in the process of becoming, history is not a static past; it is active in shaping our identity, and, as Nakayama (2004) simply put, situates us in our communication with others. The question of what stories of the past are widely known and what stories are still hidden has a powerful implication for our communication. Understanding the identity construction of Nikkei during the war is not merely a look into how Nikkei in the past constructed themselves and were constructed; it is also about how we might engage and renegotiate identities based on the historical constructions that are unfolded.

The current article contributes to critical intercultural communication scholarship on immigration and identity in a few important ways. First, drawing specific examples from Japanese diaspora, I have attempted to show how diasporic theorizing provides a more complex, relational, and often unpredictable articulations of immigrant identity than the cross-cultural adaptation models. Particularly, this study paid attention to three themes of diaspora – transnational relationships, double consciousness, and (re)production of culture (Vertovec, 1997) as sites where the tensions between the nationstates and diasporas (Drzewiecka and Halualani, 2002) are articulated. Some critical intercultural communication scholars have already drawn attention to the limitations of the social science models of cultural identity (Drzewiecka and Halualani, 2002; Hegde, 1998). This essay crystallizes such critiques by underscoring differential power relations in which immigrants are situated. According to cross-cultural adaptation theories, immigrants are to leave their home culture behind and become part of their host culture through their communicative efforts (Kim, 1988, 1995, 2001; Gudykunst and Kim, 1992). However, as I have shown, this linear, location-bound, autonomy-focused identity formation is inadequate when structural forces prevent immigrants from being integrated into the host society. In this regard, cross-cultural adaptation models may be said to work well for immigrants who come from racially and socioeconomically privileged backgrounds but not for those who do not have such resources. My study, then, suggests that critical intercultural communication research through diasporic theorizing, such as the one I adopted here, can shed light on the role of states in differentially racializing and classing immigrants and how such practices influence their identity formations.

Second, this study makes a case for the usefulness of analyzing diasporic identity in multiple sites surrounding one critical event. Analysis of a diasporic group across geopolitical borders can reveal how structural and cultural dialectics manifest themselves in identity articulations similarly or differently in response to one significant event. In this study, similarities are more pronounced than differences. For example, both Brazilian Nikkei and Canadian Nikkei creatively linked key Japanese cultural symbols or notions to Brazilianness or Canadianness as a way to enact their cultural identities in response to the hostile environments of World War II. The specific forms of the linking are different, but they were both articulations based on the belief that Japaneseness is continuous with these identities at their core. These commonalties indicate that Nikkei identity is neither geographically fixed as modernism suggests or free-floating as the postmodern impulse urges. Rather, it is formed through the power struggles between structural forces and agency. Examining the identity in multiple states, thus, provides insights into how its formation occurs in relation to global and local politics.

Another notable parallel across nationstates is that Nikkei were represented by the dominant societies similarly; they were construed as "yellow perils" in all four countries (Peru, Brazil, Cananda, and the United States) through federal laws, dominant media, and powerful national leaders. This illustrates global – rather than locally specific or contained – repression of Japaneseness as a diasporic identity. Japanese national loyalty, whether it is imagined, real, or forced, was used by the states as a justification for their marginalization. In short, this study gives support to the claim that states must be recognized as ever-present in diaspora (Drzewiecka and Halualani, 2002; Tölölyan, 1996) and suggests the need for closely examining the role of nationstates in studying identity formation and politics through and after immigration. While not a commonalty across nationstates, the global presence of nationstates was also evident in another notable way. The case of Peruvian Nikkei illustrated that diasporas can be marginalized by multiple states due to the global politics involving the homeland's political position in the world. Multiple states – the United States, Peru, and, to some extent, Japan – all benefitted from the incarceration and deportation of Latin American Nikkei. The multiple vested interests in repressing diaspora suggest that diaspora studies may need to pay attention to more than the relationship between the homeland and the nation of settlement in understanding a diasporic group but locate the group in global webs of political and economic interests.

Notes

1 According to Lesser (2007), 189 000 Japanese immigrated to Brazil between 1908 and 1941, followed by 50 000 more after World War II.

2 According to Befu (2002), thousands of Japanese stayed behind, including civilians and servicemen in China, Thailand, the Malay Peninsula, Vietnam, and Indonesia. Yet, because the majority returned or died after the war, the Japanese diaspora in Asia and Micronesia has been forgotten.

3 The statistics is from their population report of 2004. The total number includes Nikkei in North and Latin America.

4 As a result of a class-action lawsuit, the US government issued an official apology, but it was not until 2007 that the US government expressed interest in investigating the unjust incarceration. On June 13, 2007, the Senate Committee on Homeland Security and Governmental Affairs voted in favor of S. 381/H.R. 662, a bill that proposed a creation of a commission to investigate the facts surrounding the abduction, incarceration, and deportation of Latin Americans of Japanese descent during World War II. As of September 2008, the bill still awaits hearing by the Subcommittee on the Immigration, Citizenship, Refugees, Border Security, and International Law. For more details, visit Campaign for Justice, www.campaignforjusticejla.org/whoweare/index.html (accessed May 27, 2010)

5 Peru did not declare war against Japan until February 1945.

6 When Japan joined the United Nations in 1957, the Japanese government invited representatives of Nikkei in Americas to Tokyo to show appreciation for their assistance for rebuilding postwar Japan and to acknowledge and honor the kinship between Japan and diasporic Japanese. The convention led to the formation of the Association of Nikkei and Japanese Abroad and their annual convention.

References

Adachi, N. (2007) Racial journeys: Injustice, internment and Japanese-Peruvians in Peru, the United States, and Japan. *Japan Focus*, http://japanfocus.org/products/details/2517 (accessed May 27, 2010).

Agnew, V. (2005) Introduction, in *Diaspora, Memory, and Identity: A Search for Home*, (ed. V. Agnew), University of Toronto Press, Toronto, Canada, pp. 3–17.

Althusser, L. (1971/2001) *Lenin and Philosophy and Other Essays*, (trans. B. Brewster), Monthly Review Press, New York.

Anthias, F. (1998) Evaluating "diaspora": Beyond ethnicity. *Sociology*, 32 (3), 557–581.

Artz, L., and Murphy, B.O. (2000) *Cultural Hegemony in the United States*, Sage, Thousand Oaks, CA.

Azuma, (2002) Introduction to part one, in *New Worlds, New Lives: Globalization and People of Japanese Descent in the Americas and from Latin America in Japan*, (eds L.R.

Hirabayashi, A. Kikumura-Yano and J.A. Hirabayashi), Stanford University Press, Stanford, CA, pp. 1–4.

Befu, H. (2002) Globalization as human dispersal: Nikkei in the world, in *New Worlds, New Lives: Globalization and People of Japanese Descent in the Americas and from Latin America in Japan,* (eds. L.R. Hirabayashi, A. Kikumura-Yano and J.A. Hirabayashi), Stanford University Press, Stanford, CA, pp. 5–18.

Berry, J.W., Kim, U., and Boski, P. (1987) Psychological acculturation of immigrants, in *International and Intercultural Communication Annual, Vol.11: Cross-Cultural Adaptation: Current Approaches,* (eds Y.Y. Kim and W.B. Gudykunst), Sage, Newbury Park, CA, pp. 62–89.

Clifford, J. (1997) *Routes: Travel and Translation in the Late Twentieth Century,* Harvard University Press, Cambridge, MA.

Cohen, R. (1997) *Global Diaspora: An Introduction.* University of Washington Press, Seattle.

Collier, M.J., Hegde, R.S., Lee, W. *et al.* (2002) Dialogue on the edges: Ferment in communication and culture, in *Transforming Communication about Culture,* (ed. M.J. Collier), Sage, Thousand Oaks, CA, pp. 219–280.

Di Biase, L. (2000) Japanese Canadian Internment. *Information at the University of Washington Libraries and Beyond,* www.lib.washington.edu/subject/Canada/internment/intro.html (accessed May 27, 2010).

DiscoverNikkei (2008) www.discovernikkei.org/en (accessed May 27, 2010).

Drzewiecka, J.A., and Halualani, R.T. (2002) The structural-cultural dialectic of diasporic politics. *Communication Theory,* 12, 340–366.

Gardiner, C.H. (1975) *The Japanese and Peru,* 1873–1973. University of New Mexico Press, Albuquerque.

Gardiner, C.H. (1981) *Pawns in a Triangle of Hate: The Peruvian Japanese and the United States,* University of Washington Press, Seattle and London.

Gilroy, P. (1993) *The Black Atlantic: Modernity and Double Consciousness,* Harvard University Press, Cambridge, MA.

Gudykunst, W.B., and Kim, Y.Y. (1992) *Communicating with Strangers: An Approach to Intercultural Communication,* McGraw-Hill, New York.

Gupta, A., and Ferguson, J. (1997) Beyond "culture": Space, identity, and the politics of difference, in *Culture, Power, Place: Explorations in Critical Anthropology,* (eds A. Gupta and J. Ferguson), Duke University Press, Durham, NC, pp. 33–51.

Hall, S. (1985) Signification, representation, ideology: Althusser and the post-structuralist debates. *Critical Studies in Mass Communication* 2, 91–114.

Hall, S. (1996) Introduction: Who needs identity?, in *Questions of Cultural Identity,* (eds S. Hall and P. D. Gay), Sage, London, pp. 1–17.

Halualani, R.T. (2008) "Where exactly is the Pacific?": Global migrations, diasporic movements, and intercultural communication. *Journal of International and Intercultural Communication,* 1 (1), 3–22.

Hegde, R.S. (1998) Swinging the trapeze: The negotiation of identity among Asian Indian immigrant women in the United States, in *Communication and Identity Across Cultures,* (eds D.V. Tanno and A. González), Sage, Thousand Oaks, CA, pp. 34–55.

Hirabayashi, L.R., Kikumura-Yano, A., and Hirabayashi, J.A. (eds) (2002) *New Worlds, New Lives: Globalization and People of Japanese Descent in the Americas and from Latin America in Japan,* Stanford University Press, Stanford, CA.

Iino, M. (2002) Licensed agencies for relief in Asia: Relief materials and Nikkei populations in the United States and Canada, in *New Worlds, New Lives: Globalization and People of Japanese Descent in the Americas and from Latin America in Japan*, (eds L.R. Hirabayashi, A. Kikumura-Yano and J.A. Hirabayashi), Stanford University Press, Stanford, CA, pp. 59–75.

Iino, M. (2005) The identity of Nikkei Canadians seen in the Buddhist Church, www.discovernikkei.org/en/people/clip.php?id=523 (last accessed February 14, 2008).

Kim, Y.Y. (1988) *Communication and Cross-Cultural Adaptation: An Integrated Theory.* Multilingual Matters, Clevedon, UK.

Kim, Y.Y. (1995) Cross-cultural adaptation: An integrative theory. *Intercultural Communication Annual*, 19, 170–193.

Kim, Y.Y. (2001) *Becoming Intercultural: An Integrative Theory of Communication and Cross-Cultural Adaptation*, Sage, Thousand Oaks, CA.

Konno, T., and Fujisaki, Y. (1994) *Iminshi Nanbei hen*, Shinsensha, Tokyo.

Laclau, E., and Mouffe, C. (2001) *Hegemony and Socialist Strategy*, 2nd edn, Verso, London.

Lavie, S., and Swedenburg, T. (1996) Introduction: Displacement, diaspora, and geographies of identity, in *Displacement, Diaspora, and Geographies of Identity*, (eds S. Lavie and T. Swedenburg), Duke University, Durham, NC.

Lesser, J. (1999) *Negotiating National Identity: Immigrants, Minorities, and the Struggle for Ethnicity in Brazil*, Duke University Press, Durham, NC.

Lesser, J. (2001) In search of the hyphen, in *New Worlds, New Lives: Globalization and People of Japanese Descent in the Americas and from Latin America in Japan*, (eds L.R. Hirabayashi, A. Kikumura-Yano and J.A. Hirabayashi), Stanford University Press, Stanford, CA, pp. 37–58.

Lesser, J. (2007) *A Discontented Diaspora: Japanese-Brazilians and the Meaning of Ethnic Militancy*, Duke University Press, Durham, NC.

Lowe, L. (1991) Heterogeneity, hybridity, multiplicity: Making of Asian American differences. *Diaspora*, 1, 24–44.

Martin, J.N., and Nakayama, T.K. (1999) Thinking dialectically about culture and communication. *Communication Theory*, 9, 1–25.

Marx, A.W. (1998) *Making Race and Nation: A Comparison of the United States, South Africa, and Brazil.* Cambridge University Press, Cambridge.

Masterson, D.M. (2004) *The Japanese in Latin America.* University of Illinois Press, Urbana.

Mendoza, S.L., Halualani, R.T., and Drzewiecka, J.A. (2002) Moving the discourse of identities in intercultural communication: Structure, culture, and resignification. *Communication Quarterly*, 50 (3/4), 312–327.

Moon, D.G. (1996) Concept of "culture": Implications for intercultural communication research. *Communication Quarterly*, 44 (1), 70–84.

Nakayama, T.K. (2004) Dis/orienting identities: Asian Americans, history, and intercultural communication, in *Our Voices: Essays in Culture, Ethnicity, and Communication*, 4th edn, (eds A. González, M. Houston, and V. Chen), Roxbury, Los Angeles, pp. 26–31.

Nikkei Net Association (2006) Anti-Japanese racism in Peru – past and present, http://www.discovernikkei.org/forum/en/node/1068 (last accessed February 14, 2008).

Ono, K.A. (1998) Problematizing "nation" in intercultural communication research, in *Communication and Identity across Cultures* (eds D.V. Tanno and A. González), Sage, Thousand Oaks, CA, pp. 193–202.

Reichl, C.A. (1995) Stages in the historical process of ethnicity: The Japanese in Brazil, 1908–1988. *Ethnohistory*, 42 (1), 31–42.

Safran, W. (1991) Diasporas in modern societies: Myths of homeland and return. *Diaspora*, 1, 83–99.

Shibayama, A. (2003) Denied redress as a Japanese Peruvian. www.discovernikkei.org/en/people/clip.php?id=377andnf=1 (last accessed February 14, 2008).

Shome, R. (2003) Space matters: The power and practice of space. *Communication Theory*, 13 (1), 39–56.

Takaki, R. (1998) *Strangers from a Different Shore: A History of Asian Americans*, Back Bay Books, Boston, MA.

The Association of Nikkei and Japanese Abroad (2004) *Kaigai nikkeijin suu* (The Number of Nikkei Population) www.jadesas.or.jp/aboutnikkei/index.html (accessed May 27, 2010).

The Commission on Wartime Relocation and Internment of Civilians. (1997) *Personal Justice Denied*. University of Washington Press, Seattle.

The Ministry of Foreign Affairs (2008) www.mofa.go.jp/mofaj/index.html (accessed May 27, 2010).

Tölölyan, K. (1996) Rethinking *diaspora(s)*: Stateless power in the transnational moment. *Diaspora*, 5 (1), 3–36.

Vertovec, S. (1997) Three meanings of "Diaspora," exemplified among South Asian Religions, *Diaspora*, 6 (3), 277–299.

Ward, W.P. (1990) *White Canada Forever: Popular Attitudes and Public Policy Toward Orientals in British Columbia*, 2nd edn, McGill-Queen's University Press, Montreal.

Yanagida, T. (ed.) (2002) *Laten amerika no Nikkeijinjin: Kokka to esunicitii* [Japanese Descendants in Latin America: State and Ethnicity], Keio Gijuku Daigaku Shuppankai, Tokyo.

Yep, G.A. (2002) My three cultures: Navigating the multicultural identity landscape, in *Readings in Intercultural Communication*, 2nd edn, (eds J.N. Martin, T.K. Nakayama, and L.A. Flores), McGraw Hill, Boston, pp. 60–66.

30

Placing South Asian Digital Diasporas in Second Life

Radhika Gajjala

Who has not known, at this moment, the surge of an overwhelming nostalgia for lost origins, for "times past?" And yet, this "return to the beginning" is like the imaginary in Lacan – it can neither be fulfilled nor requited, and hence is the beginning of the symbolic, of representation, the infinitely renewable source of desire, memory, myth, search, discovery – in short, the reservoir of our cinematic narratives.

(Stuart Hall, 1993, p. 236)

In this essay, I extend existing work that examines how technologically mediated diasporas occur at online/offline intersections specifically in relation to "South Asian," "digital" and "diasporic." This is done through a personal, affective engagement within these spaces. My narrations privilege personal routes, drawing first from my experience as a "nomad" in predigital times (offline) to illustrate what I mean by "communicative spaces of diaspora" and second, from a cultural route through Second Life that follows Indian looking clothing stores, dance clubs linked with South Asian remix, Bollywood music, and related symbolism to examine "digital diaspora" in virtual worlds. In doing so, I also explore and discuss how the ways in which mediated spaces of diaspora have made a subtle shift from post 1960s "imagined community" to "digital diasporic networks."

Stuart Hall (1993) has noted how nostalgia and affect form the foundation for building narratives of identity and belonging. In the quote above, he refers to "cinematic narratives." In this present article I look at how we build "reservoirs" of mediated narratives in communicative spaces of diaspora. This is illustrated through the examples. The first describes offline predigital communicative spaces of diaspora based in post-1960s flow of professional, mostly upper caste and upper caste, western educated labor away from South Asia towards modernity, internationalization,

The Handbook of Critical Intercultural Communication, edited by Thomas K. Nakayama and Rona Tamiko Halualani.   © 2010 Blackwell Publishing Ltd.

and development. The second takes us through some scenarios on Second Life with built environments appealing to South Asian affect.

Identities produced within digital contexts enabled by computer software and hardware, are made possible through the coproduction of sociocultural digital place and global networks involving time-space compression. These sociocultural contexts are coproduced by inhabitants who access these contexts. The sociocultural literacies of these inhabitants determines the kinds of free labor (Terranova, 2004) they contribute towards the building of these spaces. The continued inhabiting of these spaces leads to a reorganization of social space and everyday practice similar to that experience by call center workers from India who are tuned-in to time-zones and cultural practices in the Western worlds as described by Ananda Mitra in his work on outsource call center workers (Mitra, 2008). Therefore they experience a social, affective transformation that orients them towards life in global multicultural communities similar to those encountered by those in diaspora. Further these online residents also experience displacement and disorientation similar to that produced in social encounters within diaspora. However this is still not the same as that encountered by traveling bodies. Thus, while the digital diasporas produced through online encounters of global environments can affectively simulate diasporic life and even actually change the everyday praxis of offline bodies the experience is not fully that of those in diaspora. Simultaneously, the digital spaces are also inhabited by younger generations from various diasporas the world over. Contact zones of geographical dispersed diaspora from South Asia are produced in the encounter between these differently located digital subjects. Thus, these spaces can be considered transitional places orienting digital subjects towards a particular kind of multicultural globalization. They provide the entry point for new and emerging digital forces connecting from nonglobal geographical areas of South Asia that are not quite fully rural but neither are they fully urban and global in the way in which scholars such as Sassen (1996) have described global cities.

These present generations of global workers thus live in a:

> dynamic moment in history [when] the First and Third Worlds are involved in a major confrontation of cultures, while the Third World and its myriad diasporas in the West are engaged in an attempt to reframe their cultural identities to stave off the threat of "cultural genocide," through the effects of a rampant globalization (Rajgopal, 2003).

There are several entry points into online South Asian digital formations. Some privilege the cultural and social practices, some privilege the economic routes. The several "routes" crisscross in layers. Neither the cultural nor the economic routes are mutually exclusive. The cultural entry point tends to precede the economic layer sometimes and the economic quest for jobs tends to precede cultural transformations. These digital places and global networks become potential transitional places (Naficy, 2001) and contact zones for the formation of transnational subjects able to work within the increasing digital global economy through sociocultural processes facilitating the further intellectualization of labor (Bratich, 2008).

Post-1960s imagining of community, for instance, materialized through communicative spaces of diaspora, where "home" was a romanticized, frozen place remembered through nostalgic storytelling and through radio, LP records, slides, photographs, home movies and occasionally televised and screened movies from the subcontinent. Diasporic affect based in nostalgia for a geographical location of home fostered connections between diasporic groups that identified as originating from the South Asian sub-continent with sub-groups formed along nation, religion, language, and sometimes even caste. Post-1960s migration from the South Asian subcontinent was also a response to international modernization. The United Nations (and related global nongovernmental organizations) and the IMF came to be seen as global facilitators of development and upliftment of "underdeveloped" nations, while the United States rose to the status of superpower. It is well known that the 1965 immigration act was a result of US labor needs as well as the political need to be perceived as more open than before.

In the post-1960s waves of migrations, "South Asian" group identities were more strongly forged than in previous generations as a response to the professional and social expectations of that time. In cosmopolitan international social gatherings, such as those attended by a growing number of UN officials from the subcontintent, exclusive identification along national, religious or caste identities (as in "Pakistani", "Indian", "Hindu", "Muslim", "Brahmin" and so on) were discouraged through social cues pointing to the nonmodern nature of such ways of identifying. Rather, religious and linguistic diversity was celebrated as part of world cultures. Further, this Modern space was urban-centric. The rural could be romanticized when spoken of, but South Asian "third-world" rural practices in everyday living were considered unhygienic, backward, and primitive – the opposite of Modern. The professional class and their families therefore learned to police themselves into the appropriate cosmopolitan, modern socio-cultural behaviors expected of them in such public international spaces. Religious, regional, and rural based everyday practices, if they persisted, were contained in the private space of the home, where the woman became the keeper of culture.

Digital Diaspora

"Digital diasporas" occur at the intersection of local/global, national/international, private/public, offline/online, and embodied/disembodied. In digital diasporas, a multiplicity of representations, mass media broadcasts, textual and visual performances, and interpersonal interactions across geographical locations occur. The material and discursive shapings of community through such digital encounters indicate nuanced and layered continuities, discontinuities, conjuctures and disjunctures between colonial pasts and a supposedly postcolonial present. Thus, digital diasporas occur within racially, geographically, culturally, ecologically, and socioeconomically marked configurations of the local which in turn exist within a power structure that conflates a certain specific sociocultural, urbanized way of living as "global." Various transnational traveling subjects as they travel through cyberspace – through mouse-clicks and keyboard taps, multitasking between various online and offline activities, conversations and "windows" – negotiate an online existence within such technological environments in different ways.

The digital encounters of interactive meaning-making in these digital diasporic spaces produce not only social and digital spaces of cultural representation but also contact zones of cultural contestation. Mary Louise Pratt defines her contact zone as "social spaces where disparate cultures meet, clash, and grapple with each other, often in highly asymmetrical relations of domination and subordination" (1992, p. 4) These contact zones are "the space[s] of colonial encounters, the space[s] in which peoples geographically and historically separated come into contact with each other and establish ongoing relations, usually involving conditions of coercion, radical inequality, and intractable conflict" (p. 6). This notion of a contact zone is predicated on the unequal power structures of colonial encounter that usually involves (white) Westerners and nonWestern cultures in the era of colonization. The asymmetrical relations between the West and the East, United States and India, NRI (nonresident Indian) and RI (resident Indian) and so on are also lived via digital diasporas in the age of digitization, circulation and globalization of specific kinds of cultural and material capital embedded in sociocultural processes of meaning making shaped through the social and economic logics driving the proliferation of digital technologies and labor.

Digital Diaspora as Transitional Place

In post-1990s globalization, digital diasporic space functions as a transitional *place* (Naficy, 2001, p. 5)[1] and a cybernetic place (Mitra, 2006) where transnational corporate workforces are produced through an interplay of identity, sociocultural practice and layered literacies. Note that when I speak of digital diaspora – I am not limiting myself to talking only of South Asians in diaspora who are online. Drawing on Ananda Mitra's work on call centers and outsourced labor from India, where he looks specifically at the process of outsourcing call center work to India and finds that although workers in globalized call centers do not physically "travel" to a new "real" place, their job description makes it imperative that they adapt themselves to a new culture when they are in their workspace – that is, they have to "talk the talk" and "walk the walk" of their clients. Call center employees are exposed to similar struggles (of race, oppression, Otherness, etc.) that diasporas traditionally face, despite the absence of movement from one place to another (Mitra, 2008). Therefore, the South Asian digital diaspora that I describe includes all those who connect to online space from South Asia.

I am not claiming that the experience of the digital diasporic subject replicates literally the offline embodied experience of diasporic populations as they negotiate offline placed relations. The experience of the veiled South Asian Muslim body traveling with body through transitional places such as airports and through global cities such as New York is certainly a far different experience than that of the veiled Muslim woman who sits in Hyderabad, India and connects to digital space via her avatar in Second Life (whether or not the avatar is in fact veiled or dressed in non-western attire). So I once again emphasize that the two – digital diaspora and offline embodied diaspora – must not be considered as one and the same. However, neither should digital diaspora be considered as not real or not embodied – life online is real and we do not "leave behind" the body when we use computers to immerse ourselves online. An aching back, carpal tunnel, dry eyes, and other bodily reactions attest to our different experiences of embodiment at and in the computer interface as we inhabit virtual worlds.

In the business sector, the concept of digital diaspora has been taken up – since the late-1990s – to mobilize digital labor. In 2000, there was a digital diaspora initiative sponsored by the United Nations that focused on trying to mobilize Nonresident Indians of the educated and professional classes to help bridge technology gaps. These diasporic Indians were drawn into the service of connecting India to globalization processes by training and educating labor in addition to investing capital into mostly information technology related businesses in India (DeHart, 2004). Monica DeHart notes that:

> The Digital Diaspora projects were modeled after the IndUS Entrepreneurs (TiE) network, a partnership of South Asian technology-industry professionals who organized a non-profit organization in 1994 to foster entrepreneurship and development throughout the Indian diaspora (DeHart, 2004, p. 253).

Thus at this time what was emerging as an online presence of "South Asians" in diaspora that began to be referred to by some as "South Asian digital diasporas" became more of an "Indian Digital Diaspora."

This Indian digital diaspora became a site – a space – of transition for work forces to get trained socially, culturally, and technically to be part of the digital global economy. The present article extends existing literature on Indian digital diasporas through a critical lens, by looking at particular South Asian and Indian presences in the three-dimensional virtual world[2] known as Second Life (see www.Second Life.com). A central continuing concern that shapes the article is the question of how South Asian Diaspora as well as people from the geographical sub-continent of South Asia connect with and use digital technologies, digital media, digital networks, digital space, and digital place.

Thus, while both kinds of diasporas that I refer to in this article are based in economic migration and founded on economic quests for upward mobility or survival, each of these groups is socialized into the work and social environment as ideal worker, native informant and model immigrant through different sociocultural processes, requiring different kinds of sociocultural literacies and different types of laboring.

In this essay, therefore, I extend existing work that examines how technologically mediated diasporas occur at online/offline intersections specifically in relation to "South Asian", "digital" and "diasporic" by examining how South Asian/Indian presences are manifested in the virtual world known as Second Life. These are topics that have been studied by scholars who examine South Asians socio-cultural formations online since the early-1990s have included issues of nation, gender, class, caste, and sexuality in relation to technological environments and globalization (Rai 1995, Lal 1999). Much of my research for this essay comes through ongoing immersive ethnographies at online/offline intersections, through rural and urban travel, and through cyberethnographies. In doing my offline ethnographies, I follow traditions based in feminist postcolonial anthropology (Visweswaran, Narayan, Abu-Lughod) and critical ethnography (Madson). In doing cyberethnographies I draw upon mostly cultural studies based research traditions developed through the past 10 years of online research.

Online Ethnography

Early researchers of cyberculture (especially in early 1990s) faced the internet with a certain amount of bewilderment in terms of method for studying what was happening online. Several were caught up in the sheer fascination of being online and mere descriptive writing about the Internet and euphoric claims about the potential of hypertext were the theme in much of that writing. However that was also the time that several researchers began to pose questions about the nature of the communication enabled and social spaces produced within this human-machine continuum. Researchers such as Lucy Suchman, Katherine Hayles and Donna Haraway are already been writing about the human technology encounter in ways that seem suitable for what the researchers of Internet based communication were seeing when they approached the Internet as culture. Thus scholars such as Don Slater, Nancy Baym, Annette Markham, Lisa Nakamura, and Lori Kendall, reached for ethnography as a way to study these online cultures by living in both online and related offline environments. Thus critical questions raised were as basic as:

> How do ethnographic practices and the ethnographer evolve in an online context?
> How are they revolutionized? What constitutes the field and how do we define the
> boundaries of the field? Further, can we transpose concerns that arise out of RL (real-
> life) anthropology or face-to-face ethnography onto the study of virtual communities
> without seriously considering the very important differences in the nature of face-to-
> face interaction and virtual interaction and thus confuse the issues? When can RL
> anthropological and critical issues be considered relevant to online ethnography?
> (Gajjala, 2004, p. 29).

Ethnography as a way to research online environments in present times is an established and authorized method and continues plays a key role in communication and cultural studies scholarship (Bell, 2001). Christine Hine (2000), for instance, uses the label of "Virtual Ethnography" to describe her approach to the study of cyberculture and examines cyberspace both as a culture, social space, and as a cultural artifact. Thus, the Internet as cyberspace is simultaneously a product of culture and is produced by people with contextually situated goals and priorities. Thinking about the Internet as culture, thus allows us to approach the human-machine continuum through everyday practice. Further ethnography, to use Susan Leigh Star's (1999) characterization, is "tempting" (p. 383) for those of us interested in studying online interactions as communicative environments. Ethnography allows us to examine contradictions and diverse meaning-making practices by connecting speech, action within socio-cultural, political, and economic contexts. Currently, multiple examples of studying the Internet through ethnography exist (e.g., Hine, 2000; Markham, 1998; Miller and Slater, 2000; Turkle, 2005).

In order to examine digitally mediated sociocultural activity, it is necessary to "obtain" both online and offline data. This is an important point to note as, later, I discuss digital diaspora and attempt to differentiate between *digital* diasporas and *offline* embodied, place-based diasporas.[3] In addition, the researcher struggles to stay focused on trying to articulate everyday practices of weaving in and out of online and offline states of being, on a continuum based in everyday life in order to point to the nuanced relational nature at online/offline intersections.

Therefore, in order to gain fuller understandings of situations at online/offline and global/local intersections, the researcher is compelled to continually *live* both online and offline – viewing online/offline and global/local as continuums and not as binaries. Researchers such as Boellstorff (2008) have made the argument that Second Life is a place for residents of Second Life, that is those who own avatars that live and participate in the various activities in Second Life. This argument can be understood through a living within and affective engagement with various communities within Second Life which engenders an affective sense of belonging and placement as the human using the online avatar gets drawn into the ownership of real estate, building of homes, and participation within neighborhoods.

My preferred methodology, as a consequence, is what we might call a deep "hanging out" in various places simultaneously online and offline[4] as well as fully offline, in order to understand how practices of daily life in these environments shape meaning making practices in our world today. Thus, the research in this current article is also based in cyber(auto)ethnographies, offline ethnographies and especially in epistemologies of doing (Gajjala, Rybas and Altman 2007). The economic, cultural and social always intersect with the personal in some way and as a critical feminist scholar, my stated point of entry into any project is through a revealed personal location.

Communicative Spaces of Diaspora

My journey into communicative spaces of diaspora has always been initiated through a search for community. My physical journeys away from my country of origin began at age three, and, although I have always had a home address in India that I returned to there, and although most of my schooling happened in that geographic location, "community" for me has always been built - never taken for granted – put together from those around me and from memories, things, media and communication tools. As far back as I can remember I have always had to work at being a community member or at gaining community support for myself. So I have never thought of community as existing without my participation in it in some form. Much of my early knowledge of a "home" in India came to me through letters from my siblings – read out loud (before I could read) by my father. It was the active reading of these letters and the enacting of emotion through his narration that brought my siblings' worlds into mine. They existed because of the letters and because the content of the letters were communicated to me by parents who were invested in my connecting with my siblings and their community. Likewise, through stories about my parents experience with the Gandhian way of life, their investment in a nation free from British Rule was conveyed to me. But their investment in remaining connected to that nation was visible to me in everyday life through observing their media consumption patterns and through consuming the same media as they did (since there were no i-pods in those days, I had no choice but to share in these acts of consumption unless I was outdoors climbing trees).

Thus my envisioning (which to this day remains mostly an envisioning) of Bombay (I say Bombay rather than Mumbai because that is the place in my memory) came from black and white photos, stories narrated by my parents, and from the letters written by my siblings. My affective understanding of "home," at that time, came from my mother's singing, my father's reading and chanting of Sanskrit and Telugu texts, from the nostalgic stories they narrated, the long-playing records of varieties of music from India, and from radio broadcasts on a shortwave radio from "All-India Radio." In the 1960s and 1970s, the television, radio, news reports, letters, telegrams, and the telephone were some of the ways in which we would connect to some sort of "community" from "home." Yet, for a child who had spent more time outside of this home-nation than within it during her first 16 years of life – home and community were always clearly mobile and always in the affective space of imagination constructed through other peoples' memories.

In embodied form, this "community" came together in Indian/South Asian potluck parties with their aromas, incense, and multiple tongues spoken while some form of music from that continent played in the background. Very early in life, then, I learned community must be built – through choice and circumstance. Circumstance determined where I was physically placed. Choice allowed me to choose or be chosen to engage in specific social, educational, and economic activities that made me part of a community.

So when the Internet and the notion of emailing messages became a possibility in my adult life, it was but logical that I looked actively for "community" through that screen as well. Since the teleology of events had always been disjointed and nonlinear in a sense, community was always to be put together in the day-to-day through active participation, production and redefinition of self through consumption and communication. Therefore, constructing community in Internet space, as scattered bytes that came together to form messages, seemed a logical way of seeing the world. Thus in 1992, the first thing I sought to do through this communication medium was to build community through encounters and collaborative meaning-making with the people I came in touch with.

My past and continuing research quests come from this urge to build and connect to "community" through multiple locations. Therefore my work has involved building, joining, and participating in online communities while also engaging in extended periods of offline ethnographies in different "locals" (Northwest Ohio and South India). I continue to examine online formations that are referred to as virtual communities and digital diasporas through the lenses enabled by what I learn in these online and offline journeys.

Looking for "India" on Second Life: 2003 to 2008

Prior to encountering "Second Life", my experience with three-dimensional communicative environments came from having tried out what was known as "Alphaworld" in 1997, and from watching my son play computer games in the late-1990s and early-2000s. My experience with text-based MOOs and MUDs allowed me to understand the logic of building selves and worlds within online multiuser environments. In 2003, I got an account on Second Life mostly because I needed something that functioned like a MOO but also had a graphical user interface for use in my class assignments. In my classes on performing digitally mediated identities I had been using MOOs (specifically Linguamoo and PMC moo) to make my students understand the notion of constructing identity and community in online settings. The use of MOOs pedagogically allowed me to make them see how identity and context functioned together and how existing hierarchies shape such identities and contexts. In addition MOOs provide a way to map the social codes, practices, and cues inherited by web 2.0 social networking systems and instant messaging practices.

Once I entered Second Life the best way for me to learn more about this environment was to explore by looking for anything that seemed Asia-like, while trying to make my avatar look more ethnic. Apart from a place called Sone Ki Lanka with a Buddhist stupa like structure and pillars with textures made of images that looked very much like the Sculptures from the temples at Belur and Halebid in Karnataka, I found very little non-European looking environments there. Nor was I able to modify my avatar to look properly raced or ethnic.

In those initial months, however, Second Life was comparatively slow and had very little social life for me to explore. Later, in 2004, I reinvented myself and got another avatar and gained some more insight into the communicative environment. It was not until 2006 when I reinvented myself yet again as "rad Zabibha" and went looking for Bollywood, that I actually found "India" on Second Life. India on Second Life took various forms – appeared in various symbols, clothes, avatars and places in Second Life. This time I decided I was going to live there for a longer time and even set up my own business in selling "handloom." In what follows I draw on rad Zabibha's explorations, experiences and observations on Second Life. In order to maintain confidentiality and adhere to the Second Life codes I will not use any real names – neither the first life real names nor the Second Life real names. I will also try not to use the names of actual Second Life locations when the mention of such might reveal either the Second Life identity or first life identity (or both) of any of the Second Life avatars I refer to here. However, some locations and Second Life characters are Second Life celebrities – public figures – and it is likely that I will use actual Second Life names.

Second Life as Transitional Place

If Second Life is viewed as a transitional place – then the work and play activities within this virtual world become infused with more meaning than when it is viewed as a world unconnected to the real where horny adolescents play out sexual fantasies. The social, cultural, and technical activities come under the categories of skills development and free labor. Bollywood becomes an ambassador of digital worlds rather than a mere multicultural identity marker or a signifier of difference within an otherwise "white" cyberspace. In order to lay out some context for my Second Life based narrative, I need to show the reader a few quick discursive snapshots of "desi" living on Second Life. Contrary to popular belief, Second Life is not a white male space. Nor is it just a North American or even a Western space even the software and hardware based three-dimensional environment is an initial product of western cultures and the company – Linden Labs – is located in the United States. For instance, a news article from the Indian Express states that:

> About 90 per cent of the accounts registered from Delhi are engaged in some serious financial investments ... One of the more common ways of investing in Second Life is to buy virtual real estate. Then, like in the real world, the user can wait for property prices to escalate, before selling at a profit. The entire transaction is carried out in Linden Dollars, which can be converted into real world currencies on the exchange.[5]

Second Life Bollywood: A New World Beckons

In 2007, Indusgeeks produced a machinima called India in Second Life – shot on location on Bollywood Island.[6] "A new world beckons" is the very first line that appears on the screen, while young men and women from all vocations are shown rising up in a trance and running towards what turns out to be Bollywood Island in Second Life. While the exoticization of the Indian is a very obvious point to note and may not carry much significance in itself in a place like Second Life that is fashioned around the production of exoticized selves, what was striking to me was that there was potter dressed in village garb who was one of the entranced group of people running to Second Life.

This notion of new world resonates with a discourse that is emerging regarding "Bollystan" as "India's diasporic democracy" (Khanna, 2005) with the likes of Aishwarya Rai (who's profile on myspace emerged around the time that Rupert Murdoch bought the social networking site) and Sharukh Khan being proclaimed as ambassadors of Bollystan. In this mediated environment, where Bollywood becomes representative of "India" for much of the second and later generations of diasporic Indians.

While it is true that mobile generations of south Asian youth hang out in social network systems and blogs such as LiveJournal, Facebook, Orkut and hi5 (masked in semi-anonymity) and even remix videos posted on YouTube blur notions of transnational sexuality and notions of "Indianness," as they hide behind and digitally manipulate Bollywood and other pop icons and music, this particular video with its characterization of a "new world" beckoning in Second Life in fact recodes these transgressions through the heteronormative perfection of three-dimensional imagery. In other Web 2.0 venues there is a continuing play on gender and identity as the Bollywood icons produced in such communities are subjected to a gaze that blurs the boundary between heteronormative idolization of Bollywood stars and queer pleasure, while also producing uncertainty about geographic location as they appear to multitask between work, fun, and offline/online formations of friends.

However, the characterization of a Bollywoodized 3d new world, evident in the machinima described above, re-instates hierarchies and binaries while also reproducing a very specific euphoric vision of development. It is not within the scope of the current article to discuss and elaborate on how youtube and other web 2.0 social networking tools are used in South Asian digital diasporas. There is work being done on how fan communities and remix Bollywood music performs South Asian digital diasporas (see for instance Zuberi, 2008), but my focus in this section of the article is on Second Life and south Asian digital diasporas. Even as, in actuality, there is much gender-bending and "cross-dressing" of avatars with great ease, the actual avatars produced – whether or not their owners sitting at the computer are of the same sex/gender – are made to look, dress, and behave in a highly heteronormative way following a post-1995 Bollywood notion female and male embodiment. So who is this vision of Bollystan-Second Life being presented to? And who is presenting it? Where are these future visions emerging from in relation to Second Life? As these kinds of re-presentations attempt to showcase status quo heteronormativity and westernized development in this "new world," how, if at all, are these codings and reinstating of norms being negotiated?

Second Life Desi Dancing Clubs – Re-mixing Digital Diasporas

In her article on "Henna and Hip Hop", Sunaina Maira writes:

> The youth subculture created by South Asian American youth in New York City is based
> on remix music that was first created by British-born Asian youth in the 1980s and that
> layers the beats of bhangra … It mixes a particular reconstruction of South Asian music
> with American youth popular culture, allowing ideologies of cultural nostalgia to be
> expressed through the rituals of clubbing and dance music. … This remix subculture
> includes participants whose families originate from other countries of the sub-continent,
> such as Bangladesh and Pakistan, yet these events are often coded by insiders as the
> "Indian party scene" or "desi scene," where the word "desi" signifies a pan-South Asian
> rubric that is increasingly emphasized in the second generation, and which literally
> means "of South Asia," especially in the context of the diaspora (Maira, 2000, p. 240).

On Second Life, several such dance clubs exist, where young men and women of
South Asian descent and their non-South Asian friends "hang out". At least so it
appears to the Second Life avatars who visit these clubs.

Here I draw my analysis from visits to dancing environments and the observations
are based on my experience of them. I must make clear that my understanding of these
comes from a "deep hanging out" in various dancing clubs on Second Life in order to
understand some apparently sociotechnically scripted codes for behavior in such environments. Thus, I have visited dancing clubs that self-describe as Hispanic clubs, as
Middle-Eastern, as Reggae, as Jazz, as "desi", as Bollywood focused and so on.

I describe these environments based on specific visits that I made to a few Indian
and South Asian themed dance clubs. In Second Life – no "place" stays static for
long. Groups and individuals are continually rebuilding and relocating – therefore
the dance club experiences I discuss here can only be located in my affective experience and memory of the events and on snapshots and various YouTube videos taken
by various Second Life residents as they visit these clubs.[7] Thus, my own reading of
performative cues are what I rely on as I describe these clusters of activities.

All these dancing clubs have basic scripted objects[8] – a dancing ball, or a floor with
dance scripts – to animate the avatars. They all have streaming media set up – where
the songs are streamed from a server (such as shoutcast or something else) onto the
Second Life location. Most of them have tip balls or some form of money collecting
scripted objected and some also have exploding objects that are scripted to allow
visitors to enter into a competition to win the jackpot by making a money contribution. Some clubs have themed dances and competitions for dancers to enter (this is
also done through scripted object), where fellow dancers get to vote for the "best
dressed female in pink" or something such theme decided by the club owners.

In dance clubs focused on Indian interests, there is often a stock set of Bollywood
remix music (and sometimes even video) streaming in. The Second Life avatars in
these clubs are dressed in a variety of clothes but more and more of them (since 2007)

are dressing in ethnic seeming garb modeled mostly after Bollywood characters' dresses. Since 2007 Second Life residents and business owners have noticed more and more sari designers, for instance.

Since the practice of designing of a sari using photoshop requires a certain amount of dedicated patience and continued effort in trying to get the detail and shape just right so as to make it look like a sari that an Indian from India would recognize as a sari – this increased production of saris, to me, indicates at least an increased interest in the consumption of such attire by Second Life avatars.

While the Goreans, a role-playing group that inhabits Second Life (see http://en.wikipedia.org/wiki/Gorean for a quick description of the Goreans), are interested in saris, they have not been as particular about how "Indian" sari-like it should be. The Second Life avatar of Indian origin tends to be more knowledgable of a particular set of practices around sari wearing and this seems to influence what they consider to be apparel worthy of the name "sari." This is reflected in their consumption and production of saris and comments about saris when their avatars are wearing them. Interestingly, then this female attire becomes a certain symbol of "authenticity" of Indianness at the same time as it is still exotic and sexualized through its use by the Goreans on Second Life.

There are of course instances where both the Gor market and the Indian market are targeted by a sari producer. Second Life avatar LP, for instance, has at least one store in a Gorean focused Mall and a store in at least one India focused dance club and shopping center. She also sells her creations at the now famous House of Style owned by the clothes designer OT. In 2006, O, L and one or two others were the only sari and Indian apparel designers easily found on Second Life. Now there are several – both well known and not so well known. However, the perception of authenticity of saris on Second Life has more to do with the offline practice of making the sari through digital imaging and textures from the original textile based sari material than it does with the authentic Indianness of the Second Life avatar wearing the sari or the person behind the avatar. However, I digress – the investigation of the authenticity of saris and Indianness on Second Life in relation to sari wearing is a topic to be explored more in depth in other writing.

As far as the dancing clubs with Bollywood music is concerned – Indianness is established mainly through familiarity with the music being played and a basic minimum knowledge of Hindi which is demonstrated in conversation among avatars in the club as they dance on. "Where are you from?" seems to be a question often asked of newcomers in an attempt to connect to some kind of South Asian origin story. Bollywood is invoked as representative of India in such mediated environments but also serves as an apolitical and safe common language.

Is She "More" Real Because I "Know" Her On Orkut?

In 2007, I met a young lady (or so the avatar said she was) who told me she was on Second Life because she had heard of the jobs you could get on Second Life and had seen an advertisement in a regional vernacular news essay in India. She started to type to me in a roman script version my mother tongue saying she felt more "at home" on Second Life now that she had found someone who understood the same vernacular Indian language as the one she spoke in her everyday offline. When she told me where she was logging on from I was more than mildly surprised. Not that the region she was logging on from was remote or rural but it was not one of the Hi-tech cities like Bangalore and Hyderabad or the more elite cosmopolitan cities like Mumbai, Delhi, Kolkatta, or Chennai. She had found a job on Second Life that would pay her about the equivalent of a dollar a week. She was annoyed at all the male type avatars that kept asking her for sex, she said. She thought all that was silly and ridiculous. She wanted to learn all there was to learn about scripting and building in Second Life. Along the way she was certainly making some interesting friends. She has visited many India centric places and has confessed to not feeling too comfortable in the dance clubs. She did not say clearly why.

Certainly – if we are to believe the avatar's story – here is a person behind the avatar who is clearly in diasporic space through Second Life and not because she has physically traveled outside her home region. She was encountering versions of "America", "China", "Netherlands" and even "Australia" as she interviewed for jobs. Some of these interviews were done through the voice feature on Second Life and the accents of the people behind the avatars came through to her and that was her way of identifying where they were from based on her knowledge of the geographic location of such an accent (gleaned from exposure to other media such as television and film).

Do I believe the "truth" of the story about this young lady I met on Second Life? What are the truths I believe about her and why? Does the fact that she linked to my profile on Orkut where she has several friends from the region she claims to hail from and that they all seem to think she is a young woman mean that she is "real"?

What is real in this instance? My experience and her experience are certainly real. That I chatted with someone who understands my mother-tongue is real. That there was an advertisement in the regional essay the avatar mentioned is real (I found a copy of the news essay on the Internet – so it must be real). The fact that she is working for Linden dollars in Second Life and building a shop and designing saris and jewelry is real ... So why should her stories about her offline life not be real? But that in itself does not matter to the present essay and our understanding of digital diasporas in this framework. That the avatar has certain specialized knowledge of a specific geographic context and has language skills specific to a region attest to a certain kind of authenticity. S/he is a real Indian. Does it matter if she may be a he or that she may be someone who has recently traveled physically away from the region she claims to be from? Not for the understanding of digital diasporas in the framework I write from. But certainly it is of great importance that she is authentic in terms of Indian origin and that she is looking to make Linden dollar money on Second Life. Certainly it is important information that she has given me when she tells me that Second Life is being advertised in various media in India. Further, it is important and relevant since this information can be verified.

What all these truths about this Indian woman's presence on Second Life point to is the Economic pull of Second Life for young IT interested people living in India. This makes sense in relation to all the talk about crowd sourcing and outsourcing via Second Life. Businesses such as Wipro and IBM India have moved into Second Life to recruit and train. A visit to these areas reveals that they are fairly deserted at the moment, but the very fact that these big companies have announced their presence in Second Life draws more young job seeking Indians and other Asians into Second Life, thus changing the cultural, visual, and interactive climate within this three-dimensional reality. As digital diasporas from these regions increase in size the demographics and practices in Second Life will shift. In future work, I will be exploring these issues along with an examination of globalization and multiculturalism in Second Life.

Conclusion

I have attempted to show a shift in conceptualization of diaspora from "imagined community" and "digital diaspora" through a examination of social life in Second Life. Through stories based in personal experience of travel through embodied diaspora and through online ethnographies in digital diaspora, I have tried to show this difference. While the socio-cultural environments and communicative spaces in post-1960 South Asian diaspora were conducive to the kinds of labor needed for the modern internationalization of the world, the sociocultural environments in digital diaspora serve as transitional places that shape and discipline digital workforces for an emerging digital transnational economy. Implicitly, this contribution urges us to continue to ask how the issues from past generations of travel based in global economic structural mobilization of labor, play into the production of digitally diasporic identities in the virtual worlds such as Second Life. It is important therefore that we do not examine the digital space and place as outside of or opposed to real place and space.

Notes

1 Hamid Naficy gives the example of borders, airports, tunnels, seaports and so on – I view online places produced within Second Life as one such transitional place.
2 For a working definition of "virtual world" see Sarah (Intellagirl) Robbins' definition of virtual worlds at www.slideshare.net/intellagirl/aoir-robbins-presentation (accessed May 27, 2010).
3 Digital diasporas are embodied through human computer interaction and practice at the interface therefore I use phrases such as offline embodiment and offline place to make distinctions as needed rather than resort to the binary that positions embodiment as offline and disembodiment as online.
4 Based on the understanding that we are never just "online" for our bodies have not yet been drawn completely into cyberspace – contrary to popular ways of storying online existence, we have not left the body behind.

5 The full article is available at www.indianexpress.com/news/Investing-virtually:-
   New-Delhi-is-India%92s-First-City-on-Second-Life-%09%09%09%09—/220104/
   (accessed May 27, 2010).
6 See www.youtube.com/watch?v=GIg4XMhh14Y&feature=related] (accessed May 27,
   2010).
7 See www.youtube.com/watch?v=y2w2p3v7WSE&feature=related (accessed May 27,
   2010) for a quick idea of how this scene looks. However, it should be noted that merely
   viewing the video or images does not give us a sense of how it actually feels when
   immersed in the environment.
8 Kelly's world blog (www.kgadams.net/2006/06/11/my-second-life-deflowering)
   (accessed May 27, 2010) describes scripted objects as follows "Objects a user creates can
   have scripted behaviors – a table could have a fold out extension, or those ears I mentioned could wiggle. Even more intriguing, an objects behavior could be based on something outside the game: virtual weather in an area could be based on real-world weather
   reports, for example- or a soccer ball could move based on telemetry from a real-world
   soccer ball."

References

Bell, D. (2001) Community and cyberculture, in *An Introduction to Cybercultures*,
   Routledge, New York, pp. 92–111.
Boellstorff, T. (2008) *Coming of Age in Second Life: An Anthropologist Explores the Virtually
   Human*, Princeton University Press, Princeton, NJ.
Bratich, J. (2008) From embedded to machinic intellectuals: Communication studies and
   general intellect. *Communication and Critical Cultural Studies*, 5 (1), 24–45.
DeHart, M. (2004) "Hermano entrepreneurs!" Constructing a Latino diaspora across the
   digital divide. *Journal of Transnational Studies*, 13 (2/3), 253–277.
Gajjala, R. (2004) *Cyber Selves: Feminist Ethnographies of South Asian Women*, AltaMira
   Press, New York.
Gajjala, R., Rybas, N., and Altman, M. (2007). Epistemologies of doing: E-merging selves
   online. *Feminist Media Studies*, 7 (2), 209–213.
Hall, S. (1993) Cultural identity and diaspora, in *Colonial Discourse & Postcolonial Theory:
   A Reader*, (eds P. Williams and L. Chrisman), Harvester Wheatsheaf, New York.
Hine, C. (2000) *Virtual Ethnography*, Sage, London.
Khanna, P. (2005) *Bollystan: India's Diasporic Diplomacy*, Foreign Policy Centre, London,
   UK.
Lal, V. (1999) The politics of history on the internet: Cyber-diasporic Hinduism and the
   North American Hindu diaspora. *Diaspora*, 8 (2), 137–172.
Maira, S. (2000) Henna and hip hop: The politics of cultural production and the work of
   cultural studies. *Journal of Asian American Studies*, 3 (3), 329–369.
Markham, A.N. (1998) *Life Online: Researching Real Experience In Virtual Space*, AltaMira
   Press, Walnut Creek, CA.
Miller, D., and Slater, D. (2000) *The Internet: An Ethnographic Approach*, Berg, Oxford.
Mitra, A. (2006) Towards finding a cybernetic safe place: Illustrations from People of Indian
   Origin. *New Media and Society*, 8 (2), 251–268.
Mitra, A. (2008) Working in cybernetic space, in *South Asian Technospaces*, Peter Lang,
   New York.

Naficy, H. (2001) *An Accented Cinema: Exilic and Diasporic Filmmaking*, Princeton University Press, Princeton, NJ.

Pratt, M.L. (1992) *Imperial Eyes: Travel Writing and Transculturation*, Routledge, London and New York.

Rai, A.S. (1995). India on-line: Electronic bulletin boards and the construction of diasporic Hindu identity. *Diaspora: A Journal of Transnational Studies*, 4, 31–57.

Rajgopal, S.S. (2003) The politics of location: Ethnic identity and cultural conflict in the cinema of the South Asian diaspora. *Journal of Communication Inquiry*, 27 (1), 49–66.

Sassen, S. (1996) Cities and communities in the global economy: Rethinking our concepts. *American Behavioral Scientist*, 39 (5), 629.

Star, S.L. (1999) The ethnography of infrastructure. *American Behavioral Scientist*, 43, 377–391.

Terranova, T. (2004) *Network Culture: Politics for the Information Age*, Pluto Press, London, Ann Arbor, MI.

Turkle, S. (2005) *The Second Self, Computers and the Human Spirit*, 20th edn, MIT Press, Cambridge, MA.

Zuberi, N. (2008) Sampling South Asian music, in *South Asian Technospaces*, (eds R. Gajjala and V. Gajjala), Peter Lang, New York, pp. 49–69.

31

"The Creed of the White Kid"
A Diss-apology

Melissa Steyn

Introduction

The flow of history deposits us in positions relative to others – social spaces of greater or lesser power, privilege or disadvantage, spaces of collective honor or shame, hope or despair, ascendency or decline. Our communication is shaped within such historical legacies – we speak out of, and into, those contexts. The way we construct meaning about our social identities is not innocent, but rather infused with the drive to position ourselves, and those we see as "us," as we believe is best within the currents and tides of contemporary history. We seek to influence the discourses of our place and time such that we are comfortable with the subjectivities they enable for us within the politics of our locations. To illustrate some of these dynamics, this chapter considers the way in which some young white South Africans in postapartheid South Africa are presenting their situation. It discusses a blog posting, *The Creed of the White Kid*, which was circulated by email in March 2008, probably written by a young white Afrikaans-speaking blogger (Chris, 2008) It spread like wild fire across the local Internet, finding its way on to several Internet sites, both celebratory and critical (Dellie, 2008; Ben-Ariel, 2008; Rosenberg, 2008), enjoying postings on social sites such as Facebook, even appearing on the South African page on the white pride website, Stormfront (World Wide White, 2008; Kruger, 2008) It was discussed on TV and radio current affairs programs, where some participants said it gave voice to sentiments many feel, but would normally be unwilling to express.

The critical perspective that informs this chapter is postcolonial theory, which situates its analyses within the unequal racialized and gendered conditions that are the legacy of Western colonization, and often perpetuated by contemporary forms of imperialism. Postcolonialism is an interdisciplinary lens that seeks to "unsettle"

The Handbook of Critical Intercultural Communication, edited by Thomas K. Nakayama and Rona Tamiko Halualani. © 2010 Blackwell Publishing Ltd.

the global and local hegemonies established by the original acts of settlement, conquest, domination, and oppression established as (Western) Europe expanded and consolidated its reach, eventually controlling approximately 85% of the globe. The objective of postcolonialism is to create knowledge differently, affording full recognition to the marginalized, overcoming legacies of exclusion and silencing, and correcting misrepresentations of subordinated people so as to create a fairer, freer world (Castle, 2001; Ashcroft, Griffiths and Tiffen, 1995; Quayson and Goldberg, 2002; Venn, 2006) Critical Communication scholars working in the postcolonial tradition pay particular attention to the meaning constructions which, through the interrelated effects of language, power, and subjectivity within unequal material relations, act as instruments of psychological and political control. They seek to expose how partisan interests are served by dominant ways of thinking about things, and they give "voice" to alternative, subjugated knowledges and alternative possible worlds (Hasian Jr., 2001; Hegde, 1998; Shoma, 1996; Supriya, 1996)

Postcolonialism

The extension of European domination was aggressive and violent, accompanied by slavery, genocide, political subjugation, and economic and cultural exploitation on an unprecedented scale. An important aspect of the colonizing machinery was the cultural, discursive, and linguistic formations that provided the legitimating meaning systems for the imperial project, thus making European global domination seem natural, inevitable, and in the best interests of all, even for those who were undermined and disseminated by the empires. As these constructions in the symbolic realm accompanied physical expansion, European hegemony was established across the globe, and the unequal, inherently conflictual state of affairs was rendered invisible, and other, dissenting voices were increasingly silenced.

While colonial discourses were inflected within particular contexts, adapted and evolved to effect specific tasks in various local settings, certain general contours can be discerned that shaped the grand narratives of colonialism, recognizable as modern, European Enlightenment knowledge. This includes a particular notion of history, which sees Europe "ahead" of the other peoples of the world who have to follow the European trajectory if they, too, are to "progress," often needing to be subjugated in order to imbibe the superior European religious, linguistic, cultural, artistic values, and political systems, or possibly even having to disappear completely if they were "too far" behind to "catch up." Europeans were understood to also lead the world in rationality – science, especially medical science, and technology was constructed as quintessentially European and Western. The borrowings by Europe from other cultural traditions such Eastern and African bodies of knowledge were repressed and even forgotten. At an individual level, it was held that Europeans, especially European men, were able to reach levels of rationality that made them eminently suited to government, management, controlling economic assets and production, and extracting natural resources from the earth and use value from labor.

Postcolonialism and Africa

In this overall scheme of understanding, Africa was constructed with ease of colonization in mind. As the part of the globe regarded as most Other and least capable of developing on its own, it was seen as territory in need of control and conquest (Magubane, 1999). Its vast population was constructed as naturally suited to physical labor, thus rendering the trade in slaves an obvious application. Its abundance of natural resources, to which the Europeans believed they were entitled by virtue of their inherent superiority, offered unlimited opportunity for wealth creation. The scramble for Africa remains one of the greatest "land grabs" in history. The territories divided among the European nations were never intended to be other than resources to their "owners," and their colonial subjects were homogenized into undifferentiated masses through racializing discourses. Unlike the nationstates of Europe, therefore, which were developed by the logic of the nationalist movements of powerful ethnic groups, providing a territorial base for regional ethnic, linguistic, and cultural groups, the African nations that achieved independence through the post-World War II postcolonial period had no internal coherence, and heterogeneous ethnic groups still to some extent struggle for power and recognition within these states. Postcolonial scholars examine these dynamics of the post-colony, but they also show that notions of a homogenous nation or of "pure" cultural groups always have been myth, consisting of complex layerings of multiple pasts, memories, and imagined spaces. The impression of the "coherent whole" is perpetuated through the exclusion of the histories of those less desired as part of the nation, or of those whose narratives would challenge the dominant version.

An important element in securing colonial advantage was the notion of "race," which played itself out in particularly pernicious ways on the African continent. It naturalized the relative positions of superiority and inferiority in Europe's relationship with its global others, casting Africa as the "darkest" place of all. Since the revulsion caused by Nazism, particularly, fewer people are willing to engage in overt racist discourse and discrimination. Yet the weight of history and practice positions people of European descent in positions of privilege that are experienced as normal, and reproduced through every day systems and habits of entitlement that are not necessarily perceived as the operations of privilege, but rather simply as normal ways of going about things. This is the space of whiteness, where racial privilege is rendered unremarkable.

The work of one of the earliest postcolonial theorists, Franz Fanon (1967/1952; 1965/1961), explored the unconscious processes of Othering that lock colonizer and colonized, whiteness and blackness in complex psychological patterns of enmeshment.

While formal colonial relations may no longer be practiced anywhere in Africa, subjectivities continue to be shaped through racially inflected discourses operating within unequal social positioning. The colonial unconscious may continue to operate within the social spaces of whiteness, maintaining the fantasies and stereotypes that sustain racialized social relations (Cash, 2004; López, 2001; Stokes, 2001).

Postcolonial, Postapartheid South Africa

The modern South African nationstate was established through an early history not very dissimilar from that of the United States, New Zealand, Australia, or Canada: the colonial invasion, conquest and annexure by European powers vying for foreign dominions previously occupied by indigenous peoples. South Africa differed from these other deep settler states, however, in that the numbers of settlers were relatively small[1] and thus the indigenous population groups generally were able to survive despite the dispossession of land, economic oppression, decimation of social fabric, and the concomitant processes of loss of culture. It also differed from other colonies in Africa, however, in that the settlement was nevertheless permanent, practicing a form of internal colonialism through white state control and oppression of the black majority. In later years, racist white control took the form of a grand plan for large scale segregation along ethnic and tribal lines, known as apartheid.

On the African continent, South Africa was the last to achieve a full postcolonial status when the protracted political struggle, waged both internally and externally of the country's borders, ended white minority rule and brought about the demise of the apartheid government. The first democratic elections were held in 1994.

Postapartheid South Africa

The young democracy, as any society in transition, has experienced its fair share of challenges. Chief among these has been the need to address the legacy of centuries of racial discrimination: the racially skewed nature of the economy, characterized by extreme inequality and high levels of poverty and unemployment; educational discrimination and infrastructural backlogs; unequal access and opportunity in work and the professions; residential segregation and inadequate or no housing for the poor; poor health services for the majority black population; lack of social cohesion – to name some. The entire legal framework of the country needed to be overhauled in accordance with the new constitution, and more humane labor conditions needed to be established, especially for the most vulnerable workers such as domestic and farm workers. All of this has had to happen within both the context of the country re-entering the globalizing international community with the lifting of sanctions, as well as large scale migration within the country as people from the rural areas moved to the cities to seek better life opportunities, now unfettered by influx control.[2]

In this context, white South Africans have generally done very well. The liberalization of the economy has suited business, and the standard of living for most whites is high. There is a trend to live in gated communities, where only those black people who are able to assimilate to the dominant lifestyle can buy property.

The Department of Labor's statistics show very slow transformation of the private sector, with little change in the racial composition of particularly management positions. Responses to events in national life still appear to be very highly bifurcated along racial lines (Foster, 2006)

The score card for the postapartheid government has been mixed. The payment of social grants is one of the highest in the world, as is the percentage of GDP spent on education, and electricity, water, and sanitation have been extended to the greater part of the population. Yet the country still has one of the highest Gini coefficients in the world (Statistics South Africa, 2008a), this is despite the growth of a fairly substantial black middle class, and a very small number of wealthy black business people. Unemployment levels remain very high.[3] The crime rate is concomitantly high, showing increases especially in organized crime – like bombings of bank ATMs and cash-in-transit heists – and tends to be accompanied by violence. While somewhat democratized, crime is still overwhelmingly concentrated in the poor black areas.

Postcolonial Apologies, South African Reconciliation

In contexts where colonizing groups live among the descendents of those they conquered or enslaved, such as South Africa, Australia, the United States, Canada and New Zealand, postcolonial theorists argue for the need to renegotiate the terms of interracial relationships (Cash, 2004) Such processes of reconciliation, in general, require a willingness to create an honest footing on which to build, a full recognition of the extent and depth of the pain experienced by the subjugated people, and sincere acts of restitution. In Australia, the plea for an apology to the aboriginal people fell on deaf ears for many years under the Howard administration, but one of the first acts of the new Prime Minister, Kevin Rudd, was to propose a motion of apology in the Australian parliament (Rudd, 2008) In New Zealand, the Prime Minister, Helen Clark, oversaw a $317 million settlement to the Maoris in compensation for historic injustices committed in violation of the founding Treaty of Waitangi, signed with European settlers in 1840 (The Associated Press, 2008)

In South Africa, by contrast, issues of restitution and redress have been a priority for the new nonracial government, but are highly contested within the general population. The South African Truth and Reconciliation Commission provided evidence of gross violations of human rights under Apartheid by operatives of the apartheid government, but fell short of engaging with the systemic nature of racial oppression, from which all white South Africans benefited. Attempts to start a groundswell movement of apology have met with little support.[4] The moral imperative of an apology from white South Africa as a gesture of reconciliation, albeit late, was raised again by the chairperson of the Human Rights Commission, Jody Kollapen, in February 2008 (Kassiem, 2008) His statement came in the wake of a series of racist incidents that had shocked the society and raised the emotional temperature.

In one incident in mid-February, a young white Afrikaner youth from the North Western Province, Johan Nel, went on a shooting rampage in a neighboring informal settlement area, Skierlik, killing four black people and injuring seven more (Hawkey, 2009) Seemingly, he has shown no remorse for his egregious deed (SAPA, 2008a, 2008b) The incident caused widespread shock and outrage, raising fears of deteriorating racial attitudes and hardening sentiment among moderate South Africans.

Shortly thereafter, another incident occurred at the University of the Free State, which is situated in an area of conservative white politics. The university had announced at the end of 2007 that all residences at the university were to be integrated, a step which enraged those white students who had been insisting on their right to "freedom of association" in segregated residences. A group of students from the Reitz residence produced an amateur video for a residence "cultural evening" in February 2008, "demonstrating" the residence's initiation (fazing) procedures and concluding with the text, "*This Is What We Think of Integration*" (fuzzyskwerl, 2008) It depicts a mock initiation of five black cleaning staff, four females and one man, in which they perform a series of humiliating acts, culminating in eating, while on their hands and knees, revolting food[5] that the "pranksters" had previously filmed being urinated on.[6] The incident was widely reported on in the international media (CNN, 2008) Yet despite the extensive fury at their actions, the young men seemed to have little grasp of what the vehement response was about, insisting that they were not racist, and that it was just a bit of fun, satirical "play-acting" (Wolmerans and SAPA, 2008), understood as such by others of their age and culture.

The chairperson of the Human Rights Commission was speaking into this highly charged atmosphere when he made his appeal for whites to still seek amends for the racist legacy the country has to confront. His plea was also one of the immediate spurs for the *Creed*.

The other immediate prompt for the *Creed of the White Kid* blog was the proposal by the Minister of Education, Naledi Pandor, for a creed, based on the values of the Constitution,[7] to be recited by children at school assemblies.[8] The stated intention was to build national cohesion, to instill a sense of shared future, common values, and civic consciousness:

> *We the youth of South Africa,*
> *recognising the injustices of our past,*
> *honour those who suffered and sacrificed for justice and freedom.*
> *We will respect and protect the dignity of each person, and stand up for justice.*
> *We sincerely declare that we shall uphold the rights and values of our constitution,*
> *and promise to act in accordance with the duties and responsibilities*
> *that flow from these rights.*
> *! KE E: / **XARRA** // KE[9]*
> *Nkosi Sikelel' iAfrika.[10]*

The Diss-apology

This was prefaced by the following statement:

Now the following is someone who thinks the Pledge should rather be said like this ...

Creed of the white kid

We are sorry that our ancestors were intelligent, advanced and daring enough to explore the wild oceans to discover new countries and to conquer and develop these.

We are sorry that those who came before us took you out of the bush and taught you that there was more to life than beating drums and chasing animals with sticks and stones.

We are sorry that they planned, funded and developed roads, towns, mines, factories, airports, all of which you now claim to be your long deprived inheritance so you have full right to change and rename these at your discretion.

We are sorry that our parents taught us the value of small but strong families, to not breed like rabbits and end up as underfed, illiterate shack dwellers living in poverty.

We are sorry that when they provided you with schools, you decided it looked better without windows or in piles of ashes. We happily gave up those bad days of getting spanked in our all white schools for doing something wrong, and much prefer these days of freedom where problems can be resolved with knives and guns.

We are sorry that it is hard to shake off the bitterness of the past when you keep on raping, torturing and killing our friends and family members, and then hide behind the fence of 'human rights' with smiles on your faces.

We are sorry that we do not trust the government. We have no reason to be so suspicious and short sighted seeing that there has never been a case where any of these poor hard working intellectuals were involved in any form of corruption or irregularities.

We are sorry that we do not trust the police force and although they have openly admitted that they have lost the war against crime and criminals, we should not be so negative and just keep on hoping for the best.

We are sorry that we basically flung open our border posts, and now left you competing for jobs against illegal immigrants from our beautiful neighboring countries. All these countries that have grown so strong after kicking out the "settlers", you should follow their excellent example and grow big and strong like them!

We are sorry that we don't believe in witchcraft, beetroot and garlic, urinating on street corners or trading woman for cattle, maybe we just grew up differently.

So sorry that when we are forced into sharing the same establishments, sometimes we loose our temper, that is totally uncalled for.

We are sorry that your medical care, water supplies, roads, and your electrical supplies are going down the toilet because skilled people who could have planned and resolved these issues had to be shown away because they were of the wrong ethnic background and now has to work in foreign countries where their skills are more needed.

We are so sorry and should really try harder to be more tolerant and learn to get along with EVERYBODY around us, one big happy family.

The Dumb White Kid

The next section of this chapter will analyze the discursive tropes that shape the *apology*. In highlighting these discursive patterns, the analysis shows how some of the underlying assertions that structured white subjectivity in the past are reconfigured in an unreconstructed racist imagination in the present: the writer responds to changed circumstances with unchanged expectations of self and other, the colonial lingers in the postcolonial.

White mythologies

The "apology" clearly establishes a "western" subject by recycling the founding myth of the South African nation, as told by the dominant group through four centuries of colonial rule and apartheid. This version of the early encounter between the indigenous people and the settlers employs the ideological binary of the advanced European bringing civilization, and heathen/primitive African unable to move beyond a stone age, except by submission to European tutelage delivered under conditions of labor. In this account, conquest is conflated with development, and the benefits of white supremacist rule are reframed as logical rewards for a system benevolently exercised to everyone's advantage. The "whites only" schools of the past were not so much about privilege and exclusion as training for "the white man's burden." Any hardship that black South Africans suffered was just some "collateral damage" in the greater scheme of things.

White knowledge

Framing his subject position as the heir to western knowledge systems, the "apologist" repeats the colonial construction of African knowledges/customs as either superstitious distortions, or ignorance – even of basic hygiene (the reference to urinating on street corners has to be highly ironic in the light of the University of Free State incident referred to above) The broadside on *labola*, the African practice of paying bride price, reflects the strategy of demonizing the Other through presenting one's "own" group as the rescuers of the vulnerable and/or oppressed in the Other's society (Kapur, 2005) Antipathy is created against African society by portraying them as backward in gender relations, thus also establishing the purportedly superior values of the cultural background of the writer, the "white" subject.

White nation, White ownership

Closely allied to the above, the *creed* reflects the belief that all advancement, especially technological, technical, scientific, and infrastructural is attributable white entrepreneurship and competence, which means the benefits remain their entitlement. All ownership logically belongs those best able to extract value and manage the resources; all the wealth accrued to them has been earned through their superior capacities. In the absence of white ownership, the wage is self-destruction. The self-congratulatory subject owes no debt to Others, as the labor on which the country's wealth was built is rendered invisible, or inconsequential. Because the legitimate nation is seen to be white, the freedom for others to come into their own is a corrupting invasion of the spaces of authority, trespassing by noncitizens. By extension, all Africans from other countries on the continent living in South Africa are "illegal." Racism and xenophobia neatly dovetail.

White determination

The apology assumes that social, political and economic terms should be set by whites. By this logic, the program of transformation is a kind of theft, fuelled by illegitimate greed and replete with spite. Far from justifiable action to rectify earlier injustices, transformation entails the confiscation of legitimate white entitlements. A key entitlement is the right to define, expressed particularly in the right to maintain the names of cities, towns, airports and such like that honor the heroes of Afrikaner history. That the majority population should be insulted by living in places whose names commemorate their previous oppressors is not seen to be problematic, whereas the removal of these signifiers of control and ownership of public spaces is seen to be an outrageous displacement and even obliteration of Afrikaner identity.

The political freedom of black people, the right to political self-determination, is cynically caricatured as piracy, the conversion and reversal of a legitimate order into rampant lawlessness, destruction, and criminality. One cannot but be struck by the extraordinary insinuation that relations were proper in the past, "forgetting" how the South African Security Forces used arms against fellow South Africans, and destabilized the surrounding countries in Southern Africa.

White revisionism

The creed reflects a trend to rewrite the history of the political struggle for freedom. The desperate riots of the suppressed people during apartheid are recast as willful, wanton acts of vandalism, whereas the apartheid regime is recast as a benevolent, appropriately disciplined/ing dispensation, which maintained law and order against the difficult odds presented to them by the insubordination and ungovernability of the black population.

Significantly, the negotiated outcome of the struggle prior to the establishment of democracy is similarly misrepresented in the phrase, "We gave you freedom." The collapse of the old regime – cast as an act of generosity on the part of white South Africa, a liberality verging on regrettable self-sacrifice and not the only option available to a failing regime – has disastrously unleashed the innate "Africanness" of the continent, leading to inevitable decline. Revisionist history whitewashes apartheid, now constructed as a benevolent time by comparison with the present. The denial is accompanied an astonishing ignorance – the author of *the creed of the white kid* has learnt nothing from the past, and white South Africa remains the "hope" for "sanity," redemption.

White grievances

The implication of the "apology" is that white South Africa has nothing to say sorry for; if anything the debt lies the other way round. The attempts at developing Africa have been unappreciated, and the civilizing mission has proved futile. White South Africans are now trapped in a country in invidious circumstances not of their own making, whereas Africans are getting what they deserve – their poverty is a just measure of their (lack of) worth, their moral depravity and lack of intelligence to grasp the basics of modernity. By contrast with this moral abyss, white value systems are seen as contemporary. Transformation, which seeks to afford recognition to all cultural traditions, is not only illogical, but also morally topsy-turvy, leaving all decency in disarray. This is illustrated particularly in the appeal to western, middle class family structures as the norm, implying a lesser attachment to loved ones in African society,[11] and emphasizing the victimization of innocent family life by the brutality now "legitimized" by the new order.

By inversion of logic, then, it is the white population that holds legitimate grievances not only in the present, but even for the past. From the dizzy moral highground, it is they who need to be forgiving, who carry the baggage of unpunished injustice, and are the recipients of gross violations, violence, and disappointment at being thwarted in their attempts to enact a noble mission in the third world.

White vindication

The prevalent stereotypes of black men as rapists, naturally crimenogenic, and now out of control – these important tropes of the racist imagination position whites as victims, and reveal a desire for more repressive measures, for harsher punishments directed at black people. The real miscarriage of justice/order occurs in that whites cannot act with impunity and carry out "proactive strikes," an orgy of racial revenge.

By means of further racist inversions, the necessity for power to rest with whites is "demonstrated." Power in the hands of black people is dangerous. Black people with power, almost by definition, are untrustworthy. They are corrupt, self-enriching, and lack the intellectual capacity for leadership. The idea of a black intellectual is a contradiction in terms. Political freedom for black people is to court lawlessness. Laws and constitutional rights for black people are seen as misguided. Legal protection renders them immune to "justice" – they cannot be dealt with as harshly as they deserve. The extension of rights to all is a miscarriage of justice, leading to triumphant smirking, and a refusal to take responsibility. These rights curb informal means of dispensing white power, and open the doors for state apparatuses to be misused. All of this, of course, is highly ironic, given that in the past, the state was the primary source of terror for the majority black population, and that the rights of white citizens are guaranteed by the current government.

The White Burden Endures

The familiar trope of Africa as the hopeless continent clearly underpins the "apology." The writer sees the Southern African region as a neighborhood sinking into a state of irredeemable chaos. He has an undifferentiated view of the complex and far from homogenous region, and gloats at difficulties experienced. He attributes problems to the exodus of white settlers, which he constructs as forced, rather than the continuation of the pattern of white flight seen in all African countries after independence. The only bastion of "progress" and good economic management in the region, by this account, was the Old South Africa. Again, this is an irony given the high growth rates in some of these African countries, including South Africa which has had its longest period of sustained economic growth in the period since 1994. His reference to "breeding like rabbits" recalls the manner in which racial competition in the country was cast as a battle of demographics during the apartheid years, the fear always being that "they" would "outbreed" the white population.

What is clear is that whites now have to concede defeat in their attempt to maintain 'civilization' against all odds – not through any fault of their own, but as a result of the sheer irredeemable lack of aptitude of black South Africans.

White Flight

The exodus of white South Africans through emigration is seen to be the simple result of affirmative action, further explained by infrastructural deterioration and crime. Whites are seen as playing/having played no role in the nation's current problems. There is no recognition that the old regime catered for only 3 million (white) people in its delivery of services, whereas the infrastructure has to be extended to serve the full 50 million of the population. Under current circumstances, the apologist suggests, white's skills are "more needed" in other countries. Within this rhetoric of injured self-righteousness, the choice to leave the country is a proper unwillingness to contribute to a society that is not "their" problem, a kind of noble banishment, the curse of a superior race misrecognized by their those not able to appreciate their value. By virtue of the European ancestors, though, such exiles can see themselves as a diaspora of a white racial community (Steyn, 2005). It is this connection which underwrites their legitimacy, and which extends a life line. They can reunite with their ancestral kin.

The final line of the apology refers to the growing pressure for racial integration in residences, and the general thrust towards desegregation of the society. The *Apology* casts this as an unreasonable expectation, an indignity, and clearly shows that he and those he identifies with are unwilling participants. In the scathing sarcasm of the "one big happy family" the blogger concludes by suggesting the impossibility of association, the outrageousness of expecting any common identification across the chasms of otherness he has demonstrated in his text. Reconciliation is fundamentally outside the realm of reasonableness, a new subjectivity is roundly rejected.

Conclusion

The intransigent *Apology* certainly does not represent the only answer to Lopéz's (2001) question: "What happens to whiteness, in other words, when it loses its colonial privilege?" In its blatancy, this *Apology* is probably quite shocking to many, possibly most, white South Africans. Yet it does contain discursive elements that are present in much *White Talk*, "common sense" generally couched within discourse that takes greater care with self-presentation (Steyn and Foster 2008) Peter's (2008) comment gives an example of how these accepted narratives need not sound reactionary:

> The essential problem is that the "creed" is correct, but not nice. So, that's something quite difficult to reconcile. Dealing with the not nice aspect alone is a lie and is incomplete. Any enduring reconciliation is going to have to find a way to integrate the reality of white accomplishment (Peter, 2008)

The *Creed* reveals a great deal about the subjectivity of this young white person, and of the "we" he purports to speak for. It is a subjectivity that remains trapped within the discourses of victim-aggressor, enabled by colonial expectations of white entitlement and even white supremacy. The world from which he speaks is white-identified, and white-centered (Johnson, 2001) even as white domination has waned. Despite the blatant racism present in the discourse, the subjectivity maintains a kind of racial innocence through the refusal to take responsibility, to engage with history and understand how he is positioned through colonial and apartheid legacy. All the discomfort, which he clearly feels, is attributable to the undesirable behavior of blacks, whereas any implication in injustice is deflected through denial and revision of the apartheid legacy. The multiple and complex causes of the challenges that face the society, many of which lie in the past brutalization and dehumanization of the population, and high levels of structurally induced poverty are absent from this mindspace. Pervasive belligerence, an aggression reconstituted as victimhood, which in turn allows a "retaliatory" aggression to be justified, and nursed, characterize the text. Indeed, the suggestion emerges that white aggression is needed to prevent decline and to defend innocent white people from the excesses of black abuse of power.

It seems sad that despite the fact that young people like the blogger were probably born as apartheid ended, they have no signifiers with which to imagine fundamentally different narratives about self, no tools with which to forge new relationships, or make sense of their positioning in hopeful ways. For these children of the apartheid-supporting generation, transformation is still the Other. Despite the (official) context of national reconciliation, the curious processes of intergenerational remembering the past that Jansen (2009) calls "bitter knowledge," foreclose the future for them. Within this limited horizon of possibility, only two prospects are rendered thinkable: alienation within, or "exile" outside the land of their birth.

Notes

1 In the 1960s white South Africans were approximately 20% of the total population. Currently they are estimated at 9.2% (Statistics South Africa, 2008b)
2 Influx control was an apartheid measure designed to keep black Africans separate and in "their own" areas. They could only enter white urban areas with a special permit to work as temporary migrant laborers, and would then be confined to living in townships outside the city. People found to be in violation of these laws were forcibly removed or imprisoned.
3 Depending on which measure you take, anywhere from 25–50% of the population.
4 The "Home for All" campaign, which attempted to get whites to sign an apology is a case in point.
5 It looks like a stew. The commentary provided by the students making the video is that as they were preparing this for "previously disadvantaged" (black) people, they need some nutrition, and therefore it is meat.
6 The students who made the video afterwards claimed that it was not urine, but in fact water from a hidden bottle that had been poured into the "food."
7 Similar to the American Oath of Allegiance.
8 According to the announcement in the government gazette on February 22, 2008, the objectives of the Pledge are:
   a To promote civic participation and responsibility among young people;
   b To evoke national pride and unity; and
   c To promote social cohesion and nation-building.
9 The motto on the South African Coat of Arms, which is in the language of one of the San groups, who are the original inhabitants of Southern Africa and have First Nation status.
10 The prayer, *God Bless Africa*, which is a refrain in the South African national anthem.
11 For example, in 2008 the journalist David Bullard wrote a column in the *Sunday Times* in which he attributed brutish lack of family feeling to pre-colonial African society. His column was withdrawn after public outcry, but he retains his popularity among white South Africans, especially.

References

Ashcroft, B., Griffiths, G., and Tiffen, H. (1995) *The Post-Colonial Studies Reader*, Routledge, New York.
Ben-Ariel, D. (2008) *Hillary Clinton*. Hillary Clinton: The dumb white kid, March 10, http://clintonhillary.blogspot.com/2008/03/dumb-white-kid.html (accessed May 27, 2010).

Cash, J. (2004) The political/cultural unconscious and the process of reconciliation. *Postcolonial Studies*, 7 (2), 165–175.

Castle, G. (2001) *Postcolonial Discourses: An Anthology*, Blackwell, Oxford.

Chris (2008) The new pledge for SA school KIDS. The Dumb White Kid, March 6, http://blogs.24.com/ViewComments.aspx?blogid=b3d88ca0-dcf3-4005-a4fd-4cd46a8e519dandmid=358bcfa9-7640-4a3b-b565-d3d80ef2d451 (last accessed March 30, 2008).

CNN (2008, February 28) Whites tricked blacks into consuming urine, university says, CNN.com/world, www.cnn.com/2008/WORLD/africa/02/27/saf.racist.video/index.html#cnnSTCText (accessed May 27, 2010).

Dellie (2008) The dumb white kid, March 3, Dellie se Dinge, http://delliesedinge.wordpress.com/2008/03/03/the-dumb-white-kid/ (accessed May 27, 2010).

Fanon, F. (1965/1961) *The Wretched of the Earth*, (trans. C. Farrington), Penguin Books, London.

Fanon, F. (1967/1952) *Black Skin, White Masks*, (trans. C.L. Markmann), Grove Press, New York.

Foster, D.H. (2006) Social change and contact: Macro-political considerations. Unpublished keynote address, Contact 50 Conference, Ithala Game Lodge, KwaZulu-Natal, July, 6–9.

fuzzyskwerl (2008) *The "RACIST" University video South Africa!! Full Un-edited*, YouTube, February 28, www.youtube.com/watch?v=e8N-h8anSuEandfeature=related (last accessed October 15, 2008).

Hasian Jr., M. (2001) Rhetorical Studies and the future of postcolonial theories and practices. *Rhetoric Review*, 20, 1/2, 22–28.

Hawkey, K. (2009) The day the devil got into Johan Nel. *The Times*, January 19.

Hegde, R.S. (1998) A view from elsewhere: Locating difference and the politics of representation from a transnational feminist perspective, in *International and Intercultural Communication Annual*, 21, 11–33.

Jansen, J. D. (2009) *Knowledge in the Blood: Confronting Race and the Apartheid Past*, Stanford University Press, Stanford, CA.

Johnson, A.G. (2001) *Privilege, Power and Difference*, New York: McGraw-Hill.

Kapur, R. (2005) *Erotic Justice: Law and the New Politics of Postcolonialism*, Glass House Press, London.

Kassiem, A. (2008) It's not too late, say sorry for apartheid. *Independent Online*, February 28, http://www.iol.co.za/index.php?set_id=1andclick_id=13andart_id=vn20080228034 706653C206125 (last accessed October 10, 2008).

Kruger, B. (2008) This was read and talked about on radio this morning, stormfront.org, March 17, http://www.stormfront.org/forum/showthread.php?p=5258547 (accessed May 27, 2010).

Lopéz, A.J. (2001) *Posts and Pasts: A Theory of Postcolonialism*, SUNY Press, Albany, NY.

Magubane, B. (1999) The African Renaissance in historical perspective, in *The African Renaissance: The New Struggle*, (ed. M.W. Makgoba), Tafelberg, Cape Town, pp. 10–36.

Peter (2008) musings-in-mzansi-racism-cyberspace. *History Matters*: a blog promoting citizenship and democracy in South Africa, http://historymatters.co.za (accessed May 27, 2010).

Quayson, A., and Goldberg, D.T. (2002) Introduction, in *Relocating Postcolonialism*, (eds A. Quayson, and D.T. Goldberg), Blackwell, Oxford, pp. xi–xiii.

Rosenberg, L. (2008, Aug 14) Musings in Mzansi: Racism in cyberspace. *History Matters: A blog promoting citizenship and democracy in South Africa*, August 14, http://historymatters.co.za/2008/08/14/musings-in-mzansi-racism-cyberspace/ (accessed May 27, 2010).

Rudd, K. (2008, February 13) *Apology to Australia's Indigenous Peoples*, Prime Minister of Australia, http://www.pm.gov.au/media/speech/2008/speech_0073.cfm (last accessed February 20, 2008).

SAPA (2008a) Anger as Skierlik shooting accused referred to Weskoppies. *The Cape Times*, February 13, p. 4.

SAPA (2008b) Skierlik accused pleads innocence. *Pretoria News*, April 15, p. 1.

Shoma, R. (1996) Postcolonial interventions in the Rhetorical canon: An "other" view. *Communication Theory*, 6, 40–59.

Statistics South Africa (2008a) *Income and Expenditure of Households 2005/2006*, Statistics South African, Pretoria.

Statistics South Africa (2008b) *Mid-year Population Estimates 2008*. Statistics South African, Pretoria.

Steyn, M. (2005) White talk: White South Africans and the strategic management of diasporic whiteness, in *Postcolonial Whiteness*, (ed. A. Lopéz), SUNY Press, Albany, NY, pp. 119–136.

Steyn, M., and Foster, D. (2008) Repertoires for talking white: Resistant whiteness in post-apartheid South Africa. *Ethnic and Racial Studies*, 31 (1), 25–51.

Stokes, M. (2001) *The Color of Sex: Whiteness, Heterosexuality, and the Fictions of White Supremacy*, Duke University Press, Durham and London.

Supriya, K. (1996) Confessionals, testimonials: Women's speech in/and contexts of violence. *Hypatia*, 11, 92–106.

The Associated Press (2008) New Zealand gives Maori tribes forest in largest-ever settlement, June 25, *International Herald Tribune: Asia-Pacific*, http://www.iht.com/articles/2008/06/25/asia/maori.php (accessed May 27, 2010).

Venn, C. (2006) *The Postcolonial Challenge: Towards Alternative Worlds*, Sage, London.

Wolmerans, R., and SAPA (2008, February 28) Free State four: We didn't urinate on meat, February 28, *Mail and Guardian Online*, http://www.mg.co.za/article/2008-02-28-free-state-four-we-didnt-urinate-on-meat (accessed May 27, 2010).

World Wide White (2008) Stormfront South Africa, stormfront.org, June 24, http://www.stormfront.org/forum/showthread.php/reponse-not-too-late-say-500811.html (last accessed October 21, 2008).

32

A Critical Reflection on an Intercultural Communication Workshop
Mexicans and Taiwanese Working on the US-Mexico Border

Hsin-I Cheng

I arose early. It was a big day. After double-checking my I-20 and passport, I was on my way to Juárez Mexico. Riding along with Mr. Lee, the Managerial Director and my relative in the company's Toyota Avalon, we approached the border. Entering Mexico from El Paso Texas by car entailed passing through the traffic-light-like device with red and green lights. The red light went on, so Mr. Lee parked the car to the side and opened the trunk with only two laptop carriers inside. I then realized why Mr. Lee had told me to put all my carry-ons in the trunk. The officer glanced at the bags, the light switched to green, and we drove away. It was a stress-free process as Mr. Lee said "they just need to take a quick look. They know we're here to work, and won't give us any trouble." About 20 minutes into Mexico, we arrived at a bluish-gray building surrounded by a white metal fence. The guard waved at us while opening the gate for us. Mr. Lee said "Buenos Dias" to him as we drove in. It was around 8:20 am and a few cars, mostly Toyotas were in the parking lot already. The total land area of the plant was 205 555 sq ft and the building area was 106 000 sq ft. We went directly upstairs to the office area with approximately 25 desks adjacent to each other. There was virtually no decoration on the off-white walls. A few potted plants sat around the corner right in front of the restrooms. A few managers were getting ready for the day by making tea or coffee. After introducing me to the managers, I was shown to a conference room. It was quiet there except for pounding of keys at computer stations and the noise of coffee being brewed. A Taiwanese manager Tom brought me a cup of coffee and said "Have a cup. It's good; I only drink Starbucks." The aroma permeated the office area where the managers worked.

The Handbook of Critical Intercultural Communication, edited by Thomas K. Nakayama and Rona Tamiko Halualani. © 2010 Blackwell Publishing Ltd.

Border Factories

With the implementation of the North American Free Trade Agreement (NAFTA) in 1994 and a treaty between the US, Canadian and Mexican governments that eliminates tariffs on products and offers easier restrictions on the mobility of business executives and professionals (Myers, 1998), the faces on the border have become much more diverse. This treaty also increased the involvement of Pacific Rim countries in the US-Mexico borderlands. With close to 3000 assembly plants, more than 328 000 people are employed and trade between the United States and Mexico had exceeded US$121 billion in 2001 (*Report to Congressional Requesters* 2003). There are more than 400 gated plants in Chihuahua, Mexico like the one I entered. Every morning, vehicles travel through the border checking point like the one that I crossed. These *maquiladoras* not only create more economic contacts between various countries, but also intercultural interactions.

Taiwan is among the Asian countries including Japan and South Korea that have established *maquiladoras* – assembly factories that enjoy special duty-free status. Pac Tide is one of these Taiwanese-based electronic multinational companies (MNC).[1] The company was founded in the late 1970s and established itself in Asia, Europe, and North America within two decades. At the turn of the twenty-first century, Pac Tide established its first plant in Juárez, Mexico, with approximately 300 employees. The mission for the *maquiladora* at Juárez was to provide immediate service for the US customer, benefited by its geographical immediacy. The company included a training department that developed various training programs for building job skills and language capabilities.

In mid-2002, I was contacted by a relative Mr. Lee, who was assigned as a Managerial Director (MD) at the Juárez plant. After sharing his frustration with the communicative problems between the Taiwanese and Mexican managers, I agreed to design an intercultural workshop. The goal for the workshop was, in the Cargile and Giles (1996) sense, to "teach people to think and behave as individuals from different cultural groups might think and behave" (p. 386). In the following, I will first briefly describe the development and content of the intercultural workshop to illustrate the theoretical perspective. A reflection based on Foucauldian discipline and critique of neoliberalism will address what occurred during my visit as a facilitator of the workshop. It invites interrogation of ways in which multilayered power is expressed, articulated, and struggled in daily communication at the *maquiladora* owned by a Taiwan-based MNC in the world of globalization.

Designing an Intercultural Communication Workshop

In October 2002, I started to gather information from the managers with surveys to understand better the general perceptions and attitudes held in this multinational company. Until then, much of the intercultural/cross-cultural training research focused on intercultural communication between US or European employees working in Latin

American or Asian countries as a consequence of the rapid economic growth of Pacific Rim counties (Bhagat and Prien 1996). There was scarce scholarship on interactions in multinational corporations where people from Latin and Asian nations work together on daily basis.

Black and Mendenhall (1989) commented that previous research of intercultural training methods suggests that the degree to which trainees are required to interact with the host culture and the similarity between their native culture and the new culture are two foci in an intercultural training program. Such programs expose trainees to domains such as simple factual knowledge, applicable skills, and participatory engagements. However, Bhagat and Prien (1996) pointed out that such a framework assumes that knowledge acquisition leads to a change in attitudes. They provided a new theoretical approach that facilitates attributes on the individual-level (e.g., cognitive flexibility, familial support); job-level (e.g., training for complicated skills); organizational-level (e.g., integration of the overall institutional missions and strategies); and cultural-level (e.g., differences between the host and the native country). This model provides a more comprehensive adjustment to a novel environment.

Knowledge of both the subjective culture (e.g., norms and belief systems) and norms the objective culture (e.g., foods, infrastructures, and clothing) in the host country facilitates the expatriates' adjustment to the new environment. However, as Chang and Holt (1997) and Lindsley (1999a) suggested, intercultural (mis) communication is never ahistorical nor decontextualized. Any intercultural training program needs to consider the impact of unbalanced power relations on both individual and institutional levels. Chang and Holt wrote:

> complicating factors such as power, attributions, stereotypes, and ingroup/outgroup distinction are less matters of cultural difference (such elements are generally acknowledged to be universal) than outgrowths of historical conflict and struggle that are worked out in contexts in which interactions take place ... through the focus provided by immediate contact between members of two cultures, power and politics originating in sociohistorical context are brought into the present situation. Therefore, a satisfactory explanation of intercultural interaction must push further into the realms of power and political reality (1997, p. 225).

Chang and Holt contend the necessity of incorporating issues of power in the intercultural training program where questions such as "what do people do about these cultural differences and why?" are addressed (1997, p. 223). Such practice is however difficult to carry out, for the possible danger of creating an uncomfortable atmosphere in the training process (Chang and Holt, 1997; Foeman, 1997; Leeds-Hurwitz, 1997). Lindsley (1999a) proposed a layered model in which socio, political and historical factors were contextualized during her examination of problematic interactions at a US-owned *maquiladora* in Mexico. These layers include (1) macrocontext such as group and intergroup histories; (2) individual's (in)competencies such as cultural knowledge, language skills and stereotypes that underlie the problematic interactions; (3) the dyadic communicative behaviors that negotiate individual and organizational cultural identities; and (4) the attribution of perceptual, metaperceptual, and metarelational meanings in intercultural encounters. Lindsley (1999a) concluded that these four interlocking layers address the roots of problematic communication in which more factors than simply the lack of cultural knowledge could explain. Her model in some sense addressed Chang and Holt's concerns about the consequences of omitting power as a factor in intercultural training programs. The significance of looking at how power plays as a presupposition (e.g., stereotypes, historical and political inequality, unbalanced economical status, identity negotiation) that affects intercultural interactions may shed light on how cultural differences can be discussed in the training process.

These perspectives delineate a picture that when expatriates come to a host culture, they need to acquire the ability to appreciate novelty, to learn the skills to perform the job, to obtain cultural knowledge of native culture(s), and to gain perspectives as to why these cultural differences may lead to undesired communicative outcomes with attention paid to the attribute of power inequality. Thus, the focus on expanding the participants' perceptions toward the historical and political backgrounds of their cultural counterpart is as important as the focus on equipping individuals with the ability and awareness to adjust to the new environment.

In order to identify issues affecting managers at the Pac Tide plant in Juárez, a survey was distributed to gain basic demographic information and cultural knowledge and perceptions of the Mexican and Taiwanese managers toward their counterparts. Their feedback suggested prevalent misconceptions toward each other. For example, conflicting statements were issued such as "Mexicans are stubborn" by a Taiwanese manager and "Mexicans are open to learn" by a Mexican manager. Another example is "Mexicans are lazy and slow" from a Taiwanese manger while a Mexican manager wrote "Mexicans are present oriented." Misunderstanding also existed in how Taiwanese were understood such as "Taiwanese are disciplined and follow the rules" by a Mexican manager while "Taiwanese are flexible" by a Taiwanese manager. Furthermore, only a few mentioned heterogeneity within groups classified by nationalities. Drawn from the responses, two domains were constructed to address perceived intercultural communicative issues: (1) major cultural themes of both Mexican and Taiwanese cultures; and (2) critical instances to practice knowledge learned. The workshop was to combine cognitive information with behavioral exercise.

Mexican cultural themes

It has been long argued that cultures are not merely static entities which can be analyzed without contextualization (Drzewiecka and Halualani, 2002; Halualani, 2008; Lindsley, 1999a; Martin and Nakayama, 1999; Moon, 2002; Ono, 1998). Contemporary Mexican lives are influenced by multiple cultural and political sovereignties (Covarrubias, 2002; Gannon, 2001b; Martínez, 2001; Ortíz-González, 2004). Spanish rule in the 1500s introduced Roman Catholicism and exacerbated the existing hierarchical structure in Mayan civilization (600–900 BCE) and the Aztecs (1100s–1500s CE). These influences remain prevalent in today's Mexico. Following

Spain, the French occupied Mexico (1830–1860) where the stratified hierarchy was further reinforced. Since the war between the United States and Mexico from 1846–1848, the US has been influential in political and material involvement in Mexico such as the plethora of American-owned *maquiladoras* in the border area after 1964. Throughout Mexico's long history, there have been foreign powers influencing its culture, society, politics and consequently, their communication. These influences produced interrelated characteristics in which Mexicans show a strong belief in hierarchy and *palanca*. Interpersonal relationships and stability are highly valued with a present orientation (Albert, 1996; Archer and Fitch, 1994; Gannon, 2001b; Levine, 1997; Lindsley, 1999b; Lindsley and Braithwaite, 1996, 2003). A brief discussion of this cultural salience offers a glimpse into the working environment at this *maquilla*.

The concept of *padrinazgo* is a recurrent theme across research. According to Archer and Fitch (1994) and Gannon (2001b), the historical *patrón* (owner of the workers) system is inherited from the colonial era. Within the patrón system, the workers lack resources compared to their upper class *patrones*. A *palanca* serves as a connection to help the worker to achieve individual objectives. The workers then exchange favors such as labor in return. Gannon (2001b) points out that Mexicans tend to hire their relatives and friends over strangers. This illustrates the web of human relations that stems from Mexican social and political history throughout the centuries. The sense of building personal connections via giving, receiving, or returning favors indicates the informal information flow in the Mexican culture.

The importance of connections in human relationships creates an emphasis on communication competency. Gannon (2001b) explains that "Mexicans tend to view success in terms of affiliation rather than achievement ... A manager should rarely, if ever, criticize a subordinate in front of his or her friends or family" (p. 358). Such inscriptions echoes Albert's (1996) explanation that Mexican children are socialized with the traditional values of respect and criticism or insults are perceived as a great lack of respect for another person's dignity. Mexicans place high value on how to treat people with respect in all contexts (Lindsley and Braithwaite, 2003). The focus on relationships strengthens the concept of *confianza* or trust in Mexican culture. By adhering to the cultural merit that focuses on people, good relationships are built and *confianza* is earned. People from outside the culture can gain trust from the Mexicans by paying close attention to both nonverbal and verbal behaviors to cultivate a stable relationship. Family is prioritized as it provides stability in peoples' lives (Lindsley, 1999b; Lindsley and Braithwaite, 2003). The aforementioned *padrinazgo* system and the concept of *palancas* exemplify the stable relationships where the distinction between familial and organizational roles is often blurred in Mexican culture. By building trust and confidence through an interconnected network such as managers giving employees favors (e.g., help for gaining accesses, financial loans), a stable and family-like organizational relationship is established to reduce uncertainty in economic and political structures. Religious institution plays another significant role in providing stability for relationship building. With strong religious influence, the Mexican concept of time is as something present to be lived and enjoyed instead of controlled (Levine, 1997).

Taiwanese cultural themes

A sociopolitical perspective would also enhance an understanding of Taiwanese cultural salience, which was inevitably brought into the working environment at the US-Mexico border. Located just off the southeast China coast facing its Fu-Jien Province separated by the Taiwan Strait, Taiwan is an island that stretches nearly 245 miles long and approximately 90 miles wide. Since the sixteenth century, Taiwan has been the target of colonizers for its strategic and mercantile location (Chen and Reisman, 1972; Cooper, 2003). It had been occupied by the Spaniards, Dutch, Chinese, and Japanese. After WWII, its political identity has been a struggle even until now. The issues of "two Chinas" remain unsolved (Chan and Cheng, 2002; Chang and Holt, 1996; Cooper, 2003; Davison, 2003; Lee and Barnett, 1997; Ng, 1998). Due to Taiwan's ambiguous political status, Taiwanese business conduct has been indirect and circumscribed.

Regardless of Taiwan's ambivalent status, Taiwan has achieved economic success (Chang and Holt, 1997; Chen and Chung, 1994; Gannon, 2001a, b; Hofstede and Bond, 2001; Lee and Barnett, 1997; Williams and Bent, 1997). Chen and Chung (1994) articulated the relationships between the economical success of Asian countries and Confucian cultural teachings. Confucianism stresses the importance of each individual to recognize his/her role in society and relationships, because relationships are key to maintaining stability and harmony in society (Williams and Bent, 1997). Four characteristics including hierarchy, responsibility, trust, and harmony exist in Taiwanese culture that occur in "relationships" during everyday conduct.

There are five major hierarchical relationships, *Wu Lun*,[2] that regulate human behaviors in all contexts. The importance of the family is revealed as four of the five relationships occur within the family and can be perceived as the basis in Chinese managing philosophy (Chen and Chung, 1994). According to Chang and Holt (1996) this so-called "family orientation" of including the employee's family members in Taiwanese business practice illustrates that employers value interconnection (*guanxi*) highly which consequently secures the working environment. It is a way to create workers' loyalty and responsibility to the company as it is not just the individual employee that makes a commitment to the company but also family members. If the employee fails the task, it would be the face of her/his family members or very close friends that is at risk. As Yu (2000) states "the workplace is a web of strong interrelated and interdependent interpersonal relationships throughout the levels of the organizational hierarchy" (p. 124). By achieving the goals assigned to them, the employees fulfill the obligations to their managers. It is seen as helping out a family member or close friend. This makes it difficult for workers to separate their personal and professional lives.

As a culture with distinct boundaries between ingroups and outgroups (Samovar and Porter 2003), Chinese in Taiwan would feel responsibility for all their relationships, that is, the groups they are in. Achieving the assigned tasks shows not only loyalty but also of being a *jun tze* who is responsible for all the interconnected relationships of her/his groups (Yu, 2000). As Williams and Bent (1997) suggest, Chinese people would put their personal interests after the collective goals and trust group members with personal material resources or information. In showing trust and loyalty by prioritizing group goals, harmony is kept within the group. As Gannon (2001b) points out, Taoism and Buddhism, in some ways, complement Confucian teaching such as rejecting any form of assertiveness and competition and seek no individual desires in order to keep group harmony. These philosophical and religious beliefs influence how Chinese in Taiwan may approach work, interpersonal relationships, and being. However, Lee and Barnett (1997) remind us of the possibility that there are some young managers who are probably less influenced by these ways, for "Taiwanese organizations have always been bombarded by American and Japanese cultural influences" (p. 406). With the cultural influences of MNCs in Taiwan, it is important to keep in mind that the Taiwanese organizational culture may have incorporated both the old and new.

When Mexican and Taiwanese managers work together

Lindsley's (1999a) layered model reminded and rendered explanations as to why problematic communication occurs rather than a fixed formula with these conflicts. Based on the historicized cultural patterns discussed above, several overlapping areas are incorporated into designing activities for the workshop. There is a shared emphasis on: (a) family oriented organizational structure; (b) developing trusting interpersonal relationships; and (c) harmony and stability as the foundation of all matters. This is not to claim that there is no difference between these two cultural outlooks. Rather, similar values are indeed practiced and carried out in different ways. For example, Taiwanese were perceived as putting work before family needs. However, for Taiwanese, it might be the very reason to work diligently in order to provide for and bring honor to the family in an ambivalent sociopolitical environment. In a similar vein, the interpretation of Mexicans as lazy and less aggressive workers omitted their strong values of spending quality time with family members in the present when other events are out of personal control. It was the overlapping yet contradicting contextualized values that the workshop intended to address. However, unequal past and present geopolitical power permeates inside and outside the maquila in which intercultural learning is intertwined with the macrostructural parameter. Consequently, a critical reflection is imperative to rethink the meaning of working together in a multinational company on the US-Mexico border.

Between Developing and Delivering the Workshop

The workshop was scheduled at 1.00 pm. Before the workshop, I had an opportunity to converse with Jiménez, the HR manager. Jiménez was educated in Mexico and had several years of work experience at another MNC owned by a US/European company. Appearing to be in his 50s with Anglo features, he said "most of our on-line operators are young girls, an average of 16, 17 years old. They came from southern Mexico looking for a golden opportunity to marry some Americans and then move to America. We offer English and GED equivalent programs for them to have at least a high school degree. I told them to have an education, but very few attend, they just want to find someone to marry and move to America."

After our conversation, I went back to my room and stared at my paper where I explained the concept of simpatía with a quote from a manager in a previous study:

> If a person is an assembly line operator, they may not think that they achieve a great future. They may not be very motivated in their jobs because they think they will be doing this same thing all their lives. What you intended to do is to teach the employee how to have a better life. Ask them to stay after work, with no pay, to teach [them] other skills. Train them for a new position after work or encourage the employee to go to school, improve their education. This is what helps motivate employees (Lindsley, 1999b p. 17).

Deep in my thinking, Mr. Lee came to invite me for lunch at the cafeteria. I was led downstairs where the on-line operators worked. There were more than a hundred of them in their uniform of white coat, blue hair cap, clear goggles, and gloves. Walking parallel to the assembling lines, I learned that "the Mexican government has strict labor laws to protect their workers. We are required to have transportation, food, and on-site medical care. We have to provide breakfast and lunch daily. Mexican workers have it better than even those in Taiwan. They also know their rights very well. If we don't comply, someone would tell on us (laugh)."

I probably appeared disoriented as I tried to comprehend his words amid the Spanish radio music and machine noise. The MD tried to help me to reorient myself. "Up there is management offices" he said while pointing to the area above my head. There is a huge tinted glass window from which the managers could look down at the operators but not the other way around. The operators were aware of this uni-directional glass. We moved along to the cafeteria where a television played novellas. I later learned that whenever the on-line production meets expectations, music is played for the workers for ten minutes as a reward.

Soon, it was workshop time. During a simulation with a case study on communicating criticism, a Taiwanese manager Peter called on another manager Herman. As Herman was sharing the way to provide suggestions in private, suddenly, Peter interjected "Herman, you have an American passport right? So are you a Mexican or an American?" Herman did not respond. The silence lasted for some seconds as I was figuring out a way to redirect the conversation back to the discussion.

Finally, the workshop was done. Several Mexican (American) managers stayed and talked with me for quite some time. I received thanks and also information on how Mother's Day is "the holiday" to be celebrated. After packing up, I was happy overall with the outcome of the workshop since I had received immediate invitations for more in the coming summer. Going downstairs toward the exit, which was a different door from the entrance, I saw a security guard by the metal detector. Not knowing what to do, I followed other managers. First, I took out my laptop. Then I took out all items in my pocket and placed them on the table and opened my bag for inspection. Last, he waved the metal wand around my arms and legs. It was explained to me that this inspection was added after several thefts during the past few months. The company lost many CPUs that are tiny in size but great in value.

Layered Control via Multiple Gaze

Throughout the visit, I witnessed "transparency as discipline" as Foucault (1980) explicated. These on-line operators encountered the power of gaze in their daily work. On the floor, there were supervisors walking around to ensure production and provide assistance. In addition to the bodies of the supervisors, the operators were conscious of the gaze from behind the tinted glass. This "all-seeing power" (Foucault, 1980, p. 152) is integrated into the physical space in which double vision was performed in a different fashion (Dreyfus and Rabison, 1983). Although the plant is not structured with windows on both sides, in fact there are no windows to the outside, the visibility on the operators is immense. In that space each operator occupies a particular spot/machine which translates her into a numeric symbol serving to achieve the utmost economical production power. Under this highly detailed and calculative "micropower" the disciplined docile body is created. Through repeated actions of arm/finger movements, the on-line operator's body turns into an object that simultaneously engages in generating greater power for this disciplinary machine. Their fingers and arms are inseparably integrated and fixed in the position to the assembling lines which produce a maximum amount of computer chips. When this happens, the music blasts as if the operators' fingers push the play button. All this seems to function flawlessly in a self-sustaining fashion without much apparent interference. The on-line workers are isolated and confined to the area under constant watch. When they physically leave their work for home, the final gaze is performed in the security checkpoint as a reminder of the kind of power the MNC holds over their bodies. The disciplinary technique is realized in meticulous calculation, control, examination, and surveillance.

This dominance is not to be viewed as omniscient or complete. The capitalistic division on gendered labor has been the focus of much poststructural feminist critique. The imperialistic ideology of how women's bodies and temperament are more suited for assembling factories is under much challenge (Lim, 2003; Ong 1991; Salzinger, 2003; Wright, 2003). The hierarchical patriarchic dichotomy between the emotional and less-skilled female body versus the rational minds of their counterparts is created for subjugation as Ong (1991) asserts that "transnational capitalism has produced ... discourses that naturalize the subordination of women in industrial enterprise" (p. 291). After the conversation with Jiménez described above, I was perplexed as to how to make sense of what I read from previous research and heard from others' experiences. Jiménez proclaimed that the young female workers lacked interest in attending educational programs offered free at cost outside their work time. Rather, they hoped to settle down North of Cd. Juárez. Under the mentality of *padrinazgo* where managers played the role of upper class *patrones*, they would practice *simpatía* and *palanca* to help the worker to achieve her/his objectives such as jobs, services, or authorizations. What Jiménez wanted for the operators was justifiable. However, it might be over-simplistic to position them as too young and naïve to know their best interests. This view overlooks the young women's ability to assert resistance to the exploitation that they experience on a daily basis.

Women factory workers demonstrate their agency in ways that are often omitted (Lim, 2003; Ong, 1991; Shi, 2008; Vila, 2003). In the eyes of both Jiménez and the manager in Lindsley's (1999b) study, education such as English and higher skill-focused literacy is the imperative route for these young female employees. To stray from this path may be self-destructive or innocent at best. However, as the MD shared, the on-line operators are knowledgeable about their rights and would "turn the management in" to the Labor Department if there is a violation on the employer's part. Some researchers have reported that the employees in *maquilas* are informed about their rights offered by the Mexican Federal Labor Law (Dawlatshahi, 2001; Sargent and Matthews, 1999). Hence, these young women are not ignorant of their conditions. Lim (2003) and Ong (1991) both detailed how young factory female workers in less capitalistic societies assert their subjectivity in ways that might not be recognizable in the traditional class or gender consciousness. They perform "embodied desires" (Ong, 1991, p. 296) in which a stronger sense of self is expressed through doubting the management, tactically manipulating stereotypes of being female, and even their appearance to show their autonomy (see Wright, 2003, 2006). The ways in which female *maquila* workers engage and experience in the multilayered exploitative systems can only be unpacked by viewing transnational corporations as not only the perpetrators but also a product of neoliberalism. In the multilayered system of exploitation and resistance various imperial, patriarchic, and capitalist forces simultaneously feed in and detract from one another (Bourdieu, 1998; Harvey, 2005; Larner, 2006; Lim, 2003; Ong, 1991).

The transnational managers in the workshop are not merely workers at a *maquila* in Cd. Juárez. Whether being a manager of Mexican, Taiwanese, or American nationality, their identity is to be viewed in relation to the deterritorialized structure of an economic-politically connected global market. In the awkward moment when Peter who was on a temporary US working visa pointed out Herman's flexible status as someone who has both Mexican and US nationalities, identity as an intersected and fluid zone was in contestation. Any treatment toward a manager based on his/her nationality neglects the complexity of identities. Furthermore, the notion of host culture versus that of the newcomers is ever more volatile in this context. Sorrell (2008) lucidly argued for interactive dynamism in the globalized world where both travelers and residents engage in intercultural learning and adaptation. On this particular territory of maquila much movement occurs on a daily basis. Highlighting cultural salience based on national characteristics and traditions for the workshop runs the risk of essentializing the exceedingly interactive culturing processes. In so doing I left out a significant terrain of forces such as capitalist practices and ideology which was actively engaged in and resisted at various times and degrees. Under the mentality that economic agency leads to social mobility the managers of all nationalities in this MNC may share a similar attitude toward management or career goals. Some may believe what Sargent and Matthews (1999) found in their research on how employees in the Cd. Juárez and Cd. Chihuahua view the relative attractiveness of the maquila jobs. They reported that many employees were positive overall toward the benefits of transportation, food, onsite medical care, and the considerably high minimum wage provided by multinational corporations. Regardless of how applicable this finding is to the particular maquila I visited, each individual holds multiple positionalities that may be altered with new experiences. The MNC plant is a microcosm of a globalized world where histories, politics, and economic imbalance is interactive with identities and relationship formations.

Conclusion

This essay provides a prolegomenon where I reflect on an intercultural workshop designed and delivered to facilitate better intercultural communication between managers working together at a Taiwan-based MNC. Due to the global economic policies, the Mexican electronic industry has lost business to Asian and Central American countries because of cheaper labor (Hall, 2002; Millman, 2002). This new competition has led to massive layoffs as the Mexican authority states: "more than 350 maquiladoras have been shuttered, many of them bound for Asia.... At least 240 000 maquiladora jobs [which was a fifth of the total workforce in the Mexico economy] have been lost" since 2001 (Hall, 2002). Such a condition suggests the importance of generating more intercultural understanding in MNCs that established *maquiladoras* without much previous economic, social, or political contact with Mexico in hopes of more sustainable relationships. More specifically, this intercultural training aimed to build understanding between two cultural groups, Mexican and Taiwanese, to decrease their communicative problems at Pac Tide in Juárez, Mexico. Since previous studies focused mostly on generating intercultural competence for members from the two ends of the continuum between the eastern collectivistic cultures and the individualistic west,[3] this study initiates a dialogue in which two cultures, both classified as collectivistic (Hofstede and Bond, 2001), encounter each other in an organizational global context. In showing how homogenous and heterogeneous these employees at the MNC are historically, socially, politically, and economically this study intends to demonstrate the intricacy and complexity of the intercultural communicative process which cannot be easily simplified by a do and do not list based on any essentialized identification.

This is not to deny that certain memberships do carry actual privileges and material impacts on the less resourceful, particularly the on-line operators. Rather it points to the contradictory, fragmented, and overlapping economic, social, and cultural current present in intercultural engagements.

Although the actual effects of intercultural trainings are yet to be proven, the failure of expatriate assignments represents larger problems and complexities in the macro (e.g., sociohistorical contexts) and micro (e.g., individual adapting abilities) levels of intercultural communication (Lindsley 1999b) and therefore, this needs to be carefully investigated. In the process of preparing and delivering the workshop, I realized that in addition to asking who works together at the company, questions such as "What parameters do people work under?" and "What end do people work toward?" need to be raised. I envisioned with the assumption that by designing a workshop where individual, sociohistorical, and cultural issues are addressed knowledge and behavioral adjustment would be likely to follow. Yet the *maquiladora* is, in a way, a "transcultural contact zone" (Pratt, 1999) where new agency is cultivated and shifted in daily interactions. Treating participants based on either national or gender identity risks missing an opportunity to address undercurrent influences and structures present in daily interactions. Treaties such as NAFTA supported by multiple neoliberal governments have implications on workers unbound by nation states as Bourdieu (1998) describes. A workshop intending to improve intercultural communication cannot neglect the fundamental arrangement of a multinational corporation based on meticulous calculations and micro control of human labor/energy. As I experienced in the intercultural workshop this structure permeates the air breathed by all.

Notes

1 Pac Tide is a pseudo name for the company in order to maintain confidentiality.
2 The five relationships of Wu Lun are: ruler/subject, father/son, husband/wife, older brother/younger brother, and between friends. These relationships are unequal and complementary in keeping social order and harmony: the rulers are to show justice, subjects to show loyalty; fathers to show love, sons to show filial piety; husbands to show initiation, wives to show obedience; older brothers to show brotherly love, younger brothers to show reverence; and friends to show mutual trust. They serve as basic rules that apply to all human relationships.
3 For example, Domsch and Lichtenberger's (1991) study on German MNCs' employees in China and Brazil; Gregersen and Black's (1992) studies on various organizations in Europe and Asia; Harrison's (1992) study on employees of US military in Japan; Thomas and Ravlin's (1995) study on US employees work at Japanese-owned firms; Earley's (1987) study on US electronics firm in Korea; Bhagat and Prien (1996) pointed to Naumann's study of employees in US MNCs in Hong Kong, Korea, Taiwan, and China. Kim and Paulk's (1994) study investigated Americans working with Japanese. Based on Hofstede and Bond (2001) scores, these studies seem to have the countries of individualism and those of collectivism in comparison for amending intercultural misunderstanding.

References

Albert, R.D. (1996) A framework and model for understanding Latin American and Latino/ Hispanic cultural patterns, in *Handbook of Intercultural Training*, (eds D. Landis and R.S. Bhagat), Sage, Thousand Oaks, pp. 327–348.

Archer, L., and Fitch, K. (1994) Communication in Latin American multinational organizations, in *Communicating in Multinational Organizations*, (eds R.L. Wiseman and R. Shuter), Sage, Thousand Oaks, CA, pp. 75–93.

Bhagat, R., and Prien, K. (1996) Cross-cultural training in organizational contexts, *Handbook of Intercultural Training*, (eds, D. Landis and R.S. Bhagat), Sage, Thousand Oaks, pp. 216–230.

Black, S., and Mendenhall, M. (1989) Practical but theory-based framework for selecting cross-cultural training methods. *Human Resource Management*, 28, 511–539.

Bourdieu, P. (1998) *Practical Reason*, Stanford University Press, Stanford.

Cargile, A., and Giles, H. (1996) Intercultural communication training: Review, critique, and a new theoretical framework, *Communication Yearbook*, 19, 385–423.

Chan, K., and Cheng, H. (2002) One country, two systems: Cultural values reflected in Chinese and Hong Kong commercials, *Gazette*, 64, 385–400.

Chang, H.C., and Holt, R. (1996) An exploration of interpersonal relations in two Taiwanese computer firms. *Human Relations*, 49, 1489–1517,

Chang, H.C., and Holt, R. (1997) Intercultural training for expatriates: Reconsidering power and politics, in *Politics, Communication and Culture*, (eds A. González and D. Tanno), Sage, Thousand Oaks, pp. 207–230.

Chen, G.-M., and Chung, J. (1994) The impact of Confucianism on organizational communication. *Communication Quarterly*, 42, 93–105.

Chen, L.-C., and Reisman, W.M. (1972) Who owns Taiwan: A search for international title. *The Yale Law Journal*, 81, 599–671.

Cooper, J.F. (2003) *Taiwan: Nation-State or Province?* Westview, Boulder.

Covarrubias, P. (2002) *Culture, Communication, and Cooperation: Interpersonal Relations and Pronominal Address in a Mexican Organization*, Rowman & Littlefield Publishers, Inc., Lanham, MD.

Davison, G.M. (2003) *A Short History of Taiwan: The Case for Independence*, Praeger, Westport.

Dawlatshahi, D. (2001) Managing a labor strike in a maquilladora industry: A case study. *International Journal of Operations and Production Management*, 5/6, 728–748.

Domsch, M., and Lichtenberger, B. (1991) Managing the global manager: Predeparture training and development for German expatriates in China and Brazil. *Journal of Management Development*, 10, 41–52.

Dreyfus, H., and Rabinow, P. (1983) *Michel Foucault, beyond Structuralism and Hermeneutics*, University of Chicago Press, Chicago.

Drzewiecka, J., and Halualani, R.T. (2002) The structural-cultural dialectic of diasporic politics. *Communication Theory*, 12, 340–366.

Earley, P.C. (1987) Intercultural training for managers: A comparison of documentary and interpersonal methods. *The Academy of Management Journal*, 30, 685–698.

Foeman, A. (1997) The problem with power: Reflections on Chang and Holt, in *Politics, Communication and Culture*, (eds A. González and D. Tanno), Sage, Thousand Oaks, CA, pp. 237–243.

Foucault, M. (1980) *Power/Knowledge: Selected Interviews and Other Writings 1972–1977*, (ed. C. Gordon), Pantheon, New York.

Gannon, M. (2001a) *Cultural Metaphors: Readings, Research Translations, and Commentary*, Sage, Thousand Oaks, CA.

Gannon, M. (2001b) *Understanding Global Cultures: Metaphorical Journeys through 23 Nations*, Sage, Thousand Oaks, CA.

Gregersen, H.B., and Black J.S. (1992) Antecedents to commitment to a parent company and a foreign operation, *The Academy of Management Journal*, 35, 65–90.

Hall, K. (2002, April 25) Mexico loses factory jobs to China, Central America. *Knight Ridder Tribune Washington Bureau*, http://0-web.ebscohost.com.sculib.scu.edu/ehost/detail?vid=6&hid=105&sid=4e6233f9-1666-4c60-a76e-32d3f38eb0e3%40sessionmgr 104#db=nfh&AN=2W61733708808#db=nfh&AN=2W61733708808 (accessed May 31, 2010).

Halualani, R. (2008) "Where exactly is the Pacific?": Global migrations, diasporic movements, and intercultural communication. *Journal of International and Intercultural Communication*, 1, 3–22.

Harvey, D. (2005) *A Brief History of Neoliberalism*, Oxford University Press, New York.

Hofstede, G., and Bond, M. (2001) The Confucius connection: From cultural roots to economic growth, in *Cultural Metaphors: Readings, Research Translations, and Commentary*, (ed. M. Gannon), Sage, Thousand Oaks, CA, pp. 31–50.

Harrison, J.K. (1992) Individual and combined effects of behavior modeling and the cultural assimilator in cross-cultural management training, *Journal of Applied Psychology*, 77, 952–962.

Kim, Y., and Paulk, S. (1994) Intercultural challenges and personal adjustments: A qualitative analysis of the experiences of American and Japanese co-workers, in *Communicating in Multinational Organizations*, (eds R.L. Wiseman and R. Shuter), Sage, Thousand Oaks, CA, pp. 117–140.

Larner, W. (2006) Neoliberalism: Policy, ideology, and governmentality, in *International Political Economy and Poststructural Politics*, (ed. A.D. Goede), Palgrave, New York, pp. 199–218.

Lee, M., and Barnett, G. (1997) A symbols-and-meaning approach to the organizational cultures of banks in the United States, Japan, and Taiwan. *Communication Research*, 24, 394–412.

Leeds-Hurwitz, W. (1997) Introducing power, context, and theory to intercultural training: A response to Chang and Holt, in *Politics, Communication and Culture*, (eds A. González, and D. Tanno), Sage, Thousand Oaks, CA, pp. 231–236.

Levine, R. (1997) *Geography of Time: The Temporal Misadventures of a Social Psychologist*, Basic Books, New York.

Lim L.Y.C. (2003) Capitalism imperialism, and patriarchy: The dilemma of Third-World women workers in multinational factories, in *Feminist Theory Reader: Local and Global Perspectives*, (eds C. McCann, and S.-Y. Kim), Routledge, New York, pp. 222–230.

Lindsley, S.L. (1999a) A layered model of problematic intercultural communication in U.S.-owned maquiladoras in Mexico. *Communication Monographs*, 66, 143–167.

Lindsley, S.L. (1999b) Communication and "The Mexican Way": Stability and trust as core symbols in maquiladoras. *Western Journal of Communication*, 63, 1–31.

Lindsley, S.L., and Braithwaite, C.A. (1996) You should "wear a mask": Facework norms in cultural and intercultural conflict in maquiladoras. *International Journal of Intercultural Relations*, 20, 199–225.

Lindsley, S.L., and Braithwaite, C.A. (2003) U.S. Americans and Mexicans working together: Five core Mexican concepts for enhancing effectiveness, in *Intercultural Communication: A Reader*, (eds L.A. Samovar, and R.E. Porter), Wadsworth/Thomson Learning, Belmont, pp. 293–299.

Martin, J.N., and Nakayama, T.K. (1999) Thinking dialectically about culture and communication. *Communication Theory*, 9, 1–25.

Martínez, O. (2001) *Mexican-Origin People in the United States: A Topical History*, University of Arizona Press, Tuscon.

Millman, J. (2002) Mexican border workers suffer as plants relocate south. *Wall Street Journal*, 59, March 26, A20.

Moon, D. (2002) Thinking about "culture" in intercultural communication, in *Readings in Intercultural Communication: Experiences and Contexts*, (eds J.N. Martin, T.K. Nakayama, and L. Flores), McGraw Hill, Boston, pp. 13–20.

Myers, J. (1998) In praise of open markets. *Canadian Business*, 71, 132.

Ng, F. (1998) *The Taiwanese Americans*, Greenwood Press, Westport.

Ong, A. (1991) The gender and labor politics of postmodernity. *Annual Review of Anthropology*, 20, 279–309.

Ono, K. (1998) Problematizing "nation" in intercultural communication research, in *Communication and Identity across Cultures*, (eds D.V. Tanno, and A. González), Sage, Thousand Oaks, CA, pp. 193–202.

Ortíz-González, V. (2004) *El Paso: Local Frontiers at a Global Crossroads*, University of Minnesota Press, Minneapolis.

Pratt, M. (1999) Arts of the contact zone, in *Resources for Teaching Ways of Reading: An Anthology for Writers*, (eds D. Artholomae and A. Petrosky), Bedford/St. Martin's, New York, pp. 1–10.

Report to Congressional Requesters (2003) United States General Accounting Office, July.

Salzinger, L. (2003) Re-forming the "traditional Mexican woman": Making subjects in a border factory, in *Ethnography at the Border*, (ed. P. Vila), University of Minnesota Press, Minneapolis, pp. 46–72.

Samovar, L.A., and Porter, R.E. (2003) *Intercultural Communication: A Reader*, Wadsworth/Thomson Learning, Belmont, CA.

Sargent, J., and Matthews, L. (1999) Exploitation or choice? Exploring the relative attractiveness of employment in the maquilaoras. *Journal of Business Ethics*, 18, 213–227.

Shi, Y. (2008) Chinese immigrant women workers: Everyday forms of resistance and "coagulate politics." *Communication and Critical/Cultural Studies*, 5, 363–382.

Sorrell, K. (2008) Crossing borders in the context of globalization. National Communication Association Annual Convention, International and Intercultural Communication Division, San Diego.

Thomas, D.C., and Ravlin, E.C. (1995) Responses of employees to cultural adaptation by a foreign manager. *Journal of Applied Psychology*, 80, 133–146.

Vila, P. (2003) *Ethnography at the Border*, University of Minnesota Press, Minneapolis.

Williams, G., and Bent, R. (1997) Developing expatriate managers for Southeast Asia, in *Handbook of Intercultural Training*, (eds D. Landis, and R.S. Bhagat), Sage, CA, Thousand Oaks, pp. 383–399.

Wright, M. (2003) The politics of relocation: Gender, nationality, and value in a Mexican maquiladora, in *Ethnography at the Border*, (ed. P. Vila), University of Minnesota Press, Minneapolis, pp. 23–45.

Wright, M. (2006) *Disposable Women and Other Myths of Global Capitalism*, Routledge, New York.

Yu, X. (2000) Examining the impact of cultural values and cultural assumptions on motivational factors in the Chinese organizational context: A cross-cultural perspective, in *Chinese Perspectives in Rhetoric and Communication*, (ed. D.R. Heisey), Ablex, Stamford, pp. 119–138.

33

"Quit Whining and Tell Me About Your Experiences!"
(In)Tolerance, Pragmatism, and Muting in Intergroup Dialogue

Sara DeTurk

An important concern of contemporary communication scholarship has been muting, both of marginalized groups in society, and of individual members of marginalized groups in interpersonal communication. Research has demonstrated that institutional policies, cultural norms, stereotypes, prejudice, discrimination, and differences in communication styles all serve to reinforce perspectives of powerful groups, while silencing those of racial, sexual, national, religious, and other minorities. When these voices of marginalized group members are listened to, it is often for very specific purposes that also serve the interests of the dominant groups and their members.

Occasionally, in institutional settings, communication is carefully structured to relieve some of these power dynamics. One such forum is intergroup dialogue. Increasingly, schools, businesses, and community groups are creating structured dialogue programs to improve communication and understanding across social/ cultural groups, with the assumption that clear ground rules and skilled facilitation can mitigate some of the power imbalances and distortions of everyday interaction. Little empirical data, though, is available to either support or reject this assumption. The intent of this study, therefore, is to explore what actually happens in a voluntary, structured intergroup dialogue program, and how such dialogue reinforces and/or challenges extant power relations. This is important not only for what it reveals about structured intergroup dialogue *per se*, but to the extent that it sheds light on structural constraints on communication more generally, including how power is manifested discursively.

Findings of the current study suggest that structured dialogue can help to mitigate muting. Even communication situations that have been carefully structured to do so, however, are governed by underlying cultural ideologies that are often wielded by dominant group members to justify discursive closure. The framing of dialogue as education, and of "diversity" as being about "minorities," furthermore,

The Handbook of Critical Intercultural Communication, edited by Thomas K. Nakayama and Rona Tamiko Halualani. © 2010 Blackwell Publishing Ltd.

positions minority group members as subject-matter experts or educational providers, and majority group members as consumers. Structured intergroup dialogue, then, while it offers important potential for intercultural understanding and social change, is not immune to the reproduction of cultural power relations.

Review of Literature

Silencing marginalized groups

Much extant communication scholarship addresses the role of social power in silencing members of marginalized groups. Deetz (1992), for example, argues that some communication is systematically (and often unconsciously) distorted to reproduce meaning by blocking communicative challenges to the political status quo. Deetz enumerates several forms of "discursive closure" that serve to suppress conflict and mute perspectives that challenge those of people with authority. *Disqualification*, for example, occurs when groups are denied the right of expression ostensibly because they lack certain expertise, do not express themselves "appropriately," or have standpoints not considered to represent the interests of the majority. *Naturalization* is the discursive process by which social and historical processes are removed from view and their resulting subjective constructions are reified. Cultural assumptions, in other words, are unchallenged and taken for granted. *Neutralization* is the presumption of value-laden positions to be value-free, in part by ignoring the selectiveness of language use. A fourth form of discursive closure is the *avoidance* of topics which might challenge the status quo. "These prohibitions may be motivated to enhance propriety and order, but they often function to preclude a discussion of the values that define propriety and order and the benefits that certain groups acquire from them" (p. 192). *Subjectification* of experience is the dismissal of issues as matters of personal opinion. *Denial* and deniability refer to defenses that what was interpreted was not what was meant, or a refusal to take responsibility for one's discourse. *Legitimation* is the appeal to higher order explanatory devices such as the Protestant work ethic to rationalize values such as hard work. *Pacification*, finally, is the process by which conflicts are diverted by discounting their significance or the possibility of any solution. Problems, in other words, are labeled as either too big or too small to be dealt with.

Philomena Essed (1991) gives an example of how Black women are excluded from decision making through what she calls repressive tolerance: "They can say what they have to say. But then what they say is not considered to be of any consequence" (p. 236). One of her research participants elaborates:

> In meetings with my colleagues it often happens that one *does not understand what you are saying*, being a Black person ... In particular this is the case when you look at things from an alternative perspective. You make your point, they *look at you weird*, they steamroll your point, or, and this is the crucial thing, *your point is not taken down in the minutes* because they do not understand what you are saying, therefore, they cannot restate it, they do not see the relevance of what you are saying. It may also be

the case that they exclude your point from the minutes on purpose, because what is in the minutes counts in the process. Therefore they do not take it up. (p. 236)

Silencing, then, occurs frequently as a result of systemic power dynamics and, as Essed (1991) illustrates, out of insufficient skill in communicating interculturally. Muted Group Theory (Ardener 1975, Ardener, 1978) explains that, in societies with structural inequalities, more powerful groups will have greater influence over socially acceptable modes of communication than less powerful groups, and these modes will, as a result, privilege the experiences and worldviews of those powerful groups. Members of these dominant groups are thereby socialized *only* into these particular modes of communication, such that other perspectives, concerns, and communication styles fail to make sense to them. As a result, even when less powerful groups gain access to influential communication channels, their discourse is dismissed as inarticulate, irrelevant, or wrong. While the theory originally focused on women as a muted group, communication scholars such as Orbe (1998) have also applied the theory to "people of color ..., gays, lesbians, bisexuals, people with disabilities, lower and working class, and the young and elderly" (p. 21).

Similarly to Essed's observation, Parker (2002) demonstrates that the ideas of African American women in organizational meetings tended to be ignored or coopted, even when these women were senior executives. Hendrix (2002) offers empirical evidence of muting in academia, not only of black women and their points of view, but of white allies to black faculty. She quotes an interviewee who observes that:

> even the most supportive administrators ultimately succumb to the pressures applied by their peers. One dean constantly fighting three or four others (in support of a person of color) generally leads to the single individual giving up at some point. ... My department chair ... was ostracized for his support of Black faculty in his division and, ultimately, was embarrassed and punished by being transferred to another position within the institution (with less prestige).

Goldberg (1993) explains that such discursive manifestations of racism are part of a cultural system that celebrates universalism, individualism, and equality, thereby failing to recognize group-based differences in either culture or power. Racial logic, he points out, is established and maintained through institutions which include language, values, norms, rules, and principles of social organization. Communication may be argued to be the central mechanism by which some social groups are empowered while others are marginalized: "It is not just that the limits of our language limit our thoughts; the world we find ourselves in is one we have helped to create, and this places constraints upon how we think the world anew" (Goldberg, 1993, p. 204).

Possibilities of dialogue

Power, of course, is neither static nor monolithic, and many scholars and practitioners have envisioned what Habermas (1971) called the "ideal speech situation," in which all participants have equal voice and communication is free from systematic distortions or other constraints. Habermas, Buber, and others often use the term "dialogue" to refer to this ideal speech situation. Dialogue, for Buber (1958), implied a state wherein all parties were mutually committed to asserting their own perspectives as faithfully as possible, each person listened fully and openly to the other(s), and each viewed the other as a "Thou" rather than an "It" – recognizing, in other words, the other person's full humanity. Also central to Buber's conception of dialogue was the notion of the "between" – that which is common to dialogue participants as a function of the intersubjectivity of dialogue itself, and which is cocreated in their relationship to one another. Zamora (2002) created a conceptual framework enumerating seven themes and three tenets of dialogue in its purest or most ideal form. The themes are presence, openness, multivocality, reciprocity, responsiveness, emergence, and inclusion, and the tenets are the participants, the content, and the between. Zamora summarizes her model by stating:

> true dialogic interaction can be said to be taking place in those interactions where participants are fully engaged as their own unique and authentic selves (presence) while also being fully willing to experience the unique and authentic self of the other (openness) without requiring those selves, or their values and ideas, to merge or be dominated by one or the other of the participants. (p. 6)

Cissna and Anderson (2002) argue that dialogue, according to Buber's conception, is essentially momentary and fleeting. This ephemeral quality of dialogue has important implications. The dialogic moment is characterized by "radical availability to otherness" (Cissna and Anderson, p. 6), and sheds itself of ego concerns such as social status. As each person "turns toward" the other,

> both mutually perceive the impact of each other's turning. It is a brief interlude of focused awareness and acceptance of otherness and difference that somehow simultaneously transcends the perception of difference itself ... At that moment, and in a sense only for that moment, dialogue levels the communicative field (Cissna and Anderson, p. 186).

Anticipating a postmodern perspective, Buber (1958) called attention to the "near, dialectical, fluctuating, interpersonal, immediate, and momentary" nature of truth (Cissna and Anderson, p. 201), and to the potential of dialogue for destabilizing power relations, if only for that dialogic moment.

Scholarship about dialogue is not merely theoretical. Many schools, organizations, and community groups have established programs aimed at fostering such dialogic moments. Many of these are specifically aimed at improving intergroup relations. By definition, intergroup dialogues bring together individuals who are diverse in regard to race, gender, religion, and/or other social identity categories. Increasingly, people in the United States are participating in intergroup dialogue groups, which generally consist of approximately 12 to 15 people who meet regularly and voluntarily to discuss diversity issues with the assistance of one or two trained dialogue facilitators. Typically, the content of discussion is largely open-ended, though facilitators introduce varying amounts of structure through the introduction of discussion topics and activities. They may be guided by a loose curriculum that has a series of progressive goals emphasizing mutual learning and intergroup understanding; usually, though, these are much broader and more open-ended than those of typical training or educational programs (see Guarasci and Cornwell, 1997; Schoem *et al.*, 2001; Zúñiga and Nagda, 2001). Hurtado (2001) cites research indicating that, in fact, students reporting interaction with diverse peers demonstrate complex thinking associated with discussion of social issues, openness to diverse perspectives, and willingness to challenge their own views.

In terms of *participants'* interests, the current study revealed a variety of motives influenced by the cultural and historical context. In general, participants joined the dialogue program under investigation with the hope of promoting intergroup harmony and social justice. For those who framed their participation through lenses of their subordinate identities (e.g. Muslim or Mexican American), these goals were particularly important, and were pursued by gaining voice and educating members of the Christian, white mainstream. For their Christian, white counterparts, participation in the program was primarily a way to gain "communicative competency" in an environment with increasing political, professional, and demographic pressures toward pluralism and integration of culturally different others. (These findings are discussed elsewhere in more detail (DeTurk, 2004). This study, additionally, sought to investigate the *meaning* of dialogue for participants of one municipal intergroup dialogue program. The current paper explores the nature of intergroup dialogue participants' orientation to dialogue with one another, including their communicative norms, values, and behavior.

Methodology

In the spring of 2003, I acted as a participant-researcher in a municipal intergroup dialogue program in the Southwest. I had volunteered as a group facilitator in the program for the two previous years, and was active in facilitator training sessions and other meetings to improve and expand the program and to enhance its connections to the city government and other interested local organizations. During one of these meetings, other stakeholders articulated qualitative, contextually-rooted research as a necessary component of program improvement, and accepted my offer to pursue such research as my doctoral dissertation.

I began by collecting background information about the program and the local context by consulting the city's website, planning and recruitment documents, local newspapers, and other program participants and stakeholders. Then, once registration for the 2003 program was underway, I recruited 10 coresearchers for three stages of in-depth interviews. In addition to acting as a participant in one of the three dialogue groups, I conducted interviews with coresearchers before, during, and after the six-week program. The first two rounds were one-on-one, while the third took the form of a focus group (though some participants opted out of the focus group in preference for a third one-on-one interview). Finally, I transcribed the interviews and analyzed them according to a three-step phenomenological process of description, reduction, and interpretation.

Description, which constitutes the first stage of phenomenological analysis, consists of "horizontalizing" the phenomena under investigation by striving to describe it without privileging any particular perspective or imposing theoretical assumptions (Ihde, 1986). This requires, first, a reflexive process of bracketing, or invoking the *epoché*, by carefully articulating one's own perspectives and assumptions. In this case, I then consolidated each coresearchers interview transcripts into first-person accounts, or narratives, and submitted these to the coresearchers for feedback.

Reduction is the process of identifying themes that emerge across narratives. The reduction, or second-order analysis, is accomplished through "imaginative free variation," which implies consideration of each element of a phenomenon as present or absent in order to establish which features are essential (Lanigan, 1988).

Interpretation, finally, is a third-order analysis, whereby a second reduction is performed in order to: (1) find further meanings not apparent in the initial reduction; (2) identify relationships among these themes; and (3) associate the themes with the original research questions. The interpretation, according to Ihde (1986), accounts for the condition for the possibility of the phenomenon, thereby designating it as essential, and establishing a claim to significance.

Findings

The meaning of intergroup dialogue, for the participants of this program, was tightly intertwined with the meaning that diversity held for them, and with their motivation to participate in the first place; these questions are addressed elsewhere in more detail (DeTurk, 2004, 2005, 2006). In sum, many of the Christian, heterosexual, Anglo-American participants joined the dialogue program, in large part, for exposure to voices of "diversity," which they saw as a characteristic of Muslims, people of color, and members of other marginalized groups. They sought access to voices of these "others" in the interests of "authentic" relationships, professional efficacy, intergroup harmony, and social justice activism. Jim, for example, said:

> I sometimes meet people that I realize I don't know enough about, and I feel like I need more exposure to different cultural perspectives on issues … I often wonder how Asian immigrants to the city are received, especially Arabs since September 11. I think about what it must be like for them, and would like to hear some of their points of view. I always try to understand situations from other people's perspectives. Some of this is just curiosity, and some of it is practical; I feel that the more I understand about

other people, the better I can help them. I don't want to be hypersensitive, but I think it's important to be aware of other people's feelings and some of the harsh experiences they've been through.

Jim's narrative was typical in its expression of (1) not knowing enough about groups on the margins of US society, and (2) wanting to help others for personal, professional, civic, and humanistic reasons. It can be read simultaneously as a marker of liberatory social change *and* as an example of a hegemonic relationship as articulated by Said (1978), wherein members of the dominant culture view others as objects for their educational purposes. Muslims and people of color, on the whole, shared aims related to social justice and intergroup harmony, but also viewed intergroup dialogue as a forum in which to have their perspectives heard and understood by the cultural mainstream.

Participants' faith in the program as a means to these ends rested on their ideals and assumptions about the nature of dialogue. Their comments about what they had expected, what they enjoyed, and what frustrated them about the dialogue sessions offer considerable insight into norms of communication that reflect wider cultural values, assumptions, and power relations. Phenomenological analysis manifested six themes in regard to their orientation to dialogue: hermeneutic listening and perspective taking; tolerance; dialogue as therapy and confession; direct, honest talk; pragmatism; and dialectical tensions in regard to knowing and understanding others. Together, these themes reveal important elements of the larger culture in which the program was situated.

Hermeneutic listening and perspective taking

Not surprisingly, given the very definition of dialogue, participants valued their group experiences to the extent that they were characterized by "hermeneutic listening," or listening, with the entire self, in order to fully understand the other. Several commended the spirit of mutual presence and ethic of caring and emotional support that they found in their groups, and others bemoaned their absence. Tony (a Mexican American man), for example, said:

> The culture of the group is one that is educational, very accepting, and that celebrates differences. The setting is intimate, where one person is talking, and everyone else is listening, and absorbing everything that person's saying ... where you're able to let your guard down, say what you gotta say, and everyone listens. Everyone's very attentive, you know, everyone kind of takes a step back and listens, truly listens, to try to understand.

This "listening to understand" is reflective of Gadamer's definition of hermeneutic listening (from Kimball and Garrison, 1998), which Kimball and Garrison note is also dynamic and interactive, and has the potential to generate a new, shared reality for dialogue participants.

Leila described the impact of listening with all of her ears, mind, eyes, and heart:

> One person in our group is African American. And he talked about visiting Alabama
> when he was a little kid, and how when he got on a bus, his mother grabbed him and
> shoved him to the back. I mean I've seen that kind of thing on television before, but
> to actually see someone with their eyes welling up a little bit, and talking about it, and
> you *know* it's true; it's not an actor. You know that they're sincere, and you can feel
> their emotion. I felt like I was that little kid being yanked by my mom in the back of
> the bus. How many times have I heard the stories of African Americans having to sit
> in the back of the bus? But yet I really didn't *feel* it. But when I sat with this person,
> I actually felt, I actually felt his pain.

Leila's claim to having felt the pain of another highlights the problem of empathy.
Writers as diverse as Buber (1958), Arnett and Nakagawa (1983), Broome (1991),
Houston (1994), and Sontag (2003) have pointed out that claims of understanding the feelings of others are both untenable – particularly from different social or
cultural standpoints – and potentially colonizing.

It is clear, though, that hermeneutic listening allowed dialogue participants to
understand better the experiences of people whose social identities were different
from their own. They did this through perspective taking, or trying to imagine the
other's experience while at the same time recognizing the limitations of their own
social locations. Jim, for example, described listening to a female group member's
story of sexual harassment:

> Listening to her tell her story made me realize that it's still a reality, and it got me
> thinking about how that kind of experience would wear you down, and wear you
> down, and wear you down … If you read an article about discrimination, you just
> think, "oh, that's just rhetoric." But if you hear somebody talking about it, you realize
> that it's a real experience and it has real consequences.

Jim also made it clear that he recognized the limits of perspective taking: "hearing
these stories first-hand makes me realize that, just because something wouldn't be
offensive to me, doesn't mean it wouldn't be to somebody else. For somebody
else, that might just really hit home."

Leila (a Muslim woman) talked about seeing perspective taking occurring in others: "I think other people are learning, too. Sometimes you'll see people talking,
and you'll see someone where the little light bulb goes on: 'hmm, I never thought
about it that way before.'"

Coresearchers, in general, indicated either that they valued the mutual presence,
hermeneutic listening, and perspective taking experienced in their groups, or that
they wished there were more of it. At least two participants framed this in ways that
echoed certain definitional characteristics of dialogue. Leila noted that all participants were there to express their points of view, as opposed to preaching or debating: "We're not trying to win anybody over to our side. My goal is just to have
people open up their eyes and their minds and their hearts … Just point 'em in the

right direction, and just let 'em know that there is a different point of view, and they'll investigate it on their own."

Tolerance

If learning through hermeneutic listening and perspective taking was the goal of dialogue, freedom of expression was one of its conditions. In evaluating their dialogue experiences, participants had praise for the extent to which they found autonomy, flexibility, freedom of self-expression, and emotional support in their groups.

Several coresearchers articulated nonjudgmentalness as a marker of moral autonomy. Jack said, "You may not *like* what they do. That's beside the point. You can understand it, and tolerate it." Angela, in reference to a palm reader, said, "Now I'm opposed to that. But she has a right to live in society. Who am I to really say that what she's doing is wrong, other than my belief?" She made this point in connection with her feelings about gay people, which were echoed by Leila: "I don't believe in homosexuality. However, I do believe in accepting the person, because only God can judge people." These comments, collectively, suggest a celebration of individual autonomy.

An interaction that I observed occurred during the initial dialogue session, during which facilitators presented ground rules to participants (see Appendix B), and various group members inquired or commented about them. One person verbally expressed resistance to this structure, arguing that since we were all adults we should not need rules. Everyone else in the group appeared to disagree with him, but some, including the facilitators, praised him for expressing his view, and declared that such differences of opinion were what made intergroup dialogue valuable.

Several coresearchers spoke of how they valued, or wanted to see more of, this freedom of expression. Some observed that there was a nice combination of structure and flexibility regarding topics of conversation and equality of voice, and others used words like "easygoing," "open," "comfortable," and "free-flowing" to describe the dialogue sessions.

These comments reflect what Carbaugh (1990) refers to as "righteous tolerance" – a norm that explicitly differentiates tolerance from acceptance and that celebrates the autonomy of the individual: "persons are treated as individual beings, as separate and separable entities" (p. 136). Carbaugh's analysis reveals the construction of a model " 'self,' who is compelled to communicate, to be aware of its internal qualities, and to think and act independently" (p. 136). Coresearchers enjoyed their dialogue groups when they felt them to be tolerant of a variety of opinions and flexible in regard to styles of participation. Underlying these values are ethics of freedom and individualism that cuts to the core of US American ideology and identity.

A consequence of this conception of tolerance, as articulated by St John and Shepherd (2004), is that it is "enacted in ways that assume a view of the other as permanently other" and "defines good interaction as the absence of any interaction that might impinge upon self-oriented aims or desires" (p. 169), Tolerance as thus framed, they argue, is in conflict with pragmatic, communitarian notions of civic engagement. Chesler (2001), too, articulates the concern that the outcome of intergroup dialogue may be limited to individual consciousness raising. "And when new individual behaviors are not translated into action with others, in forms of collective action, fundamental social structures maintaining privilege and oppression go unchecked" (p. 294).

Dialogue as therapy or confession

Peck (1994) demonstrated that the American ideology of individualism, when applied to communication about race, often takes on a religious and therapeutic flavor. Such a therapeutic discourse, she notes, frames racism (and other "isms") in terms of individuals' cognitive, affective, attitudinal, and behavioral shortcomings suggesting that intergroup conflict and injustice is best resolved by changing individuals' perceptions, rather than through structural change. Angela's comments during the focus group illustrate this emphasis on personal transformation through confession. Talking about her desire to stare at people who look strange to her, she says, "I'm not proud of it. I'm admitting it because that's what I'm supposed to do, in this circle. But I will look ..." Later in the same conversation, she reflects, "I have to really make sure that I care, and I understand, and I learn more, and I try and be more aware."

The religious flavor of much of this discourse, furthermore, condemns anger in preference for unity, thereby weakening political possibilities for social criticism. Two other themes – direct, honest talk, and pragmatism – also reflect the individualism that permeates US American culture.

Direct, honest talk

Despite the ethic of tolerance noted above, conflict avoidance and "beating around the bush" were criticized, and participants expected each other to speak out about their experiences and perspectives as representatives of various social identity groups. Christian, Anglo-Americans, especially, were frustrated when their questions about others were not answered directly, or when potentially productive controversy was avoided. Jack, for example, said:

> You know, if you're going to have a group of people taking up an hour and a half, let's get down to the nitty gritty. Let's get it out on the table, let's learn something. But I guess maybe people are afraid they're gonna get their feelings hurt. But how else can you learn about other people, and other cultures – other *anything* – unless we have direct, pointed questions, and hear people's opinions?

True dialogue, for these participants, is characterized by high levels of self-disclosure and a forthright, low-context communication style. These characteristics reflect (1) an association of dialogue with therapy, (2) mainstream American communication style preferences, and (3) assumptions that freedom and equality are present for all parties and everyone is entitled to satisfy their curiosity about others.

Pragmatism (no whining)

Despite an expressed desire to hear others speak honestly about their experiences, some participants expressed disapproval when members of marginalized groups did so. Angela, for example, lamented that "there's too much griping":

> Most of the people in the group, I would say, are either very silent and just sit there, or they want to vent and let their pain out, and show people how they're suffering ... And a lot of people seem to be pushing their own personal agendas, as opposed to making a cohesive group that really learns to appreciate each other and take informa-tion about that group, and utilize it appropriately elsewhere. Here's what I'd like to see ...[to] identify an actual issue, and go to work on it.

Angela's perspective reflects two cultural phenomena. One is an American ten-dency toward action-orientation, which implies that for every problem there is a solution that can, and should, be pursued. Many of the dialogue participants were most satisfied when they felt that their group experiences led to some kind of action. They enjoyed conversation that was characterized by efficient communica-tion, specific information, and resolution of issues. Their ideal visions of the pro-gram included brainstorming, action planning, and communicating policy recommendations to decision makers in the local government or media.

The other thing revealed in Angela's complaint is a cultural norm against whin-ing that has evolved to protect dominant groups from unpleasantness. At least for white Americans, Angela's perspective is much more typical than Leila's satisfac-tion at "feeling the pain" of another. Carrillo Rowe (2003), for one, found that white women tended to establish relationships with and perceptions of women of color that were relatively abstract, impersonal, and stereotypical, which allowed them to avoid their pain. Dace (1994), similarly, noted that "at least where racial issues are concerned, European Americans expect persons of color to communicate in ways that are friendly, comfortable, and absolving" (p. 25). Discourse that exposes social problems without including solutions, therefore, is censured.

Nedra, a Muslim woman referring to some other Muslims, observed critically that "sometimes people are looking to be offended." This suggests that, while one effect of the "quit whining" discourse is to uphold the status quo and deflect guilt away from its defenders, another is to mark injured parties as complainers, or trans-gressors of polite discourse. Not only, then, are their objections not heard, but their credibility and social desirability are diminished. The current climate, too, disciplines even would-be allies who are excessively "politically correct," as reflected in Jim's concern to avoid being "hypersensitive." Thus many dialogue participants condemn and make special efforts to avoid "complaining," "bringing it on themselves," or "playing the race card," and pose these communicative acts in opposition to "addressing real problems constructively." This neutralization of complaints against injustice is even codified in the program's prohibition against "venting" (see Appendix B).

Some participants' discourse about dialogue is characterized by what de Certeau (1984) and Nakayama and Krizek (1995) described as "strategic rhetoric." De Certeau defined a strategy as an apparatus of power that has become transformed into an organizing principle, such that it becomes invisible and taken for granted. Strategic rhetoric, then, is rhetoric that reflects and reproduces power relations. It incorporates not only available discursive moves, but also the rules and conditions that make those moves possible and meaningful. De Certeau invokes the following metaphor: "A 'strategy' … is the equivalent of 'taking a trick' in a card game: it depends both on the deal (having a good hand) and on the way one plays the cards (being a good cardplayer)." "Playing the race card," for example (as Tony observed during one interview), is against the rules. Also against the rules is whining, as Leila noted in her tactics for confronting discrimination against Muslims:

"The problem with focusing on the negative," she said, "is that if you're sitting up there just 'wah, wah, wah, wah, wah,' then that's what it becomes. You get turned off. Nobody's going to listen, because they just think you're up there whining." Whereas dialogue participants expect each other to share their experiences, feelings, and opinions, then, their tolerance for griping, whining, or complaining is limited. The distinction between sharing and whining, though, is ambiguous, and this ambiguity leaves room for criticism of anything participants do not want to hear – including challenges to their self-images as virtuous allies to Muslims, Jews, homosexuals, or other groups. Griping, in such a cultural environment, is an implied demand, and a threat to the ontological security of dominant group members. As such, it is invalidated, and therefore silenced, through discursive closure.

Knowing and understanding others

As noted above, many of the dialogue participants whose social identities reflected the American mainstream came to the program in order to learn – specifically, to be exposed to the standpoints of those to whom they lacked access in their everyday lives. This lack of access may be explained, on one hand, by various forms of muting, and, on another, by a lack of everyday interaction between Christians and Muslims, or between Anglo-Americans and people of color. Some of this lack of contact was structural, such as a certain amount of de facto racial segregation of neighborhoods. Some of it may also be explained by fear or prejudice, as indicated by Tony's remark that "I haven't had much interaction with Muslims around here besides just 'hi,' or 'good afternoon,' even though I'm near the Muslim Cultural Center." Tony revealed that he came into the program with a stereotype of Middle Eastern Muslims as potential terrorists, though his interaction with Muslims in the dialogue group eventually eradicated this stereotype and motivated him to reach out to Muslims in his everyday interactions.

For some participants, though – particularly those who were Christian, Anglo-Americans – their desire to know and understand others was limited by, and specific to, their own interests. Angela, for example, wanted to know what kinds of racial or ethnic labels were acceptable to others. Krysia, similarly, wanted to be able to categorize people so as to understand how their standpoints reflected their cultural experiences. She conveyed frustration that "I'm not getting my answer," and explained her desire for understanding as follows: "I always have been for the weaker person, you know, the underprivileged – those who are less fortunate than some ... I [hope] we can actually teach them that they don't have to have that chip on their shoulder all the time." Krysia also criticized members of minority groups who expressed anger or bitterness in ways that she found to be aggressive: "You don't always have to be confrontational," she said.

Some of this criticism undoubtedly reflects defensiveness on the part of members of privileged racial, sexual, and age groups, who would rather not be confronted with the ugly realities of racism, homophobia, and ageism as experienced by real people, or their own possible roles in upholding them. Carrillo Rowe (2003) reflected on white women who seek to get to know women of color in order to learn from their experiences. They want, she argued, to be "transformed by their affective ties to women of color" and yet do "not seem to recognize that [they are] imposing particular modes of relating and conditions for bridge possibilities in ways that may preclude the kind of intimate connections" (p. 64) they seek. Dace (1994), too, illustrated how whites in her study demanded "disclosure, trust, and communication that affirmed their liberal attempts to work on [racism]" (p. 21). These dynamics were evident in the current study, as well.

Carol, for her part, expressed a desire to advocate for members of oppressed groups by "giving them a chance to show me their individuality." This comment suggests an assumption that such an opportunity is her right and responsibility to give. Carol also expressed a need for personal self-disclosure from others in order to be a more supportive friend:

> I need to know, um, or what means a lot to me, what I value, is when people share what's going on for them ... I need to know – I mean, when you take the chance to share that with me, it just puts it into a greater context of understanding for myself. I need to know when someone – if someone's sexuality, for example, is at the top of their mind. If they share that with me, I can be closer to them. Similarly, if you're wrestling with health issues, I would hope that you could share that with me, so that I can be closer to you.

Angela, too, wanted to learn on her own very specific terms:

> I guess I just want to hear people present their issues in a dispassionate way, rather than a complaining, whining way. And then work on it. The homosexual man, for example, I'd like to know what struggles he has with his own homosexuality. I wanna know that, so that I can help him work through it, maybe. Or see if they're the same struggles that *I* have in understanding him.

Underlying many dialogue participants' interest in learning about and "helping" others in this manner are desires to shape society according to one's own values, to assuage feelings of guilt based in social privileges, and to learn about others for purposes of control or mastery of one's social environment. Many Christian, Anglo-American participants, in sum, expect Muslims and participants of color to answer their questions and to embrace their communication styles, assumptions, and goals, transforming the dialogic "Thou" into an "it." Often, they tend to frame dialogue about diversity in ways that – however well-meaning – place them-selves in positions of authority, serve their own personal interests, and make unreasonable demands of people that they are ostensibly trying to empower. Jackson (2002) describes this orientation to communication as a "ready-to-sign" contract, in which interlocutors present each other with conditions of discourse. This is in contrast to "quasi-completed" contracts, which are somewhat protec-tive of individuals' own ontological security, but also partially committed to rela-tional coordination; and "cocreated" contracts, which imply openness, "full acknowledgment and validation of cultural differences ... and unconditional appreciation and valuation of the other person" (p. 185). The current findings support Jackson's conclusion that "[d]ominant groups almost instantaneously, and often subconsciously, present ready-to-sign contracts to marginalized group members" (p. 184). Because the dominant culture is their own, Jackson explains, dominant group members are never required to shift their worldviews, and often feel no incentive to do so.

Jackson's typology of cultural contracts echoes what Yoshikawa (1987) refers to as a "control mode" of communication, as well as Habermas's (1985) concept of instrumental rationality. Participants' approaches to dialogue, though, can sel-dom be characterized strictly as one type of contract/rationality or another. Instead, participants alternate between the two, as the simultaneously seek cogni-tive complexity and ontological security. Carol, for one, articulated a desire to "tackle her prejudices" and "shut off" her tendency to want to categorize people. She recognized, though, that openmindedness entails risks of uncertainty and challenges to her worldview. For people whose worldviews are rarely challenged and whose cultures rationalize their position at the top of a social hierarchy, such a risk is considerable.

People who volunteer to participate in intergroup dialogue almost inevitably seek to complicate their worldviews. This quest for cognitive complexity, though – especially for members of dominant social groups – occurs in fits and starts, and alternates with efforts to confirm their already existing standpoints.

Conclusion

Dialogue in general, and intergroup dialogue in particular, have been hailed as communicative forms that can interrupt relations of domination, overcome the muting of subordinate groups in society, and foster mutual understanding and even collective action. Communication scholars continue to grapple with the promise dialogue holds for improving the human condition, though, perhaps because dialogue comprises inherent tensions. By its very nature, dialogue involves a tension between difference and commonality; it *requires* both the presence of different perspectives and the transcendence of differences in the interest of common understanding. The way in which dialogue tends to be conceptualized and promoted in the United States, moreover, celebrates cultural values of tolerance and pragmatism – values which inhibit as well as facilitate the goals described above, especially as they exist in tension with one another. On one hand, if dialogue succeeds at "letting 'em know that there's a different point of view," then such a process might lay the groundwork for broader participation in social change efforts. On the other hand, an individualistic orientation and tolerance for different perspectives seems to inhibit potential for collective action; for many of us, its ability to "destabilize power relations *only for that dialogic moment*" is insufficient.

In the current study, too, this tension sometimes facilitated muting and discursive closure, even when dominant group members sought to learn from their subordinate-group counterparts. Anglo-Americans (in particular) simultaneously tried to understand and to silence the "other," as a result of tensions between their interests in ontological security and cognitive complexity, and between privilege and equality. This dynamic, of course, reflects the broader cultural problem of muted groups being asked to educate dominant groups about their perspectives and experiences precisely because their voices have been muted in the first place.

Dialogue, then, becomes not just a communication event, but an educational one – one in which dominant group members can be understood as the learners, or consumers, while members of racial and religious minority groups are framed as teachers, or tools to serve their educational ends. One subsequent danger – in addition to the burden of cultural "others" to serve the needs of the dominant group – is that the framing of white, Anglo-Saxon Christians as consumers leaves members of this dominant group free to accept or reject the others' teachings. When we are confronted with perspectives that we do not wish to hear, we invoke legitimation, disqualification, and other tools of discursive closure to protect our ontological security and positions of power.

Authentic dialogue requires that its participants overcome the systemic distortions that characterize most communication. The current study suggests that structured facilitation and goodwill on the part of participants are helpful but insufficient conditions; even in communication situations that have been carefully constructed to encourage ideal dialogue, cultural norms, values, and assumptions often function to privilege dominant groups and silence those who would challenge the cultural status quo.

One limitation of this study is a certain amount of strategic essentialism that was employed in order to tease out the role of power relations in communication; within this group of coresearchers, Muslims and Mexican Americans tended to frame their discussions around their marked social identities, whereas Christians and Anglo-Americans tended to speak from their dominant identities. This does not, of course, mean that their religion always conveyed relative power, nor that their communication was unaffected by other identities such as gender or sexual orientation. I recognize, too, that the current analysis focuses primarily on the consciousness of dominant group members as potential allies, and under-analyzes the perspectives of subordinate group members. Additional studies, therefore, will be important both to explore perspectives of people who represent other racial, religious, sexual, and economic identities, and in contexts where different dimensions of identity may be more salient.

Another limitation is the primary reliance on interviews at the expense of direct observation of communicative micropractices. Future research would be profitable to the extent that it offers additional empirical descriptions of such practices in a variety of contexts, including social change organizations and movements. Also extremely valuable would be investigations of tactical responses to muting, not only by its targets, but also their allies. This must, of course, include attention to our own discourse as communication scholars.

Appendix A

Interview guide

Before first dialogue session:
- How did you hear about Diversity Dialogues?
- Tell me about the process of deciding to do it.
- What do you hope to achieve or get out of it?
- Why is it valuable enough to spend 2–3 hours/week of your time?
- What else do you give to it?
- What situational/community factors play a role?
- What do you think makes you different from people who may have heard about the program but don't choose to participate?
- What does "diversity" mean to you?
- How do you see yourself relative to other participants (in terms of similarities and differences)?
- Are there other things you'd like me to know?

During course of dialogue sessions:
- How is your dialogue group going for you?
- Tell me about a typical session, an especially memorable one, or a particularly memorable moment in one.
- What does it mean to you to be participating in this group?
- What value does it have for you? Do you feel you're getting what you'd hoped out of it?
- To what extent would you say your attitude is shared by other group members?
- How do you see yourself in relation to other participants?

➤ How would you describe the culture of your group (e.g. norms, communication styles, values, beliefs, idiosyncrasies, traditions)? Of the project as a whole?

➤ What effects, if any, has participation in the dialogue group had on you (beliefs, attitudes, knowledge, behavior, relationships)?

➤ I asked you this during our first interview, but for the sake of comparison, tell me again what diversity means to you.

➤ Are there other things you'd like me to know?

After last dialogue session:

➤ How did the Diversity Dialogues experience go for you, all in all?

➤ What effects, if any, has participation in the dialogue group had on you (beliefs, attitudes, knowledge, behavior, relationships)?

➤ What changes, if any, have you noticed in your fellow group members? In the group as a whole?

➤ How, if at all, has the process of participating in my research affected you?

➤ Are there other things you'd like me to know?

Appendix B

Group dialogue ground rules

The following ground rules are necessary to produce constructive dialogue and a safe environment for all participants. Please read all ground rules carefully.

Confidentiality
In order to create a climate of open and honest dialogue, confidentiality must be maintained at all times.
I AGREE NOT TO REVEAL NAMES, PERSONAL EXPERIENCES, OR PERSONAL INFORMATION TO PEOPLE OUTSIDE THE GROUP.

Climate for Productive Dialogue
The purpose of the dialogue is to achieve understanding about and between different individuals and groups on campus. Thus, the dialogue should include questions that seek to understand and gain insight, rather than convince someone about a particular point of view.
I AGREE TO REFRAIN FROM VENTING OR ENGAGING IN DEBATES WITH OTHER GROUP MEMBERS.
I AGREE TO DIRECT MY QUESTIONS AND ANSWERS IN A WAY THAT WILL GENERATE GREATER UNDERSTANDING AMONG PARTICIPANTS.

Conflict Management
Managing conflict during the intergroup dialogues is critical to having a productive and successful group in which people learn from each other and gain greater insight

into their own group as well as others. If at any point in time during the dialogues a participant is having a difficult time because of tension, conflict, or psychological or emotional distress, she or he can request one of the following: a "sit-out," a "time-out," or group departure.

I ACKNOWLEDGE THAT AT ANY TIME I MAY ASK FOR A SIT-OUT, TIME-OUT, OR GROUP DEPARTURE.

IN THE INTEREST OF MAINTAINING SAFE AND PRODUCTIVE DIALOGUE GROUPS, I AGREE THAT FACILITATOR(S) MAY ASK ME TO TAKE A SIT-OUT, TIME-OUT, OR GROUP DEPARTURE.

Respect for Each Other

It is important that group members treat each other with respect. Name-calling, accusations, verbal attacks, sarcasm, and other negative exchanges are counter-productive to successful dialogue groups.

I AGREE TO MAINTAIN RESPECT FOR ALL GROUP MEMBERS AT ALL TIMES.

Participant-suggested guidelines

By participating in these discussions, I agree to abide by all the ground rules stated above, as well as others added by consensus in my dialogue group.

References

Ardener, E. (1978) Some outstanding problems in the analysis of events, in *The Yearbook of Symbolic Anthropology*, (ed. G. Schwinner), Hurst, London, pp. 103–121.

Ardener, S. (1975) *Perceiving Women*, Malaby, London.

Arnett, R.C., and Nakagawa, G. (1983) The assumptive roots of empathic listening: A critique. *Communication Education*, 32, 368–377.

Broome, B.J. (1991) Building shared meaning: Implications of a relational approach to empathy for teaching intercultural communication. *Communication Education*, 40, 235–249.

Buber, M. (1958) *I and Thou*. Scribner, New York.

Carbaugh, D. (1990) Communication rules in *Donahue* discourse, in *Cultural Communication and Intercultural Contact*, (ed. D. Carbaugh), Lawrence Erlbaum Associates, Hillsdale, NJ, pp. 119–149.

Carrillo Rowe, A. (2003) Bridge inscriptions: Transracial feminist alliances, possibilities, and foreclosures, in *Intercultural Alliances: Critical Transformation*, (ed. M.J. Collier), Sage, Thousand Oaks, CA, pp. 49–80.

Chesler, M. (2001) Extending intergroup dialogue: From talk to action, in (eds D. Schoem and S. Hurtado), *Intergroup Dialogue*, University of Michigan Press, Ann Arbor, pp. 294–305.

Cissna, K., and Anderson, R. (2002) *Moments of Meeting: Buber, Rogers, and the Potential for Public Dialogue*, State University of New York Press, Albany, NY.

Dace, K. (1994) Dissonance in European and African American communication. *The Western Journal of Black Studies*, 18, 18–26.

de Certeau, M. (1984) *The Practice of Everyday Life* (trans. S. Rendell), University of California Press, Berkeley, CA.

Deetz, S. (1992) *Democracy in an Age of Corporate Colonization*, State University of New York Press, Albany.

DeTurk, S. (2004) "I need to know": Conditions that encourage and constrain intercultural dialogue. Paper presented at the National Communication Association, Chicago, IL.

DeTurk, S. (2005) "When I was white": Semiosis of whiteness, race, and sociocultural diversity in contemporary U.S. culture. *Journal of Intergroup Relations*, 32 (1), 40–60.

DeTurk, S. (2006) The power of dialogue: Consequences of intergroup dialogue and their implications for agency and alliance building. *Communication Quarterly*, 54, 33–51.

Essed, P. (1991) *Understanding Everyday Racism: An Interdisciplinary Theory*, Sage, Newbury Park, CA.

Goldberg, D. (1993) *Racist Culture*, Blackwell, Malden, MA.

Guarasci, R., and Cornwell, G. (1997) *Democratic Education in an Age of Difference*, Jossey-Bass, San Francisco, CA.

Habermas, J. (1971) *Knowledge and Human Interests*, Beacon Press, Boston, MA.

Habermas, J. (1985) *The Theory of Communicative Action, Volume 1: Reason and the Rationalization of Society*, Beacon Press, Boston, MA.

Hendrix, K. (2002) The undaunted spirit of black female professors: Stories from the war zone. National Communication Association, New Orleans, LA.

Houston, M. (1994) When black women talk with white women: Why dialogues are difficult, in *Our Voices*, (eds A. González, M. Houston, and V. Chen), Roxbury, Los Angeles, CA, pp. 133–139.

Hurtado, S. (2001) Research and evaluation on intergroup dialogue, in *Intergroup Dialogue*, (eds D. Schoem and S. Hurtado), University of Michigan Press, Ann Arbor, MI, pp. 22–35.

Ihde, D. (1986) *Experimental Phenomenology*, SUNY Press, Albany, NY.

Jackson, R. (2002) Cultural contracts theory: Toward an understanding of identity negotiation. *Communication Quarterly*, 50, 359–367.

Kimball, S., and Garrison, J. (1998) Hermeneutic listening in multicultural conversations, in *Affirming Diversity through Democratic Conversations*, (eds V.R. Fu and A.J. Stremmel), Prentice-Hall, Upper Saddle River, NJ.

Lanigan, R. (1988) *Phenomenology of Communication*, Duquesne University Press, Pittsburgh, PA.

Nakayama, T., and Krizek, R. (1995) Whiteness: A strategic rhetoric. *Quarterly Journal of Communication*, 81, 291–309.

Orbe, M. (1998) *Constructing Co-Cultural Theory*, Sage, Thousand Oaks, CA.

Parker, P. (2002) Negotiating identity in raced and gendered workplace interactions: The use of strategic communication by African American women senior executives within dominant culture organizations. *Communication Quarterly*, 50, 251–268.

Peck, J. (1994) Talk about racism: Framing a popular discourse of race on *Oprah Winfrey*. *Cultural Critique*, 89–126.

Said, E. (1978) *Orientalism*, Vintage Books, New York.

Schoem, D., Hurtado, S., Sevig, T. *et al.* (2001) Intergroup dialogue: Democracy at work in theory and practice, in *Intergroup Dialogue*, (eds D. Schoem and S. Hurtado), University of Michigan Press, Ann Arbor, MI, pp. 1–21.

Sontag, S. (2003) *Regarding the Pain of Others*, Farrar, Straus & Giroux, New York.

St John, J., and Shepherd, G.J. (2004) Transcending tolerance: Pragmatism, social capital, and community in communication. *Communication Yearbook*, 28, 167–187.

Yoshikawa, M. (1987) The double swing model of intercultural communication between the East and the West, in *Communication Theory: Eastern and Western Perspectives*, (ed. D.L. Kincaid), Academic Press, New York, pp. 319–329.

Zamora, A. (2002) Does dialogue really matter for learning? An investigation of the presence of dialogue in students' accounts of successful learning experiences. National Communication Association, New Orleans, LA.

Zúñiga, X., and Nagda, B. (2001) Design considerations in intergroup dialogue, in *Intergroup Dialogue*, (eds D. Schoem and S. Hurtado), University of Michigan Press, Ann Arbor, MI, pp. 306–327.

34

A Proposal for Concerted Collaboration between Critical Scholars of Intercultural and Organizational Communication

Brenda J. Allen

Box 34.1

Multicultural teams	Outsourcing	Diversity plan
Glass ceiling	Critical pedagogy	Cultural competence training
Globalization	Identity politics	Service learning
Affirmative action	Assimilation	Transnational communities
Difference	First nation	Study abroad programs
Cultural bias	Immigration policy	Intergroup dialogue

Due to their political implications, the terms in Box 34.1 represent contemporary issues that merit attention from critical intercultural communication scholars as they seek to make the world more equitable. These terms also allude to organizational contexts where humans encounter and negotiate power dynamics. Examples of such settings include corporations (national, international, multinational, and transnational), educational institutions, nonprofit groups, government agencies, volunteer organizations, health care facilities, and religious institutions. Thus, these terms also imply areas of study for critical organizational communication scholars. Based on the obvious point that overlap exists between critical studies of intercultural and organizational communication, this essay calls for more proactive collaboration between those two fields. I know this is not a new idea. After all, scholars from both areas of study have worked together already, and many of us enjoy supportive, collegial relationships. We also often refer to and rely upon information and insight from each other for research, teaching, service, and consulting practices. However, if scholars from these two areas of study engage in more

The Handbook of Critical Intercultural Communication, edited by Thomas K. Nakayama and Rona Tamiko Halualani. © 2010 Blackwell Publishing Ltd.

concerted, systematic efforts, they can facilitate and expedite accomplishing their mutual goal of effecting change related to persistent, pressing social issues around the world.

To explore this proposal, I begin with a brief overview of critical organizational communication, after which I describe similarities between the two areas of study, including interests, foci, and challenges. I also share examples of overlapping scholarship. I conclude with a few preliminary ideas for how critical scholars of intercultural and organizational communication might collaborate more deliberately.

"Organizational communication" refers to processes that humans use to share meaning in goal-oriented social collectivities such as the types of organizations listed above. As organizations are ubiquitous and significant to everyday life, organizational communication scholars strive to describe, understand, critique, and improve communicative practices within and across these varied contexts (Seibold *et al.*, 2009). They also contend that communication constitutes organizations (Ashcraft and Allen, 2009).

As the field has grown, increasing numbers of scholars have committed to critical approaches which: (1) characterize power as an ongoing, entrenched aspect of organizing; and (2) expose organizations as pivotal sites/systems of domination and resistance where people "enact, reinforce, or challenge various power relations endemic to society at large" (Allen, in press-b). They also contend that organizations are key sites of identity (re)construction where humans indoctrinate one another about dominant notions of social identities (Alvesson, Ashcraft and Thomas, 2008). Finally, due to the dynamic nature of power relations and the fluidity of identity constructions, critical organizational communication scholars believe that their efforts can emancipate humans from systems of oppression (Deetz and Mumby, 1990).

In the past decade or so, critical organizational communication studies has advanced by heeding calls for empirical research about routine, everyday political practices (Mumby 1993a, 1993b). Among areas for improvement, scholars have specified a need to increase scholarship on international and multicultural organizations (Cheney and Barnett, 2005), and to develop more complex conceptions of power dynamics (e.g., Ganesh, Zoller and Cheney, 2005; Johnson, Bhatt and Patton, 2007; Shugart, 2003; Taylor, 2005).

Two recent developments in critical organizational communication studies are especially relevant to this volume because they coincide with current issues in critical intercultural communication studies. First, scholars in both areas have critiqued tendencies to focus on microlevel, interpersonal interactions (Ganesh *et al.*, 2005; Halualani, Mendoza, and Drzewiecka, 2009). A group of intercultural researchers challenged tendencies to depict "intercultural communication as mostly individual-based skills and practices that need to be merely improved based on standards of competency for 'effective' and 'smooth' intercultural outcomes" (Halualani *et al.*, 2009, p. 27). Similarly, organizational communication scholars solicited research that moves beyond interpersonal, mundane, and routine situations of "individuals in individual workplaces" in the United States to studying larger contexts (Ganesh *et al.*, 2005, p. 174). The latter approach can help us explore how individual acts of resistance might be related to transformation or collective change – pivotal goals of critical work. Basically, scholars from both areas have stressed a need to contextualize research at macro levels, and to acknowledge effects of history, culture, and politics on microlevel interactions.

Both areas of study have also increased their focus on "difference" as a complex concept that encompasses numerous, intersecting aspects of social identity that can vary, according to socio-historical context (Allen, in press-b; Johnson *et al.*, 2007; Mumby, in press). Some organizational communication scholars strive to theorize relationships between power dynamics in organizations and discourses about social identity categories to interrogate "mundane politics of difference" (Ashcraft and Allen, 2009). They have moved away from one-dimensional conceptions of identity (especially gender) and power to acknowledge that most people simultaneously embody identities associated with privilege *and* oppression. Thus, they have responded to critiques that organizational communication studies often conflates "cultural identity" with "national identity," which overlooks other important aspects of social identity that matter in contemporary organizations (Ashcraft and Allen, 2003).

Similarly, critical intercultural communication scholars have called for more complex framing of aspects of identity such as gender, race, and class. Also noting a tendency to conceptualize culture as a nation-based variable, they recommend returning to 1970s' conceptualizations of identity in intercultural communication studies that included race, social class, and gender (Halualani *et al.*, 2009).

These two topics exemplify a nexus of critical intercultural and organizational communication studies where scholars in both areas might benefit from sharing insights and information. In addition, other precedents point to potential contexts and topics for joint efforts. For instance, several chapters in a recent volume of the *International and Intercultural Communication Annual* ("Communicating within/across Organizations") detail critical approaches to studying issues related to diverse organizational contexts around the world (Allen, Flores, and Orbe, 2007). Consider this sampling of titles: "Tempered radicals: Organizational and intercultural communication practices of Kenyan women leaders" (Ngunjiri and Lengel, 2007); "Grassroots agendas and global discourses: Tracking a planning process on children's issues [in Goa, India] (Ganesh, 2007); "Towards a critical organizational approach to civil society contexts: A case study of the difficulties of transnational advocacy [in the Amazon rainforest]" (Dempsey, 2007); "The way I work: Cross-country [China and the United States] comparisons of women's conceptualization of their gender and career identities" (Wang and Buzzanell, 2007). Authors of these chapters provide contextual information about social, cultural, and historical factors related to their projects.

Three of the chapters examine power dynamics and identity construction in higher education in the United States (Hendrix, Hebbani and Johnson, 2007; Hopson, 2007; Johnson *et al.*, 2007). They focus on the concept of privilege to illuminate complexities of power dynamics associated with various academic roles and intersections of social identity. For instance, Johnson *et al.* (2007) analyze intersections of race, gender, and sexuality to illustrate how intercultural interactions can simultaneously reproduce and challenge hegemony in the academy. As I discuss next, these chapters imply an area rich with promise for immediate, sustained impact.

As scholars from critical intercultural and organizational communication studies contemplate joining forces, I urge us to begin where we are: in the academy (Allen, 2002). We can apply critical perspectives to critiquing, (re)developing, and implementing curricula, pedagogy, research, and service related to contexts of higher education. To respond to concerns about contextualizing critical scholarship on communication, we can situate our work in critical studies of higher education in the United States (e.g., Maher and Tetreault, 2007) and around the world, as well as sociohistorical knowledge about the discipline of communication in general, and intercultural and organizational communication specifically. We also can focus explicitly on the topic of "difference" to investigate complexities of power dynamics associated with intersections of social identities of diverse stakeholder groups in specific locales of higher education. Moreover, we can compare our findings and experiences to inform practice and theory-building.

As a starting point, we can develop and share resources to optimize our pedagogy to accomplish goals of critical scholarship. To accomplish this, we can refer to the budding field of critical communication pedagogy, which highlights the constitutive role of communication in a specific context of organizing (education), and emphasizes relationships among power, identity, and culture (Allen, in press-a; Ashcraft and Allen, 2009; Fassett and Warren, 2007; Sprague, 1994). For example, we can help students to understand how power operates, and therefore prepare them for life after college, by teaching them to interrogate power dynamics *in their experiences as students*, while also modeling our own self-reflexivity regarding those dynamics (Ashcraft and Allen, 2009). In this approach to teaching power and communication:

> Classroom interactions conscientiously refer to knowledge about power dynamics as they unfold within the classroom, rather than referring to external, more abstract examples of power. The goal is to facilitate classrooms that are sites of resistance and empowerment, where students acquire critical perspectives and skills that cannot only reform the classroom and higher education, but also translate into other contexts. ... The common ground of education among participants can serve as a pivotal source for collaboration and learning as they observe and analyze how relations of power develop contextually. (Allen, in press-a)

I recently experimented with this approach to teach a master's course in communication entitled "Difference matters in organizational communication: Power in the ivory tower" (see Allen, in press-a).

We also should collaborate to interrogate and transform textbooks and other materials that "'discipline' students into a field's key interests while acculturating teachers who use them" (Ashcraft and Allen, 2009, p. 24). Resources to consult include critical analyses of textbooks in intercultural communication (Rodriguez and Chawla, 2008) and organizational communication (Ashcraft and Allen, 2003). Authors of these critiques stress the significance of textbooks for maintaining or transforming dominant perspectives on subject matter. Also, an edited volume entitled *Organizing Difference: Research, Pedagogy, and Practice* investigates differences as phenomena that humans construct through communicating, and examines relationships between organizing processes, discourse, and intersections of social identities (Mumby, in press). Of course, this handbook on critical intercultural communication is a great exemplar of how to provide alternative perspectives on intercultural communication.

As we apply critical perspectives to various aspects of teaching intercultural and organizational communication, we should also orient and socialize current and future scholars. Basically, we should aspire to conscientiously develop critical intercultural and organizational communication studies into substantive, transformative areas of study.

To guide our efforts, we can refer to the wealth of scholarship on power dynamics in higher education that already exists in communication studies (see, for example, Alexander, 1999, 2004; Alexander and Warren, 2002; Allen, 1998, 2000; Allen, Orbe and Olivas, 1999; Ashcraft and Allen, 2003, 2009; Carillo Rowe and Malhotra, 2006; Chawla and Rodriguez, 2007; Collier *et al.* 2001; Hendrix, Jackson, and Warren, 2003; Hendrix, Hebbani and Johnson, 2007; Hopson, 2007; Johnson, Rich and Cargile, 2008; Johnson *et al.*, 2007; Johnson and Bhatt, 2003; Nicotera, 1999; Patton, 2004; Simpson and Allen, 2006). Many of these publications illuminate experiences of faculty, administrators, and students who are "outsiders within" (Collins, 1986) the academy. Although this body of work "has been essential for developing a deeper understanding of how oppression works, injustice and oppression continue to influence the lived experiences of many within academic organizations" (Johnson *et al.*, p. 24). Our concerted efforts can help to mitigate such experiences in US institutions of higher education, with important implications for other contexts, including universities across the world. As applied communication scholar John Parrish-Sprowl (2009) observes, "Educational quality is a global issue because universities operate in an increasingly international context; therefore, educational practices around the world benefit from greater study" (p. 271). Critical intercultural and organizational communication scholars should be involved in those and related types of research endeavors.

Of course, in addition to studying and seeking to transform higher education, scholars can engage in research and practice within and related to other organizations and institutions to address issues such as those listed at the beginning of this essay and implied in the chapters I cited. For instance, they might consult the growing body of work in organizational communication on engaged scholarship "in which theory and practice are mutually transformative" (Seibold *et al.*, 2009, p. 346). This type of scholarship corresponds with the enduring intent of critical intercultural and organizational studies to delve into practice and theory, while also highlighting the interplay between them.

Regardless of what they focus their efforts upon, scholars in both areas of study can collaborate to merge their teaching, research, service, or practice. Or, we simply could commit to consulting our respective bodies of work to bolster one area of study with insights and information from the other. To be more proactive and systematic, at the very least, we should develop resource websites, and plan formal occasions (e.g., conference sessions or online discussion groups) to share with one another. We should also invite critical scholars from other areas within and external to the discipline of communication to join us.

In closing, I hope that the ideas I have outlined will inform whatever plans you have made or intend to develop for engaging in critical communication scholarship. Through communal, conscientious, and concerted effort, we really can make the world a better place.

References

Alexander, B.K. (1999) Performing culture in the classroom: An instructional (auto) ethnography. *Text and Performance Quarterly*, 19 (4), 307–331.

Alexander, B.K. (2004) Racializing identity: Performance, pedagogy, and regret. *Cultural Studies Critical Methodologies*, 4 (1), 12–27.

Alexander, B.K., and Warren, J.T. (2002) The materiality of bodies: Critical reflections on pedagogy, politics and positionality. *Communication Quarterly*, 50 (3&4), 328–343.

Allen, B.J. (1998) Black womanhood and feminist standpoints. *Management Communication Quarterly*, 11 (4), 575–586.

Allen, B.J. (2000) "Learning the ropes": A Black feminist critique, in *Rethinking Organizational and Managerial Communication from Feminist Perspectives*, (ed. P. Buzzanell), Sage, Thousand Oaks, CA, pp. 177–208.

Allen, B. J. (2002). Translating organizational communication scholarship into practice: Starting where we are. *Management Communication Quarterly*, 16, 101–105.

Allen, B.J. (in press-a) Critical communication pedagogy as a framework for teaching difference and organizing, in *Organizing Difference: Research, Pedagogy, and Practice*, (ed. D.K. Mumby), Sage, Thousand Oaks, CA.

Allen, B.J. (in press-b) *Difference Matters: Communicating Social Identity*, 2nd edn, Waveland Press, Long Grove, IL.

Allen, B.J., Flores, L., and Orbe, M.P. (eds) (2007) Communicating within/across organizational contexts. *International and Communication Annual*, 30, National Communication Association, Washington, DC.

Allen, B.J., Orbe, M.P., and Olivas, M.R. (1999) The complexity of our tears: Dis/enchantment and (in)difference in the academy. *Communication Theory*, 9 (4), 402–429.

Alvesson, M., Ashcraft, K.L., and Thomas, R. (2008) Identity matters: Reflections on the construction of identity scholarship in organization studies. *Organization*, 15 (1), 5–28.

Ashcraft, K.L., and Allen, B.J. (2003) The racial foundation of organizational communication. *Communication Theory*, 13 (1), 5–33.

Ashcraft, K.L., and Allen, B.J. (2009) Politics even closer to home: Repositioning CME from the standpoint of communication studies. *Management Learning*, 40, 11–30.

Carillo Rowe, A., and Malhotra, S. (2006) (Un)hinging whiteness. *International and Intercultural Communication Annual*, 29, 166–192.

Chawla, D., and Rodriguez, A. (2007) New imaginations of difference: On teaching, writing, and culturing. *Teaching in Higher Education*, 12, 697–708.

Cheney, G., and Barnett, G.A. (2005) *International and Multicultural Organizational Communication*, Hampton Press, Cresskill, NJ.

Collier, M.J., Hegde, R.S., Lee, W. *et al.* (2001) Dialogue on the edges: Ferment in communication and culture, in *Transforming Communication about Culture: Critical New Directions*, (ed. M.J. Collier), Sage, Newbury Park, CA, pp. 218–280.

Collins, P.H. (1986) Learning from the outsider within: The sociological significance of black feminist thought. *Social Problems*, 33, 14–32.

Deetz, S., and Mumby, D.K. (1990) Power, discourse, and the workplace: Reclaiming the critical tradition, in *Communication Yearbook, 13*, (ed. J. Anderson), Sage, Thousand Oaks, CA, pp. 18–47.

Dempsey, S. (2007) Towards a critical organizational approach to civil society contexts: A case study of the difficulties of transnational advocacy, in *International and Intercultural Communication Annual, 30*, (eds B.J. Allen, L.A. Flores, and M.P. Orbe), National Communication Association, Washington, DC, pp. 317–339.

Fassett, D., and Warren, J. (2007) *Critical Communication Pedagogy*, Sage, Thousand Oaks, CA.

Ganesh, S. (2007) Grassroots agendas and global discourses: Tracking a planning process on children's issues, in *International and Intercultural Communication Annual, 30*, (eds B.J. Allen, L.A. Flores, and M.P. Orbe), National Communication Association, Washington, DC, pp. 289–316.

Ganesh, S., Zoller, H., and Cheney, G. (2005) Transforming resistance, broadening our boundaries: Critical organizational communication meets globalization from below. *Communication Monographs*, 72 (2), 169–191.

Halualani, R.T., Mendoza, L.S., and Drzewiecka, J. (2009) "Critical" junctures in intercultural communication studies: A review. *The Review of Communication*, 9 (1), 17–35.

Hendrix, K., Hebbani, A., and Johnson, O. (2007) The "other" TA: An exploratory investigation of graduate teaching assistants of color, in *International and Intercultural Communication Annual, 30*, (eds B.J. Allen, L.A. Flores, and M.P. Orbe), National Communication Association, Washington, DC, pp. 51–82.

Hendrix, K., Jackson II, R., and Warren, J. (2003) Shifting academic landscapes: Exploring co-identities, identity negotiation, and critical progressive pedagogy. *Communication Education*, 52 (3/4), 177–190.

Hopson, M.C. (2007) Negotiations of organizational whitespace: Critical reflections on bodies of power, privilege and intercultural (in)sensitivity within academia, in *International and Intercultural Communication Annual, 30*, (eds B.J. Allen, L.A. Flores, and M.P. Orbe), National Communication Association, Washington, DC, pp. 1–20.

Johnson, J.R., and Bhatt, A.J. (2003) Gendered and racialized identities and alliances in the classroom: Formations in/of resistive space. *Communication Education*, 52 (3/4), 230–244.

Johnson, J.R., Bhatt, A.J., and Patton, T.O. (2007) Dismantling essentialisms in academic organizations: Intersectional articulation and possibilities for alliance formation, in *International and Intercultural Communication Annual, 30*, (eds B.J. Allen, L.A. Flores, and M.P. Orbe), National Communication Association, Washington, DC, pp. 21–50.

Johnson, J.R., Rich, M., and Cargile, A.C. (2008) "Why are you shoving this stuff down our throats?": Preparing intercultural educators to challenge performances of white racism. *Journal of International and Intercultural Communication*, 1 (2), 113–135.

Maher, F.A., and Tetreault, M.K.T. (2007) *Privilege and Diversity in the Academy*, Routledge, New York.

Mumby, D.K. (1993a) Critical organizational communication studies: The next ten years. *Communication Monographs*, 60, 18–25.

Mumby, D.K. (ed.) (1993b) *Narrative and Social Control: Critical Perspectives*, Sage, Newbury Park.

Mumby, D.K. (ed.) (in press) *Organizing Difference: Research, Pedagogy, and Practice*, Sage, Thousand Oaks, CA.

Ngunjiri, F.W., and Lengel, L. (2007) Tempered radicals: Organizational and intercultural communication practices of Kenyan women leaders, in *International and Intercultural Communication Annual, 30*, (eds B.J. Allen, L.A. Flores, and M.P. Orbe), National Communication Association, Washington, DC, pp. 117–146.

Nicotera, A.M. (1999) The woman academic as subject/object/self: Dismantling the illusion of duality. *Communication Theory*, 9 (4), 430–464.

Parrish-Sprowl, J. (2009) Managing a world of problems: The implications of globalization for applied communication research, in *Routledge Handbook of Applied Communication Research*, (eds L.R. Frey and K. Cissna), Routledge, New York, pp. 257–279.

Patton, T.O. (2004) Reflections of a black woman professor: Racism and sexism in academia. *Howard Journal of Communications*, 15, 185–200.

Rodriguez, A., and Chawla, D. (2008) Locating diversity in communication studies, in *International and Intercultural Communication Annual, 31*, (eds L.A. Flores, M. Orbe and B.J. Allen), National Communication Association, Washington, DC.

Seibold, D.R., Lemus, D.R., Ballard, D.I., and Myers, K.K. (2009) Organizational communication and applied communication research: Parallels, intersections, integration, and engagement, in *Routledge Handbook of Applied Communication Research*, (eds L.R. Frey and K. Cissna), Routledge, New York, pp. 331–354.

Shugart, H.A. (2003) An appropriating aesthetic: Reproducing power in the discourse of critical scholarship. *Communication Theory*, 13 (3), 275–303.

Simpson, J., and Allen, B.J. (2006) Engaging difference matters in the classroom, in *Engaging Communication, Transforming Organizations: Scholarship of Engagement in Action*, (eds J. Simpson and P. Shockley), Hampton Press, Cresskill, NJ.

Sprague, J. (1994) Ontology, politics, and instructional communication research: Why we can't just "agree to disagree" about power. *Communication Education*, 43 (4), 273–290.

Taylor, B.C. (2005) Postmodern theory, in *Engaging Organizational Communication: Theory and Research*, (eds S. May and D.K. Mumby), Sage, Thousand Oaks, CA, pp. 113–140.

Wang, Z., and Buzzanell, P. (2007) The way I work: Cross-country comparisons of women's conceptualization of their gender and career identities, in *International and Intercultural Communication Annual, 30*, (eds B.J. Allen, L.A. Flores, and M.P. Orbe), National Communication Association, Washington, DC, (pp. 147–174).

Part IV

Critical Visions of Intercultural Communication Studies

35

Conclusion
Envisioning the Pathway(s) of Critical Intercultural Communication Studies

Thomas K. Nakayama
and Rona Tamiko Halualani

Le seul véritable voyage, le seul bain de Jouvenance, ce ne serait pas d'aller vers de nouveaux paysages, mais d'avoir d'autres yeux, de voir l'univers avec les yeux d'un autre, de cent autres, de voir les cent univers que chacun d'eux voit, que chacun d'eux est.

Marcel Proust, (1954, p. 258)

The only true voyage of discovery, the only really rejuvenating experience, would be not to visit strange lands but to possess other eyes, to see the universe through the eyes of another, of a hundred others, to see the hundred universes that each of them sees, that each of them is.

Marcel Proust, (1981, p. 260)

At the outset of this handbook, we noted that we stand at an important crossroads in the development of critical intercultural communication. We urge critical scholars not to think about crossroads as a singular moment through which we move and close off other options, or the other roads not taken. We will be faced with many, and unending, crossroads as we move ahead. We cannot always see the path clearly, nor foresee world events, but we must move forward with critical engagement of these issues.

Throughout the course of this reader, critical intercultural communication scholars have engaged multiple approaches, theories, concepts, and methods in an attempt to understand the complexity of the world in which we live. We do indeed live in a multilayered world with no easy answers to the challenges confronting us. In this brief conclusion, we want to point to some directions that a critical intercultural communication project might head. Our call is to point to some of the challenges that face this project.

The Handbook of Critical Intercultural Communication, edited by Thomas K. Nakayama and Rona Tamiko Halualani. © 2010 Blackwell Publishing Ltd.

Perspective, Agency, and Form

There is no unified critical intercultural communication project and this fact represents a key strength of a critical perspective. As critical scholars, we come to this project from multiple approaches and perspectives with different agenda and goals in mind. Humans, cultures, history, power, and knowledge are infinitely complex as Proust noted.

Any attempt to be reductionist in understanding intercultural interaction is destined to failure. Yet, we cannot let this complexity render us without agency or paralyze us into separate, disparate projects with no connection to or impact on one another (or any sense of collective responsibility on issues and projects). We can and we must act to create a better and more just world for all.

Despite the many perspectives that we take to understand the world, we urge critical scholars to think otherwise, to view the world in new, unexplored ways. We must move beyond the ways that we "know" about others, as human experience is far too complex for the tools we have been given to generate knowledge. Part of the challenge of the critical project is to create new tools and ways of knowing that will help us take on very different kinds of projects.

As we develop new ways of looking at the other, we must also acknowledge the grasp that the past has on us. As we learn about the plight of albinos in Tanzania whose lives are endangered due to "a growing criminal trade in albino body parts" (Gettleman, 2008) believed to be magical, or the recently proposed, "Anti-Homosexuality Bill of 2009 which would sentence HIV positive homosexuals to death for having sex, and severely punish any homosexual with up to life imprisonment" (Hughes, 2009), can critical scholars be a force for social change? As critical scholars located in the West with connections to others around the globe, do we remain fearful of charges of colonialism, cultural imperialism, or ethnocentrism, if we speak out against such abuses? What kinds of agency do we have and under what conditions? How best can we activate and maximize such agency to be impactful across all influential contexts (contexts of learning, governmentality and regulation, economy and commerce, popular culture and media, and communities)?

We must also become more open to the forms through which our critical projects and scholarship take shape; whether as critical praxis demonstrations, policies, interventional programs, popular cultural forms, performances and narratives, and organized groups. To discount any of the possibilities or options that enact new perspectives and forms of agency would be to diminish the dynamic range, flexibility, and room for critical intercultural work to be consequential, forceful, targeted, and transformative. This is an especially urgent reminder (as underscored by the contributors of this handbook) for all scholars and practitioners in the West (and in the academy) to cross boundaries, contexts, and available tools and forms. We anxiously await how scholars will take up such a call.

Globalization

We live in a world fraught with contradictory intercultural tensions. These dialectics must be kept in mind as we navigate a global perspective. The emergence of third wave thinkers about globalization highlights the "reality of globalization today and undermines skeptics' claims that we, at best, live in an era of internationalization rather than on a new global plane above and beyond the international" (Martell, 2007, p. 193). Globalization is changing the world in ways that are significant. While there "are global flows of media, communications, technology, and finance," nations have been "stricter in controlling immigration, that is, the movement of people" (p. 194). These all have to be understood within the specific contexts of the "local, regional, national, and international" (p. 194). These changes have far reaching impacts that we can only begin to imagine.

Globalization drives us into tighter and tighter economic relationships. While globalization increases intercultural contact within a specific frame, it also highlights ways that cultures impact each other and always have (albeit in disproportionate ways). The more entwined our economics become, the more world economic waves can impact people around the world. In the recent downturn, on the one hand, smaller economies have been devastated or are facing tremendous challenges, such as Dubai, Iceland, and Ireland. On the other hand, globalization is driving technological changes that may lead to improved everyday life. For example, "technology is the core of Rwanda's plan to transform its economy by 2020. The country seems ready to back its ambition with money and policies. By 2012, for instance, Rwanda wants every child in the country between the ages of nine and 12, 1.3 million children in all, to have a laptop with an Internet or intranet connection to download free educational software and electronic books" (Upgrading the children, 2009, p. 60). Although Rwanda is still technologically behind some of its fellow African nations, rapid changes may help to transform Rwanda and other African nations in the coming years.

Still, protests against globalization continue unabated. Protests at WTO meetings, G-7, G-8 meetings and the like seem to have no end. The myriad of concerns of the protesters who represent a range of political positions and concerns, highlight the complexity of globalization and the complexity of its impact around the globe. Marwan Kraidy (2005) highlights the formation of hybridity, but are there other ways that cultures influence each other?

Globalization also drives cultural contact which can create and solve problems at the same time. Recently, for example, Uganda has discussed the death penalty for gays and lesbians, while at the same time outlawing female genital mutilation (female circumcision). The influence of Christian evangelical rhetoric and ex-gay movement discourse on these decisions has been dramatic. Combined with colonial era anti-gay laws, "within Uganda deeply-rooted homophobia, aided by a US-linked evangelical campaign alleging that gay men are trying to 'recruit' schoolchildren, and that homosexuality is a habit that can be 'cured,' has ensured widespread public support for the bill" (Rice, 2009). The ongoing influence of the West on the rest and the impossibility of discrete cultures in a global world is highlighted by these exchanges with disturbing results. Thus, as one of the major premises of a critical intercultural communication perspective, "inter"cultural encounters, relations, and exchanges need to be examined in all of their forma-tions, inflections, invocations, and inequalities (over/under positionings) as wrought by historical context and economic and political influence. The intersectional collisions of identity and culture (for example, a discourse that is simultaneously anti-gay and pro-female) adds a complex dimension to how we view, engage, and confront (with counter-hegemonies) intercultural relations and dynamics. The globalized (a term and or attribute that changes on a daily basis in terms of its movement, scope, influence, and outcome) nature of our world may finally propel us to re-theorize and reconceptualize what "inter"cultural communication means, with "inter" standing as a more historical term of reference to earlier work but nonetheless one that requires a re-spatialization and re-territorialization of "inter" (as argued by scholars like Stuart Hall and Kuan-Hsing Chen) as between, across, within, and underneath every aspect of culture and power among interactants, groups, countries, structures and institutions, and contexts. We will only gain from the bold ("no looking back") reconstruction of our theoretical terms and naming logics to accurately reflect and capture the complexity and unwieldiness of the phenonmena, interactions and relations, and discourses that we interrogate.

Religion

Religion has been a major force for unification and division throughout the centu-ries. As people become more mobile, they come into increasingly more frequent and sustained contact with members of other religions. These encounters can be learning experiences for exploring other ways of being spiritual, but they can also incite religious conflict. One Rand Corporation report notes: "After September 11th, it almost goes without saying that religious violence in the name of a holy cause has escalated. Killing in the name of God constitutes a major driver of violent conflicts today" (Treverton *et al.*, 2005, p. xi). Yet, we have a very difficult time discussing, analyzing, and understanding religion, whether from the fear of tread-ing on ideologically protected ("sacred") ground or the daunting challenging of engaging a force that is so historically and ideologically engrained and connected to the forces of Empire and the State. Where there is great fear, potential resist-ance, and hesitation definitely signals for us territory that needs to be traversed, carefully and deliberately. With religious conflict standing as one of the major influ-ences on intercultural relations in the world, it is a wonder that our field has not fully spoken to this issue. It is time to employ a critical perspective – one that is well suited to this issue – to engage religion, religious identity, and its connection to historical memory, ethnic and national identity, and the forming of a people (in addition to the relationships surrounding gender, sexuality, regionalism, ethnicity, race, class status, and educational standing).

Critical intercultural communication scholars need to devise a new vocabulary for engaging with religion. Religion has remained an unexplored area of intercultural interaction, but probably not blindly so. Religion is difficult to discuss and even more difficult to analyze from the tools that we currently have as academics. The more we examine religious beliefs, the more elusive they seem to be. Our critical language and tools do not yet have the ability to grasp how to understand religion. Yet, the increasing importance of religion in this world means that critical scholars must develop ways of understanding and analyzing the place of religion in society and the world.

We live in a world with increased opportunities to interact with people around the globe. Communication has played a key role in both making the global economy possible, as well as emerged as a vital part of resistance to it. This dialectical tension opens up enormous challenges for critical intercultural communication scholars, as well as all of us who live in this new global world. There is no turning back, only the facing of what has been, what is, and what will become. We hope that this collection is but one step in moving toward a serious critical engagement with this world which presents new and historically present challenges everyday. Our collection is meant to reveal all of the significant work being done in this vein and to push us all to continue to do more as a diverse and intercontinental network of scholars, advocates, and teachers who are deeply committed to justice, liberation, transgression, transformation, and the surpassing of conditions that have been deemed as "natural," "right and good," "inevitable and necessary," and "the way it has always been."

References

Gettleman, J. (2008) Albinos, long shunned, face threat in Tanzania. *New York Times*, June 8. www.nytimes.com/2008/06/08/world/africa/08albino.html?pagewanted=1&_r=1 (accessed May 24, 2010).

Hughes, D. (2009) Africa's culture war: The fight over Uganda's anti-gay bill. *ABC News*, December 14. http:// blogs.abcnews.com/theworldnewser/2009/12/africas-culture-war-the-fight-over-ugandas-antigay-bill.html (accessed May 24, 2010).

Kraidy, M. (2005) *Hybridity, or the Cultural Logic of Globalization*, Temple University Press, Philadelphia.

Martell, L. (2007) The third wave in globalization theory. *International Studies Review*, 9, 173–196.

Proust, M. (1954) *La prisonnière. A la recherché du temps perdu*, Vol. III. Librarie Gallimard, Paris. Originally published 1923.

Proust, M. (1981) *The Captive. Remembrance of Things Past*, Vol. III, (trans. C.K.S. Moncrieff, T. Kilmartin and A. Mayor), Random House, New York. Originally published 1923.

Rice, X. (2009) Uganda considers death sentence for gay sex in bill before parliament. *The Guardian*, November 29. www.guardian.co.uk/world/2009/nov/29/uganda-death-sentence-gay-sex (accessed May 24, 2010).

Treverton, G.F., Gregg, H.S., Gibran, D.K. *et al.* (2005) Exploring religious conflict, Rand Corporation, Santa Monica, CA. www.rand.org/pubs/conf_proceedings/2005/RAND_CF211.pdf (accessed May 24, 2010).

Upgrading the children (2009) *The Economist*, December 5, p. 60.

Index